BARRON'S

GRE

PSYCHOLOGY

Graduate Record Examination in Psychology

7TH EDITION

Laura A. Freberg, Ph.D.
Professor of Psychology
California Polytechnic State University,
  San Luis Obispo
San Luis Obispo, California

Edward L. Palmer, Ph.D.
Watson Professor
Department of Psychology
Davidson College
Davidson, North Carolina

Sharon L. Thompson-Schill, Ph.D.
Professor of Psychology
Class of 1965 Term Chair
Center for Cognitive Neuroscience
Department of Psychology
University of Pennsylvania
Philadelphia, Pennsylvania

BARRON'S

All inquiries should be addressed to:
Barron's Educational Series, Inc.
250 Wireless Boulevard
Hauppauge, New York 11788
www.barronseduc.com

Library of Congress Catalog Card Number: 2015944080

ISBN: 978-1-4380-0573-7

PRINTED IN THE UNITED STATES OF AMERICA

9 8 7 6 5 4

10%
POST-CONSUMER
WASTE
Paper contains a minimum
of 10% post-consumer
waste (PCW). Paper used
in this book was derived
from certified, sustainable
forestlands.

CONTENTS

Preface

Welcome! We're glad you've joined us on this prep journey toward GRE Psychology Test success. It's not an easy journey and there aren't any shortcuts, but if you allot yourself sufficient study time, bring along a current major introductory textbook, take the diagnostic test, focus on your weak areas, and follow-up with more practice tests and weak area reviews, you will be ready when the time comes to head in for the test that counts. Our work with you will resemble that of a coach. In a book like this, **we can't give you all the answers you'll need, but we can tell you how and where to find them and we can give you some test-taking strategies.**

SOME INTRODUCTIONS

There are a number of GRE Psychology Test preparation books on the market, and of course we're very happy that you have chosen ours. So who are the people behind the scenes of this book?

Laura Freberg, the author of this current revision, is Professor of Psychology at California Polytechnic State University, San Luis Obispo. She received her bachelor's, master's, and doctoral degrees from UCLA, specializing in learning and behavioral neuroscience. She conducted her dissertation research with Robert Rescorla of the University of Pennsylvania. Freberg is the author of two editions of an introductory psychology textbook, *Discovering Psychology: The Science of Mind*, with John Cacioppo of the University of Chicago and three editions of a behavioral neuroscience textbook, *Discovering Behavioral Neuroscience: An Introduction to Biological Psychology*.

Two eminent psychologists prepared previous editions of this book, which formed the basis for the current revision. Edward L. Palmer is Watson Professor Emeritus in the Department of Psychology in Davidson College, located in North Carolina. Palmer has written extensively on the topic of children and television. Sharon L. Thompson-Schill is Christopher H. Browne Distinguished Professor of Psychology and Department Chair at the Center for Cognitive Neuroscience at the University of Pennsylvania. Her research investigates the neural basis of human memory and language.

WHAT TO EXPECT IN THIS BOOK

Because we're psychologists, and psychological science has a great deal to say about the best practices in learning and memory, we're hoping that you'll find this material even more useful than other test preparation books you might have used in the past.

Here is a quick chapter-by-chapter summary of what you will see in this book:

- **CHAPTER 1** provides you with a basic outline of the testing process and what you can expect to see in the GRE Psychology Test, including the amount of emphasis on specific topics. You will also learn about the purpose of the test, how to register, and some useful ETS websites where you can find further information. Chapter 1 also discusses preparation and test-taking strategies based on psychological principles. A special section highlights the important changes between DSM-IV-TR and DSM-5. Finally, this chapter provides recommended books and websites for further topic-specific background study.

- **CHAPTER 2** provides you with a full-length diagnostic version of the GRE Psychology Test. What does it mean to have a diagnostic version? One major difference between this version and the real thing is the ordering of questions. In this diagnostic version, the questions related to a specific topic are grouped together (e.g., ten questions in a row on biological psychology), whereas in the real test, the topic areas are randomized. The diagnostic version contains scoring information, correct answers, and the rationale for the correct answers. This allows you to identify your strengths and weaknesses in both test-taking skills (Did you finish on time?) and subject areas (Did you answer all of the clinical questions correctly while struggling with the developmental questions?).

- **CHAPTER 3** includes a comprehensive review of the main topic areas covered by the GRE Psychology Test. The structure of this chapter follows the outline of the topic areas found in Chapter 1. This chapter is not a substitute for a more thorough study of the material using an introductory psychology textbook, but it helps highlight some of the key points you can expect to see on the test.

- **CHAPTER 4** includes another full-length diagnostic test that will let you see how much your weak areas identified by the first diagnostic test have improved so far.

- **CHAPTER 5** presents three full-length versions patterned after the GRE Psychology Test, which means that the topic areas are randomized instead of appearing in order as they did in the diagnostic tests. These tests not only pick up on any remaining weaknesses you have in the subject areas but they should build your confidence. When you finally see the real test, there shouldn't be too many surprises.

Used properly, this *Barron's GRE Psychology* prep book should help you do your very best on the GRE Psychology Test. The materials included in this book have been selected to help you make the most of your precious preparation time. We would love to know any feedback you have during your prep process or after the test. Please feel free to e-mail *lfreberg@calpoly.edu* or message on Twitter at *@lfreberg*.

Acknowledgments

It has been an honor and privilege to update and revise the work of two such distinguished psychologists, Edward L. Palmer and Sharon L. Thompson-Schill. Their previous editions of this test preparation book provided a marvelous template for my work. I am also indebted to Kristen Girardi and Veronica Douglas for their invaluable support and guidance throughout this project.

My family, including my husband, Roger, and daughters Kristin Saling, Karen Freberg, and Karla Freberg, provided many moments of patience and encouragement. I would also like to thank my very dear friends Steph and John Cacioppo for helping me see psychology in many new ways.

Finally, a thank you goes out to those of you who have entrusted me with your preparation for this important next step in your academic and professional careers.

The GRE Psychology Test | 1

ABOUT THE TEST

The GRE Psychology Test, developed by the Educational Testing Service (ETS) is administered to approximately 6,000–7,000 people just like you each year. You have plenty of company!

People take the GRE Psychology Test for a number of reasons. Most are applying to graduate programs in psychology. Not all graduate programs require the GRE Psychology Test, but many either require or recommend the test. If a program "recommends" the test, students are usually putting themselves at a disadvantage if they do not take it. Even if the test is not recommended or required by a program, Kuncel, Hezlett, and Ones (2001) suggest sending the test report anyway, as this conveys a student's enthusiasm and mastery in the field of psychology.

Like all standardized admissions tests, the GRE Psychology Test provides a measuring stick for comparing students who have studied at institutions that vary in rigor. Graduate programs differ widely in what they consider to be an "acceptable" score, so it is important for prospective students to investigate program requirements carefully. A meta-analysis by Kuncel et al. (2001) showed that the subject matter test was a better predictor of students' grades and their probability of earning a graduate degree than the comprehensive GRE.

The GRE Psychology Test has other uses in addition to admissions. Some scholarships and fellowships for graduate students in psychology require the test. Increasingly, senior psychology majors enrolled in capstone courses are being required to take the GRE Psychology Test to meet administration requirements for assessing program success.

How to Register for the Test

As we go to print, the test is paper based rather than computer based and is offered three times per year: September, October, and April. A worldwide list of the test centers is available here: *www.ets.org/s/gre/pdf/gre_pbt_center_lists.pdf*. Not all test centers are available on all dates, so careful planning can be helpful. The test is written in English only. Accommodations for test takers with disabilities and health-related needs can be requested by following the procedures outlined in this document: *www.ets.org/s/disabilities/pdf/bulletin_supplement_test_takers_with_disabilities_health_needs.pdf*. Test takers with special needs do not register online.

Online registration begins at this portal: *https://mygre.ets.org/greweb/login/login.jsp*. The current cost for the GRE Psychology Test is $150 USD, and online payments can be made using PayPal or major credit cards.

General Structure and Scoring of the GRE Psychology Test

The current test contains approximately 205 questions to be completed within 2 hours and 50 minutes (170 minutes). Items are developed for the test by a committee of six faculty members. Committee members evaluate new proposed items each year, which are then reviewed by the GRE Sensitivity Committee. The Sensitivity Committee rejects items that are potentially offensive. Analysis of test-taker performance on all items is conducted following each administration of the test.

Most of the questions on the test will look rather familiar to you, as they are likely to be similar to multiple-choice questions you have seen in exams in your psychology courses. However, the GRE Psychology Test also contains sets of "Analysis of Evidence" questions. These items begin with a description of a research study. Following the description are two to five questions about the conclusions that can be drawn from the study, weaknesses of the study, or ways to improve the study. If you have downloaded the 2015 version of the ETS Practice Book, examples of these questions can be seen in numbers 91–96 on pages 26–27 and numbers 166–169 on page 42. These questions depend less on your knowledge of specific areas of psychology, but rather test your ability to think about research design and analysis. If this is not your strong suit, don't worry. We'll work on these skills as well.

Scores on all GRE subject matter tests range from a low of 200 to a maximum of 990. Scoring begins with a raw score, which is the total number of questions you answered correctly minus one-fourth of the number you answered incorrectly. We discuss the implications of the scoring of incorrect answers on guessing strategies in a later section. ETS converts your raw score to a scaled score in a process designed to equalize scores across different editions of the test.

According to ETS, the mean score for test takers between 2010 and 2013 on the GRE Psychology Test was 616 with a standard deviation of 102. The following table provides percentiles related to scaled scores:

Scaled Score	Percentile
820	99
740	88
700	76
660	61
640	53
620	46
600	39
560	27
520	17
480	10
360	1

Topics Covered by the Test

In addition to a total score, the results of the Psychology Test are divided into subscales: the Experimental subscale (40%), the Social subscale (43%), and the Other Areas subscale (17%). The outline below gives you more specific topics and their weightings on the typical test.

Be sure to pay careful attention to the weightings of each area, which will allow you to prioritize your study time. You might be surprised by some of the weightings. For example, your professors might have spent a great deal of time on personality (Sigmund Freud included), yet personality makes up a relatively small 3–5% of the GRE Psychology Test. Many psychology majors are not required to take a course in sensation and perception, yet 5–7% of the GRE Psychology Test features this material.

Most psychology majors are comprehensive, but it is difficult to take courses in all aspects of psychology and graduate in a reasonable amount of time. Most students specialize to some extent in their choice-of-study plan. As a result, some material may be relatively unfamiliar to you, such as the language topics and industrial/organizational psychology. Do not despair. Psychology is a heavily integrated field, so what you already know about psychology, its history, its methods, and its theoretical approaches will help you to learn about the "gaps" in your undergraduate education.

I. Experimental Subscale (40% or approximately 82/205 questions)

    A. Learning (3–5% or approximately 6–10 questions)

        1. Classical Conditioning

        2. Instrumental Conditioning

        3. Observational Learning and Modeling

        4. Theories, Applications, and Issues

    B. Language (3–4% or approximately 6–8 questions)

        1. Units (Phonemes, Morphemes, Phrases)

        2. Syntax

        3. Meaning

        4. Speech Perception and Processing

        5. Reading Processes

        6. Verbal and Nonverbal Communication

        7. Bilingualism

        8. Theories, Applications, and Issues

    C. Memory (7–9% or approximately 14–18 questions)

        1. Working Memory

        2. Long-term Memory

        3. Types of Memory

        4. Memory Systems and Processes

        5. Theories, Applications, and Issues

    D. Thinking (4–6% or approximately 8–12 questions)

        1. Representation (Categorization, Imagery, Schemas, Scripts)

        2. Problem Solving

        3. Judgment and Decision-Making Processes

    4. Planning and Metacognition

    5. Intelligence

    6. Theories, Applications, and Issues

E. Sensation and Perception (5–7% or approximately 10–14 questions)

    1. Psychophysics and Signal Detection

    2. Attention

    3. Perceptual Organization

    4. Vision

    5. Audition

    6. Gustation

    7. Olfaction

    8. Somatosenses

    9. Vestibular and Kinesthetic Senses

    10. Theories, Applications, and Issues

F. Physiological/Behavioral Neuroscience (12–14% or approximately 25–29 questions)

    1. Neurons

    2. Sensory Structures and Processes

    3. Motor Structures and Functions

    4. Central Structures and Processes

    5. Motivation, Arousal, and Emotion

    6. Cognitive Neuroscience

    7. Neuromodulators and Drugs

    8. Hormonal Factors

    9. Comparative and Ethology

    10. States of Consciousness

    11. Theories, Applications, and Issues

II. Social Subscale (43% or approximately 88/205 questions)

A. Clinical and Abnormal (12–14% or approximately 25–29 questions)

    1. Stress, Conflict, and Coping

    2. Diagnostic Systems

    3. Assessment

    4. Causes and Development of Disorders

    5. Neurophysiological Factors

    6. Treatment of Disorders

    7. Epidemiology

    8. Prevention

    9. Health Psychology

    10. Cultural and Gender Issues

    11. Theories, Applications, and Issues

B. Life Span Development (12–14% or approximately 25–29 questions)

1. Nature–Nurture
2. Physical and Motor
3. Perception and Cognition
4. Language
5. Intelligence
6. Social and Personality
7. Emotion
8. Socialization and Family and Cultural Influences
9. Theories, Applications, and Issues

C. Personality (3–5% or approximately 6–10 questions)

1. Theories
2. Structure
3. Assessment
4. Personality and Behavior
5. Applications and Issues

D. Social (12–14% or approximately 25–29 questions)

1. Social Perception, Cognition, Attribution, and Beliefs
2. Attitudes and Behavior
3. Social Comparison and Self
4. Emotion, Affect, and Motivation
5. Conformity, Influence, and Persuasion
6. Interpersonal Attraction and Close Relationships
7. Group and Intergroup Processes
8. Cultural and Gender Influences
9. Evolutionary Psychology, Altruism, and Aggression
10. Theories, Applications, and Issues

III. Other Areas (17% or approximately 35 questions)

A. General (4–6% or approximately 8–12 questions)

1. History
2. Industrial/ Organizational
3. Educational

B. Measurement and Methodology (11–13% or approximately 23–27 questions)

1. Psychometrics, Test Construction, Reliability, and Validity
2. Research Designs
3. Statistical Procedures
4. Scientific Method and the Evaluation of Evidence
5. Ethics and Legal Issues
6. Analysis and Interpretation of Findings

TEST-TAKING STRATEGIES

One of the advantages psychology students have over students taking GRE subject tests in other areas is a strong understanding of learning and memory. If you remember what you have learned about these processes and apply these principles to your preparation for taking the GRE Psychology Test, you should perform very well!

Studying for the Test

1. DO NOT EVEN THINK ABOUT CRAMMING.

If you recall your study of information processing and memory, you will probably recognize the terms *spaced trials* and *massed trials*. Massed trials refer to cramming, or trying to learn material in a very short amount of time. As per a large body of research, spaced, or spread-out learning, is superior to massed trials.

Many students are in the unfortunate position of managing their graduate school applications during the fall term of their senior year. This term usually features many distractors. You might be working on a capstone course or senior thesis, or you might be spending many hours at an internship. Your senior-level course work is likely to be challenging. Asking professors for letters of recommendation, preparing statements of purpose, and taking required tests on top of regular course work can seem overwhelming.

2. TO HELP YOU MANAGE YOUR TIME, PLAN.

- Set out your study plan 6 to 8 weeks ahead of your scheduled test.
- Your plan should be as detailed as possible. Set up specific tasks (e.g., take diagnostic test, review material on personality in intro psych textbook) and schedule a time for them. Google Calendars might be particularly helpful, as you can color code tasks and set up reminders for yourself.
- Use checklists for tasks. There is something inherently rewarding about checking off a completed task.

3. USE THE SELF-REFERENCE EFFECT (SRE).

Psychologists have discovered that material that is relevant to the self is easier to recall. As you work your way through your review of the material, see if you can think of a way to apply each concept to your own experiences or to things you already know. For example, when you're studying classical conditioning, think about experiences you might have had with taste aversion (being unable to eat a food that you once ate prior to feeling ill), and apply the key terms (*conditioned stimulus*, etc.) to this personal experience.

4. USE EFFECTIVE STUDY TECHNIQUES.

- Repetition works. There is no substitute for going over material many times. However, be aware of one trap. Repeated reading of material can make the material easier to read independent of any true understanding of the concepts in the section. Just because something looks familiar does not mean that you understand it or can recall it. You might just be glossing over your reading without really thinking about it. Stay engaged. Take frequent breaks when it becomes difficult to concentrate.

- The PQRST method works for many students. **P**review the material you want to cover in a study session first, by scanning for key terms and headings, reading learning objectives, and viewing illustrations and their captions. Think of a **Q**uestion that might be answered in the passage you're about to read. What do you expect to learn? **R**ead a section in depth, making sure you understand each concept and example. **S**elf-recite to put the material in your own words (most instructors are amazed at how easy it is to remember detailed material after lecturing about it a few times). **T**est yourself by going back through the headlines to see how much you remember about a topic.
- Before you can succeed on tests in any field of study, you need to know the language of the field. Barron's also publishes a set of 500 flash cards by Robert McEntarffer (2013) titled *Barron's AP Psychology Flash Cards, Second Edition.* Although designed for high school students preparing for the Advanced Placement (AP) Psychology Test, psychology vocabulary is still psychology vocabulary. This card set enjoys very positive user reviews on *Amazon.com.*
- Take tests. Roediger and Karpicke (2006) presented compelling evidence for a "testing effect." Not only do tests assess what you know, but they aid in retention of the material. Prior testing, in their studies, produced "substantially greater retention" than studying. We are not arguing for skipping your studying of course, but we recommend that you make full use of the practice tests supplied in this book.
- Recite. See if you can explain the key concepts you're studying in your own words in mini-lectures. Talking about a topic tells you very quickly if you really understand it, so this is a great check for finding areas that you don't know as well as you think you do.

PREPARING FOR TEST DAY

You're planning to go to graduate school, so we can assume that you have already sailed through many difficult exams with success. However, we have a few reminders of good strategies that might be new to you.

1. CONTEXT-DEPENDENT LEARNING

Research suggests that the more similar your practice and performance situations are, the better your recall will be. Participants learning lists of words underwater (with scuba gear, of course) or on dry land performed better on memory tests for those lists when tested under the same circumstances as the one in which they studied. Changing from underwater to land or vice versa produced poorer performance.

Think about the testing center where you will be asked to perform. If it's close, visit it and find your way around. Where are the restrooms? Where can you get a coffee or snack? If possible, find out if you can peek into the testing room itself (these are often classrooms).

When you study, see if you can recreate aspects of the testing situation in terms of seating and lighting. Avoid distractions, such as your cell phone or television. This is particularly helpful when you are taking the practice tests.

Some of the strongest context-dependent effects occur with psychoactive substances, including caffeine. If you are a regular coffee or tea drinker, and you study while sipping your favorite beverage, by all means, enjoy your normal beverages before the test. However, if you are not accustomed to coffee or tea or other caffeinated beverages, drinking several energy drinks right before the test is a really bad idea.

2. PRACTICE GOOD STRESS MANAGEMENT

As we mentioned earlier, you are very likely to be taking the GRE Psychology Test during a very busy time of your life. It becomes that much more important to maintain good stress management habits. Eat a healthy diet and do your best to get adequate sleep. A half-hour of daily aerobic exercise, even if it's just a brisk walk around your neighborhood, is important. Researchers are beginning to report that practicing mindfulness or other forms of meditation can be beneficial. You might find it helpful to learn how to do progressive relaxation, which is helpful not only while studying, but also during the test itself. Several protocols are available online, including this one from the American Medical Students Association: *www.amsa.org/healingthehealer/musclerelaxation.cfm*

TAKING THE TEST

Now the big moment has arrived! Be sure to attend to and follow the test monitor's instructions very carefully.

Research on social facilitation suggests that a person's "dominant" behavior will emerge in the presence of other people. This means that in the presence of others, a well-practiced behavior will be more likely to appear than an infrequently or poorly practiced behavior. Remind yourself about all the hours of hard work you put in to prepare for this moment. You are like an athlete or musician who has trained diligently for a big performance, and this is your chance to shine!

Another line of psychological research that predicts performance is the classic Yerkes-Dodson law. If you are engaged in a complex behavior, such as taking the GRE Psychology Test, the relationship between arousal and performance should take the shape of an inverted *U*. With too little or too much arousal, performance will suffer. Your job is to find that middle range of arousal that will elicit your peak performance. This is another reason why completing the practice tests is so important. After having taken several of these under varying conditions, you probably have a good idea of how much arousal is "too much." Test-takers viewing the materials for the very first time are likely to have overwhelming amounts of arousal, which are likely to interfere with their ability to remember the material.

TIPS FOR TEST DAY

1. Arrive early. This gives you time to park, grab a last-minute coffee, take a restroom break, and find the testing room.
2. Find a seat in the classroom that feels comfortable to you. If you're easily distracted, perhaps choose a seat away from the windows or doors.
3. Remember that everyone else in the room is likely to be somewhat nervous, which can be contagious. Be friendly before the test if this is your style, but try to tune out people who are raising your anxiety.

If you feel yourself becoming too stressed or keyed up during the test, close your eyes, take a few deep breaths, and do a few shoulder shrugs to relax those muscles. If you practiced progressive relaxation during your test preparation, this might be a good time to relax your body. Now that you're refreshed, sit up straight and get back to work.

Approaching the Test

Again, we understand that most of you are already very experienced and successful test takers, but there might be a few strategies you haven't tried so far in your academic career.

1. THE "THREE-PASS" SYSTEM

Finishing 205 questions in 170 minutes means that you have 1.2 minutes per question. Many people achieving top scores are unable to answer all of the questions. What is important is that you make time to answer the questions that you are most likely to answer correctly. Remember that all questions are weighted equally. The easy ones count as much as the difficult ones. Wasting time on a difficult question that then prevents you from answering easier questions is not a great strategy.

The three-pass system will provide you with a strategy for prioritizing your work on the questions. Be sure to practice this approach as you complete your practice and diagnostic tests in this book so it is very familiar to you by test day.

Pass One

As you evaluate each question the first time through the test, divide the questions into three categories:

A. Easy questions: You are quite certain you know the answer to these.
B. Moderate questions: The material seems familiar to you, but the answer does not immediately come to mind.
C. Difficult questions: The questions are complex or do not seem immediately familiar to you.

On this first pass, answer all of the easy questions as you go. Put a single mark next to the moderate questions and a double mark next to the difficult questions and move on.

Pass Two

Go through the test a second time. Work on all of the questions that you marked as moderate. If during this second reading you don't make much progress on a moderate question, mark it instead as difficult and move on.

Pass Three

Now that you have completed all of the questions that you are most likely to answer correctly, use the remaining time in the test to work on the difficult questions.

2. GENERAL STRATEGIES FOR MULTIPLE-CHOICE QUESTIONS

Multiple-choice questions tap into some general verbal comprehension skills in addition to factual, conceptual, and analytical skills. Following these strategies can help you interpret the questions effectively.

Place Your Hand Over the Answers

Each question in the GRE Psychology Test has five possible answers: the correct answer and four distractors. Wrong answers on multiple-choice tests are called "distractors" for a good reason—they're designed to look like good possible answers even though they are incorrect. Many students get truly distracted as they evaluate the possible accuracy of each of the five items. Their thinking goes off on tangents triggered by the answers. By the time they read all five, they might even forget what the question is asking!

To avoid being distracted by the distractors, try covering all five answers while you read the question "stem." Think to yourself, or even jot a quick note on scratch paper, what is the likely answer to this question? This changes your task to a true recognition task. Instead of wondering if each answer is true or not, all you have to do is find the answer that is most similar to the answer you already have in your head or in your notes.

Read Stems and Answers Together

Most students read a multiple-choice stem, and then they proceed to read each of the possible answers in turn. This runs the risk of forgetting what the stem really says by the time you get to the last answer.

Instead, try reading the stem before EACH answer to form complete sentences. If the stem says something like "Damage to the hippocampus results in reduced" followed by answers like "ability to form long-term declarative memories" or "ability to pay attention," you should read "Damage to the hippocampus results in reduced ability to form long-term declarative memories" and "Damage to the hippocampus results in reduced ability to pay attention." Evaluating complete thoughts is easier than evaluating isolated bits of thoughts.

Evaluate Writing Style

The multiple-choice questions in the GRE Psychology Test are written by college faculty members who have extensive experience in test construction. Nonetheless, they are human beings. When professors sit down to write a multiple-choice item, they have a correct answer in mind. Then they need to find the right number of reasonable-sounding wrong answers. Because the correct answer is the most salient and well thought out, it is likely to be the one that "sounds" the best. When you read the answers, the one that seems to be the best written is likely to be correct. This strategy is not too helpful when the answers are all single words (e.g., Which of the following structures participates in the evaluation of threat?), but for longer, more complex answers, this might be helpful.

Sweeping Generalizations

As advanced psychology students, you are now aware that we are rarely able to use words like *always, never, only, must, completely, totally,* or *necessarily* when describing behavior. If you see answers with these terms, they are very likely to be incorrect. At the same time, the inclusion of words such as *often, sometimes, perhaps, may,* or *generally* might indicate a very likely correct answer.

3. SHOULD I GUESS?

According to the scoring rules described earlier in the chapter, you get 1 point for every question you answer correctly, 0 points for a question you do not answer, and minus ¼ point for a question you answer incorrectly. What implications do these scoring rules have on your use of guessing?

For questions about topics you do not recognize at all, and you pick an answer at random, you would have a 20% chance of success. This probably does not justify a guess. However, if you can reject even one answer as incorrect, the rules change. For any question for which you can reject one or more options, it is probably to your advantage to guess. The more options you can reject, the better your odds of success will be. If you are trying to select among two or three potential answers, using the strategies outlined above should help narrow your choices even further.

SPECIAL SECTION ON CHANGES FROM DSM-IV TO DSM-5

As you probably know, the newest version of the *Diagnostic and Statistical Manual of Mental Disorders* or DSM-5 was published by the American Psychiatric Association in May 2013. This manual forms the backbone of study into clinical and abnormal psychology in the United States. The GRE Psychology Test has already adapted to the new criteria and labels of the DSM-5, so it is important to familiarize yourself with any changes. This is particularly important if you used a textbook for your abnormal psychology and other clinical courses that was published earlier than 2015. Most textbooks and their revisions are in the works for at least 18 months to 2 years, so it has taken time for the textbooks to become current. Hopefully, your professor was updating you in spite of any lags in your textbook, but to make sure you are current, please review this section carefully.

Because you are pursuing a graduate degree in psychology, this might be the time to invest in your own copy of the DSM-5. It is a terrific resource to have on your bookshelf. The American Psychiatric Association does a very thorough job of protecting its copyrighted materials, so do not expect to find what you need to know about DSM-5 on Wikipedia or Google books.

The following material is a summary of the chapter on "Highlights of Changes from DSM-IV to DSM-5" that is found on pages 809–816 of DSM-5. This is not meant to be an exhaustive list of changes. For the purposes of this study guide, we have focused on the changes that are particularly likely to be covered by the GRE Psychology Test. For more detail, please consult DSM-5 directly. One of the large overall changes is the abandoning of the previous multi-axial system. Note, too, that the ordering of disorders within the book has changed.

I. Neurodevelopmental Disorders

    A. *Intellectual disability* is the new term replacing *mental retardation*.

    B. Autism spectrum disorder replaces separate categories for autism, Asperger's disorder, childhood distintegrative disorder, Rett's disorder, and pervasive developmental disorder not otherwise specified. Symptoms are now divided into two domains: communication/social interaction and restricted, repetitive patterns of behavior, interests, and activities.

    C. Age factors for attention-deficit/hyperactivity disorder (ADHD) have changed; comorbid diagnosis with autism spectrum disorder is allowed; and management of subtypes has been changed.

II. Schizophrenia Spectrum and Other Psychotic Disorders

    A. Criteria A symptoms: two are now required, with one being delusions, hallucinations, or disorganized speech.

    B. Schizophrenia subtypes were replaced with a severity spectrum.

    C. Catatonia is clarified.

D. Schizoaffective disorder is reconceptualized to recognize its similarities to schizophrenia, bipolar disorder, and major depressive disorder.

III. Bipolar and Related Disorders

A. Bipolar is no longer grouped with major depressive disorder under a "mood disorders" heading, but takes this position as a "bridge" between schizophrenia and major depressive disorder.
B. Criteria changes include changes in mood and changes in activity/energy.
C. Most cases previously diagnosed as bipolar disorder in children are now likely to be diagnosed with disruptive mood dysregulation disorder.

IV. Depressive Disorders

A. The bereavement exclusion found in DSM-IV has been omitted.
B. Premenstrual dysphoric disorder has moved from the appendix of DSM-IV to this section in DSM-5.
C. Dysthymia is now referred to as persistent depressive disorder.

V. Anxiety Disorders

A. Obsessive-compulsive disorder, posttraumatic stress disorder (PTSD), and acute stress disorder are no longer grouped in this chapter.
B. Social anxiety disorder has replaced social phobia.
C. Panic disorder and agoraphobia have been unlinked.
D. Separation anxiety disorder and selective mutism are now grouped in this chapter.
E. Adults over 18 years of age are no longer required to recognize that their anxiety is unreasonable.

VI. Obsessive-Compulsive and Related Disorder: This is a new chapter that also includes hoarding disorder, trichotillomania (hair-pulling disorder), and body dysmorphic disorder.

VII. Dissociative Disorders

A. Depersonalization has been expanded by adding derealization to make derealization/depersonalization disorder.
B. Dissociative fugue is no longer a separate category, but instead is a specifier for dissociative amnesia.
C. Disruptions of identity in dissociative identity disorder can now be reported as well as observed, and gaps in recall may occur for all events, not just traumatic events.

VIII. Somatic Symptom and Related Disorders

A. Somatic symptom disorder replaces the somatoform disorder label.
B. The number of subtypes has been reduced to avoid overlap.

IX. Feeding and Eating Disorders

A. Feeding disorders of childhood are now included in this chapter.
B. The requirement of amenorrhea in anorexia nervosa was deleted.
C. A new category, binge-eating disorder, describes cases of binge eating that are not accompanied by efforts to compensate.

X. Gender Dysphoria

  A. Criteria emphasize "gender incongruence" rather than cross-gender identification.

  B. Separate criteria are provided for children, adolescents, and adults.

XI. Disruptive, Impulse-Control, and Conduct Disorders

  A. This new chapter combines oppositional defiant disorder, conduct disorder, and their variants.

  B. Antisocial personality disorder appears here and in a later chapter on personality disorders.

XII. Substance-Related and Addictive Disorders

  A. New categories have been added for gambling disorder, cannabis withdrawal, and caffeine withdrawal.

  B. Disorders are not separated into abuse and dependence categories.

XIII. Neurocognitive Disorders

  A. Dementia and amnestic disorder are now parts of major neurocognitive disorder (NCD).

  B. Mild NCD is also now recognized.

  C. New, separate criteria are added for frontotemporal NCD, NCD with Lewy bodies, and NCDs due to traumatic brain injury, substance/medication, HIV infection, prion disease, Parkinson's disease, and Huntington's disease.

XIV. Personality Disorders: Criteria for personality disorders have not been changed.

BACKGROUND RESOURCES

Many students today rent their textbooks, use e-books, or resell their textbooks after class is over. Even if your bookshelves are bare, the good news is that a small investment in background reading materials should be sufficient for your success.

Textbooks

Many of the GRE Psychology Test questions can be answered using information from a good introductory psychology textbook, such as the following:

Cacioppo, J. T., and L. A. Freberg (2016). *Discovering Psychology: The science of mind* (2nd ed.). San Francisco, CA: Cengage.

Of the topics covered on the GRE Psychology Test, the one that has the most questions but is least likely a course students have taken is sensation and perception. If your finances can stand the purchase or rental of another textbook, the following is a very solid survey of key sensation and perception topics:

Goldstein, E. B. (2013). *Sensation and Perception*. Belmont, CA: Cengage.

Whichever texts you choose to review, **do not rely on older editions**. One of the biggest recent changes in psychology was the May 2013 publication of DSM-5. The GRE Psychology Test uses DSM-5 labels and diagnostic criteria. Because it takes some time for textbook authors to prepare new editions, any books published prior to 2015 are unlikely to have the information you need to succeed. As long as you're planning to attend graduate school in psychology, you might as well invest in a copy of DSM-5. Amazon lists copies to rent at about $13 and to buy starting at $30 for a used copy.

When you are considering purchasing an introductory psychology textbook for the purpose of studying for the GRE Psychology Test, be sure to compare the table of contents and index of the textbook to the topic list above. You might find that a few topics, such as test construction, are not covered in very much detail in your introductory psychology textbook. You can augment the textbook information with a carefully selected website. Beware of Wikipedia. Although some psychology topics are covered rather well in Wikipedia, others are not. If a topic is relatively new to you, it will be difficult for you to determine whether the Wikipedia article is accurate and current.

Websites

In addition to your introductory psychology textbook(s), the following websites can provide useful background for many psychology topics.

1. **GENES TO COGNITION**

   www.g2conline.org

   This comprehensive website produced by Cold Spring Harbor Laboratory literally takes the reader from the genetic level up through advanced cognition. Included on the site are up-to-date discussions of major psychological disorders, cognitive processes, and research approaches. Best of all, the site features a 3-D brain, which can also be downloaded as a smartphone app. The 3-D brain allows you to search for structures and read brief but accurate accounts of a structure's functions and implications for health and disease.

2. **SOCIAL PSYCHOLOGY NETWORK**

   www.socialpsychology.org/social.htm

   This is another very large site, but the link above is a hub for social psychology topics. For example, if you feel like you need more information on cultural or gender psychology (which is ideally interwoven within relevant topics rather than located in standalone boxes in most introductory psychology textbooks), there is a link on this site to further reading.

3. **RESEARCH METHODS KNOWLEDGE BASE**

   www.socialresearchmethods.net/kb/index.php

   William Trochim of Cornell University has developed one of the most complete and understandable resources for mastering the basics and nuances of research design. While there is much more detail here than you will need for the GRE Psychology Test, you might want to bookmark this for your future graduate studies!

4. **ALL EVENTS IN THE TIMELINE OF THE HISTORY OF PSYCHOLOGY**

   http://resources.iupsys.net/iupsys/index.php/timeline-all

   This searchable timeline provides a convenient way to check your knowledge of important people and events in the history of psychology. It takes a more international view than that featured in most introductory psychology textbooks or the GRE Psychology Test, but this can be interesting and useful for your future graduate studies.

CHAPTER SUMMARY AND NEXT STEPS

This chapter introduced you to the basic format of the GRE Psychology Test and some strategies and resources for maximizing your success. Be sure to come back occasionally and review these materials as you continue your preparation. Hopefully, the testing process is starting to look more familiar and less uncomfortable.

Chapter 2 contains a Diagnostic Test, which is a practice version of the GRE Psychology Test. The main difference between the diagnostic and real tests is that the topic areas are clustered in the Diagnostic Test. This makes it easier to identify your strengths and weaknesses, but it also makes it easier to succeed. When items linked to the same topic are presented together, your thinking about one question is likely to help you answer similar questions, too. We do not have this luxury in the real test, however, so don't get complacent. Your results on the nondiagnostic tests in this book are likely to be more similar to the results you can expect to see on your real test.

Diagnostic Test 1 for Review Analysis

2

The purpose of this diagnostic test is to help you spot areas of weakness so that you can focus your review time and effort most efficiently. The test will have a normal GRE Test length and timing, and its area coverages will be representative. In this chapter you will familiarize yourself with the test areas and procedure while discovering where you need to do your most concentrated review.

PREPARATION FOR TAKING THE DIAGNOSTIC TEST

For best results, treat this diagnostic test as the real thing. Make a copy of the answer sheet that appears on the next page, sharpen your pencil, find a professional environment in which to work (library cubicles are not bad; avoid your favorite coffee shops), and set your timer.

Should you study before taking this test? That depends. If you think your current knowledge of some parts of psychology is a bit stale, and you might feel discouraged by a poor performance, by all means take time to do some review first. However, if you just want to jump ahead and see where you stand today, go ahead and take the test.

DO make use of the three-pass system described in Chapter 1. The more times you practice this method, the more comfortable you will be with it when it is time to take the real exam. It probably is a good idea to avoid wild guesses. If you can narrow your choices down to two answers, a guess is probably appropriate for diagnostic purposes. If you guess more liberally, you might actually succeed in an area where you really need more work.

Keep in mind that the diagnostic tests are grouped by topic, but in the real test, the topic areas will be scrambled.

About the GRE Grid Form

They landscape the first page, and you'll be cautioned to use only soft, black, No. 2 pencils.

Upper left, you'll bubble in your name.

Lower left, you'll print your name, mailing address, the test center location, and write your signature.

Across the bottom of the landscaped page, you'll print and bubble in your date of birth, social security number, registration number, title code (from the back cover of your test book), and your test name, form code, and test book serial number (also from the back cover of your test book).

The upper center and right of this page will be the bubble-in area for the first 114 questions of your test. Side 2 will be numbered from 115 to 242. Don't panic! They never use all those numbers—205 is the average. We do not put in all those spaces, but we want you to have a good sense of what you will find on the test.

One other thought before you head into the Diagnostic Test: For diagnostic ease in scoring, we group our questions by topic. The actual test will have them scrambled topically.

We do some scrambling later on, but for diagnostic purposes, we want to keep scoring ease as our priority.

ANSWER SHEET
Diagnostic Test 1

1. Ⓐ Ⓑ Ⓒ Ⓓ Ⓔ
2. Ⓐ Ⓑ Ⓒ Ⓓ Ⓔ
3. Ⓐ Ⓑ Ⓒ Ⓓ Ⓔ
4. Ⓐ Ⓑ Ⓒ Ⓓ Ⓔ
5. Ⓐ Ⓑ Ⓒ Ⓓ Ⓔ
6. Ⓐ Ⓑ Ⓒ Ⓓ Ⓔ
7. Ⓐ Ⓑ Ⓒ Ⓓ Ⓔ
8. Ⓐ Ⓑ Ⓒ Ⓓ Ⓔ
9. Ⓐ Ⓑ Ⓒ Ⓓ Ⓔ
10. Ⓐ Ⓑ Ⓒ Ⓓ Ⓔ
11. Ⓐ Ⓑ Ⓒ Ⓓ Ⓔ
12. Ⓐ Ⓑ Ⓒ Ⓓ Ⓔ
13. Ⓐ Ⓑ Ⓒ Ⓓ Ⓔ
14. Ⓐ Ⓑ Ⓒ Ⓓ Ⓔ
15. Ⓐ Ⓑ Ⓒ Ⓓ Ⓔ
16. Ⓐ Ⓑ Ⓒ Ⓓ Ⓔ
17. Ⓐ Ⓑ Ⓒ Ⓓ Ⓔ
18. Ⓐ Ⓑ Ⓒ Ⓓ Ⓔ
19. Ⓐ Ⓑ Ⓒ Ⓓ Ⓔ
20. Ⓐ Ⓑ Ⓒ Ⓓ Ⓔ
21. Ⓐ Ⓑ Ⓒ Ⓓ Ⓔ
22. Ⓐ Ⓑ Ⓒ Ⓓ Ⓔ
23. Ⓐ Ⓑ Ⓒ Ⓓ Ⓔ
24. Ⓐ Ⓑ Ⓒ Ⓓ Ⓔ
25. Ⓐ Ⓑ Ⓒ Ⓓ Ⓔ
26. Ⓐ Ⓑ Ⓒ Ⓓ Ⓔ
27. Ⓐ Ⓑ Ⓒ Ⓓ Ⓔ
28. Ⓐ Ⓑ Ⓒ Ⓓ Ⓔ
29. Ⓐ Ⓑ Ⓒ Ⓓ Ⓔ
30. Ⓐ Ⓑ Ⓒ Ⓓ Ⓔ

31. Ⓐ Ⓑ Ⓒ Ⓓ Ⓔ
32. Ⓐ Ⓑ Ⓒ Ⓓ Ⓔ
33. Ⓐ Ⓑ Ⓒ Ⓓ Ⓔ
34. Ⓐ Ⓑ Ⓒ Ⓓ Ⓔ
35. Ⓐ Ⓑ Ⓒ Ⓓ Ⓔ
36. Ⓐ Ⓑ Ⓒ Ⓓ Ⓔ
37. Ⓐ Ⓑ Ⓒ Ⓓ Ⓔ
38. Ⓐ Ⓑ Ⓒ Ⓓ Ⓔ
39. Ⓐ Ⓑ Ⓒ Ⓓ Ⓔ
40. Ⓐ Ⓑ Ⓒ Ⓓ Ⓔ
41. Ⓐ Ⓑ Ⓒ Ⓓ Ⓔ
42. Ⓐ Ⓑ Ⓒ Ⓓ Ⓔ
43. Ⓐ Ⓑ Ⓒ Ⓓ Ⓔ
44. Ⓐ Ⓑ Ⓒ Ⓓ Ⓔ
45. Ⓐ Ⓑ Ⓒ Ⓓ Ⓔ
46. Ⓐ Ⓑ Ⓒ Ⓓ Ⓔ
47. Ⓐ Ⓑ Ⓒ Ⓓ Ⓔ
48. Ⓐ Ⓑ Ⓒ Ⓓ Ⓔ
49. Ⓐ Ⓑ Ⓒ Ⓓ Ⓔ
50. Ⓐ Ⓑ Ⓒ Ⓓ Ⓔ
51. Ⓐ Ⓑ Ⓒ Ⓓ Ⓔ
52. Ⓐ Ⓑ Ⓒ Ⓓ Ⓔ
53. Ⓐ Ⓑ Ⓒ Ⓓ Ⓔ
54. Ⓐ Ⓑ Ⓒ Ⓓ Ⓔ
55. Ⓐ Ⓑ Ⓒ Ⓓ Ⓔ
56. Ⓐ Ⓑ Ⓒ Ⓓ Ⓔ
57. Ⓐ Ⓑ Ⓒ Ⓓ Ⓔ
58. Ⓐ Ⓑ Ⓒ Ⓓ Ⓔ
59. Ⓐ Ⓑ Ⓒ Ⓓ Ⓔ
60. Ⓐ Ⓑ Ⓒ Ⓓ Ⓔ

61. Ⓐ Ⓑ Ⓒ Ⓓ Ⓔ
62. Ⓐ Ⓑ Ⓒ Ⓓ Ⓔ
63. Ⓐ Ⓑ Ⓒ Ⓓ Ⓔ
64. Ⓐ Ⓑ Ⓒ Ⓓ Ⓔ
65. Ⓐ Ⓑ Ⓒ Ⓓ Ⓔ
66. Ⓐ Ⓑ Ⓒ Ⓓ Ⓔ
67. Ⓐ Ⓑ Ⓒ Ⓓ Ⓔ
68. Ⓐ Ⓑ Ⓒ Ⓓ Ⓔ
69. Ⓐ Ⓑ Ⓒ Ⓓ Ⓔ
70. Ⓐ Ⓑ Ⓒ Ⓓ Ⓔ
71. Ⓐ Ⓑ Ⓒ Ⓓ Ⓔ
72. Ⓐ Ⓑ Ⓒ Ⓓ Ⓔ
73. Ⓐ Ⓑ Ⓒ Ⓓ Ⓔ
74. Ⓐ Ⓑ Ⓒ Ⓓ Ⓔ
75. Ⓐ Ⓑ Ⓒ Ⓓ Ⓔ
76. Ⓐ Ⓑ Ⓒ Ⓓ Ⓔ
77. Ⓐ Ⓑ Ⓒ Ⓓ Ⓔ
78. Ⓐ Ⓑ Ⓒ Ⓓ Ⓔ
79. Ⓐ Ⓑ Ⓒ Ⓓ Ⓔ
80. Ⓐ Ⓑ Ⓒ Ⓓ Ⓔ
81. Ⓐ Ⓑ Ⓒ Ⓓ Ⓔ
82. Ⓐ Ⓑ Ⓒ Ⓓ Ⓔ
83. Ⓐ Ⓑ Ⓒ Ⓓ Ⓔ
84. Ⓐ Ⓑ Ⓒ Ⓓ Ⓔ
85. Ⓐ Ⓑ Ⓒ Ⓓ Ⓔ
86. Ⓐ Ⓑ Ⓒ Ⓓ Ⓔ
87. Ⓐ Ⓑ Ⓒ Ⓓ Ⓔ
88. Ⓐ Ⓑ Ⓒ Ⓓ Ⓔ
89. Ⓐ Ⓑ Ⓒ Ⓓ Ⓔ
90. Ⓐ Ⓑ Ⓒ Ⓓ Ⓔ

91. Ⓐ Ⓑ Ⓒ Ⓓ Ⓔ
92. Ⓐ Ⓑ Ⓒ Ⓓ Ⓔ
93. Ⓐ Ⓑ Ⓒ Ⓓ Ⓔ
94. Ⓐ Ⓑ Ⓒ Ⓓ Ⓔ
95. Ⓐ Ⓑ Ⓒ Ⓓ Ⓔ
96. Ⓐ Ⓑ Ⓒ Ⓓ Ⓔ
97. Ⓐ Ⓑ Ⓒ Ⓓ Ⓔ
98. Ⓐ Ⓑ Ⓒ Ⓓ Ⓔ
99. Ⓐ Ⓑ Ⓒ Ⓓ Ⓔ
100. Ⓐ Ⓑ Ⓒ Ⓓ Ⓔ
101. Ⓐ Ⓑ Ⓒ Ⓓ Ⓔ
102. Ⓐ Ⓑ Ⓒ Ⓓ Ⓔ
103. Ⓐ Ⓑ Ⓒ Ⓓ Ⓔ
104. Ⓐ Ⓑ Ⓒ Ⓓ Ⓔ
105. Ⓐ Ⓑ Ⓒ Ⓓ Ⓔ
106. Ⓐ Ⓑ Ⓒ Ⓓ Ⓔ
107. Ⓐ Ⓑ Ⓒ Ⓓ Ⓔ
108. Ⓐ Ⓑ Ⓒ Ⓓ Ⓔ
109. Ⓐ Ⓑ Ⓒ Ⓓ Ⓔ
110. Ⓐ Ⓑ Ⓒ Ⓓ Ⓔ
111. Ⓐ Ⓑ Ⓒ Ⓓ Ⓔ
112. Ⓐ Ⓑ Ⓒ Ⓓ Ⓔ
113. Ⓐ Ⓑ Ⓒ Ⓓ Ⓔ
114. Ⓐ Ⓑ Ⓒ Ⓓ Ⓔ
115. Ⓐ Ⓑ Ⓒ Ⓓ Ⓔ
116. Ⓐ Ⓑ Ⓒ Ⓓ Ⓔ
117. Ⓐ Ⓑ Ⓒ Ⓓ Ⓔ
118. Ⓐ Ⓑ Ⓒ Ⓓ Ⓔ
119. Ⓐ Ⓑ Ⓒ Ⓓ Ⓔ
120. Ⓐ Ⓑ Ⓒ Ⓓ Ⓔ

ANSWER SHEET
Diagnostic Test 1

121. Ⓐ Ⓑ Ⓒ Ⓓ Ⓔ
122. Ⓐ Ⓑ Ⓒ Ⓓ Ⓔ
123. Ⓐ Ⓑ Ⓒ Ⓓ Ⓔ
124. Ⓐ Ⓑ Ⓒ Ⓓ Ⓔ
125. Ⓐ Ⓑ Ⓒ Ⓓ Ⓔ
126. Ⓐ Ⓑ Ⓒ Ⓓ Ⓔ
127. Ⓐ Ⓑ Ⓒ Ⓓ Ⓔ
128. Ⓐ Ⓑ Ⓒ Ⓓ Ⓔ
129. Ⓐ Ⓑ Ⓒ Ⓓ Ⓔ
130. Ⓐ Ⓑ Ⓒ Ⓓ Ⓔ
131. Ⓐ Ⓑ Ⓒ Ⓓ Ⓔ
132. Ⓐ Ⓑ Ⓒ Ⓓ Ⓔ
133. Ⓐ Ⓑ Ⓒ Ⓓ Ⓔ
134. Ⓐ Ⓑ Ⓒ Ⓓ Ⓔ
135. Ⓐ Ⓑ Ⓒ Ⓓ Ⓔ
136. Ⓐ Ⓑ Ⓒ Ⓓ Ⓔ
137. Ⓐ Ⓑ Ⓒ Ⓓ Ⓔ
138. Ⓐ Ⓑ Ⓒ Ⓓ Ⓔ
139. Ⓐ Ⓑ Ⓒ Ⓓ Ⓔ
140. Ⓐ Ⓑ Ⓒ Ⓓ Ⓔ
141. Ⓐ Ⓑ Ⓒ Ⓓ Ⓔ
142. Ⓐ Ⓑ Ⓒ Ⓓ Ⓔ

143. Ⓐ Ⓑ Ⓒ Ⓓ Ⓔ
144. Ⓐ Ⓑ Ⓒ Ⓓ Ⓔ
145. Ⓐ Ⓑ Ⓒ Ⓓ Ⓔ
146. Ⓐ Ⓑ Ⓒ Ⓓ Ⓔ
147. Ⓐ Ⓑ Ⓒ Ⓓ Ⓔ
148. Ⓐ Ⓑ Ⓒ Ⓓ Ⓔ
149. Ⓐ Ⓑ Ⓒ Ⓓ Ⓔ
150. Ⓐ Ⓑ Ⓒ Ⓓ Ⓔ
151. Ⓐ Ⓑ Ⓒ Ⓓ Ⓔ
152. Ⓐ Ⓑ Ⓒ Ⓓ Ⓔ
153. Ⓐ Ⓑ Ⓒ Ⓓ Ⓔ
154. Ⓐ Ⓑ Ⓒ Ⓓ Ⓔ
155. Ⓐ Ⓑ Ⓒ Ⓓ Ⓔ
156. Ⓐ Ⓑ Ⓒ Ⓓ Ⓔ
157. Ⓐ Ⓑ Ⓒ Ⓓ Ⓔ
158. Ⓐ Ⓑ Ⓒ Ⓓ Ⓔ
159. Ⓐ Ⓑ Ⓒ Ⓓ Ⓔ
160. Ⓐ Ⓑ Ⓒ Ⓓ Ⓔ
161. Ⓐ Ⓑ Ⓒ Ⓓ Ⓔ
162. Ⓐ Ⓑ Ⓒ Ⓓ Ⓔ
163. Ⓐ Ⓑ Ⓒ Ⓓ Ⓔ
164. Ⓐ Ⓑ Ⓒ Ⓓ Ⓔ

165. Ⓐ Ⓑ Ⓒ Ⓓ Ⓔ
166. Ⓐ Ⓑ Ⓒ Ⓓ Ⓔ
167. Ⓐ Ⓑ Ⓒ Ⓓ Ⓔ
168. Ⓐ Ⓑ Ⓒ Ⓓ Ⓔ
169. Ⓐ Ⓑ Ⓒ Ⓓ Ⓔ
170. Ⓐ Ⓑ Ⓒ Ⓓ Ⓔ
171. Ⓐ Ⓑ Ⓒ Ⓓ Ⓔ
172. Ⓐ Ⓑ Ⓒ Ⓓ Ⓔ
173. Ⓐ Ⓑ Ⓒ Ⓓ Ⓔ
174. Ⓐ Ⓑ Ⓒ Ⓓ Ⓔ
175. Ⓐ Ⓑ Ⓒ Ⓓ Ⓔ
176. Ⓐ Ⓑ Ⓒ Ⓓ Ⓔ
177. Ⓐ Ⓑ Ⓒ Ⓓ Ⓔ
178. Ⓐ Ⓑ Ⓒ Ⓓ Ⓔ
179. Ⓐ Ⓑ Ⓒ Ⓓ Ⓔ
180. Ⓐ Ⓑ Ⓒ Ⓓ Ⓔ
181. Ⓐ Ⓑ Ⓒ Ⓓ Ⓔ
182. Ⓐ Ⓑ Ⓒ Ⓓ Ⓔ
183. Ⓐ Ⓑ Ⓒ Ⓓ Ⓔ
184. Ⓐ Ⓑ Ⓒ Ⓓ Ⓔ
185. Ⓐ Ⓑ Ⓒ Ⓓ Ⓔ
186. Ⓐ Ⓑ Ⓒ Ⓓ Ⓔ

187. Ⓐ Ⓑ Ⓒ Ⓓ Ⓔ
188. Ⓐ Ⓑ Ⓒ Ⓓ Ⓔ
189. Ⓐ Ⓑ Ⓒ Ⓓ Ⓔ
190. Ⓐ Ⓑ Ⓒ Ⓓ Ⓔ
191. Ⓐ Ⓑ Ⓒ Ⓓ Ⓔ
192. Ⓐ Ⓑ Ⓒ Ⓓ Ⓔ
193. Ⓐ Ⓑ Ⓒ Ⓓ Ⓔ
194. Ⓐ Ⓑ Ⓒ Ⓓ Ⓔ
195. Ⓐ Ⓑ Ⓒ Ⓓ Ⓔ
196. Ⓐ Ⓑ Ⓒ Ⓓ Ⓔ
197. Ⓐ Ⓑ Ⓒ Ⓓ Ⓔ
198. Ⓐ Ⓑ Ⓒ Ⓓ Ⓔ
199. Ⓐ Ⓑ Ⓒ Ⓓ Ⓔ
200. Ⓐ Ⓑ Ⓒ Ⓓ Ⓔ
201. Ⓐ Ⓑ Ⓒ Ⓓ Ⓔ
202. Ⓐ Ⓑ Ⓒ Ⓓ Ⓔ
203. Ⓐ Ⓑ Ⓒ Ⓓ Ⓔ
204. Ⓐ Ⓑ Ⓒ Ⓓ Ⓔ
205. Ⓐ Ⓑ Ⓒ Ⓓ Ⓔ

DIAGNOSTIC TEST 1

TIME: 170 MINUTES
205 QUESTIONS

> **Directions:** Each of the questions or incomplete statements below is followed by five suggested answers or completions. Select the one that is best in each case and then fill in the corresponding space on the answer sheet.

QUESTIONS 1–7, LEARNING

1. In one experiment, pigeons were rewarded with food every 15 seconds regardless of their behavior. At the end of the hour, one pigeon was observed to bob its head more frequently than at the beginning of the session and another pigeon flapped its wings more frequently. Which of the following phenomena is responsible for these changes in behavior?

    (A) generalization
    (B) superstitious behavior
    (C) discrimination
    (D) classical conditioning
    (E) modeling

2. Two groups of rats are exposed to a flashing light followed by an electric shock. Rats usually respond to electric shock by freezing. In the first group, no shock occurs unless it is immediately preceded by the light. In the second group, lights are always followed by shock, but some shocks occur in the absence of light. Which of the following describes what will happen after training when both groups of rats are shown a test trial consisting of the flashing light without a shock?

    (A) The first group of rats will be more likely to freeze than the second group of rats, because the flashing light was a better predictor of shock for that group.
    (B) The second group of rats will be more likely to freeze than the first group of rats, because the flashing light was a better predictor of shock for that group.
    (C) The two groups of rats will be equally likely to freeze, because both experienced flashing lights that preceded shocks.
    (D) Neither group of rats will freeze, because the temporal contiguity between the light and shock are equal for both groups.
    (E) The first group of rats will be more likely to freeze than the second group, because the temporal contiguity between the flashing light and shock is less for the first than the second group.

GO ON TO THE NEXT PAGE

3. A new theory of personality development and change suggests that people's expression of personality traits such as extraversion/intraversion is influenced by the feedback they obtain from peers. This theory is closest to the work of which of the following individuals?

(A) Sigmund Freud
(B) B. F. Skinner
(C) Ivan Pavlov
(D) Carl Rogers
(E) Abraham Maslow

4. Which of the following is an example of a fixed-action pattern?

(A) A cat runs into the kitchen upon hearing the sound of the can opener.
(B) Following a large earthquake, people are more jumpy in response to loud noises.
(C) A person is less disturbed by unfamiliar city noises during the second night spent in a hotel than during the first.
(D) A baby goose emerging from its shell follows the first object it sees.
(E) A person stops eating peanut butter after becoming ill while consuming peanut butter cookies.

5. A parent frustrated with a teen's messy room declares that unless the room is clean by the start of the weekend, the teen will not be allowed to go out with friends. Which type of consequence is the parent applying?

(A) positive reinforcement
(B) negative reinforcement
(C) positive punishment
(D) negative punishment
(E) shaping

6. An obstetrician working for a large medical practice receives a standard fee for every caesarean section that is performed. Which of the following schedules of reinforcement best describes this payment system?

(A) continuous reinforcement
(B) fixed ratio schedule
(C) variable ratio schedule
(D) fixed interval schedule
(E) variable interval schedule

GO ON TO THE NEXT PAGE

7. Some individuals faint at the sight of blood, and must be restrained during regular blood tests to avoid injury. Which of the following best explains the role of classical conditioning in this situation?

(A) The sight of blood has taken on the role of a conditioned stimulus for distress.
(B) The pain resulting from being stuck with a needle becomes a conditioned stimulus for distress.
(C) Fainting is an unconditioned stimulus that signals pain.
(D) The sight of blood becomes a conditioned response to fainting.
(E) The sight of blood becomes an unconditioned response to pain.

QUESTIONS 8–13, LANGUAGE

8. Which of the following types of words are most likely to be among the first fifty words used by young language learners?

(A) words describing common objects in their environment
(B) words that are used frequently by their parents
(C) words that describe their internal mental states, such as "I'm feeling sad"
(D) words that describe the past or future rather than the present
(E) no observable trends in the type of words used by young language learners have been established; the process appears to be random

9. English speakers say "the brown dog," while Spanish speakers say "the dog brown" (el perro marrón). Which of the following language terms refers to this difference?

(A) morphemes
(B) phonemes
(C) syntax
(D) semantics
(E) linguistics

10. Individuals with autism spectrum disorder often experience communication difficulties, including problems with pragmatics. Which of the following statements illustrates the pragmatics of language?

(A) taking turns during a conversation
(B) producing clear speech sounds, so that a listener can distinguish similar-sounding words
(C) using word endings appropriately to designate plurals and past tenses
(D) using words in the correct order in a sentence
(E) using the correct vocabulary word to express a thought

GO ON TO THE NEXT PAGE

11. How many phonemes are in the word *cat*?

    (A) none
    (B) one
    (C) two
    (D) three
    (E) four

12. Which of the following statements is consistent with Benjamin Lee Whorf's hypothesis of linguistic relativity?

    (A) A critical mutation in the *FOX-P2* gene is responsible for human speech.
    (B) The number of phonemes in a language decreases with distance from Africa along human migratory pathways.
    (C) Children learn more language in face-to-face situations than they do from screen time (television, tablets, etc.).
    (D) Multilingual individuals appear to enjoy more cognitive reserve in old age.
    (E) A psychology student who understands more key terms in psychology is better prepared to think about the results of psychological research.

13. Paul Broca's autopsy of Louis Leborgne, known as "Patient Tan," demonstrated damage in which of the following areas?

    (A) an area of secondary motor cortex known to be involved with language production
    (B) an area adjacent to the primary auditory cortex known to be involved with language comprehension
    (C) a pathway connecting the visual cortical areas of the occipital lobe with the auditory cortex in the temporal lobe
    (D) a pathway connecting speech comprehension areas to speech production areas of the brain
    (E) a pathway connecting areas of the brain involved in language to areas involved with semantic memories

QUESTIONS 14–32, MEMORY

14. Which of the following is an example of a recognition test of memory?

    (A) "How do you define the term *mode*?"
    (B) "Is this one of the words that you read in the list I just showed to you?"
    (C) "Can you list the cranial nerves in order?"
    (D) "In the list I just showed you, which words began with the letter *b*?"
    (E) "What did you do last weekend?"

GO ON TO THE NEXT PAGE

15. The following experiment uses two groups of participants. The first group studied two lists of words, each for 3 minutes. The second group worked on a crossword puzzle for 3 minutes then studied the second list of words for 3 minutes. Which of the following describes the likely results of this experiment?

(A) Both groups would perform similarly on the second list.
(B) The first group would recall more words than the second group due to anterograde interference.
(C) The second group would recall more words than the first group due to anterograde interference.
(D) The first group would recall more words than the second group due to retrograde interference.
(E) The second group would recall more words than the first group due to retrograde interference.

16. Which of the following is an example of an episodic memory?

(A) remembering what you ate for breakfast
(B) remembering the capital city of California
(C) remembering how to troubleshoot a problem with word processing software
(D) remembering the name of the city in which you were born
(E) remembering the name of your fourth-grade teacher

17. According to information processing models of memory, which part of the memory system is characterized by a very large capacity for data, yet very short durations of memory storage?

(A) sensory memory
(B) short-term memory
(C) working memory
(D) procedural memory
(E) long-term memory

18. Which of the following is an example of a stimulus that would probably be held in memory as a haptic code?

(A) the characteristic sound of a friend's voice
(B) the feel of a cat's fur when you pet it
(C) the sight of your "name" that you wrote using a sparkler at a fireworks display
(D) the memory of the first few notes of the introduction to your favorite song
(E) the meaning of a vocabulary word you are trying to learn in a language class

GO ON TO THE NEXT PAGE

19. While reaching for her phone, a student repeats the phone number her friend just told her. The student is using which of the following memory strategies?

    (A) chunking
    (B) consolidation
    (C) maintenance rehearsal
    (D) elaborative rehearsal
    (E) priming

20. Will is studying for a neuroanatomy test by breaking long-structure names, like the ventromedial hypothalamus, into bits that he recognizes: ventral, medial, hypo, thalamus. Will is using which of the following memory strategies?

    (A) chunking
    (B) consolidation
    (C) maintenance rehearsal
    (D) elaborative rehearsal
    (E) priming

21. Which of the following is *not* a part of working memory as proposed by Alan Baddeley and his colleagues?

    (A) central executive
    (B) visuospatial sketch pad
    (C) phonological loop
    (D) semantic memory
    (E) episodic buffer

22. In information processing models of memory, which type of memory features virtually unlimited duration and unlimited capacity?

    (A) sensory memory
    (B) working memory
    (C) short-term memory
    (D) procedural memory
    (E) long-term memory

23. According to levels of processing theory, which of the following is an example of shallow processing?

    (A) using a vocabulary word in a sentence
    (B) considering how a vocabulary word describes a personal experience
    (C) observing how many syllables a vocabulary word has
    (D) thinking of how many meanings a vocabulary word has
    (E) remembering when you first learned a vocabulary word

GO ON TO THE NEXT PAGE

24. Richard's roommates call him while he's just about to order pizza to tell him which items they want (mushrooms, pepperoni, bell peppers, pineapple, sausage), but Richard did not write them down because he is proud of his good memory. According to research on the serial position curve, which of the following ingredients is Richard most likely to remember?

(A) mushrooms and sausage
(B) mushrooms and pepperoni
(C) pineapple and sausage
(D) bell peppers and pineapple
(E) pepperoni, bell peppers, and pineapple

25. Which of the following is an example of a declarative memory?

(A) a classically conditioned taste aversion
(B) a trial that indicates priming on a lexical decision task
(C) the ability to remember how to ice skate in spite of not having done this for years
(D) the ability to define the term *conditioned stimulus*
(E) the ability to drive a car with a manual transmission

26. Which of the following types of memory is organized as a timeline?

(A) procedural memory
(B) episodic memory
(C) semantic memory
(D) implicit memory
(E) nondeclarative memory

27. People with a rare condition known as hyperthymesia demonstrate which of the following behaviors?

(A) They are unable to learn new procedural memories, although other types of memories are intact.
(B) They retain memories from childhood, but are unable to form new memories.
(C) They retain the ability to complete difficult visuospatial puzzles, but are unable to learn new vocabulary words.
(D) They are unable to remember their own identities.
(E) They form highly detailed episodic memories.

GO ON TO THE NEXT PAGE

28. Anna has had a lifetime of alcohol abuse, which her physicians note has resulted in bilateral damage to the hippocampus in both hemispheres. Which of the following describes a likely symptom of Anna's condition?

(A) She experiences few memory problems, but her balance and coordination are impaired.

(B) She can remember her childhood, but has difficulty learning new facts, such as current events.

(C) She can remember current information, but is unable to remember much about her childhood.

(D) She can solve visuospatial puzzles, but struggles to learn the names of people she meets.

(E) She can achieve high scores on explicit tests of memory, but her performance on implicit tests of memory is impaired.

29. Tom smokes while he studies, but obviously, he is not allowed to smoke while taking his exams. Which of the following is the most likely result of Tom's habits on his test performance?

(A) His test performance will be better than if he smoked during exams, because nicotine interferes with memory retrieval.

(B) His test performance will be worse than if he smoked during exams due to context-specific memory effects.

(C) His test performance will be worse than if he smoked during exams due to the effects of spreading activation.

(D) His test performance will be worse than if he smoked during exams due to anterograde interference.

(E) His test performance will not be affected.

30. Which of the following is the most accurate statement regarding eyewitness testimony?

(A) Preliminary testimony is usually improved during follow-up questioning.

(B) Attorneys can influence eyewitness accounts by using particular wordings.

(C) Hypnosis improves eyewitness recall and testimony.

(D) Errors do not occur in eyewitness testimony unless the eyewitness is intentionally changing an account.

(E) Eyewitness testimony is almost always accurate and reliable.

31. Dr. Martinez wants to assess how many vocabulary words his advanced Spanish students recalled following the winter break. Which of the following methods would give him the most accurate results?

(A) a savings test

(B) a recognition test

(C) a matching test

(D) an essay test requiring use of the vocabulary words

(E) a fill-in-the-blanks test

GO ON TO THE NEXT PAGE

32. Anthony is legally required to send child support checks to his ex-wife, a task that he finds upsetting. He often forgets to send the checks on time. Which of the following is the most likely reason for Anthony's forgetfulness?

(A) retroactive interference
(B) proactive interference
(C) confabulation
(D) motivated forgetting
(E) decay

QUESTIONS 33–43, THINKING

33. When considering the roots of aggression in children, a cognitive psychologist would most likely agree with which of the following statements?

(A) Children identify with their same-sex parent and adopt the level of aggression expressed by him or her.
(B) Children are reinforced for displaying certain levels of aggression.
(C) Children learn to be aggressive by observing other people or media.
(D) Children conform to their schemas related to appropriate levels of aggression.
(E) Children's aggression is heavily influenced by their genotypes.

34. Which of the following is *not* a feature of a parallel distributed processing (PDP) model such as that proposed by Rumelhart, Hinton, and McClelland (1986)?

(A) Each unit has an output function.
(B) Units are isolated from the network and can operate independently.
(C) The system operates within an environment.
(D) Rules govern the propagation of activity through a network.
(E) The system has a current state of activation.

35. Which of the following represents an example of a mental representation?

(A) Alexandra can name the friends who attended her last birthday party.
(B) Jasmine views the pathway to the nearest coffee shop on her map app.
(C) Madison enjoys the taste of her ice cream.
(D) Allison studies the features of a van Gogh painting very carefully for her art history exam.
(E) Chelsea paints a unicorn for her niece's bedroom.

36. When hearing the word *cat*, Daniel immediately thinks of the large, orange cat named Tommy that he had as a child. Tommy serves as which of the following for Daniel's concept of cat?

(A) a prototype
(B) an exemplar
(C) a model
(D) a schema
(E) a template

GO ON TO THE NEXT PAGE

37. Research participants respond more quickly to the question "Is an apple a fruit?" than they do to the question "Is an avocado a fruit?" This is most likely due to which of the following?

    (A) Avocados are not, in fact, fruits.
    (B) Apples are closer to a prototypical fruit than avocados are.
    (C) Avocados are more likely to be exemplar fruits than apples are.
    (D) Apples have more overlapping characteristics with a fruit concept than avocados do.
    (E) Avocados are closer to prototypical vegetables than apples are.

38. Michelle comes to her introductory psychology class the first day and sees a young woman dressed in jeans and a sweatshirt at the front of the class. She assumes that the young woman is another student, and is surprised when the woman stands up at the start of class and introduces herself as Dr. Lawrence, their professor. Michelle's confusion is most likely due to the differences she sees between Dr. Lawrence and the "average" of professors she has taken courses from in the past. Which of the following terms most precisely refers to Michelle's "average professor" way of thinking?

    (A) exemplar
    (B) schema
    (C) feature detector
    (D) prototype
    (E) mental representation

39. Which of the following represent the four steps of problem solving in their correct order?

    (A) understand the problem, plan, carry out the plan, evaluate the plan
    (B) plan, carry out the plan, evaluate the problem, understand the problem
    (C) plan, define the problem, understand the problem, evaluate the problem
    (D) research options, identify an algorithm, carry out the algorithm, evaluate the plan
    (E) plan, define the problem, evaluate the plan, carry out the plan

40. Brandon is concerned about his weight gain over the last term, and he believes becoming more physically active could solve his problem. However, he has never been athletic, so he does not believe that he would be capable of sticking to a workout plan. Brandon's evaluation is best described as a problem with which of the following?

    (A) framing a problem
    (B) defining a problem
    (C) generating solutions
    (D) self-efficacy
    (E) evaluating a problem

GO ON TO THE NEXT PAGE

41. Rachel is having difficulty with her statistical software package license, and her data analysis is due the next day. Her roommate suggests that she add the statistics package into her Excel program, which would allow her to complete the same analyses as her statistical software. Rachel rejects the suggestion, though, because she believes that Excel is only good for recording data, not conducting statistical analyses. Rachel's attitudes reflect which of the following?

    (A) the availability heuristic
    (B) the representativeness heuristic
    (C) functional fixedness
    (D) the use of algorithms
    (E) the recognition heuristic

42. Zach is making a difficult choice between two cars that he really likes. Finally, he chooses one that he tells his friend is "just cooler" than the other. Zach is most likely using which of the following strategies?

    (A) the availability heuristic
    (B) the recognition heuristic
    (C) the representativeness heuristic
    (D) utility theory
    (E) the affect heuristic

43. Dr. Walsh tells Lucy that her new medication is likely to help 75% of patients. He tells Martha that 25% of patients taking the drug experience no benefits. Lucy fills her prescription, but Martha does not. This situation is an example of which of the following?

    (A) the affect heuristic
    (B) utility theory
    (C) a framing effect
    (D) a cost-benefit analysis
    (E) the recognition heuristic

QUESTIONS 44–55, SENSATION AND PERCEPTION

44. A person who is unable to recognize faces is likely to be diagnosed with which of the following disorders?

    (A) Wernicke's aphasia
    (B) Rasmussen's syndrome
    (C) Prosopagnosia
    (D) Akinetopsia
    (E) Neglect syndrome

GO ON TO THE NEXT PAGE

45. Two radiologists are reviewing mammograms and identifying those that require follow-up testing. Although the radiologists have very different hit rates and false alarm rates, their d' scores are identical. What can we conclude about the relative sensitivity of these two physicians to potential problems in mammograms?

   (A) We cannot conclude anything because d' is not relevant to sensitivity.
   (B) We can conclude that the physician with the higher hit rate is more sensitive.
   (C) We can conclude that the physician with the lower false alarm rate is more sensitive.
   (D) Because d' allows us to judge sensitivity, we can conclude that both physicians are equally sensitive.
   (E) Although d' gives us a starting place to judge sensitivity, we need the physicians' ROC curves as well to make an accurate conclusion.

46. Which of the following sensory systems rely on the movement of hair cells to transduce information?

   (A) the visual and tactile systems
   (B) the gustatory and visual systems
   (C) the tactile and olfactory systems
   (D) the auditory and tactile systems
   (E) the auditory and vestibular systems

47. A novice stargazer was having difficulty finding a dim star on a dark, moonless night. Her mentor suggested that she focus her vision slightly to the side of the coordinates where the star was expected to appear. Why is this likely to be a successful strategy?

   (A) By looking to the side, the stargazer is focusing dim light on her rods rather than her cones, and rods are much more sensitive than cones to dim light.
   (B) By moving her focus, the stargazer is readjusting her criteria for reporting a signal.
   (C) By looking to the side, the stargazer is focusing dim light on her cones instead of her rods, and the greater acuity made possible by the cones will help her find a small star.
   (D) This strategy is actually an ineffective urban myth, but the greater confidence produced by using a strategy suggested by a trusted mentor might help the stargazer see her target.
   (E) Looking to the side results in more visual input being transmitted to a single hemisphere, enhancing visual processing.

48. What information is provided by a comparison of arrival times of sounds at the two ears?

   (A) equal loudness contours
   (B) difference thresholds
   (C) pitch
   (D) the location of a sound source
   (E) the distance of a sound source

GO ON TO THE NEXT PAGE

49. You are much faster at recognizing your friend in the crowd outside a coffee shop if you expected to meet her there than if it is a chance meeting. This experience illustrates which of the following concepts?

(A) bottom-up processing
(B) top-down processing
(C) Weber's law
(D) simultaneous contrast
(E) interposition

50. Phantom pain following the amputation of a limb probably results from which of the following?

(A) a distortion in the gate control of pain
(B) a depletion in substance P in the spinal cord due to the amputation
(C) an increase in the number of neurons responding to the now-missing limb
(D) the need for the brain to reorganize its representation of the body following amputation
(E) posttraumatic stress disorder due to the amputation

51. The process of transforming information from the environment, such as light energy, into signals processed by the nervous system is known as

(A) refraction
(B) transduction
(C) reduction
(D) construction
(E) signal detection

52. Which of the following does Stevens's power law describe?

(A) the relationship between the magnitude of a physical stimulus and its perceived intensity
(B) the relationship between attention span and reaction time
(C) the ratio of hits to misses in signal detection
(D) the absolute threshold for a stimulus
(E) the difference threshold between two stimuli

53. The human sensory homunculus

(A) is nearly identical to those of other mammals
(B) emphasizes the processing of information from the torso, arms, and legs
(C) emphasizes the processing information from the hands and face
(D) becomes "fixed" or relatively unchangeable during infancy
(E) matches the amount of cortical area used to process a body part to the relative size of the body part

GO ON TO THE NEXT PAGE

54. Dr. Wills is conducting a single-cell recording experiment of a center-on surround-off retinal ganglion cell while shining various lights on a screen. Dr. Wills observes that the lowest rate of responding occurs under which of the following circumstances?

(A) A light fills about 25% of the center.
(B) A light fills the entire center but covers none of the surround.
(C) A light fills the entire center and about 25% of the surround.
(D) A light fills both center and surround completely.
(E) A light fills the surround but none of the center.

55. Eagles have cones but no rods in their retinas. Which of the following describes the implication of this fact for eagle vision?

(A) Eagles should see equally well in bright and dim light conditions.
(B) Eagles cannot see color.
(C) Eagles should be especially sensitive to the movement of prey.
(D) Eagles should see color and fine detail, but only under very bright light conditions.
(E) Eagles should see well in dim light, but only if a stimulus is focused onto the periphery of the retina.

QUESTIONS 56–81, PHYSIOLOGICAL/BEHAVIORAL NEUROSCIENCE

56. Selective serotonin reuptake inhibitors (SSRIs) block the reuptake of serotonin. Which of the following is the most likely immediate outcome of SSRIs?

(A) Production of serotonin will increase.
(B) Production of serotonin will decrease.
(C) The effects of serotonin in the synapse will be prolonged.
(D) Storage of serotonin in vesicles will be less efficient.
(E) More serotonin will be released in response to each action potential.

57. Parkinson's disease, which is a movement disorder characterized by difficult initiation of voluntary movement, results most directly from which of the following?

(A) a degeneration of substantia nigra, leading to fewer signals reaching the basal ganglia
(B) a degeneration of the basal ganglia, leading to fewer signals reaching the motor cortex
(C) a degeneration of the substantia nigra, leading to fewer signals reaching the alpha motor neurons of the spinal cord
(D) an overactivity in the basal ganglia, leading to tremors that interfere with smooth, voluntary movement
(E) an overactivity of the substantia nigra, leading to greater inhibition in the basal ganglia

GO ON TO THE NEXT PAGE

58. Which part of the nervous system is primarily responsible for telling your heart to speed up as you climb a hill?

(A) somatic nervous system
(B) enteric nervous system
(C) autonomic nervous system
(D) limbic system
(E) default mode network

59. Where does saltatory conduction take place?

(A) along the length of an unmyelinated axon
(B) along the length of a myelinated axon
(C) across the synaptic gap separating two neurons
(D) at gap junctions
(E) from the farthest reaches of the dendrites to the axon hillock

60. Damage to which of the following structures is associated with difficulties in learning and managing emotional responses, particularly in the case of negative events?

(A) hypothalamus
(B) mammillary bodies
(C) hippocampus
(D) amygdala
(E) cingulate gyrus

61. Which of the following serves as insulating material on some axons?

(A) dendrite
(B) myelin
(C) mitochondrion
(D) soma
(E) axon

62. A new drug produces changes in activity at the neuromuscular junction in skeletal muscles. With which of the following neurochemical systems is the new drug most likely to interact?

(A) dopamine
(B) norepinephrine
(C) glutamate
(D) acetylcholine
(E) serotonin

GO ON TO THE NEXT PAGE

63. Which of the following imaging technologies would allow a cognitive neuroscientist to observe brain activity associated with decision making?

(A) positron emission tomography (PET) or computerized tomography (CT) scans

(B) positron emission tomography (PET) or repeated transcranial magnetic stimulation (rTMS)

(C) positron emission tomography (PET) or functional magnetic resonance imaging (fMRI) scans

(D) computerized tomography (CT) or functional magnetic resonance imaging (fMRI) scans

(E) functional magnetic resonance imaging (fMRI) or repeated transcranial magnetic stimulation (rTMS) scans

64. Bilateral damage to the hippocampus is most likely to result in which of the following memory problems?

(A) difficulty encoding new declarative memories

(B) difficulty retrieving childhood memories

(C) difficulty learning new procedural memories

(D) difficulty forming classically conditioned associations

(E) difficulty performing a priming task successfully

65. Adult neurogenesis, or the growth of new neurons in the adult

(A) does not occur in the brain of mammals

(B) occurs throughout the adult brain of mammals

(C) results in new neurons in the olfactory bulbs and hippocampus

(D) results in new neurons in the cerebral cortex

(E) results in new neurons in the amygdala and thalamus

66. The "rise" phase of an action potential results from which of the following?

(A) Sodium ions move into the neuron.

(B) Potassium ions move out of the neuron.

(C) Calcium ions move into the neuron.

(D) Potassium ions move into the neuron.

(E) Sodium ions move out of the neuron.

67. Damage to which of the following structures is likely to produce deficits in balance and motor coordination?

(A) thalamus

(B) amygdala

(C) anterior cingulate cortex (ACC)

(D) orbitofrontal cortex

(E) cerebellum

GO ON TO THE NEXT PAGE

68. Which of the following functions is typically processed in the left hemisphere to a greater extent than by the right hemisphere?

(A) emotion
(B) intuition
(C) spatial relations
(D) music
(E) language

69. The basal ganglia, substantia nigra, and red nucleus are important for which of the following functions?

(A) memory
(B) emotion
(C) movement
(D) vision
(E) olfaction

70. People with posttraumatic stress disorder (PTSD) often feel hypervigilant, or unable to relax even when they're perfectly safe. Which of the following neurotransmitters might be implicated in the production of this unusual state?

(A) Serotonin
(B) GABA
(C) Norepinephrine
(D) Glutamate
(E) Dopamine

71. Which type of glial cells form the myelin found in the central nervous system?

(A) microglia
(B) Schwann cells
(C) astrocytes
(D) oligodendrocytes
(E) ependymal cells

72. Lesions in which of the following areas abolishes administration of addictive drugs in research animals?

(A) locus coeruleus
(B) nucleus accumbens
(C) area postrema
(D) raphe nucleus
(E) amygdala

GO ON TO THE NEXT PAGE

73. Dr. Kirk is recording the activity of a squid axon and finds that a larger than normal depolarizing shock is necessary to produce a new action potential. What is the most likely explanation for Dr. Kirk's observations?

   (A)   The squid axon is an artificial laboratory preparation, so its behavior is not very predictable.
   (B)   Dr. Kirk probably applied the shock during a relative refractory period.
   (C)   Dr. Kirk probably applied the shock during an absolute refractory period.
   (D)   The squid preparation generally requires larger than normal shocks to produce action potentials.
   (E)   The squid preparation has been used for too long a time in the laboratory, and its responsiveness is reduced.

74. Fetal alcohol syndrome occurs

   (A)   only in cases where the mother drinks heavily at the outset of the pregnancy
   (B)   only in cases where the mother drinks heavily at the end of the pregnancy
   (C)   only with heavy drinking (four to five drinks daily) throughout the pregnancy
   (D)   with any instance of heavy drinking (four to five drinks at one sitting) at the end of the pregnancy
   (E)   even in cases where the mother drinks only moderate amounts of alcohol

75. Which of the following structures is considered to be the "master clock" for setting circadian rhythms?

   (A)   the preoptic area of the hypothalamus
   (B)   the pineal gland
   (C)   the suprachiasmatic nucleus
   (D)   the interstitial nuclei of the anterior hypothalamus (INAH)
   (E)   the organum vasculosum

76. Which of the following occurs during non-rapid eye movement (NREM or slow-wave) sleep but not during rapid eye movement (REM) sleep?

   (A)   activity of the sympathetic nervous system
   (B)   muscle paralysis
   (C)   release of human growth hormone
   (D)   PGO spikes
   (E)   very low levels of serotonin and norepinephrine activity

77. The EEG recordings during the deepest stages of non-REM (NREM or slow-wave) sleep feature large amounts of which of the following waveforms?

   (A)   alpha waves
   (B)   beta waves
   (C)   gamma waves
   (D)   theta waves
   (E)   delta waves

GO ON TO THE NEXT PAGE

78. Maria has just been diagnosed with diabetes 2, which is associated with insulin resistance. Prior to treatment, which of the following describes Maria's symptoms best?

    (A) She is likely to feel very hungry in spite of high levels of circulating glucose, because insulin moves glucose out of the blood supply and into cells.
    (B) She is likely to feel no hunger, as her blood glucose levels remain very high even between meals.
    (C) She is likely to feel very hungry, because high levels of insulin keep her blood glucose low.
    (D) She is likely to feel no hunger, because her low insulin activity results in few signals to the lateral hypothalamus, which initiates feeding.
    (E) She is likely to feel very hungry, because her low insulin activity interferes with the action of leptin.

79. Anna discusses her recent decrease in sexual desire with her physician, who suggests trying a hormone patch as treatment. Which of the following hormones is most likely to increase Anna's sexual desire?

    (A) estrogen
    (B) progesterone
    (C) testosterone
    (D) follicle stimulating hormone (FSH)
    (E) luteinizing hormone (LH)

80. The New Zealand national rugby team, the All-Blacks, perform a traditional Maori haka, or prewar ritual, to "psych up" before a game. In other words, the players use the aggressive movements and vocalizations to produce a cognitive state of arousal. With which of the following theories is this practice most consistent?

    (A) the James-Lange theory of emotion
    (B) the Cannon-Bard theory of emotion
    (C) Freud's catharsis theory
    (D) cognitive attribution theory
    (E) the elaboration likelihood theory

81. A patient experienced trauma to the anterior cingulate cortex and orbitofrontal cortex as the result of a traffic accident in which his head hit the windshield of the car. What behavioral changes might the patient expect to experience?

    (A) The patient will experience difficulties with language.
    (B) The patient will begin to make impulsive, poor decisions.
    (C) The patient will have trouble with coordinated movement.
    (D) The patient will hallucinate.
    (E) The patient will have problems with vision.

GO ON TO THE NEXT PAGE

82. Which of the following is an important distinction between bipolar disorder and major depressive disorder?

   (A) Genetic contributions to major depressive disorder are substantial, but none have been identified for bipolar disorder.
   (B) Psychotic symptoms occur in cases of bipolar disorder, but not in cases of major depressive disorder.
   (C) Effective medications have been developed for the treatment of bipolar disorder, but not for the treatment of major depressive disorder.
   (D) Major depressive disorder and bipolar disorder share symptoms of depression, but only bipolar disorder is characterized by symptoms of mania.
   (E) Individuals with major depressive disorder often experience intense anxiety, but those with bipolar disorder do not.

83. Which of the following disorders occur when an individual experiences physical symptoms that do not have an underlying medical cause?

   (A) somatic symptom disorder
   (B) factitious disorder
   (C) anxiety disorder
   (D) major depressive disorder
   (E) dissociative disorder

84. Which of the following correctly pairs a disorder with an empirically supported intervention for treating it?

   (A) borderline personality disorder—dialectical behavior therapy
   (B) attention-deficit/hyperactivity disorder (ADHD)—exposure therapy
   (C) autism spectrum disorder—stimulant medication
   (D) social anxiety disorder—lithium medication
   (E) panic disorder—sodium lactate medication

85. Which of the following approaches to treatment of psychological disorder is most closely related to learning theory?

   (A) psychoanalysis
   (B) applied behavior analysis
   (C) object relations therapy
   (D) client-centered therapy
   (E) rational-emotive therapy

GO ON TO THE NEXT PAGE

86. Individuals with autism spectrum disorder display which of the following types of behavior?

    (A) separation anxiety when separated from caregivers
    (B) unusually large vocabulary
    (C) inability to focus on a detail of the environment
    (D) unusual social extraversion
    (E) intolerance of change

87. Mary has an identical twin who has been diagnosed with schizophrenia. How do her risks of developing schizophrenia compare with the following individuals?

    (A) Her risk is higher than a person who has a nontwin sibling with schizophrenia.
    (B) Her risk is lower than a person who has one parent with schizophrenia.
    (C) Her risk is about the same as a person with two parents with schizophrenia.
    (D) Her risk is about the same as a person whose fraternal twin has schizophrenia.
    (E) Her risk is lower than a person married to an individual with schizophrenia.

88. A patient complains of checking faucets to see if they are leaking so frequently that there is very little time for other activities. This behavior is an example of

    (A) an obsession
    (B) a compulsion
    (C) a delusion
    (D) a hallucination
    (E) psychosis

89. Which of the following patients is most likely to benefit from medication with a selective serotonin reuptake inhibitor (SSRI)?

    (A) a small child who has difficulty remaining seated in an elementary classroom
    (B) a young adult who complains of hearing voices
    (C) a middle-aged adult who is convinced that others are intent on doing him harm
    (D) a teen who is feeling that life is hopeless and worthless
    (E) a child who engages in repetitive, stereotypical play and whose language development is substantially delayed

90. Exposure therapy is most likely to be used with people diagnosed with which of the following disorders?

    (A) schizophrenia
    (B) major depressive disorder
    (C) conduct disorder
    (D) dissociative identity disorder
    (E) specific phobia

GO ON TO THE NEXT PAGE

91. Which of the following clinicians is most likely to endorse the use of existential therapy?

(A) a therapist who believes that many psychological disorders have their origin in chemical imbalances in the brain

(B) a therapist who believes that most psychological conflicts arise from an understanding of our own mortality

(C) a therapist who believes that the key to improving a person's psychological state lies in accessing content from the unconscious mind

(D) a therapist who believes that causality of disordered behavior is not important; all one needs to know is how the person's behavior is being reinforced

(E) a therapist who believes that confronting a person's illogical ideas is the key to improvement

92. Shawn feels very discouraged about his performance on an important exam. Which of the following is the best example of a positive emotion-focused coping response by Shawn?

(A) He goes out with friends and has several beers.

(B) He goes for a long, exhausting run.

(C) He stays at home alone and drinks wine.

(D) He goes to a friend's house to watch some favorite comedy movies.

(E) He goes to the gym and works out on the punching bag.

93. Which of the following individuals represent the Type A person most likely to have heart disease?

(A) Michael, a thrill seeker who loves participating in extreme sports

(B) Jessica, who works hard on her studies, but hates to do any type of exercise

(C) Tyler, who regularly pulls all-nighters to get his work done on time

(D) Amanda, who moves from job to job because she struggles with important projects

(E) Andrew, whose witty but often cruel and hostile behavior toward others does not make him popular at work, in spite of his considerable talents

94. Which of the following is the best example of delusional behavior?

(A) checking your windows at night so many times that you have little time to actually sleep

(B) demanding frequent cosmetic surgery procedures to correct physical flaws

(C) rushing away from a lunch with friends at a nice restaurant because of feelings of extreme fear

(D) believing that physicians implanted technology in the brain during a recent hospitalization that allow them to control your thoughts

(E) hearing voices that do not actually exist that accuse you of having committed a crime

GO ON TO THE NEXT PAGE

95. Six-year-old Ben has more difficulty than his peers when asked to stay seated in the classroom and complete his worksheets. Ben's behavior is typical of individuals diagnosed with

(A) attention-deficit/hyperactivity disorder (ADHD)
(B) early-onset schizophrenia
(C) autism spectrum disorder
(D) generalized anxiety disorder
(E) intellectual disability

96. Emily's language is delayed and she rarely makes eye contact with others. When she skinned her knee on the pavement, she tried to put a Band-Aid on it herself instead of seeking help from her parents. Emily's behavior is typical of individuals diagnosed with

(A) attention-deficit/hyperactivity disorder (ADHD)
(B) early-onset schizophrenia
(C) autism spectrum disorder
(D) generalized anxiety disorder
(E) intellectual disability

97. Which of the following hypotheses regarding the causes of autism spectrum does *not* have any empirical, scientific support?

(A) Genetics play a role in the development of autism spectrum disorder.
(B) Parental age plays a role in the development of autism spectrum disorder.
(C) The mother's use of some antidepressants around the time of pregnancy might increase the risk of having a child with autism spectrum disorder.
(D) Common vaccination practices are responsible for recent increases in the prevalence of autism spectrum disorder.
(E) Some viral infections contracted by the mother during pregnancy might influence the risk that her child will have autism spectrum disorder.

98. Medications used to treat attention-deficit/hyperactivity disorder (ADHD) have their main effects on brain systems using which of the following neurochemicals?

(A) serotonin
(B) dopamine
(C) glutamate
(D) GABA
(E) adenosine

GO ON TO THE NEXT PAGE

99. Hallucinations, delusions, and disorganized thought patterns are characteristic of which of the following disorders?

   (A) autism spectrum disorder
   (B) specific phobia
   (C) schizophrenia
   (D) major depressive disorder
   (E) dissociative identity disorder

100. Patients diagnosed with schizophrenia show unnaturally low levels of activity in the

   (A) frontal lobes
   (B) parietal lobes
   (C) occipital lobes
   (D) temporal lobes
   (E) entire cerebral cortex

101. Psychotic symptoms, such as the hallucinations and delusions experienced by patients with schizophrenia, also occur under which of the following circumstances?

   (A) in patients with traumatic brain injuries to the frontal lobes
   (B) in individuals who use drugs that increase the activity of dopamine in the brain
   (C) in individuals who use drugs that increase the activity of glutamate in the brain
   (D) in individuals with untreated Parkinson's disease
   (E) in individuals who consume excess amounts of caffeine

102. Which of the following statements best describes the relationship between schizophrenia and socioeconomic status (SES)?

   (A) There is no systematic relationship between SES and rates of schizophrenia, because schizophrenia is due to genetic factors.
   (B) Schizophrenia is more common in lower-SES populations, but we don't know if low SES is a risk factor or if people ill with schizophrenia move into low SES due to unemployment.
   (C) Schizophrenia is more common in higher-SES populations, but we don't know if this simply reflects better access to health care and diagnosis of problems.
   (D) Schizophrenia is more common in lower-SES populations because communication patterns between parent and child, which are worse in low-SES environments, are the main risk factor for schizophrenia.
   (E) Schizophrenia is more common in higher-SES populations, because these individuals are more likely to experience high stress levels due to demanding careers.

GO ON TO THE NEXT PAGE

103. According to DSM-5, what is the relationship between the depression found in bipolar disorder and the depression found in major depressive disorder?

(A) The same criteria are used to evaluate depression in both disorders.

(B) Appetite disturbances are characteristic of bipolar disorder but not major depressive disorder.

(C) Appetite disturbances are characteristic of major depressive disorder but not bipolar disorder.

(D) Loss of pleasure is characteristic of major depressive disorder but not bipolar disorder.

(E) Feelings of hopelessness are characteristic of major depressive disorder but not bipolar disorder.

104. Which of the following is a correct description of the role of gender in major depressive disorder?

(A) Females with depression outnumber males with depression throughout the life span.

(B) Males with depression outnumber females with depression throughout the life span.

(C) There are no gender differences in the prevalence of major depressive disorder.

(D) Males and females are about equally likely to be diagnosed with major depressive disorder prior to puberty, but from that point forward, females are more likely than males to be diagnosed with depression.

(E) Females are more likely to be diagnosed with major depressive disorder in adolescence and young adulthood, but males are more likely to be diagnosed in old age.

105. Individuals with major depressive disorder

(A) always sleep far more than is normal

(B) experience more rapid eye movement (REM) sleep than is normal

(C) are unable to enter rapid eye movement (REM) sleep at all

(D) experience more non-REM sleep than is normal

(E) are less likely to experience interruptions in their sleep than people without major depressive disorder

GO ON TO THE NEXT PAGE

106. Which of the following is a correct statement about panic disorder?

(A) Panic disorder should be diagnosed in any person who experiences at least one panic attack.

(B) Panic disorder is more common among males than among females.

(C) The experience of one or a few panic attacks is not sufficient for diagnosing an individual with panic disorder.

(D) People who do not have panic disorder respond to injections of sodium lactate by experiencing a panic attack, but people with panic disorder show no effect of the injections.

(E) Symptoms of a panic attack are easily distinguished from those of a heart attack in older adults.

107. According to DSM-5, a person who is highly anxious about being in an open space is likely to be diagnosed with

(A) obsessive-compulsive disorder

(B) social anxiety disorder

(C) agoraphobia

(D) separation anxiety disorder

(E) generalized anxiety disorder

108. Ellen is constantly seeking cosmetic surgery procedures to correct perceived flaws in her appearance, even though her friends and family try to reassure her about her beauty. Ellen might be diagnosed with

(A) generalized anxiety disorder

(B) borderline personality disorder

(C) body dysmorphic disorder

(D) bipolar disorder

(E) specific phobia

109. Nick's therapist works to encourage him to see the "glass as half full rather than half empty" and to reward himself whenever he meets a therapeutic goal. It is likely that Nick's therapist considers herself to be using

(A) psychoanalysis

(B) client-centered therapy

(C) applied behavior analysis

(D) cognitive-behavioral therapy

(E) existential therapy

GO ON TO THE NEXT PAGE

110. Longitudinal and cross-sectional research designs can be used to study how behavior changes as a function of age. Which of the following is more of a disadvantage of the longitudinal design than of the cross-sectional design?

    (A) inability to use random assignment to conditions
    (B) cohort effects
    (C) the necessity of using small sample sizes
    (D) inability to consider socioeconomic status
    (E) participant attrition

111. Which of the following is an example of social referencing?

    (A) Children watch a teacher's reaction to a snake that was brought to class.
    (B) Children attempt to develop attitudes that are similar to the peers they admire.
    (C) Children measure their self-esteem by comparing their achievement levels to those of their peers.
    (D) Children select friends from among others having similar demographic characteristics.
    (E) Children pay attention to the social status of their peers.

112. Lawrence Kohlberg and Carol Gilligan both developed theories of moral development. Which of the following terms is more central to Gilligan's theory than to Kohlberg's?

    (A) rationality
    (B) justice
    (C) care
    (D) conservation
    (E) motivation

113. Which of the following examples illustrates the concept of animism?

    (A) A child is convinced that the number of a row of candies increases when the row is spread out.
    (B) A child fails to search for an object that is suddenly hidden from view.
    (C) A child is convinced that the amount of fluid changes when poured into a glass with a different shape.
    (D) A child is comfortable with the idea of an acorn growing into an oak tree, but struggles with the concept that the oak tree originated with an acorn.
    (E) A child is convinced that the moon is hiding behind the clouds.

114. Private speech was first reported by which of the following developmental psychologists?

    (A) Jean Piaget
    (B) Erik Erikson
    (C) Lev Vygotsky
    (D) Mary Ainsworth
    (E) John Bowlby

GO ON TO THE NEXT PAGE

115. According to proponents of birth order effects, which of the following characteristics is more likely in a firstborn child than in later-born members of the family?

    (A) conscientiousness
    (B) openness
    (C) agreeableness
    (D) rebelliousness
    (E) submissiveness

116. Children with autism spectrum disorder display much less spontaneous symbolic play than typically developing children do. Which of the following is an example of this kind of play?

    (A) A child pretends that a banana is a cell phone.
    (B) A child sweeps out a playhouse with a toy broom.
    (C) A child bangs a truck against the floor.
    (D) A child pretends to serve tea from a small toy tea set.
    (E) A child spins the wheels of a truck in different light conditions.

117. Which of the following statements is most closely related to the concept of object permanence?

    (A) A bird in the hand is worth two in the bush.
    (B) Birds of a feather flock together.
    (C) Out of sight, out of mind.
    (D) A penny saved is a penny earned.
    (E) Better late than never.

118. Which of the following children are engaged in parallel play?

    (A) Two children are playing in different corners of a sandbox and are engaged in different actions.
    (B) Two children are playing and conversing in a sandbox, and one is talking about panning for gold while the other is talking about making sand pies.
    (C) Two children are building a sand castle together.
    (D) Two children are making the same movements through the sand with their bulldozers.
    (E) Two children are talking about one of the other children while one plays with a shovel and bucket and another is playing with a bulldozer.

119. A startled newborn appears to wave her arms and cry. Which of the following is the most likely reason for this behavior?

    (A) the rooting reflex
    (B) the Babinski reflex
    (C) the Moro reflex
    (D) the stepping reflex
    (E) habituation

GO ON TO THE NEXT PAGE

120. Dr. Jackson is studying child soldiers of Africa, and focuses on the effects of poverty and lack of educational opportunity on the phenomenon. Dr. Rogers is looking at child soldiers in the context of the obedience and sense of immortality common to young teens in all environments. Which of the following best captures the distinction between Dr. Jackson's and Dr. Rogers's perspectives on life-span development?

(A) Dr. Jackson takes a nurture view of development, while Dr. Rogers takes a nature view.

(B) Dr. Jackson takes a continuous view of development, while Dr. Rogers takes a discontinuous view.

(C) Dr. Jackson takes an ecological view of development, while Dr. Rogers takes a universal view.

(D) Dr. Jackson takes a universal view of development, while Dr. Rogers takes an ecological view.

(E) Dr. Jackson supports the theories of Jean Piaget, while Dr. Rogers supports the theories of Lev Vygotsky.

121. During the embryonic stage of development, which germ layer differentiates into neural tissue?

(A) ectoderm

(B) mesoderm

(C) endoderm

(D) thermoderm

(E) optoderm

122. Newborn humans show an innate preference for

(A) salty tastes over sweet tastes

(B) looking at faces

(C) low-contrast stimuli

(D) high-pitched sounds

(E) pastels over bright colors

123. We speak of motor development in terms of proceeding from medial to lateral. Which of the following is consistent with this view?

(A) crawling before walking

(B) sitting before standing

(C) reaching before grasping

(D) raising the head before sitting

(E) hopping before walking

GO ON TO THE NEXT PAGE

124. Megan learned about a newly discovered species of butterfly in her biology class. The butterfly had many overlapping characteristics with the other butterflies that the class was studying. According to Piaget, Megan will respond to information about the new butterfly by engaging in the process of

    (A) accommodation
    (B) assimilation
    (C) conservation
    (D) concrete operations
    (E) formal operations

125. Josh is observing parents day at the campus preschool as part of a class assignment. He notices that many of the children interact with their parents by running off to explore the preschool environment and periodically returning to the parents to "check in." Josh believes that these children are most likely to have

    (A) secure attachments to their parents
    (B) avoidant attachments to their parents
    (C) disorganized attachments to their parents
    (D) insecure attachments to their parents
    (E) anxious-ambivalent attachments to their parents

126. Ashley, age five, thinks it is funny when one of her teachers asks her if one row of five candies has the same amount as another row of five candies that is more spread out on the table. She tells the teacher that of course they both have the same number, because spreading them out doesn't change anything. It is likely that Ashley is in which of the following stages of development, according to the theories of Piaget?

    (A) sensorimotor
    (B) preoperational
    (C) preconventional
    (D) concrete operational
    (E) postconventional

127. According to the classic theories of Erik Erikson, adolescents face the challenge of

    (A) establishing autonomy
    (B) finding intimacy
    (C) discovering identity
    (D) avoiding stagnation
    (E) achieving integrity

GO ON TO THE NEXT PAGE

128. When Ryan was a little bit younger, his parents could distract him from an undesirable activity like playing with electrical outlets by showing him a new toy. Lately, Ryan has become much harder to distract. Even when his parents block the electrical outlet with a piece of furniture, he tries to find a way to reach it. About how old is Ryan likely to be?

(A) about six months of age
(B) nearing his first birthday
(C) about two years of age
(D) about six years of age
(E) about twelve years of age

129. Which of Piaget's concepts is most similar to the development over time of theory of mind?

(A) assimilation
(B) accommodation
(C) object permanence
(D) conservation
(E) egocentrism

130. A child's ability to anticipate when a toy will reappear between two blocks without having had experience with similar tasks is known as

(A) conservation
(B) a naïve theory
(C) object permanence
(D) concrete operations
(E) animism

131. According to Mary Rothbart, which of the three dimensions of temperament are visible within the first few months of life?

(A) agreeableness, activity, and resilience
(B) neuroticism, extroversion, and delayed gratification
(C) surgency, affect, and effortful control
(D) conscientiousness, empathy, and agreeableness
(E) neuroticism, openness to experience, and empathy

132. According to classic studies by Harry Harlow, which type of interaction is most likely to enhance the bonding between parent and child?

(A) providing good food
(B) using plastic seats to hold children while the parents watch television
(C) providing reliable contact comfort
(D) teaching autonomy by letting the child "cry it out" at night
(E) avoiding picking a child up just because he or she cries

GO ON TO THE NEXT PAGE

133. Kaitlyn's parents are very supportive, but they establish firm household rules and administer consequences if a rule is broken. Kaitlyn's parents are using which of the following parenting styles?

    (A) authoritarian
    (B) authoritative
    (C) indulgent
    (D) neglecting
    (E) overly involved

134. Which type of intelligence is most likely to decrease over the life span?

    (A) Crystallized intelligence
    (B) Emotional intelligence
    (C) General intelligence
    (D) Fluid intelligence
    (E) Verbal intelligence

135. According to the Baltimore Longitudinal Study of Aging (2000), healthy aging is accompanied by

    (A) gradual deficits in cognition beginning in midlife
    (B) eventual dementia, although age of onset varies from person to person
    (C) mild cognitive changes, most of which occur very late in life
    (D) abrupt decreases in cognitive abilities, some of which can be remediated with proper treatment
    (E) no changes in any cognitive domain

QUESTIONS 136–145, PERSONALITY

136. How do trait theories of personality differ from type theories?

    (A) Trait theories assume that individuals can differ in the degree to which they have a trait, such as extraversion, whereas type theories categorize people as having a trait or not.
    (B) Type theories feature smaller numbers of personality attributes than trait theories.
    (C) Type theories separate central traits from cardinal traits, but trait theories do not make this distinction.
    (D) Situational variables play a more significant role in type theories than in trait theories.
    (E) The mathematical models of type theories are much more complex than those for trait theories.

GO ON TO THE NEXT PAGE

137. While taking a personality test based on the "Big Five" theory, a participant consciously avoids answering in ways that will result in a high neuroticism score, even though she believes that she is a genuinely anxious person. Which of the following statements is the best explanation for this behavior?

(A) The participant is attempting to compensate for bias in her introspections.
(B) The participant is responding in socially desirable ways.
(C) The participant's explicit understanding of her neuroticism differs from her implicit understanding.
(D) The participant desires to be seen as unique.
(E) The participant does not believe the test is valid.

138. According to the classic theories of Sigmund Freud, which component contains the internalized rules of a person's society?

(A) the id
(B) the ego
(C) the superego
(D) the preconscious
(E) the collective unconscious

139. Brittany burst into tears when a police officer pulled her over for speeding. Freud might suggest that Brittany was using which of the following defense mechanisms?

(A) projection
(B) displacement
(C) reaction formation
(D) regression
(E) repression

140. According to Carl Rogers, which of the following is essential for the achievement of self-actualization?

(A) congruence
(B) empathy
(C) self-discrepancies
(D) unconditional positive regard
(E) rewards for positive behavior and negative consequences for negative behavior

141. Samantha is very trusting and kind. If she has a fault, it is that she is sometimes taken advantage of by some people. According to the Big Five trait theory of personality, it is likely that Samantha would score

(A) high on openness to experience
(B) high on agreeableness
(C) low on conscientiousness
(D) high on neuroticism
(E) low on extroversion

GO ON TO THE NEXT PAGE

142. David and John both did very well on their GRE Psychology Test. David told their friends that the key to his success was his hours of hard work and preparation. John told their friends that he was very lucky that the prep test he studied was very similar to the real test. It is most likely that

(A) both David and John have an internal locus of control
(B) both David and John have an external locus of control
(C) David has an internal locus of control and John has an external locus of control
(D) David has an external locus of control and John has an internal locus of control
(E) John scores higher on Big Five tests of conscientiousness than David does

143. Which of the following is *not* an example of a projective test of personality?

(A) the Rorschach Inkblot Test
(B) the Thematic Apperception Test
(C) the Draw-a-Person Test
(D) the Minnesota Multiphasic Personality Inventory
(E) the Sentence Completion Test

144. The Minnesota Multiphasic Personality Inventory

(A) compares test takers' responses to the responses of people with known psychological disorders
(B) assesses the test taker's personality using the Big Five trait theory
(C) requires the test taker to respond to ambiguous pictures by telling a story
(D) uses 7-point Likert scales
(E) has limited validity and reliability

145. H. J. Eysenck's theory of personality is similar in some respects to the Big Five personality theory. Which of the following dimensions do the two types of theories share?

(A) extroversion and psychoticism
(B) neuroticism and psychoticism
(C) openness to experience and extroversion
(D) extroversion and neuroticism
(E) agreeableness and conscientiousness

GO ON TO THE NEXT PAGE

146. In the classic studies conducted by Stanley Milgram and his colleagues, which of the following variables produced the greatest effects on rates of obedience?

(A) The study was conducted in a rented storefront in Bridgeport, Connecticut, instead of in a Yale laboratory.

(B) Female participants were used instead of male participants.

(C) The degree of demographic similarity (age, gender, ethnicity, etc.) between the "teacher" and "learner" was varied from highly similar to highly dissimilar.

(D) The experimenter (authority figure) was in the same room or in a remote location relative to the "teacher."

(E) The proximity of the "teacher" and "learner" was varied from being in the same room to being unable to hear or see each other.

147. The empathy-altruism hypothesis would predict which of the following?

(A) A homeless person asking for money is likely to receive more money if he or she is accompanied by a child or pet.

(B) People are more likely to render aid to a person whose situation has been evaluated as objectively as possible.

(C) People are less likely to render aid in situations similar to those they have experienced personally.

(D) People are more likely to render aid to a person who is a genetic relative.

(E) People are more likely to help when people do not identify with the person in need.

148. Which of the following situations best illustrates the use of exemplification?

(A) A student argues for a higher grade by stating that the poor grade will result in being expelled from school.

(B) An employee stays later than required to help clean up the store.

(C) A person being interviewed for a job uses flattery to impress the interviewer.

(D) A salesperson pressures a buyer by stating that the deal will only last a short time.

(E) One employee helps another employee cover a shift because he or she might need a shift covered in the future.

149. After an intense workout in the gym, Steve returns to the parking lot to find he has a flat tire on his car. Steve's workout partner, Sarah, thinks that his reaction to the flat tire is not characteristic of him. He is usually a calm person, but he starts cursing and kicking the tire. Which of the following concepts might account for Steve's uncharacteristic behavior?

(A) excitation transfer

(B) cognitive dissonance

(C) correspondence bias

(D) availability heuristic

(E) actor-observer bias

GO ON TO THE NEXT PAGE

150. In one experiment, people arriving in an international airport were given the choice of a free pen. The choice was to be made from a set of five that contained four of the same color and one of a unique color. People chose either the common or unique pen in systematic ways. Which factor was most important in determining an individual's choice of pen?

(A) the person's level of implicit self-esteem
(B) the person's level of explicit self-esteem
(C) whether the person was from an individualistic or collectivistic culture
(D) the person's gender
(E) the person's age

151. A psychologist is convinced that people behave in gender-appropriate ways because they have developed schemas about how people of a particular gender should act. This psychologist's work is most representative of which of the following approaches?

(A) social learning or modeling
(B) social cognitive
(C) psychoanalytic
(D) humanistic
(E) behaviorist

152. Harold Kelley and John Thibaut developed an interdependence theory of social relationships. Which of the following statements best illustrates this theory?

(A) Close relationships usually occur in people who are very similar to each other.
(B) Close relationships go through a series of stages featuring differing levels of personal disclosure.
(C) Relationships are characterized by different levels of rewards and costs.
(D) Opposites usually attract.
(E) Relationships vary in terms of passion, intimacy, and commitment.

153. Which of the following theories proposes that intention to behave is the result of a combination of attitudes, social norms, and perceived control?

(A) the theory of planned behavior
(B) the elaboration likelihood model
(C) schemata theory
(D) cognitive dissonance theory
(E) social exchange theory

GO ON TO THE NEXT PAGE

154. Which of the following statements is consistent with a social learning view of aggression in children?

(A) Children become aggressive or not as a result of genetic predispositions.
(B) Children become aggressive because they learn scripts for using aggression in certain situations.
(C) Children learn to be aggressive by watching aggressive models, such as parents or media characters.
(D) Children learn to be aggressive when they are positively reinforced for engaging in aggressive behavior.
(E) Children become aggressive in response to peer pressure and expectations.

155. Evolutionary psychologists assume that altruism evolved in humans because of which of the following processes?

(A) People behaving in altruistic ways experience changes in their underlying DNA that is passed on to their offspring.
(B) People are more likely to behave altruistically toward their genetically related relatives.
(C) People are more likely to imitate the altruistic behaviors of their genetic relatives.
(D) People who sacrifice themselves for others tend to be more fertile.
(E) People who are not willing to behave altruistically are rejected as reproductive partners, leaving only those who are altruistic with opportunities to reproduce.

156. Psychologists have argued that people with high levels of achievement motivation also possess which of the following characteristics?

(A) high tolerance for risk
(B) external locus of control
(C) dislike of precise goal setting
(D) high tendency to take responsibility for own behaviors
(E) preference for familiar over innovative tasks

157. Which of the following examples best illustrates reciprocal determinism?

(A) While waiting for a difficult exam, an anxious student shares concerns with others nearby, who then become anxious. Seeing the other students' anxiety increases the anxiety of the first student.
(B) An anxious student selects an easier course over a difficult course that would prepare the student better for graduate school.
(C) Through an interview process, a graduate school committee selects students who appear to be the least anxious.
(D) A student is very anxious at school but is very relaxed when socializing with friends and family.
(E) A professor discusses an upcoming exam as being the most difficult one students will likely experience in their entire academic careers. The students become very anxious.

GO ON TO THE NEXT PAGE

158. Which of the following individuals is most likely to be using a downward comparison for self-enhancement?

(A) A tennis player reviews the latest rankings in his division and counts how many players are ranked ahead of him.

(B) A student compares her score on a midterm with her classmates', and reassures herself that she is ahead of the majority.

(C) A salesperson on commission compares her annual earnings with the average earnings in her organization.

(D) A newly diagnosed breast cancer patient compares her case with others in her support group who are in remission.

(E) A figure skater criticizes the performance of the winner of a competition.

159. Which of the following situations best illustrates social exchange theory?

(A) A person who receives an expensive birthday gift from a friend feels obligated to buy that friend an equally expensive gift.

(B) A person makes a generous public donation to impress a new friend.

(C) A person shares her class notes with other students.

(D) A person stops to help a stranded driver with a flat tire, because he would want help if he were the one with the flat tire.

(E) A parent works an extra job to help a child attend a better school.

QUESTIONS 160–163 REFER TO THE INFORMATION BELOW.

Courtney is waiting in line at the campus bookstore, and she's late for her first class. While reaching for his wallet, the man in front of her loses his balance and steps on her foot, causing quite a bit of pain. In turn, Courtney steps backward onto the feet of the student behind her. The man at the front of the line apologizes to Courtney and the student behind her. As she hurries to class, Courtney tries to understand what happened in the bookstore.

160. Courtney wonders if her stepping on the student behind her was a result of her being upset about being late for class rather than anything that was happening at the moment. Based on her study of Freudian theory, she thinks Freud would attribute her behavior to which of the following?

(A) displacement
(B) repression
(C) rationalization
(D) identification
(E) reaction formation

GO ON TO THE NEXT PAGE

161. Courtney recalls her professor's discussion of the correspondence bias. If she is subject to the correspondence bias, how might she attribute the man's stepping on her foot?

(A) as an accident
(B) because of his being crowded in line
(C) because of his being a generally clumsy person
(D) because of the warm temperature in the bookstore
(E) because of her having stood too closely to him in line

162. If Courtney falls prey to the actor–observer bias, how would this affect her thinking about the bookstore incident?

(A) She would view the man's stepping on her foot because of his clumsiness, but her stepping on the person's foot behind her because of her situation.
(B) She would view the man's stepping on her foot because of his situation, but her stepping on the person's foot behind her because of her clumsiness.
(C) She would predict that the man's apology to her was because of his general courtesy, but that his apology to the student behind her was because of peer pressure.
(D) She would view her stepping on the person's foot behind her because of the situation, but her nice apology to the person would be because of her nice personality.
(E) She would assume that the man who stepped on her foot would interpret the situation exactly as she had done.

163. Courtney related her experience to a classmate, who tended to be rather aggressive and hostile. The classmate is more likely to interpret the man's stepping on Courtney's foot as

(A) situational
(B) accidental
(C) intentional
(D) global
(E) consensual

164. Thomas is outgoing and loud around his peers, but quiet and respectful when he visits his grandfather in a nursing home. These variations in Thomas's behavior can be described as resulting from his

(A) personal self
(B) collective self
(C) relational self
(D) independent self
(E) cultural self

GO ON TO THE NEXT PAGE

165. Hermione is constantly forming crushes on men who are excellent dancers, but who otherwise have little in common with her. It is likely that Hermione is being influenced by

    (A) situational attributions
    (B) the correspondence bias
    (C) halo effects
    (D) the self-serving bias
    (E) the actor-observer bias

166. Kayla had her heart set on attending her first-choice graduate program, but she didn't get accepted. Instead, she will attend her second choice program. At first, she was disappointed, but later she began telling her friends that the first-choice school really wasn't as good as it was advertised to be. Kayla's changing attitudes likely reflect the effects of

    (A) social exclusion
    (B) the actor-observer bias
    (C) the self-serving bias
    (D) cognitive dissonance
    (E) halo effects

167. The late Emmy award-winning news producer Leroy Sievers, who got his start working in an Oakland, California, local station after graduating from UC Berkeley, loved to tell the story about how he was hired sight unseen by a major news network in New York. His new coworkers were shocked to see that Leroy from Oakland was not the African-American they expected to see, but instead a tall, blonde with family from Sweden. The news executives' mistake is an example of

    (A) prejudice
    (B) stereotyping
    (C) discrimination
    (D) cognitive dissonance
    (E) actor-observer bias

168. Claude Steele and his colleagues told one group of students that the test they were about to take usually resulted in higher scores for Asians than white students. A second group of students was given the test without this introduction. Which of the following outcomes would be predicted by the concept of stereotype threat?

    (A) White students in both groups would perform the same way, but Asian students in the first group would perform better than Asian students in the second group.
    (B) Asian students in both groups would perform the same way, but white students in the first group would perform better than white students in the second group.
    (C) Asian students in both groups would perform the same way, but white students in the first group would perform worse than white students in the second group.
    (D) The two groups would perform exactly the same, as white and Asian students do not show significant responses to stereotype threat.
    (E) Both Asian and white students in the first group would outperform their counterparts in the second group.

GO ON TO THE NEXT PAGE

169. Justin is the first person to admit that he is prejudiced against people who participate in sororities and fraternities. Which of the following experiences is most likely to reduce Justin's prejudice?

   (A) He lands an ideal job working for a supervisor who belonged to a sorority in college.
   (B) He rents an apartment in a building where many fraternity members live, and he runs into them in the lobby and laundry room on occasion.
   (C) He works on a group project with several members of sororities and fraternities.
   (D) He visits a friend on another campus who belongs to a sorority.
   (E) He participates in a student government position where he helps approve funding for sorority and fraternity activities.

170. Harry is investigating the purchase of a new broom for the next Quidditch season. He studies the specs of the latest models and reads online reviews. According to the elaboration likelihood model, Harry is most likely to be persuaded by which of the following sales approaches when he goes to the store?

   (A) The store hires very attractive salespeople.
   (B) The store offers pamphlets featuring terrible accidents that happened to people who bought other brands of brooms.
   (C) The store serves Harry snacks while he listens to a sales pitch.
   (D) The store provides a detailed video of the important features of the broom, supported by laboratory testing.
   (E) The store advertises testimonials by professional Quidditch players.

171. A local charity sends out appeals asking people to buy $1,000 tables at an upcoming fund-raiser. The appeal states that if a person can't afford a table, perhaps he or she can still help the cause by sending in a $25 or $10 donation. This appeal is using which of the following persuasive strategies?

   (A) foot in the door
   (B) door in the face
   (C) lowball
   (D) conformity pressure
   (E) elaboration likelihood

QUESTIONS 172–180, GENERAL

172. Which of the following theories is most closely linked to Edward Tolman?

   (A) the law of effect
   (B) connectionism
   (C) recapitulation
   (D) sign-Gestalt theory
   (E) pragmatism

GO ON TO THE NEXT PAGE

173. Which of the following theorists proposed that we have a collective unconscious in addition to a personal unconscious?

(A) Sigmund Freud
(B) Carl Jung
(C) Erich Fromm
(D) Karen Horney
(E) Erik Erikson

174. Which of the following psychologists is *least* likely to write in depth about conscious mental activity?

(A) B. F. Skinner
(B) Sigmund Freud
(C) Edward Titchener
(D) Albert Ellis
(E) Ulric Neisser

175. A third-grade teacher, frustrated by low reading performance by students, decides to reward students by paying them $1 for each library book completed. Which of the following outcomes is most likely?

(A) All students will begin to read more, even when the monetary reward is no longer available.
(B) All students will begin to read even less, because extrinsic rewards can reduce the effects of intrinsic rewards.
(C) The students who were already reading the most will continue to do so, but the less active readers will decrease their performance.
(D) The least active readers will read more, but the extrinsic rewards might interfere with the intrinsic motivation of the best readers, possibly reducing their motivation to read.
(E) The results will be highly variable from student to student, because the extrinsic monetary reward will have no systematic effect on the amount of reading completed.

176. Which of the following theoretical perspectives is most likely to endorse the idea that behavior depends on people's beliefs and expectations?

(A) behaviorism
(B) psychoanalytic theory
(C) cognitive psychology
(D) clinical psychology
(E) functionalism

GO ON TO THE NEXT PAGE

177. A professor demonstrates the proper use of a microscope, and carefully supervises students for the first few lab sessions. Over time, the professor provides less and less guidance to the students about their skills with the microscope. This approach best illustrates which of the following educational techniques?

(A) modeling
(B) scaffolding
(C) discovery
(D) scripting
(E) learn by doing

178. Sam began his new job with great enthusiasm, but because of salary cuts, few opportunities for promotion, and reduced benefits, he no longer feels as motivated to work. Sam's change in motivation is best described by which of the following theories?

(A) Maslow's hierarchy of needs
(B) Herzberg's two-factor model
(C) equity theory
(D) expectancy theory
(E) job characteristics model

179. Strict behaviorism is most closely associated with which of the following psychologists?

(A) John B. Watson
(B) Kurt Lewin
(C) Jean Piaget
(D) Erik Erikson
(E) Carl Rogers

180. Which of the following is most likely to view employment as a "calling?"

(A) Levi, who entered the family computer software business, but would prefer to be a high school teacher
(B) Harry, who works as a social worker at a nursing home, and loves helping the residents and their families solve difficult problems
(C) Jane, who finds her work as a corporate attorney repetitive, but who appreciates her very high salary and what she can do with that
(D) Naomi, an office clerk whose rather boring job provides lots of free time
(E) Austin, who became an aeronautical engineer because his parents thought that was the best use of his talents

GO ON TO THE NEXT PAGE

181. A thesis adviser gently tells a student that it appears that the student committed a Type I error. What does this mean?

(A) The student has failed to reject a false null hypothesis.
(B) The student has proved that the null hypothesis is true.
(C) The student rejected the null hypothesis, but the null hypothesis is actually true.
(D) The student rejected an experimental hypothesis that was actually true.
(E) The student failed to come to any conclusions regarding the experimental and null hypotheses related to the thesis.

182. A group of students decided to take the GRE Psychology Test twice without doing any further study or review between the two tests. Their scores on the two tests were positively correlated, $r = .95$. What can the students conclude about the GRE Psychology Test?

(A) The test has strong content validity.
(B) The test has strong reliability.
(C) The test has weak divergent validity.
(D) The test has weak face validity.
(E) The test has weak reliability.

183. A researcher asked a group of individuals known to be color deficient to name a set of color chips. Which of the following types of scale is the researcher using?

(A) a nominal scale
(B) an ordinal scale
(C) an interval scale
(D) a ratio scale
(E) a Likert scale

184. A researcher found an insignificant negative correlation of –.15 between the amount of tea consumed by participants and their body mass index (BMI). What should the researcher conclude from this finding?

(A) Increased consumption of tea does not produce a decrease in BMI for most people.
(B) People with higher levels of tea consumption tend to have a lower BMI than people who drink less tea, but it is impossible to say which is the cause and which is the effect.
(C) Most of the people with lower BMI drank the most tea.
(D) The relationship between tea consumption and BMI is likely to be curvilinear.
(E) No significant relationship between tea consumption and BMI was observed.

GO ON TO THE NEXT PAGE

185. A prospective employee learns at an interview that the salaries offered by the employer range from $40,000 per year to $250,000 per year. To obtain the best picture of the salary opportunities available in this organization, the employee might ask to know which of the following?

   (A) the mean
   (B) the median
   (C) the mode
   (D) any of the three measures (mean, median, mode), as all are equally useful
   (E) none of the measures, as none provide any useful information in this case

186. A researcher is interested in rates of college attendance among different ethnic groups. To enhance the researcher's ability to generalize the results, which of the following sampling techniques would be best?

   (A) simple random sampling
   (B) stratified random sampling
   (C) nonrandom sampling
   (D) simple convenience sampling
   (E) convenience sampling with quotas

187. Results of certain tests are often given in T scores to make them easier to interpret. If a child receives a T score of 70 on the Spence Children's Anxiety Scale (SCAS), what can we conclude?

   (A) The child's score is 2 standard deviations above the normal score of age and gender peers.
   (B) The child's score is 200% above that of age and gender peers.
   (C) The child's score is 2% above that of age and gender peers.
   (D) Scores by age and gender peers are about twice as high as the child's score.
   (E) The T score does not provide adequate information for assessing the child's score.

188. When constructing a new test, researchers often compute a measure known as correlation alpha or Cronbach's alpha. One new test has an alpha of 0.85. What does this measure indicate about a test?

   (A) The test demonstrates strong cross-validation.
   (B) The test produces weak normative data.
   (C) The test shows weak internal validity.
   (D) The test demonstrates acceptable internal validity.
   (E) The test's subscales group together in a manner consistent with the theory behind the test.

GO ON TO THE NEXT PAGE

189. Which of the following describes the use of a double-blind procedure?

(A) A schoolteacher takes notes about the behavior of a student who has just begun treatment with a stimulant medication for attention and hyperactivity problems.

(B) A researcher provides children with fruit juice that either contains food additives or no food additives, but does not know which children received which juice until the experiment is complete.

(C) A person keeps a journal about mood changes after beginning to take antidepressant medication.

(D) A researcher asks a group of medical marijuana users if smoking marijuana gives them superior results compared with taking prescription THC pills.

(E) A therapist observes that a child using neurofeedback seems to be paying better attention to schoolwork.

190. Research has shown that preschoolers who watch more violent television are more likely to be physically aggressive on the playground. Why are we unable to conclude on the basis of these data that watching violent television leads to physical aggression?

(A) The study does not include a wide enough age range.

(B) The study is influenced by experimenter bias.

(C) We cannot make causal conclusions based on correlational data.

(D) The study does not include appropriate control groups.

(E) Most preschoolers are physically aggressive, so there is little variance to explain.

191. Evidence for the unconscious nature of priming can be demonstrated most clearly by which of the following procedures?

(A) comparing patients with amnesia and healthy participants on a word-completion priming task

(B) observing the performance of healthy individuals on a lexical decision task

(C) asking participants to answer multiple-choice questions about a passage they read

(D) asking participants to summarize a passage they just read in their own words

(E) asking participants to read an essay several times and note any new information that they describe after each reading

GO ON TO THE NEXT PAGE

A researcher is curious about whether a new drug prevents deteriorating performance on memory tasks in patients with traumatic brain injury (TBI). She advertises for patients who are newly diagnosed with TBI and obtains twenty volunteers. She instructs them to take the new medication once per day for six months. She then recruits an additional group of twenty patients with TBI who will serve as the control group because they decided not to take any medication for their condition. Both groups of patients take the same memory tests at the end of the six-month treatment period. The researcher finds that the patients who took the medication perform better than those who did not, and concludes that the new drug prevents deterioration in memory performance in patients with TBI.

192. Which of the following changes would make this procedure into a true experiment?

   (A) Compare the performance of the patients taking medication to patients without TBI.
   (B) Analyze the range of symptom severity to see if the new drug was more effective in more severe cases.
   (C) Randomly assign patients with TBI to medication and control groups.
   (D) Vary the doses of the new drug given to the medication group.
   (E) Measure memory throughout the six-month period to assess any changes.

193. Which of the following describes the potential confound produced by the demand characteristics of this study?

   (A) Participants in the two groups might not be matched according to severity of symptoms.
   (B) The experimenter's knowledge of who was and was not using medication might have biased her interpretation of the memory test results.
   (C) The participants taking the medication expect to perform better, so they might have put more effort into their memory tests.
   (D) The researcher had no way of knowing whether the medication group complied with her instructions to take the new drug daily.
   (E) The new drug only produces improvement in people with TBI, and some of the participants might have been misdiagnosed.

194. What change in procedure would make this study into a double-blind procedure?

   (A) Participants would not be told that the drug improves the symptoms of TBI for many people.
   (B) Add a control group of patients who have stroke rather than TBI.
   (C) Use the same design, but instruct the patients that the new drug is designed to improve mood.
   (D) Provide the control group with a placebo pill, and do not allow either participants or researchers to know who is taking the active medication or the placebo until after the experiment is complete.
   (E) Administer a pretest in addition to the existing posttests for both groups.

GO ON TO THE NEXT PAGE

195. If the researcher administered a pretest, which of the following outcomes would support the idea that the new drug prevents progressive declines in memory function in patients with TBI?

(A)
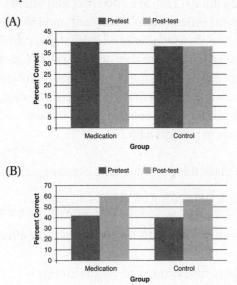

(B)
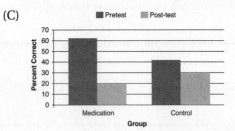

(C)

(D)
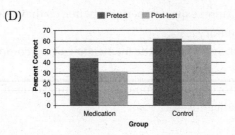

(E)
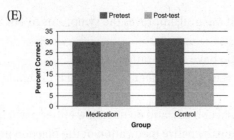

GO ON TO THE NEXT PAGE

196. Which of the following changes would *not* improve this research design?

   (A) random assignment of students to medication and control groups
   (B) provide a pretest to assess changes in functioning
   (C) provide a better system for monitoring compliance with the instruction to take the medication daily
   (D) ensure that the participants do not know whether they are taking medication or placebo
   (E) ensure that the more severe cases of TBI are given medication that might help them

197. Because of all the problems associated with this research design, the researcher decides to run a second study. She recruits a group of thirty-six patients with TBI based on physician referral. The physicians have already prescribed the new drug for half of the patients, but the others have not been prescribed any medications. This type of research design is known as

   (A) a double-blind placebo-controlled design
   (B) a within-subjects design
   (C) a multivariate design
   (D) a quasi-experimental design
   (E) a factorial design

198. A group of researchers was investigating two dose levels of a new medication for depression. The participants included a group of adolescents and a group of adults ages sixty-five and older. The following table shows the participants' scores on a test of depression in which higher scores indicate more severe symptoms.

	Adolescents	Older Adults
Low dose	80	45
High dose	55	40

   A statistical analysis showed a statistically significant interaction between the participants' age group and the efficacy of the two dose levels of the new drug. Which of the following statements would be the best interpretation of this interaction?

   (A) The new drug was equally effective for both age groups.
   (B) There were large individual differences in the participants' response to the new drug.
   (C) Adolescents are more resistant than older adults to the effects of medication for depression.
   (D) Adolescents showed more benefit from the higher dose than older adults did.
   (E) The higher dose produced little benefit for the older adults, but seemed to have produced substantial benefits for the adolescents.

GO ON TO THE NEXT PAGE

199. When a hypothesis is demonstrated to be false using appropriate research methods, what is the best course of action?

    (A) Other researchers should attempt to replicate the original study.
    (B) The hypothesis should be modified or rejected.
    (C) The researchers should try different statistical methods to see if any of the results are significant.
    (D) Data that did not fit the hypothesis should be discarded as outliers.
    (E) Results that are close to being significant should be reported as trends.

200. The original taste aversion study by John Garcia and Robert Koelling (1966) was initially rejected for publication because its results were so different from the prevailing thinking in the field at the time. However, when a number of investigators were able to reproduce the results, the study gained in credibility and eventually became quite influential. This process underscores the importance of

    (A) being cautious about reporting data that do not fit contemporary trends
    (B) replicating work that features unexpected results
    (C) understanding that peer reviewers rarely make mistakes
    (D) realizing that prestigious journals are the most likely to publish novel results
    (E) discarding any work that is not accepted by the first journal to which it is submitted

201. Although case studies involve very small numbers of participants, which limits generalization, they can be very useful in which of the following ways?

    (A) They can provide the basis for rejecting a hypothesis.
    (B) They are quick and easy to do.
    (C) They are easier to publish than research involving more participants.
    (D) They do not present any ethical concerns.
    (E) They provide the basis for proving that a hypothesis is correct.

202. Which of the following is an advantage of using the survey method of research?

    (A) People are usually honest on surveys, because they are confidential.
    (B) Surveys provide large amounts of data quickly and cheaply.
    (C) Surveys involve very few ethical constraints.
    (D) Surveys provide insight into natural, real-world behaviors.
    (E) Constructing good survey questions is relatively easy.

GO ON TO THE NEXT PAGE

203. Dr. Ross was curious about the effects of sleep deprivation in college students on their caloric intake. She assigned participants to different levels of sleep deprivation and then measured their caloric intake over the next few days. In this experiment, which of the following serves as the independent variable?

(A) sleep deprivation
(B) calories consumed before the beginning of the experiment
(C) calories consumed during the experiment
(D) typical sleep habits before the experiment
(E) attending college or not

204. Researchers have found that scores on the GRE Psychology Test do a better job than scores on the general GRE of predicting some aspects of performance in graduate psychology programs. These results suggest that

(A) the general GRE is more reliable than the GRE Psychology Test
(B) the GRE Psychology Test is more reliable than the general GRE
(C) the general GRE is more valid than the GRE Psychology Test
(D) the GRE Psychology Test is more valid than the general GRE
(E) the reliability and validity of the two tests is about the same

205. Amber is conducting a survey for her senior thesis and she is offering a drawing for a free dinner as an incentive for participation. To manage the drawing for the dinner, she asks participants to provide their contact information on the top of the survey. Amber's thesis adviser tells her that this plan has ethical problems. For which of the following reasons is the adviser likely to object to Amber's plan?

(A) The incentive of the drawing for the dinner is excessive.
(B) The drawing for the dinner is too deceptive.
(C) Including contact information along with the data does not provide adequate confidentiality.
(D) Surveys are by their very nature ethically deficient.
(E) Amber needs to tell the participants to put their contact information at the very end of the survey, not at the beginning.

STOP

If there is still time remaining, you may review your answers.

ANSWER KEY
Diagnostic Test 1

1.	D	36.	B	71.	D	106.	C	141.	B
2.	A	37.	B	72.	B	107.	C	142.	C
3.	B	38.	D	73.	B	108.	C	143.	D
4.	D	39.	A	74.	E	109.	D	144.	A
5.	B	40.	D	75.	C	110.	E	145.	D
6.	B	41.	C	76.	C	111.	A	146.	E
7.	A	42.	E	77.	E	112.	C	147.	A
8.	A	43.	C	78.	A	113.	E	148.	B
9.	C	44.	C	79.	C	114.	C	149.	A
10.	A	45.	D	80.	A	115.	A	150.	C
11.	D	46.	E	81.	B	116.	A	151.	B
12.	E	47.	A	82.	D	117.	C	152.	C
13.	A	48.	D	83.	A	118.	B	153.	A
14.	B	49.	B	84.	A	119.	C	154.	C
15.	C	50.	D	85.	B	120.	C	155.	B
16.	A	51.	B	86.	E	121.	A	156.	D
17.	A	52.	A	87.	A	122.	B	157.	A
18.	B	53.	C	88.	B	123.	C	158.	B
19.	C	54.	E	89.	D	124.	B	159.	A
20.	A	55.	D	90.	E	125.	A	160.	A
21.	D	56.	C	91.	B	126.	D	161.	C
22.	E	57.	A	92.	D	127.	C	162.	A
23.	C	58.	C	93.	E	128.	B	163.	C
24.	A	59.	B	94.	D	129.	E	164.	C
25.	D	60.	D	95.	A	130.	B	165.	C
26.	B	61.	B	96.	C	131.	C	166.	D
27.	E	62.	D	97.	D	132.	C	167.	B
28.	B	63.	C	98.	B	133.	B	168.	C
29.	B	64.	A	99.	C	134.	D	169.	C
30.	B	65.	C	100.	A	135.	C	170.	D
31.	A	66.	A	101.	B	136.	A	171.	B
32.	D	67.	E	102.	B	137.	B	172.	D
33.	D	68.	E	103.	A	138.	C	173.	B
34.	B	69.	C	104.	D	139.	D	174.	A
35.	A	70.	C	105.	B	140.	D	175.	D

176.	C
177.	B
178.	C
179.	A
180.	B
181.	C
182.	B
183.	A
184.	E
185.	B
186.	B
187.	A
188.	D
189.	B
190.	C
191.	B
192.	C
193.	C
194.	D
195.	E
196.	E
197.	D
198.	D
199.	B
200.	B
201.	A
202.	B
203.	A
204.	D
205.	C

EVALUATING YOUR PERFORMANCE

How did it go? If you find at this point that you were pushed for time and did not finish in the 170 minutes, finish the questions still remaining. The point right now is review and analysis of weak spots. As you refresh your mind on the subject matter and take further sample tests, you will find your speed improving. In the sample tests, you will also find it helpful to answer the questions you know and note those you were not sure about so you can return to them when you have completed a particular test. Even then, spend only a minimal amount of time on each question—eliminating the answer choice or choices you can, making your best guess, and moving on.

Scoring Diagnostic Test 1

Now that you have completed Diagnostic Test 1, follow the directions below to score your test. Study the correct answers carefully as you go, as these will help you understand any questions on which you guessed wildly or missed. Use the feedback on your test to help prepare your review.

To score your first diagnostic test, please compare the answers on your answer sheet with the answers below. Place a check mark next to questions you answered correctly. Place an "X" next to questions you answered incorrectly. Leave questions you did not answer blank.

Answer Explanations

Learning

_____ 1. **(B)** B. F. Skinner reported that any behavior just preceding a reward would be reinforced.

_____ 2. **(A)** Contingency, or predictive ability, produces strong conditioning.

_____ 3. **(B)** B. F. Skinner would argue that consequences determine the frequency of behaviors in the future.

_____ 4. **(D)** Imprinting is an example of a fixed-action pattern (sometimes called an instinct).

_____ 5. **(B)** Negative reinforcement increases target behavior (cleaning room) by removing something of value from the environment (unable to go out with friends).

_____ 6. **(B)** Ratio schedules count the number of times a behavior occurs to obtain a reward, and the required number in a fixed schedule does not change.

_____ 7. **(A)** Sight of blood becomes a learned signal for further distress.

Learning Summary	
Number Correct	
Number Incorrect	
Number Blank	

Language

_____ 8. **(A)** Common objects form most of a child's first vocabulary words.

_____ 9. **(C)** Syntax, or the rules of grammar, organize word order.

_____ 10. **(A)** Pragmatics are the "practical" rules of using language.

_____ 11. **(D)** c–a–t

_____ 12. **(E)** Whorf believed that the more words you knew about a topic, the more ideas you can have about a topic.

_____ 13. **(A)** This area is now known as Broca's area.

Language Summary	
Number Correct	
Number Incorrect	
Number Blank	

Memory

_____ 14. **(B)** You have just seen the list; now you must recognize what you have seen.

_____ 15. **(C)** Learning something before target learning can produce anterograde interference.

_____ 16. **(A)** Episodic memories are formed from personal experience.

_____ 17. **(A)** Sensory memory has large capacity but short duration.

_____ 18. **(B)** Haptic codes refer to touch.

_____ 19. **(C)** Repeating material is maintenance rehearsal.

_____ 20. **(A)** Chunking in memory can expand capacity by grouping data into more manageable bits.

_____ 21. **(D)** The other four are part of Baddeley's system.

_____ 22. **(E)** Long-term memory does not have limited duration or capacity.

_____ 23. **(C)** You don't need to think about the meaningfulness of an item using shallow processing.

_____ 24. **(A)** The first and last items on a list are the easiest to remember, although for different reasons.

_____ 25. **(D)** Declarative memories are conscious, explicit memories that are easy to verbalize.

_____ 26. **(B)** Time is an important cue for organizing episodic memory.

_____ 27. **(E)** These individuals can recall remarkable detail about a specific day.

_____ 28. **(B)** Damage to the hippocampus results in anterograde amnesia, or difficulty forming new declarative memories.

_____ 29. **(B)** Keeping practice and performance situations similar enhances memory due to context-dependent effects.

_____ 30. **(B)** Elizabeth Loftus and her colleagues have demonstrated the ease with which memories are changed through the use of carefully worded questions.

_____ 31. **(A)** By reteaching material and comparing the rate of learning with the original rate, we can estimate how much information had been "saved" in memory.

_____ 32. **(D)** Motivated forgetting suggests our memories can serve our personal needs.

Memory Summary	
Number Correct	
Number Incorrect	
Number Blank	

Thinking

_____ 33. **(D)** Schemas or scripts are very important to cognitive explanations of behavior.

_____ 34. **(B)** Units are always enmeshed in the system.

_____ 35. **(A)** The friends are not present anymore, but Alexandra has a mental model of who attended.

_____ 36. **(B)** An exemplar is a "best example" of a concept based on your personal experience.

_____ 37. **(B)** For many people, apples serve as a more "average" version of a fruit than an avocado does.

_____ 38. **(D)** The word "average" is a clue that we're talking about prototypes here.

_____ 39. **(A)** This is a classic problem-solving model.

_____ 40. **(D)** Brandon is having trouble feeling confident that he can implement a good solution.

_____ 41. **(C)** Rachel sees only one purpose for her Excel program instead of the full range of possibilities.

_____ 42. **(E)** Zach is making an emotional or "gut" decision.

_____ 43. **(C)** This is a modification of the famous Asian disease problem proposed by Tversky and Kahnemann to illustrate framing effects.

Thinking Summary	
Number Correct	
Number Incorrect	
Number Blank	

Sensation and Perception

_____ 44. **(C)** Prosopagnosia results from damage to the fusiform face area of the inferior temporal lobe.

_____ 45. **(D)** The physicians have the same d', which indicates their sensitivity is also the same.

_____ 46. **(E)** Hair cells in the cochlea and semicircular canals respond to movement in their surrounding fluids by producing action potentials.

_____ 47. **(A)** Rods are more prevalent in the peripheral areas of the retina.

_____ 48. **(D)** Sound from the side impacts one ear before the other. Sounds directly in front or behind the head are difficult to distinguish because arrival times are similar.

_____ 49. **(B)** Expectations about what you should perceive improve perception.

_____ 50. **(D)** The somatosensory cortex is "plastic," which means it can reorganize in response to changes in input.

_____ 51. **(B)** This is the formal definition of transduction.

_____ 52. **(A)** This is the formal definition of Stevens's power law.

_____ 53. **(C)** The sensory (and motor) homunculi provide more processing space to body parts requiring precise feedback and fine motor movement.

_____ 54. **(E)** Light filling the surround but not the center should inhibit the cell's response nearly completely.

_____ 55. **(D)** The photopigments contained in cones are broken down, which begins the process of visual transduction, only in bright light conditions. Cones process color and fine detail.

Sensation and Perception Summary	
Number Correct	
Number Incorrect	
Number Blank	

Physiological/Behavioral Neuroscience

_____ 56. **(C)** If the process of reuptake is inhibited, more molecules of a neurochemical will remain in the synaptic gap where they can continue to interact with receptors.

_____ 57. **(A)** Degeneration in the substantia nigra leading to further degeneration in the basal ganglia forms the basis for Parkinson's disease.

_____ 58. **(C)** The autonomic nervous system sends commands to glands and organs, including the heart.

_____ 59. **(B)** Saltatory comes from the Latin word _saltare_, which means to dance or jump. This describes the propagation of action potentials from node to node in a myelinated axon.

_____ 60. **(D)** Lesions of the amygdala abolish previously learned classically conditioned fear responses and prevent the learning of new ones.

_____ 61. **(B)** This is a definition of myelin.

_____ 62. **(D)** Acetylcholine is the major neurotransmitter found at the neuromuscular junction.

_____ 63. **(C)** Both PET and fMRI provide information about brain activity. CT cannot distinguish between a dead or living brain as it provides no data on activity. Repeated TMS bombards the cortex with magnetism but does not record activity.

_____ 64. **(A)** This result is especially evident in the case of Henry Molaison, the famous amnesic patient "H. M."

_____ 65. **(C)** These areas show the most compelling evidence of adult neurogenesis.

_____ 66. **(A)** As the positively charged sodium ions enter a neuron, the recording of an action potential shows a "rise," or depolarization.

_____ 67. **(E)** Although the cerebellum is involved with many more complex behaviors than balance and motor coordination, damage to this structure will produce these deficits.

_____ 68. **(E)** One of the most thoroughly lateralized functions in the human brain is language. However, people who are left-handed or somewhat ambidextrous can show atypical lateralization of language.

_____ 69. **(C)** All three structures have major roles in motor functions.

_____ 70. **(C)** Norepinephrine activity is associated with alertness and vigilance, making this neurochemical one of interest in cases of PTSD.

_____ 71. **(D)** This is by definition.

_____ 72. **(B)** Although addiction has many complex sources, it is abolished in animals by lesioning the nucleus accumbens. We do not use this as a "cure" for human addicts, as the nucleus accumbens has many other important contributions to normal functioning.

_____ 73. **(B)** During the relative refractory period, the neuron is hyperpolarized. It can fire, but needs more than the usual amount of depolarization in order to reach threshold.

_____ 74. **(E)** The amount and pattern of alcohol use required to produce symptoms of fetal alcohol syndrome remain unknown, prompting advice to pregnant women to completely abstain from all alcohol.

_____ 75. **(C)** The suprachiasmatic nucleus has been shown to maintain independent circadian rhythms even when isolated in a petri dish. It is considered to be the body's "master clock."

_____ 76. **(C)** The vast majority of human growth hormone is released during the deepest stages (Stages 3 and 4) of NREM sleep.

_____ 77. **(E)** Alpha, beta, and gamma waves are recorded during waking. Theta waves are recorded in lighter NREM sleep, and delta waves are characteristic of deeper stages of NREM sleep.

_____ 78. **(A)** Diabetes requires modification of a simple blood glucose level explanation for hunger in favor of a glucose availability hypothesis. People with diabetes can be very hungry because their cells are not receiving nutrients trapped in the circulation.

_____ 79. **(C)** For both males and females, testosterone levels are most closely related to sexual desire.

_____ 80. **(A)** The James-Lange theory of emotion proposes that subjective awareness of an emotional state follows and is dependent on a precisely defined set of physical symptoms. When the athlete becomes aware of his physical arousal, he subjectively feels more aroused and aggressive.

_____ 81. **(B)** Clinical studies indicate that damage to these two areas of the brain is often associated with sudden reductions in the ability to make logical decisions.

Physiological/Behavioral Neuroscience Summary	
Number Correct	
Number Incorrect	
Number Blank	

Clinical and Abnormal

_____ 82. **(D)** According to DSM-5, the symptoms of depression used to diagnose major depressive disorder and bipolar disorder are identical. What differs between the two disorders is the presence of mania in bipolar disorder.

_____ 83. **(A)** The DSM-5 label for what used to be known as a somatoform disorder is now somatic symptom disorder.

_____ 84. **(A)** Linehan's dialectical behavior therapy has demonstrated significant efficacy in treating cases of borderline personality disorder.

_____ 85. **(B)** Applied behavior analysis (ABA) is the newer preferred term for what used to be known as behavior modification. It is a direct application of the principles of classical and operant conditioning to treatment.

_____ 86. **(E)** One of the hallmark problems of individuals with autism spectrum disorder is a ritualistic need for sameness. Change in the environment or in a routine might elicit a strong, negative response by the individual.

_____ 87. **(A)** The concordance rate for schizophrenia in identical twins is about 50%, meaning that having a twin with schizophrenia gives you about a 50% chance of also being diagnosed. The concordance rate for siblings is much lower.

_____ 88. **(B)** Obsessions are repetitive thoughts while compulsions are repeated, ritualistic behaviors. Checking is a common type of compulsive behavior in patients with OCD.

_____ 89. **(D)** SSRIs are used for a variety of psychological disorders but more commonly for people with symptoms of depression.

_____ 90. **(E)** Exposure therapy has been shown to be efficacious in the treatment of specific phobias.

_____ 91. **(B)** Existential therapy is endorsed by therapists who believe many problems originate in the human ability to question the meaning of life.

_____ 92. **(D)** Shawn is counteracting possible negative mood by engaging in an activity that generally is associated with positive mood. Doing so within his social network is likely to produce even better results.

_____ 93. **(E)** Type A personality on its own shows little correlation with health outcomes. However, hostility, with its negative impact on social connectivity, is associated with higher risk for cardiovascular disease.

_____ 94. **(D)** This is an example of a delusion of control.

_____ 95. **(A)** Difficulty staying seated when staying seated is expected is one of the diagnostic criteria for ADHD.

_____ 96. **(C)** Autism spectrum disorder is characterized by communication and social deficits like those described in this question.

_____ 97. **(D)** Unfortunate misinformation has led to the urban myth that vaccinations may be the cause of autism spectrum disorder in spite of the complete lack of empirical support for this hypothesis.

_____ 98. **(B)** Ritalin (methylphenidate) and Adderall (amphetamine salts) function as dopaminergic reuptake inhibitors.

_____ 99. **(C)** This cluster of symptoms is associated with schizophrenia.

_____ 100. **(A)** Patients with schizophrenia show dramatically reduced levels of activity in the frontal lobes.

_____ 101. **(B)** It is very challenging to distinguish between a patient with schizophrenia and a person with "stimulant psychosis" resulting from the use of cocaine, methamphetamine, and other dopamine agonists on the basis of clinical observation alone.

_____ 102. **(B)** Correlations show that schizophrenia is more common in lower-SES communities. Being poor might be a risk factor for schizophrenia, schizophrenia might prevent a person from maintaining economic security, some third factor might lead to both outcomes, or all of the above.

_____ 103. **(A)** The same criteria are used to describe depression found in both disorders.

_____ 104. **(D)** Beginning at puberty, rates of major depression in males and females begins to diverge, leading to females accounting for two-thirds of adult patients.

_____ 105. **(B)** Serotonin and norepinephrine suppress REM sleep. With less activity of these two neurochemicals, abnormally high levels of REM occur.

_____ 106. **(C)** Diagnosing panic disorder requires the occurrence of multiple, frequent attacks accompanied by distress at the thought of having another attack.

_____ 107. **(C)** Agoraphobia is named after the Greek agora, or marketplace.

_____ 108. **(C)** People with body dysmorphic disorder see "flaws" in their appearance that others do not notice.

_____ 109. **(D)** Cognitive restructuring and use of reward are central to the application of cognitive-behavioral therapy.

Clinical and Abnormal Summary	
Number Correct	
Number Incorrect	
Number Blank	

Life Span Development

_____ 110. **(E)** People do drop out of longitudinal studies. Because cross-sectional studies are usually conducted on a single occasion, dropout is not a problem.

_____ 111. **(A)** Social referencing refers to watching the emotional response of others. We can assume that the teacher would either be calm or distressed at the sight of the snake, which could influence the emotional response of the students.

_____ 112. **(C)** Gilligan emphasized care as a major component of morality, whereas Kohlberg did not.

_____ 113. **(E)** The ability to hide is characteristic of living things, while the moon is inanimate. Attributing the abilities of living things to inanimate objects is animism.

_____ 114. **(C)** Private speech was incorporated into the developmental theories of Vygotsky.

_____ 115. **(A)** This finding was reported by Sullaway, but has not been consistently replicated.

_____ 116. **(A)** Symbolic play is defined as the use of one object to represent another.

_____ 117. **(C)** Prior to the achievement of object permanence, objects are forgotten as soon as they disappear. After the achievement of object permanence, a child understands that the object still exists and is likely to look for it.

_____ 118. **(B)** In parallel play, children are near each other but do not influence the other's activities.

_____ 119. **(C)** This is the classic Moro reflex response.

_____ 120. **(C)** The ecological view focuses on behavior within a particular niche, whereas the universal view takes more of a species-wide approach to development.

_____121. **(A)** The ectoderm develops into the nervous system, skin, and in appropriate animals, things like horns and hooves.

_____122. **(B)** Human infants seem preprogrammed to engage with social stimuli like faces.

_____123. **(C)** Infants control the arms before the hands, which are lateral (away from the midline) relative to the arms.

_____124. **(B)** If you do not need to change a concept in response to learning about a new instance of the concept, you can assimilate the new instance into the existing concept. If you have to change the concept, accommodation occurs.

_____125. **(A)** Securely attached children explore the environment at age-appropriate distances and return occasionally to interact with caregivers.

_____126. **(D)** The achievement of conservation of number is more typical of children in the concrete operational stage than of those in the preoperational stage. The borderline of age for these stages is about six years of age, so Ashley is just on the young side for making this transition.

_____127. **(C)** Erikson viewed the challenge facing adolescents as achieving identity or experiencing identity role confusion.

_____128. **(B)** Object permanence in human infants occurs in the latter half of the first year of life, usually around 9 or 10 months of age.

_____129. **(E)** Piaget used the term *egocentrism* to describe the young child's relative difficulties in taking the view of other people. Children who have not yet achieved theory of mind also cannot take the viewpoint of others, as demonstrated in the classic Sally-Anne task.

_____130. **(B)** Very young children startle when a moving toy does not appear between two blocks when they expect it to do so, indicating that basic knowledge about the movement of objects in reality is present at very early points in human life.

_____131. **(C)** Rothbart's temperament theories focus on these three attributes.

_____132. **(C)** Harlow's work suggested that bonding is influenced by touch and comforting.

_____133. **(B)** The authoritative parenting style combines high support for the child with high levels of behavioral regulation. This style is associated with the best outcomes for children.

_____134. **(D)** Fluid intelligence, or reasoning that does not require prior knowledge, tends to decrease in adulthood with age.

_____135. **(C)** In the absence of disease states such as dementia, cognitive changes are mild and tend to occur toward the end of life.

Life Span Development Summary	
Number Correct	
Number Incorrect	
Number Blank	

Personality

_____ 136. **(A)** Type theories put individuals in boxes—you are an introvert or an extrovert. Trait theories add the dimension of the strength of a characteristic. You are *very* extroverted or *mildly* extroverted.

_____ 137. **(B)** Being highly neurotic may not seem like a very attractive way to be, so the test taker is trying to skew her results in a more socially acceptable direction.

_____ 138. **(C)** This is by definition.

_____ 139. **(D)** Regression is a Freudian defense mechanism characterized by returning to a less mature level of behavior. Children cry frequently, whereas adults do not. By acting in a childlike way, Brittany might expect to be treated more kindly.

_____ 140. **(D)** With conditional positive regard (say, like the consequences of operant conditioning), Rogers believes people will develop guilt and shame and be unable to achieve self-actualization.

_____ 141. **(B)** Agreeableness measures trust, kindness, and sympathy.

_____ 142. **(C)** People with an internal locus of control see most of their outcomes as being the result of their talents and efforts. People with an external locus of control are more likely to view their outcomes as a result of luck, chance, and opportunity (being in the right place at the right time).

_____ 143. **(D)** The other four are examples of projective tests, while the MMPI is not.

_____ 144. **(A)** This statement describes the way the test is normally interpreted.

_____ 145. **(D)** Eysenck's third trait is psychoticism, which does not appear in the Big Five.

Personality Summary	
Number Correct	
Number Incorrect	
Number Blank	

Social

_____ 146. **(E)** While many of the variations Milgram studied produced small changes in outcomes, the proximity of the teacher and learner usually had a large effect. The closer the two were in proximity, the less likely the teacher was to continue to administer shocks.

_____ 147. **(A)** When we feel sorry for another or empathize with another's situation, we are more likely to behave altruistically.

_____ 148. **(B)** Exemplification refers to efforts to make yourself appear virtuous. By staying later than required, the employee wishes to be viewed as "extra good."

_____ 149. **(A)** Arousal in one domain can promote arousal in other domains.

_____ 150. **(C)** People from individualistic cultures such as the United States. chose the single pen, while individuals from more collectivistic cultures, such as Korea, chose a pen with the more common color.

_____ 151. **(B)** Schemas or scripts are important parts of cognitive explanations of behavior.

_____ 152. **(C)** Interdependence theory is one of several social exchange theories of interpersonal relationships based on perceived gains and losses associated with a relationship.

_____ 153. **(A)** The theory of planned behavior added perceived behavioral control as a construct to the earlier theory of reasoned action. Both theories are associated with Fishbein and Ajzen.

_____ 154. **(C)** Bandura described social learning as learning purely through observation. While the presence of positive reinforcement in choice D might sound like learning, Bandura argued that you don't need to go through the actions in order to learn.

_____ 155. **(B)** A person sacrificing him- or herself for others appears counterproductive to reproductive success, unless the sacrifice is directed to saving those who carry some of the same genes. There are many other explanations of altruism, but this one is favored in evolutionary psychology.

_____ 156. **(D)** Taking personal responsibility is associated with high achievement motivation, while the other choices are the opposite of characteristics shown by people with high achievement motivation.

_____ 157. **(A)** Bandura proposed that a person's behavior affects the environment, which in turn shapes the person's behavior.

_____ 158. **(B)** A downward comparison involves looking at those whose performance is considered below your own.

_____ 159. **(A)** Social exchange theory looks at the impact of perceived fairness on relationships. If you receive an expensive gift, you might damage a relationship by responding with an unfair exchange.

_____ 160. **(A)** The Freudian defense mechanism of displacement suggests that we "pass it along." Courtney is upset about something she can't easily control, so she takes out her frustration on the person behind her in line.

_____ 161. **(C)** According to the correspondence bias, we make dispositional attributions even when we are fully aware of the power of the situation. Courtney might have been fully aware of the difficult circumstances of the man ahead of her in line, but she is likely to focus on his personal characteristics (Note: Contemporary social psychologists DO make a distinction between the correspondence bias and the fundamental attribution error, but the GRE Psychology Test questions may not have caught up with that yet. The questions in the real test might use the terms interchangeably, which is not correct. Please refer to the review section on this issue for more guidance.)

_____ 162. **(A)** The actor-observer bias suggests we use situational attributions more in explanations of our own behavior while continuing to depend on dispositional explanations for the behavior of others.

_____ 163. **(C)** Hostile people tend to make stronger dispositional attributions than others.

_____ 164. **(C)** Thomas's behavior is elicited by the situation in which he finds himself. He has one self with his friends and another facet of self with his grandfather.

_____ 165. **(C)** When forming first impressions, we might place too much emphasis on a small number of desirable attributes, overlooking other more important things.

_____ 166. **(D)** Being rejected from her first-choice school produces discomfort in the form of dissonance. To resolve the dissonance, Kayla cannot change the rejection, but she can change her attitude about the school. By downgrading the school, she resolves her feelings of dissonance.

_____ 167. **(B)** This is actually a true story about my brother. Stereotypes are cognitive. We form categories and expectations based on those categories. Most of us dislike being put in boxes, and of course, the boxes provide an incomplete description of the individual in most cases.

_____ 168. **(C)** Steele has published many demonstrations of the stereotype threat effect in which performance actually conforms to stereotyped beliefs.

_____ 169. **(C)** Simple proximity does not seem to affect prejudice much. However, cooperative activities with individuals who are perceived as typical representatives of their groups and who are peers can reduce prejudice.

_____ 170. **(D)** Harry is clearly using the central route to persuasion in selecting his next broom, which will make him relatively immune to the more peripheral cues related to speaker characteristics, the emotional tone of the message, and the presentation of the message in a pleasant setting.

_____ 171. **(B)** This is a classic door-in-the-face approach. The charity does not really expect to receive the big donation very often, but by making people feel obligated to the charity because they let them down, the charity can expect to receive quite a few small donations.

Social Summary	
Number Correct	
Number Incorrect	
Number Blank	

General

_____ 172. **(D)** Tolman developed the sign-Gestalt theory, which suggests that three aspects of learning work together as a "gestalt": the goal of the behavior, the signal for action, and "means-end relations."

_____ 173. **(B)** The collective unconscious was contributed by Jung in response to his seeing similar cultural attributes during his wide travels.

_____ 174. **(A)** Although the idea that Skinner thought cognition was rubbish is usually vastly overstated in many textbooks, of the psychologists listed here, mental activity would have the least interest for Skinner.

_____ 175. **(D)** The work of economist Roland Fryer of Harvard shows very clearly that paying low-income children to read quickly improves their academic performance. However, educational psychologists worry that paying children who enjoy reading to read will make reading a less satisfying "job."

_____ 176. **(C)** Beliefs and expectations are key terms for cognitive explanations of behavior.

_____ 177. **(B)** Educational psychologists use the term _scaffolding_ to the gradual removal of supervision as a skill is mastered.

_____ 178. **(C)** Industrial/organizational psychologists suggest that the perception of unfair distribution of resources has a damaging effect on employee motivation.

_____ 179. **(A)** It's hard to find a more strict behaviorist than Watson.

_____ 180. **(B)** Workers work for many reasons, including pay, but a person who values the actual work that is done for pay is likely to view it as a calling.

General Summary	
Number Correct	
Number Incorrect	
Number Blank	

Measurement

_____ 181. **(C)** The dreaded Type I error suggests that you need to go back to the drawing board. If the null hypothesis is true, you must reject or modify your experimental hypothesis instead of proceeding with your report.

_____ 182. **(B)** This is an example of strong test-retest reliability. Most of the ETS tests share this feature, so retaking the test without changing your preparation is unlikely to be helpful.

_____ 183. **(A)** The nominal scale consists of putting things in categories without order or structure.

_____ 184. **(E)** An insignificant outcome is an insignificant outcome. We take this no further.

_____ 185. **(B)** To best describe the central tendency of the salary structure of an organization, the median (point where half of the instances are above and half below) might work best. You are likely to have one or a few senior executives making very large salaries and lots of minions making much less.

_____ 186. **(B)** If you used simple random sampling, you might not obtain enough individuals in the ethnic groups of interest to make your analysis useful. If you set out your categories, then randomly sample within those categories, you are more likely to obtain the results you need.

_____ 187. **(A)** For many tests, raw scores are converted to _T_ scores such that the mean is 50 and each change of 10 indicates 1 standard deviation. So a score of 70 would represent a score that is 2 standard deviations (20 divided by 10) above the mean of 50.

_____ 188. **(D)** Correlation alphas provide a measure of internal validity. The usual acceptable minimum is .70.

_____ 189. **(B)** The first "blind" is that of the children, who do not know which juice they are drinking. The second "blind" is that of the observer, who does not know which children are receiving the active substance and which are receiving the placebo until the experiment is complete. The double-blind placebo-controlled design is the "gold standard" of treatment efficacy designs.

_____ 190. **(C)** It is likely that your instructors have drilled this into your head, but it is still tempting to wish to make a causal conclusion based on correlational data. The data simply do not support this, however.

_____ 191. **(B)** The lexical decision task is a classic method for studying priming. Using reaction time as the dependent variable, word pairs are presented and the participant must indicate whether the second word is a "real" word (*flame*) or not (*plame*).

_____ 192. **(C)** Without random assignment, we do not have a true experiment.

_____ 193. **(C)** Participants often seem to want to second guess an experiment, which may lead them to consciously or unconsciously conform to the expected outcome.

_____ 194. **(D)** Again, providing a placebo control and making both participants and observers blind to the condition of each participant until the experiment is complete is the gold standard of treatment efficacy design.

_____ 195. **(E)** The medication group showed no change, indicating that they did not experience any further declines in performance while taking the experimental drug. The control group, however, performed more poorly on the posttest than they had done on the pretest. If these differences turn out to be statistically significant, they would provide evidence supporting the ability of the new drug to prevent deterioration of performance on a memory test in patients with TBI.

_____ 196. **(E)** In some cases, our ethical impulses make for bad science. It is important to randomly assign participants to groups. The informed consent for the experiment should alert potential participants to the fact that they may receive a placebo instead of a drug that might help them. Usually, this type of study is done against the background of "conventional treatment" for both experimental and placebo groups so that nobody goes untreated.

_____ 197. **(D)** By definition, an experiment that does not include random assignment to groups is quasi-experimental. This weakens the conclusions we can draw, because without random assignment, there might be influential differences between the participants in the two conditions.

198. **(D)** A graph of the two lines (low dose/high dose) with age on the *x*-axis and depression test score on the *y*-axis would show that the lines were not parallel. This confirms the interaction effect.

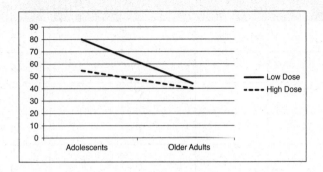

Knowing that the interaction is significant allows us to say that the decrease in scores for adolescents is greater than the decrease in scores for older adults, or that adolescents showed more benefits from the drug than older adults did.

199. **(B)** We cannot prove a hypothesis to be true, but we can certainly prove one to be false. Under these circumstances, the hypothesis must be modified or completely rejected.

200. **(B)** Being able to replicate scientific research is one of the cornerstones of good methodology.

201. **(A)** If you have a hypothesis stating that school shooters play violent video games, you must reject the hypothesis if you have a case study of a school shooter who does not play violent video games.

202. **(B)** Surveys remain a useful tool for obtaining fast, relatively cheap results.

203. **(A)** The independent variable is the one that is manipulated by the researcher.

204. **(D)** Validity refers to the ability of a test to assess what it is supposed to assess. If a test is designed to predict graduate school performance and then it actually delivers that result, its validity is good.

205. **(C)** This is a common rookie error seen by institutional review boards. No connections should be made between identifying information and data. If Amber wants to offer her drawing, she can collect contact information that remains separate from data.

Measurement Summary	
Number Correct	
Number Incorrect	
Number Blank	

Now transfer the data you collected for each section into the chart below for easy reference.

	Number Correct (C)	Number Incorrect (I)	Number Blank	C-(I/4)	75th Percentile Target	Maximum Possible
Learning					5	7
Language					5	6
Memory					12	19
Thinking					8	11
Sensation Perception					8	12
Physio/BN					18	26
Clinical/ Abnormal					18	28
Life Span					18	26
Personality					7	10
Social					18	26
General					6	9
Methods					16	25

Computing Your Total Score	
Add up the totals of the C and I rows above and fill in the total number correct, total number incorrect, and C-(I/4) below. The ETS rounds up for .5 and above, and down for .1 to .4.	
Total Number Correct	
Total Number Incorrect	
Total Raw Score C – (I/4) =	

For copyright reasons, we cannot provide a chart for converting raw scores to scale scores. In addition, the scaled scores differ a bit from one version of the test to another. Please review the latest *GRE Psychology Test Practice Book*, which is free from ETS, to get an idea of how the scaled scores (which are the ones reported to your programs) will look.

We can, however, give you some representative ranges.

Raw Score	Scaled Score	Percentile
175+	800–880	99
163	760	95
154	730	90
147	710	85
138	680	75
134	670	70
125	640	60
117	615	50

PLANNING YOUR STUDY

Review your C-(I/4) scores for each of the topic areas in your results chart. We are assuming that you would like to score as high as possible, but your chances of being admitted to a competitive graduate program are better if you score in the 75th percentile or above. We are using that as an initial target. The relevant C-(I/4) scores for each topic area appear at the bottom of the columns in bold.

Compare your C-(I/4) scores with the target scores. Do you see a pattern? Are there some areas where you are stronger than others? Are your scores consistent across all topic areas? Can you identify any weak areas?

Keeping your strengths and weaknesses in mind, it is time to review! To make the best use of your efforts, tackle your weak areas first and give them the most time and attention.

Review of Psychology $\Big|$ 3

ABOUT THE REVIEW

Now you know how well your introductory psychology notes and the underlining and notations in your book prepared you for the GRE. Naturally, there is work to be done, and this section is designed to help you in your comprehensive review.

Start by reading through the entire section, spending more time in the areas that were weak in your Diagnostic Test 1 analysis. Keep a current general psychology book handy (see listings in Chapter 1), and use it frequently as you review. After you have finished reviewing, take Diagnostic Test 2. Evaluate your score using the same procedures you did with Diagnostic Test 1. This will tell you which areas need still more review; return to those sections for additional work.

As stated in Chapter 1, the subject areas covered by the Psychology Test and included in this review are the following:

Learning
Language
Memory
Thinking
Sensation and Perception
Physiological/Behavioral Neuroscience
Clinical and Abnormal
Life Span Development
Personality
Social
General
Measurement and Methodology

Topics in this review are arranged in this same order, which is also the same order used in Diagnostic Test 1. Hopefully, this will facilitate your ability to focus on the areas that need the most work. Even if you did very well on an area, however, we recommend that you spend time on the corresponding review section. Each area covers quite a bit of ground, and the 205-question diagnostic and practice tests can only scratch the surface of the possible questions.

During your review, keep in mind that for each subject area you will be expected to exhibit a mastery of basic principles and concepts (theories and laws, if the area has any), names of persons associated with the better-known concepts and research, and primary research findings. By concentrating on these aspects in each review area, you will soon gain a clearer understanding both of the individual areas and of the science of psychology as a whole.

To facilitate your review, each topical section will include a brief, descriptive introduction to the area. An outline of basic principles, concepts, personalities, and terms will follow the introduction. Don't panic when you view an outline and find little or nothing familiar. That's why we're here—to get acquainted with the area. You'll soon be quite familiar with those strange-looking outlines! A comprehensive general psychology text will serve as a helpful reference and for clarification throughout your review.

Think of it this way: The outline is a road map to the area. It tells you the major routes, the cities and towns along the way. The general psychology text resembles a close-up of a particular area on the map as well as an atlas for reference and clarification. Between them, you definitely will know where you're going!

LEARNING

Organisms have three ways of responding to the environment. They can respond with reflexes, instincts (fixed-action patterns), or with learned responses. Reflexes and instincts are relatively inflexible, but learning allows organisms to adapt to new circumstances, providing an enormous advantage in the game of survival.

Learning is defined by psychologists as a relatively permanent change in behavior because of experience. In this section, we explore a number of types of learning. For example, you might be able to think of a food that you couldn't possibly imagine eating again because you ate it once and became ill.

You will come to know this type of learning as classical conditioning—the conditioning of an expectation by way of a stimulus or cue. We have learned similar signals and signs in our backgrounds and environments, and may have developed a whole repertoire of positive feelings or fears related to them. As we "discover" within a given environment—finding that a given behavior leads to a positive outcome while another behavior does not—we engage in another kind of learning known as operant or instrumental. It is, in effect, the "school of trial and error learning," from which we will preserve and strengthen those behaviors that bring us positive outcomes and very likely will drop or change those behaviors that do not so reward us. The settings in which we learn are virtually limitless and endless—as a child interacting with parents, as a student interacting with classroom material and study habits, as a brother and sister interacting with each other, as a loving couple in the midst of spring. Welcome to the field of learning and to its terms that literally affect all of us daily.

The human glimpse may seem brief in this discussion of basic learning principles, but you will soon find that we have headed for practical applications of these principles that will affect all of us. Subsequent sections will cover cognition and complex human learning as well as developmental psychology and other areas of the discipline. In order not to flounder in those sections, you must master the basic learning principles. There are numerous terms and concepts you will need to know, so take a deep breath and plunge in.

Learning Outline

Concepts	Names	Terms
Forms of learning		Habituation
		Sensitization
	Pavlov	Classical conditioning (also called Respondent or Type-S)
	Skinner, Watson	Operant conditioning (also called Instrumental or Type-R)
Classical conditioning terminology		Conditioned stimulus (CS)
		Unconditioned stimulus (UCS)
		Conditioned response (CR)
		Unconditioned response (UCR)

		Temporal relations between CS and UCS
		    Forward pairing (delayed or trace)
		    Backward pairing
		    Simultaneous pairing

		Second-order conditioning
		Discrimination and generalization
Operant conditioning terminology	Thorndike	Law of effect
		Positive reinforcement
		Negative reinforcement
		Types of reinforcers
		Appetitive stimulus
		Aversive stimulus
	Hull	Drive-reduction theory
	Premack	Premack's principle
	Skinner	Shaping
		Successive approximation
		Cumulative record
		Discriminative stimulus
Learning curve terminology		Acquisition
		Plateau/asymptote
		Extinction
		Spontaneous recovery
Schedules of reinforcement		Continuous vs. partial reinforcement
		Partial-reinforcement effect
		Fixed interval
		Variable interval
		Fixed ratio
		Variable ratio
Aversive conditioning		Escape and avoidance behavior
	Mowrer	Two-process theory
		Punishment

Concepts	Names	Terms
Neural basis for learning		Long-term potentiation
	Hebb	Hebb's law
Evolutionary perspectives on learning		Equipotentiality principle
		Biological constraints
	Garcia and Koelling	Belongingness
		One-trial learning
Clinical applications of conditioning		Behavior therapy
		Conditioned emotional response
		Phobias
		Compensatory reaction/tolerance
		Drug addiction
		Compulsive behavior
	Seligman	Depression
Cognitive learning	Rescorla/Wagner	Contiguity vs. contingency
		Blocking effect
	Seligman	Learned helplessness
	Tolman	Latent learning
		Cognitive map
	Köhler	Insight ("aha" phenomenon)

Outline Terms Elaborated

FORMS OF LEARNING

Learning can be broadly defined as any long-lasting change in an individual's behavior that results from experience. This definition distinguishes learning from fatigue or hunger (a short-lived change in behavior), from maturation (a change that does not depend on experience), and from evolution (a change that is seen across generations). The simplest forms of learning are changes in a reflexive response caused by mere repetition of a stimulus: A decrease in responsiveness is *habituation* and an increase in responsiveness is *sensitization*. *Classical conditioning* results in a new association being formed between a previously neutral stimulus and a stimulus that elicits a reflexive response—this is the form of learning that Pavlov's salivating dogs exhibited. *Operant conditioning* pairs a response with a consequence in order to change the likelihood of that response; this form of learning is most associated with behaviorists *Watson* and *Skinner*.

CLASSICAL CONDITIONING TERMINOLOGY

Classical conditioning starts with an *unconditioned stimulus (UCS)* that already elicits an *unconditioned response (UCR)*. During learning, a *conditioned stimulus (CS)* is repeatedly paired with the UCS, and eventually the CS will elicit a *conditioned response (CR)* that is similar in type to the UCR. In Pavlov's case, the UCS was the food, the CS was the bell, and the UCR and the CR were the salivation. Animals will show *generalization* of the CS to similar stimuli and *discrimination* between the CS and different stimuli. The temporal relation between the UCS and CS can vary: The CS can precede the UCS (*forward pairing*), it can occur at the same time as the UCS *(simultaneous pairing)*, or it can even follow the UCS *(backward pairing)*. Forward pairing produces the best conditioning and backward, the absolute worst. *Second-order* conditioning occurs when a new CS is paired with a previously learned CS (instead of with a UCS) during learning.

OPERANT CONDITIONING TERMINOLOGY

In contrast to classical conditioning, where the response or behavior of interest is automatically elicited with the appropriate stimulus, in operant conditioning, the response may or may not be produced. The goal of operant conditioning is to change the likelihood with which the organism produces the response. The ability to change behavior with consequences in an animal was first demonstrated when Edward *Thorndike* taught a hungry cat to press a lever or pull a wire in a *puzzle box* in order to get out and obtain a food reward. His description of the cat's behavior formed the basis for his *Law of Effect*, which became the foundation for operant conditioning. There are a number of different categories of consequences that can be used in operant conditioning: Reinforcement is any consequence that increases the probability of a response. *Positive reinforcement* involves the presentation of an *appetitive stimulus* (e.g., the cat's food) as a consequence; negative reinforcement involves the termination of an *aversive stimulus* (e.g., the cat's freedom from the confining box). (Note that negative reinforcement is not the same as punishment.) Clark *Hull* described a reinforcer as anything that reduces a *drive* for a biological need (hunger, thirst) in his *drive-reduction theory*. The *Premack principle* states that any preferred response can be a positive reinforcer. In many cases, learning must begin by a period of *shaping*, in which the animal is taught what the correct response is through a series of *successive approximations*. The total number of responses that an animal has made is often plotted in a *cumulative record* of performance. In operant conditioning, stimulus discrimination can still occur even though the response is not elicited from a stimulus (as with classical conditioning): *discriminative stimuli* in this setting can provide a context for responding.

LEARNING CURVE TERMINOLOGY

A *learning curve* is a graph of the change in the response over time (usually magnitude of a response in classical conditioning and probability of a response in operant conditioning). Learning curves have the same general shape: During *acquisition* the response increases gradually until improvement finally levels off at an *asymptote*. It remains here until the learning situation changes (the CS is no longer paired with the UCS or an operant response is not rewarded), causing the response to decline during the *extinction* period. In classical conditioning, an extinguished response may occasionally *spontaneously recover* only to be extinguished again.

SCHEDULES OF REINFORCEMENT

These describe how often an animal is rewarded for an operant response. During operant conditioning, rewards can be administered on a *continuous reinforcement* schedule or on a *partial reinforcement* schedule. The *partial-reinforcement effect* describes the resistance that partial reinforcement schedules have to extinction; in other words, they are more effective at maintaining a behavior in the long run. The four types of partial reinforcement schedules are: Fixed interval (reward every *n* seconds), variable interval (on average reward every *n* seconds), fixed ratio (reward every *n* responses), variable ratio (on average reward every *n* responses). Ratio schedules give reinforcement on the basis of the number of responses made and interval schedules give reinforcement on the basis of time. Variable ratio schedules produce very high levels of responding.

AVERSIVE CONDITIONING

Aversive conditioning modifies responding using aversive stimuli. *Punishment* involves the administration of some aversive stimulus in order to decrease responding; the effectiveness of punishment as a consequence is debatable. Removal of an aversive stimulus can be an effective reinforcer to increase responding: Allowing an animal to *escape* from an unpleasant stimulus (typically a shock) or to *avoid* it altogether is an effective way to change behavior. Punishment and escape consequences are straightforward, but *avoidance learning* is more complicated, because there is no clear reinforcer. *Mowrer* explained this phenomenon with a *two-process theory* that includes both classical conditioning (of a fear response to a neutral stimulus) and instrumental conditioning (of a response that reduces the fear).

NEURAL BASIS FOR LEARNING

For any of the laws of learning to be effective, something in the brain must be modifiable by experience. For several decades now, scientists have believed those modifications occur at the *synapse*, the small gap between neurons. Donald *Hebb* first suggested the idea that "neurons that fire together wire together." He speculated that simultaneous activity in any pair of neurons would strengthen the synapse between those neurons; hypothetically, such a process could explain classical conditioning associations. Hebb's ideas have recently received support from neurobiologists, who have documented that experience can cause a *long-term potentiation* (or increase) in the responsiveness of a neuron. The long-lasting nature of this phenomenon makes for a tantalizing comparison to learning processes, and researchers in this area are closely examining the possibility that long-term potentiation is the cellular mechanism underlying learning.

EVOLUTIONARY PERSPECTIVES ON LEARNING

John *Locke* used the term *tabula rasa* to describe the mind—infants are born with a "blank slate" onto which learned associations are written. It is not much of a leap to claim that any conditioned stimulus could be associated with any conditioned response, or any response with any reinforcer. This claim is called the *equipotentiality principle*, and was popular in the early days of behaviorism. However, much research now points to the *biological constraints* on what a species can learn. *Garcia* demonstrated that a rat could learn to associate a taste with an illness and a light with a shock, but could not associate a taste with a shock or a light with an illness. Garcia termed this *belongingness*—some associations are easier to learn, others are harder, and still others are impossible. Some associations are so easy to learn that *one trial* is enough to affect behavior. A classic example of this is food aversions. It is easy to see the selection pressures that favored certain one-trial learned associations (such as food with illness) in evolution!

CLINICAL APPLICATIONS OF CONDITIONING

These range from phobias to drug addiction, from compulsive behavior to depression. *Behavior* therapy is used to treat a wide range of clinical disorders using learning principles; and the formation of these disorders is often well explained by simple classical and instrumental conditioning. For example, the *conditioned emotional response* between an aversive stimulus and fear may explain extreme *phobias*, and treatment of phobias often involves an attempt to extinguish the learned association. *Compensatory reactions* to drugs (creating higher *tolerance*) can be explained by classical conditioning, as can cravings associated with *drug addiction*. The *two-process* theory of avoidance learning may explain the development of *compulsive* behaviors. And contingency theory could be related to feelings of helplessness and *depression*.

COGNITIVE LEARNING

Cognitive learning focuses on the knowledge that is learned and not the behavior that is modified. Robert *Rescorla* and Allan *Wagner* described the knowledge about *contingency* (versus mere *contiguity*) that is acquired during classical conditioning. Leon *Kamin* illustrated the role that surprise plays in learning contingencies with the *blocking effect* of redundant information. Martin *Seligman* documented that the absence of contingencies (reinforcements unrelated to responses) can lead to *learned helplessness*, which may be related to *depression*. Edward *Tolman* moved away from behaviorism by distinguishing between learning and behavior; one context in which he demonstrated so-called *latent learning* was in the formation of a *cognitive map* through exploration of an environment. Wolfgang *Köhler* studied learning that was not gradual (like conditioning) but instead that was *insightful*.

Learning Summary

In our review of learning, you have been reminded of some of the powerful principles that govern much of animal and human changes in behavior. We have moved from Pavlov's dogs and Thorndike's cats, to an appreciation of some of the complex human phenomena—phobias, depression, and drug addiction—that may have their roots in these principles. However, we have also had a foreshadowing that we must move beyond the study of behavior to truly understand learning: With scientists like Wagner, Tolman, and Köhler pushing the focus onto what we *know* and not just how we *behave*, psychology moved beyond behaviorism into a fuller study of complex cognition. In a later section, we will see how much further this new approach can take us toward our understanding of the mind.

If you did not reach your target score in the Learning area on Diagnostic Test 1, and if the preceding review has left you with more questions than answers, we recommend that you turn to some of the many specialized texts in this area. A good, up-to-date textbook is *The Principles of Learning and Behavior* (6th edition) by Domjan (Cengage, 2010). Finally, *Cognition, Evolution, and Behavior* (Oxford University Press, 1998) is an excellent book that places learning research in a more ecological context when discussing animal behavior and cognition.

LANGUAGE

Linguistic Analysis Levels

The field of linguistics is concerned with characterizing the structure of language. A major goal of this field is to describe a set of rules, also known as a *grammar*, that is able to account for the vast number of different utterances that are possible in a language as well as the regularity that these utterances possess. One of the major blows to behaviorism was its inability to account for these facts about language. A grammar consists of three major types of rules that govern language production: *Syntax* (word order and inflection), *semantics* (meaning), and *phonology* (sound structure). Because violations to all three of these types of rules occur often in normal language use, it is important to keep in mind a distinction between *linguistic competence* and *linguistic performance*. This distinction becomes particularly relevant in studies of language development. The relationship between competence and performance has been the subject of heated debates.

Components of Language

The smallest structural element of spoken language that distinguishes meaning is the *phoneme*, which corresponds to a single sound; the English language has forty phonemes. Phonemes vary from language to language, and our ability to discriminate between phonemes of other languages is very poor. Phonemes are joined together into *morphemes*, which correspond to a single meaning. A word can have one morpheme (e.g., bus) or it can have more than one morpheme (e.g., sing + ing). Morphemes like "ing" that add meaning or grammatical information to another morpheme are called *bound morphemes*. Morphemes are joined into words, which are joined together to form *propositions*, which are units of meaning in a sentence. A proposition has a *subject* and a *predicate*. Propositions are incorporated into sentences that vary in structure and even meaning (e.g., shifting emphasis in the proposition by using a passive construction). *Phrase structure analysis* is an important method in understanding language processing.

Language Comprehension

One of the challenges facing computer scientists is to make a computer program that can understand language—real language, as opposed to a series of simple commands. The fact that this problem has yet to be solved illustrates how difficult the task of language comprehension is, even though we do it effortlessly all the time. One of the most important steps in successful language comprehension is *parsing*, whereby words in a spoken or written message are transformed into a mental representation of the meaning of the message. There are rules that guide this transformation, and in order to apply these rules, we break sentences into smaller units, called *constituents*. For example, in the preceding sentence, a constituent would be "we break sentences into smaller units." People process the meaning of sentences one constituent at a time. How do psychologists know this? One technique psycholinguists use to study sentence processing involves interrupting people as they are reading passages and asking them to write down everything they remember. This is called an *off-line* measure of sentence processing, because it requires an interruption to measure performance. One *on-line* measure of sentence processing (one which does not require interrupting the person) uses the reader's eye movements to study parsing. Another on-line technique uses neural responses obtained from ERPs (see the review of methods in Biological Foundations for more information about this technique) to infer the time course of availability of different types of information during sentence processing. In order to interpret the meaning of a sentence, we use syntactic clues (e.g., word order and inflection) and semantic clues (e.g., the plausible interpretations of a word) to guide our comprehension. ERP studies have found that semantic and syntactic anomalies in sentences affect processing at different points in time and in different areas of the brain. One thing that makes language comprehension so difficult is the occurrence of ambiguities in sentences. There can be ambiguities in the meaning of single words—when you go down to the bank, are you depositing money or taking a walk by the river? There can also be ambiguities that are present in a sentence, but which are ultimately resolved. For example, if you start to read "The child painted . . ." you might begin to imagine a budding young artist in front of her canvas, until you finish the sentence: "The child painted by the artist was sleeping." Sentences that suggest one interpretation that turns out to be wrong are called *garden-path sentences*. Psychologists study how people read these sentences to understand the parsing process.

Language Acquisition

This is the remarkable process whereby a child achieves near mastery of a language in just a few brief years. The *behaviorists* explained language acquisition as just another example of *instrumental conditioning*; however, examination of exchanges between adults and young children revealed very few instances of correction or *reinforcement* that could lead to conditioning. An alternative hypothesis is that children are born equipped with a language capacity, not specific to any particular language, of course, but rather for *language universals*. Noam *Chomsky* argued that such an innate ability to extract the rules of language is required to overcome the *"poverty of the stimulus"* that is presented to babies. Chomsky also broke from behaviorism by distinguishing between language *competence* and language *performance*. The ability to learn a language seems to peak during a *critical period*, which is most evident when comparing first and second language acquisition. Anne *Fernald* has studied a universal way in which parents speak to children, called *Motherese*, which may help the young language learner mark word and sentence boundaries. The earliest language exposure also determines which sounds an infant is capable of discriminating; by six months there are changes in phoneme discrimination (a decrease in sensitivity to foreign contrasts). The ability to understand language precedes the ability to produce language. Early language production begins with single words, followed by two-word, *telegraphic* speech. Between two and three, children begin to produce *overregularization errors* that were not present earlier, as they learn rules (such as adding –ed to the past tense, which might produce the error "eated").

Relationship Between Language and Thought

Another contested issue is the relationship between language and thought. Perhaps the best known stance on this issue is the *Whorfian hypothesis*, which states that language determines the way in which a person thinks and perceives the world. For example, do Americans, who have eleven basic color words (green, yellow, etc.) perceive colors differently than the Dani (a native Indonesian culture), who have just two basic color words? For this question, the evidence does not support the Whorfian hypothesis; the Dani and Americans perceive colors in a similar way. In fact, most of the research in this area suggests that language does not determine the way we think or the way in which we perceive the world. An important extension of this conclusion is called the *modularity* position, most often associated with philosopher Jerry *Fodor*, which holds that language is independent from other cognitive systems (e.g., perception). Fodor further claims that the principles that govern language acquisition and use are different than those that govern the rest of cognition. This claim has been particularly influential in the study of language acquisition: Is language acquisition governed by the same learning principles that apply to other cognitive skills? The jury is still out on this issue. As psychologists have grappled with this question, a number of important principles have been discovered. Some of these are reviewed in the pages dealing with Developmental Psychology.

Language in Nonhuman Species

This is perhaps the most controversial issue in the field of psycholinguistics. Theories of language learning (behaviorism versus innate grammar) clearly make different predictions about the ability of nonhuman species to truly acquire language. In this debate, language must be distinguished from speaking—a parrot that speaks may not be using language, whereas an animal that cannot speak may be able to use a different form of language. This latter possibility has been investigated in chimpanzees using symbol-languages *(Rumbaugh)* and gesture *(Gardner)*. Chimps can learn words with these systems, but there is disagreement about whether they can learn syntax and whether they produce novel constructions. While the jury is still out, it is clear that even the most advanced chimp's language is less advanced than that of the typical three-year-old child.

Brain and Language

In most people, the *left* hemisphere is dominant for language function. Paul *Broca* first described the relation between an area in the left frontal lobe, now called *Broca's area*, and language production, in his report of a patient who could only utter the sound "tan-tan" after sustaining brain damage in that area; despite this impairment the patient could understand language normally. Karl *Wernicke* described the converse pattern of language dysfunction following brain damage at the border of the temporal lobe and parietal lobe of the left hemisphere, in an area that we now call *Wernicke's area*. These patients can produce fluent utterances that are devoid of meaning, and they have grossly impaired language comprehension.

Language

Concepts	Names	Terms
Linguistic analysis levels		Phonological (phonemes)
		Grammatical (morphemes and syntax)
		Semantic (word and sentence meaning)
Components of language		Phonemes
		Morphemes
		Words
		Propositions Subject and predicate
		Phrases and sentences

Concepts	Names	Terms
Language comprehension		Parsing
		Constituents
		Ambiguity/"garden-path" sentences
		On-line vs. off-line measurement
Language acquisition	Skinner, Mowrer	Reinforcement
	Chomsky	Inborn competence

		Stages of acquisition
		    Prelinguistic
		    Linguistic

		Motherese
		Comprehension vs. production
Relationship between language and thought	Whorf	Whorfian hypothesis (language determines thought)
	Brown	Thought determines language
	Fodor	Modularity position
Language in nonhuman species	Chomsky	Unique human ability
	Gardner, Rumbaugh	Animal language
Brain and language function	Broca	Language production/Broca's area
	Wernicke	Language comprehension/Wernicke's area

MEMORY

Types of Memory

In the nineteenth century Hermann *Ebbinghaus*, a German psychologist, used the *nonsense syllable* (consonant-vowel-consonant, e.g., DAX) to study association and learning in a revolutionary way. His famous curve of retention and forgetting demonstrated that material is forgotten rapidly in the first few hours after learning—then forgetting occurs more and more slowly as time passes. There are several distinctions in the study of memory that we can draw by way of comparison to the work of Ebbinghaus. First, Ebbinghaus was studying material for memory that was *intentionally* learned. Memory can also be tested for material learned *incidentally,* that is, without making an attempt to study something for a later test. Second, Ebbinghaus used nonsense syllables to study memory for items devoid of meaning or other associations. Although this artificial situation allows for a better understanding of basic memory principles, in the past few decades psychologists have shifted their focus to more natural learning situations, for words, pictures, stories, and events. Third, Ebbinghaus assessed his memory by measuring how long it took him to relearn the same set of words day after day. This test, which Ebbinghaus called the *savings method,* or relearning, is now described by psychologists as *implicit memory*, learning that improves your performance on a task (also called *repetition priming*) without intent to recollect the information consciously. Although the study of implicit memory is currently enjoying a resurgence in the field, for most of this century psychologists have studied *explicit memory*, the conscious recollection (either *recall* or *recognition*) of prior experiences. When you try to remember a phone number or the name of your third-grade teacher, you are explicitly trying to recall a memory. Prospective memory refers to remembering to remember something in the future. The terms *procedural* and *declarative* memory are nearly synonymous with implicit and explicit memory. Fourth, Ebbinghaus studied learning of an event in his own experience. So-called *episodic memory* of events for particular occurrences (or episodes), like what you ate for breakfast this morning or what grade you got on your last history test, was distinguished by Endel *Tulving* from generic memory of facts, called *semantic memory*, like what foods are suitable breakfast foods and the names and dates of the major battles of the Civil War.

Memory Processes

For all types of memories, successful remembering requires three mental processes. *Encoding* is the process by which an external stimulus (e.g., a face or a word) is attended to, identified, studied, and incorporated into memory. This memory must then be retained, or *stored*, for some period of time. Finally, at *retrieval* the stored information must be recovered. Psychologists have studied each of these processes in detail.

Stages of Memory

The process of encoding has been described with an *information-processing model* of three stages or memory systems: *sensory memory*, *short-term memory*, and *long-term memory*. Sensory memory, roughly speaking a mental afterimage, lasts for only a second, just long enough to allow attention and identification of a visual (*iconic* memory) or auditory (*echoic* memory) stimulus needed for later processing. The duration and capacity of the sensory store was first illuminated by George *Sperling*, who described the accurate storage by rapid rate of decay of letters flashed very briefly. With attention to information in the sensory store (or sensory register), information can be transferred to the *short-term store*, which can hold small amounts of information for about twenty seconds. Depending on the extent to which this information is further processed, some memories will be retained for longer periods of time in the *long-term store*. When you remember a phone number just long enough to dial it once, but then realize you have forgotten it when you encounter a busy signal on the line, that is a case of information that was in short-term memory but not transferred to long-term memory. The capacity of short-term memory is described in terms of units of information called *chunks*, which are defined in terms of meaning and not size. For example, the list of letters C-I-A-M-T-V-F-B-I would be nine bits, or chunks, of information unless the letters were grouped into three larger but meaningful chunks: CIA – MTV – FBI. George *Miller* established the capacity of short-term memory as 7 ± 2 chunks. In recent years the description of short-term memory has been modified to include any information that is in conscious awareness, whether from the sensory store or from older, long-term memories. Because this information is thought to be actively processed (i.e., thought about) while in consciousness, this form of memory has been called *working memory* by Alan *Baddeley*, who describes multiple working memory *buffers*, including one for verbal information and one for visuospatial information.

Factors That Influence Memory

Many factors influence how likely we are to remember some event. Memory for items on a list is affected by the order of those items: This *serial position effect* describes the advantage in memory of items at the beginning and end of the list. Memory may be better for unusual or novel things (the *von Restorff effect*) or for some emotionally charged events *(flashbulb memories)*. The method of studying, or *rehearsal*, of information also affects how likely we are to remember something. Things we make vivid through imagery or rich associations *(elaborative rehearsal)* are processed more deeply and are better remembered than things we merely repeat by rote *(maintenance rehearsal)*: The *levels of processing effect* illustrates that there is superior memory after deep processing than after shallow processing. Additionally, the *encoding specificity principle* states that memory will improve if the context at the time of retrieval closely resembles the context during encoding. When this context describes an emotional or physical state, this effect is called *state dependence*.

MNEMONICS are learning aids or strategies that train a person to use elaboration to make information more memorable. Do you know the order of notes on the treble staff? If you thought "Every Good Boy Does Fine" to remember E-G-B-D-F, you used a mnemonic device to elaborate that information. *Chunking* is a form of *recoding* information into fewer but more meaningful units to remember. A very effective mnemonic strategy is to elaborate with *mental imagery*. One such technique is called the *method of loci*, in which to-be-remembered words are imagined in different spatial locations in a familiar place. To remember, you need only take a mental tour of that location! Another effective mnemonic device is verse: "Thirty days have September, April, June, and November . . ." This falls into the larger category of *natural language mediators* that use sounds, patterns, and meanings of words already known to assist learning new information. The principle behind all of these techniques is meaningful elaboration.

Forgetting

Even with all of these mnemonic devices at our disposal, our memories will still fail us. As time passes, our memories for older events can seem to fade away. But most psychologists no longer believe that memories simply *decay* with time. Rather, *interference* from other memories may be responsible for most of what we forget. *Proactive interference* is the negative effect that old information we know has on new things we are trying to learn; when you try to learn a new language or a new computer program, you may experience proactive interference. *Retroactive interference* is the effect that new learning has on information we learned before. If you can't remember your last telephone number, that's retroactive interference. Sigmund *Freud* introduced the idea of *motivated forgetting* or *repression* of particularly painful memories. One special form of forgetting, *infantile amnesia*, may be explained by changes in retrieval contexts and cues, according to the encoding specificity principle.

CONSTRUCTIVE MEMORY views memory as a more active process than words like *storage* would suggest. New memories are interpreted, elaborated upon, and organized based on prior knowledge, or frameworks called *schemas*, in a constructive memory process first described by Sir Frederic *Bartlett* in the 1930s. This constructive process can lead to distortions in memory. Elizabeth *Loftus* has described the ways in which memories reported in *eyewitness testimony* can be distorted by things that happen or that are said after the event occurred; this is the *misinformation effect*.

Neurobiology of Memory

While everyone forgets things in daily life, some people have a profound impairment in the ability to remember. There are many causes for *amnesia*, most of which affect a structure in the brain called the *hippocampus*. As a result, a person will be unable to learn new information *(anterograde amnesia)* and may have some loss of memories for a period of time before the onset of trauma or disease *(retrograde amnesia)*. What about the movie portrayal of amnesics unable to remember their names, families, and entire childhoods? Although a convenient plot device, accidents and diseases do not result in the complete loss of long-term memories. Psychologists are beginning to understand more about different memory systems by looking at what amnesics are and are not able to learn. Memory for how to do things *(procedural memory)* is unaffected by amnesia, which devastates memory for new events *(declarative memory)*. Additionally, amnesics show *implicit memory* for events when improved performance following learning is assessed *(repetition priming)* in the absence of *explicit memory* for those events. The hippocampus is probably involved in the *consolidation* of new memories. Other regions of the brain may have different functions for memory; for example, the *frontal lobe* may play an important role in working memory. At a cellular level, the mechanism for learning in the neurons of the brain has been described as a process of *long-term potentiation* of new activity at the synapses between neurons. Some psychologists try to understand more complicated cognitive functions by constructing computational *neural networks* based on the behavior of neurons.

Categorization

Whereas the study of episodic memory has focused on encoding and retrieval processes, it is the storage or organization of knowledge that has dominated investigations of semantic memory. A major avenue of investigation in this area has centered on the formation and representation of *concepts*. The *critical feature* theory of concept representation defines concepts in terms of necessary and sufficient features. Eleanor *Rosch* argued, instead, for a less rigid representation of a concept, based on similarity to a representative *prototype* of a concept (e.g., a robin is a prototype bird). She also described a hierarchical organization of concepts, centered on a *basic level* at which we tend to categorize things.

Imagery and Visual Memory

Thus far, our entire discussion has focused on verbal memory. Because many of the same principles apply to memory for pictures, some psychologists have asserted that visual and spatial memories are stored as *propositions*, just as are verbal memories. However, the work of Roger *Shepard* and Steven *Kosslyn* suggests that visual thought is different from verbal thought, and that people are capable of rotating, scanning, and manipulating visual memories or *images* in ways similar to how they manipulate actual pictures. Spatial memories may be organized as *mental maps* that represent but often distort physical reality. *Paivio* suggested that we use a *dual code* of both visual and verbal memory whenever possible.

Memory

Concepts	Names	Terms
Types of memory	Tulving	Semantic vs. episodic
		Intentional vs. incidental
		Verbal vs. nonverbal
	Schachter	Implicit (procedural)
	Ebbinghaus	Relearning/savings method
		Repetition priming
	Squire	Explicit (declarative) Recall Recognition
		Prospective memory
Memory processes		Encoding
		Storage
		Retrieval
Stages of memory (information-processing)	Sperling	Sensory store (iconic, echoic)
	Miller, Baddeley	Short-term store/Working memory
		Long-term store
Factors that influence memory		Serial position effect
		von Restorff effect
		Flashbulb memories
		Elaborative vs. maintenance rehearsal
	Craik & Lockhart	Levels of processing effect
	Tulving	Encoding specificity principle
		Context and state dependence
Mnemonics		Method of loci
		Visual imagery
		Chunking
		Natural language mediators
Forgetting		Decay vs. interference
		Retroactive interference
		Proactive interference
		Motivated forgetting
		Infantile amnesia
Constructive memory	Bartlett	Schemas
	Loftus	Misinformation effect/ eyewitness testimony

Concepts	Names	Terms
Neurobiology of memory		Anterograde amnesia
		Retrograde amnesia
		Hippocampus (consolidation)
		Frontal lobe (working memory)
		Long-term potentiation
	Rumelhart, McClelland	Neural networks
Categorization		Critical features vs. prototypes
	Rosch	Hierarchies and basic levels
		Schemas and scripts
Imagery and Visual Memory		Propositional vs. analog
	Shepard, Kosslyn	Mental rotation
	Farah	Visual imagery
	Paivio	Dual-code, picture-superiority effect
		Mental maps

THINKING

During the heyday of behaviorism, words like *cognition* and *thought* were taboo. As learning theorists began to think about thought, and move away from strict behaviorism, the atmosphere was ripe for a major paradigm shift. This move was spurred by two historical events that, on the surface, have little to do with psychology. The first was World War II, which brought with it a number of applied problems, like how to train fighter pilots to read all of the information on a complex instrument panel. Psychologists like Donald *Broadbent* found that answers to these problems gave birth to the field of *information theory* or information processing, which persists today in studies of perception, attention, and memory. The second event was the advent of the computer age, which led to questions about how computers behave intelligently. Led by Allen *Newell* and Herbert *Simon*, cognitive psychologists and computer scientists began to ask similar questions about information processing, using the language of "buffers" and "storage" to describe their ideas. The focus on information—and not on behavior—became the foundation for *cognitive psychology*.

Perhaps the final nail in the behaviorist coffin was struck by linguists, led by Noam *Chomsky*, who challenged the notion that the laws of behaviorism had much to offer by way of understanding language. The field of *psycholinguistics* has taken off in its own right, which focuses on issues of language production, comprehension, structure, and development. Of all our many cognitive abilities, one of the most impressive and most unique is the human capacity for language. If you stop to contemplate some of the wonders of language—the seemingly infinite number of utterances that you are able to produce and comprehend without effort—or if you have ever spent any time with a young child who is just learning to speak, you should get a sense of the myriad of questions that psychologists who study language try to address. Work in the related fields of linguistics and computer science has also been enormously influential in the psychology of language.

The study of higher mental processes such as memory, language, and thought, form the heart of cognitive psychology today. This review may remind you of all of the wonderful and exciting capacities that make humans so special and the mind so thrilling a topic to explore.

THOUGHT

INFORMATION PROCESSING (Donders, Sternberg) (the time required to do each mental operation in a fixed sequence)

ATTENTION AND CONTROLLED OPERATIONS (each proceeding serially with conscious attention required), automatic processes (several proceeding simultaneously with no conscious attention required), dichotic listening and shadowing task (different messages sent to each ear simultaneously)

TYPES OF REASONING, including *inductive* (generalizing from a specific instance), *deductive* (applying a logic-based rule to new, specific situation for single-solution) (carries two error potentials: content [conclusion undesirable] and form [conclusion invalid]), *decision making* (with its heuristics [rules of thumb, focusing on likely solution-points], in which decisions are based on recent experiences producing the most readily available information). This decision-making approach can fall prey to the conjunction or "gambler's" fallacy (e.g., that if you have just rolled "snake eyes" with dice four times in a row, you will overestimate or underestimate [far above or below random or chance probabilities] that the event will occur again). Another approach—*problem solving*—uses *productive* (new or novel approach to a problem) and *reproductive* (applying old rule to new problem) thought processes, encompasses incubation (problem-mulling while engaged in nonproblem-based activities). The reproductive can at times block creativity through the rigidity of functional fixedness (e.g., hammers are only used for hammering) and mental set (applying old problem-solving strategies).

REPRESENTATIONS of the world and our experiences in it are the stuff of thought. A central question for cognitive scientists is the extent to which a particular proposed mental representation is analogical or symbolic. Analogical representations share some features or characteristics of the things to which they refer. For example, a picture of a guitar is not a real guitar, but a representation of a guitar, yet it has some guitar-like features. In contrast, symbolic representations have no such resemblance to the things they stand for; the relation is arbitrary. The word *guitar* is a symbolic representation of the object guitar; the appearance or sound of the word bears no resemblance to the appearance or sound of a guitar. One area where this question has been actively debated concerns the nature of the representations of mental images of objects and spatial configurations.

ARTIFICIAL INTELLIGENCE AND ITS COMPUTER SIMULATION OF HUMAN MENTAL OPERATIONS through two approaches—*algorithms* (proceeding systematically, step-by-step, toward solution) and *heuristics* (proceeding more rapidly than algorithms by going to most likely solution areas and utilizing subgoal analysis [defining the problem as discrete subgoals, each addressed individually])

HEURISTICS AND BIASES The human ability for reasoning and decision making differs from, say, a computer algorithm, and the cognitive constraints on human thought give rise to a number of interesting errors. Two of the leading figures in this area of research are the late Amos Tversky and his long-time collaborator Daniel Kahneman, who received a Nobel

Prize for this research in 2002. They and others have characterized the cognitive basis for common human "errors" that result from heuristics and biases in reasoning and decision making. During inductive reasoning, humans typically apply heuristics in order to reach a solution with maximum efficiency. If the problem requires an estimation of the frequency of some event, a common strategy is to employ the availability heuristic: the easier it is to think of an example of an event, the more frequently that event occurs. This is a good, but not perfect, strategy, because frequency is not the only factor that affects availability. If the problem involves reaching a generalization based on a specific example, we might apply the representativeness heuristic to draw conclusions about a group based on a single case, or to make inferences about a single case based on knowledge about the group. One specific reasoning error that can result from this heuristic is called the base rate fallacy that is illustrated in this example: A patient may have symptoms that closely match a very rare disorder, but the likelihood that the patient has that disorder is still lower than the likelihood that he has a more common disorder (with a less perfect symptom match). This error is captured by the saying, "If you hear hooves, think horse, not zebra." Another bias with serious implications for inductive reasoning is the confirmation bias, which describes our tendency to seek out, attend to, and remember evidence that supports our beliefs (compared to evidence that does not). In the study of decisions that people make, Kahneman and Tversky also pointed out ways in which human decisions depart from those predicted by utility theory. For example, when contemplating risky decisions, humans show loss aversion. As such, framing effects can occur in which a person will reach two different decisions based on the same set of facts, if those facts are presented in different reference frames (e.g., saving lives or costing lives). Some theorists propose that humans have dual systems for reasoning—one that is fast and automatic and one that is slower and more effortful—in these terms, heuristics and biases characterize the former (also referred to as the intuitive system).

Thought

Concepts	Names	Terms
Information processing	Donders, Sternberg	
Measurement		Attention and controlled operations
		Automatic processes
		Dichotic listening and shadowing task

Types of reasoning		Inductive
		  Representativeness heuristic
		  Availability heuristic

		Deductive (e.g., syllogisms)
		Decision making
		Problem solving
Artificial intelligence and computer simulation		Algorithms
		Heuristics
		Expert systems
Theories and principles	Hull Spence	Continuity Theory
	Krechevsky Lashley	Noncontinuity Theory
	Bruner	Inductive Reasoning

Concepts	Names	Terms

Mental representations	Galton	Analogical
		   Mental images
		   Eidetic imagery
		   Spatial thinking
		Symbolic
		   Episodic memory
		   Generic memory
		    Semantic

Models		Hierarchical network model in semantic memory
		Spreading activation model
		Parallel distributed processing (PDP) models
Problem solving		Hierarchical organization with subroutines
		Automatization
	Newell and Simon	Artificial intelligence and problem-solving strategies such as working backward through the logic sequence
	Kosslyn, Holyoak	Mental image manipulation of visual information
Barriers to problem solving		Stroop effect
		Mental set (fixation)
		Functional fixedness
Facilitators to problem solving		Restructuring Incubation

Representative research evidence	Shepard	Analogical
		   Mental rotation
		   Image scanning

		Symbolic Semantic priming
Reasoning and problem solving		Deductive vs. inductive reasoning
		Algorithm, heuristic
	Newell and Simon	Search and representation
		Mental sets
		Functional fixedness
	Holyoak	Analogy
Heuristics and biases	Tversky	Confirmation bias
	Kahneman	Availability heuristic
		Representative heuristic Base-rate fallacy
		Dual-process theory
		Utility theory
		Loss aversion
		Framing effects

Intelligence

In any study of the mind, language, or thinking, you will inevitably encounter the concept of intelligence quotient (IQ). No review of the discipline of psychology could be complete without a discussion of this term and an attempt to convey a basic understanding of intelligence and its relationship to problem-solving and creativity. A definition of intelligence generally includes three elements: the ability to profit from experience, the ability to learn new information, and the ability to adjust to new situations. Theoretical work in the area has concentrated on the general nature of intelligence and whether it is a general, unitary factor or a combination of several specific factors. Scholarly work on this question began just after 1900 with *Spearman's Two Factor Theory* (a general-type factor and a specific-type factor). The next major name was *Thurstone*, who postulated seven factors in intelligence, and intelligence theory reached its peak of complexity with *Guilford's Structure of Intellect* (120 factors in three general classifications).

Two recent theoretical approaches have sought to broaden the definitional perspective of intelligence. Sternberg defines intelligence as a number of components that allow one to adapt to, select, and shape one's environment. His triarchic theory of intelligence includes more traditional notions of intelligence (componential intelligence, of linguistic and logical-mathematical skills) as well as contextual intelligence ("street smarts") and experimental intelligence (creative insight). Gardner expands on the notion of multiple intelligences to include seven domains of intelligence: linguistic, musical, logical-mathematical, spatial, bodily-kinesthetic, interpersonal, and intrapersonal. These different types of intelligence can be seen in the genius of experts from composers (musical) to dancers (bodily-kinesthetic), from teachers (interpersonal) to poets (linguistic). Both Sternberg and Gardner view intelligence not as a single or biologically determined factor, but as a number of domains that represent the interaction of the individual's biological predispositions with the environment and cultural context. From the emergence of these theories we come to know and appreciate the complexity of the term "intelligence."

In some respects, it is easier to measure intelligence than to discuss it theoretically.

Measurement began with *Binet and Simon* (French contemporaries of Spearman). Commissioned by the French minister of public instruction, they developed a test to determine which children could not profit from elementary instruction in the public schools. Their end product, later translated into English by *Terman* and named the *Stanford-Binet*, launched an era of intelligence testing in this country. In addition to creating the pioneering intelligence test, Binet and Simon gave prominence to the IQ concept and established a method for IQ computation. Other names and concepts important to the intelligence area (e.g., Wechsler) are cited here:

Intelligence Outline

Concepts	Names	Terms
Individual intelligence tests	Terman	Stanford-Binet
	Wechsler	WAIS-III (adult)
		WISC-III (children)
		WPPSI-R (preschool)
Group intelligence tests		Otis
		Lorge-Thorndike
		California Test of Mental Maturity

Concepts	Names	Terms
Theories of intelligence	Spearman	Two-factor
	Thurstone	Seven-factor
	Guilford	Structure of intellect (120 factors in 3 classifications)
	Sternberg	Triarchic theory
	Gardner	Multiple intelligences
Intelligence quotient	Binet	IQ = MA/CA × 100

Practical intelligence (tacit)	Wagner	Information-processing (subtheories)
		    Componential
		    Experiential
		    Contextual

Multiple intelligences	Gardner	Linguistic
		Logical-mathematical
		Spatial
		Musical
		Bodily-kinesthetic
		Interpersonal and intrapersonal

Classifications	Terman	Giftedness (135 and above)
		    Longitudinal study
		 Retardation
		    Mild (50–70)
		    Moderate (35–55)
		    Severe (20–35)
		    Profound (below 20)
		    (Current term is intellectually challenged)

History	Darwin	Species variability
	Galton	Individual differences Correlation coefficient

Test-related concepts		Reliability
		    Test-retest
		    Alternative-form
		    Split-half
		 Validity
		    Predictive
		    Construct
		    Concurrent
		    Face
		    Content

Nature/Nurture issues and controversies	Plomin, DeFries, McClearn	Twin studies, family studies
	Jensen	Between-group and within-group differences

Concepts	Names	Terms

Statistical concepts		Central tendency and variability
		    Mean
		    Standard deviation

		Normal curve
		Frequency distribution
Prenatal and postnatal influences		Environmental factors present during pregnancy and after birth (e.g., maternal drug use, smoking, alcohol use, malnutrition, AIDS, and health-related aspects of the early childhood setting)

Intelligence Summary

Although interest in intelligence measurement initiated the testing movement, applications of the technique spread quickly to the areas of aptitude, achievement, vocation, and personality. *Aptitude* is a narrower, more specific term than intelligence, and aptitude tests seek to measure much more specialized abilities (e.g., mechanical aptitude, musical aptitude, and so on) than general intelligence tests. To extend the distinction one step further, aptitude differs from achievement in that *aptitude* means *potential for successful performance* and *achievement* means *actual performance.* One could say that, on the basis of their test scores, two particular individuals are more *apt* to do well in mechanical tasks than two others. None of them has performed the tasks or become mechanically proficient as yet, but the test does predict their future performance. Your knowledge in the area should include moderate acquaintance with:

SAT (Scholastic Assessment Test)

Vineland Social Maturity Scale

Kuder Preference Test

Strong-Campbell Vocational Interest Test

California Achievement Tests

Sequential Tests of Educational Progress

Stanford Achievement Test

Later, as you get into personality and clinical and applied areas, you will look at some representative tests in these areas and make critical distinctions between objective and subjective approaches to testing. For now, it is sufficient to note that intelligence testing "started something" that proliferated into many other areas. In addition to the introductory textbooks, Anastasi's *Psychological Testing* (New York: Macmillan, 1989), Cronbach's *Essentials of Psychological Testing* (New York: Harper Collins, 1990), Kaplan and Saccuzzo's *Psychological Testing* (Pacific Grove, Calif.: Brooks/Cole, 1993), and the October 1981 issue of the *American Psychologist* ("Testing: Concepts, Policy, Practice, and Research") would be excellent sources. If you really are into this area, have the time, and want to do some exploring in depth, you could check into Sternberg's *Handbook of Human Intelligence* (New York: Cambridge University Press, 1982).

Problem Solving and Creativity

If you were to take the expression "thinking and _____" and ask your listeners to fill in the blank, many of them would immediately say "problem solving." Much of the time we spend in thought is directed toward problem solving; thus, the process is a logical target for psychological inquiry. Several species engage in some form of problem solving—rats, cats, pigeons, monkeys, and humans among them—and the complexity level of solution varies markedly across species. If you put a cat or a rat in a puzzle box, you would find that its method of problem solving would be strictly trial and error. Literally by accident, it would bump into the response that gained the desired result and would learn to repeat that response in a similar future situation. Much of our own learning falls into this category, but humans and monkeys also demonstrate a phenomenon that *Kohler* found comparable to *insight*. We also seem to develop a capacity for solving problems that we have never encountered in the past, and it is this capacity that *Harlow* termed *learning set*. Although set is our best friend in some problem-solving instances, it can be a barrier in others. Persistence of set, "functional fixedness" and deeply ingrained rules can sometimes prevent us from attaining the fresh, imaginative approach that some problems may require.

The next step in the problem-solving sequence is *creativity* or creative problem solving. Creativity is a phenomenon that most people can detect far more easily than they can define. "That was a creative idea!" and "She's imaginative and creative!" are much more familiar to us than "Creativity is _____." D. Krech, R. Crutchfield, and N. Livson (*Elements of Psychology*, rev. ed. [New York: Knopf, 1976], pp. 134–35) express the belief that the determinants of creative problem solving lie within (1) the stimulus pattern, (2) knowledge, and (3) the personality. They feel that the stimulus pattern, however, can cause individuals to become too rule-oriented and stimulus-bound so that their minds may tell them, as they approach a solution, that "A hammer can only be used for hammering," or "A yardstick can only be used for measuring." Creativity implies the capacity to go beyond the conventional and traditional. But if one becomes stimulus-bound, individual problem-solving methods are automatically limited to the conventional and unimaginative.

It is not surprising that knowledge can serve as both a help and a hindrance to creative problem solving. Everyone needs a certain amount of knowledge to solve a problem, but too many facts may lock us into the conventional. In the third area—personality—it appears that the creative person needs the ability to tolerate both frustration and ambiguity. Generally speaking, creativity presents an important field of investigation, which currently contains more questions than answers. Haimowitz and Haimowitz (*Human Development* [New York: Crowell, 1960], pp. 44–54) demonstrated an early awareness of the fascination held by the field—along with its unanswered questions.

Current work in the field includes several fascinating avenues of inquiry. *Amabile* cites *three cognitive/personality characteristics* she considers essential ingredients for creativity—expertise in the field; creative skills such as persistence, divergent thinking, and breaking down a problem into its component parts; and internal motivation (e.g., personal satisfaction) rather than external motivation (e.g., money or recognition). *Simonton* points to middle adulthood (46–65) as a time of peak creativity and achievement. *Csikszentmihalyi* underscores the vital importance of parental interaction with their children (e.g., reading to and talking with them, warmly supporting them, and challenging them to develop their talents). *Sternberg and Lubert* consider it essential that the creative person be firmly rooted within the society, its realities and needs, and the experience and knowledge of friends and associates. *Gardner* addresses creativity within the context of multiple intelligences outlined elsewhere in our review—linguistic, logical-mathematical, spatial, musical, body-kinesthetic, and personal. He notes that the "conventional" ways of testing only sample the first three rather than the diversity that includes musical, body-kinesthetic, and personal.

Research studies of creative people have discovered five key elements.

1. They have prominent knowledge and expertise within their field.
2. Their imaginative thinking ability perceives things differently and in more novel ways than most of us.
3. They have a venturesome personality that can tolerate what is ambiguous and of risk.
4. They're highly motivated—intensely interested and intrigued by the challenge.
5. They function in a creative environment. Contrary to our usual picture, they do not work alone but rather interact and network with colleagues.

Problem Solving and Creativity Outline

Concepts	Names	Terms
Gestalt	Kohler	Insight
Learning	Harlow	Learning set (i.e., learning a creative approach to new problem settings)

Cognitive/Personality characteristics in creativity	Amabile	Essential elements:
		    Expertise in the field
		    Creative skills (persistence, divergent thinking, breaking down a problem into component parts)
		    Internal motivation

Life-cycle	Simonton	Middle adulthood as peak time of creativity and achievement
Societal relationship	Sternberg and Lubert	Creative individual's firm rooting within the societal context, its realities, and the input of friends/associates
Creativity within multiple intelligences	Gardner	Moves beyond the conventionally tested realms of linguistic, logical-mathematical, spatial, into the unconventional musical, body-kinesthetic, and personal
	Maslow	Creativity within self-actualization
Tests of creativity	Guilford	Divergent thinking
	Mednick	Remote associations
	Barber and Wilson	Creative Imagination Scale

Problem Solving and Creativity Summary

Two of our time-tested maxims get revised in the area of creativity. Don't say them too loudly around grandma or grandpa (or perhaps even mother and dad!):

"Practice makes blindness."
(The idea here being that as you practice a given solution-attempt to a problem, you dig a rut similar to the car wheel that spins in the mud. The more you spin, the lower the likelihood that you'll see creative—and likely more efficient—problem-solving alternatives beyond that "rut.")

"If at first you don't succeed, don't try again."
(In a manner similar to the above, continual trying can create a dead-end rut. Getting away from it and coming back to it later can lend fresh perspective.)

Creativity is a fun area to talk about and an even more fun thing to possess. We wish you the best in your creative review!

As you can see, creativity and intelligence are not synonymous—a fact demonstrated vividly by M. Wallach and N. Kogan in *Modes of Thinking in Young Children: A Study of the Creativity-Intelligence Distinction* (New York: Holt, Rinehart & Winston, 1965). For additional depth in the area of creativity, look into one of these: Kaufman, J. C. *Creativity 101.* (New York: Springer, 2009). Kaufman J. C., and R. J. Sternberg *Cambridge Handbook of Creativity.* (New York: Cambridge University Press, 2010).

Thinking Summary

We have come a long way since World War II, the development of computers, and a linguist named Noam Chomsky who gave birth to ideas that converged on the field of cognitive psychology. As you test your encoding and retrieval processes and fight off the effects of decay and interference on forgetting, you may find it helpful to do some elaborative rehearsal with some additional reading on the topics of memory, language, and thought.

While you review this material, notice the many connections between the study of complex cognition and almost every other facet of psychology: Your review of psycholinguistics will pay off when we reach our discussion of child development, just as your review of reasoning and decision making will be useful when considering topics in social cognition and behavior. The threads of complex cognition are woven into every square inch of this beautiful psychology tapestry.

For reading beyond your introductory textbook, the following works provide additional depth on the topics we have briefly reviewed above: A good place to begin is with a comprehensive textbook on cognitive psychology that will review the topics of language, attention, memory, thinking, and decision making. A classic in the field is Sternberg's *Cognitive Psychology* (5th edition, Wadsworth Publishing, 2008), although there are many good alternatives. To focus on memory research, a slightly dated classic in the field is *Essentials of Human Memory* by Baddeley (Taylor & Francis, 1999). It would be well paired with the very readable *Seven Sins of Memory: How the Mind Forgets and Remembers* by Schacter (Houghton Mifflin, 2002). If you need to delve deeper into research on language, consider *The Psychology of Language: From Data to Theory* (3rd edition) by Harley (Psychology Press, 2008). A lively and thought-provoking account of psycholinguistics (and other topics in cognitive psychology) can be found in any of the fascinating books by Steven Pinker, such as *The Language Instinct*

(2007) or *Words and Rules: The Ingredients of Language* (2000). To review the literature on reasoning and decision making, turn to the classic text in this area, Baron's *Thinking and Deciding* (4th edition, Cambridge University Press, 2007). A fascinating tour through the world of inductive reasoning is provided by *Heuristics and Biases: The Psychology of Intuitive Judgment*, edited by Gilovich (Cambridge University Press, 2002).

SENSATION AND PERCEPTION

Sensation is the process of informing the brain about some experience occurring outside the central nervous system. These experiences can be classified into seven types, or senses: visual, auditory, somatosensory (touch, temperature, pain, and proprioception), olfactory, gustatory, kinesthetic (movement), and vestibular (orientation). Although the message in each of these senses is quite different, the messenger, or the way of communicating with the brain, is very similar. In fact, in 1826 Johannes *Müller* published his *doctrine of specific nerve energies*, which stated that qualitative differences between the sensation of sounds and lights, for example, are not due to differences in the neural signals but to differences in the structures that the neural signals excite. In all types of sensation, a set of *receptors* is responsible for the *transduction* of the physical stimulus energy into an electrical, neural signal. Stimulus dimensions (e.g., pitch, hue) are coded, or translated, into neural signals that are relayed to the appropriate projection area in the brain. In your review of sensation, pay particular attention to the unique ways in which each sense transduces, or codes information about a stimulus, and to the route that information travels before reaching its final destination in the brain.

Because sensation is, in effect, an extension of the physiological aspects of psychology, an understanding of the basic terms and concepts in the section of Physiological/Behavioral Neuroscience will be essential. The physiology of sensory systems provides an essential foundation for understanding thresholds and general psychophysical concepts. This foundation consists of knowledge of neural pathways and the ways in which sensory information is processed within them.

The eye, a thoroughly researched sensory system, demonstrates the area and some of its basic concepts. When light energy reaches photoreceptors (rods and cones), neural signals are sent through the visual system, producing sensations. The travel route includes the neural layers through which the light must pass before being absorbed by the photoreceptors. A photochemical reaction is triggered in the photoreceptors, producing neural signals that are transmitted first to the bipolar cells and then to the ganglion cells. Neural signals then travel along retinal ganglion cells' axons to the lateral geniculate nucleus of the thalamus. Cells in the lateral geniculate nucleus relay the signal to the occipital lobes of the brain. All of the neurons along this path have a specific *receptive field*, which is defined as the part of space that the given neuron responds to. Furthermore, the neurons are organized into systematic maps (called *retinotopic maps* in the visual system) such that neighboring neurons have neighboring receptive fields.

Of necessity, the above example has been oversimplified, but it provides a basic orientation that you will want to use for each sensory system. Although the specific terminology will vary from one sense to another, you will discover some common themes that hold across all of the sensory systems, such as sensory coding, thresholds, and receptor specificity. And with each level of understanding will come a renewed awareness and appreciation for the senses and their moment-by-moment service to us all.

Beyond the essential understanding of physiology and neural information processing, basic familiarity with a number of fundamental psychophysical terms and concepts will also be important.

Sensation Outline

Concepts	Names	Terms
Dimensions of sensation		Quality (what kind)
		Intensity (how much)
		Duration (how long)
Threshold (or limen)		Absolute threshold
		Difference threshold
	Weber's Law (and formula)	Just noticeable difference (j.n.d.)
	Fechner's Law (Weber's elaborated)	
	Stevens' Law	Magnitude estimation and power
Methods of measurement		Method of limits
		Method of constant stimuli
		Magnitude estimation
Signal-detection theory		Cognitive bias or expectations of sensing person
Receiver-operating-characteristics (ROC) curves		Proportion of times a signal is reported when presented and when not presented
Sensory code		Neural representation of a given sensory experience
Doctrine of specific nerve energies	Müller	Differences in experienced quality are not stimulus-based but nervous-system-based
Specificity theory vs. across-fiber theory		Specificity: Quality-specific neurons—given neurons signal or fire for given qualities
		Across-fiber: Quality comes from overall pattern of neural firing
Senses: What they are		Vision (Sight)
		Audition (Hearing)

		Chemical
		    Gustation (Taste)
		    Olfaction (Smell)

		Skin
		    Pressure
		    Temperature
		    Pain

		Kinesthetic
		    Limb movement feedback
		    Balance (vestibular)

Outline Terms Elaborated

- Dimensions of sensation—*quality* (what kind of sensation), *intensity* (how much of a sensation), *duration* (how long a sensation)
- Threshold (or limen)—*absolute threshold* (minimum physical energy that will result in a sensory experience); *difference threshold*—j.n.d. (just noticeable difference)
- Laws and procedures—*Weber's Law* (and formula) for j.n.d., *Fechner's Law, Stevens' magnitude estimation procedure*, and his *power law*
- Methods of measurement—the *method of limits* (using a stimulus such as light, alternating intensity direction with each presentation), the *method of constant stimuli* (stimuli of specific intensities are presented sequentially, the measurement being whether detection occurs), *magnitude estimation* (two stimuli of different intensities are presented to a person who is then asked to compare the two and express a numerical ratio of their relative magnitudes ("First was twice as bright as the second," and so on)
- *Signal-detection theory* (the cognitive bias or expectations of the sensing person) and *ROC* (receiver-operating-characteristic) *curves* (the proportion of times a signal is reported when presented and the proportion of times a signal is reported erroneously when none was presented, and the variation found in these proportions as a function of "conservative reporting" versus "liberal reporting" instructions given to the subjects)

Vision and Audition

In terms of psychological emphasis, vision has been the most heavily studied modality in the sensory area, and audition has been next in prominence. Other sense modalities also receive attention, but not to the extent of these two. In keeping with this emphasis, we will begin with a review of vision and audition, then move on to other sensory modes.

In studies of visual sensation, the retina assumes primary importance—specifically the rods and cones. You will need to know the many distinctions between rods and cones (being able to compare them on such grounds as approximate numbers and distribution on the retina, shape, sensitivity to color and light, visual acuity, and neural connections). With such information, you will then be prepared to understand phenomena such as dark adaptation.

VISION

- Eye-related terms such as lens, iris, pupil, cornea, retina, photoreceptors, rods (achromatic, functioning in dim light, "party line" [sharing a bipolar cell] neural connections to the brain), cones (color sensitive, requiring brighter light, "private line" [each cone having its own bipolar cell] neural connections to the brain), cells (amacrine, bipolar, ganglion, horizontal), blind spot, fovea, optic nerve
- Visual functioning terms such as accommodation, convergence (summation, antagonism), retinal disparity, myopic, hyperopic, astigmatism, adaptation (dark, light)
- Brain-related visual terms such as columnar organization of cells (Hubel and Wiesel), ocular dominance columns, orientation columns, simple/complex/hypercomplex cells, lateral geniculate nucleus (LGN), primary visual (striate) cortex, occipital lobe

- Wave properties (frequency, amplitude, complexity), their color-vision expressions (hue, saturation, brightness), and their audition expressions (pitch, loudness/intensity [measured in decibels], timbre)

Not surprisingly, studies of sensory modalities have reached beyond the modalities themselves to the nature of the stimuli impinging upon them. In the case of vision, the most prominent "reach beyond" has encompassed color mixing and vision theory. Again, these are among the general outline terms and concepts that you will need to understand.

- Color mixing—general understanding of where, for instance, violet, blue, green, yellow, and red are located within the wavelength spectrum; distinction between subtractive and additive color mixing and knowledge of the primaries within each; ability to distinguish the terms hue, saturation, and brightness
- Color-related terms such as color solid, color circle, color mixing (additive [pigment], subtractive [light]), color primaries and complementaries
- Vision theories such as the Young-Helmholtz Trichromatic Theory (which postulates that there are three types of cones in the retina, each having primary sensitivity to a different part of the color spectrum) and Hering's proposed Opponent-Process Theory, which describes antagonistic interactions that occur in three "opponent channels" (red/green, yellow/blue, and black/white). Hurvich and Jameson provided quantitative evidence for the opponent-process theory almost a century after Hering proposed it.

Vision Outline

Concepts	Names	Terms

Parts of the eye		Front chamber
		  Lens, iris, pupil, cornea
		Rear chamber
		  Retina
		  Photoreceptors
		    Rods and cones
		  Bipolar cells
		  Ganglion cells

Vision in the brain		Magno and parvo cells
	Hubel and Weisel	Simple cells
		Complex cells
		Occipital lobe
		Primary visual cortex (V1)
	Ungerleider	"What" and "where" pathways
Visual depth		Retinal disparity
		Convergence
Near-sighted/Far-sighted		Accommodation
Dark adaptation		Rod-cone vision
Purkinje effect		

Color vision
  Additive mixing
  Subtractive mixing
		Light: primaries = blue, green, red

		Pigment: primaries = blue, yellow, red

Concepts	Names	Terms
Properties		Frequency = hue (the color)
		Amplitude = saturation (color purity)
		Complexity = brightness (color shade)
Theories (cortical)	Hubel and Weisel	Neural firing to vertical lines
Theories (color)	Young-Helmholtz	Trichromatic
	Hurvich-Jameson	Opponent-process
Theories (contrast)	Hering	Contrasts at line junctions
	Mach	Mach bands
Negative after-image		

Audition has similar aspects, mastery of which will be essential. In addition to background familiarity with neural information processing, the following will also be important:

HEARING

- Auditory components—three parts of the ear: outer—pinna, the visible structure plus the ear canal; middle—three-part bone structure (ossicles) including hammer, anvil, and stirrup; inner—oval window (actually a kind of "front door" letting in messages); cochlea (basilar membrane, hair cells of Organ of Corti, auditory nerve, round window); understanding of the general hearing process as it relates to the above parts; familiarity with the work of Georg von Bekesy
- Auditory functioning of each basic area: outer as the initial point of entry; middle as a transformer converting large sound waves in the air into more forceful vibrations of smaller amplitude (the stirrup acting like a piston to transform the eardrum pressure into twenty-two times greater pressure on the fluid in the inner ear); inner making the conversion to neural transmission
- Auditory functioning terms such as audiometric function (lowest audible threshold energy for each frequency) and our normal audiometric hearing range and pain threshold, decibel (loudness measure, the term itself honoring Alexander Graham Bell), and a recognition familiarity with the tone oscillator and sound spectrogram ("voice print")
- Distinction between nerve deafness and ossification and their differential effects on hearing and on the prognosis for recovery of hearing function
- Audition wave properties (briefly mentioned within vision discussion): pitch/frequency (measured in hertz), loudness/amplitude/intensity (measured in decibels), and timbre (wave complexity, overtones)
- Audition theories such as Helmholtz' Place ("Piano") Theory (proposing that a given place on the basilar membrane is responsive to a specific pitch), Rutherford's Frequency ("Telephone") Theory (proposing that the entire basilar membrane vibrates, much like the diaphragm of a telephone or microphone), and Wever-Bray's Volley Theory
- Localization of sounds is based on differences between the two ears both in timing (for low frequency sounds) and loudness (for high frequency sounds). Different species have evolved to be sensitive to those frequencies that can be most easily localized (which varies with head size)

- Auditory phenomena—general hearing range sensitivity (in cycles per second); functions and threshold distinctions between "boilermaker's ear" (nerve deafness) and deafness attributable to burst eardrum or bone ossification; stimulus-related terminology: pitch, loudness, and timbre; understanding of tones, beats, and masking

Audition Outline

Concepts	Names	Terms
Parts of the ear		Outer: 　Pinna 　Ear canal Middle: 　Eardrum 　Ossicles 　　Hammer 　　Anvil 　　Stirrup Inner: 　Oval window 　Cochlea (w/ basilar membrane, hair cells of Organ of Corti, auditory nerve, round window)
Properties		Frequency = pitch
		Amplitude = loudness
		Complexity = timbre
Measurement units		Pitch = cycles per second (hertz)
		Loudness = decibels
Theories (pitch)	Helmholtz	Place ("piano")
	von Bekesy	Wave-like motion of the basilar membrane (location of peaks varying with pitch)
	Rutherford	Frequency ("telephone or telegraph") (entire membrane vibration, frequency of vibration establishes pitch)
	Wever-Bray	Volley (modification of Rutherford—neural firing in volleys rather than all-at-once)
Deafness		Nerve-based (inner ear)
		Bone-based (middle ear)

The Chemical Senses

The chemical senses of taste and smell become our prominent concerns within this heading. The receptor cells for taste are located in clusters of cells known as the taste buds. Taste sensitivity is dependent upon a two-stage process that involves (1) the chemical stimulus penetrating the taste bud and (2) the chemical reaction that prompts the nerve impulse. Taste buds are served by branches of three cranial nerves (VII, IX, X), all of which terminate in the medulla or pons. The taste pathway subsequently reaches the posteroventral nucleus of the thalamus and terminates in the face somatic area of the cortex. Some of the most detailed work in this area has been done by Pfaffmann; his work entitled "Taste, Its Sensory and Motivating Properties" in *American Scientist* (52, 1964; pp. 187–206) is among the most basic in this area.

In smell sensitivity, the olfactory receptors are located in the roof of the nasal cavity. The olfactory epithelium contains columnar, basal, and olfactory cells; and the epithelium itself is bathed in mucus fluid—meaning that gases and mucus must be soluble in order to excite olfactory receptors. From the olfactory epithelium, axons extend to the olfactory bulb (a complex entity with its brain-destined networks of fibers and its reverberatory circuits). The final portion of the "journey" is via the olfactory tract to the cortex. What has been termed the primary olfactory cortex is actually a number of points in the ventral surface region. The region varies in size among species, depending on the relative importance of olfaction for the given species. Compared with other species, the area is notably small in humans. As you review the chemical senses, the following should be important to you:

- Taste-related terms such as gustation (formal name for taste), the taste primaries (bitter, sour, salt, sweet) and their tongue locations, and the gustatory system (including papillae, taste buds, receptor cells)
- Note that the list of four primary tastes you've known for years has now been expanded by one: umami. Coming from the Japanese word meaning "savory," umami is a taste linked to the activation of a glutamate receptor on the tongue. Glutamate is found in meats, some cheeses and mushrooms, and protein-heavy foods.
- Smell-related terms such as olfaction (formal name for smell), elements in the olfactory system (including nasal cavity, olfactory hair cells, nerve fibers, and olfactory bulb), and the function of pheromones

Chemical Senses Outline

Concepts	Names	Terms

Gustation (taste)		Primaries
		    Sweet
		    Salt
		    Sour
		    Bitter
		    Umami

Adaptation		With exposure time
Contrast effect		Sweet followed by sour
Age effects		Decreasing sensitivity
Taste bud anatomy		
Taste system neuroanatomy		
Olfaction (smell) System parts and neuroanatomy		Olfactory bulb
		Olfactory epithelium and types of cells
		Nasal cavity
		Turbinate bones
Relationship of olfactory system to other structures in the brain		

Concepts	Names	Terms
Cues		Pheromones
		Menstrual synchrony
Interaction with gustation		The child who holds her nose while she drinks her prune juice

Attempts to formulate theories of smell have not met with notable success. However, the work of Crozier, Moncrieff, and Adey demonstrates the theoretical progression that has occurred in the field.

The Skin Senses

In the late nineteenth century, experimenters observed that the human skin is not uniformly sensitive to different types of stimuli. In further investigations, areas of skin were circumscribed and, for instance, a cold stimulus was systematically applied to determine at what points a person would report feeling coldness. Similar mapping of the identical skin area was conducted for stimuli warmer than skin temperature. It became apparent that coldness and warmth were not being felt at the same points on the skin surface. Similar mapping was conducted with touch and pain stimuli, and again the sensations were not felt at identical points on the skin surface. Woodworth and Schlosberg (*Experimental Psychology* [New York: Holt, Rinehart & Winston, 1954]) give details of experiments that were conducted in this area. These experiments led to conclusions that there were at least four primary qualities of cutaneous sensation—touch, pain, cold, and warmth. Müller's doctrine of specific nerve energies, advanced fifty years earlier, was being supported. For review purposes, we will discuss the skin senses in the general categories of pressure, temperature, and pain. Receptor categories that will be important throughout this section will be (1) free nerve endings, (2) hair follicles, and (3) encapsulated end organs; and, as was true for the previous review sections, a general knowledge of neuroanatomy will also be important.

- Touch (pressure)-related terms such as epidermis (outer layer) and dermis (hair cells, blood vessels, oil and sweat glands, receptor cells), differential touch sensitivity in different areas of the body (e.g., extremities most sensitive, back least sensitive), and cross-sensory potentials such as the capacity to "project" a visual image through tactile pressure on the back of a blind person, enabling the individual to "see" it
- Temperature-related terms such as heat receptors, cold receptors, and the sensation of paradoxical warmth or paradoxical cold, which occurs when, for example, a warm receptor is contacted with a cold stimulus or a cold receptor is contacted with a warm stimulus
- Pain-related terms such as receptors, substance effects upon pain sensation (e.g., opiates blocking pain information transfer to the brain), substance effects upon emotional response to pain sensation (e.g., tranquilizers such as Valium not affecting the sensation but dulling the emotional reaction), body-produced opiate-type hormones (endorphins and enkephalins)
- Pain-related theory such as the gate-control theory of Melzack and Wall, suggesting a "pain gate" in the spinal cord

PRESSURE

Geldard formally defines pressure sensation as "tissue distortion, or the mechanical deformation of skin tissue." Pressure intensity is measured in grams per millimeter. As with other senses, the level of pressure sensitivity is different in different parts of the body. In general, the closer to the extremity, the more sensitivity there will be (making the center of the back, for instance, one of the least pressure-sensitive parts of the body). To understand pressure sensitivity fully, you should also look into such terms and concepts as the types of pressure receptors (encapsulated end organs, and so on) and touch blends (cold pressure, "wetness," and so on). Your goal should be a general understanding of the area and an acquaintance with its problems.

TEMPERATURE

As mentioned previously, evidence supports the suggestion of two receptor systems—one for warmth, one for coldness. Your knowledge in this area should include an awareness that cold receptors apparently are the smaller and more numerous. In addition, you should know something about cold and heat sensitivity in different parts of the body and the "three bowl" adaptation experiment of Weber.

PAIN

There are many questions relating to the nature of pain and how to stop it effectively. Initial thought that pain was a direct function of tissue damage was quickly proven to be incorrect (when, for instance, it was found that major tissue damage could go hand in hand with minor pain sensation).

PROPRIOCEPTION

In addition to touch, temperature, and pain, the sensory receptors in our skin give rise to the sense of proprioception, which refers to our sense of the relative position of our body parts. This is related to the kinesthetic sense, which we describe below—some people use the terms interchangeably—but the kinesthetic sense relates more to the perception of movement of the limbs. Proprioception depends both on the receptors in the skin that we have been discussing, and the receptors in the inner ear (our vestibular sense).

The following outline provides concepts you will need to understand. In addition, you should be familiar with aspects such as the differential effects, and apparently very different pain-relieving functions, of aspirin versus a colleague anesthetic such as morphine.

Skin Senses (Cutaneous Senses) Outline

Concepts	Names	Terms
Qualities of cutaneous sensation	Müller	Specific nerve energies
	von Frey	Four primary cutaneous senses: pressure, cold, warmth, and pain
Pressure		

Receptors: various		Among them:
		   Merkel's disk
		   Meissner's corpuscle
		   Free nerve endings
		   Digital nerve
		   Pacinian corpuscle

Sensitivity		General rule: the closer to the extremity, the more sensitive (e.g., least sensitive is the back).
Temperature		
Receptors		Cold Small and more numerous than warmth receptors
		Warmth Larger than cold receptors, less numerous
Pain		
Gate Theory	Melzack and Wall	Pain messages pass through a "gate" in the spinal cord enroute to the brain. In effect, pain messages may or may not be sent depending upon other sensory experiences and the moment's attention and activity.
Reducing pain		Endorphins (countering the "pain messenger" neurotransmitter "substance P")
		Attention distraction (e.g., Lamaze method in childbirth)

Every sensory receptor discussed to this point has had the quality of being stimulated from outside the body and providing knowledge of events external to the body. In his well-known scheme, *Sherrington* classified such senses as *exteroceptors*, in contrast to *interoceptors* and *proprioceptors*. Neither of the latter two categories receives direct stimulation from outside the body. The sensory field of the interoceptors is the gastrointestinal tract (making them the organic or visceral sensors), and the "in-betweens" (receptors in subcutaneous tissue, deep-lying blood vessels, muscles, tendons, and bone coverings) are the proprioceptors—having the common characteristic of being stimulated mainly by actions of the body itself. Among the proprioceptors Sherrington includes the labyrinthine balance function of the inner ear. This labyrinthine sense is unique in that no other sense can make good on a claim to yield no sensations of its own. If you feel dizzy, the sensations that you experience are kinesthetic, pressure, visceral—but not labyrinthine. The kinesthetic sense (which tells you where your appendages are and what they are doing) is also among the proprioceptors. Within these general areas, there are some novel and classic studies with which you should be familiar, including *Boring's "balloon" study of the gastrointestinal tract* and the *Cannon-Washburn technique* for studying *hunger sensation*.

Internal Senses Outline

Concepts	Names	Terms
Kinesthetic		
Function		Provide feedback on limb positions and movement via muscles, joints, and tendons
Balance (Vestibular)		
Location and function		Inner ear semicircular canals contain fluid which, moving with head rotation, triggers vestibular nerve impulses. Process is critical to balance

Control center for all the sensory phenomena you've reviewed is the twelve cranial nerves. We include them simply to convey that sense of awe at this remarkable universe we carry with us daily.

Cranial Nerves Outline

Concepts	Names	Terms
I. Olfactory	Afferent	Smell
II. Optic	Afferent	Vision
III. Oculomotor	Predominantly efferent	Eye muscles
IV. Trochlear	Predominantly efferent	Eye (proprioception)
V. Trigeminal	**Mixed:**	
	Afferent	Face, teeth, tongue (mostly tactile, some temperature and pain)
	Efferent	Muscles of the mouth/tongue
VI. Abducens	Predominantly efferent	Eye (proprioception)
VII. Facial	**Mixed:**	
	Afferent	Taste, salivation, some sense of pressure and position (from facial muscles)
	Efferent	Facial nerve (motor) and intermediate nerve
VIII. Auditory/ Vestibular-Cochlear	**Two part:**	
	Cochlear—afferent	Transmits signals from Organ of Corti; serves inner ear for equilibrium and position orientation
	Vestibular—mostly afferent	

Concepts	Names	Terms
IX. Glosso-pharyngeal	Mixed:	
	Afferent	Sense of taste from posterior tongue; sensations from pharynx, eustacian tube, tonsils, soft palate
	Efferent	Muscles of pharynx, larynx, and upper esophagus (sing well!)
X. Vagus	Mixed:	
	Afferent	Pain and temperature sensation from ear; also, pharynx, larynx, esophagus, thoracic and abdominal viscera such as heart and intestines
	Efferent	Abdominal and thoracic viscera (inhibit heart rate, stimulate gastric and pancreatic activity, gastrointestinal action)
XI. Spinal accessory	Predominantly efferent	Cardiac and laryngal nerves, et al.
XII. Hypoglossal	Efferent	Voluntary movements of neck and tongue; perhaps also teams with V in sucking, chewing, and swallowing reflexes

Sensation Summary

In studying sensation, an experimenter characteristically begins with a given stimulus (e.g., light), then varies some property of the stimulus, such as the intensity or the duration. Because human receptor cells are not infinitely sensitive, the term *threshold* becomes prominent. *Absolute threshold* deals with the minimum physical energy that will result in a sensory experience; *difference threshold* deals with the minimum *change* in physical energy that will result in a sensory-detected change. For instance, absolute threshold involves the questions "Do you see it?" and "Do you hear it?" in either/or terms. In the difference threshold study the question revolves around how much additional light or sound will be required before one can detect a change from the initial stimulus (in this case, the initial light or sound). Weber's classic work and formula ($\Delta I/I = K$) pioneered in this area, and you will need to understand his work and be prepared for questions relating to it. The symbol ΔI represents the detectable change in a stimulus, while I is the initial stimulus intensity, and K is a constant. *Fechner's Law* was an extension of Weber's work and suggested that the relationship between physical stimulus intensity (I) and the strength of sensation (S) is logarithmic ($S = c \log I$), c being a constant based on the unit of intensity. *Stevens' magnitude estimation procedure* would present a stimulus to the subject and assign it an intensity number. When the second stimulus was presented, the subjects would be asked to assign it a number based on their judgment of its intensity compared with the first stimulus. His general way of characterizing these relationships is known as *Stevens' power law* ($S = kI^b$), which says, in effect, that sensation (S) is proportional to stimulus intensity (I) raised to a power (b), k being a constant based on the unit of measurement.

You now have gone through the spectrum of sense receptors. To the extent that you understand their neuroanatomy, physiological bases, and functioning, you are now prepared for a knowledgeable review of perception.

Perception

You'll have fun reviewing this section. It's all about how we see things and how they fool us. Our senses are all primed and ready to receive input, and our past experiences and learning determine what we truly perceive. You've already had a brief dose of perception without realizing it. In the pain area, for instance, we mentioned how the perception of pain varied for different folks based on their experiences and expectations. There's the child who screams bloody murder when getting a shot at the doctor's office, while another child considers it no big deal. Expectations and past experiences make all the difference.

Sensation is physiologically based, and perception builds a bridge to our upcoming review of learning. The learning factor makes a critical difference between what comes to us through our senses and what we individually *perceive* as having been received by those senses.

Hermann von Helmholtz studied visual perception in the nineteenth century, and his discussions of unconscious inference are still very influential in the field today. Helmholtz began with a simple observation: The quality of sensory coding in the eye is very poor. Our complex visual experience should not be possible with this as our only input! Thus, Helmholtz reasoned that our perceptual experience must be the result of unconscious inferences: We combine the incomplete data we receive from our eyes with assumptions based on our experiences in the world in order to reach a hypothesis about what we are seeing. Today, Bayes' theorem is a formalism used by vision scientists to characterize this inference process for deriving a perception from sensory information.

In contrast to what is actually received and transmitted, perception is our *mental organization* of what is out there. It is what we *say* we saw, heard, felt, and so on—as distinct from what actually was received. Perception, therefore, contains both the sensory element (bottom-up processes) and the past experience that we bring to every situation (top-down processes). Vision again comes to the fore, and a school of thought known as Gestalt is responsible for the body of information concerning visual perception.

Whereas a thorough understanding of the term *stimulus* was relatively incidental to our previous discussions, it is essential both for perception discussions and our subsequent look at the learning area. Most definitions state that a stimulus is a physical agent that (given sufficient strength) activates one or a group of sensory receptors. Witnesses to an explosion, for instance, will find the explosion both a visual and an auditory stimulus. With such things as a traffic light, however, the stimulus will be in only one sensory modality. Having digested this all-important term, we can now take a look at the material on perception that you will need to review for the GRE.

The study of perception invariably calls for a distinction between "illusion" and "hallucination." For clarity, you can think of illusion as misperception of a stimulus and hallucination as response in the absence of any external stimulus. Inevitably, the discussion will go one step further, into extrasensory perception (ESP), and again some distinctions will be important.

- Definitional aspects of extrasensory perception—mental telepathy, clairvoyance, precognition
- Psychokinesis (or telekinesis)

Historically, J. B. Rhine's lab at Duke University served as the principal location for ESP research in the United States, and it was Rhine who developed the ESP cards used frequently in these research studies. Extrasensory perception is not a generally respected or accepted area within psychological research, but some familiarity with it is appropriate. When you've mastered the following outline you'll be a perceptual genius!

Perception Outline

Concepts	Names	Terms
Views of perceptual processes	Gibson	Ecological—Using information from the environment to support actions (e.g., driving)
	Rock, Helmholtz	Constructionist—Constructing a representation of the environment from sensory fragments (e.g., figure closure)
	Green	Computational—Explaining complex computations within the nervous system that translate sensory stimulation into representations of reality (e.g., the brain's capacity to clear up retinal blood vessels, and so on, so we see clearly)
Depth perception	Gibson	Monocular cues 　Relative size 　Linear perspective 　Interposition 　Texture gradient 　Good form 　　Height in picture plane 　　Shading 　Binocular cues 　　Retinal disparity (stereopsis) 　　Convergence 　Motion cues 　　Motion parallax 　　Optic flow
Perceptual constancies		Size
		Shape
		Brightness
		Color
Illusions	Muller-Lyer	Muller-Lyer
	Ponzo	Ponzo
	Zollner	Zollner
	Wundt	Wundt
	Ebbinghaus	Ebbinghaus twisted cord
	Poggendorf	Poggendorf moon
	Necker	Necker cube
	Ames	Distorted room
	Ames	Trapezoidal window
	Gestaltists	Phi phenomenon/stroboscopic movement (apparent motion)
		Autokinetic effect
		Induced movement
		Cross-cultural differences

Concepts	Names	Terms
Impossible figures	Escher	Classic drawings
Laws of perceptual organization	Gestalt:	Law of Pragnanz
	Wertheimer,	Proximity

	Koffka, Kohler	Similarity
		   Continuity
		   Common fate
		   Closure/subjective contours

	Helmholtz	Maximum-Likelihood Principle
	Palmer	Common region
Perceptual expectation		Perceptual set
		Schemas
Theories	Ames	Transactional
	Brunswick	Probabilistic
ESP/Parapsychology	Rhine	Mental telepathy
		Clairvoyance
		Precognition
		Psychokinesis/Telekinesis

Outline Terms Elaborated

DEPTH PERCEPTION

How do we perceive a three-dimensional world from the two-dimensional image on our retina? There are a number of cues that we use to infer the missing dimension of depth. *Monocular cues* are those that can be used by a single eye to suggest depth (linear perspective, relative size, interposition); these are cues that artists have been using for centuries to convey depth in a two-dimensional painting. Binocular cues are those that require both eyes, such as the *binocular disparity* between the slightly different images that fall on each eye. There is evidence for innate and learned aspects of depth perception; for example, the ability to use binocular disparity to perceive depth develops during a critical period early in life and can be disrupted by congenital conditions that cause a misalignment of the images on the eyes (e.g., cross-eyed).

PERCEPTUAL CONSTANCIES

Our visual world is constantly changing. When our perception is unaltered by environmental changes that affect properties of a stimulus, this is referred to as a *perceptual constancy*. For example, if you look at the pages of this book inside under fluorescent light, then later outside under natural light, and finally at dusk as the sun is setting, you will still perceive the pages as white despite the fact that their color is actually changing. A number of constancies have been identified—lightness and color (changes in illumination do not alter the perception of brightness or color), size (perceived size does not vary with depth), shape (perceived shape does not vary with orientation).

ILLUSIONS

Illusions are fun, but they are also informative about how perception normally proceeds. For example, to see the effect that perceived distance has on size perception (the basis for size constancy), consider the Müller-Lyer, Ponzo, or moon illusions. In all of these illusions, perceived distance is misleading our perceptual system.

LAWS OF PERCEPTUAL ORGANIZATION

In a complex visual scene, how do we determine which pieces go together? This is the problem of *perceptual organization* or segregation. A long list of factors that influence perceptual organization was first described by Max *Wertheimer*, the founder of the *Gestalt* school of psychology, and these laws of perceptual organization are on your outline.

Perception Summary

Were the terms familiar to you? If so, you are all set to move on. Realistically, catch any "loose ends" first if you need to. And, at this point, stop for a minute to reflect on the distance you have come. Taking inventory, you have been through the very difficult basic review sections on physiology/neuroscience, comparative, sensation, and perception. Now that you have these basics, you will see them come together. In the sections that follow, you will begin to get glimpses of the "whole person" and of total human development. Already you have begun to sense (maybe even perceive!) these intricate innerworkings. Take, for instance, the relationship between motivation and perception. We are all familiar with the expression "You see what you want to see!" This phrase suggests that we are motivated to see certain things and perhaps not to see others. Signal detection theory and concepts such as pain and perceptual defense have already given us clues that we clever humans are all experienced professionals in selectively attending and selectively perceiving—part of the fascination in studying us critters and our capacities to belie, mold, and shape the incoming raw data from our senses. You will see many instances of this selectivity as we review further. Reserve for yourself the right to be fascinated as you review and refresh your knowledge. Humans and their behavior are indeed a fascinating landscape.

PHYSIOLOGICAL/BEHAVIORAL NEUROSCIENCE

As a budding student of psychology, you of course know that the goal of the discipline is to understand the forces that shape our behavior and thought. Toward this end, a biological perspective can help explain who we are, how we think, and what we do. We can study proximate (immediate) biological explanations: How do the actions of our nervous and endocrine systems give rise to our behaviors and cognitions? These questions are the focus of the fields of behavioral and cognitive neuroscience, and this is where our review begins. We can also study ultimate (distant) biological explanations: How has our evolutionary past shaped our psychological present? Here, we turn to the interrelated fields of evolutionary biology and psychology, comparative psychology, and ethology.

Much is happening in the study of the biological foundations of psychology today, and it is impossible to be in on the excitement unless you know the playing field and the game rules. Mastery of this material will prepare you to share in the action and perhaps even contribute to it—as well as tell the Educational Testing Service that you know what it's all about. When you have completed this section of the review, you should be familiar with such names as

Sherrington and Penfield, and terms like *myelin, pituitary gland, acetylcholine, allele,* and *fixed-action pattern.* You can expect approximately 12–14 percent of the questions on the Psychology Test to touch on biological foundations, although for many students, far more than 14 percent of their studying time is devoted to firming up their fluency with the terms, definitions, relations, and scientists we review here. At times, you might feel like you are learning a foreign language, with a mountain of new vocabulary ahead of you. And, just as fluency in a foreign language opens you to new cultural worlds, fluency in biological terminology opens you to a new scientific world! If you didn't hit your target for the Biological Foundations subscore on Diagnostic Test 1, let's get to work doing just that.

Behavioral and Cognitive Neuroscience

Welcome to the incredible "hidden universe," the human brain. Like Mt. Everest, it has challenged the curiosity and inquiry of the brightest people over several centuries. One must admire the brilliance of early "brain explorers." Working with only the crudest of research tools—or, in many instances, no tools at all—they formulated concepts and a legacy for other explorers who would follow. And as the research tools and methods became all the more sophisticated across the centuries, we gained an even deeper respect for the early explorers and their insights. In the seventeenth century, Descartes formulated the concept of reflex action. In what has become a famous drawing, one can see a kneeling figure with his foot near the fire. Sketched from the brain and extending down the left leg is a nerve tube. The fire's heat begins a process up the nerve tube that opens a cavity in the brain from which animal spirits flow through the nerve tube to the muscles, which pull the foot from the fire. We can smile a bit at all Descartes's assumptions, but his reflex action concept has stood the test of time.

At the turn of the twentieth century, the Spanish medical researcher, Santiago Ramon y Cajal, was making histological discoveries destined to be generally recognized and honored throughout the world. In 1906, he was accorded Nobel Prize recognition in medicine and physiology. A marvel of Ramon y Cajal's work was that given the primitive state of the field he was able to work only with structure, and from it he advanced concepts of neural function. His description of the structure and function of neurons, his view of the central nervous system as many separate but communicating nerve cells, and his descriptions of the direction of neural conduction and of neural regeneration all earned him the "father of present-day physiology" title and acknowledgment.

In the early twentieth century, Sir Charles Sherrington (British physiologist) corrected a misconception relating to the reflex pathway. Until that point, researchers envisioned nerve tissue as a long, continuous, wire-like design along which the neural impulse traveled. Sherrington introduced the concept of the synapse—a gap between neurons across which they had to communicate. Several years later, Otto Loewi demonstrated that the basis of communication across the synapse was chemical, thereby paving the way for the discovery of what are now known as neurotransmitters. Like Descartes and Ramon y Cajal before them, the conceptual legacy of Sherrington and Loewi was destined to stand the test of time and technological sophistication. The concept of neural transmission would now be forever envisioned in a new and different way. The synaptic gap concept gave rise to a vast new conceptual landscape, one that would bring with it concepts such as threshold, summation, neurotransmitters, and many more.

There have been many explorers on this challenging expanse of hidden universe, and we haven't the time or space to name them all here. One of the leading researchers into the neuronal substrates of behavioral plasticity has been Richard F. Thompson. Best known for his work on the neural mechanisms of habituation and sensitization, he and W. Alden Spencer developed the generally accepted criteria for habituation, demonstrating that the basic process is a form of synaptic depression that occurs presynaptically. Thompson more recently has investigated the neuronal substrates of associative learning, identifying two critical systems—the hippocampus and the cerebellum. Eric Kandel is among the researchers investigating the link between proteins, synapses, and the formation of long-term memories. Specific proteins have demonstrated the capacity to strengthen synaptic connections basic to one's long-term memory storage. It's an exciting field with implications for Alzheimer's sufferers. James L. McGaugh has physiologically addressed the question of why emotionally arousing events are so memorable. McGaugh concludes that emotionally arousing events stimulate norepinephrine synapses (B-adrenergic), which enhance memory storage. These emotionally arousing events also arouse the sympathetic nervous system, which converts glycogen into glucose and raises the blood-glucose level. Since glucose is the brain's "petrol," increasing levels facilitate brain functioning.

You can readily see the excitement within current explorations of our "hidden universe," and there comes a deep, abiding respect for the many who are contributing to this field and to each of us.

The brain, as "mission control" in the central nervous system, works very closely with muscles and glands. Thus, the function and contribution of each to the total picture is critically important. To familiarize you with mission control, any of the comprehensive introductory textbooks mentioned earlier will be helpful. With so much material to cover, it would be easy to get bogged down in a mountain of names, functions, and small details. You will not, of course, be expected to have a Ph.D.'s competence in physiology in order to pass the Psychology Test, but you should understand the basics and the function of physiology within behavior.

We think, feel, act, enjoy, laugh, cry, and—yes—even write papers and books. At this very moment many elaborate, complex activities are occurring within your body—some in response to incoming stimuli, others to maintain bodily processes and their balance, and so forth. Most of this elaborate functioning is geared toward taking care of you. Psychology, by definition, studies human behavior, so it is essential and natural that a field of psychology (physiological/behavioral neuroscience) is directed toward the behaving organism and the physiological structures and elements that underlie behavior. As we head for this aspect of your review, a helpful sequence will be to read carefully and absorb this outline section and your introductory textbook chapter on the brain and biological bases of behavior. Pay special attention to outline headings, parts, systems, functions, and groupings. The more you can bring meanings and relationships to the material, the easier it will be for you to remember names and groupings. Then check yourself out on the following terms and concepts, so that you will know how prepared you are to move on.

Behavioral and Cognitive Neuroscience

Concepts	Names	Terms
Neurons and basic elements	Descartes	Neuron
	Ramon y Cajal	Glia Cell body (soma) Dendrites Axon Axon terminal Myelin sheath and nodes of Ranvier
	Sherrington	Synapse
The nerve impulse		Resting potential Action potential Threshold All-or-none law Saltatory conduction Ion channels Spatial and temporal summation
Synaptic transmission and the function of the synapse		Neurochemicals

	Loewi	Acetylcholine
		Biogenic Amines
		  Serotonin
		  Catecholamines
		    Dopamine

	McGaugh	Norepinephrine
		  Epinephrine (Adrenalin)
		Amino Acids
		  Glutamate
		  GABA Glycine
		Peptides (Neuromodulators)
		  Substance P
		  Endorphins Oxytocin
		Receptors
		Lock-and-key model
		Excitatory post-synaptic potential (EPSP)
		Inhibitory post-synaptic potential (IPSP)
		Breakdown and reuptake

Nervous system and its two major divisions		Central (CNS)
		  Brain and spinal cord
		  Sensory (afferent) neurons
		  Motor (efferent) neurons
		Peripheral
		  Somatic
		  Autonomic
		    Sympathetic
		    Parasympathetic
		    Enteric

Concepts	Names	Terms

Brain divisions and their functions		Brainstem
		  Hindbrain
		    Medulla
		    Pons
		  Midbrain
		  Cranial nerves
		  Reticular formation
		Cerebellum
		Forebrain
		  Thalamus
		  Basal ganglia
		  Limbic system
		    Hypothalamus
		    Amygdala
		    Hippocampus
		Cerebral cortex
		  Sulcus and gyrus
		  Hemispheres
		    Right (nonverbal) and left (verbal)
		    Corpus callosum
		  Lobes
		    Occipital (vision)
		    Temporal (audition, language, Wernicke's area)
		    Parietal (somatosensation, spatial ability)
		    Frontal (motor control, planning, Broca's area)

Endocrine system of glands		Hypothalamus Pituitary Thyroid Parathyroid Adrenal cortex Adrenal medulla Pancreas Pineal Ovaries and testes
Hormones		Adrenalin and noradrenalin (adrenal medulla) Growth hormone (pituitary) Insulin (pancreas) Leptin (fat tissue) Oxytocin (pituitary) Cortisol (adrenal cortex) Testosterone (testes) Estrogens and progesterone (ovaries) Melatonin (pineal gland)

Concepts	Names	Terms

Methods for measuring brain function		Recording techniques
		  Electrical
		    Single-cell recording
		    Electroencephalogram (EEG)
		    Event-related potentials (ERP)
		  Metabolic, hemodynamic

	Raichle, Petersen	Positron emission tomography (PET)
		    Functional magnetic resonance imaging (FMRI)
		  Diffusion tensor imaging (DTI)
		  Structural
		  Computerized axial tomography (CT)
		  Magnetic resonance imaging (MRI)

	Olds	Electrical stimulation

	Penfield	Motor and sensory homunculus
		Transcranial magnetic stimulation (TMS)
		Lesion/brain damage
		  Chemical, electrical lesions, cryolesions
		  (reversible)

	Phineas Gage	Natural injury (stroke, trauma, disease)
	Sperry, Gazzaniga	Surgical ablation, callosotomy (split-brain)

Sleep and sleep disorders		Stages of sleep
		  Light sleep (stages 1 and 2)
		  Deep sleep (stages 3 and 4)
		  Rapid-eye movement (REM) sleep
		    REM rebound
		    Muscle atonia
		Reticular formation
		Suprachiasmatic nucleus (SCN) of hypothalamus
		Sleep disorders
		  Polysomnogram
		  Sleep apnea
		  Insomnia
		  Narcolepsy

Neural plasticity	Thompson	Synaptic modification
	Kandel	Long-term potentiation Collateral sprouting
	Ramachandran	Cortical reorganization Interaction of environment/behavior with brain

Mood/behavior altering drugs (see outline pages 149–150)		Agonists
		Antagonists
		Blood-brain barrier
		Classification
		  Depressants
		  Stimulants
		  Narcotics/opiates
		  Antipsychotics
		  Hallucinogens/psychedelics

Outline Terms Elaborated

The next few pages embellish the outline a bit with more detail. From there your work with a strong "intro psych" book will give you the confidence you need to master this outline and move on to the next topic. Study tip: Overwhelmed by the terminology? Learning the Latin or Greek roots to the words can be a useful mnemonic (memory aid, from the Greek *mnemonikos*). For example, amygdala comes from the Greek *amygdale*, which means "almond" (because of the shape of the brain structure). Form an image of a scary "almond attack" (or whatever works for you) to remember that the amygdala is involved in emotions, especially fear. Where is the substantia nigra? Derived from the Latin words meaning "black substance," you can now picture a dark or dirty basement to remember that the substantia nigra is in the brain's basement—the brain stem. You get the idea.

NEURONS AND BASIC ELEMENTS

There are two kinds of cells in the nervous system: Neurons, or nerve cells, transmit information in the form of electrochemical changes. Glial cells perform a variety of other functions but do not transmit information (e.g., one type of glial cell forms the myelin sheath mentioned below). Our nervous systems contain hundreds of billions of neurons varying in size, shape, function, and response speed. The prototypical neuron has three parts—cell body, dendrites, and axon. As you view any drawing of a neuron, you will see branches seeming to grow from what looks like an egg, sunny-side up. The branches are the dendrites (from the Greek for "tree"), which receive signals from other neurons and send them to the cell body. The egg-resembling part is the cell body, or soma, which collects and sums these incoming signals to determine whether the neuron should initiate its own signal. The stem-like corridor is the axon, which transmits the neuron's signal to the dendrites of other neurons, and the process begins again. In many neurons, the axon is wrapped in an insulating covering called the myelin sheath; deterioration of myelin is seen in a disease called Multiple Sclerosis (MS). Myelin is formed by a type of glial cell, and periodic breaks in the myelin are called nodes of Ranvier. The color of myelin is what gives rise to the name white matter when referring to portions of the central nervous system composed of myelinated axon bundles. There is a tiny gap, called a synapse, between the ending of the axon of one neuron (the axon terminal) and the dendrites of the next neuron. There are two kinds of communication used by all neurons: electrical and chemical. Electrical changes result in the propagation of a neural signal from the dendrites to the axon terminal. Chemical changes result in the transmission of the signal from one neuron to the next. These two processes are discussed in more detail below.

THE NERVE IMPULSE

The entire neuron is surrounded by a membrane that carefully regulates the passage of molecules between the inside of the neuron and the outside of the neuron. The passage of charged particles called ions—especially sodium and potassium—through ion channels in this membrane is responsible for the electrical life of the neuron. When a neuron is at rest, this membrane maintains a constant electrical differential between the inside and outside of the neuron; this difference is called the cell's resting potential. When a neuron is communicating information, this differential changes, and is referred to as an action potential, also known as an impulse, a signal, or firing. When incoming signals to a neuron, pooled by numerous dendrites, via the processes of spatial and temporal summation, reach a certain threshold, the cell body initiates an action potential, which then propagates down the axon to the axon terminal. Because the action potential is always of the same amplitude, it is referred to as an all-or-none event. However, the speed of an action potential can vary: In axons surrounded by myelin, the action potential reaches the axon terminal quickly because the action potential "jumps" down the axon, from one node of Ranvier to the next (saltatory conduction). In all neurons, the arrival of the action potential at the axon terminal initiates a chemical reaction that leads to synaptic transmission of the neural signal.

SYNAPTIC TRANSMISSION AND FUNCTION OF THE SYNAPSE

When an action potential reaches the axon terminal of a neuron, it causes that neuron to release chemicals that fill the synapse. These chemicals are collectively called neurotransmitters. These neurotransmitters attach to receptors in the membrane of the dendrites of another neuron, in a specific lock-and-key fashion. This can result in one of two effects: Binding of an excitatory neurotransmitter to a receptor can move that neuron closer to its threshold for having an action potential, by causing an excitatory post-synaptic potential (EPSP). Conversely, binding of an inhibitory neurotransmitter to a receptor can move that neuron further from its threshold for having an action potential, by causing an inhibitory post-synaptic potential (IPSP). In contrast to the action potential, EPSPs and IPSPs are referred to as graded potentials, because (like grades) they can vary in amplitude. All of these inputs are summed by the cell body of the neuron, much the way credits and debits are summed on an accountant's ledger sheet, and if the net result is above threshold, the neuron fires an action potential. After a brief period of time, the neurotransmitter is either broken down (by other chemicals) or taken back up into the neuron that released it. There are dozens of neurotransmitters used by the brain. Three major neurotransmitter categories are biogenic amines (dopamine, norepinephrine, epinephrine, serotonin, and acetylcholine), amino acids (glutamate, GABA), and peptides (substance P, endorphins). Those in the latter group are often considered to be neuromodulators, because their effects are in some ways closer to those of hormones than true neurotransmitters. This distinction is not a sharp one.

NERVOUS SYSTEM AND ITS TWO MAJOR DIVISIONS

Central (CNS), consisting of the brain and the spinal cord (with its sensory [afferent] neurons carrying information into the CNS and its motor [efferent] neurons carrying information away from the CNS); and peripheral, consisting of the somatic (transmitting information from sense organs to CNS to voluntary, skeletal muscles) and the autonomic (controlling the viscera [smooth muscles of the blood vessels, digestive system, and glands] and the cardiac [heart] muscles).

The autonomic has two divisions: the sympathetic (activating organs and glands "in sympathy" with emotions, and mobilizing the body's resources for "fight-or-flight" emergencies), and the parasympathetic (opposing the sympathetic and conserving body resources and energy). The autonomic nervous system is the link between the nervous system and the endocrine system, which we review in more detail below. It is worth learning some of the opposing effects of the two branches of this system; for example, activation of the sympathetic branch speeds up the heart rate and slows down digestion, and activation of the parasympathetic branch does the reverse.

BRAIN DIVISIONS AND THEIR FUNCTIONS

The brain consists of three major divisions—the hindbrain, the midbrain, and the forebrain. The hindbrain begins where the spinal cord ends, and has three structures: the medulla, the pons, and the cerebellum. The medulla and pons contain entry and exit points for most of the twelve cranial nerves and control vital functions such as digestion, heart rate, and respiration. They also contain the reticular formation, or reticular activating system (RAS), which controls general arousal (sleep, waking, and attention). The cerebellum controls functions of balance and coordination of motor movement and may also contribute to skill learning. Just above the hindbrain sits the midbrain, which contains more cranial nerves, parts of the reticular formation, and important relay stations for sensory information. The midbrain also contains a group of neurons called the substantia nigra, which produce dopamine and which degenerate in Parkinson's disease. The midbrain, the pons, and the medulla are collectively known as the brainstem. The largest division of the brain in humans is the forebrain, which consists of all of the following structures: The thalamus relays sensory information to the cerebral cortex. The basal ganglia are involved in movement, speech, and other complex behaviors. Parts of the basal ganglia are damaged in Parkinson's disease and Huntington's disease. The hypothalamus works with both the central nervous system and the endocrine system and has a key role in motivated behaviors such as eating, drinking, sexual behavior, and aggression. The hippocampus is essential for learning and memory. The amygdala is involved in emotional expression. The hypothalamus, the amygdala, and the hippocampus, along with a few other structures, are collectively called the limbic system. All of the preceding brain structures are termed subcortical structures, in contrast to the rest of the forebrain, called the cerebral cortex. The cerebral cortex (Latin for "brain bark") is the convoluted surface of hills (gyri) and valleys (sulci) that you probably picture when you think of the brain. The cerebral cortex is divided into two nearly symmetrical hemispheres (with the left processing language and calculation and the right handling spatial and nonverbal functions in most people), which can each be further subdivided into four lobes: the occipital lobe in the rear, the parietal lobe on top, the frontal lobe in the front, and the temporal lobe on the bottom. The two hemispheres are connected by a bundle of nerve fibers called the corpus callosum. Regions of the cerebral cortex are often functionally subdivided into the projection areas that receive sensory input (vision in the occipital lobe, audition in the temporal lobe, somatosensation in the parietal lobe) or initiate motor commands (frontal lobe) and the association areas that make up the remaining 80% of cortex and subserve functions like planning and organization (frontal lobe), speech production (Broca's area in the frontal lobe), speech comprehension (Wernicke's area in the temporal lobe), and spatial organization (parietal lobe).

ENDOCRINE SYSTEM OF GLANDS AND THEIR ASSOCIATED HORMONES

Including the hypothalamus (which serves as the glandular system "control center" and produces the hormones oxytocin and antidiuretic); the pituitary (which stimulates bone growth and produces the hormones: growth (somatotropin), prolactin, thyroid-stimulating, adrenocorticotropic (ACTH), follicle-stimulating, and luteinizing); the thyroid (which has a major role in metabolism stimulation/maintenance and produces the hormones thyroxin and calcitonin); the parathyroid (which has a calcium-related role and produces the hormone parathyroid); the adrenal cortex (which functions in metabolism [carbohydrate, protein, lipid] and in the system's salt/water balance, producing the hormones cortisol and aldosterone); the adrenal medulla (which increases heart rate, dilates and constricts blood vessels, and increases blood sugar and produces the hormones epinephrine and norepinephrine); the pancreas (which regulates enzyme discharge into the intestines and produces the hormone insulin); the ovaries/testes (which affect sex characteristics development/ maintenance and produce the hormones estrogen/progesterone [in female, ovaries] and testosterone [in male, testes]). The pineal gland produces melatonin (in response to daylight signals that go from the eyes to the hypothalamus to the pineal gland); melatonin plays an important role in circadian rhythms.

METHODS FOR MEASURING BRAIN FUNCTION

Recording techniques measure changes in neural activity in the functioning brain. The most direct measure of brain activity comes from animal studies, in which a small electrode is placed next to a neuron and is able to record individual action potentials as they occur. So-called single-cell recording is not possible in humans, because of its invasiveness, although there are a number of techniques that are suitable for use with humans that provide a measure of neural activity. The closest parallel is the electroencephalogram (EEG), which records electrical changes across the brain with electrodes placed on the scalp. The EEG shows you a fluctuating picture of voltage changes. The EEG is known to vary predictably with the arousal level of the individual being recorded: When awake and active, the waveforms have a high frequency and a low amplitude (beta waves); when relaxed, the waveforms have a lower frequency and a higher amplitude (alpha waves); during sleep, the waveforms change with different stages of sleep. The EEG can also be used diagnostically, to reveal abnormal electrical patterns such as those observed in epilepsy. Although these EEGs can look like nothing more than jerky scribbles at first glance, there is a lot more we can learn about brain function by taking a closer look. Buried in these complex waveforms lie hidden treasures—voltage changes that depend on neural responses to stimuli in the environment. The examination of EEGs in relation to an experimental stimulus event goes by the name event-related potentials (ERPs) or evoked potentials. ERPs are simply averaged EEGs over many periods of time that are locked to (that is, that immediately follow) a stimulus of interest, such as a flash of light or a spoken word. There are other electrophysiological recording techniques that measure eye movement (EOG—electrooculogram), muscle tension (EMG—electromyogram), heart rate (EKG—electrocardiogram), and respiration. One area of research, which you may know as "biofeedback," enables people to monitor some of their own bodily functions, such as blood pressure and heart rate and control functions that were previously thought to be entirely involuntary. Neal Miller and his associates have had surprising success with experiments in this area.

In recent years a number of indirect measurements of neural activity in humans have been developed. All of these techniques rely on the coupling of neural activity and blood flow: Neurons that are firing lots of action potentials increase their demand for oxygen and glucose found in blood. One such technique is the positron emission tomography (PET) scan procedure, which injects a radioactive isotope tracer into the blood. As brain cells take up the tracer, they emit radiation that is recorded by detectors placed around the head. The more active a cell is, the more radiation it will emit. Raichle and Petersen conducted seminal studies of reading and speech processes using PET. A related technique is functional magnetic resonance imaging (fMRI), which makes use of the observation that hemoglobin bound to oxygen has different magnetic properties than hemoglobin not bound to oxygen. In other words, fMRI uses a tracer that is endogenous to our bodies! PET and fMRI scans are both methods for looking at the function of different parts of the brain. These differ from methods that only provide pictures of the structures of the brain. Two such methods are the computerized axial tomography (CAT or CT) scan, which performs multi-angle brain X-rays that are then computer-analyzed to produce a picture of each "slice" of the brain; and the magnetic resonance imaging (MRI) scan, which creates magnetic fields and records signals that occur when brain molecules respond to these fields. Remember: CAT and MRI scans depict brain structures while PET and fMRI scans analyze brain functions.

Electrical stimulation is the application of small levels of electrical current to part of the brain via an implanted electrode. Olds and Hess did pioneering work with electrical stimulation in animals, and Delgado and Penfield explored the effects of electrical stimulation in humans. Olds investigated pleasure centers in the hypothalamus, finding that a rat will happily self-administer electric current to these centers hour after hour. In humans, Delgado raised the possibility of helping people avert depression or aggressive behavior, for instance, by teaching them to recognize signals that accompany the onset of these problems and to stimulate their own brains via implanted electrodes. Other researchers have used electrical stimulation to examine the control of feeding and drinking, sexual behavior, and emotional responses. Hoebel produced eating behavior in completely satiated animals; similar drinking behavior has been produced by Miller et al. Fisher was able to obtain mating and maternal sexual behaviors in male animals, and Delgado convincingly demonstrated that the dominant animal in a colony can become quite submissive under certain conditions. Among other key researchers, Valenstein has worked with brain stimulation and psychosurgery and Magoun has worked with the reticular formation. Wilder Penfield used electrical stimulation to "map the cerebral cortex" in humans prior to brain surgery. Because the brain has no pain receptors, electrical stimulation could be applied to the brain of a fully conscious patient; using this technique, Penfield and his colleagues identified a systematic mapping of the body in motor and sensory cortex (for example, regions that control finger movement are adjacent to regions that control wrist movement) that is sometimes referred to as a homunculus. George Ojemann used electrical stimulation to map language areas throughout the brain. Clinically, this technique is important in identifying language and motor areas in each patient that can then be avoided during brain surgery. New on the scene is transcranial magnetic stimulation, a noninvasive cortical stimulation technique that uses magnetic fields to alter the electrical activity of neurons. This procedure shows promise both as a research tool and as a clinical tool (where it is currently being developed as a treatment for severe depression, as a safer alternative to electroconvulsive therapy).

Lesion and brain damage enables researchers to study how behavior is changed when some part of the brain is removed. The experimental lesion method in animals was pioneered by Charles Sherrington, who severed nerve fibers in dogs to study the importance of sensory feedback in motor control. Today, lesions are made with chemical and electrical techniques that allow remarkable precision. Of course, these techniques cannot be used in humans, although scientists do study the effects of naturally occurring brain damage on behavior. Some patients develop lesions, or tissue damage, following accidental head trauma, stroke, tumors, hemorrhage, infections, or disease. Perhaps the most famous head trauma case ever reported is that of Phineas Gage, the young construction worker who sustained a head injury after dynamite propelled an iron rod through his head. Gage's survival, and subsequent behavior changes, provided the first clues as to the function of the frontal lobes in regulating personality and emotion. Diseases that affect the brain are often tied to disruptions in one or more neurotransmitter systems. Alzheimer's disease, a degenerative memory loss resulting from widespread cortical atrophy, has been linked to a deficiency in the neurotransmitter acetylcholine; Parkinson's disease, a degenerative loss of motor control, results from the loss of neurons in the substantia nigra that produce the neurotransmitter dopamine; schizophrenia symptoms such as hallucinations are hypothesized to result from an excess of dopamine. Other patients are given therapeutic lesions to control neurological disorders, most typically to reduce or eliminate epileptic seizures. For example, to reduce the severity of seizures, the corpus callosum (the communication "link" between the two hemispheres) can be severed, thus providing a fascinating and unique way to study the differential functioning of the left and right hemispheres. Sperry pioneered this field first in animals and then in humans, and Gazzaniga continues to productively study these so-called split-brain patients to understand hemispheric differences.

SLEEP AND SLEEP DISORDERS

There are five distinct stages of sleep that have specific EEG profiles, ranging from Stage 1 light sleep (some alpha wave activity) to Stage 2 sleep (higher amplitude, lower frequency activity with some evidence of "spikes" called K-complex) to the deeper Stage 3 and Stage 4 sleep ("slow wave" sleep with a prevalence of delta wave activity) and finally to Rapid Eye Movement (REM) sleep (irregular brain wave pattern). Measurement of these patterns has revealed that the typical sleep pattern includes 4–5 REM cycles, when leaving deep sleep and moving back toward Stage 1 sleep, with each REM stage getting progressively longer as the night goes on. If REM sleep is disrupted one night, the following night REM sleep will occur earlier and more often the next night (REM rebound). Other characteristics of REM sleep include irregular breathing and heart rate, dysregulation of body temperature, penile erections and clitoral enlargement, and loss of muscle tone (muscle atonia). When awakened during REM sleep, people often report vivid dreams. Less coherent dream-like activity is reported when awakened from other stages of sleep (although it can be very difficult to wake someone from deep sleep). Sleepwalking, sleeptalking, and night terrors are all associated with deep sleep. Recordings of EEGs during sleep are one part of a comprehensive sleep test known as polysomnography. This test can be used to diagnose a variety of sleep disorders, including insomnia (difficulty falling asleep or staying asleep), narcolepsy (difficulty staying awake), and sleep apnea (interruptions in breathing during sleep). Sleep disorders may result from dysfunction of some of the brain structures involved in sleep and circadian rhythms, including the reticular formation, the pineal gland, and the suprachiasmatic nucleus (SCN) of the hypothalamus. The optimal amount of sleep (and the ratio of REM to non-REM sleep) changes across the life span.

NEURAL PLASTICITY

Plasticity refers to the flexibility that neurons have in their organization, connectivity, and function. In some regards, the brain exhibits remarkable plasticity, both during prenatal development (all neurons start out as the same type of stem cell, and look what happens!) and even into adulthood. For example, learning is thought to reflect the modification of synaptic connectivity; one process that has been studied for its relation to learning is called long-term potentiation of a synapse. However, in other regards the brain is decidedly non-plastic. The inability of the adult brain to grossly re-organize is the reason why brain damage can have such devastating, permanent effects. However, scientists are studying conditions and limitations on reorganization that could relate to recovery of some types of functions.

Collateral sprouting is a mechanism whereby neurons make connections to new areas to change their connectivity. Cortical reorganization can also be seen in the sensory and motor maps, in response to amputation of limbs or even learning. Changes in the brain have also been observed in certain regions in response to changes in the environment, such as social dominance status in animals.

EPIGENETICS

Francis Galton, Darwin's cousin, is credited with the phrase "nature *versus* nurture," which implies that environmental factors and biology act as separable influences. Nothing could be further from the truth. Today's collaborations between behavioral neuroscience and genetics demonstrate conclusively that nature and nurture are always inextricably entwined.

The field of epigenetics studies reversible changes in the performance of genes that do not involve changes to the underlying DNA. In other words, genes can turn on and off. In development, we see this in the differences between a muscle cell, skin cell, or neuron. All three types of cells contain the same DNA, but different genes are turned on (expressed) in a cell to make it look and behave like a neuron instead of a muscle cell.

Epigenetic effects are not restricted to early development. Throughout our whole lifetimes, what we eat, whether we smoke or drink alcohol, or the amount of stress we experience can tell our genes to turn on or off, leading to different outcomes of disease or health. You might know pairs of identical twins. As small children, they are remarkably alike. As they age, their accumulated, diverse experiences might make them quite different.

A dramatic example of epigenetics can be found in the Jirtle lab, which studies the effects of the plastic component BPA in mice. Identical, cloned mouse embryos are implanted in mother mice. Mother mice fed a diet containing BPA give birth to offspring that are obese and have yellow fur. Mother mice fed a diet that does not contain BPA have offspring that have brown fur and normal weight.

Does this happen to humans, too? Avshalom Caspi thinks so. He and his colleagues have published a number of articles that suggest that life experience with stress interacts with genes related to serotonin function to influence an individual's risk for major depressive disorder. Caspi also believes that exposure to child maltreatment interacts with genes to produce violent, aggressive behavior in some victims of child abuse but not others.

While new details are emerging about epigenetic processes on a daily basis, it is safe to assume that discussions of nature versus nurture are no longer relevant to psychologists.

MOOD/BEHAVIOR ALTERING DRUGS

All drugs have their effects at the synapse, by mimicking or changing the amount of neurotransmitter released by a presynaptic neuron or by modulating the effectiveness of a neurotransmitter on the postsynaptic neuron. In general, drugs that enhance a neurotransmitter's effect are called agonists while drugs that diminish the effect are called antagonists. Not every chemical can have an effect on the brain because not all chemicals have access to the brain and thus to the synapses; the blood-brain barrier is a mechanism that controls the passage of chemicals through the capillaries in the brain. The blood-brain barrier regulates which chemicals can enter the brain and how quickly they do.

Mood/behavior altering drugs fall into several major categories. We will give a narrative outline "intro" to drugs and their classification and will then follow with a quick-reference table. With that combination you'll have a strong grasp of the different categories, the characteristics of the category, and properties of specific types of drugs within each given category. Throughout this narrative we will be using the medical classification system (drug-effect-based) rather than the legal classification system, which is abuse-based. Where some drugs, for example, medically might not be classified as narcotics, a legal classification system might give them this label because they carry high abuse potential. What follows will be a medical classification.

Depressants

Depressants slow the CNS (central nervous system) functioning, reducing heart rate and breathing, and impairing motor functioning (e.g., the drunk person who staggers and would be lethal behind the wheel of a car). A depressant's crowning achievement is to put the person to sleep.

- **ALCOHOL** (ethanol) is our nation's most frequently used and abused depressant. With its physically addictive characteristics, a person developing a tolerance often will increase intake steadily to get the same "high." It's a vicious circle that compounds itself in many ways, including the person's capacity to function and the family's pain and dysfunction. The common, popular misnomer about alcohol is that it heightens sexual functioning when, in truth, it depresses this functioning and, alas, puts the person to sleep! Because it is addictive, the individual will experience withdrawal symptoms ranging from irritability and sleeplessness to seizures, heart attacks, and death. Its deleterious effects upon the body include destruction of brain cells and destruction of neurons in the CNS, liver damage, and damage to other organs of the body. Individual effects vary. Where one person will be drunk on one beer, another may take four or five before he or she appears intoxicated. These differences depend upon such factors as body weight, how quickly your body metabolizes and eliminates alcohol, and the level of tolerance developed through previous alcohol use/abuse.
- **BARBITURATES** generally carry "al" endings. Phenobarbital, Pentothal, Nembutal, and Seconal are among this cadre of depressants called "downers." Once prescribed as "sleeping pills," this group carries the same risks and dangers inherent to alcohol. When an intoxicated person takes barbiturates, the risks increase dramatically because the effects of taking alcohol and barbiturates together multiply exponentially. The combined user can easily overdose. It literally can be a deadly accident.
- **ANXIOLYTICS**, once called tranquilizers or *anti-anxiety* drugs, function to reduce anxiety feelings, calming and relaxing a person. Like alcohol and barbiturates, they also can produce sleep. Where meprobamate (Miltown) in small doses can reduce anxiety, larger doses can produce sleep or even death. *Benzodiazepine anxiolytics* such as Valium (diazepam class), Librium (chlordiazepoxide class), Xanax (alprazolam class), and Klonapin (clonazepam class) carry anxiety-reducing potential and frequently are used to treat anxiety disorders such as panic disorder and obsessive-compulsive disorder. Benzodiazepines produce less sedation than Miltown. Anxiolytics carry the same risks of psychological and physical dependence present with barbiturates, and the withdrawal process here can be every bit as painful.

Narcotics/Opioids

Narcotics/opioids such as *opium*, its *derivatives* (*codeine, heroin, morphine*), and the *synthetics* (e.g., *methadone*) function as painkillers. Like the depressants, they produce temporary feelings of euphoria, and bring on drowsiness and sleep. Narcotics are very highly addictive and carry a very high death-risk from overdose. Withdrawal also tends to be excruciating in its physical craving, pain, and suffering. AIDS and hepatitis are often transmitted by narcotics users through needle-sharing and blood-contact. Beyond these transmission risks, the bodily damage from narcotics/opiates surprisingly is less than that from alcohol abuse.

- **OPIUM**, coming from the poppy plant, is the "father or mother opiate." Its "offspring derivatives" are morphine; its derivative, heroin; and codeine. Heroin is three times more powerful than its "parent," morphine, and it brings intensely pleasurable reactions. Because it functions within a narrow range, a user can easily overdose, with devastating consequences including death. All opium derivatives produce euphoria and pain-control, and all are very highly addictive—both physically and psychologically.

- **METHADONE**, a synthetic narcotic/opioid, holds a unique place and function within this group. While it has pain-control properties, it produces very little euphoria. With this blend of properties, it is frequently used in narcotics treatment programs (methadone maintenance programs). Because it, too, is very highly addictive, its use in treatment programs has been highly controversial. The recovering narcotics addict is, in effect, trading one addiction for another.

Psychedelics

Psychedelics (*hallucinogens* or *psychotomimetics [mimicking psychosis]*) are perception, emotion, and mood-altering. Body images may become distorted (the user feeling God-like or ant-like), identity may become confused (much like amnesia), and the loss of reality may include dream-like fantasies and hallucinations.

The two "major players" in the psychedelic realm are *LSD* and *marijuana*.

- **LSD (LYSERGIC ACID DIETHYLAMIDE)** was synthesized from a rye fungus by a Swiss chemist, Albert Hofmann, in 1938. When he accidentally swallowed a bit of it and "tripped out," he became vividly aware of its bizarre qualities. Timothy Leary became the LSD guru in this country. As a serotonin agonist, LSD enhances the action of serotonin across the synapse. Minds can leave bodies, sounds can become visual, and time can become distorted. Trips are entirely unpredictable. They can be very pleasurable or very, very bad. LSD is not addictive, but its prolonged use has been linked with short-term memory loss, nightmares, paranoia, panic attacks, and flashbacks. Such side effects can prove lasting . . . consequently, the nickname, "acid heads."

- **MARIJUANA ("POT," "DOPE," "REEFER," "WEED")** and its active ingredient (*tetra-hydro-cannabinol, THC*) is a blend of crushed leaves, flowers, and stems from the hemp plant (*Cannabis sativa*). THC can be inhaled and quickly absorbed by the body and the brain. Senses and sensory experience are enhanced, and the user may feel dreamy, carefree, floating, and blissful. The effect lasts for a few hours. Like alcohol, it can impair muscle movement and coordination, and motor impairment can persist for an extended period after the enhanced state has dissipated. Frequent users can have lasting impairments to reasoning and memory.

"Minor players" include *mescaline, psilocybin,* and *PCP (phencyclidene).*

- **MESCALINE** occurs naturally in peyote cactus. The "trip" begins after the cactus buttons are chewed and the juice swallowed. It's a four-to-six-hour trip and, the user hopes, a blissful one.
- **PSILOCYBIN** comes from certain mushrooms. They, too, are chewed and the juice swallowed. The trip resembles that of mescaline.
- **PCP (PHENCYCLIDENE, "ANGEL DUST")** is a synthetic originally used as an anesthetic. It can be ingested or smoked with trip qualities and dangers similar to those outlined above.

Stimulants

Stimulants literally live up to their name. They increase activity in the CNS, heightening arousal and energy level. More than one student has called upon an aluminum can of their favorite stimulant to "pull an all-nighter" or two . . . not you, of course, but some of your peers! Virtually all stimulants carry the "ine" ending—amphetamines (Benzedrine ["bennies," "speed"], Dexedrine ["uppers"], Methedrine ["ice"]), methamphetamines ("crystal meth") and derivatives (MDMA ["ecstasy" or "X"]), cocaine ("coke" and "crack"), caffeine, nicotine, and convulsants (strychnine).

- **AMPHETAMINES** stimulate the brain and the sympathetic nervous system. Heart rate and blood pressure elevate, blood vessels constrict, mucous membranes shrink, and appetite is reduced. This latter property made amphetamines popular for weight control in the 1950s and 1960s.
- **METHAMPHETAMINES ("CRYSTAL METH")** and *derivatives* (*MDMA* [*"ecstasy"* or *"X"*]) have amphetamine-like properties. "Crystal meth" is a powder that can be "snorted" or injected. For quite obvious reasons, MDMA is short for 3,4-Methylene-dioxymethamphetamine (impress your date with that one!). Also known as "Ecstasy" or "X," it produces both stimulant and psychedelic effects. Effects are similar to those produced by amphetamines and cocaine. All is not ecstasy, however, because the user may experience jaw muscle spasms ("lockjaw") and "day after" muscle aches, depression, and fatigue.
- **COCAINE** has properties and effects similar to amphetamines, increasing norepinephrine and dopamine activity. With its rapid onset and short duration, it is very highly addictive; and "crack," the purified, smokable form is all the more powerful, addictive, and dangerous. While use can temporarily stimulate self-confidence and a sense of well-being, the long-range effects include nausea, hyperactivity, insomnia, hallucinations, depressive "crashes," sexual dysfunction, and seizures. The "roller-coaster" carries an exceptionally high price tag, and breaking an addiction is exceedingly difficult. A minimum of one year in treatment carries the greatest hope of success and, even then, recidivism runs disturbingly high. Buprenorphine, an opiate antagonist, may hold treatment promise; but all treatment results have been mixed. "Cocaine babies" carry severe and permanent intellectual/behavioral problems that provide no small societal challenge.
- **CAFFEINE** is, without a doubt, the world's most popular drug. At one time or another we all have encountered it in our chocolates, coffee, tea, and sodas; and a surprising number of us have liked it and continued its use. While it temporarily fights drowsiness, and heightens physical work and problem-solving, it also keeps us headed to the toilet

frequently and brings a packet of unwelcome "guests" like anxiety, headaches, craving, fatigue, and the "shakes." Like alcohol, the user can build a tolerance as well as a physical dependence.

- **NICOTINE** powerfully stimulates the autonomic nervous system and carries many psychoactive effects such as mood elevation and increased attention. The U.S. Surgeon General equates its physically addictive properties with those of heroin and cocaine, while others make reference to psychological dependence. Mark Twain once said, paraphrased, "Stopping smoking is the easiest thing in the world to do. I've done it many times." Many would-be abstainers from smoking can readily identify with Twain's comment about stopping. Smoking is an exceedingly difficult habit to break. Many women develop the habit for weight control, trying to attain the body image of "Virginia Slim," and weight gain is one of the notable effects for those who stop smoking, along with irritability, craving, and anxiety.

- **CONVULSANTS** (strychnine) are a rough and "one-way-ticket" way to stimulate. Beyond "who done it?" mystery novels, we wouldn't recommend your spending much time on this one.

Now we come to the "anti's"—*antidepressants* (*thymoleptics*), *antimanics* (*thymoleptics*), and *antipsychotics* (*neuroleptics*). Technically, the anxiolytics are "anti's," too, but we covered them earlier within our antianxiety discussion.

Antidepressants

Depression has been called the "common cold" of our generation—highly present and pervasive within our society. Consequently, *antidepressants* are very frequently prescribed mood elevators. There are three major categories—*tricyclics, monoamine oxidase (MAO) inhibitors,* and *serotonin reuptake inhibitors.* All three categories prolong the activity of the neurotransmitters dopamine, norepinephrine, and serotonin. This prolonged activity stimulates receptors on the postsynaptic neuron. Tricyclics prevent the reabsorption of dopamine, norepinephrine, or serotonin; MAO inhibitors block the enzyme monoamine oxidase from breaking down neurotransmitter molecules; and serotonin reuptake inhibitors prevent the reabsorption of serotonin. In each instance, more neurotransmitter crosses the synapse to the postsynaptic neuron. Tricyclics and MAO inhibitors were the earlier generation of antidepressants, and serotonin reuptake inhibitors are the exciting "new kids on the block."

- **TRICYCLICS (TCAS)** are a potent category of antidepressants frequently prescribed for a person suffering from severe depression. Two of the commonly prescribed tricyclics are *imipramine* (*Tofranil*) and *amitriptyline* (*Elavil*). These drugs carry fewer side effects and potential medical complications than MAO inhibitors.

- **MAO INHIBITORS (OR MAOIS)** are less frequently prescribed because of their unwelcome side effects. When mixed with the food substance tyramine (present in sharp cheeses, dinner wines, and chicken livers), severe hypertension results. A newer version of MAOIs have mitigated many of these side effects.

- **SEROTONIN** *reuptake inhibitors* are the so-called "second generation" of antidepressants. This is the "land of *Prozac, Zoloft,* and *Paxil.*" With few side effects, these drugs allow many depression sufferers to function effectively outside the hospital setting. More than 60 percent of current antidepressant prescriptions now come from this category, and one of the current controversies revolves around the risk of overprescribing—something of a "designer drug" use rather than a prescribed use for depression.

Antimanics

Antimanics (*thymoleptics*) relieve the symptoms of bipolar (manic-depressive) disorders. As the name implies, they are especially effective in relieving the manic phase. There is truly only one effective entry in this group, *lithium carbonate*, but several other entries round out the group, including *valproic acid* and *carbamazepine*.

- **LITHIUM CARBONATE** is a mineral salt whose calming properties for bipolar disorders were discovered in the early 1970s. Drug company interest was understandably mute because it was a naturally occurring substance. Lithium is effective in approximately 80 percent of manic disorders, and dosage level is critical. While too little produces no effect, too much produces nausea or, in extreme instances, death. Like the antidepressants, time is required to build up the desired blood level before any effective relief is apparent.
- **VALPROIC ACID** and *carbamazepine* are two other entries in this class. From their names you can readily conclude that, unlike lithium, they are manufactured rather than naturally occurring.

Antipsychotics

Antipsychotics (*neuroleptics*) entered the mental health scene in the early 1950s and revolutionized the treatment of mental disorders. With their use the schizophrenic's hallucinations, delusions, mental incoherence, and fragmented thought patterns were notably ameliorated. This was the first wave of drug treatment in the mental health movement. The most frequently prescribed drugs in this group are the following:

- **PHENOTHIAZINES (CHLORPROMAZINE [THORAZINE], TRIFLUOPERAZINE [STELAZINE], FLUPHENAZINE [PROLIXIN], AND THIORIDAZINE [MELLARIL]).**

Other entries include the:

- **BUTYROPHENONES (HALOPERIDOL [HALDOL])** and the
- **ATYPICALS (CLOZAPINE [CLOZARIL] AND RISPERIDONE [RISPERDAL]).**

Like the antidepressants, dosage level is critically important, and prolonged use of antipsychotics can result in irreversible CNS disorders such as involuntary repetitive movements or tics.

Well, you've been thoroughly drugged at this point, and along the way we introduced the terms *agonist* and *antagonist* within our definitions. Let's pause for a moment to understand more fully what this means. Think of a receptor dendrite as though it were your electrical outlet on the wall. When neurotransmitters are functioning normally, they cross the synapse and "plug into" the receptor dendrite much as your plug for the radio or stereo would. When neurotransmitters are abnormally functioning, either too much or too little is crossing the synapse to the receiving dendrite. Where the problem is too little crossing the synapse, an agonist "plugs in" and establishes a normal flow. Where the problem is too much crossing the synapse, an antagonist blocks flow similar to those clever little plastic inserts we place in outlets to keep toddlers from getting toasted. Of necessity the example is oversimplified, but we wanted you to know and understand these terms.

Now let's summarize at-a-glance what we've just been through.

Mood/Behavior Altering Drugs Outline

Function	Class	Chemical and/or Trade and Street Name
Depressants	Alcohol	Ethanol ("booze")
	Barbiturates ("al" endings)	Phenobarbital ("downers" or "sleeping pills")
		Pentothal
		Nembutal
		Seconal
		Tuinal
	Hypnotics	Methaqualone
		Glutethimide
Pleasure/Euphoria/ Pain-relief	Narcotics/Opiates	Opium Morphine (Percodan, Demerol) Heroin ("junk," "smack")
		Codeine
	Synthetics	Methadone
Psychedelics	Hallucinogens or	LSD ("acid")
	Psychotomimetics	Marijuana (cannabis) (THC) ("pot," "dope," "reefer," "hashish")
		Mescaline
		Psilocybin
		PCP (phencyclidene, "angel dust")
Stimulants ("ine" endings)	Amphetamines	Benzedrine ("bennies," "speed")
		Dexedrine ("uppers")
		Methedrine ("ice")
	Methamphetamines Derivatives	"Crystal meth"
		MDMA ("ecstasy," "X")
	Others	Caffeine
		Cocaine ("coke," "crack")
		Convulsants (strychnine)
		Nicotine ("smokes," "weeds," "coffin nails")
The "Anti's"		
Antianxiety (anxiolytics)	Benzodiazepines	Diazepam (Valium)
		Chlordiazepoxide (Librium) Alprazolam (Xanax)
		Clonazepam (Klonapin)
	Other	Buspirone (Buspar)

Function	Class	Chemical and/or Trade and Street Name
Antidepressant (thymoleptics)	Tricyclics	Amitriptyline (Elavil)
		Imipramine (Tofranil)
		Nortriptyline (Pamelor)
		Desipramine (Norpramine)
		Doxepin (Sinequan)
		Clomipramine (Anafranil)
	Monoamine oxidase (MAO) inhibitors	Phenelzine (Nardil)
		Tranylcypromine (Parnate)
	Serotonin reuptake inhibitors	Fluoxetine (Prozac)
		Sertaline (Zoloft)
		Paroxetine (Paxil)
		Fluvoxamine (Luvox)
Antimanic (thymoleptics)	Lithium carbonate	Lithium (Eskalith, Lithobid, Lithonate)
	Other	Valproic acid (Depakene)
		Carbamazepine (Tegretol)
Antipsychotic (neuroleptics)	Phenothiazines	Chlorpromazine (Thorazine)
		Trifluoperazine (Stelazine)
		Fluphenazine (Prolixin)
		Thioridazine (Mellaril)
	Butyrophenones	Haloperidol (Haldol)
	Others	Clozapine (Clozaril)
		Risperidone (Risperdal)

Behavioral and Cognitive Neuroscience Summary

Now that you have thought through your outlines and have thoroughly reviewed your introductory psychology textbook chapter in the biological bases of behavior, check yourself out on the following sample of basic concepts and information. If they feel familiar to you, move on in your review. If they feel very spotty, strengthen your review-grasp before heading on.

- Neuron and its components: dendrites, soma, axon, synapse
- Distinction between central nervous system and peripheral nervous system
- Major neurotransmitters and the distinction between excitatory effects and inhibitory effects
- Distinction between receptors and effectors (and corresponding words such as sensory, afferent fibers and motor, efferent fibers)
- Autonomic nervous system (and its subdivisions into sympathetic and parasympathetic)
- Brain hemispheres and the four lobes within each—frontal, temporal, parietal, and occipital—with knowledge of what general behavioral functions each area encompasses
- Subcortical structures including cerebellum, basal ganglia, medulla, pons, midbrain, thalamus, hypothalamus, amygdala, hippocampus

- Terms such as sulcus, gyrus, corpus callosum, reticular formation, limbic system, acetylcholine, epinephrine, norepinephrine, serotonin, dopamine, blood-brain barrier, action potential, myelin
- Distinction among striated (voluntary), smooth (visceral), and heart muscles
- Location and function of endocrine glands—pineal, anterior and posterior pituitary, thyroid, parathyroid, thymus, adrenal medulla and adrenal cortex, and ovaries/testes
- Relationships between hormonal secretions and behavior
- The neuroendocrine system
- The physiology and neuroanatomy of sexual behavior
- The uses of and differences between EEG, ERP, CAT, PET, MRI

Note—you need not spend time and energy on terms such as brachial plexus, ventral nerve root, and the like. Your time is limited, and your goal is basic understanding.

- Alpha, beta, delta, and theta waves (the types of activity and the general wave frequency associated with each)
- Stages of sleep (their sequence and frequency)
- Dreams (their relationship to sleep stages, their frequency, and bodily functioning, such as REM, that accompanies them)
- Basic brain function activity in relation to sensory input and the effects of hormones and drugs
- Drug categories and their behavioral effects: depressants, stimulants, narcotics/opiates, antipsychotics, hallucinogens/psychedelics
- Neurotransmitters and their implications in depression (norepinephrine and serotonin) and schizophrenia (dopamine) as well as their function in memory trace (see Donald A. Norman's *Learning and Memory* [1995] for an excellent orientation, if needed; Lindsay and Norman's chapter entitled "Neural Basis of Memory" you may find especially helpful).
- Epigenetics

Within your review you probably sensed the vibrance, pace, and excitement of this pioneering, rapidly moving field. With technological breakthroughs such as the CAT scan (computerized axial tomography), PET scan (positron emission tomography), and the MRI scan (magnetic resonance imaging), *the study of brain structure and activity has taken a quantum leap.* Just sixty years ago, links between brain structure and function were made only by following patients with specific behavioral or cognitive deficits to autopsy and forming crude post-mortem descriptions of their brain damage. Now it is possible to "take a picture" of the brain of a living, healthy volunteer who is speaking, reading, solving problems, remembering, or performing any other complex task under a psychologist's control. This opens an exciting, vast expanse for future research into the intricate inner workings of brain and memory. A related area—the developmental study of neural activity in the brain—also has limitless potentials stemming from these new technologies. As we discover how neurally and chemically active is the brain of the two-year-old in comparison with the brain of the six-year-old, for instance, we stand on the threshold of studying the "birth of learning." What we have seen to date is just the tip of the iceberg in these research potentials and the contribution they will make to our lives and our future.

If you need or want more in-depth reading before moving on, refer to one of the recent introductory textbooks mentioned at the end of Chapter 1 and delve into some of the readings recommended there. If you want more detailed information and explanations than you find in your introductory textbook, you might turn to more specialized resources. *Discovering Behavioral Neuroscience* (3rd edition) by Freberg (Cengage, 2016) should provide the background detail you need.

EVOLUTIONARY AND COMPARATIVE PSYCHOLOGY

Our review of biological foundations of psychology has, thus far, focused on the proximate biological bases of behavior and cognition. However, we can also ask about the ultimate causes of our psychology on an evolutionary time scale: How is human biology and psychology similar to and different from that of other species, and how can those differences be understood as the product of evolution by natural selection? How are these changes encoded in our biological blueprint, our genes? In this next section of our review, we focus on the comparative approach to understanding the biological foundations of behavior and thought, and we review some basic terms about genetics. This approach has touched every area of psychology, as our understanding about the complex interplay between our genes and our experiences advances with every passing year.

No discussion of evolutionary or comparative psychology could take place without mention of Charles Darwin, so we might as well begin there. In 1859, Darwin published his theory of evolution in the seminal book, *On the Origin of Species*. This was not the first developed theory of evolution; decades earlier Jean-Baptiste Lamarck published a theory of evolution that described the important role of the environment in this process. However, unlike Darwin, Lamarck argued that the environment could change behavior or structures in an individual, who could then pass on those changes to his or her offspring. Darwin's theory of evolution focused on how the environment affects evolution through the process of natural selection: those traits that are adaptive in an environmental niche are favored in evolution, and the diversity of species reflects the variations in their environmental ecology.

Darwin developed his theory through careful observation, without the benefit of our current molecular knowledge. He knew there was a mechanism for passing traits to offspring, but did not know what that mechanism was. His contemporary, Gregor Mendel, sometimes called the father of genetics, documented patterns of inheritance of traits in pea plants, and introduced the notion of dominant and recessive alleles. But the structure of these alleles (or gene variations) would have to wait for almost a century, until the publication of the first accurate model of DNA structure by James Watson and Francis Crick in 1953. Today, a detailed characterization of the human DNA sequence is known, and we have begun to learn more about the relationship between genetic variations and patterns of psychological traits and abilities, both typical and pathological.

The study of evolution began with an appreciation of the similarities and the differences among distinct species, and the environmental factors that shaped these patterns. Today, this comparative approach is evident in disciplines known by the names evolutionary biology, evolutionary psychology, comparative psychology, and ethology (animal behavior). Dewsbury and Rethlingshafer defined comparative psychology as "the systematic study of everything every species does or is capable of doing." Phew—that's no small task! Through reasonable limitations upon the number of organisms studied, however, comparative psychology has become "a broad, but manageable, science of behavior." Within this framework, researchers attempt to describe and explain species differences and similarities with regard to all aspects of behavior, including communication, sexual and aggressive patterns, social interactions, learning and instinct, and so on. All of these behaviors can be characterized in terms of interactions between an animal and its environment. This approach had its historical mooring and primary foundation within classical European ethology. Given impetus and direction through the pioneering work of Tinbergen, Lorenz, and von Frisch, research in the field of ethology focused upon instructive behavior and its observation within the natural habitat of the species. Comparative psychologists in the American tradition have placed their major emphasis upon observations of animal behavior under controlled laboratory conditions. These two approaches—field observations and laboratory experimentation—complement each other and communication between those involved in these orientations is frequent and constructive.

As outlined by Niko Tinbergen, the four areas of study in animal behavior are development, mechanism, function, and evolution: Development is concerned with genetic determinants of behavior and their interaction with environmental determinants. Mechanism deals with the interaction between behavior and physiological systems, and function places emphasis upon the adaptive value of a behavior for the animal's survival and reproduction. Evolution provides the unifying central theme and cohesive focus for all aspects of the field. Development and mechanism explore proximate explanations of behavior, whereas questions about function and evolution explore ultimate explanations.

Recently, the study of human psychology—our behaviors, preferences, and emotions—has been viewed through this same evolutionary lens, in a field called evolutionary psychology. Extending the work of sociobiologists, such as Edward Wilson, who discussed the evolutionary advantages of social behavior (territorialism, mating patterns, and so on), evolutionary psychologists (e.g., Buss, Tooby, and Cosmides) seek both proximate and ultimate explanations of human psychology: What aspects of our minds can be understood as adaptations to our ancestral environment?

These topics—evolution, genetics, ethology and animal behavior, and evolutionary psychology—comprise the last piece of our review of biological foundations.

Evolutionary and Comparative Psychology Outline

Concepts	Names	Terms
Evolution	Lamarck	Inheritance
	Darwin	Adaptation
		Natural selection
		Species
		Fitness
	Galton	Eugenics
Behavioral genetics	Mendel	Genotype
		Phenotype
		Allele
		Dominant gene
		Recessive gene
		Heritability

	Plomin	Twin study
		  Monozygotic/dizygotic
		  Common/unique environments

		Nature/nurture

Concepts	Names	Terms
Molecular genetics	Watson	DNA

	Crick	Chromosomes (23 pairs)
		   Autosomes
		   Sex chromosomes (XX/XY)

		Gene
		Diploid
		Nucleotides
		Mutation
		Genome
Ethology/Animal behavior	Tinbergen	Proximate/ultimate mechanisms
	Lorenz	Imprinting
		Critical period
		Species-typical behaviors
		Fixed-action pattern
		Innate releasing mechanism
		Releasing (sign) stimulus
Sociobiology/ Evolutionary psychology	Wilson Buss	Altruism Kin selection theory
	Tooby/Cosmides	Ancestral environment
	Pinker	Domain-specific
	Dawkins	Memes

Outline Terms Elaborated

- As reviewed above, the first well-articulated theory of evolution is generally attributed to French biologist Jean-Baptist Lamarck, who developed a theory of the inheritance of acquired characteristics (now referred to as Lamarckian evolution). Charles Darwin disagreed with this aspect of Lamarck's proposal, and instead advanced a theory of evolution that described adaptations as the result of random mutations and not individual efforts to change in their environment. In his famous book *On the Origin of Species*, Darwin explained how natural selection led to the divergence of species, which can be defined as a group of organisms who can reproduce and produce fertile offspring. Natural selection favors traits that enhance the reproductive fitness of an organism (i.e., their genetic contribution to future generations). Adaptations are structures and functions that enhance the fitness of an organism in its specific environment. Two controversial extensions of these ideas are called social Darwinism and eugenics, which refers to selective breeding in order to enhance the human gene pool; the latter term was coined by Francis Galton, and his interest in improving human abilities through eugenic practices motivated his research on the heritability of psychological traits.

- Galton's publication of *Hereditary Genius* anticipated the field now known as behavioral genetics. Behavioral genetics has as its foundation the work of Gregor Mendel, the Austrian scientist now referred to as the father of genetics. Based on his experimentation with pea plants, Mendel developed his Laws of Inheritance, which describe how inherited characteristics are transmitted from parent to offspring. He introduced the idea that there are alternate versions of each gene, called alleles. Humans have two copies of each gene: if the two copies are identical we say the individual is homozygous for that gene, if not, heterozygous. The notion of dominance describes the relation between the genotype (genetic blueprint) and the phenotype (observable characteristics) of an individual: a recessive version of the gene will be expressed only in the presence of another recessive allele, whereas the dominant version of the gene will be expressed regardless. In behavioral genetics, traits that appear to arise from a single locus (as Mendel described) are referred to as Mendelian traits. Of course, many other factors also affect an individual's phenotype, and the interaction of genes and environment is a fundamental issue in psychology. One of the core methods for teasing these factors apart is the twin study in which the psychological traits of monozygotic (identical) and dizygotic (fraternal) twins are assessed in an effort to tease apart the heritable influences and the environmental influences on a given behavior or ability, also referred to as the nature–nurture distinction. Robert Plomin is well known for making the distinction between two types of environmental influences: common and unique.

- Contemporary research on heritability benefits from advances in molecular genetics. We now know that our genes are made of molecules of this deoxyribonucleic acid (DNA). As a diploid organism, humans have two copies of every gene, which Mendel already knew; they are stored (in humans) on 23 pairs of chromosomes: 22 pairs of autosomes referred to as a number and one pair of sex chromosomes (XX for girls and XY for boys). Each chromosome has many genes (typically referred to with either a number indicating the location on a chromosome or by a name indicating the putative function). The variation in the alleles is, at a molecular level, related to differences in the sequence of nucleotides (adenine, guanine, thymine, and cytosine). Mutations in this sequence can give rise to variations in traits, and these variations are the target of natural selection. The complete catalog of this sequence of nucleotides is our genome, and the catalog of the human genome was completed in 2001.

- Much of the history and emphasis of the related fields of ethology and animal behavior was reviewed above. Here, we remind you of a few key ideas and terms that have arisen from those traditions. Konrad Lorenz, sometimes called the father of ethology, has been memorialized in a classic picture of imprinted geese following him across a field. In his studies of imprinting, Lorenz introduced the notion of a critical period for learning, which we return to in our review of child development. Lorenz also introduced the term fixed-action pattern to describe the species-typical behaviors that occur instinctively in response to an environmental cue. These patterns are indivisible (once initiated they run to completion) and are caused by an innate releasing mechanism. Lorenz, along with Tinbergen (who we met earlier) studied fixed-action patterns in waterfowl, who will roll a displaced egg (or any egg-shaped object) back to the nest. Tinbergen also studied aggression and courtship behaviors in stickleback, a fish species. The red underbelly of a male stickleback during the breeding seasons serves as a releasing (or sign) stimulus for aggressive behaviors in other sticklebacks. Tinbergen characterized the proximate and ultimate causes of this response.

- The term sociobiology was popularized by Edward Wilson in his 1975 book Sociobiology: The New Synthesis. In this book, Wilson described the search for ultimate explanations for social behaviors such as altruism, aggression, and nurturance by considering the adaptive value of these behaviors for the fitness of an individual. For example, a prominent hypothesis for altruistic behavior—kin selection theory—is that it increases an individual's fitness when the behavior helps a relative (with shared genes). The same approach is taken by *evolutionary psychologists*, a term coined by coworkers John Tooby and Leda Cosmides and also advanced by David Buss. Much of their (and related) work characterizes the domain-specific mechanisms that evolved as adaptations to the human ancestral environment. Prominent psychologist Steven Pinker has taken this approach to the study of language. Another idea to emerge from this field is that natural selection operates not only on genes but also on aspects of culture, called memes by Richard Dawkins.

Evolutionary and Comparative Psychology Summary

As you can see from the difference in review coverage, you can expect many more questions on the GRE based on the neuroscientific approach than on the comparative approach. Balance your own study time accordingly. If you would like to read more about these topics, there are a number of specialized books to consider. For an excellent introduction to evolutionary biology, Richard Dawkins' 30th anniversary edition of *The Selfish Gene* (Oxford, 2006) is an update on a classic if not *the* classic work in this area. Alcock's *Animal Behavior: An Evolutionary Approach* (Sinauer, 8th edition, 2005) is a very good introduction to that field, and could be usefully followed up with Krebs and Davies' *Behavioural Ecology: An Evolutionary Approach* (Wiley-Blackwell, 1997) which, though a little older, remains a resource of choice for the interested student. Probably no one is better positioned to comment on humans in the context of the principles of behavioral ecology than Irenaus Eibl-Eibesfeldt—*Human Ethology* (Aldine Transaction, 2007) is a challenging but worthwhile entry point into the area. There are now a number of texts available in evolutionary psychology, the modern application of principles of evolutionary biology to humans, probably the best known and most traditional of which is David Buss's *Evolutionary Psychology: The New Science of the Mind* (Allyn & Bacon, 2007), now in its third edition. There are two other textbooks, *Human Evolutionary Psychology* by Barrett, Dunbar, and Lycett (Palgrave Macmillan, 2002), and *Evolutionary Psychology* by Gaulin and McBurney (Prentice Hall; 2nd edition, 2003), both of which give excellent overviews of the field. Steve Pinker's award-winning *How the Mind Works* (Norton, 1999) is a lengthy but very readable book at the intersection of evolutionary and cognitive psychology.

CLINICAL AND ABNORMAL

Extensive NIMH Research revealed that one out of every seven persons in the United States has had a significant mental illness in the past year. Equally striking is the fact that, at any given moment, half of all hospital beds in the United States are occupied by persons suffering from emotional disturbances. Moreover, it is estimated that 30 percent of all Americans have emotional disturbances not severe enough to require hospital care, yet severe enough to interfere significantly with their life adjustment. There is much emotional pain in our midst and, consequently, much attention centered in the area of psychopathology.

What is normal? What is abnormal? And how do we know we *are* normal or abnormal? These are difficult questions—not simply for us but for professionals in the field as well. There are several approaches we could take to such questions. One would be the *subjective*, which is demonstrated by the Quaker saying, "Everyone's weird 'cept me and thee, and sometimes I wonder about thee." It says, in effect, "I'm normal, and I will now measure everyone else by the yardstick of my own normality." The *normative* approach would take perfection as normal—meaning that each of us would strive but never fully measure up. A *cultural* approach would begin from the assumption that what the majority of the people are doing is normal. The *statistical* approach would design a test and then interpret normality on the basis of scoring at or near the mean (generally scoring within one standard deviation). And the *clinical* approach to normality would be based on the assessment rendered by a trained professional in the field. That assessment might use statistical measures, but it also would use the professional's insights regarding the individual's capacity to interact, to function, and to cope in the environment. Behaviors that are bizarre and extreme (e.g., hallucinations, uncontrolled violence), behaviors that interfere with the well-being of others (e.g., spousal abuse, child molesting), emotional extremes (e.g., uncontrollable mania or depression), and behavior that interferes with daily functioning (e.g., self-destructive patterns) would be considered abnormal. The more formal expression of abnormal behavior or psychopathology is a classification system (*Diagnostic and Statistical Manual or DSM*) developed by the American Psychiatric Association. The DSM is now in its fifth edition, known as DSM-5, which was published in May 2013. In Chapter 1, you will find a section that highlights the major changes between DMS-5 and the previous ediction, known as DSM-IV-TR.

Five major models encompass current attempts to understand and address abnormality. The *biomedical model* takes the position that abnormality is an illness of the body. The *psychodynamic model* believes abnormality is a product of hidden personality conflicts. The *behavioral model* sees abnormality as learned maladaptive behaviors that can be changed through the learning of adaptive behaviors. The *cognitive model* sees abnormality as stemming from disordered thinking about oneself and the world. And the *existential-humanistic model* relates abnormality to a person's inability to successfully confront and address ultimate life questions such as the meaning of life, how you can live up to your fullest potential, and how you can face death.

The *Diagnostic and Statistical Manual (DSM-5)* has its roots in psychiatry and the biomedical model, and as you review you will appreciate the difficulty and complexity of classifying abnormal behavior. To reduce the complexity of your DSM introduction, we will turn the calendar back a bit.

This classification system is a bit like B.C. and A.D. in our calendar perspective on time. B.C. in their classification system was DSM-II (*Diagnostic and Statistical Manual of Mental Disorders*, 2nd ed., American Psychiatric Association). From your viewpoint it is unfortunate that it is not the current classification system—it did have the beauty of simplicity. It classified behaviors in the two general categories of psychoneurotic and psychotic disorders. The psychoneurotic disorders (sometimes called simply "neurotic") had the common characteristic of anxiety (a painful state of tension). The psychoneurotic person remained behaviorally and cognitively in contact with his environment. Psychotic disorders, on the other hand, were more severe cognitive, emotional, and behavioral disturbances characterized by hallucinations and delusions.

As diagnostics have become sharper and more focused, and as given pathologies and problems have become more prevalent and pressing, the diagnostic system itself has changed to keep pace. So let's jump right into our review of DSM-5, using it as the framework for our preparation in psychopathology.

Place yourself, for a moment, in the role of a therapist. A client comes to see you with a problem. As you interact with the client, you will use DSM-5 to classify the individual.

Neurodevelopmental Disorders

This group is characterized by appearance during childhood. Intellectual disability refers to statistically low IQ (below a standarized IQ of 70 or two standard deviations below the mean) and difficulties in life skills. Autism spectrum disorder is characterized by communication problems, social relatedness problems, and unusual rituals or interests. Attention-deficit/hyperactivity disorder features either inattentiveness or hyperactivity or both that is inconsistent with developmental age.

Schizophrenia Spectrum and Other Psychotic Disorders

Schizophrenia is what most people think about when they consider mental illness. An individual with this disorder might hallucinate, experience delusions, demonstrate disorganized thinking or speech, and experience movement disturbances. In addition, negative symptoms such as social withdrawal, lack of motivation, and emotional disturbance can occur.

Bipolar and Related Disorders

Now in their own category (they were grouped with major depressive disorder in previous editions of the DSM), the bipolar disorders feature mania, or periods of unrealistically elevated mood. The person might feel little need for sleep, talk incessantly, or make impulsive, unwise decisions. Although classic bipolar disorder features cycling between manic periods and depressive episodes, which uses the same diagnostic criteria as major depressive disorder, a patient no longer needs to show depression to be given a diagnosis of bipolar disorder. Because of the genetic similarities between schizophrenia and bipolar disorder (one case study of identical triplets finds two that have schizophrenia and one who has bipolar), bipolar now occupies a "bridge" position between schizophrenia and the depressive disorders.

Depressive Disorders

Major depressive disorder features depressed mood or lack of pleasure (anhedonia) along with sleep disturbances, appetite disturbances, lethargy or restlessness, difficulty concentrating, and feelings of hopelessness and worthlessness. Seasonal affective disorder (SAD) is now categorized as a subtype of major depressive disorder with seasonal pattern.

Anxiety Disorders

Anxiety is the anticipation of danger. People with anxiety disorders have exaggerated responses to objects or situations that can be disabling. These disorders come in many forms, and patients often have more than one type.

Obsessive-Compulsive and Related Disorders

Now in its own category outside the anxiety disorders, obsessive-compulsive disorder combines repetitive disturbing thoughts (obsessions) with ritualistic, repetitive behaviors (compulsions). The DSM specifies spending one hour or more per day in compulsive behavior as indicating problematic behavior.

Trauma- and Stressor-Related Disorders

These are the only disorders in the DSM that feature a firm causality—the experience of a traumatic event. Posttraumatic stress disorder (PTSD) is frequently in the news in conjuction with military veterans, and combat remains one of the stressors most likely to produce the disorder. However, PTSD can result from a variety of traumatic experiences, including natural disasters and automobile accidents that produce injury. Individuals with PTSD are troubled by recurrent flashbacks and nightmares accompanied by a state of hypervigilance.

Dissociative Disorders

This classification includes dissociative identity disorder, formerly known as multiple personality disorder. Psychologists no longer believe that it is likely that multiple personalities can coexist within the same person without the person's conscious awareness.

Somatic Symptom and Related Disorders

Somatic symptom disorder occurs when a person is distressed by somatic symptoms, usually pain, that either result from normal body functions or are not associated with a medical condition. Psychologists treat the distress, which is real for these patients, regardless of the nature of the underlying causes.

Feeding and Eating Disorders

Anorexia nervosa is one of the few psychological conditions that can result in death. Individuals with this disorder do not maintain a healthy body weight and have a distorted body image leading to the belief that they are overweight when they are actually abnormally thin. Some individuals show symptoms of both anorexia nervosa and bulimia nervosa. Bulimia nervosa refers to the regular consumption of large amounts of calories at a sitting, leading to feelings of guilt and loss of control and followed by efforts to purge the calories by use of vomiting, laxatives, and so on. The new condition in this category is binge-eating disorder, which is similar to bulimia nervosa, but without the compensating purging activities.

Elimination Disorders

These disorders typically occur in children and involve inappropriate patterns of urination and defecation.

Sleep-Wake Disorders

These disorders feature disruption in the quality, amount, or timing of sleep.

Sexual Dysfuntion

These conditions represent disruptions in an individual's ability to perform or enjoy sexual behaviors.

Gender Dysphoria

This new chapter identifies a state of gender dysphoria as occurring when an individual's experienced or expressed gender is not congruent with his or her assigned gender. The DSM is sensitive to the controversies surrounding this topic, and emphasizes the remediation of the individual's distress.

Disruptive, Impulse-Control, and Conduct Disorders

These disorders involve externalizing, acting-out behaviors that are often harmful to other people. The DSM recognizes that conduct disorder in children often transitions to a diagnosis of antisocial personality disorder in adulthood.

Substance-Related and Addictive Disorders

This chapter features a long list of substances that can either lead to substance-use problems or problems that are induced by substances, such as withdrawal syndromes. A new entry in this category is gambling disorder, in recognition of the similarities between people who have addictions to substances and people who are unable to stop gambling.

Neurocognitive Disorders

Remember that the DSM is written by the American *Psychiatric* Association, so some of the disorders it covers have a distinct medical etiology. However, the cognitive outcomes of these disorders blur the boundaries among psychiatry, neurology, and neuropsychology, both in assessment and treatment. The DSM recognizes that other disorders, such as schizophrenia, produce profound distortions of cognition, but the disorders in this category, such as Alzheimer's disease, are primarily distinguished by their cognitive correlates.

Personality Disorders

Psychologists define personality as stable patterns of thinking and behaving that can be used to compare individuals. A personality disorder involves stable, maladaptive ways of thinking and behaving. These patterns might be evident earlier, but personality disorder is typically not diagnosed prior to adulthood. Some of these disorders show gender differences. More males than females are diagnosed with antisocial personality disorder and more females than males are diagnosed with borderline personality disorder.

Paraphilic Disorders

Several of the disorders in this category, such as pedophilic disorder and exhibitionist disorder, are disturbing to others and hence are considered illegal, at least in the United States. Other disorders in this category might cause personal distress, for which an individual might seek treatment.

Overview of Psychological Disorders

There is no substitute for reading through the diagnostic criteria of DSM-5 in preparation for answering questions on this material. Because you are planning to attend graduate school, this is probably a good time to purchase a copy.

Major Category	Disorders	Main Features
Neurodevelopmental Disorders	■ Intellectual Disability ■ Autism Spectrum Disorder ■ Attention-Deficit/Hyperactivity Disorder	Neurodevelopmental disorders have an onset during the developmental period.
Schizophrenia Spectrum and Other Psychotic Disorders	■ Schizophrenia ■ Schizoaffective Disorder	These disorders feature abnormalities in delusions, hallucinations, disorganized thinking, motor behavior, and negative symptoms.
Bipolar and Related Disorders	■ Bipolar I Disorder ■ Bipolar II Disorder ■ Cyclothymic Disorder	Bipolar disorders form a bridge between the schizophrenia spectrum and the depressive disorders in terms of symptoms, family history, and genetics.
Depressive Disorders	■ Major Depressive Disorder ■ Persistent Depressive Disorder (Dysthymia) ■ Premenstrual Dysphoric Disorder	These disorders are characterized by sad, empty, or irritable mood accompanied by somatic and cognitive changes.
Anxiety Disorders	■ Separation Anxiety Disorder ■ Specific Phobia ■ Social Anxiety Disorder (Social Phobia) ■ Panic Disorder ■ Agoraphobia ■ Generalized Anxiety Disorder	These disorders share the presence of excessive fear and anxiety.
Obsessive-Compulsive and Related Disorders	■ Obsessive-Compulsive Disorder ■ Body Dysmorphic Disorder ■ Hoarding Disorder	These disorders are grouped together now in recognition of their similar features.
Trauma- and Stressor-Related Disorders	■ Reactive Attachment Disorder ■ Posttraumatic Stress Disorder	Exposure to a traumatic or stressful event is required for the diagnosis of these disorders.
Dissociative Disorders	■ Dissociative Identity Disorder ■ Dissociative Amnesia ■ Depersonalization/Derealization Disorder	These disorders feature a disruption in the integration of consciousness, memory, identity, emotion, perception, body representation, motor control, and behavior.
Somatic Symptom and Related Disorders	■ Somatic Symptom Disorder ■ Illness Anxiety Disorder ■ Conversion Disorder	These disorders feature prominent somatic symptoms.
Feeding and Eating Disorders	■ Anorexia Nervosa ■ Bulimia Nervosa ■ Binge-eating Disorder	These disorders feature a persistent disturbance in eating or eating-related behaviors.
Elimination Disorder	■ Enuresis ■ Encopresis	These disorders feature an inappropriate elimination of urine or feces.

Major Category	Disorders	Main Features
Sleep-Wake Disorders	▪ Insomnia Disorder ▪ Narcolepsy ▪ Sleep Apnea ▪ Sleep Terrors ▪ Rapid Eye Movement ▪ Sleep Behavior Disorder ▪ Restless Legs Syndrome	These disorders impact the quality, timing, or amount of sleep.
Sexual Dysfunction	▪ Delayed or Premature Ejaculation ▪ Erectile Disorder ▪ Female Orgasmic Disorder	These disorders involve a disturbance in a person's ability to respond sexually.
Gender Dysphoria	▪ Gender Dysphoria	Gender dysphoria refers to distress due to incongruence between experienced/expressed gender and assigned gender.
Disruptive, Impulse-Control, and Conduct Disorders	▪ Oppositional Defiant Disorder ▪ Conduct Disorder ▪ Pyromania ▪ Kleptomania	These disorders feature problems with self-control over emotions and behavior.
Substance-Related and Addictive Disorders	▪ Substance Use Disorders ▪ Substance-Induced Disorders ▪ Gambling Disorder	These disorders involve the use of psychoactive substances or gambling behavior.
Neurocognitive Disorders	▪ Alzheimer's Disease ▪ Parkinson's Disease ▪ Traumatic Brain Injury ▪ Prion Disease ▪ Huntington's Disease ▪ Due to HIV ▪ Due to Vascular Disease ▪ Delirium ▪ Frontotemporal Disease ▪ With Lewy Bodies	The core features of these conditions produce cognitive impairment.
Personality Disorders	▪ Schizoid Personality Disorder ▪ Schizotypal Personality Disorder ▪ Antisocial Personality Disorder ▪ Borderline Personality Disorder ▪ Histrionic Personality Disorder ▪ Narcissistic Personality Disorder	These disorders feature enduring patterns of inner experience and behavior that deviate from expectations of the individual's culture, are stable, and lead to distress or impairment.
Paraphilic Disorders	▪ Voyeuristic Disorder ▪ Exhibitionist Disorder ▪ Frotteuristic Disorder ▪ Sexual Masochism Disorder ▪ Sexual Sadism Disorder ▪ Pedophilic Disorder ▪ Fetishistic Disorder ▪ Transvestic Disorder	These are sexual behaviors that typically constitute criminal offenses or cause significant distress to the person engaged in the behavior.

Clinical Psychology

Clinical psychology, is, in effect, treatment psychology. Not surprisingly, treatment approaches reflect the viewpoints held by professionals in the areas of theory, measuring instruments, and psychopathology. To get acquainted with this whole area, a logical starting point is to examine the ways in which each theoretical viewpoint approaches the clinical aspect. For purposes of clarity, you should take your initial glimpse via the outline used in the personality discussions.

PSYCHOANALYSIS

The assumption is made in psychoanalysis that the *personality's core elements* are established in the first few years of life. Treatment, therefore, is oriented toward reaching back into those early years and "laying bare" the guilt and conflict in the situations where they occurred initially. In the classical approach to treatment, the method used for this uncovering process is *free association* (subject lies on his back on a couch with instructions to say everything that comes to mind). It is assumed that the relaxed setting and these instructions will enable the person both to become aware of and reveal thoughts that have been kept from awareness by the usual *psychological defense system* prominent within daily life. *Dream interpretation* is central to this process—dreams being considered, in Freud's words, "the royal road to the unconscious." In addition to dream interpretation, the Rorschach Test is frequently used as another means of probing the unconscious. Complete psychoanalysis can require several years (and, obviously, a sizable sum of money). It also requires a patient with a reasonable degree of intelligence and some capacity for thought and insight. The assumptions underlying such treatment are that a change in personality can occur only through return to "the scene of the crime" (that is, the source of guilt and conflict) and that the "laying bare" process will enable the person to initiate a desirable change.

EGO ANALYSIS

Followers of this method believe that they have modified the classical psychoanalytic approach in the way Freud himself might have done if he were alive today. As the title suggests, this approach frees the individual from a "slavery" to id urges and promotes the importance of ego. Although free association and dream interpretation are still important parts of this view, the play-by-play "laying bare" process within early childhood is relieved somewhat by the ego emphasis. A primary goal of this treatment is an understanding of child-based conflicts, coupled with a wholesome strengthening of the person's ego.

PSYCHODYNAMIC ANALYSIS

In this and the above two approaches, the therapist talks with the subject in a one-to-one setting. However, psychodynamic treatment is less formal than psychoanalysis, and treatment does not include free association and the necessity for several years of treatment. Again, the goal is insight and self-understanding as the means of initiating behavior change. Specific methods used to reach this goal reflect the unique aspects of a given theoretical position. For instance, *Adler's* approach to insight might include replacing inferiority feelings with self-respect and social interest, but *Jung's* approach might feature a balance among the psychological functions of sensing, thinking, feeling, and intuiting. We could expect *Sullivan* to use spadework directed toward removal of lingering parataxic cognitions still present and problematic in our adult thinking. *Horney* would emphasize adjustment to one's culture and the development of effective modes of relating within it. *Fromm's* method stresses relationships that carry within them a love between equals and emphasizes a personality strong in relatedness, creativeness, brotherliness, individuality, and reason. As they begin to build the learning-theory bridge, *Dollard* and *Miller* seek to grant a person learning-based understanding of early childhood conflicts. Because of its learning base, the heart of this treatment approach rightfully belongs in the next section.

BEHAVIORIST AND LEARNING THEORY

The general emphasis of this approach is to remove faulty learning and replace it with learning that enables the subject to function and cope effectively. Virtually all the terms that you encountered in classical and operant conditioning come into play here because of the learning principles that are utilized. *Dollard* and *Miller* speak of the process as *counterconditioning* (i.e., running an effective response in direct and strong competition with the person's current ineffective one). Because this theory is a bridge between psychotherapy and learning theory, emphasis is given to insight—the ability to realize how faulty learning occurred in the early years and the learning capacity to change current problem behavior on the basis of this knowledge.

Behavior theorists place little importance on insight. They view psychopathology as one or a combination of several noncoping behaviors, and their goal is to change those behaviors. The method for doing so is to establish a learning situation or, in some instances, a complete environment, within which predetermined behaviors can be systematically encouraged through reinforcement, and other behaviors (considered problem behaviors) can be either ignored or punished (depending on the approach). This spectrum of approaches follows, generally, one of the subsequent classifications.

The *behaviorist-learning theory* techniques provide the most readily demonstrable results in behavior change. Such techniques operate on the premise that the primary goal must be to change the current, maladaptive behavior and that a time-consuming, expensive return to one's childhood for purposes of unraveling and new insight is not important. Behaviorists believe that a person does not need insight into childhood conflicts in order to effectively change current behaviors. It is a "now" orientation based on systematic structuring of stimuli and responses. The technique initially identifies the problem behaviors and develops a conditioning program to change the responses customarily given to problem stimuli. It lives up to its name—placing emphasis on observable behavior without concerning itself with intrapsychic constructs such as id.

Desensitization

Watson pioneered in this method when he created within a child intense fear of white rats and then proceeded to remove the fear by a systematic procedure containing gradual steps (white objects at a distance, then moved closer to the child and approximating the feared object more and more in each successive treatment session). What Watson instituted was a *desensitization process*. This approach is widely used in cases of intense fear and phobia. Suppose, for instance, that you had an intense fear of butterflies and you were a summer lifeguard at an outdoor pool. Butterflies would no doubt appear and might well cause you both problems and embarrassment. To desensitize you, a professional might first have you read about butterflies in general, then later about the species that bother you the most. Next, you might be asked to collect pictures of them. And, to pass your "final exam," you might be given a butterfly net with instructions to catch a butterfly and return it to the therapist. The entire procedure would constitute desensitization. A prominent, controversial name in the field is that of Wolpe. Wolpe's treatment approach begins with development of an anxiety stimulus hierarchy (careful listing of most-to-least anxiety-producing situations). He then teaches the subject to relax all the muscles in his body. Desensitization begins as Wolpe introduces one or two of the least anxiety-producing situations and asks the person to relax (a response in direct conflict with the individual's normal behavior in these situations). Subsequent sessions move systematically toward the more severe anxiety-producing situations, again with instructions to the subject to relax.

Implosion Therapy (Flooding)

Stampfl's flooding or implosion therapy forms a direct contrast to the systematic desensitization approach. Rather than gradually exposing the person to the feared object or situation, this approach "floods" the person with feared-object or idea exposure suddenly and all-at-once. Because our sympathetic nervous systems cannot maintain this high level of arousal for an extended period of time, the person inevitably will "come back down" and feel more relaxed somewhere along this sequence. It's as though "I went through the worst possible. I made it through, and I'm OK." What once threatened to overwhelm has now been gone through at its worst, and the "worst" didn't prove as bad as the expectation.

Observational Learning

This approach relies on observation as a means of relieving intense fear and anxiety. Suppose you were intensely afraid of dogs. If this approach were used in treating you, you would be asked to observe someone with whom you could identify closely as this person moved gradually closer and closer to the feared object (a dog). Because you would be observing from a safe place, the initial threat of direct contact would be greatly reduced. Eventually (in the final stage of observation), however, you would be called upon to join your model in petting a dog. *Bandura* developed this approach and continues to be the most prominent name in the area.

Conditioned Aversion

Anyone who has seen the movie *A Clockwork Orange* is familiar with facets of this approach, which is used in cases where the subject finds great pleasure and positive reinforcement in some problem behavior. Sexual problems such as fetishism and transvestism are among the behaviors treated by this method. Generally speaking, it is a method utilized when other methods have failed; and the subject must have advance knowledge of and give consent for any treatment. For example, suppose a man achieved great sexual satisfaction and orgasm while wearing women's undergarments. The treatment would involve his wearing the undergarments at the same time that a drug-induced nausea was making him feel quite ill. The pairing of his former source of great pleasure with the drug-induced nausea would continue. Over a period of time, the drug level could be reduced, but the thoughts and feelings of nausea would continue to accompany the former pleasure objects. In other cases, the stimulus object might be nude child photos (pedophilia), a drink of Scotch whiskey (alcoholism), and so on. The major objective is to develop the nausea response as dominant over the former pleasure response, thus discouraging the problem behavior.

Changing Behavior Consequences

This technique emphasizes the manipulation of positive reinforcement. In general, it involves the withdrawal of positive reinforcement from maladaptive behaviors and the association of reinforcement with appropriate, adaptive behaviors. Suppose that problem child George frequently screams and kicks, uses derogatory language, and takes off his clothes. Normally, each of these situations gets his mother's attention (in effect, a positive reinforcement). Under this technique, however, the consequence of George's problem behavior would change because George's mother would be instructed to signal George when his behavior was disruptive. If the behavior continued he would be put in a dull, drab isolation room and brought out only when the behavior ceased. He would, of course, be praised whenever a behavior occurred that was appropriate and desirable. The technique involves all the specifics of the shaping process familiar to you from the learning section review. It is this type of procedure that is generally being referred to when you hear the term behavior modification.

Therapeutic Communities

In certain instances, a person's entire environment can be set up with systematic reinforcement contingencies. The mental hospital and the prison setting are two environments having such contingencies, and behavior modification techniques in these instances would seek to change reinforcements and consequences in such a manner that desired behaviors would be encouraged and motivation toward such behaviors would be prompted. In effect, a therapeutic community involves a total-environment usage of behavior modification techniques and the changing of behavior consequences. Ethics controversies enshroud some of these usages. Currently, questions such as whether prisoners can be forced to rehabilitate within such a modification program are being raised. Such controversies can be expected to continue, as there are no simple solutions to them.

PHENOMENOLOGICAL

Perhaps the least systematic collection of views are those found under this heading. The main idea holding this collection together is an emphasis on individual perception. In the perception discussions earlier in this book, it was indicated that perception combined the sensory experience (what is received physiologically) with past learning (what one expects to receive). Two people can wake up at the same hour on the same morning with very different outlooks on the day. These two people may encounter virtually the same events during the day, and yet one may have a positive outlook and exhibit optimism toward these events, and the other may demonstrate a negative outlook and pessimism. Phenomenologists believe that the essential goal of a clinical technique is to change the subject's perception of himself and his environment. Where such perception is hampering a person, the technique seeks to free the individual to be what he can be. As *Maslow* once stated, "What a person can be, he must be." Translated into actual settings, the approach uses therapist-person discussions on a one-to-one basis. For persons such as Rogers, Berne, and Harris, various approaches to group therapy are also important techniques. Group techniques are less expensive for the individual, and they provide clients with an opportunity to see how other people will respond to them and to what they are saying in a safe, controlled setting. The basic premise throughout this approach is that if you can change perception, behavior will change as a consequence.

Fixed Role Therapy

Kelly believes the critical role of the therapist is to act as a validator for the client's experience. Within this process—through the Role Construct Repertory Test (REP Test)—the therapist becomes familiar with the client's faulty constructs and helps the client to break down the faulty and reconstruct adaptively. The therapist's role is to serve as validator of the client's new constructs.

Client-Centered Therapy

Carl *Rogers* founded this approach and the term *client*, which we have used frequently within other therapeutic descriptions. In Rogers's view, the person who comes for therapy is a client (an equal) who has engaged the services of the therapist as a consultant. This perspective is vastly different from the patient-therapist scenario in which roles are distinctly unequal and the therapist is the expert provider of mental health knowledge and procedures. Rogers's therapy is premised on giving the client unconditional positive regard and acceptance, clarifying what the client says by reflecting it back, and helping the client to get in touch with feelings. Where conscious self-structure from one's past is notably different from sensory visceral experience in one's present, the process will seek to bring the conscious self-structure more closely aligned with present experience.

Logotherapy

Founded by Viktor *Frankl*, this approach is premised on paradoxical intent. The client may say, "I think I am going to faint." The therapist may respond, "Go ahead, faint." And when the eventuality doesn't happen, the therapist and client share the humor of this nonhappening and build on the distinction between thought and reality.

Gestalt Therapy

Fritz *Perls* formulated this approach to therapy. It stems from the premise that our words frequently say very different things than our bodies are expressing, and the therapist seeks to bring out the bodily expressed message—pointing out the duality and contrast. Perls believed frustration to be an essential ingredient of growth, and within the therapy session he sought to frustrate the client (e.g., "What is your hand doing now?" "What is your foot doing now?" and so on). Perls believed we disown major parts of our personality (frequently aspects relating to sex), and it is the therapist's role to help us reown those disowned parts, becoming whole once again.

Rational-Emotive Therapy

Founded by Albert *Ellis*, this approach targets the irrationality in many of our thoughts and beliefs that carry negative psychological consequences. Ellis points to the eleven universally inculcated irrational thoughts or values he perceives as prevalent in Western societies. Among these eleven are the beliefs that we must be liked by everyone, we must be perfectly competent, we should be dependent and must have someone stronger on whom to rely, there's always a right or perfect solution to every problem, and it's easier to avoid certain difficulties and responsibilities than to face them. In therapy Ellis seeks to target and point out the irrational, replacing it with rational, adaptive thoughts and beliefs.

Cognitive Therapy

Aaron *Beck*'s cognitive therapy focuses on faulty cognitions—especially among those who are depressed. He believes depressed people have a "negative cognitive triad of depression" containing automatic thoughts that feed on themselves in a destructive cycle. The self messages within the triad are "I am deprived or defeated. The world is full of obstacles. The future is devoid of hope." With this triad cycling, the depressed person has little option but to sink deeper into the trough. Beck seeks to substitute more favorable beliefs for those in the destructive triad.

Cognitive-Behavior Therapy

Cognitive-behavior therapy blends aspects of behavior therapy and cognitive therapy. Like the behavior therapist, cognitive-behavior therapists such as *Meichenbaum* (founder and principal spokesperson) set behavior-change-based goals for their clients, but in contrast to behaviorists, the cognitive-behavior therapist puts more emphasis on a person's interpretation of his situation. Within past as well as present events, the therapist illumines the person's interpretive distortions and helps the client to reinterpret more accurately and adaptively.

Multi-modal Therapy

Richard *Lazarus* points out that how much a given event stresses a given individual depends on how the individual interprets the event and what action options they see for themselves within it. The pregnant, unmarried 14-year-old is likely to experience far greater stress than the pregnant, married 30-year-old. Situations and perceptions of options are vastly different. The element of familiarity with a potentially stressful situation is central to Lazarus, and part of his approach is to help the client anticipate potentially stressful situations and formulate response-options within them.

DRUG THERAPY

One of the most exciting breakthrough areas in treatment has been the area of drug therapy. The "straight-jackets," chains, and shackles of yesteryear have been replaced by a battery of drug therapies that promote behavioral balance and functionality while enabling the individual to work on underlying problems. These drugs exist across virtually the entire spectrum of disorders, and new pharmacology discoveries are entering the line-up constantly. Among the most exciting new entries have been the second-generation antidepressant drugs. The suspects in depression have been norepinephrine and serotonin neurotransmitters, and the goal has been to help neurotransmitter activity. Until recently, two classes of drugs—monoamine oxidase (MAO) inhibitors and tricyclic antidepressants—had been called upon for this mission. Now serotonin reuptake inhibitors, among them Prozac, Zoloft, and Paxil, largely have replaced their tricyclic predecessors. There's a prediction that somewhere in the not-distant future these drugs will be available over-the-counter. They are among the most prevalently prescribed and used among our population today. Antimanic medications include lithium carbonate (Eskalith), and Valium and Librium rank among the front runners in treating anxiety. Antipsychotic drugs include haloperidol (Haldol), chlorpromazine (Thorazine), clozapine (Clozaril), and resperidone (Resperdol). Attention-Deficit Disorder (ADD) and Attention-Deficit/Hyperactivity Disorder (ADHD) have been effectively treated with Ritalin and Cylert.

As mentioned earlier, drug therapy may be a mixed blessing. On the one hand, behavior is controlled, paving the way for other therapeutic interventions. The infamous straight-jacket has long ago been discarded and extreme behaviors are being drug-controlled. Many who could not function outside the institutional setting can now function effectively and hold jobs. These are no minor or insignificant strides. On the other hand, drugs are over-prescribed—often for individuals who do not need them and do not have a disorder—and the jury is still out on long-term effects of drug usage. As for the automobile industry, the general public tests the long-term effects, and many years down the road we could make discoveries of long-term effects that are irreversible. For example, the long-term use of anti-psychotic drugs has been linked with symptoms similar to those found in Parkinson's disease ("pseudo-parkinsonianism"). Current users, for the most part, see present benefits as over-riding long-term potential risks. It is difficult at this juncture to predict what chemotherapy's future will be—whether it will become the clinical mainstream or simply one of many tech-niques in prominent usage. For now and the foreseeable future, it is very much with us.

Electroconvulsive Therapy (ECT)

Another technique used within the institutional setting for specific types of depression and manic disorders is electroconvulsive therapy (ECT). After anesthesia and a muscle relaxant, a light electric current is sent across the patient's temples for a split-second, producing a convulsion. Treatment for a severely depressed patient typically requires 6 to 12 treatments within a one-month time period. Anesthesia wears off within an hour or so of treatment, as does the immediate amnesia. Recovery from memory loss generally occurs within six months or a year, and the treatment itself has been found effective with severely depressed patients.

Because our image of this treatment resembles "Big Brother," brainwashing, or mind-pro-gramming, it is understandably controversial. The state of California at one point outlawed it, and for some time it was the unwanted stepchild within the public psyche. Responding to concerns, the National Institute of Mental Health (NIMH) named a panel to evaluate ECT. They confirmed its effectiveness in treating severe depression and found side effects minimal and complications exceedingly rare. Risks were no greater than those for anesthesia itself. After having been the little-utilized stepchild for many years, there has been a recent resur-gence in ECT use.

Transcranial Magnetic Stimulation (TMS)

Transcranial magnetic stimulation (TMS) is the most recent approach to profoundly depressed patients. It carries fewer side effects in memory loss than its ECT predecessor. This noninvasive procedure uses magnetic fields to stimulate nerve cells in the brain's frontal lobe. When other treatments have failed, therapists often turn to TMS. In the procedure, a large electromagnetic coil is placed against the scalp near the forehead. Painless electric currents stimulate nerve cells central to mood regulation and depression. From *www.mayoclinic.com/ health/transcranial-magnetic-stimulation/MY00185/UPDATEAPP=false&FLUSHCACHE=0*, Accessed October 9, 2008.

Pragmatic Therapy

Steeped in the psychoanalytic tradition, Otto *Rank* advanced the therapeutic premise that "if it works, use it." His approach had a major impact upon one of his younger child-guidance-clinic colleagues, Carl Rogers. Rogers integrated this conceptual approach into the development of his own theoretical views and approach to therapy.

Primal Therapy

Primal therapy of *Janov* takes us back to the very beginnings of our life-journey. One must make and experience the primal scream. In some groups, they lay out a carpet-runner across the floor and an individual lies on it at one end, pushing across while other members of the group support, encourage, and spur the individual on. The point is to recreate the birth process and to experience the primal scream and joy upon entry to the outer world. Controversial? Perhaps a bit.

Transactional Analysis

Founded by *Berne*, it is based on the premise that people play destructive games with one another. All of us have the entities of Parent, Adult, and Child within us, and a challenge for us as adults is to "turn off the shoulds" of the Parent and get in touch with our feelings and spontaneity within the Child. *Harris* frames this latter challenge within the context of finding and maintaining an "I'm OK–You're OK" life position as distinct from the "I'm Not OK–You're OK" position we naturally inherited from childhood life among those adult, seemingly giant figures.

Reality Therapy

Founded by *Glaser*, a key aspect of reality therapy is the formation of a contract agreement between the client and the therapist. By signing the contract, we have signed and sealed our commitment to the therapeutic process and to the change-goals set within it. Ignoring the typical DSM categories, this approach seeks to make the client more proactive in his life and environment, actively pursuing adaptive and fulfilling goals.

Psychodrama

It has often been said, "if we could only see ourselves as others see us." *Moreno's* approach provides this self-enlightenment opportunity within the framework of role-play and role-reversal. As we see how we're perceived by others, the message can be a startling one, which spotlights aspects of ourselves we may have ignored or denied. Within this supportive setting, we have the opportunity to work toward change. In the broader context, this approach takes the view that the more roles we become familiar with, the better prepared we are for any future eventualities and role-expectations that may come our way.

Family Therapy

The overriding premise within all of family therapy is that an individual does not have a problem. Rather, the individual reflects symptoms of an interactive system problem. Therefore, the system needs to be treated and restructured. Taking this as our definitional baseline, there are *four major schools* within family therapy. *Object relations theory*, traced to *Melanie Klein*, sees the purpose of interpersonal interaction being self-development, as distinct from instinctual need fulfillment. *Bowen theory*, from *Murray Bowen*, posits the triangle as the basic construction within a flawed family-interaction system. The goal of this approach is to differentiate oneself from the family, attaining a stand-alone, solid, individual identity. *Structural family theory*, associated with *Salvador Minuchin*, focuses on the present family interactive patterns rather than their past roots. The goal is to realign the family members within their structural system, thereby changing their experience of one another. *Communication theory* stems directly from the work of *Bateson* and the concept of the double-bind. It views family pathology as a communication problem. Like Minuchin, the present is emphasized and the goal is to change the communication rules within the system. *Conjoint Family Therapy*— Virginia Satir's first book—launched her renowned family therapy career and contributions to the field. Through her extensive clinical studies she created the Satir change process model that has been prominently embraced by organizations embarking upon communication, structural, and managerial change.

EVIDENCE-BASED TREATMENT

Evidence-based treatment (EBT)—also known as evidence-based practice (EBP) and empirically supported treatment (EST)—has moved from the medical community to the mental and behavioral health community. EBP seeks to weed out therapeutic approaches that are ineffective and identify those that have scientific, empirical research in support of their effectiveness. When medicine, psychology, and psychiatry at times had practiced on the basis of loosely held and shared knowledge, there was no definitive way to know whether a given approach was effective. Quackery and fake "cures" were not uncommon. EBP has been adopted as the tool and the scientific process designed to identify effective practices— optimally through randomized treatment group research wherever feasible. The American Psychological Association strongly encourages its members to conduct well-designed research and to continue building the knowledge base that identifies the best evidence-based practices. The close relationship between the psychological and the medical communities also has led to the granting of selective prescription privileges for clinical psychologists in several states. The privilege is generally focused exclusively toward prescriptions relating to ADD/ADHD or mood disorders/depression.

Clinical Psychology (Treatment) Outline

Concepts	Names	Terms
Psychoanalysis	Freud	Free association (revisiting and working through early childhood conflicts)
Ego analysis	Hartmann, White	Free association (with emphasis on ego rather than early childhood)
Psychodynamic	Adler, Sullivan, Horney, Jung	One-on-one interaction with the person—goal being self-insight and understanding
	Jung	Discovering an individual's complexes and working through them
Behaviorist		
Changing behavior consequences (shaping)	Skinner	Behavior modification by reinforcing desired responses and ignoring maladaptive ones

Concepts	Names	Terms
Observational learning	Bandura	Reduction of fear through observation of another person with whom one identifies approaching the feared object
Desensitization	Watson, Wolpe	Within a familiar, positively reinforcing environment, gradually move the person step-by-step toward the feared object or stimulus (countering fear with relaxation en route)
Implosion (flooding)	Stampfl	Suddenly and intensely expose the person to the feared stimulus, knowing the panic response can only last briefly
Conditioned aversion	Wolpe et al.	Change the outcome of a previously pleasurable problem behavior (e.g., pedophilia) to one of drug-induced nausea
Therapeutic communities	Skinner	Outline behavior contingencies and reinforce desired behaviors within a controlled setting (e.g., hospital or prison)
Phenomenological		
Fixed role	Kelly	Validate the client's experience in trying out new, adaptive constructs
Client-centered	Rogers	Provide unconditional positive regard for the client, reflect back to the client, and help him get in touch with feelings
Logotherapy	Frankl	Utilize paradoxical intent to demonstrate and change unrealistic thoughts
Gestalt	Perls	Focus on bodily movements and expressions, enabling clients to gain synchronicity between their feelings (nonverbal) and their words (verbal)
Rational-emotive	Ellis	Illuminating a client's irrational thoughts (e.g., everyone must like me) and moving him toward effective, rational thought
Cognitive	Beck	Focus on faulty cognitions— especially the "negative triad" within depressed persons—and substitute favorable cognitions
Cognitive-behavior	Meichenbaum	Set behavior-change goals for the client, emphasizing a person's interpretation of his life situation
Multi-modal	Lazarus	Help the client anticipate potentially stressful situations and formulate response-options within them

Concepts	Names	Terms
Medical		Medical interventions (drug therapy or ECT)
Drug therapy		Use of drugs to moderate and control behaviors. Among the applications: For antidepression: MAO inhibitors, tricyclics, and serotonin reuptake inhibitors (Prozac, Zoloft, et al.) For antimanic:Lithium carbonate (Eskalith), Abilifi, and Lamictal For antianxiety: Valium, Librium, and Xanax For antipsychotic: Halperidol (Haldol), Chlorpromazine (Thorazine), Clozapine (Clozaril), and Resperidone (Resperdol) Zyprexa and Seroque For ADD/ADHD: Ritalin and Cylert Straterra and Adderall (also used for narcolepsy)
Electroconvulsive		Split-second shock to the temples with resulting convulsion. Used for severe depression and mania.
Transcranial magnetic stimulation		Large electromagnetic coil on scalp and forehead sends painless electric currents to stimulate nerve cells central to mood regulation and depression
Eclectic		A blend of theoretical approaches
Pragmatic	Rank	"If it works, use it"—drawing from a variety of theoretical backgrounds
Primal	Janov	Revert to the primal scream and, in effect, the first moment of daylight (simulating emergence from the birth canal) as an emotionally cleansing and liberating exercise
Transactional analysis	Berne/Harris	Point out crossed lines of communication among the Parent/Adult/Child entities in our interactions with others. Work toward an "I'm OK-You're OK" life position.
Reality	Glasser	Eschews the diagnostic categories— placing people in the generally happy/generally miserable categories. Helps the miserable to be more proactive in their lives, selecting behaviors that will fulfill their innate needs and goals. Client makes a signed "contract" with the therapist.

Concepts	Names	Terms
Psychodrama	Moreno	Focuses on role-play and role-reversal. Takes the premise that the more roles an individual becomes familiar with and can assume, the better prepared the individual is for the requirements of any future situation.
Family	Klein, Bowen, Minuchin, Bateson et al.	Treats the family as an interactive system rather than treating an individual. Seeks to restructure the interactive patterns within the system.

Having viewed the range of clinical techniques, from the couch and free association to chemotherapy and electroconvulsive shock, you now have an idea of the variety of methods that are directed toward the common objective of changing maladaptive behavior. We are a long distance from rebuilt-brain transplants, and, in the meantime, people need emotional help. Clinical techniques seek to provide such help and relieve the accompanying emotional pain.

LIFE SPAN DEVELOPMENT

Developmental psychology, one of the most sweeping topical areas in the discipline, encompasses the psychological study of the child, that is, the child's physiological, comparative, sensory, perceptual, and learning characteristics. Thus, the study of child development actually involves everything we have been or will be talking about. For the sake of time and space, however, we will confine our discussion only to those concerns generally included in a course on the topic.

As Papalia and Olds point out in their introductory comments, child development centers upon the *quantitative and qualitative* ways in which children change over time. Not surprisingly, the quantitative changes are more easily measured because they are readily observable. The child's "quantity" changes in both weight and height, and in each instance the change can be systematically recorded. Qualitative changes pose greater problems for the would-be observer. For instance, how can one monitor a child's intellectual, emotional, social, and moral growth? And how does one determine the presence of creativity? Such questions quickly lead away from the straightforward instruments and answers that investigators rely upon in quantitative measurement.

The instruments and techniques necessary for *qualitative* measurement take various complexions. In the *naturalistic approach*, the investigator uses the method of Tinbergen and Lorenz, observing the child in his natural habitat. Large numbers of children are watched systematically at different ages, and these observations yield such data as the average age for walking, talking, parallel play, the presence of conscience, sexual interest, and so forth. *Gesell* and his associates compiled enormous amounts of observational data that enabled them to develop and publish a widely revered work and numerous articles on the average age for the emergence of specific skills and abilities in children.

Another technique, the *clinical method* of child observation, came into prominence with *Piaget*. With this method, the agenda is no longer strictly the child's in the sense that specific, open-ended questions are asked and responses are carefully studied. Whereas no intervention or structure is imposed under naturalistic observation, some intervention is evident in the clinical method—although individual freedom of response continues to be preserved. Piaget was able to use the clinical method to provide insightful glimpses into child thought processes, which previously had been totally unexplored.

A third, and most structured, measurement setting is known as the *experimental approach*. With this method, children may be grouped according to some established basis (e.g., age or socioeconomic status) and be "measured" by means of a standardized procedure, thus permitting response comparisons between groups. Statistical analysis of results enables the investigators to determine whether groups of children differ significantly on the skill or ability being measured. Everyone who has taken a school-administered IQ test has participated to some extent in a standardized, potentially experimental approach.

The development of a child begins at the point of conception, and *prenatal development* is divided into three *stages—germinal* (fertilization to two weeks), *embryonic* (two to eight weeks), and *fetal* (eight weeks to birth). Specific events are associated with each stage. During the germinal stage, there is rapid cell division and implantation on the uterine wall. In the embryonic stage, rapid differentiation of major body systems and organ development make the embryo particularly vulnerable to influences upon the prenatal environment. Because the mother is, in effect, the prenatal environment, the available research deals with such critical questions as the effects upon the embryo of maternal diet, drug and alcohol intake, and emotional state. Equally critical are considerations relating to illness, exposure to radiation, and mother-embryo blood compatibility. In the systematic, sequential development that is characteristic of humans and animals, impaired development during the embryonic stage is major and permanent. Nature provides no opportunity for compensatory "makeup" work later in pregnancy. In the final stage, the body systems and organs of the fetus that were formed and differentiated during the preceding embryonic stage have the opportunity to grow.

At *birth*, new questions come into focus. Among them are concerns regarding the child's adjustment to the cold, bright, noisy environment beyond the womb. Physiologically, reflexes and sensory capacities are studied, and socially and emotionally, the mother-child relationship is carefully examined for possible links between the child's emotional adjustment and characteristics such as mode and schedule of feeding, maternal warmth, and the like.

Motor Development

During the *first two years*, the child's motor development is of primary import. Have the child's crawling, walking, and so on occurred on schedule? Invariably "the schedule" used as the reference point is the one created by Gesell.

If motor development proceeds without difficulties, language development begins to steal the spotlight. One of the most exciting days for parents is the day their child says her first word, and if that word proves to be in the "socially acceptable" category (ma-ma, da-da, and so on) the day is a joy indeed. Language development is equally exciting for child psychologists. It is obvious that a child receives and understands many words long before she can produce them, and, given the appropriate technology, the reception area may someday become an important exploration ground. For the moment, however, research emphasis centers on the accessible—language production.

Language Development

Two broad categories in language production are prelinguistic (first year) and linguistic. E. and G. Kaplan ("Is There Such a Thing as a Prelinguistic Child?" in *Human Development and Cognitive Processes*, ed. J. Eliot [New York: Holt, Rinehart & Winston, 1970]) have further defined the prelinguistic category as encompassing the basic cry (first three weeks), sound variety beyond the basic cry (three weeks to four or five months), and babbling (last half of the first year). Babbling consists of vowel-like and consonant-like sounds articulated with imitations of adult intonation. One of the questions that fascinates theorists is whether the transition from babbling to recognizable words is a leap or a sequential step. A related question deals with exactly how the monkey differs from the human in the language area. At one time, *language* use was considered the standard by which humans were rated above monkeys and their relatives, but surprising and convincing studies with chimps have begun to erode that standard. Names with which you should be familiar in this area include: *Kellogg and Kellogg* (early study with "Donald" and "Gua"), *Gardner and Gardner* (work with "Washoe" and the American Sign Language for the Deaf), *Premack* ("Sarah" and "plastic sentences"), and *Rumbaugh* (the fascinating, computer-based Lana project).

Cognitive Development

Two prominent voices in opposition to the intelligence test movement were *Jean Piaget* and *Lev Vygotsky*. Piaget's keen theoretical mind, penchant for observing children, and background in Binet's laboratory equipped him for the unique contribution he made to the field of cognition. His basic disagreement with Binet centered on the notion of structuring the response possibilities for a child. Piaget preferred to let the child be "in charge" of the situation, and he merely observed and sought to systematize what he saw. In short, he attempted to get a glimpse of the child's mental world and how it functioned. His experiments and observations have yielded a wealth of insights into the cognitive capacities of the young mind and the nature of cognitive development. Piaget's world of the child was a physical world, whereas Russian psychologist Vygotsky's focus was the social world. To him, the mind was a product of its social/cultural history and the interactions that mind had with other minds. The absence of such interaction would leave the child animal-like (e.g., the Wild Boy of Aveyron). The presence of such interaction through parents, teachers, and other key persons in the child's life and experience—socializes the child into the culture. Current research (e.g., Nelson) has taken Vygotsky's premises and studied them in the context of children's social routines. In North American culture, for example, such routines include trips to the mall, McDonald's, birthday parties, and such. In other cultures the routines would be very different—perhaps pottery-making, carrying water from a common well, and so on.

One of the major *concepts* stemming from Piaget's work has been *conservation*—a child's capacity to recognize equivalences when a specific form or arrangement changes. For example, if you took two identical glasses of lemonade and poured the contents of one of them into a thinner, taller glass, a five-year-old might tell you that there was more lemonade in the taller glass than in the original one. On the other hand, a seven-year-old who had witnessed the pouring procedure might chime in that both glasses really contained equal amounts, that the taller glass just appeared to have more lemonade in it. The seven-year-old has cognitively attained conservation in relation to such a demonstration, but the five-year-old has not yet reached such a point in cognitive development. In addition to this concept, you should further acquaint yourself with the following:

Piagetian Terms Outline

Concepts	Names	Terms
Conservation		Number
		Substance
		Length
		Area
		Weight
		Volume
General conservation sequence		Ballpark age of acquisition
Assimilation		Environment is interpreted in terms of the child's existing schema
Accommodation		Child's schema changes through interaction with the environment (i.e., "accommodates" to the environment)
Distinction between stage theory and continuity learning theory		Stage: step-like
		Continuity: gradual, like an inclined plane (Piaget's is a stage theory)
Stages		Sensorimotor (first 2 years)
		Preoperational (2–7 years)
		Concrete Operations (7–11 years)
		Formal Operations (11–15 years)

Phillips' *The Origins of Intellect: Piaget's Theory* (San Francisco: W. H. Freeman, 1975) is an authoritative source in this area.

Social Development

Social and personality development become prominent research concerns as the child moves beyond the immediate family to the peer group, and obvious questions relate to the effects that early family influences have had upon the child's personality and social adjustment. Several personality theorists have spoken to these early years and their potential influence. Among the most prominent is Erikson, whose psychosocial theory suggests that foundations for basic trust, autonomy, and initiative are laid during the first five years of life. Freud's earlier theory took a sexual view, suggesting the possibilities of narcissism and fixations and the presence of Oedipal love characteristics. Dollard and Miller sought to combine the Freudian concept with learning principles, indicating that early experiences of hunger and crying in a child's dark bedroom could be the basis for later fear of the dark, overreaction to slight pain, apathy, and overeating. Many child psychologists who have a learning orientation concern themselves primarily with the present behavior of the child and the stimuli that prompt a given behavior. Nevertheless, few psychologists would be willing to defend a position that these early years are unimportant to the child's personality development and social adjustment.

For the *preschool* child—typically viewed as the three- to five-year-old—mental development becomes an important concern. The effects of stimulus-enriched environments both in and beyond the home take on major importance, and most personal vocabularies now include the terms *public kindergarten, private kindergarten,* and *day care center.* Research has convinced several state school systems to develop kindergarten facilities for all five-year-olds, and the preschool years are being increasingly viewed as a time for learning as well as for social adjustment.

As the child *begins school,* she enters what child psychologists call middle childhood. Stretching from ages six to twelve, middle childhood is a critically important time for physical, mental, personality, and social development. Understandably, the development areas are complexly interwoven. A girl who grows quickly and is taller than her male peers, for instance, can expect a social experience that is quite different from that of a girl who is shorter. Erikson sees this period as a time when the child's energies are directed toward "industry" (i.e., school achievement). For many, this involvement leads to the frustration of failure and to feelings of inferiority. It also raises the question of a child's moral development strength in the wake of achievement pressure and competition. This developmental stage terminates with the onset of puberty.

Adolescence begins with the onset of puberty—a time of rapid physical and sexual development accompanied by conflicts and feelings that can make the young person's life difficult and trying. Growth spurts, concern about physical appearance, nocturnal emissions, menstruation, and masturbation are among the factors combining to form the adolescent's complex adjustment picture. Erikson sees the young person at this stage as an individual making a search for identity; he also sees successful achievement of self-identity as essential for meaningful love relationships. A search for identity is, in part, a search for values; and the young person's parental and peer group relationships become dominant factors in this search.

The preceding is a chronological approach to developmental psychology. Now let's review the outline.

Developmental Psychology Outline

Concepts	Names	Terms
Research methods		Cross-sectional (comparing children of various ages simultaneously)
		Longitudinal (studying the same children across an extended time span)
	Based on Tinbergen/Lorenz utilized by Gesell	Naturalistic approach
	Piaget	Clinical method (partially structuring a naturalistic setting)
		Experimental (highly structured laboratory setting)
Prenatal development stages		Germinal (fertilization to two weeks) (zygote)
		Embryonic (two to eight weeks)
		Fetal (eight weeks to birth)
Teratogens		Substances producing malformations in a fetus (e.g., maternal alcohol intake, smoking, stress, drug use [tranquilizers, cocaine, marijuana], moods [depression])

Concepts	Names	Terms
Patterns of development		Cephalocaudal (head most fully developed first, i.e., a "top-down" pattern)
		Proximodistal (torso center toward extremities)
		General to specific (large motor before fine motor movement)
Reflexes in the newborn		Babinski (toes outward and upward to a sole-of-the-foot touch)
		Moro (outstretched arms, legs, and crying to a sudden change in environment or loud noise)
		Rooting (head-turn toward a mild lips/cheek stimulus [e.g., breast or hand])
		Sucking (response to objects touching the lips)
		Grasping (response to objects touching hand or fingers)
		Plantar (toes curl under to a finger-press against ball of the foot)
		Eye blink (to flashed light)
Infant perceptual preferences	Fantz' "viewing box"	Complex over simple; curved over straight; human faces over random patterns or mixed features
Imprinting	Lorenz Hess Scott Harlow	Across-species pattern of following (i.e., bonding with) a moving object present during the critical period for imprinting
Bonding		Emotional attachment between newborn and primary caregiver(s) immediately after birth
Separation anxiety		Fear response when primary caregiver is absent (occurs in 8-to-15-month age range)
Heritability of temperament	Kagan	Shyness
	Emde	Identical twins (temperament)
Stage theories	Piaget	Cognitive
	Kohlberg	Moral
	Freud	Psychosexual
	Erikson	Psychosocial
	Gesell	Physical maturation
Piagetian Stages		See stage-listing, earlier chart
Kohlberg Stages/Levels		Premoral
		Conventional morality
		Moral principles
	Gilligan	(Extension of Kohlberg, gender differences in caring)

Concepts	Names	Terms
Major studies	Berkeley	Berkeley Growth Studies
	White	Harvard Early Education Project (early childhood cognitive/intellectual development)
	Kagan	Heritability of temperament; cross-cultural study of relationship between environmental stimulation and child intelligence
Testing infant development	Fantz	"Viewing box" and early childhood sensation/perception
	Gesell Cattell Bayley	Scales
Classic studies	Gibson/Walk	Visual cliff
	Sears	"Conscience of a child"
	Bandura	Social learning
Determinants of development		Developmental level = heredity × environment × time (heredity × time is maturation; environment × time is learning)
Six classes of factors in behavioral development	Hebb	Genetic
		Chemical, prenatal
		Chemical, postnatal
		Sensory, constant
		Sensory, variable
		Traumatic
Brain development	Thompson	
Continuity vs. stage theory approach to development		
Sensory capabilities at birth		A "blooming, buzzing confusion"? Color vision? No pain in male circumcision? (Check it out!)
Genetic terminology	Tryon	Singly determined vs. multiply determined characteristics (stemming from "maze-bright/maze-dull" work);
	Mendel	Genetics law and distinction between dominant and recessive traits
		Distinction in twins (monozygotic [identical] vs. dizygotic [fraternal])
Comparative-systems development patterns		Neural (earliest-developing)
		Reproductive
		Somatic (general body growth)

Concepts	Names	Terms
Abnormalities/ Disorders		Dwarfism
		Acromegaly
		Down syndrome
		Klinefelter syndrome
	Lovaas	Autism spectrum disorder
		Aphasia
		PKU (phenylketonuria)
		Attention-deficit/hyperactivity disorder (ADHD)

Though the preponderance of work in the developmental field has been directed toward children, a look at the entire life span has become increasingly prevalent. The "prime time" and passages of midlife, as well as the adjustment challenges and strengths of the elderly, are far more central in focus than they were ten years ago. Myths about decline in intellectual and sexual activity are being disconfirmed through research, and there is hope that one of our nation's most valuable natural resources—the experience and the insight of the retired person—can be respected and meaningfully shared. The role of the actual or surrogate grandparent in the development of young children is being acknowledged and studied.

The sex stereotypes accompanying aging have been very blatant and identifiable. In both the media and the general societal spectrum, women "age" far more quickly than men. Television drama and the print media perpetuate this inequity and its effects.

Another major focus within developmental psychology stems from the rapid increase in two-parent working households and single-parent families. The impact of both upon the child has been more and more upon the minds of researchers, reflecting, undoubtedly, a prominent uncertainty within the nation itself. Hetherington, for instance, has studied the effect of divorce upon children, an effect extending well beyond the event itself to the prospect of parents' remarrying.

As you review the areas of adolescence, adulthood, and aging, you will notice fewer terms and concepts than you found in the child development area. This distinction is partly a function of the areas themselves, and partly due to the relative recency of work in the life span area. We have outlined a few of the basic terms and names. In your review you likely will discover others. In apportioning your study time, spend more on child development than on life span.

Specifying age-markers for each period is somewhat arbitrary, but if they're used as guidelines rather than absolutes, they can be meaningful. Levinson outlined four eras. He based his outline on longitudinal research with forty men. Mercer, Nichols, and Doyle (1989) observed that the stages for men lacked relevance for women because motherhood, career-reentry, etc., were frequently a woman's experience. To acknowledge that difference, they carefully studied women's transitions and came up with a five-stage developmental sequence. Neither Levinson nor Mercer, Nichols, and Doyle subdivide the period beyond age 66. Gerontology researchers now speak in terms of young-old and old-old, further subdividing this age-range. A rough timeline for old-old is 80+.

Life Span Outline

Concepts	Names	Terms
Four eras (male-based)	Levinson	Adolescence (11–17)
		Early adulthood (18–45)
		Middle adulthood (46–65)
		Late adulthood (66+)
Five eras (female-based)	Mercer, Nichols, Doyle	Launch to adulthood (16–25)
		Leveling (26–30)
		Liberation (36–60)
		Regeneration/redirection (61–65)
		Creativity/destructiveness (66+)
Erikson's Relevant Stages	Erikson	Identity vs. role diffusion
		Intimacy vs. isolation
		Generativity vs. stagnation (or self-absorption)
		Integrity vs. despair
Peck's stage elaboration	Peck	Generativity vs. Stagnation: Valuing wisdom vs. valuing physical powers Socializing vs. sexualizing in human relationships Cathectic flexibility vs. cathectic impoverishment (ability to shift one's emotional investments from one activity and person to another)
		Ego Integrity vs. Despair: Ego-differentiation vs. work-role preoccupation Body transcendence vs. body preoccupation Ego transcendence vs. ego preoccupation
Physical, sensory, and intellectual functioning with aging		
Terminology		Secondary sex characteristics (puberty)
	Bem	Androgynous (incorporating equality and interchangeability in gender roles)
		Social clock (self-outlined developmental schedule for accomplishment)
		Ageism (prejudice and discrimination toward the elderly)
Gender schema theory	Bem Maccoby	That children and adolescents use gender and gender-specific roles as their way of organizing and perceiving the world

Concepts	Names	Terms
Changing lifestyles	Hetherington	Effects of divorce on children (generally speaking, less impact on younger children and an adjustment period of approximately two years)
Dementia types		Reversible 　Alcoholism 　Malnutrition 　Toxic
		Irreversible 　Alzheimer's disease 　Multiple infarct (small-stroke-related)

Life Span Summary

For heading beyond your introductory textbook and exploring across the life span or given parts of it, obtain a copy of Sigelman and Rider, *Life Span Human Development*, 8th ed., New York: Cengage.

PERSONALITY

You have all heard at one time or another the expression that someone "has personality," and you have no doubt given thought to your own personalities at times. It is easier to spot personality than to define it, but the many definitions of the term carry the common elements of: (1) relatively enduring qualities in our behavior; (2) uniqueness; and (3) comprehensiveness. "Jan swats a fly" says nothing about Jan's personality, because it is a statement about a behavior of the moment that has an automatic quality about it. In addition, everyone swats flies (even cows), so it really says nothing to distinguish Jan from anyone else. On the other hand, someone might say that "Jan reacts quickly and defensively to criticism." That person has said something about her personality—something that defines a relatively enduring characteristic distinguishing her from other people and having the comprehensive quality of being part of a total view of "Jan the person."

Review of this area logically centers on two categories: theory and measurement. *Personality theory* actually began with the work of the early Greek philosophers. With expressions such as "Know thyself" (Socrates) and "Control thyself" (Cicero), these early, brilliant minds were exploring the realm of personality. With all due respect to personality theorizing among the early philosophers (e.g., Plato, Socrates, Aristotle, and Epictetus), we will begin our review focus in the mid-nineteenth century.

Freud stunned nineteenth century Vienna when he wrote *The Interpretation of Dreams*, suggesting that our behaviors are unconsciously motivated and that dreams are the "royal road to the unconscious." His Vienna Psychoanalytic Society included many professionals who, using this as their theoretical starting points, either extended his psychoanalytic views or developed theories of their own notably different from—and in reaction to—psychoanalysis. In the following lists and narratives, you will meet these theorists and their views, and you will move beyond them to the many who never had psychoanalysis as their starting points. Here's a quick, bird's-eye view of the fascinating and lush theoretical landscape that lies just ahead.

Psychoanalysis says, "You are your instincts." In this picture, each of us is sitting on a huge dynamo of instinctual drive energy that wants immediate gratification. As we bump along the road of life with this huge dynamo whirring under us, our challenge is to stay on the civilized, narrow road. *Ego-analysis* and the *psychosocial* moved beyond Freud's view that instinct is the sole driving force. The ego-analysts believed our personalities have ego-based energy that is free from instinctual control; and the psychosocial approach of *Erikson* reinterpreted Freud's psychosexual stages in a psycho-social context—creating the well-known eight stages in the life cycle. As you will readily see in the following table, the *psychodynamic* theorists held a variety of perspectives. *Adler*, for example, believed our basic, underlying drive was not instinctual/sexual but, rather, a drive for superiority born of early inferiority feelings. Many of his therapy patients were circus performers and he noted repeatedly that the area in which they now were superior was an area in which they were inferior as children. *Jung* created the theoretical basis for what we know today as the Myers-Briggs Text—those four "magic letters" on your forehead that tell whether you're an introvert or extrovert, sensing or intuiting, thinking or feeling, and perceptual or judging. Other major names among psychodynamic theorists include *Sullivan*, with his emphasis on interpersonal relationships; *Horney*, with her perspectives on the role of culture in personality; and *Fromm*, with his distinctions in types of love. *Dollard and Miller* took psychoanalytic concepts and defined them in learning theory terms, creating a bridge to the behavioristic view that follows. It's a rich psychodynamic landscape. Note the uniqueness of each theoretical contributor and enjoy the ride.

Behaviorists say, "You are your learned behaviors." Based on the early views of John Locke, this perspective suggests that we are born "blank tablets," and the environment then writes upon our tablets. These writings begin from "Day 1," and contributors include our families, our friends, our schoolmates, our teachers, and anyone else with a "pencil or pen" who makes a mark upon us as we grow and develop. *Radical behaviorists* (e.g., *Watson, Skinner*) need to see and observe behaviors. They confine themselves to what we observably do. *Social or cognitive behaviorists* (e.g., *Bandura, Rotter*) include our expectancies and values relating to given behaviors. Where we might not play the piano for the kids on our block because they'd laugh at us, we may ride bicycles with them.

Phenomenologists say, "You are your perceptions." Jill and Jan may look out the very same window at the very same morning. The images upon their retinas may be virtually identical and yet Jill says, "What a beautiful day!" while Jan says, "What a crappy day!" The difference is not in the view. It's in how they perceive it. *Kelly* stated this difference in terms of personal constructs (i.e., the different set of glasses we wear as we look out upon our worlds). Taking a more *humanistic* view, *Rogers* spoke about the importance of our feelings and those notable moments when our rational mind has made a decision and we get that sick feeling in the pit of our stomachs. He believed our feelings are often wiser than our intellects, and we need to be in touch with those feelings. Other humanistic perspectives include *Maslow*'s view of our needs hierarchy, with the optimal attainment being self-actualization, and *Frankl*'s view of life-meaning coming through our pursuit of exciting goals.

Trait theorists say, "You are your underlying, basic characteristics." Just as we can think of different breeds of dogs and say, "That one's aggressive!" "That one's gentle and good with children!" our traits and temperaments are seen in similar terms. We are seen to have a small, select group of characteristics or traits that are basic to our personalities. *Sheldon* thought such traits were related to body types—an historical perspective to note, but a view no longer held. *Allport* believed our cardinal traits can be seen in virtually all our behavior (e.g., our quest for power, our reverence for nature). Central traits reflect in much of our behavior but are not as all-pervasive as cardinal traits. Another class, the peripheral, he terms secondary traits. Much of the significant work in trait theory has come through factor analysis—testing large groups of people, conducting multiple correlations, and finding clusters of characteristics that correlate highly together. Key work in this area has been done by Cattell and Eysenck. *Cattell's* data come from three sources—a person's life record (L data) as gleaned from those who have known him, a person's own self-report (Q data), and objective test input (T data). Source traits are those underlying factors responsible for a highly correlating cluster. Say, for instance, that we found a highly correlating cluster of humor, gregariousness, and generosity. The source trait might be termed friendliness. The 16 PF (16 Personality Factor) Scale is the best-known instrument from Cattell's factor-analytic work. Where his 16 PF Scale encompasses normal traits, his Clinical Analysis Questionnaire (CAQ) assesses abnormal traits. *Eysenck's* work raises the criterion threshold for identifying traits. Not only must they correlation-cluster, but they must be heritable, make sense theoretically, and have social relevance. Using these criteria, Eysenck's typology includes introversion-extroversion, stability-neuroticism, and impulse control-psychoticism. The "*Big Five*" theory of personality—first proposed by *Norman*—has now been embraced by many different personality researchers, both in and outside the trait-theory "camp." As you read the "Big Five" you'll notice the roots from which several of them have come—neuroticism (Eysenck), extroversion (Jung, Eysenck), openness, agreeableness, conscientiousness. Not all current theorists sign on to the "Big Five" train. The interactionists take a different view.

Interactionist theorists note that traits do not predict a person's behavior in a given situation. For them, the critical "mix" blends the interaction of the person and the situation. We bring our unique traits to any given situation, and the interaction between our traits and that setting will determine our behavior. As an extrovert, you will behave very differently in a large, gala reception than will an introvert, and you likely will feel a sense of happiness and satisfaction that will elude the introvert. Early roots of this approach can be found in Rotter and Bandura's work. Studying our development from early infancy, *Thomas and Chess* have identified nine characteristics of temperament (e.g., activity level, adaptability, approach/withdrawal) and believe the key determinant of our personality is the match between our temperament and our environment. Mischel, Bem, Allen et al. weigh in prominently.

Now that you've had a bird's-eye view of this lush, theoretical landscape, let's look a bit more closely at those fascinating fields we just flew over. The following outline will be a helpful tool and reference point.

Personality Outline

Concepts	Names	Terms
Personality Theories		
Psychoanalytic	Freud	Personality as instinct-driven
Ego-analytic	Hartmann, Erikson	Less emphasis on id. More central role for ego.
Psychosocial	Erikson	Eight stages in life-cycle
		Emphasis on identity
Psychodynamic		
Individual	Adler	Basic drive is superiority-striving
Analytic	Jung	Four perceptual approaches to the environment: sensing, thinking, feeling, and intuiting
Interpersonal	Sullivan	Interpersonal relationships are the defining elements of personality
Cultural	Horney	Three ways of relating to people: moving toward, moving away from, moving against
Sociopsychoanalytic	Fromm	Five types of love: brotherly, motherly, erotic, self, and supernatural
Learning interpretation of psychoanalytic	Dollard-Miller	Translates psychosexual stages into learning-theory terms
Behaviorist		Personality as learned behaviors
Radical	Watson/Skinner	Focus on stimulus-response, observable behavior
Social	Bandura/Rotter	Focus on expectancies and values of behavioral outcomes. Stimulus-Organism-Response (as distinct from radical's S-R)
Reciprocal inhibition	Wolpe	Pair a problem behavior with an adaptive one, making it impossible to do both
Phenomenological		Personality is one's perceptions.
Personal construct	Kelly	We view the world through our own set of glasses (personal constructs)
Client-centered	Rogers	"Listen to your feelings." Often they're wiser than your intellect.
Self-actualization	Maslow	Hierarchy of needs—physiological, safety, belongingness/love, esteem, self-actualization
Logotherapy	Frankl	Will to meaning (setting goals and working toward them rather than pursuing a will to power or a will to pleasure—both of which are self-defeating)

Concepts	Names	Terms
Transactional analysis	Berne/Harris	"Games People Play" (all of which are self-defeating and destructive)
		Parent/Adult/Child and the importance of parallel rather than crossed communication (goal of an "I'm OK, You're OK" life position)
Trait		
Functional autonomy	Allport	Traits that once had a survival function (e.g., hunting) now take on a self-perpetuating life of their own. Counters psychoanalysis with a positive view of human nature.
Factor analysis	Cattell/Eysenck	Correlational clusters enable us to identify specific personality traits.
	Cattell	Source trait identification and the Clinical Analysis Questionnaire
	Eysenck	Typology premised on introversion-extroversion, stability-neuroticism, and impulse control-psychoticism
"The Big Five"	Norman	Neuroticism (emotional stability)
	Costa	Extroversion
	McCrae	Openness
	Goldberg	Agreeableness
	Eysenck	Conscientiousness
Temperament	Thomas and Chess	Activity level
		Rhythmicity (bio-cycle regularity)
		Approach/withdrawal
		Adaptability
		Reactivity threshold
		Reaction intensity/energy
		Dominant mood quality
		Distractibility
		Attention span/persistence
Personology	Murray	Motivation's effect on personality. A taxonomy of needs including achievement, affiliation, dominance, play, sex, understanding, et al.
Interactionist		
	Mischel, Bem, Allen	Interaction between a given personality trait and a given situation
	Thomas and Chess	Interaction between a temperament characteristic and a situation
Positive psychology		
	Seligman	Three pillars: Positive emotions Positive character Positive groups/communities

Theory

A reasonable question at this point would be: Why don't personality theorists get together on a single, unified theory? The reason is that research in the field is not far enough along for the investigators to be in that enviable position. Dealing with and theorizing about the whole person is a complex task. The theorists themselves are well trained, thoroughly experienced clinical psychologists or psychiatrists who have dealt firsthand with people's adjustment problems. Their theories reflect their observations and the commonly recurring themes that they have encountered. Each theorist, in his own way, gets at important aspects of personality. All current theoretical views will at some point in the future seem as weird and archaic as early maps of the world seem now. But people's problems are occurring now, and efforts to systematize and understand in order to help must be made now, too.

In the following outline you'll visit with each of the major theorists, sharing key elements in their work.

Theory Outline

Concepts	Names	Terms
Psychoanalysis	Freud	
Divisions of psyche		Id (biological/instinctual)
		Ego (executive)
		Superego (social/perfection)
Cathexis and anticathexis		Investing emotional energy in another person (bonding) (positive feeling = cathexis, negative feeling = anticathexis)
Defense mechanisms		Repression, reaction formation, isolation, undoing, denial, projection, identification, regression and fixation, displacement, sublimation
Psychosexual stages		Oral (passive-sadistic)
		Anal (retentive-expulsive)
		Phallic (Oedipus complex and castration fear; Electra complex and penis envy)
		Latency
		Genital
Conscious, preconscious, and unconscious		Premise = our behavior is unconsciously motivated (id-driven)
Thanatos/Eros		Death/Life instinct (drive)
Parapraxes and wit		Slips of the tongue (betraying unconscious motivations)
		Wit = vehicle for getting the forbidden (sexual or aggressive) past the defense mechanisms
Dreams		"Royal road to the unconscious"
Dream interpretation		Manifest (reported) and Latent (underlying meaning)
Free association		Method of therapy

Concepts	Names	Terms
Ego Analysis	Hartmann/Erikson et al.	
Ego as conflict-free sphere	Hartmann	Not beholden to the id for borrowing its energy
Eight stages in life	Erikson	Basic trust vs. basic mistrust
		Autonomy vs. shame/doubt
		Initiative vs. guilt
		Industry vs. inferiority
		Identity vs. identity diffusion
		Intimacy vs. isolation
		Generativity vs. stagnation
		Integrity vs. despair
Psychodynamic		
Individual	Adler	Inferiority feeling/superiority striving
		Social interest as a determinant of mental health
		Family constellation (birth order and personality)
		Predisposing situations for mental illness—organ inferiority, pampering, neglect
Analytic	Jung	Archetype
		Collective unconscious
		Extroversion-introversion
		Persona
		Anima/Animus
		Shadow
		Four psychological functions: sensing, thinking, feeling, intuiting

Interpersonal	Sullivan	Modes of cognition:
		   Prototaxic
		   Parataxic
		   Syntaxic

		Emphasis on schizophrenic patients
		Dynamisms
		Personifications
Cultural	Horney	Role of culture in defining normality

		Modes of relating:
		   Moving toward
		   Moving away from
		   Moving against

		Womb envy (male counterpart to Freud's penis envy concept)

Concepts	Names	Terms

Sociopsychoanalytic	Fromm	Five types of love:
		  Brotherly
		  Motherly
		  Erotic
		  Self
		  Supreme being

		Five human needs:
		  Relatedness vs. narcissism (love need)
		  Creativeness vs. destructiveness (transcendence need)
		  Brotherliness vs. incest (rootedness need)
		  Individuality vs. conformity (identity)
		  Reason vs. irrationality (frame of orientation/devotion need)

Behaviorist/Learning Theory

Concepts	Names	Terms
Radical	Watson/Skinner	Larnyx movements and muscle twitches (Watson)
		Operant conditioning
		Shaping techniques
		Positive reinforcement
		Inadequacy of punishment as a behavior controller
Social	Bandura/Rotter	Expectancies and values
		Perceived value of reinforcers
		Observational learning
		Situational emphasis (in contrast to early childhood emphasis within psychoanalysis)
Reciprocal inhibition	Wolpe	Reactive inhibition
		Reciprocal inhibition
		Systematic desensitization

Phenomenological

Concepts	Names	Terms
Client-centered	Rogers	Organized and goal-directed behavior
		Conscious self-structure and sensory-visceral experience
		Basic striving to actualize, maintain, and enhance
		Importance of listening to one's feelings

Hierarchy of needs	Maslow	Five levels of needs:
		  Physiological
		  Safety
		  Belongingness/Love
		  Esteem
		  Self-actualization

		Centrality of self-actualization

Concepts	Names	Terms
Logotherapy	Frankl	Existential vacuum
		Existential frustration
		Collective neurosis
		Life will and meaning—will to meaning vs. will to power and will to pleasure
Personal constructs	Kelly	Constructs and contrasts
		Constructive alternativism
		C-P-C cycle (circumspection, preemption, control)
		Role Construct Repertory Test ("Rep" Test)
Transactional analysis	Berne/Harris	Script
		Parent/Adult/Child
		Contract
		Life-positions (four)
		Games
Trait		
Dispositional	Allport	Dispositional traits: Cardinal (basic core trait[s]) Central (present throughout personality) Secondary (occasional traits, not centrally defining)
Factor analysis	Cattell	L, Q, and T-data (life record, questions regarding self, objective tests)
		Trait elements
	Eysenck	Personality dimensions: Introversion-extroversion Neuroticism Psychoticism
"The Big Five"	Norman Costa McCrae Goldberg	Five basic personality traits: Neuroticism (emotional stability) Extroversion Openness Agreeableness Conscientiousness
Temperament	Thomas and Chess	Nine basic characteristics of temperament: Activity level Rhythmicity (bio cycle regularity) Approach/withdrawal Adaptability Reactivity threshold Reaction intensity/energy Dominant mood quality Distractibility Attention span/persistence

Concepts	Names	Terms
Personology	Murray	Person-environment forces (needs and press)
		Viscerogenic (primary) needs and psychogenic (secondary) needs
		Specific psychogenic needs including achievement (later pursued by McClelland), social approval, et al.
Interactionist		
	Mischel, Bem, Allen	Personality's key ingredient is the interaction between one's personal trait and a given situational environment.
	Thomas and Chess	Personality's key ingredient is the interaction between one's temperament characteristic and a given situational environment.

The preceding list will provide quick reference and rapid feedback regarding the personality theory aspects of your review.

Measurement

The second portion of this personality discussion centers on measurement—the use of formal instruments to tell psychological investigators about their subjects. Instruments in this collection vary from the highly objective to the highly subjective, and it might be helpful at this point to take a look at the various devices within that broad range and some major names within the different categories.

"Dean" of the *objective measuring instruments* is the *Minnesota Multiphasic Personality Inventory (MMPI)*. Developed by *McKinley and Hathaway* in 1942, it stands as a milestone in objective personality measurement. The standardization process for the inventory was conducted with a wide range of persons judged to have specific psychological abnormalities, and as a person answers the 567 statements, his response patterns can be compared with those of the large standardization sample. Obviously, such comparison means that the inventory is oriented toward detecting abnormality. The current version—the MMPI-2—has ten clinical scales closely following the original scales. It also has seven validity scales. Both MMPI and its offspring (MMPI-2) stand as hallmarks of objective testing in the field of personality and psychopathology. Another frequently used objective scale is a real tongue-twister—the Millon Clinical Multiaxial Inventory (MCMI). Millon designed it to closely parallel the categories of psychological disorders with the American Psychiatric Association's DSM-IV-TR. Similar scales patterned after the MMPI (e.g., *Gough's California Psychological Inventory*) have been standardized on normal individuals and thus emphasize normality. In each of these tests, the scales are organized around the true-false statement—the test taker reads each statement and marks it either true or false. The subject's responses to the large number of statements then enable the psychologist, utilizing established procedures (or perhaps computer analysis), to develop a response profile. Objective tests of this nature have the advantage of ease of administration to large numbers of people simultaneously and ease of objective scoring.

Nevertheless, the structured format of such tests does not allow unique individual expression.

Subjective measuring instruments are often described as projective techniques. In the projective technique a person is shown an ambiguous stimulus or life situation, and is asked to give his observations concerning it. The test format makes it relatively easy for a person to relate his or her own thoughts, concerns, and problems to the stimulus (generally without realizing that he is doing so). The term *projection* suggests casting upon something (or someone) "out there" that which is within. Were you depressed and lonely, for instance, you might see depression and loneliness in every life-situation picture presented to you, although the pictures did not specifically suggest such feelings. You would be, in effect, projecting onto the pictures the feelings that you have. Such techniques enable therapists to observe recurring themes and trends among subjects' responses, allowing them to get at major facets of their patients' concerns and thoughts.

The "dean" of *projective techniques* is the *Rorschach Inkblot Test,* a series of ten ambiguous-stimulus plates presented to a respondent. A life-situation instrument employing the projective-technique format is the *Thematic Apperception Test (TAT)* developed by *Murray.* Variations on each technique have been incorporated into subsequent measuring instruments (e.g., the Blacky Pictures Technique). These and additional test names are mentioned here for purposes of familiarity and quick reference.

Personality Test Outline

Concepts	Names	Terms
Objective Tests		
Minnesota Multiphasic Personality Inventory (MMPI) now in MMPI-2 rev	McKinley and Hathaway	Standardized on diagnosed abnormal clinical subpopulations.
Millon Clinical Multiaxial Inventory (MCMI)	Millon	Closely parallels current diagnostic categories.
California Psychological Inventory (CPI)	Gough	Standardized on a diagnosed normal sample from population.
16 Personality Factor Scale (16 PF) and the newly elaborated 12 factors in the Clinical Analysis Questionnaire (CAQ)	Cattell	16 bi-polar dimensions of personality. The new test (CAQ) contains 12 new scales (total of 28) and is based on the 16 PF. The 12 new factors measure psychopathology.
"Big Five" Personality Traits: Neuroticism Extroversion Openness Personality Inventory, Revised (NEO-PI-R)	Costa and McCrae Eysenck	Has a "private" and "public" dimension—first, asks the test taker's self-assessment; next, asks a person who knows the test taker well to rate her/him on several dimensions.
Manifest Anxiety Scale	Taylor	Designed specifically to measure anxiety. Items are selected from the MMPI.
Eysenck Personality Questionnaire (EPQ)	Eysenck	Measures introversion-extroversion, stability-neuroticism, impulse control-psychoticism.
Q-sort	Rogers	Measures difference between the actual and the ideal self.

Concepts	Names	Terms
Internal-External Control Scale (I-E)	Rotter	Measures extent to which a person feels internal control or being controlled by external circumstances.
Social Desirability Scale	Edwards	
Allport-Vernon-Lindzey Study of Values	Allport, Vernon, Lindzey	Based on the premise that values reflect one's underlying cardinal and central traits.
Projective Tests		
Rorschach "Inkblot"	Hermann Rorschach	Ten cards with ink-blot-like pictures. Person to "tell me what you see" (and can be expected to see several things in any given ink blot). In analysis, the therapist looks for patterns across card responses.
Thematic Apperception Test (TAT)	Murray	Several cards with pictures. The person is to tell a story—"What led up to this? What's happening now? How does it turn out?"

The list is not complete, of course, but it should be sufficient for review purposes.

In addition to the objective and projective techniques, there is a set of techniques that could best be described as behavioral or situational. The OSS—World War II predecessor to the CIA—mastered this set of techniques and utilized them prominently in their screening procedures. As an OSS applicant, one might have become involved in situational testing the moment he or she walked through the front door. Such tests were designed to judge individual performance and response in actual, structured settings—providing information essential to the OSS in its selection procedures. Understandably, there are practical limitations on broad, general usage of such a procedure. To understand individuals, professionals observe carefully and theorize—developing measuring instruments to help pinpoint specific aspects of personalities. At some point in the distant future, the theories and measuring instruments now in use may seem ridiculously humorous and weird; but for now they constitute one of the major avenues for gaining increased understanding of emotional disturbances.

SOCIAL PSYCHOLOGY

Social psychology connects sociology and clinical psychology. Whereas the sociologist is concerned with the study of groups and the clinical psychologist works with the concerns and problems of the individual, the social psychologist studies the behavior of the individual within the group and the effects of the group upon the individual's behavior. If the area sounds sweeping to you, it is! This review spotlights some of the major areas of social psychology and discusses briefly certain aspects of each. In deference to the breadth of the field and the limitations of the review, however, a list of terms, concepts, and names concludes this section.

Attitudes and Attitude Measurement

If you were asked to select the most prominent area of research within social psychology, your best bet would be to select the study of attitudes. It is estimated that approximately half the research in the field deals with some aspect of attitude formation and change. Definitionally, many researchers in the field indicate that there are three components essential to the existence of an attitude: (1) cognitive; (2) emotional; and (3) behavioral. If we know something about cars (cognitive), get a "charge" out of working on them (emotional), and frequently can be spotted under the hood of some four-wheeler (behavioral), we have an attitude about cars. Knowledge alone, without emotional feeling, does not qualify; and the only way an attitude can be detected is through some form of behavior (working on cars frequently, answering an opinion poll, and so on).

Because attitudes are a prominent concern, researchers in the field have spent quite a bit of time and effort designing and standardizing attitude measurement scales. The earliest efforts in this area were those of *Thurstone*. Following very rigorous procedures for item selection, he developed a scale technique known as "equal-appearing intervals." This term encompasses both the underlying concepts and the procedures used in developing such a scale. For example, the experimenter might ask 200 people to act as judges, whose job would be to categorize a large group of statements that had been written on a specific subject (war, for instance). They would read each statement, decide to what extent it was favorable or unfavorable (i.e., for or against war), and place it in the category corresponding to their rating. There would be twelve categories into which the judges could sort these statements. Categories 1 or 2 would receive the statements that were felt to be strongly antiwar, while categories 10 or 11 would receive strongly prowar statements. As you can imagine, it would take a long time for 200 judges to sort a large group of statements into these categories.

When the judges had completed their sorting, the weeding out and selecting of statements for the final scale would begin. The best candidates for the final scale would meet two criteria: (1) low variability among the judges (meaning that a statement did not get placed into categories 1 or 2 by some judges and 10 or 11 by others); and (2) equal representation of all statement categories (meaning that the statements in the final scale would be equally distributed across the twelve-category range). The second criterion prompts the "equal-appearing intervals" description associated with Thurstone scaling procedures. After the above series of steps, the resulting scale would be a collection of approximately twenty statements. Judges would then be asked to read those statements, checking the ones that were in agreement with their respective viewpoints on the subject. By adding the category weightings of these statements (1, 2, 4, 7, 10, 11, and so on) and obtaining a mean score, the scale administrator would be able to determine where in the twelve-category range the judges' attitudes on this subject happened to be. Scale results would indicate, for instance, whether they were prowar or antiwar.

Because the judging, categorizing, and statement-selecting procedures must be repeated for each subject on which one wishes to develop a Thurstone-type scale, it is easy to understand why attempts have been made to simplify scale-development procedures. One of the earliest and best-known attempts was that of *Likert*. Likert believed that it was important to have judges express their own attitudes on a subject rather than to ask them to make general "anti" or "pro" judgments in relation to others' attitude statements. In keeping with this belief, he developed a scaling procedure known as the "*method of summated ratings.*" The response range on a Likert scale item encompassed five categories (strongly agree, agree, no opinion, disagree, strongly disagree). A strongly "pro" response on a given item was scored as a 5, and this meant that the person with the most prominent "pro" attitude on the subject received the highest overall score on a Likert scale. Correspondingly, the person with the strongest "anti" attitude on the subject received the lowest overall score on the scale. In this procedure, called "summated ratings," it is important that a person's score on each individual item in the scale correlate positively with the person's overall score.

A number of scale measurement approaches concentrating on specific measurement purposes followed these early beginnings. One was *Guttman's unidimensional approach*, in which he sought to measure a range of depth on a given attitude dimension. In a scale itself, he arranged this depth measurement sequentially. This means that, if a subject had a very slight agreement attitude on the attitude dimension, the person would agree with the first item in the scale. If a subject had a stronger agreement attitude, the person might agree with the first two scale items, and so on. In theory, it was an approach whereby Guttman claimed the ability to discern what specific items in his scale the subject has agreed with, simply by knowing that person's overall scale score. In practice, prediction has not always been that neatly accomplished, but the method proved innovative and important.

Another specific-purpose scale was *Bogardus's "social distance scale."* This scale had a seven-phrase description range that could be used in relation to a number of different identifiable ethnic groups or nationalities. For whatever groups or nationalities that were being tested in a given situation, a person had a response range from (1) "would admit to close kinship by marriage" to (7) "would exclude from my country." Several modifications of this scale technique have been made—the best-known recent one being that of Triandis.

Osgood developed the *"semantic differential scale."* In this scale, the subject is given a concept—such as church, capital punishment, or whatever—followed by a series of bipolar adjectives (e.g., good-bad, honest-dishonest, clean-dirty, and so on). Between the two poles (good-bad, for instance) there are seven spaces, and the subject's job is to place a check in one of those spaces. A check in the spot next to "good" receives a score of 7 and, correspondingly, a check next to "bad" receives a score of 1. There are several sets of these bipolar adjectives, thus allowing for a large possible range in which scores can occur. Through factor analysis, Osgood has discovered three dimensions to be tested—evaluative, activity, potency. The first of these dimensions is tested with adjectives such as good-bad; the second with adjectives such as active-passive; and the third, with adjectives such as strong-weak. The key dimension, and the one measured most prominently within an Osgood scale, is the evaluative one.

Public opinion polling is familiar to us and constitutes another measurement approach in this area. Unlike the preceding approaches, public opinion polling seeks to obtain a response percentage figure that can serve as a base for comparison when subsequent polls are conducted on the same question or attitude dimension. The "white elephant" in this area, which served as a great lesson for subsequent pollsters, was a presidential poll conducted by the *Literary Digest* in 1936. The *Digest* used the telephone book as the source of names to be included in its samples. Conducting a poll using these names, the *Digest* predicted that Alf Landon would win the election by a landslide. When Roosevelt's strength at the ballot box smothered Landon's election hopes, it also smothered the *Literary Digest*. Because the *Digest's* managers had failed to realize that the names in the phone directory did not constitute a representative sample of the voting public, they had polled an unrepresentative sample and correspondingly had made an erroneous prediction. The *Literary Digest* went out of business, but the lesson of representative sampling was remembered well by other would-be pollsters—especially George Gallup, whose American Institute of Public Opinion has become a byword in polling. Polling techniques have become very refined, and polls are depended upon heavily by certain groups, notably politicians. Pollsters warn, however, that they are not predictors of an outcome but, instead, monitors of an opinion as it exists within a sample at a specific time.

Scaling techniques continue to develop. Among current entries on the scene is *Bem's Scale of Psychological Androgyny* (a measure of sex-role stereotypes). If your androgyny scale score were low, you would be considered high in sex-role stereotyping, and vice versa. Since current research emphases in the field provide needs for new or modified measuring instruments, the development of new scales and techniques will no doubt continue.

Attitude measurement now has ventured well into the field of physiological instruments. For a long time we have known about *galvanic skin response (GSR)* as a measure of lie detection. That time-honored device is now joined by new cousins such as the facial electromyograph (EMG), which detects subtle muscle cues of positive or negative attitudes toward a stimulus the person has just heard or seen. Cacioppo and colleagues make frequent use of the EMG and the electroencephalograph (EEG) in their attitude measurement work. We can expect more melding and blending of response scales and physiological instruments in the years ahead. Then, of course, there's that wonderful piece of impressive looking equipment that subjects are told will detect their lies and true feelings on even the most socially sensitive questions. The instrument looks convincing enough, and unwitting subjects opt toward honest responding, but in reality it doesn't measure a thing. It's called the *bogus pipeline*.

Attitude Change

Among the best-known names in the area of attitude change is *Festinger*. His *theory of cognitive dissonance* has been the source of a broad range of experimentation in this field. In effect, Festinger's theory says that there is a tendency for people to seek a state of consonance between their attitudes and their behavior. Someone is in a state of consonance when behavior in a given belief-area corresponds to one's attitude in that area. After formulating his theory, Festinger's next step was to create a dissonance between the person's attitude and behavior. Subjects were induced to behave in conflict with an attitude they held. He predicted that in order to regain the comfort that comes with consonance, the person's attitude would tend to change in the direction of the behavior that had been performed. For instance, a conscientious objector who had been forced to use a rifle in frontline army combat would begin to change his attitude in favor of this behavior.

Several researchers have refined Festinger's original theory. For example, Cialdini makes the point that a person's degree of cognitive dissonance will depend upon the strength of that person's need for consistency. Cooper and Fazio set out four steps they consider basic to the occurrence of cognitive dissonance. Will the attitude-discrepant behavior have *negative consequences*? Will the person feel *personal responsibility* for those consequences? Will the person be *physiologically aroused*? And will the person *attribute* that arousal to his or her behavior?

A significant interpretive challenge came from Darryl Bem. He took the position that what Festinger termed *cognitive dissonance* was simply the individual perceiving his or her behavior and adjusting the attitude to correspond with it.

Aronson and other researchers extended this theory to the area of initiation-type settings. If we go through some pretty unpleasant behavior in order to meet the requirements for joining a group, we justify having gone through this behavior by enhancing our valuation of the group. We say, in effect, "This is a tremendous group and well worth the initiation requirements we went through in order to join." If this seems farfetched, check with some of your friends who have joined a sorority or a fraternity recently and ask them whether they are glad they joined. Better yet, ask your dad or one of his friends whether he is glad he had the experience of basic training in the military, or ask your friend whether she is glad she went through recruit-hazing at the military academy. In each of these instances, one's tendency to say that the experience was worth the trouble is an example of cognitive dissonance—a means of self-justification.

Petty and Cacioppo have developed the Elaboration Likelihood Model (ELM), which both extends and modifies some of the original work in the field. The model states that people use either a central or a peripheral route to decision making. In the central route, people are highly motivated and give careful thought and extensive deliberation to the decision they are making. In the peripheral route, people have low motivation and give very little thought or deliberation to the decision they are making. These routes are two ends of a continuum, and different influence strategies work for central and peripheral. For example, classical conditioning techniques or simple exposure work well on the peripheral route, but would have little or no impact on the highly discerning person following the central route. Correspondingly, creating a positive mood would prominently influence the low-motivation, peripheral route person but would have little or no impact on those following the central route. The central route is influenced by promoting concepts that people value and find relevant to them. Here, slight variations in expression can make the significant difference. Rather than saying, "Society will benefit from this recycling campaign," the pronoun "*You* will benefit . . ." makes the critical difference.

MOTIVATION

Motivation generally is defined as a social or psychological condition that directs an individual's behavior toward a certain goal. Drive, on the other hand, is a biological condition that performs a goal-direction function. The distinction is that a rat probably turns right in the T-maze because it has sensations of hunger or thirst, not to preserve its self-esteem. In the cases of both motivation and drive, we have to infer that they exist on the basis of what the animal or person does. We note the relationship between a stimulus and a response and then say, "Aha, the rat was hungry!" or "I see a lot of love messages in the glances those two have been exchanging!" Each of these cases involves a stimulus (food pellet, lover) to which an organism responds (by turning right in the alley or sending affectionate glances). In short, on the basis of what we see, we infer.

To keep from switching terms in general discussion, the word drive is sometimes prefaced with "biological," "psychological," or "social." Our discussion of motivation will follow this pattern.

BIOLOGICAL DRIVES

Biological or primary drives have certain common elements, including: (1) the maintenance and preservation of the organism; (2) homeostasis (the tendency toward achieving and maintaining a state of balance); and (3) the quality of preempting all other drives. Entries in this group include hunger, thirst, pain, respiration, fatigue, body temperature, and bowel and bladder tension. The commonalities of biological drives can be easily illustrated. For example, if a person is hungry, his or her sonnet-writing and guitar-picking behavior stops temporarily (is preempted) until the hunger drive has been reduced. The tension of the drive itself creates a disturbing imbalance within the individual, requiring that the tension be relieved and balance be restored (homeostasis). The entire behavior sequence has survival at its root (maintenance and preservation of the organism).

PSYCHOLOGICAL DRIVES

These drives have the common characteristic of seeking to establish mental-emotional well-being. Psychological drives include sex, curiosity, and gregariousness. Sex seems to have many biological drive characteristics. It does not qualify as a full-fledged biological drive entity, however, because its arousal is as actively sought as its reduction (not homeostatic), and though it is essential for the survival of a species, it is not necessary for the survival of an individual organism (despite what your date may tell you!). Its power as a motivator is well known to advertisers, who utilize it as a selling aid for products ranging from magazines and entertainment to automobiles and cigarettes. Motivational research in this area has reached a point where even foods have been categorized as masculine or feminine.

The second major psychological drive—curiosity—is defined as a need to explore. Romanes, Thorndike, and Harlow have been among the early researchers who have found that monkeys will perform a task or learn a response without any tangible reward except the opportunity to explore and discover. In one instance, the curiosity reward was the opportunity to see an electric train in operation. Translated to the human level, curiosity is exemplified by our desire to know what is on the moon or on Mars or Venus. Curiosity is the penchant to explore, to discover, to know.

The third psychological drive—gregariousness—is the drive for affiliation among humans and other species. One yardstick for measuring emotional trouble in a friend might be the observation that he or she stays alone a good deal and does not mix. The capacity for interaction with others is seen as an aid in maintaining mental and emotional well-being.

SOCIAL DRIVES

Learning is the common element among drives in this category. We must learn to associate some kind of basic need gratification with these entries, or they never gain the capacity to motivate us. The normal means by which these entries gain their motivating qualities is an association with an element (food, maybe) that satisfies a primary drive. A person learns that with this element he or she can obtain whatever is necessary to satisfy biological or psychological drives. Entries in this category include money, achievement, and freedom from anxiety. You will inevitably encounter additional entries in some of the reference books you come upon. The above-mentioned entries—particularly money and achievement—will be found universally in your sources. Surprisingly, chimps have paralleled the human social drive for money. In an apparatus called a "Chimp-O-Mat," they have been known to work diligently for tokens that they could later exchange for food.

Motivation Outline

Concepts	Names	Terms
Theories		
Instinct	Darwin, Lorenz, Tinbergen	Adaptive function
Tension-reduction	Epicurean-based (hedonistic)	Maximize pleasure and minimize pain
	Psychoanalytic (Freud)	Tension builds and must be released
	Homeostasis	
	Cannon	Primary (biological) drives preempt other activities until these drives are reduced
	Hull	Hull considered this the basis of all learned behaviors.
	Needs hierarchy (Maslow)	Physiological, safety, belongingness and love, esteem, self-actualization (Note: both a tension-reduction and enhancement entity)
Arousal-enhancement	**Optimal state**	
	Berlyne	Optimal-arousal
	McClelland	Optimal-incongruity
	Intrinsic motivation	
	White et al.	Competency drive
	Opponent-process	
	Solomon	Pleasurable stimuli evoke an opposing inhibitory process
	Sensation-seeking	
	Zuckerman	Sensation-seeking personality
Acquired-type	**Need-Press**	
	Murray	Several environment-activated needs (measured by his Thematic Apperception Test [TAT])
	Expectancy-value	
	Tolman	Repetition of behaviors bringing outcomes we value
	Rotter	
	Achievement need	
	McClelland	A basic achievement motive or need to achieve (nAch)
	Atkinson	

Concepts	Names	Terms
Terminology definitions and distinctions		
Drive		Internal state of tension prompting activities designed to reduce the tension. (Drive includes the concepts of energy, activity level, arousability, and the arousal/cue functions of stimuli.)
Incentive		External stimulus catalyst for behavior. It includes reward and response predisposition based on deprivation, learning, and heredity.
Biological aspects		Homeostasis
		Eating behavior elements such as predisposition-based weight level (role of cells and the hypothalamus)
		Precipitating factors (blood glucose, stomach, taste, and external precipitators)
Homeostasis		Organism's physiological state of equilibrium
Instinctual aspects		Ethology and fixed-action patterns
		Sign stimuli
		Action specific energy
		Imprinting (and critical periods)
Physiological regulatory mechanisms		
Blood glucose level	Mayer	Regulating hunger by the level of blood glucose. (A partial, but not total explanation.) Glucostats (glucose-sensitive neurons) appear to be liver-based, sending signals to the vagus nerve and, from there, to the hypothalamus.
Hypothalamus		Central role in regulating hunger and other physiological needs. (Stimulating the rat's lateral area prompts overeating; stimulating the rat's ventro-medial nucleus stops eating behavior.)
Insulin		Secreted by the pancreas, it enables cells to extract glucose from the blood.
Nonregulatory physiological		
Sex drive	Masters and Johnson	Phases in human sexual response cycle: excitement (vasoconstriction), plateau, orgasm, resolution

Concepts	Names	Terms
Nonphysiological motives		
Affiliation	Schachter, Maslow, Bowlby, Murray, et al.	Association and bonding need (differs for extroverts [generally high] and introverts [generally low])
		Bowlby's early work with orphans and "wasting away" suggested a physiological, survival component
Intimacy	Erikson, McAdams, et al.	Warm, close dyadic relationships
Achievement	McClelland, Atkinson	Driven by mastery of the difficult challenge
Pleasure centers	Olds and Milner	Repeated electrical self-stimulation to an animal's limbic system
Dopamine hypothesis		Self-stimulation most effective when stimulating nerve fibers in the medial forebrain bundle (MFB), implicated in the release of dopamine

Outline Terms Elaborated

THEORIES OF MOTIVATION

INSTINCT (Also known as fixed-action pattern; behavior patterns "wired in" and occurring automatically in the presence of certain stimuli):

Darwin, Lorenz, Tinbergen, et al. studied the adaptive significance of instinctual behaviors.

Tension-Reduction

PLEASURE-PAIN (hedonistic) (Epicurean background): Actions are selected to maximize pleasure and minimize pain.

PSYCHOANALYTIC (hydraulic model—build-up/release) (Freud): Build-up of tension, as in a pressure-cooker or boiler, which must be released (catharsis). There are life and death instincts (eros/thanatos). Drive for sexual gratification is basically motivating and is either satisfied directly or through indirect means such as fantasy and creativity.

DRIVE (biologically based arousal states): Principle of homeostasis (Cannon). Basis of all learned behaviors (Hull).

NEEDS HIERARCHY Maslow developed a five-level needs hierarchy. The first four—physiological, safety, belongingness and love, esteem—he termed "deficit needs" (as in "filling a hole"). The fifth—self-actualization—is growth-oriented and enhancing. It is here that a person realizes her potential.

Arousal-Enhancement-Type Theories

OPTIMAL-STATE THEORIES Optimal-Arousal (Berlyne): There is an optimal arousal state for maximal efficiency. Below it we are bored, and above it we are anxious. Optimal-Incongruity

(McClelland): Each of us has a personal adaptation level and finds small deviations from it pleasant and stimulating. Large deviations are anxiety-producing.

INTRINSIC MOTIVATION (White et al.): There is an internal drive to develop our competencies and to accept challenges that will promote our individual growth. There is a related motivation to have personal control over events affecting our lives.

OPPONENT-PROCESS (Solomon): Pleasurable affective stimuli evoke one brain-process that then triggers an opposing inhibitory process. The opposing process is gradual and lasts longer than the pleasurable stimuli, having major implications for a vicious-cycle-type phenomenon for drug users and other substance abusers. As the drug user comes down from a short-term, pleasurable high, a longer-lasting depression trough lies ahead. The reverse sequence would be true in the case of unpleasurable initial affective stimuli.

SENSATION-SEEKING (Zuckerman): This approach theorizes a sensation-seeking personality trait and suggests that it has four components: (1) thrill and adventure-seeking; (2) experience seeking; (3) disinhibition; (4) susceptibility to boredom. These four components are measured in Zuckerman's Sensation-Seeking Scale.

Acquired-Type

NEED-PRESS (Murray): Developed by Murray and measured within his Thematic Apperception Test (TAT), the approach theorizes several needs and motives that are activated by the pressure of environmental stimuli (people and settings, for instance). Murray postulates an elaborate list of needs, including abasement, achievement, aggression, play, dominance, understanding, and so forth.

EXPECTANCY-VALUE (Tolman, Rotter, et al.): Based on the purposive behavior work of Tolman, this approach suggests that we come to expect certain outcomes for given behaviors and place a value on those outcomes. We are then motivated to repeat those behaviors that bring an outcome we highly value.

ACHIEVEMENT (McClelland, Atkinson): This theory postulates a basic achievement motive or need to achieve (n Ach). People high in n Ach welcome new challenges and are constantly seeking to attain high standards and to excel. (Ah, just like you as you prepare for the GRE!)

Aggression is a drive that does not classify neatly into any of the above categories but has characteristics of each of them. Psychoanalytic theory views aggression as instinctual (most of us spending much of our unconscious time trying to "throttle it"); drive theorists see aggression as the result of frustration (giving it characteristics of a psychological drive perspective); and social learning theorists consider it a response that stems from observational learning and imitation (television viewing and computer/video-game playing by children is becoming an area of major concern within this perspective). With its increasing prevalence in our social milieu, it likely will remain strong as a research concern as well. Two of the classic theoretical positions influencing this field have been the Berkowitz position that frustration leads to a readiness for aggression (whether aggression itself will occur depending upon the presence or absence of aggression-eliciting stimuli in the situation) and Bandura's observational learning of aggression (children playing aggressively after viewing a television model attacking a plastic, air-filled Bobo doll). The latter has often been cited when aggression and television concerns have been expressed with regard to children.

EMOTION

Emotion is a logical companion of motivation. When we attain (or fail to attain) a goal, words like joy, anger, delight, and depression enter the picture. We express a feeling . . . an emotion. On the physiological side, emotional expression can prompt a number of changes, including:

- Striated muscle changes controlled by the central nervous system—facial expressions, vocal expressions, muscle tension, tremors, and so on.
- Autonomic changes controlled by the autonomic nervous system and endocrine glands—heart rate, blood pressure, digestion, blood-sugar level and levels of acidity, epinephrine and norepinephrine, metabolism, breathing rate, sweating

Measurement of emotions has been prominent in the areas of:

- "Lie detector"—breathing, heart rate, galvanic skin response (GSR)
- Pupil size—increase in pupil size signifying increased interest, pleasant stimulus, heightened mental activity

A theoretical question of long standing has focused on whether the cognitive, experiential aspects of an emotion precede physiological arousal or whether, on the other hand, the emotion is experienced as a result of the physiological arousal. Theoretical positions of importance to you include:

- James-Lange Theory (emotion a result of physiological arousal)
- Cannon-Bard Theory (neurological)
- Schachter epinephrine studies

Among the cues to use in detecting someone's emotions are the following:

- Verbal (least reliable, Mehrabian)
- Facial (reliable cross-culturally for basic, simple emotions, Ekman)
- Situational context (essential to judgment of complex emotional expression, Frijda)
- Behavior

There is no doubt that prominent *learned* aspects are present in many emotional responses. For instance, a child may learn how much a cut finger hurts and how profusely to respond to such a trauma by the amount of parental fuss, alarm, and attention given similar preceding events. Where one child may cry a lot, another may hardly shed a tear—such is the parental "burden" in shaping human emotions.

Solomon's research in the *opponent-process* aspect of emotion (cited in the motivation outline) carries some far-reaching implications for the future of this field. In blatantly oversimplified form, the opponent-process theory states that our brain is oriented toward suppression of emotion—keeping our functioning at a homeostatic baseline. Consequently, an emotion being experienced prompts the brain to trigger its opposite in an effort to reinstate balance. The theory has many implications relating to abnormal psychology and the use of drugs. When a stimulant wears off, for instance, the emotional trough may be deeper than it was initially. The pattern evident with addiction—initial highs moderating over time (as the opponent process response becomes more rapid) while subsequent depression becomes more pronounced—fits this theory impressively.

Advances in brain research have provided extensive understanding of the role of brain mechanisms in emotion. We have come a long way from the days of *Phineas Gage's* railway accident in 1848, which transformed a gentle, soft-spoken man into an impulsive, irritable person with unpredictable fits of profane emotional outburst. It was then that scientists began their long road toward understanding the role of the limbic system in emotion. Subsequent understanding of brain mechanisms has revealed not only a close "working relationship" between the cerebral cortex and the limbic system, but two basic "operational loops"—one involving the cerebral cortex, the limbic sytem, and motoric (behavioral) functions, the other involving the cerebral cortex, the hypothalamus, and the autonomic nervous system (blood pressure, heart rate, skin temperature, glands, and so on). There is also convincing evidence that the right cerebral hemisphere holds primary responsibility for recognizing and mobilizing appropriate responses to emotion-eliciting stimuli and settings.

Another aspect of emotion-based research that is gaining increasing research attention and understanding is the very basic and important relationship between the emotions and physical health. With the increased pressure and complexity of American lives and lifestyles, the entire area of stress and its effects on physical health is coming under close scrutiny. *Bernard* first recognized the potential *consequences of stress*. *Cannon* was a pioneer in suggesting that we had a built-in mechanism—the *fight-or-flight reaction*—that protected us from physical danger. *Selye* further refined and extended that position, developing an understanding of the *stress-related response patterns* within the endocrine system and the autonomic nervous system. Focusing centrally on the adrenal gland, he found that a stressor prompts the organism's pituitary gland to secrete adrenocorticotropic hormone (ACTH)—this should sound familiar, based on your earlier review of the endocrine system. ACTH, in turn, signals the adrenal gland to secrete corticosterone. This hormone is key to producing the physiological changes found in the stress response. The growing area of behavioral medicine is taking a global look at the relationship between emotional and physical health. You can expect considerable spotlight in this area in the years to come.

Emotion Outline

Concepts	Names	Terms
Elements in emotion		Cognitive (subjective)
		Physiological (arousal)
		Behavioral (action)
	Plutchik	"Plutchik's Circle"—mixing emotions to produce new blends
	Lazarus	Four types: resulting from harm, loss, or threat; resulting from benefits; borderline (e.g., hope and compassion); complex (e.g., grief, bewilderment, curiosity)
	Turner and Ortony	Focus on components of emotions rather than basic emotions themselves
	Lewis and Saarni	Five basic elements: Elicitors (triggering events) Receptors (brain mechanisms) States (physiological changes) Expressions (visible changes) Experience (interpretation)
Cognitive	Ekman	The smile is universally interpreted cross-culturally

Concepts	Names	Terms
Physiological		
Nervous system		
Sympathetic		Prepares body for emergency (i.e., "fight or "flight") (e.g., dilates pupils, accelerates heart rate, inhibits digestion, releases glucose)
Parasympathetic		Controls the normal operations of the body (keeps the body running smoothly)
		Calms everything down (e.g., heart rate) after emergency
Brain-body pathways		
		Two pathways: Through the autonomic nervous system releasing catecholamine hormones mobilizing the body for emergency response Through the pituitary gland and endocrine system controlling corticosteroid hormone release, increasing energy, and inhibiting tissue inflammation
Behavioral		
Nonverbal	Ekman and Friesen	We can correctly identify seven facial expressions: happiness, sadness, anger, fear, surprise, disgust, and contempt. (Cross-cultural agreement in facial expressions of fear, disgust, happiness, and anger interpretation.)
Theories		
Physiological	James-Lange	I run, therefore I'm afraid—the action precedes the emotion. The emotion results from the physiological arousal.
	Cannon-Bard	I'm afraid, therefore I run—challenged the James-Lange Theory.
Cognitive	Schachter-Singer	Arousal and physiological change are interpreted on the basis of context (e.g., I'll "feel" what those around me are feeling).
	Valins and Reisenzein	Arousal not a prerequisite for experiencing an emotion. Cognitive processes alone can do it. Challenged Schachter-Singer.
	Frijda	Cognitive appraisal and action tendencies occur simultaneously.

Concepts	Names	Terms
Multicultural	Shaver	People universally organize their emotions with six basic categories—love, joy, anger, sadness, fear, and surprise.
Effectiveness	Yerkes-Dodson Law	Increases in motivation and arousal bring increases in emotion. A mid-range level of arousal lends to optimal performance effectiveness.
Social stimulation need	Harlow	Contact comfort (rhesus monkeys feeding on a terry cloth "mother")
	Bowlby	Early Foundling Home studies of orphans and the importance of social stimulation to survival
Measurement		Lie detector test (monitoring breathing, heart rate, and galvanic skin response [GSR])
	Holmes-Rahe	Social Readjustment Rating Scale (SRRS)
	Spielberger	State-Trait Anxiety Scale
Stress terminology		
Anxiety		Generalized fear
	Spielberger	State vs. Trait Anxiety
Stress		A nonspecific emotional response we make to real or imagined demands on us
Frustration		Resulting emotional state when a goal is thwarted or blocked
Conflict		Approach, avoidance, and approach-avoidance (the latter related to a single stimulus)
Stress and physical health	Friedman and Rosenman	Type A personality: competitive, aggressive, impatient, hostile
		Type B personality: relaxed, patient, easygoing, amicable
		Relationship to physical diseases such as rheumatoid arthritis and heart disease
		Relationship to a weakened immune system
		(Note: Both relationships are correlational and subject to controversy within the field.)

Concepts	Names	Terms
Moderating factors	Gore	Social support
	Kobasa	Hardiness (marked by commitment, control, and the excitement of challenge)
	Greenberg	Exercise
	Benson	Relaxation and mediation
	Dixon	Humor
	Spielberger	Releasing pent-up emotions
Stress syndrome	Selye	General Adaptation Syndrome (three stages): alarm, resistance, exhaustion

Emotion Summary

Spanning several decades, Selye's work has had a profound impact upon the field. He once observed that the world is comprised of "racehorses" and "turtles." The racehorses find stress exciting and are highly motivated by it. The turtles require a calm, quiet environment for their functioning.

Having completed this much of your review, you may feel both relieved and happy; that is, you may experience both a motivation and an emotion, companions throughout human existence. Motivation and emotion lead naturally into the next two areas of psychology that we shall discuss, personality and social.

Attraction and Affiliation

DETERMINANTS OF ATTRACTION

To answer the question of why persons are attracted to one another, several possible determinants have been mentioned and investigated. *Proximity* is one of the most prominent of these determinants. Whyte found that within a new housing development the single best predictor of social attraction and friendship development was the distance between houses. Friendship and social attraction were far more likely between persons living next door to each other than, for instance, between people living down the street from each other or in different blocks. Festinger and his associates did a similar study in an apartment complex containing several two-story buildings with five apartments on each floor. Social attraction and friendship patterns again were found to be most prominent in the next-door setting and weaker as one moved additional doors away from any given apartment. This finding introduced the concept of functional distance—functional because, although two or three doors away is not all that far in terms of actual physical distance, the principle of proximity still seems to hold.

A second determinant—*similarity*—has been investigated prominently by Newcomb, Byrne, and others. Newcomb put the variables of proximity and similarity in competition with each other by setting up a dormitory room assignment procedure and carefully assigning rooms on the basis of either similar or dissimilar interests and values. Of major concern was whether sheer proximity (being roommates) would determine attraction patterns or whether similarity in interests and values would be the major determinant in attraction. The outcome revealed that proximity operated short-range but that similarity determined the long-range attraction patterns. Byrne and his associates used a questionnaire technique to establish within their subjects either perceived similarity or dissimilarity to another person's attitudes. Typically, Byrne might present his subject with the results of a questionnaire that presumably had been filled out by another person—but actually had been based on the subject's responses to an earlier questionnaire. The subject's reactions yield strong evidence of attraction on the basis of perceived similarity (i.e., agreement between the subject's responses and those of the "other person"). This evidence of attraction holds even in situations where the perceived "other person" has been represented as being a member of a different ethnic group or nationality.

Aronson and Jones are among the leading researchers who have investigated a third determinant—*rewardingness* (and its ingratiation counterpart). In effect, they have found that individuals are attracted to persons who care about them (reciprocity) and will be very wary about persons whose "care" seems to have within it the possibility of an ulterior motive. Concentrating on the rewardingness aspect of attraction, Aronson and his associates have also found that persons are more likely to be attracted to individuals who have evaluated them positively than to individuals who have negatively or neutrally evaluated them. A surprising finding was that attraction was most prominent in instances where the evaluation had moved from an initially negative one to an eventually positive one. The strength of the attraction in such instances is attributed to the combined effects of negative reinforcement (removal of an aversive stimulus) and positive reinforcement (positive evaluation); and this phenomenon provides the basis for Aronson's gain-loss model, cited later. Jones, working with ingratiation, found that persons are attracted to individuals whose positive evaluation does not carry the prospect of subsequent commitment or expectation. Counterpart to this outcome is the finding that flattery or ingratiation is most effective when directed toward an area in which the recipient has never been sure of having competence but has wished for such competence.

Anderson's work deals with *personal attributes* as a basis for social attraction. He is concerned with the general question of whether there are personal traits that people collectively find attractive. Using an adjective-rating approach, he found that the highest rating among 555 adjectives was invariably given to the traits of honesty, sincerity, and trustworthiness. Correspondingly, the lowest rating was given to words connoting liar or phony. Anderson is a pioneer in this area, and his work has been prominently utilized in the categories of attribution and person perception.

Zajonc has investigated the determinant of *familiarity* and has found it to be a prominent factor in social attraction. In one of his studies, he had persons look at Turkish words (totally meaningless to the viewing persons). He offered some words only one or two times, but showed others as often as twenty-five times. Following the viewing procedures, the persons were asked to define the words they had seen. The words seen most often were accorded the most positive definitions. This generally is referred to as the *mere exposure effect*.

Research also bears out the sad reality that we favor beauty. Not only are we attracted to physically beautiful people, but we attribute to them more positive characteristics—friendly, warm, good listeners, and so on. Snyder's classic study of men thinking they were talking with either a beautiful woman or an average-appearance woman bore out this sad reality quite dramatically. The pattern extends to lengths of sentences given by judges and people's impressions of each other in job interviews, for example. But there's a downside, too. Beautiful people can never be sure whether those who interact with them are being genuine or superficial. In the relationship context, even here, the principle of similarity seems to apply. Berscheid, Feingold, and others have found a *matching hypothesis*—that those who are dating, engaged, living together, or married are equivalent in physical attractiveness.

ATTRACTION MODELS

Social psychologists have found it helpful in both their communication and their research to develop models of attraction. The following—briefly cited—are among the most prominent of these models:

Balance (A-B-X)

Developed through the work of *Heider* and the more recent theoretical concepts of *Newcomb*, this model is built upon persons A and B having attraction feelings toward each other and toward person or concept X. In the resulting A-B-X triad, the model indicates that consonance or a state of balance exists when there is an even number of negative signs. Imbalance exists where there is an odd number of negative signs. For example, suppose that Jack likes rock music, his dad does not like rock music, and Jack likes his dad. The situation within this triad is imbalance (one negative sign). Balance can be restored if Jack changes his views about either rock music or his dad (bringing a second negative sign into the triad). Obviously, all + signs in the triad also represent balance—both Jack and his dad liking rock music, and Jack liking his dad. The model is usually demonstrated as a triangularly positioned triad with signs placed between the entries. For example:

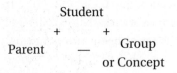

The balance model is frequently used in explaining and demonstrating a phenomenon such as cognitive dissonance.

Social Exchange Theory

Gergen is one of the most prominent names associated with this theoretical view. Simply stated, the theory puts social attraction in the context of a person's rewards from interaction divided by the person's cost incurred in the interaction. When costs outrun rewards, social attraction can be expected to decline and disappear. Moreover, the most favorable fraction (rewards/costs) will be the front-runner when a choice must occur in social attraction. If, for instance, a college student is dating back home and on the campus, the back-home relationship must be proportionately more rewarding than the on-campus one to remain comparable in strength—maintaining the back-home relationship involves more cost. According to the social exchange theory, people continually scan and evaluate reward/cost in their social relationships.

Rusbult has extended these basic social exchange principles of attraction into the area of close, committed relationships. She notes that attraction principles were developed on the premise of strangers and that important additional considerations need to be added in the area of close commitment. She proposes and has researched three categories of variables: (1) the degree of positive feeling one has about her/his partner (based on the extent to which the partner gratifies this individual's important needs in areas such as intellectual, companionship, intimacy, sexuality); (2) the quality of alternatives (other options in your region and age range); (3) level of investment (resources attached to the relationship and degree of loss if it were to end). The basic attraction principles continue to apply, but, as Rusbult vividly demonstrates, they take on important additional variables as relationships move toward closeness and intimacy.

Complementarity Theory

Winch is associated with this view, the primary application of which is in the area of extensive, intimate relationships such as courtship and marriage. This theory says, in effect, that such relationships require that aspects of personality be complementary in order for the relationship to be successful. Two people who both have strong dominance needs would be seen as heading for disaster in such a relationship. Success in the relationship would be achieved only if a strong dominance need on the part of one person were met by a low dominance need on the part of the other (in effect, complementarity). Because it is relationship-specific and symbolically "messier," this theory runs no real interference with its tailor-made prospective opponent—the balance model.

Festinger's Social-Comparison

This model demonstrates how perceived similarity and social attraction tend to interact. Essentially, *Festinger* is saying that (1) people are attracted to persons they perceive as similar to themselves; and (2) they perceive the persons to whom they are attracted as more similar to themselves than is really the case. Those "perceived similar others" take on special significance in ambiguous decision-making or opinion-forming situations. When we are faced with contradictory or ambiguous information and have to make a decision, we will rely heavily on the opinion of this "perceived similar other" person. This dynamic can be potentially disastrous in close, intimate relationship decisions, because we overlook the major differences that very likely exist between us. Yes, we very well may be "attracted to perceived similar." But beware of that next step—"perceiving those to whom we're attracted as more similar than they really are." The "snowball" effect within Festinger's concept is readily apparent—social attraction feeds perceived similarity, which feeds more social attraction, and so forth.

Aronson's Gain-Loss Model

In studies such as the one performed by *Aronson and Linder*, it was found that movement from a negative to a positive evaluation of a person led to stronger social attraction toward the evaluator by the person being evaluated than did movement from a neutral position toward positive evaluation. Aronson quotes Spinoza's observation that "hatred which is completely vanquished by love passes into love and love is thereupon greater than if hatred had not preceded it." Within this kind of situation, it has been suggested that a kind of double or compound reward operates, with (1) the removal of the aversive stimulus operating as negative reinforcement and (2) the presentation of a desired stimulus operating as positive reinforcement. Unofficially, this has been termed "Aronson's law of marital infidelity." The woman who receives a compliment from a stranger finds that compliment more rewarding than an equivalent compliment received from her husband. The husband—beginning from a general position of positive reinforcement—lacks the capacity to be as rewarding as the stranger (who begins from a neutral position). Thus, the close friend or spouse constitutes a less potent source of reward but a strong and more potent source of punishment.

The distinction between attraction and affiliation is that between positively evaluating other people (attraction) and simply being with other people (affiliation). Schachter conducted a classic series of studies on the affiliation dimension and found that, in a situation of experimentally induced stress, persons were discriminating in their choice to be with other people. Given an option of simply being with other people, being with other people experiencing the same situational stress, or being alone, those persons having only the choice of simply being with other people preferred to remain alone—and those persons having the choice of being with others in the same situational stress preferred affiliation over being alone. Schachter concluded that, in the presence of fear, misery loves miserable company. Conducting similar studies in which both unrealistic fear (anxiety) and realistic fear were introduced, Sarnoff and Zimbardo found that in high-anxiety settings persons preferred to remain alone. (This was interpreted as hesitancy to share their unrealistic fear with others because of the risk of embarrassment.) Thus, the research findings indicate that people have a tendency to affiliate with "similar situation others" in cases of high fear and a tendency to prefer being alone in cases of high anxiety.

Theories of Love

Within our models of attraction, we already have touched upon many of the dynamics relating to love relationships. Ancient writers gave us six types—ludus (game-playing, uncommitted), storge (friendship), mania (demanding, possessive), pragma (pragmatic or practical), agape (giving, altruistic), erotic (passionate). In gender comparisons, men score higher than women on ludus, while women score higher than men on storge, mania, and pragma.

As you might imagine, thoughts and theories abound in this area, but we haven't the time nor space to discuss them. Two of the best known are Rubin's distinction between liking and loving and Sternberg's Triangular Theory of Love. The points of Sternberg's triangle (going top, counter-clockwise) are Intimacy, Passion, Commitment. He then makes point-linkages such as Intimacy + Passion = Romantic Love; Intimacy + Commitment = Companionate Love; Passion + Commitment = Fatuous Love.

Communication

Two tracks operate within this heading—verbal communication and nonverbal communication. The former deals with communication via words; the latter refers to ways in which social communication occurs without words.

VERBAL COMMUNICATION

Specific communication patterns and leadership styles are prominent research concerns within this area. Their relevance is also strongly felt in organizational areas of applied psychology, though, and thus, to avoid duplicate review coverage, these topics will be considered in the Applied Psychology section. Janis introduced the concept of groupthink, which indicates the decision-making problems that can beset a group because of thought patterns that the sheer existence of the decision-making group can promote. He analyzed in detail the *groupthink* phenomena surrounding the Kennedy Administration's decisions that culminated in the Bay of Pigs invasion. Among the characteristics of groupthink are:

(1) illusions of invulnerability; (2) evolution of a rationale (justifying the group's decision); (3) belief in the morality of the group's decisions; (4) stereotyped views of the enemy; (5) conformity pressures; (6) self-censorship of critical thoughts (the individual censoring self and not expressing critical thoughts to the group); (7) mindguards (persons in the group who suppress information divergent from group opinion); and (8) illusion of unanimity (an illusion of unanimity within the group despite unexpressed individual doubts).

Janis believes that groupthink is likely to occur when (1) the decision-making group is highly cohesive, (2) the group is insulated from other, more balanced information, and (3) the leader has preconceived notions of the correct policy to follow. To prevent groupthink, Janis underscores the importance of arranging group conditions in such a manner that individual thought and expression are encouraged.

Among media effects, the following terms are generally familiar:

■ **TWO-STEP COMMUNICATION FLOW**—refers to the media communication pattern of first reaching the opinion makers in a given group or community (step 1) so that they will then influence their respective constituencies (step 2). The opinion makers need not be the "pillars" of the community, but they are those persons within any given group who have the basic opinion-reference function in that group.

■ **MEDIA ELITE**—refers to the pattern of influence associated with specific persons in a given communications medium. For instance, in television news there are certain commentators toward whom the rest of the television commentator community turn in developing their own approaches to news events. This term, therefore, refers to an influence within the medium itself.

NONVERBAL COMMUNICATION

Two avenues form the basic investigation areas here—kinesics and proxemics. *Kinesics* is the study of body language—the ways in which people unwittingly communicate through their gestures, facial expressions, body positions, and so on. Pioneering work in this area was done by *Birdwhistell.* He concentrated upon the face and the development of a notation system for each aspect of facial expression. This approach was considered *micro.* A *macro* approach was undertaken by a *Birdwhistell* associate named Scheflen. Within Scheflen's approach, general patterns of interaction over a period of time were studied. *Ekman* has concentrated upon the possibility of *universal facial expressions* and has spent much time studying the smile in various cultures. He concludes that the smile is a universal expression—a general communicator across all the cultures he has studied. Other research in this area includes the work of *Kendon* and that of *Goffman.* Possessing a theoretical mind, Goffman has been the stimulus for many research studies conducted in this area.

Proxemics deals with research relating to territoriality, that is, personal space, unseen dividing lines, and the dynamics of invading another's personal space. Key work in this field was spearheaded by *Hall,* who suggested four territorial zones—intimate, personal, social, and public. The first of these zones is believed to extend to approximately eighteen inches from the body; other zones become increasingly distant. Implications for urban crowding may be a future outgrowth of work in this area.

Persuasion

In this area, concerns relating to both noncoercive and coercive persuasion come into view. The latter includes brainwashing techniques and techniques formerly used in police interrogation; the former deals with general persuasion techniques as used in public speaking, advertising, and the like.

TECHNIQUES IN GENERAL PERSUASION

Several concepts have been advanced in this area. Among them is *McGuire's inoculation theory*, which states, in effect, that people can be "immunized" against a subsequent persuasive communication if they have been familiarized in advance with the persuasive arguments they are going to hear, and have heard counterarguments. *Freedman* introduced a *foot-in-the-door* technique that demonstrates that we are more likely to agree to a large, commitment-type request if we have agreed in advance to a smaller commitment request. This is the salesman's familiar approach of getting a small commitment now and returning to ask for a larger commitment later. Janis found an eating-while-reading effect that indicated that people were more likely to acquiesce to a request or agree with a viewpoint if it were presented during a pleasurable activity such as eating.

The *door-in-the-face* technique begins with a huge commitment potential, and relief comes when a more modest option is presented. Suppose we're preparing for Uncle Leroy's visit, so we head for the liquor store. The salesperson shows us a $150 bottle of wine and we find our throat sinking deep into our stomach. Just then the salesperson says, "However, we have this wine available for $20." Ah, relief! *Ask-and-You-Shall-Be-Given* relates to the high likelihood that a person will respond positively to our request on behalf of a charitable, worthy cause. *Low-balling* is our tendency to stay with a commitment we've made after the initially low stakes have been raised. The car salesperson initially told us we could have the car for $9,000. Then, by design, a discovery was made that $10,000 was the lowest they could go. We'll likely still spring for it.

The age-old notion that "actions speak louder than words" gets borne out within modeling. We remember once having heard that 75% of what children learn from parents, the parents did not intentionally teach. As we model positive behaviors, the message is a compelling one for others.

Additional concepts in this area include the sleeper effect (a comunication that has no immediate effect but proves to have long-range influence), the primacy-recency effect (whether first-communicator or last-communicator position in a presentation sequence is most effective), and two-sided/one-sided communication (whether persuasive communication will be most effective if both points of view are presented or if only one view is presented). In primacy-recency, the major question is how long after the communication will the audience members be making their decision. If the decision is soon or immediate, recency would apply (i.e., the last communicator in the sequence would be the most influential). If the decision is distant, primacy would be most effective. Out of necessity, we have oversimplified this area. Communicator characteristics and credibility are among the additional concerns central to investigations undertaken here.

TECHNIQUES IN COERCIVE PERSUASION

Schein is associated with the study of brainwashing techniques and has subdivided the general approach into a physical phase and a psychological phase. The physical phase occurs first and includes such things as exhaustive, forced marches at night (accompanied by sparse food, little or no medical attention, the leaving behind of those who cannot keep the rigorous pace, and captor explanation that all this is made necessary by the ruthless aggression of the captured soldiers' armed forces). The psychological phase begins upon arrival at the captors' camp facility. Leaders are separated from the group, original insignia of rank are no longer recognized, prisoners are rewarded for informing on fellow prisoners, incoming mail is read and only the unpleasant news is relayed, prisoners are rewarded for making confessions of their "wrongs" against the captors and for "admitting" the burden of guilt they feel at having engaged in such unfortunate aggressive behavior. The ultimate goal is to gain converts to the cause of the captors, but Schein has observed that the goal is seldom realized. Although a number of prisoners have been found to make confessions and testimonials, few convert.

Groups

CONFORMITY

Sherif did the earliest work in this field with something called the *autokinetic effect.* Using a small beam of light, he would ask subjects individually to make a judgment of how much it moved (ah, but the light wasn't moving at all!). Individuals would make different judgments and he would then combine groups of three who had made divergent judgments. They had to come up with an agreed-upon judgment. Later, when again asked for their individual judgments, Sherif found that the individuals had moved toward the group judgment. *Asch* introduced the *line-judgment technique* in which seven or eight persons acted as confederates in unanimously making an obvious error in judgment. Next, the unsuspecting subject was asked to respond. Findings indicate the subject's prominent tendency to go along with the obviously wrong judgment that has preceded. If confederate unanimity is broken, such conformity is far less likely.

Crutchfield developed an indirect means of imposing conformity pressure that relieves the need to have a large number of persons serve as confederates. His technique involves five individual booths, each equipped with a light panel. Via the panel, a subject presumably sees how persons occupying the other four booths have responded to questions. In actuality, each booth occupant is being given the same light-panel-response feedback from a control room. Although this technique enables every participant to be a subject, it is one step removed from the conformity pressures imposed through direct interaction.

Additional conformity influences you will pick up within your review include *informational influence* and *normative influence. Informational influence* occurs when the conforming person does so because she or he believes the others are correct in their judgment. *Normative influence* occurs when a person wishes to avoid the negative consequences or, perhaps, ostracism, of differing with the group.

Hollander felt the necessity of moving beyond a conformity-nonconformity terminology. He believed that within the nonconformity category there could be both persons who were reacting against conformity and those who were behaving independently on the basis of their own preferences (regardless of the conforming trend). To characterize this distinction, he introduced the terms *anticonformity* and *independence* (replacing *nonconformity*).

COOPERATION-COMPETITION

Sherif and Sherif did a classic field study utilizing subjects from a boys' summer camp. Through prearrangements, they established two basic groups, which they soon found to be very hostile toward each other. The only technique that the investigators found effective in reducing this hostility was the introduction of a *superordinate goal*—a desirable corporate goal that neither group could accomplish alone (e.g., finding the problem with the camp's water supply, or getting the camp's disabled food truck moving again). Whereas merely bringing the groups together only served to aggravate the hostility, the superordinate goal proved effective in hostility reduction.

In a more formalized laboratory setting, *Deutsch* has studied the dynamics of *cooperation-competition*. His Acme-Bolt Trucking Game involves two players and a single main route to their respective destinations. The game has the capacity to give each player a roadblock potential, and Deutsch has found that a player who is given such threat potential is very likely to use it.

Game decision theory (gaming) has also been prominently developed for investigating the dynamics of cooperation and competition in laboratory settings. A major distinction in this area is that between the zero-sum game and the nonzero-sum game. In the *zero-sum game*, the gains of one player are made at the direct expense of the other; the *nonzero-sum game* allows each player to make intermediate gains. The nonzero-sum game has been prominently adopted in the characteristic research on cooperation-competition. A game involves a payoff matrix. Within a matrix, each player can make one of two choices. Each player knows in advance that the payoff will depend upon the choice made by the other player. In the *"Prisoner's Dilemma,"* both players can make intermediate gains if they cooperatively refrain from trying to maximize individual gain. If they both try to maximize individual gains, they will both suffer great losses. The matrix concept allows several payoff possibilities to be established and investigated. Names prominent to this area include *Thibaut, Kelley,* and *Tedeschi*.

Violence

As a prominent social concern, violence and aggression have been natural subjects for social-psychological inquiry. Aggression can be defined as behavior intended to inflict physical or psychological injury/pain. Among boys, aggression tends to be physical—fists or weapons. Among girls, aggression tends to be verbal—the cutting remark. *Dollard and Miller* gave an early conceptual framework to the field with the *frustration-aggression hypothesis*. Their hypothesis indicates that frustration (being blocked from a goal or having the goal removed) leads to aggression. *Berkowitz* has been concerned with the effects of *aggression-eliciting stimuli* upon a potential aggressor. He has found that the presence of weapons heightens both the likelihood and the level of aggression. *Bandura* has investigated modeling effects—for instance, the effect of viewing an aggressive model on television. He finds that a child's aggression is heightened immediately following observation of a model who has been rewarded for aggressive activity. In the case of television, Siegel has suggested that a more long-range result of violence viewing is the expectation that children come to associate with specific roles in society. One of the most blatant examples of this is the role-violence differential between male and female roles as socially communicated and defined. *Wolfgang* believes that our society has, in effect, legitimized violence. Among subtle sanctions he sees in support of this position are the society's toleration of physical disciplining of children by their parents and the institutionalization of sanctioned violence through wars. *Zimbardo* investigated vandalism, violence, and his concept of deindividuation. In effect, the latter indicates that when people lose their identities or become anonymous within the larger group, they are likely to engage in aggression and violence. *Milgram* conducted perhaps one of the most frightening investigations in this area. Through a shock-administering experiment, he found that people are surprisingly obedient to commands to administer high-level shocks to other people.

Two recent models focus on the role of arousal and thought (cognition). Zillmann and Bryant link aggression to arousal and affect. To grossly oversimplify their *arousal-affect model*, if you or I have been physically aroused (perhaps just had strenuous physical activity) and someone calls us a *#@!, we're much more likely to aggress than if we had not been physically aroused prior to the insult. Berkowitz's *cognitive-neoassociation analysis* suggests that our thoughts and our feelings interact. In this context, a person interprets the situation, considers their feelings and weighs the consequences of aggressive action. In many respects, this is not far removed from the frustration-aggression hypothesis element of aggression displacement or scapegoating—not decking your boss because the consequences would be too costly, but kicking your dog when you get home.

Helping Behavior

The investigation of helping behavior grew out of the scientific interest in thought-numbing incidents of violence. The catalyst was the Kitty Genovese murder in the Forest Hills section of Queens, New York in 1964, when thirty-eight persons were known to have watched the half-hour, gruesome ordeal. What was so shocking was the fact that no one tried to help or call the police. *Darley and Latane* spearheaded early investigations and, in their laboratory studies, found the number of other persons present to be a prominent variable—with the likelihood of anyone helping decreasing as the number of bystanders increased. *Bryan, Test, and Piliavin* have found the model variable to be important. If a model of helping has preceded the incident in which a person is called upon to help, the likelihood that that person will help is greater than the likelihood present in a no-model setting. Allen has found that directness of request is also important—that there is a greater likelihood of obtaining help when the help request has been specifically addressed to the would-be helper. Another variable that has been found to be important by Darley et al. is the clarity of the helping situation—whether the person requesting help really is in an emergency situation. Batson's research adds another critical element to the likelihood of helping. If we're in a hurry and on a tight time schedule, we're far less likely to help than if we are not time-pressured.

There are ingredients for endless debate on the question of whether we are, by nature, helpful creatures or whether we help others only to satisfy our own ego needs. Batson's research supports the view that we are by nature helpful, empathic individuals. Cialdini's research suggests a *negative state relief model*—that our empathy makes us feel sad with and for the individual and helping that individual enables us to feel good—in effect, egoistic motivation rather than altruistic. The results are inconclusive. Take your choice!

Prejudice

Prejudice is defined as an attitude against an identifiable group, formed without knowledge of or familiarity with specific members of the group. The word *prejudice* gives definitional meaning and clarity to this attitude. *Allport's The Nature of Prejudice* summarized early work in the area, and *Clark and Clark* provided basic early work with young children. The latter investigators found that young black children some years ago expressed a preference to be white, but recent replications such as *Hraba and Grant's* have indicated that this preference pattern no longer exists. That turnabout may be interpreted as indicative of both personal and racial pride. Rokeach et al. experimentally pitted attitude and race similarities/differences against one another to see which would prevail. Similarities in attitude proved far more favorable in attraction and liking than similarities in race. The challenge becomes that of getting to know individuals, which serves to weaken and dilute group stereotypes. Pettigrew—one of Allport's former students—is among the most prominent research authorities in the area.

Tajfel and Turner propose *social identity theory*, which allows us to enhance our individual self-esteem by our association with the groups to which we belong. This identification creates a sense of *in-group favoritism*—in effect, "us" and "them." As Cialdini has pointed out, this also enables us to engage in "BIRGing"—"Basking in Reflected Glory" of groups with whom we identify at the same time that it creates "in-groups" and "out-groups."

Personality

Adorno's The Authoritarian Personality took a post-World War II look at the question of whether attitudes (particularly anti-Semitism) were related to general personality traits and characteristics. The large, comprehensive study uncovered a relationship between the authoritarian personality and attitudes of anti-Semitism and prejudice. The authoritarianism scale developed within this study has been widely used in other contexts and is commonly referred to as the F-scale. *Rokeach* has extended this avenue of research and introduced the concept of *dogmatism*. Also related to this general area is the term *Machiavellianism* as introduced and investigated by *Christie*. Anderson's *information integration theory* proposes that our impressions of others are formed by a combination of (1) our own personal disposition (the perceiver) and (2) a weighted average of the target person's characteristics.

Related to our helping behavior discussion is the question of whether there is an altruistic personality. Batson, Eisenberg, and others have suggested that there is, and that it is based upon a combination of empathy and an internalized, high-level of moral reasoning.

Status and Roles

In this area, we will briefly concentrate upon a handful of concepts and terms. Achieved-ascribed status distinction is between status attained on the basis of one's own achievement and status accorded on the basis of given characteristics such as family line, wealth, and so on. Interrole-intrarole conflict distinction is made between conflict experienced in meeting the expectations of two different roles (e.g., daughter and fiancée, son and fiancé) and conflict experienced in meeting expectations within a single role (e.g., professor and student differences in expectations for the role of college student). The former is "inter," the latter, "intra." Distributive justice refers to comparing your reward-minus-cost to that of another worker. If, for instance, one worker is not as well educated as another but earns more money, distributive justice does not prevail and worker discontent can be anticipated. Status congruence refers to a person's tendency to make all aspects of the individual's status congruent.

Currently, the investigation of sex roles constitutes a major research emphasis within this area. *Bem* has introduced the term *androgyny* to refer to sex equality in status and role opportunities and expectations. Her Scale of Psychological Androgyny is one of the instruments used to measure the presence of sex-role stereotypes. Williams, Bennett, and Best have made a distinction between sex roles, sex-role stereotypes, and sex-trait stereotypes—a distinction that they have built into their measurement instrument in this area. Their Adjective Checklist is used to determine the presence of sex-trait stereotypes.

Eagly underscores stereotypical tendencies within her *social role theory*—a tendency to picture women as secretaries and men as CEOs, for example. Deaux and Major believe the tendency to stereotype depends on the *perceiver*, the *target*, and the *situation*. Some perceivers are *gender schematic* and will tend to have stereotypical perceptions of women and men. Other perceivers are *gender aschematic* and will have balanced, nonstereotypic perception tendencies. Targeting persons by their appearance may trigger a given gender stereotype, and given situations and settings can trigger stereotypes as well.

Attribution Theory

A recent and growing area of investigation, attribution theory encompasses several of the topics already reviewed. The initial model in this area was *Heider's analysis-of-behavior model*:

$$\text{Behavioral effect } (E) = f(\text{environment} + \text{personal force})$$

Heider's formula states that behavioral effect is a function of environment and personal force. Research is concentrated upon determining the extent to which perceivers will attribute another person's behavior to external or internal causation. Jones and Davis have found that when external forces are strong and a person goes against those forces, the person's behavior is likely to be attributed to internal causation. Similarly, there is difficulty in attributing internal causation when the person's behavior is normative or in keeping with group behavior.

A quick look at findings in the broader spectrum indicates, for example, that when men and women perform equally well on a given task, women are seen as trying harder (Taylor, Kiesler, et al.); people tend to perceive their own behavior as situationally controlled and that of other people as internally caused (Jones and Nisbett). Hastorf et al. have found that people with unusual histories (handicap, psychiatric hospitalization, and so on) will have any non-normative actions attributed to that background. In "Lennie B" experiments concerning the severity of accidents, Walster found that there is a tendency to attribute more responsibility to the person at fault (i.e., internal causation) when the accident outcome is severe than when it is mild. Perhaps one of the most telling findings was that of Jones—discovering our tendency to attribute very high or very low performance to internal causation. Hence, the familiar comment that "the poor are poor because they're lazy and don't want to work."

To explain why people attribute internal causality to others, *Shaver* formulated a *defensive-attribution hypothesis* suggesting that the prospect of bad or unfortunate consequences occurring by chance threatens self-esteem. It therefore becomes a kind of self-defense to attribute internal causation to others. Lerner's *just-world hypothesis* indicates that people like to believe that the world is just and that individuals get what they deserve.

Theories to become familiar with include Jones' *correspondent inference theory*, which relates to our tendency to infer personality or situational causation, and Kelley's *covariation theory*. In Kelley's view, for something to be the cause of a behavior it must be present when the behavior occurs and absent when it is not. Get familiar with terms like Tversky and Kahneman's *availability heuristic* (our tendency to judge on the basis of the likelihoods that readily pop into our minds), Ross's *false consensus hypothesis* (our overestimating the extent to which others share our attitudes and opinions), and Ross's *fundamental attribution error* (our tendency to vastly overestimate the role of personal dispositional factors and vastly underestimate the role of situational factors).

Fiske and Taylor have been on the forefront of a movement called *social cognition*. It distinguishes the way people perceive things and people, and in the people context it outlines three patterns of how people are perceived. The *naïve scientist* is very methodical. The *cognitive miser* cuts corners and takes shortcuts that can head down misleading or blind alleys. The *motivated tactician* can be either very careful—perhaps even cunning—or quite careless as her or his motivations and the situation dictate.

Although it is somewhat superficial and oversimplified, we hope that this review section has given you some familiarity with the field of social psychology and its areas of research. In your further review, the concept-name-terminology sheet may provide a helpful checkpoint. As you seek mastery of concepts, names, and terminology, the following textbooks might prove valuable:

R. A. Baron Branscombe, and D. Byrne. *Social Psychology*. Boston: Allyn & Bacon, 2008 (an effective "Key Points" format throughout). Brehm S., S. Kassin, and S. Fein. *Social Psychology*. Boston: Houghton Mifflin Co., 2005 (thorough with good end-of-chapter reviews).

Social Psychology Outline

Concepts	Names	Terms
Attitude Formation and Change		
Cognitive dissonance theory	Festinger, Aronson	Attitudes move in the direction of behavior—a drive toward consistency
	Cialdini	Strength of need for consistency
	Cooper/Fazio	Four steps basic to cognitive dissonance: negative consequences, personal responsibility, physiological arousal, and arousal attribution
Elaboration likelihood model	Petty/Cacioppo	Two routes to persuasion: central (convincing content) and peripheral (attractive or expert source)
Self-perception theory	Bem	Situational inference
Reactance theory	Brehm	Motivation to reestablish one's freedom after perceived-unjust restriction
Measurement	Thurstone	Equal-appearing intervals
	Likert	Summated ratings
	Guttman	Unidimensionality
	Osgood	Semantic differential
	Bogardus	Social distance
	Remmers	Generalized Thurstone
	Gallup	Polling and quintamensional filtration
Distinction between objective and projective techniques		
Single stimulus factor	Kelley	"Warm-cold" variable

Concepts	Names	Terms
Attraction/Affiliation		
Models	Newcomb/Heider	Balance (A-B-X)
	Festinger	Social comparison
	Winch	Complementarity
	Gergen	Behavior exchange
	Aronson	Gain-loss
Attraction determinants	Whyte/Festinger, et al.	Proximity
	Newcomb/Byrne	Similarity
	Aronson/Jones	Rewardingness/ingratiation
	Anderson	Personality attributes
	Zajonc	Familiarity
Affiliation	Schachter	Stress
Intimate Relationship Attraction		
Liking/Loving Distinction	Rubin	Friends/committed lovers
Intimate Social Exchange	Rusbult	Degree of positive feeling
		Quality of alternatives
		Level of investment
Triangular Theory of Love	Sternberg	Intimacy, passion, commitment
Communication (Verbal)		
Elements	Klapper	Source
		Channel
		Audience
Source aspects		Credibility
		Attractiveness
		Power
Patterns	Bauer	Centralized: Y / chain / wheel
		Decentralized: Circle, star, all-channel
	Lewin/Lippitt/White	Autocratic/democratic
Group effects	Janis	Groupthink
Media effects	Klapper	Direct and indirect effects
		Two-step communication flow
		Media elite
		Third party

Concepts	Names	Terms
Communication (Nonverbal)		
Proxemics (territoriality)	Hall	Personal space
	Ardrey	
Kinesics (body language)	Birdwhistell	Micro
	Scheflen	Macro
	Ekman	Universal expressions
	Mehrabian	Liking
		Dominance
		Responsiveness
	Kendon	Sociological/Primal
	Goffman	
	Wilson	Sociobiological roots
Persuasion		
Advertising	Markin	Freudian vs. existential

Coercive techniques
  Brainwashing
  Interrogation
	Schein	Phases:
		  Physical/psychological
		  Structured environment and
		  intentional distortions

Groups		
Conformity (research eras)	Sherif	Autokinetic effect
	Asch	Line-judgment technique
	Crutchfield	Booth adaptation of Asch technique
	Milgram	Action (as distinct from signal) conformity, using a shock generator and implied harm to another person
Compliance-inducing techniques	McGuire	Inoculation theory
	Freedman	Foot-in-the-door
	Cialdini	Door-in-the-face
	Doob/McLaughlin	"Ask-and-You-Shall-Be-Given" (the tendency, if it's a worthy, charitable cause)
		Low-balling (sticking to one's commitment after the initially low stakes have been raised)
	Bryan/Test	Modeling positive behaviors for others
	Skinner	Incentives for performance of desired behaviors
		Primacy/recency
		Two-sided vs. one-sided communication
		Sleeper effect
Cooperation-competition	Sherif and Sherif	Superordinate goal
	Deutsch	Acme-Bolt trucking game
		Use of threat

Concepts	Names	Terms
Game decision theory (gaming)		"Prisoner's Dilemma"
		Payoff matrix
		Zero-sum and nonzero-sum
	Thibaut/Kelly	Fate and behavior control
	Tedeschi	Impression management
Risk-taking	Wallach/Kogan/Bem	
Theories of collective behavior	Smelser	
	Freud	
	LeBon	"The Crowd"
Violence		
Frustration-aggression hypothesis	Dollard/Miller	Displacement and "scapegoating"
Aggression-eliciting stimuli	Berkowitz	
Cognitive neoassociation analysis	Berkowitz	Thought/feeling interaction
Modeling	Bandura	
Arousal/Affect Model	Zillmann/Bryant	
Socialization	Wolfgang	
	Zimbardo	Deindividuation
Obedience	Milgram	Shock generator
Helping Behavior (Altruism)		
Determinants	Latane/Darley	Number of bystanders
	Bryan/Test	Model
	Piliavin	
	Allen	Directness of request
Egoistic/Altruistic Debate:		
Inherently Altruistic	Batson	Empathy a critical variable
Negative State	Cialdini	Makes us feel good
Relief Model		
Good Samaritan Model		Act is voluntary
		Act is potentially costly
		No anticipation of reward
Steps in intervention helping	Latane/Darley	Notice
		Interpret as a help-requiring situation
		Take personal responsibility
		Choose form of assistance
		Implement assistance

Concepts	Names	Terms
Concept of overload	Milgram	Adaptive responses: Less time to each input Disregard low-priority inputs Redraw boundaries Block entrance to system Filter Specialized institutions
Prejudice		
Theories	Allport	Historical
		Sociocultural
		Situational
		Psychodynamic
		Phenomenological
		Earned Reputation
Social Identity Theory	Tajfel/Turner	Enhance individual esteem through our group belonging
Basking in Reflected Glory	Cialdini	Basking in the successes and status of other group members "BIRGing"
Attitude/race dimensions	Rokeach	Attitude similarity prevails over race dissimilarity
Attitudes among children	Clark and Clark	Racial awareness
	Hraba and Grant	Racial self-identification
		Racial preference
		Racial prejudice
Personality		
Authoritarian personality	Adorno	
Dogmatism	Rokeach	The open and closed mind
Machiavellianism	Christie	
Dimensions	Rotter	Internal/external control
	McClelland	Achievement need (nAch)
	Kuhn	Self-concept
Person perception	Schlosberg/ Woodworth	Recognition of emotions
	Anderson	Additive/averaging model
Information Integration Theory	Anderson	Combination of perceiver disposition and weighted average of target person's characteristics
Perceptual defense	McGinnies	
	Bruner/Postman	
Status and Roles		
Class and class measurement	Brown	Subjective
		Reputational
		Objective (based on criteria)

Concepts	Names	Terms
Role conflict		Inter-role
		Intra-role
	Homans	Distributive justice
		Status congruence
	Bem and Bem	Androgeny
Attribution		
Definitional model	Lewin/Heider	Behavioral effect $(E) = f$ (Environment + Personal force)
Principle		The degree to which we attribute other people's behaviors to external circumstances or internal motivations
Specific attribution patterns	Jones/Davis	Nonnormative
	Steiner	Perceived freedom
	Jones/Shaver et al.	Ability
	Taynor/Deaux et al.	Sex-role
	Jones/Nisbett	Self vs. other
	Goffman/Hastorf et al.	Responsibility
	Walster	"Lennie B" experiments
	Lerner	Just-world hypothesis
Fundamental attribution Actor-observer effect		Assuming internal (motivational) causation for other people's behavior and external (situational) causation for one's own behavior
Learned helplessness	Seligman	Assuming that nothing one does can make any difference in a person's life (i.e., attributing total external causation)
Self-serving bias		"Halo"-type evaluation of one's own behavior and motives
Social cognition	Fiske/Taylor	People perceived as: naïve scientists, cognitive misers, motivated tacticians

GENERAL

History and Systems

SCHOOLS

STRUCTURALISM: *Wundt* founded the *first psychological laboratory* at Leipzig, Germany, in 1879 (a date as basic to psychology as Columbus and 1492 is to the United States). The structuralists studied the mind through *introspection* (in effect, being trained to observe your own conscious experience). *Titchener* was the major spokesperson for this school of psychology within the United States. The approach never really got a strong foothold in the United States because it *lacked objectivity*.

FUNCTIONALISM: Emphasized adaptation to one's environment (and the mind as an adaptive tool). Strongly influenced by the work of Darwin, its chief advocates were *Dewey* and *William James*. Critical of structuralism, it emphasized behavior and adjustment rather than isolated mental states.

BEHAVIORISM: A kind of "objective functionalism." Strongly influenced by the functionalist approach and the work of Pavlov, it insisted on objective observation—excluding conscious experience (the structuralism mainstay) as beyond the realm of appropriate study for scientific research. Its early advocate was *Watson*, and more recently, *Skinner* (each covered in more detail within the Personality review section).

GESTALT: A reaction to behaviorism (and its reduction of behavior to muscle-twitch elements), it emphasized studying the whole person. Its primary definitional "byline" is "The whole is greater than the sum of its parts." Its founder was *Wertheimer*. Kohler and Koffka also were key figures within this school.

PSYCHOANALYSIS: Begun with the clinical work of *Freud*, it was prevalent in Europe at the time functionalism was prevalent in the United States. It held the position that behavior was determined by unconscious motivations—many of them rooted in a child's early psychosexual development. (Further discussion of this school of thought is found within the earlier Personality review section.)

This book can provide meaningful reference in the history/systems area without heading you for five-volume detail: Kardas, E. P. *History of Psychology: The Making of a Science.* (San Francisco: Cengage, 2014).

Applied Psychology

Psychological concepts from all aspects of the field have their counterparts in practical settings, and throughout your daily experience you constantly encounter these applications. Signboards and cereal boxes utilize colors that will attract and hold attention in given intensities of light, speakers convey warmth and seek to influence opinions, newspaper ads strive to achieve the von Restorff (novel stimulus) effect, and movies appeal to motivations and emotions. Each of these methods is applied, and each is psychological. The specific intent of this applied psychology section, however, is to study industrial, human engineering, and organizational applications.

To gain a general perspective of this area, it may be helpful to concentrate briefly on each of these headings—*industrial psychology, human engineering*, and *organizational psychology*. They enable us to think of distinct concerns within the general framework of applied psychology, concerns that relate to one another like the threads of an intricate design in a woven fabric.

The term *industrial* implies production, and several aspects of this heading are product-related. Major considerations in this area include such questions as how to achieve both worker satisfaction and efficient production, how to match persons to the jobs for which they are best suited, and how to achieve high worker morale and motivation.

Human engineering relates more specifically to the work space of the individual worker. Here, some of the primary aspects can be expressed in such questions as whether the lighting, temperature, and noise levels are such that the worker can be effective. Additional concerns relate to promoting smooth work flow and eliminating bottlenecks in the production process. Within the work space of the individual employee, attention should be given to the location of equipment controls and to whether they are designed to promote both worker efficiency and safety. For obvious reasons, one work space that has been of prominent human engineering concern is the airplane cockpit. Here again, the problem is how to promote both maximal efficiency and safety.

Organizational psychology introduces concerns relating to the nature and effects of an organization's structure, communication patterns, processes in organizational decision making, and styles of leadership and leadership development. Whereas human engineering has a very specific focus upon work space, organizational psychology takes a broad-range perspective. As you proceed with this review, you will find elements from each of these headings interwoven within the context of applied psychology.

As we think of the organization and the worker, a natural emphasis at the outset is on analyzing jobs and their performance requirements and correspondingly selecting personnel whose aptitudes best match individual job descriptions. It is more than just a question of whether a person has, for instance, the finger dexterity needed to install screws quickly in automobile door handles; it is equally a question of whether the individual's personality and interests are compatible with the job and the work environment. The gardening or camping enthusiast may be discontent in a tiny office cubicle, and a basically shy radio performer may be personally unsuited for work in the television medium. In each instance, the emphasis is upon making the proper person-to-job match.

Such matching requires the use of personnel selection techniques that can produce the aptitude, personality, interest, and achievement information necessary for appropriate assessment and decision making. The required test "arsenals" are large and, in many cases, specific to the requirements of a given work setting, but among them are familiar names from your review of cognition and complex human learning. Several of the aptitude tests are prefaced with the words Purdue or Minnesota, prominent test contributors in this area. Personality tests include the Bernreuter and MMPI, and interest tests include the Strong-Campbell and the Kuder. Achievement tests range from a written test for factual knowledge to a performance test on a job-related task. Each instrument carries its unique function within the personnel selection process.

Once hired, the worker will continue to be evaluated, and the hiring organization must devise equitable, effective methods for appraising job performance. Such appraisals take on critical importance in areas such as wages and salaries, promotions, on-the-job training, and so forth. Likert-type checklist rating techniques and interview methods are among the procedures frequently employed in such appraisals. It is critical that appraisal procedures be sufficiently controlled to prevent a final evaluation based largely on the opinions of a single individual. It is equally critical to control for such elements as "halo" effect (the rater's tendency to give a totally positive evaluation to a person whom he or she likes) and constant error (the rater's general tendency toward leniency or harshness in evaluation procedures). It becomes obvious that, in order to be both effective and equitable, the components of an overall appraisal procedure must be skillfully designed and carefully implemented.

Beyond the person-centered aspects of selecting the appropriate individual and evaluating him equitably, there are major concerns relating to worker environment. In the specific work setting, these can be the human engineering questions of how to arrange equipment, knobs, lights, and traffic patterns to promote the least amount of lost motion and the most efficient worker performance. At the broader, organizational level, the question expands to that of the industry's general view of its workers.

The *industrial view toward workers* has never been a singular one that could be isolated in time and labeled unanimously scientific or consistently humanistic. Nevertheless, general climates have been evident during specific time periods in our nation's industrial history. The earliest climate, characteristic of the first quarter of the twentieth century, was one of scientific management. Within it, the emphasis was placed on production. Its principal advocates believed that work in general, and specific jobs in particular, should be defined clearly to the worker and that, given a knowledge of expectations and a product-designed work setting, reinforcements and punishments should be arranged in a manner designed to obtain highest output per worker input. This method sounds impersonal, and it is. Production emphasis, giving its attention to time-and-motion studies and piecework incentives, makes no provision for viewing the worker as a unique individual. In the purest sense, scientific management involves viewing the worker as part of the production machine.

The *human relations approach* emerged from the now classic "*Hawthorne effect*." While studying ways to improve lighting and production-oriented features of a specific work setting, management at the Hawthorne Plant of the Western Electric Company discovered that productivity was increasing in the absence of any changes in work setting. The only viable explanation for this phenomenon was the attention being given to the workers themselves, and the results provided convincing support for the view that one can increase productivity by increasing worker satisfaction. Workers were being viewed on an individual basis, and the philosophy that a satisfied worker is a productive worker gained a foothold. In some industries, counseling psychologists were hired with responsibilities for helping workers solve personal problems. Techniques were devised for making workers feel that they were participants in decision-making processes. Plant newspapers, suggestion boxes, and corporate sharing were among the changes that emerged. Industry was acknowledging the worker as a human being with feelings and needs.

Both the human relations and the scientific management approaches are currently found on the industrial scene. Also frequently used in evaluating specific organizations is the *Blake-Mouton Grid*, based on the premise that an efficient organization demonstrates strong and equal levels of concern for people and for production. This measure and several other current approaches within industry reflect an attitude to the worker environment that is both human- and production-oriented.

The human relations approach has prompted numerous psychological studies of worker satisfaction. *Katz and Kahn* have applied the level-of-involvement model and suggest that certain jobs are inherently more satisfying than others because of the degree of worker involvement characterizing them. Utilizing *Kelman*'s categories, they point to the job of guard as an example of minimal involvement in one's work. They see it as a compliance-type position that calls upon the person simply to "be there." Individuality, sense of personal worth, and involvement are lacking in the job itself. At the other end of the involvement spectrum, the manager and the creative worker have built-in opportunities to internalize their work. This means that their values and goals can be very much in keeping with the goals and objectives characterizing their work positions. Within their work responsibilities, they have a sense of personal input. One of the major challenges for management has been to take jobs such as that of guard and bring a sense of personal involvement to them. To define the situation from a slightly different perspective, *Maslow* suggested that the more a work position engages a person's potentials, the deeper the satisfaction it provides. A kind of team approach has been used successfully in several industries to enhance the worker's sense of involvement. In coal mining, the perfection of conveyor systems destroyed team feeling and interaction among workers. It was a case where implementation of an obviously more efficient scientific method led to increased absenteeism and lower production. By contrast, miners working in teams felt a sense of responsibility to those teams, could identify with team goals, and received team support for their individual contributions.

A similar kind of distinction within industry has been made between the process and product models for workers. In the *process model,* the emphasis is "plugging in" the worker to an ongoing industrial process. The *product model* seeks to identify the worker with the final product. To accomplish such identification, an organization may take assembly-line workers and rotate them among different points in the assembly process. This rotation allows the individual worker to be involved with the product at different stages of completion, enhancing the possibility of his identification with the end product toward which work is being directed.

Communication patterns and leadership styles profoundly affect the working climate and consequent satisfaction that a worker experiences. A communication pattern can promote either autocratic or democratic feeling throughout the work force and can do much to establish positions of power within the communication process. Consider briefly the following patterns of communication.

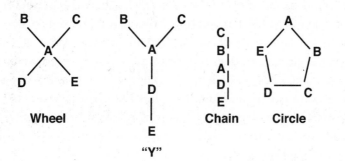

The wheel, "Y," and chain are centralized communication networks. They share the advantages of facilitating efficient performance of routine tasks, strengthening positions of leadership, and allowing for quick formation of stable patterns of interaction among group members. The most central position within each of these patterns is A, and the person occupying this position has built-in power, potential leadership, and the greatest likelihood of experiencing satisfaction. Peripheral positions such as C and E can be expected to experience the least satisfaction.

The circle is an example of a decentralized communication network. All positions have equal communication access. Although the decentralized network is less efficient than the centralized patterns, participants in such a circle-type pattern register much stronger feelings of satisfaction and seem better prepared to handle nonroutine, unpredictable situations than participants in the other patterns. One can readily see the variables in worker climate that can develop through communication network patterns.

In a specific communication setting—the interaction process of groups involved in decision making—*Bales* established analytical categories that have attained wide use and acceptance. His twelve categories are grouped in the following four areas:

(A) Positive reactions—Shows solidarity, shows tension release, shows agreement
(B) Problem-solving attempts—Gives suggestions, gives opinions, gives orientation
(C) Questions—Asks orientation, asks opinions, asks suggestions
(D) Negative reactions—Shows disagreement, shows tension increase, shows antagonism

Areas B and C are used to determine a group member's task orientation, and areas A and D are indicative of the member's sociability. Analysis centers upon the frequency of a person's interaction within each of the categories.

To point out another facet of the communication process operating within decision-making groups, *Janis* advanced the concept of *groupthink*. He believes that the highly cohesive group can foster a number of illusions among its membership. In discussing his illusion of invulnerability, Janis expresses the view that the group may decide to take risks that its members individually would not be willing to take. The illusion of morality involves the group's tendency to consider any actions that it may take as being moral. An illusion of unanimity indicates that although the group may appear to have made a unanimous decision, individual members may have censored themselves and silenced their dissent. Other factors in groupthink include shared stereotypes, rationalization, self-censorship, direct pressure, and mindguards. The cohesive group shares the benefits of high morale, but Janis points out the pitfalls that may affect such groups in their decision making.

Beyond personnel selection and the environmental factors of job satisfaction and involvement, human engineering also deals with the specific work setting and the analysis of environmental factors as they relate to worker efficiency. Such analysis deals with factors involving illumination, air flow, temperature, humidity, noise, music, number of hours in the work day, and rest periods. In addition, "human engineers" look at equipment design. In this regard, worker errors and their frequency are studied for insights that might lead to more efficient equipment design. Making dials easily readable and knobs easily accessible and distinguishable are part of the human engineering goal. As you board an airplane for some distant destination, you begin to take a strong personal interest in how well the human engineer has done his job. Efficiency in cockpit control-panel design is among the major concerns of human engineering.

Because industry cannot function without the consumers, marketing is of special corporate interest. Though some industries are meeting an already existing consumer need, other corporations must create a need among potential consumers. In either case, the marketing process must involve careful attention to consumers' attitudes, motivations, and perceptions. Instruments such as attitude surveys, questionnaires, and interviews assist the corporation in tapping consumer opinion. The relationship between sales and specific marketing techniques is carefully studied, and distinct changes in approach are made in response to generally negative attitudes from consumers and/or disappointing sales for a given product. Although marketing may seek to shape consumer behavior, it is also obvious that consumer response can shape an industry's product directions.

From the moment that you begin looking for a job, applied psychology is all around you. Personnel selection, general worker climate, specific work setting, and product sales combine to form a complex picture of which the following are among the central names and concepts:

Applied Psychology Outline

Concepts	Names	Terms
Industrial		
Production emphasis	Taylor	Scientific management
Time-and-motion		Minimize both time and motion to maximize efficiency
Piecework		Pay on the basis of number of pieces completed, setting target thresholds to be met
Process model		Focus on the process (e.g., the assembly line) rather than worker identity with product
Personnel selection		
Job analysis		Identifying job requirements
Recruitment		Methods for obtaining people to fill job requirements

Interviews
  Structured
  Situational
		Poor predictor of individual's job performance

		Prescribed set of questions
		Hypothetical work situations
Testing Assessment centers		Knowledge and skills required for a particular job
	AT&T-initiated in 1950s (Generally independent, noncompany-related facilities)	Evaluate a small number of candidates over a series of days, placing them in stressful situations, giving them a challenging "in-basket," and so on
Organizational		
Human relations approach		
Hawthorne Effect	Western Electric, 1929–32 (Mayo's research interpretation that fostered the human relations movement)	Importance of treating workers as unique and important individuals
Blake-Mouton Grid	Blake-Mouton	On a nine-point grid (vertical and horizontal axis), it evaluates the degree to which a company emphasizes process (production orientation) and human relations (worker concern)

Concepts	Names	Terms
Theories		
Need-achievement	McClelland/ Atkinson	High need to achieve (n Ach) associated with executive success
Needs-hierarchy	Maslow	The importance of attending to workers' physiological, safety, belongingness and love, esteem, and self-actualization needs
ERG	Alderfer	Relates three of Maslow's needs (existence, relatedness, and growth) to the workplace
Motivator-hygiene	Herzberg	Suggests that only meeting higher-order needs (Maslow's self-actualization) can attain worker satisfaction
Job-characteristics	Hackman/Oldham	Relates job characteristics and the individual worker's need for growth with resulting job satisfaction
Expectancy	Vroom	Reward-expectancy governs the choices and behaviors of workers in the workplace.
	Lawler-Porter Modification	Motivation, ability, and role perceptions govern worker performance
Goal-setting	Locke	Clarity and participation in goal-setting is basic to worker success and satisfaction in the workplace
Equity	Adams	Worker comparison of inputs and outcomes with those of other workers for judgment of fairness
Work-group Distinctions		
Formal		Hierarchy chart of company
Informal		Friendship and common interest groups
Work norms		Generally established within the informal work groups
Leadership		
Research eras		
Trait	Aristotle	Leaders are born with leadership traits
Leader-behavior	Hemphill (later Komaki, Lord & Maher)	Importance of studying leader-behaviors for clues to effective leadership—two basic dimensions: Initiating structure Consideration
Interaction	Fiedler (Fiedler and Garcia elaboration is termed cognitive-resource utilization theory)	Contingency Model—matching task-centered and person-centered leaders to the appropriate leadership settings (believes the match, not birth-given traits, is the key to leadership success)

Concepts	Names	Terms
Types		
Authoritarian		Leader-dominated
Democratic		Participatory
Transactional		Provide worker support to help achieve job satisfaction
Transformational		Motivate through charisma and vision to goals beyond worker expectation
Assessment	Bass & Avolio	Multifactor leadership questionnaire (MLQ)
Modes of attainment		
Appointed		From outside the group
Emergent		From within the group
Communication patterns		
Centralized		Wheel, Y, chain
Decentralized		Circle, all-channel
Group interaction process		
Categories	Bales	Positive reactions, problem-solving, questions, negative-reactions
Groupthink	Janis	Self-defeating process characteristic of cohesive groups; characterized by: Illusion of invulnerability Illusion of morality Illusion of unanimity Self-censorship Mindguards Shared stereotypes Rationalization Direct pressure
Human Factors		
Efficiency		
Ergonomics	From Greek "ergon" (work) and "nomos" (natural laws)	Matching displays and controls to natural human physiology
Applications		
Traffic safety		
Environmental	McGinnis	Brake-light position (centered and high-mounted)
Personal	Laux & Brelsford	The driving needs of an increasingly aging population
Behavioral	Ludwig & Geller	Seat belt use

Concepts	Names	Terms
Information displays		Lights vs. meters and multi-sensory (e.g., visual + audio)
Controls		Shape-coded knobs for use in aircraft cockpits; for example, standardizing the functional outcomes of a given knob, pedal, or wheel movement
Human-computer		Facilitating operator learning and minimizing stress and strain related with video display terminals (VDTs)
Space exploration		Extra-vehicular activity (EVA), its unique problems and challenges
Environmental		
Definition		Studying the impact of specific environments on behavior
Applications		
Urban density		The effects of crowding on mental health, crime, families, etc.
Noise		Effects on health and functioning, and distinctions between the effects of short-term and long-term noise exposure
School		
Roles		
Assessment		Both academic and personality
Intervention		To improve the learning environment and the experience of individual students within it
Program evaluation		Through teamwork and consultation with parents and community professionals

The preceding list is but a sampling. Beyond it, the *Journal of Applied Psychology* can give you the topically diverse flavor of the field. To review in a more systematic fashion, the following book might be helpful:

Aamodt, M. G. *Industrial/Organizational Psychology: An Applied Approach*, 7th ed. (San Francisco: Cengage, 2013).

As in the other areas of your review, you cannot expect to gain Ph.D.-level mastery of applied psychology, but acquaintance and familiarity with its primary aspects will be important to you. The field is a rapidly growing one.

MEASUREMENT AND METHODOLOGY

Because psychology is a social science, investigators in all aspects of the discipline adopt the scientific approach to new information. The scientific method is, in effect, an objective way of observing, describing, and classifying. It is quantitative, and quantitative classification must work with objectively measurable characteristics involving "more than" and "less than" relationships. Qualitative classification, on the other hand, involves simply categorizing on the basis of a specific characteristic, e.g., hair color. To gain some understanding of the distinctions, a brief look at the words *nominal, ordinal, interval*, and *ratio* can prove helpful.

Numbers used in *nominal* ways are, in effect, labels. The number on your house or apartment falls into this category. The fact that your house number is 1054 and someone else's is 1020 does not mean that your house is bigger than the other person's. The numbers simply serve a labeling, categorizing function. *Ordinal* use of numbers involves rank ordering. Judges at the county fair use numbers in this manner. A given ordinal number can indicate more of a quality than another number, but it does not indicate that the distance between first and second, for instance, is equivalent to the distance between second and third. Ordinal is rank ordering of some characteristic and does not go beyond that ordering to any suggestion of equal intervals between. The latter suggestion is reserved for the *interval* aspect of quantitative number usage. Such intervals are judged to be equal. An applied example of this type of usage involves temperature. The difference between 90 and 100 degrees Fahrenheit is considered equivalent to the difference between 70 and 80 degrees Fahrenheit. Though these differences may not seem equivalent when you are trying to find relief from the hot sun, in thermometer and interval terms they are. A psychological example that approximates interval measurement is the intelligence test. Though currently embroiled in controversy, these tests were developed on the premise that intervals were equivalent—that 15 IQ points at one point on the scale were equivalent to 15 IQ points at another point on the scale. This kind of testing provides one of psychology's strongest bids for interval use of numbers. The final type of numerical quantity, *ratio*, presumes an absolute zero point. When you have been able to establish an absolute zero, you have reached a point where you can make statements such as "twice as much as" or "three times as much as." Psychologists are certainly not yet prepared to suggest that a person having a 150 IQ is twice as intelligent as a person having a 75 IQ. This type of number usage is possible in natural science, but social scientists have not yet discovered an absolute zero and must concentrate their number usage in the ordinal and interval areas.

To maintain objectivity, the scientific method adopts an established set of procedures to be followed in the testing of hypotheses. Suppose, for instance, that you had made general observations that seemed to link the eating of carrots with reading speed. To determine whether these observations had any scientific validity, you would need to develop an hypothesis to be tested. You would be hypothesizing that carrot eating affects reading speed. As you translate this hypothesis into formally established testing procedures, this is what you would have:

Step 1: Set Up the Null Hypothesis

Null hypothesis means "no difference." Your null hypothesis would be that reading speed is not affected one way or the other by carrot eating. Actually, you believe that carrot eating has an effect on reading speed, so this hypothesis is one that you hope to disprove later in the procedure. You are hoping that the difference you find will be sufficiently great that you can disprove (reject) the null hypothesis expressed here. Note, however, that rejecting the null hypothesis does not mean you prove that carrot eating affects reading speed. A research hypothesis is never proven, per se.

Step 2: Collect the Data Sample

(A) SET UP THE EXPERIMENTAL AND CONTROL GROUPS.

Through careful thought and planning, you will need to develop your experimental design. At this point, you must familiarize yourself with such terms as *independent variable* and *dependent variable*, and learn their specific translation within your experimental situation. In this instance, the independent variable will be carrots—the stimulus element that is placed in the experimental situation to see whether it makes a difference in reading speed. The dependent variable will be reading speed—the response obtained in relation to the stimulus element introduced. To compare the responses of your experimental and control groups, you should administer carrots to the experimental group, no carrots to the control group. Because the control group will not be receiving the independent variable, this group will enable you to determine later to what extent an observed response change was a function of the carrot eating (independent variable) within the experimental group. Obviously, it is important to keep all other potential variables between the two groups the same. For example, you may want to use only girls (or boys) to remove the possibility of performance differences resulting from sex differences. The reading material that you select must be equivalent for the two groups, and you must be certain that there has been no previous familiarity with this material. It will be essential to measure the reading speeds of all subjects *before* you institute the independent variable in order to get an accurate measure of any changes in reading speed after the experimental group has gobbled its carrots. And it will be important to be sure that each person consumes the same amount of carrots. In addition, situational variables must be controlled—lighting must be equivalent for all subjects, and so on. Having proceeded with care in subject selection and control of potential variables, you can move into the second aspect of data collection.

(B) DECIDE ON A STATISTICAL PROCEDURE AND COLLECT DATA IN A FORM COMPATIBLE WITH THAT PROCEDURE.

One of the most deplorable and traumatic scenes that any statistician can relate involves the sight of someone on the doorstep who has collected a batch of data and now wants to know what he can do with it statistically. Such decisions must be made *before* the data is collected. The GRE will assume that you are very familiar with the range of statistical procedures and the experimental situations in which each should be utilized. But before you can get acquainted with the specific statistical procedures, you need a thorough understanding of the foundations upon which they are built. Therefore, take a brief look at some of the basic terms and concepts as presented below; we will also suggest books to which you can refer for additional review.

Distinction Between Descriptive and Sampling Statistics

The *descriptive-statistics* approach requires a person to specify a given population of interest and then collect measurements from *all* the members of that population. You can begin to imagine the difficulty of accomplishing this kind of measurement collection when you think of a population such as Democrats, Republicans, or Independents! The more typical situation would involve having measurement access to a smaller group selected from the larger population of interest. This smaller group is known as a sample, and the statistics used in analyzing data collected from the smaller group are known as *sampling statistics*. Analyzing the data from the sample—assuming that a sample that is representative of the population has been obtained—you can then make generalizations from the sample to the population.

Statistical Inference and the Concept of Random Sample

Statistical inference refers to sampling statistics and the process through which inference is made to whole populations through sampling procedures. Such inference requires careful attention to the concept of randomness in sampling. *Randomness* means that in selecting a sample each member of the specific population has an equal chance of being selected—that no weight or preference will enhance selection chances for some members and weaken those chances for others. As mentioned in the section on social psychology, public opinion polling relies heavily on the concept of random sampling.

Parameter-Statistic Distinction

Values obtained from populations are called *parameter*s, and values obtained from samples are called *statistics*. Parametric tests (statistical procedures) are based on the assumption that the population from which a sample has been drawn is a normal distribution. Correspondingly, nonparametric tests are not dependent upon this normal distribution assumption. Most of the statistical procedures with which you will become familiar are parametric. Among the few nonparametric procedures you will need to know is the chi-square test.

Central Tendency

In any distribution, it becomes necessary to measure central tendency. Three methods of measuring are available—mean, median, and mode. Most statistical procedures rely upon the *mean* (an average of the scores in the sample). The *median* constitutes a midpoint of the sample scores, and the *mode* is the most frequently occurring score. Use of mean can lead to problems in distributions where there are a few extremely divergent scores. Because it is an average, it tends to be prominently influenced by these extreme scores. In such instances, the median as the midpoint score (half the scores greater than, half smaller than) makes a more appropriate measure of central tendency.

You might ask what happens to the mean of a distribution when a fixed number is added to each score in that distribution. The answer is that the mean value is increased by this fixed number. In similar fashion, if each score in a distribution were to be multiplied by a fixed number, the resulting mean would be the original mean multiplied by this fixed number. Division would have a similar effect. In summary, the same effect that has occurred with the individual scores in the distribution also occurs with the mean.

Variability

Variability refers to the relationship among all the scores in a distribution. Are they clustered closely around the mean, or are they widely scattered? The terms *variance* and *standard deviation* are measures of this variability. The *standard deviation* is, in effect, the positive square root of the variance. Interpretively, if you were comparing two standard deviations (one being 3.7 and the second being 1.2), you would know that the scores in the second distribution are generally closer to the mean and less scattered than the scores in the first distribution.

If you increase or decrease each term in a distribution by a fixed amount, the variance and standard deviation remain unchanged. In effect, you have not changed the "scatter" of the distribution around the mean. If each term in a distribution is multiplied by a constant, the original standard deviation would be affected in the same manner as every other score in the distribution (the resulting standard deviation being the original standard deviation times the constant).

Because a standard deviation squared would be its corresponding variance, the effect upon variance of multiplying each score in a distribution by a constant would be that of multiplying the original variance by the square of that constant. For example, if each score in a distribution were multiplied by 2 and the original variance had been 6, the resulting variance would be 24. Squaring the constant makes it 4, and 4 times 6 equals 24. In cases of division by a constant, division by the square of the constant would yield the resulting variance.

Z-Scores

Imagine that Distribution 1 has a mean of 40 and a standard deviation of 2.5, while Distribution 2 has a mean of 40 and a standard deviation of 2.0. Now, if someone were to ask how a score of 45 in Distribution 1 would compare with a score of 46 in Distribution 2, a quick score comparison would be difficult to make, to say the least. The computation of z-scores is a way of translating these different standard deviations and different means into a common language that facilitates comparison. Computed as score minus the mean divided by the standard deviation, the z-score makes score comparisons quite simple. In the above example, for Distribution 1 a score of 45 minus 40 = 5. This 5 divided by the standard deviation of 2.5 produces a z-score of +2. In Distribution 2, 46 minus 40 = 6. This 6 divided by 2 produces a z-score of +3.0. Therefore, through the use of the z-score translation, it becomes easy to see that the score of 46 in Distribution 2 is significantly better than a score of 45 in Distribution 1. Note that the z-score in these instances was preceded by a plus sign. If the score had been below the mean, it would have been preceded by a minus sign.

Central tendency, variability, and z-scores are intricately related to the concept of a normal distribution. Because the z-score is based on the assumption of a normal distribution, it is possible to speak in terms of probabilities. In a normal distribution (which you can find outlined in table form in any basic statistics text), approximately 34 percent of the scores occur between the mean and a z-score of +1 (one standard deviation above the mean). Approximately 14 percent more occur between z-scores of +1 and +2 (between one and two standard deviations above the mean), and approximately 2 percent of the scores in the distribution occur beyond a z-score of +2. So, if we refer to Distribution 1 momentarily and ask what the probability is of a score of between 42.5 and 45, we can immediately state that probability as 14 percent. Because a normal distribution is symmetrical, exact percentages hold for scores occurring below the mean. For example, the probability of a score between 35 and 37.5 in Distribution 1 would be 14 percent. Part of the data you will receive regarding your GRE performance will involve your percentile rank. That rank will indicate the percentage of test takers scoring either the same as or below you—a computation strikingly similar to the ones made above.

Probability Type I and Type II Error

You have ten balls in your backpack. Five are red, three are green, two are yellow. Your backpack is specially designed with a ball dispenser (sure it is!), and when you shake the backpack, only one ball can come through the dispenser at a time. Since half of the entire group is red, the probability of a red ball coming through is .5; of a green ball, .3; and of a yellow ball, .2. Assuming you return all the balls to the backpack each time before dispensing, these probabilities will continue unchanged. The normal distribution discussed earlier is a bit like the colored balls. They're just stacked up in a very normal, symmetrical way. The probability of a ball being within one standard deviation of the mean is .68 (.34 on each side of the mean); between one and two standard deviations of the mean, .28 (.14 on each side of the mean); beyond two standard deviations from the mean, .04 (.02 on each side of the mean). When scientists set a significance level (as you will in Step 4 upcoming), they ask themselves, "What is the chance probability of mistakenly rejecting a null hypothesis? (Type I error) or mistakenly accepting a null hypothesis? (Type II error)." The scientists set their significance level based on the risk they're willing to take of making an erroneous rejection (Type I error) or acceptance (Type II error). We did a bit of repetition on these because they're all-too-easy to get reversed or mixed up. Do you have "RA's" (Residence [Hall] Advisers) at your institution? Just think of this as RA's—first comes the R (Type I and erroneously rejecting a null), second comes A (Type II and erroneously accepting a null). Yeah, we've repeated ourselves enough. You're ready to head on.

Percentile Rank

Got a spare piece of paper? Put it over one of those beautiful bell-shaped curves we just talked about. Now slowly move the paper to the right, little-by-little exposing the left side of the curve. What you're doing relates directly to percentile ranks. Percentiles begin at the far left side of the distribution—a zero assumed at the far left. As your paper moves farther and farther to the right, the percentile rank steadily increases. When you get to the midpoint (mean, median, and mode of this normal distribution) you have reached the 50th percentile. If your score came at the 50th percentile it would mean 50 percent of all those who took the test scored equal to or below you. As you continue to move your paper farther to the right you'll reach 60th, 70th, 80th, and 90th percentiles. Just for fun, let's move the paper just a tad farther—to the 95th percentile. This means 95 percent of all those who took the test scored equal to you or below you. And you can be very, very sure there weren't many equal to you. Has a nice ring to it, doesn't it!

At this point, you can see the intricate relationships among the concepts of central tendency, variability, z-score, normal distribution, probability, and percentiles. As you seek for more depth within one of the introductory statistics books, we suggest that you attempt to gain a basic understanding of the following concepts and terms:

Methodology Outline

Concepts	Terms
Uses of numbers	Nominal—to label
	Ordinal—to rank
	Interval—to express consistent interval values at different points in a distribution (e.g., the difference between 15 and 20 degrees Fahrenheit equivalent to the difference between 85 and 90 degrees Fahrenheit)
	Ratio—premised on an absolute zero, it can express "twice as much," "three times as much," (e.g., weight, height)
Central tendency measures (in both grouped and nongrouped data)	Mean—the average score
	Median—the midpoint score (half the distribution scores are higher than, half are lower than)
	Mode—the most frequently occurring score in a distribution
Parameter and statistic	Parameter—a descriptive measure of the population
	Statistic—a descriptive measure of a sample
Binomial distribution	Values in this distribution are either 0 or 1.
Independent and dependent variable	Independent—Experimenter puts this variable into the design within the "experimental group" (as distinct from the control group)
	Dependent—Subject response (and a comparison of differences in response between subjects in the experimental and control groups)
	For example: The Effect of Carrot-Eating on Reading Speed—Carrot-Eating = the independent variable, Reading Speed = the dependent variable. Only the experimental group will eat carrots.
Inferential statistics	Inferring characteristics of a population from a sample of data
Variability	Standard deviation—a measure of difference from the mean of a distribution (if high, it's a widely scattered distribution; if low, it's bunched closely around the mean);
	Variance—another statistical expression of difference from the mean (it's the standard deviation squared)
Frequency distribution	The "scatter-pattern" of scores

Frequency polygon and histogram	Distinction:
	    Polygon = Lines connecting points on the graph
	    Histogram = Bar graph representing score intervals

Methods of data grouping	Frequency (characteristic of the polygon)
	Interval (characteristic of the histogram)

Concept of a normal distribution	Proportions of distribution scores occurring within 1, 2, and 3 standard deviations of the mean:
	    Within 1 = 68
	    Within 2 = 96 (28 between 1 and 2 s.d.'s)
	    Within 3 = virtually all scores (4 between 2 and 3 s.d.'s)

Concepts	Terms
Concept of positive and negative skew and its effect upon location of mean, median, and mode	Negative skew = scores bunched at the right and tail off (or skew) to the left
	Positive skew = scores bunched at the left and tail off (or skew) to the right

	"Cardinal Rule"—The mean moves in the direction of the skew
	    Central tendency sequential occurrence in a negatively skewed distribution is mean, median, mode
	    Central tendency sequential occurrence in a positively skewed distribution is mode, median, mean

Percentile rank	Zero at the left side of a normal distribution, gradually increasing as one moves to the right.
Probability in relation to the normal distribution	The likelihood of a given score occurring.
Concept of risk in decision making and the distinction between Type I and Type II error	Type I Error: Mistakenly rejecting a null hypothesis
	Type II Error: Mistakenly accepting a null hypothesis
Concept of significance level as it relates to probability and types of errors	Typically set at .05 (in effect, risking that five times in 100, I'll make a Type I or Type II error)
	More stringent = .01 level (risking only one time in 100)
Difference between one-tailed and two-tailed tests	One-tailed puts the entire significance level on a designated side of the distribution
	Two-tailed evenly divides it on both sides of the distribution (e.g., if .05 level, .025 of it will be on the left, .025 will be on the right)
Degrees of freedom	The number of frequencies free to vary for any given n (e.g., if there are three brands of soda being tested with a chi square design, the df = 2 [n − 1]).
Confidence interval and confidence limits	Estimating a population mean on the basis of our sample mean, for example, and stating our level of confidence that the population mean falls within our estimate
Correlation	A co-relation between two sets of variables. If they vary in direct relation to each other, (e.g., a high score in one set is a high score in the other, a low score in one set is a low score in the other) it is a positive correlation. If they vary inversely (e.g., a low score in one set is a high score in the other, a high score in one set is a low score in the other), it is a negative correlation. Correlation range is −1.0 to +1.0 (Note: When you get a correlation of +1.5, check your calculations!)
Regression	Line drawn among a group of correlation-distribution points to represent a trend (e.g., how much Y varies when X varies by one unit).

Don't get too bogged down in concepts like degrees of freedom. You'll be in the field for several years and will still be fascinated by that concept!

With this basic statistical background, you are now ready to consider different statistical procedures and the situations in which they are utilized. Among the most prominent testing procedures are the *t*-tests for (1) the difference between sample and population means, (2) two independent means, and (3) related measures.

A typical example of the *first* instance (difference between sample and population means) would be a situation in which the researcher knows a national average for the dimensions being measured (e.g., average weight of twelve-year-olds) and now must determine whether the weight of twelve-year-olds in the sample is significantly different from the population mean (the national average).

To demonstrate the *second* instance (two independent means), suppose that a researcher wants to determine whether there is a significant difference between the IQ scores of twelve-year-old boys and those of twelve-year-old girls in a given school. The scores of the boys and those of the girls have been obtained independently and, in effect, the comparison is between two sample means. This kind of setting—a comparison of two independent means—is perhaps the most common and most often used *t*-test procedure.

In the *third* procedure (related measures) there is a relationship between the measures being obtained. For example, one might take the above group of twelve-year-old boys and give them an IQ test just before instituting an intensive educational program and then administer the IQ test again at the conclusion of the program. The *t*-test would be comparing two sets of measures obtained on the same people (before and after an experimental procedure was introduced) to determine whether significant change had occurred in their IQ scores. In addition to using this procedure to test the same people twice, it is possible to use it to compare the performances of matched groups. In such groups each member of Group 1 has been matched with a specific member of Group 2 in the critical dimensions (age, sex, background, and so on). On the rare occasions when developmental psychologists have been able to assemble a large group of identical twins, it has been the norm to assign identical twin A to Group 1, identical twin B to Group 2. By following a similar procedure for each set of identical twins, the researchers could be sure of matched groups since, for each person in Group 1, there was a person in Group 2 with identical hereditary background. The researchers could now institute an experimental procedure with one of the groups and test each group at the conclusion of the procedure to determine how much performance change was a function of the experimental procedure. Such comparisons could utilize the *t*-test for related measures.

Correlation

By its name, correlation suggests a co-relation. It is used to determine whether there is any systematic relationship between two sets of measurements or observations. The correlation coefficient used to describe such a relationship is expressed in a range from +1 to −1. A zero would indicate no relationship, a +1.0 would indicate a perfect positive relationship, a −1.0 would indicate a perfect negative relationship, and a + or −1.1 or above would indicate that a computational error had been made! Correlation coefficients never exceed 1.0. It is important to realize that the degree of correlation is expressed by the number itself and not by its sign. For example, between the numbers +0.5 and −0.7 the greatest degree of correlation is expressed by −0.7. The sign merely indicates in what direction the relationship exists, and direction will become better understood as we consider the following situation.

Spearman Rank-Order Correlation

Suppose that two judges were ranking the entries in a dog show. To simplify the outcome, imagine that the rankings looked like this:

Rankings		
Dog	Judge 1	Judge 2
A	1	5
B	2	4
C	3	3
D	4	2
E	5	1

By comparatively scanning the above rankings, one can see that the dog ranked highest by Judge 1 was ranked lowest by Judge 2, that the dog ranked next highest by Judge 1 was ranked next lowest by Judge 2, and so forth. There is definitely a systematic relationship in a negative direction. Spearman's rho formula yields a correlation coefficient of −1.0. If the rankings in Judge 2's column had been reversed (1 for dog A, 2 for dog B, and so on), there would have been a perfect positive relationship between the judges' rankings, and the resulting Spearman rho coefficient would have been +1.0. Obviously, most judges are not likely either to agree or disagree this perfectly, so correlation coefficients generally are less than 1.0.

Pearson Product-Moment Correlation

This correlation procedure applies in situations where the researcher wants to determine whether there is a relationship between two groups of paired numbers. Pairing generally means that two scores exist for the same person; thus, in a typical situation utilizing this procedure, you would expect to have two sets of scores for each of several individuals and would now want to determine whether the scores were in any way related. To illustrate, imagine that you have just obtained IQ scores and foreign-language proficiency scores for a group of college sophomores. The question now arises of whether there is any relationship between intelligence and foreign-language proficiency. To answer the question, you conduct a Pearson Product-Moment Correlation on the two sets of scores. If the resulting correlation is in the +0.6 range or above, there would appear to be a high degree of relationship between these two factors. You can begin to see how many factors and aspects of personal and social life can be examined with this method. For instance, correlations have been made between high school and college performance levels, and obviously correlations have been made between performance on the GRE and success in the graduate program.

Correlation does not mean causation. It means that a systematic relationship has been found between two factors. When government and foundation sources discovered a correlation between cigarette smoking and incidence of lung cancer, cigarette industry spokesmen were quick to remind the researchers that they had only found a relationship and could not suggest causation.

If you think for a moment, you probably will realize that this correlation involves the same basic setting described for the use of the *t*-test for related measures. The difference is that in the case of the *t*-test you are comparing the same measure (taken at two different times or in matched groups) and are looking for a significant difference instead of for a systematic relationship.

Point-Biserial Correlation

If, in the above-described correlation setting, one of the scores you obtained was dichotomous, you would need a Point-Biserial Correlation to conduct the correlation. *Dichotomous suggests "either-or"* in contrast to a score continuum. If you compare IQ scores with whether a person obtains an above-B or below-B grade-point average in college, the latter situation is dichotomous. In tabling that dichotomous situation for purposes of the correlation, you might want to represent the above-B performances by the number 1 and the below-B by 0. The IQ scores can occur in a large, continuous range, and therefore your comparison would contain one continuous and one dichotomous measure for each person. Otherwise, the basic format would resemble the one that you would establish for the Pearson Product-Moment Correlation.

Chi-square

In discussing the nonparametric area of statistics, we mentioned that chi-square was one of the most prominent methods. Chi-square seeks to determine whether two variables are independent in a population from which a sample has been obtained. Chi-square deals with variables that are discrete categories rather than continuous measurements. For example, this statistic might be used to determine whether the variables of political party registration and sex are related. In the simplest chi-square settings, you would be working with two categories for each of the dimensions (in this instance, female-male and Democrat-Republican). The question is whether sex and political party affiliation are related in the population from which the sample was drawn. Because there are two discrete categories on each of the two variables, the resulting table resembles a square, four-paned window. In the procedure itself, you will obtain a value known as a phi coefficient (similar to a correlation coefficient) which can then be used to obtain a final chi-square value. Terms you can expect to find within chi-square procedures include *expected frequency, obtained frequency,* and *degrees of freedom.* Understanding of this statistic should come after you have worked your way through several examples. One of the basic introductory books in statistics can be a valuable reference source for this purpose. From a clear, simplified, conceptual presentation standpoint, we would recommend Weinberg and Schumaker's *Statistics: An Intuitive Approach* (Belmont, Calif.: Brooks/Cole, 1980). The following is a list of other statistics:

- *F*-test and *F*-maximum test
- Analysis of variance

  Completely randomized design
  Factorial design—two factors, three factors
  Treatments-by-levels design
  Treatments-by-subjects design (repeated measures design)
  Treatments-by-treatments-by-subjects design
  Two-factor mixed design (repeated measures on one factor)
  Three-factor mixed design (repeated measures on one factor)
  Three-factor mixed design (repeated measures on two factors)

- Latin square design

With the statistics listed above, work for *general* familiarity with situations in which they would be used rather than for mastery of their fundamentals. To calm any fears that you may be having, let's say that, where the *t*-test can only handle two groups of measures simultaneously, these measures have been devised to work with more than two sets of measures simultaneously. Bruning and Kintz's section introducing the different analysis-of-variance procedures can provide further clarity (and fear reduction). With regard to statistical procedures, your main objective is knowing the settings in which they would be used. For instance, suppose that a question on the GRE outlined five experimental formats and asked which one measured learning transfer—could you identify it? Basic familiarity both here and within the area of learning transfer will prepare you to answer such questions.

Books that can assist you in this review include the following:

Peck, R. *Statistics: Learning from Data.* (San Francisco: Cengage, 2015).

White, T. L. and D. H. McBurney. *Research Methods*, 9th ed. (San Francisco: Cengage, 2013).

That may have seemed like a mammoth second step, and it was—encompassing all basic understanding in statistics. Because you have now mastered these essential concepts, however, the subsequent steps in hypothesis testing can go quickly; and as you review them you will understand their underlying rationale.

Step 3: Set a Significance Level

In psychological research, the significance level is generally either .05 or .01. The .05 level indicates that you are willing to consider significant a difference that could occur by chance only five times in each hundred cases. The .01 level is more stringent, accepting as significant a difference that could occur by chance only one time in each hundred cases. Notice that the significance level is set before statistics are computed. This sequence is essential. Otherwise, an experimenter might decide after the fact which significance level to choose—the decision then being based on the size of the difference actually found. Throughout your perusal of psychological literature, you will find expressions like "significant at the .01 level" or "significant at the .05 level." Be sure you understand both their meaning and how they relate to proportions under the normal curve and probability.

Step 4: Compute Statistics

Having selected the experimental design in Step 2 and the significance level in Step 3, you should find this fourth step self-explanatory. Depending on the design that you have selected, you may have a *t*-value, *z*-value, *F*-value, and so on. In each instance, for the *n* or *df* in your experiment (based on the number of subjects you have in each group), you will refer to the appropriate table (*z*, *t*, *F*) to determine whether the value you have obtained is larger than the value required for significance at the level selected.

Step 5: Make Decision

If the number obtained in your computation is larger than the number found in the table for your significance level (at your appropriate *n* or *df*), you can reject the null (no difference) hypothesis. As mentioned earlier, every experimenter hopes that the difference found will be large enough for such rejection of the null. On the other hand, if the number you find in computation is smaller than the table value for your established significance level, you have failed to reject the null (meaning in this case that carrot eating did not have a significant effect on reading speed). Obviously, significant results are the prime candidates for publication in experimental-professional journals; and the findings most impressive to journal editors are those involving experiments in which a large number of subjects have been used. Relating all this to your specific situation, suppose that you selected the .05 significance level and obtained a z-score of 2.05 in your statistical computation. As you move to the appropriate column in the z-table (normal distribution table), you find that the score required for significance at the .05 level is 1.96. Since your score is larger, you can reject the null hypothesis and conclude that carrot eating has had a significant effect upon reading speed. The table reference will change as a function of the statistical procedure that you have selected, but the basic reference and decision-making procedure will remain the same.

You have now been duly initiated into the scientific method. This method is utilized by researchers in all areas of psychology in their quest for information and further understanding of behavior. Because of this prominence and virtual omnipresence throughout psychology, your understanding of its various aspects should be thorough.

Diagnostic Test 2 for Review Analysis

4

Now that you've taken a very hard-core study trip through the shaky areas you found in round 1, you're getting more confident. We're betting you'll really see a difference this round. Remember the basics we talked about earlier:

- Select a comfortable, well-lit place that resembles the room you'll be taking it in. If you're in or near the actual test center, see whether there's a time when that room would be available.
- Have your sharpened No. 2 pencils at the ready.
- Briefly practice your deep breathing, and dive in.
- Set your 170 minute timer for your 205-question adventure.
- Use your "three-pass" system again.

   PASS ONE: Answer your solid bets, putting a single mark by the difficult questions you know something about and a double mark by the ones that will require more considerable thought (very likely, the A/E questions). Bubble in each answer choice as you go so that when you've finished question answering you will have finished the bubble sheet, too.

   PASS TWO: Answer the single-marked questions on which you can eliminate one of the answer choices, giving them your best guess. Bubblin' them in!

   PASS THREE: Return to the double-marked questions—ones that require more thought.

All questions are "created equal" scorewise, so you don't want to hang up on these and run out of time.

- Once again, set your timer for 2 hours, 50 minutes, and go for it!

ANSWER SHEET
Diagnostic Test 2

DIAGNOSTIC TEST 2

1. Ⓐ Ⓑ Ⓒ Ⓓ Ⓔ   31. Ⓐ Ⓑ Ⓒ Ⓓ Ⓔ   61. Ⓐ Ⓑ Ⓒ Ⓓ Ⓔ   91. Ⓐ Ⓑ Ⓒ Ⓓ Ⓔ

2. Ⓐ Ⓑ Ⓒ Ⓓ Ⓔ   32. Ⓐ Ⓑ Ⓒ Ⓓ Ⓔ   62. Ⓐ Ⓑ Ⓒ Ⓓ Ⓔ   92. Ⓐ Ⓑ Ⓒ Ⓓ Ⓔ

3. Ⓐ Ⓑ Ⓒ Ⓓ Ⓔ   33. Ⓐ Ⓑ Ⓒ Ⓓ Ⓔ   63. Ⓐ Ⓑ Ⓒ Ⓓ Ⓔ   93. Ⓐ Ⓑ Ⓒ Ⓓ Ⓔ

4. Ⓐ Ⓑ Ⓒ Ⓓ Ⓔ   34. Ⓐ Ⓑ Ⓒ Ⓓ Ⓔ   64. Ⓐ Ⓑ Ⓒ Ⓓ Ⓔ   94. Ⓐ Ⓑ Ⓒ Ⓓ Ⓔ

5. Ⓐ Ⓑ Ⓒ Ⓓ Ⓔ   35. Ⓐ Ⓑ Ⓒ Ⓓ Ⓔ   65. Ⓐ Ⓑ Ⓒ Ⓓ Ⓔ   95. Ⓐ Ⓑ Ⓒ Ⓓ Ⓔ

6. Ⓐ Ⓑ Ⓒ Ⓓ Ⓔ   36. Ⓐ Ⓑ Ⓒ Ⓓ Ⓔ   66. Ⓐ Ⓑ Ⓒ Ⓓ Ⓔ   96. Ⓐ Ⓑ Ⓒ Ⓓ Ⓔ

7. Ⓐ Ⓑ Ⓒ Ⓓ Ⓔ   37. Ⓐ Ⓑ Ⓒ Ⓓ Ⓔ   67. Ⓐ Ⓑ Ⓒ Ⓓ Ⓔ   97. Ⓐ Ⓑ Ⓒ Ⓓ Ⓔ

8. Ⓐ Ⓑ Ⓒ Ⓓ Ⓔ   38. Ⓐ Ⓑ Ⓒ Ⓓ Ⓔ   68. Ⓐ Ⓑ Ⓒ Ⓓ Ⓔ   98. Ⓐ Ⓑ Ⓒ Ⓓ Ⓔ

9. Ⓐ Ⓑ Ⓒ Ⓓ Ⓔ   39. Ⓐ Ⓑ Ⓒ Ⓓ Ⓔ   69. Ⓐ Ⓑ Ⓒ Ⓓ Ⓔ   99. Ⓐ Ⓑ Ⓒ Ⓓ Ⓔ

10. Ⓐ Ⓑ Ⓒ Ⓓ Ⓔ   40. Ⓐ Ⓑ Ⓒ Ⓓ Ⓔ   70. Ⓐ Ⓑ Ⓒ Ⓓ Ⓔ   100. Ⓐ Ⓑ Ⓒ Ⓓ Ⓔ

11. Ⓐ Ⓑ Ⓒ Ⓓ Ⓔ   41. Ⓐ Ⓑ Ⓒ Ⓓ Ⓔ   71. Ⓐ Ⓑ Ⓒ Ⓓ Ⓔ   101. Ⓐ Ⓑ Ⓒ Ⓓ Ⓔ

12. Ⓐ Ⓑ Ⓒ Ⓓ Ⓔ   42. Ⓐ Ⓑ Ⓒ Ⓓ Ⓔ   72. Ⓐ Ⓑ Ⓒ Ⓓ Ⓔ   102. Ⓐ Ⓑ Ⓒ Ⓓ Ⓔ

13. Ⓐ Ⓑ Ⓒ Ⓓ Ⓔ   43. Ⓐ Ⓑ Ⓒ Ⓓ Ⓔ   73. Ⓐ Ⓑ Ⓒ Ⓓ Ⓔ   103. Ⓐ Ⓑ Ⓒ Ⓓ Ⓔ

14. Ⓐ Ⓑ Ⓒ Ⓓ Ⓔ   44. Ⓐ Ⓑ Ⓒ Ⓓ Ⓔ   74. Ⓐ Ⓑ Ⓒ Ⓓ Ⓔ   104. Ⓐ Ⓑ Ⓒ Ⓓ Ⓔ

15. Ⓐ Ⓑ Ⓒ Ⓓ Ⓔ   45. Ⓐ Ⓑ Ⓒ Ⓓ Ⓔ   75. Ⓐ Ⓑ Ⓒ Ⓓ Ⓔ   105. Ⓐ Ⓑ Ⓒ Ⓓ Ⓔ

16. Ⓐ Ⓑ Ⓒ Ⓓ Ⓔ   46. Ⓐ Ⓑ Ⓒ Ⓓ Ⓔ   76. Ⓐ Ⓑ Ⓒ Ⓓ Ⓔ   106. Ⓐ Ⓑ Ⓒ Ⓓ Ⓔ

17. Ⓐ Ⓑ Ⓒ Ⓓ Ⓔ   47. Ⓐ Ⓑ Ⓒ Ⓓ Ⓔ   77. Ⓐ Ⓑ Ⓒ Ⓓ Ⓔ   107. Ⓐ Ⓑ Ⓒ Ⓓ Ⓔ

18. Ⓐ Ⓑ Ⓒ Ⓓ Ⓔ   48. Ⓐ Ⓑ Ⓒ Ⓓ Ⓔ   78. Ⓐ Ⓑ Ⓒ Ⓓ Ⓔ   108. Ⓐ Ⓑ Ⓒ Ⓓ Ⓔ

19. Ⓐ Ⓑ Ⓒ Ⓓ Ⓔ   49. Ⓐ Ⓑ Ⓒ Ⓓ Ⓔ   79. Ⓐ Ⓑ Ⓒ Ⓓ Ⓔ   109. Ⓐ Ⓑ Ⓒ Ⓓ Ⓔ

20. Ⓐ Ⓑ Ⓒ Ⓓ Ⓔ   50. Ⓐ Ⓑ Ⓒ Ⓓ Ⓔ   80. Ⓐ Ⓑ Ⓒ Ⓓ Ⓔ   110. Ⓐ Ⓑ Ⓒ Ⓓ Ⓔ

21. Ⓐ Ⓑ Ⓒ Ⓓ Ⓔ   51. Ⓐ Ⓑ Ⓒ Ⓓ Ⓔ   81. Ⓐ Ⓑ Ⓒ Ⓓ Ⓔ   111. Ⓐ Ⓑ Ⓒ Ⓓ Ⓔ

22. Ⓐ Ⓑ Ⓒ Ⓓ Ⓔ   52. Ⓐ Ⓑ Ⓒ Ⓓ Ⓔ   82. Ⓐ Ⓑ Ⓒ Ⓓ Ⓔ   112. Ⓐ Ⓑ Ⓒ Ⓓ Ⓔ

23. Ⓐ Ⓑ Ⓒ Ⓓ Ⓔ   53. Ⓐ Ⓑ Ⓒ Ⓓ Ⓔ   83. Ⓐ Ⓑ Ⓒ Ⓓ Ⓔ   113. Ⓐ Ⓑ Ⓒ Ⓓ Ⓔ

24. Ⓐ Ⓑ Ⓒ Ⓓ Ⓔ   54. Ⓐ Ⓑ Ⓒ Ⓓ Ⓔ   84. Ⓐ Ⓑ Ⓒ Ⓓ Ⓔ   114. Ⓐ Ⓑ Ⓒ Ⓓ Ⓔ

25. Ⓐ Ⓑ Ⓒ Ⓓ Ⓔ   55. Ⓐ Ⓑ Ⓒ Ⓓ Ⓔ   85. Ⓐ Ⓑ Ⓒ Ⓓ Ⓔ   115. Ⓐ Ⓑ Ⓒ Ⓓ Ⓔ

26. Ⓐ Ⓑ Ⓒ Ⓓ Ⓔ   56. Ⓐ Ⓑ Ⓒ Ⓓ Ⓔ   86. Ⓐ Ⓑ Ⓒ Ⓓ Ⓔ   116. Ⓐ Ⓑ Ⓒ Ⓓ Ⓔ

27. Ⓐ Ⓑ Ⓒ Ⓓ Ⓔ   57. Ⓐ Ⓑ Ⓒ Ⓓ Ⓔ   87. Ⓐ Ⓑ Ⓒ Ⓓ Ⓔ   117. Ⓐ Ⓑ Ⓒ Ⓓ Ⓔ

28. Ⓐ Ⓑ Ⓒ Ⓓ Ⓔ   58. Ⓐ Ⓑ Ⓒ Ⓓ Ⓔ   88. Ⓐ Ⓑ Ⓒ Ⓓ Ⓔ   118. Ⓐ Ⓑ Ⓒ Ⓓ Ⓔ

29. Ⓐ Ⓑ Ⓒ Ⓓ Ⓔ   59. Ⓐ Ⓑ Ⓒ Ⓓ Ⓔ   89. Ⓐ Ⓑ Ⓒ Ⓓ Ⓔ   119. Ⓐ Ⓑ Ⓒ Ⓓ Ⓔ

30. Ⓐ Ⓑ Ⓒ Ⓓ Ⓔ   60. Ⓐ Ⓑ Ⓒ Ⓓ Ⓔ   90. Ⓐ Ⓑ Ⓒ Ⓓ Ⓔ   120. Ⓐ Ⓑ Ⓒ Ⓓ Ⓔ

ANSWER SHEET
Diagnostic Test 2

121. Ⓐ Ⓑ Ⓒ Ⓓ Ⓔ	143. Ⓐ Ⓑ Ⓒ Ⓓ Ⓔ	165. Ⓐ Ⓑ Ⓒ Ⓓ Ⓔ	187. Ⓐ Ⓑ Ⓒ Ⓓ Ⓔ
122. Ⓐ Ⓑ Ⓒ Ⓓ Ⓔ	144. Ⓐ Ⓑ Ⓒ Ⓓ Ⓔ	166. Ⓐ Ⓑ Ⓒ Ⓓ Ⓔ	188. Ⓐ Ⓑ Ⓒ Ⓓ Ⓔ
123. Ⓐ Ⓑ Ⓒ Ⓓ Ⓔ	145. Ⓐ Ⓑ Ⓒ Ⓓ Ⓔ	167. Ⓐ Ⓑ Ⓒ Ⓓ Ⓔ	189. Ⓐ Ⓑ Ⓒ Ⓓ Ⓔ
124. Ⓐ Ⓑ Ⓒ Ⓓ Ⓔ	146. Ⓐ Ⓑ Ⓒ Ⓓ Ⓔ	168. Ⓐ Ⓑ Ⓒ Ⓓ Ⓔ	190. Ⓐ Ⓑ Ⓒ Ⓓ Ⓔ
125. Ⓐ Ⓑ Ⓒ Ⓓ Ⓔ	147. Ⓐ Ⓑ Ⓒ Ⓓ Ⓔ	169. Ⓐ Ⓑ Ⓒ Ⓓ Ⓔ	191. Ⓐ Ⓑ Ⓒ Ⓓ Ⓔ
126. Ⓐ Ⓑ Ⓒ Ⓓ Ⓔ	148. Ⓐ Ⓑ Ⓒ Ⓓ Ⓔ	170. Ⓐ Ⓑ Ⓒ Ⓓ Ⓔ	192. Ⓐ Ⓑ Ⓒ Ⓓ Ⓔ
127. Ⓐ Ⓑ Ⓒ Ⓓ Ⓔ	149. Ⓐ Ⓑ Ⓒ Ⓓ Ⓔ	171. Ⓐ Ⓑ Ⓒ Ⓓ Ⓔ	193. Ⓐ Ⓑ Ⓒ Ⓓ Ⓔ
128. Ⓐ Ⓑ Ⓒ Ⓓ Ⓔ	150. Ⓐ Ⓑ Ⓒ Ⓓ Ⓔ	172. Ⓐ Ⓑ Ⓒ Ⓓ Ⓔ	194. Ⓐ Ⓑ Ⓒ Ⓓ Ⓔ
129. Ⓐ Ⓑ Ⓒ Ⓓ Ⓔ	151. Ⓐ Ⓑ Ⓒ Ⓓ Ⓔ	173. Ⓐ Ⓑ Ⓒ Ⓓ Ⓔ	195. Ⓐ Ⓑ Ⓒ Ⓓ Ⓔ
130. Ⓐ Ⓑ Ⓒ Ⓓ Ⓔ	152. Ⓐ Ⓑ Ⓒ Ⓓ Ⓔ	174. Ⓐ Ⓑ Ⓒ Ⓓ Ⓔ	196. Ⓐ Ⓑ Ⓒ Ⓓ Ⓔ
131. Ⓐ Ⓑ Ⓒ Ⓓ Ⓔ	153. Ⓐ Ⓑ Ⓒ Ⓓ Ⓔ	175. Ⓐ Ⓑ Ⓒ Ⓓ Ⓔ	197. Ⓐ Ⓑ Ⓒ Ⓓ Ⓔ
132. Ⓐ Ⓑ Ⓒ Ⓓ Ⓔ	154. Ⓐ Ⓑ Ⓒ Ⓓ Ⓔ	176. Ⓐ Ⓑ Ⓒ Ⓓ Ⓔ	198. Ⓐ Ⓑ Ⓒ Ⓓ Ⓔ
133. Ⓐ Ⓑ Ⓒ Ⓓ Ⓔ	155. Ⓐ Ⓑ Ⓒ Ⓓ Ⓔ	177. Ⓐ Ⓑ Ⓒ Ⓓ Ⓔ	199. Ⓐ Ⓑ Ⓒ Ⓓ Ⓔ
134. Ⓐ Ⓑ Ⓒ Ⓓ Ⓔ	156. Ⓐ Ⓑ Ⓒ Ⓓ Ⓔ	178. Ⓐ Ⓑ Ⓒ Ⓓ Ⓔ	200. Ⓐ Ⓑ Ⓒ Ⓓ Ⓔ
135. Ⓐ Ⓑ Ⓒ Ⓓ Ⓔ	157. Ⓐ Ⓑ Ⓒ Ⓓ Ⓔ	179. Ⓐ Ⓑ Ⓒ Ⓓ Ⓔ	201. Ⓐ Ⓑ Ⓒ Ⓓ Ⓔ
136. Ⓐ Ⓑ Ⓒ Ⓓ Ⓔ	158. Ⓐ Ⓑ Ⓒ Ⓓ Ⓔ	180. Ⓐ Ⓑ Ⓒ Ⓓ Ⓔ	202. Ⓐ Ⓑ Ⓒ Ⓓ Ⓔ
137. Ⓐ Ⓑ Ⓒ Ⓓ Ⓔ	159. Ⓐ Ⓑ Ⓒ Ⓓ Ⓔ	181. Ⓐ Ⓑ Ⓒ Ⓓ Ⓔ	203. Ⓐ Ⓑ Ⓒ Ⓓ Ⓔ
138. Ⓐ Ⓑ Ⓒ Ⓓ Ⓔ	160. Ⓐ Ⓑ Ⓒ Ⓓ Ⓔ	182. Ⓐ Ⓑ Ⓒ Ⓓ Ⓔ	204. Ⓐ Ⓑ Ⓒ Ⓓ Ⓔ
139. Ⓐ Ⓑ Ⓒ Ⓓ Ⓔ	161. Ⓐ Ⓑ Ⓒ Ⓓ Ⓔ	183. Ⓐ Ⓑ Ⓒ Ⓓ Ⓔ	205. Ⓐ Ⓑ Ⓒ Ⓓ Ⓔ
140. Ⓐ Ⓑ Ⓒ Ⓓ Ⓔ	162. Ⓐ Ⓑ Ⓒ Ⓓ Ⓔ	184. Ⓐ Ⓑ Ⓒ Ⓓ Ⓔ	
141. Ⓐ Ⓑ Ⓒ Ⓓ Ⓔ	163. Ⓐ Ⓑ Ⓒ Ⓓ Ⓔ	185. Ⓐ Ⓑ Ⓒ Ⓓ Ⓔ	
142. Ⓐ Ⓑ Ⓒ Ⓓ Ⓔ	164. Ⓐ Ⓑ Ⓒ Ⓓ Ⓔ	186. Ⓐ Ⓑ Ⓒ Ⓓ Ⓔ	

DIAGNOSTIC TEST 2

TIME: 170 MINUTES
205 QUESTIONS

> **Directions:** Each of the questions or incomplete statements below is followed by five suggested answers or completions. Select the one that is best in each case and then fill in the corresponding space on the answer sheet.

QUESTIONS 1–7, LEARNING

1. Chad's young daughter throws frequent tantrums in the grocery store, a behavior he and his wife would like to extinguish. Unfortunately, in the past, they have stopped the tantrums by offering the little girl a piece of candy. Which of the following procedures should Chad follow to extinguish his daughter's tantrums?

   (A) He should show his daughter the candy but then eat it himself.
   (B) He should stop providing candy to his daughter when she throws a tantrum.
   (C) He should stop taking her to the grocery store until she is older.
   (D) He should punish her immediately for any tantrum behavior.
   (E) He should explain to his daughter that she will get a piece of candy only if she stops crying and screaming.

2. Clark Hull's drive-reduction theory would predict that learning would be most likely to occur in which of the following situations?

   (A) A hungry child finds a piece of candy hidden under a cup with a particular color more rapidly on each successive trial.
   (B) A laboratory rat will bar-press for saccharin, an artificial sweetener with no nutritive value.
   (C) A rhesus monkey will bar-press to open a window to an adjacent chamber featuring a model train set in action.
   (D) A college student who has successfully solved a problem will try to find additional solutions "just for fun."
   (E) A heroin addict experiences tolerance, or the need to use more of the drug to obtain the same subjective experience.

GO ON TO THE NEXT PAGE

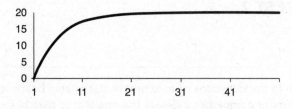

3. The figure above illustrates a learning curve predicted by the Rescorla-Wagner model, with associative strength measured on the *y*-axis and number of trials on the *x*-axis. Which of the following is a correct interpretation of this figure?

(A) Each presentation of a conditioned stimulus followed by an unconditioned stimulus produces the same increase in associative strength.
(B) More learning occurs early in training than later in training.
(C) Associative strength forms a negatively accelerated function over trials.
(D) More learning occurs on each successive trial compared to the one preceding it.
(E) Associative strength forms a linear relationship with number of trials.

4. One rat experiences an electrical shock that is signaled 60% of the time by a loud buzzer, while another rat experiences an electrical shock that is signaled 40% of the time. What can we predict about the rats' behavior in this situation?

(A) Both rats will learn to fear the buzzer at about the same rate.
(B) Neither rat will learn to fear the buzzer, because it is not a very good signal in either case.
(C) The first rat will learn to fear the buzzer faster than the second rat will.
(D) The second rat will learn to fear the buzzer faster than the first rat will.
(E) Both rats will learn to fear the buzzer on the first trial, as predicted by preparedness.

5. People form phobias about spiders and the sight of blood, but not about stimuli that bear no association with any real danger, such as chairs and coffee cups. This finding is most consistent with the work of

(A) John Garcia
(B) Ivan Pavlov
(C) John Watson
(D) Clark Hull
(E) Robert Rescorla and Allan Wagner

6. After struggling with the same statistical analysis for hours, a graduate student finally had a "eureka" moment in which she abruptly realized the solution to her problem. This experience is most likely an example of

(A) classical conditioning
(B) operant or instrumental conditioning
(C) trial-and-error learning
(D) insight learning
(E) observational learning

GO ON TO THE NEXT PAGE

7. In a series of classic experiments, dogs that had experienced uncontrollable shock failed to learn to jump over a barrier to escape shock. These experiments demonstrated

(A) learned helplessness
(B) learned optimism
(C) latent inhibition
(D) higher-order conditioning
(E) blocking

QUESTIONS 8–13, LANGUAGE

8. Which of the following statements about language learning is most consistent with a "nature" perspective?

(A) Children are rewarded when they are able to make themselves understood.
(B) Fewer phonemes are found in languages that are most distant from Africa along migration pathways.
(C) Children learn more vocabulary words from a face-to-face interaction than from listening to the same speaker on a television.
(D) The word for "no" is very similar in quite a few human languages.
(E) Children do a better job of distinguishing between the phonemes of a new language than do adults.

9. Evan, a young child with autism spectrum disorder, finds it difficult to avoid interrupting his parents and siblings when they are speaking. This behavior demonstrates a problem with Evan's

(A) pragmatics
(B) syntax
(C) stylistics
(D) morphology
(E) phonology

10. Sean, an avid skier, is trying to help Julia, a Costa Rican who is skiing for the first time, identify the different types of snow on the ski runs. Which of the following linguists introduced the idea that Sean is likely to think differently about snow compared to Julia?

(A) Noam Chomsky
(B) B. F. Skinner
(C) Benjamin Whorf
(D) Steven Pinker
(E) Michael Halliday

GO ON TO THE NEXT PAGE

11. Research using brain imaging has concluded that American Sign Language (ASL) is processed

   (A) by the right hemisphere in most people, because of its spatial qualities
   (B) by the left hemisphere in most people, because of its language qualities
   (C) equally by both hemispheres in most people, because it combines spatial and language reasoning
   (D) in the right hemisphere for about 50% of ASL speakers and in the left hemisphere for the other 50% of ASL speakers
   (E) by the right hemisphere, because of its emotional qualities

12. Sara is memorizing the meaning of her vocabulary words for her behavioral neuroscience course by using flash cards. During this process, Sara is focusing on

   (A) semantics
   (B) syntax
   (C) semiotics
   (D) pragmatics
   (E) arbitrariness

13. Which of the following distinguishes between human and nonhuman uses of language?

   (A) Nonhumans are unable to use any facet of language.
   (B) Nonhumans can use displacement, but humans cannot.
   (C) Human language demonstrates recursivity, but nonhuman language does not.
   (D) Humans learn language through imitation, but nonhumans cannot.
   (E) Human language consists of a finite set of elements, but nonhuman language does not.

QUESTIONS 14–32, MEMORY

14. In a free recall test of words that fall into categories of plants, animals, and foods, Angela responds by listing the words she remembers one category at a time. Which of the following memory principles does Angela's behavior illustrate?

   (A) massed versus spaced trials
   (B) serial position
   (C) clustering
   (D) tip of the tongue
   (E) context-dependent learning

GO ON TO THE NEXT PAGE

15. According to research on the serial position effect, what is the most likely explanation for the form of a curve plotting likelihood of recall as a function of the position of each word in the list?

    (A) Items at the beginning of the list are maintained in long-term memory, whereas items at the end of the list are maintained in short-term memory.
    (B) Items at the beginning of the list are maintained in short-term memory, whereas items at the end of the list are maintained in long-term memory.
    (C) The items at the beginning of the list are subject to proactive interference, whereas the items at the end of the list are subject to retroactive interference.
    (D) The items in the middle of the list are subject to the least amount of interference effects.
    (E) The items in the middle of the list are more likely to be subject to confabulation.

16. Kyle listens to Courtney read off a telephone number for him while he looks at the map on his smartphone. He then dials the number correctly. Kyle's behavior illustrates which of the following memory concepts?

    (A) Visual stimuli are retained in sensory memory for a longer time than auditory stimuli.
    (B) Working memory can hold different types of information simultaneously.
    (C) Retroactive interference does not affect verbal information.
    (D) Auditory information is processed more quickly than visual information into long-term memory.
    (E) Visual information can be maintained indefinitely as an echoic memory.

17. Christopher asked his psychology professor for advice about the best ways to study if the goal was long-term retention of a set of vocabulary terms. Which of the following strategies is the professor most likely to relate to Christopher?

    (A) Study each section five times, taking very short breaks between sessions, and focus on the sounds of each vocabulary term.
    (B) Study each section five times, taking very short breaks between sessions, and focus on the meaning of each vocabulary term.
    (C) Study each section five times with a few days between sessions, and focus on the sounds of the vocabulary terms.
    (D) Study each section five times with a few days between sessions, and focus on the meaning of the vocabulary terms.
    (E) Study all sections in one sitting while focusing on both the sounds and meanings of the vocabulary terms.

GO ON TO THE NEXT PAGE

18. Aaron spent the whole morning studying for his statistics exam scheduled for that same evening. To unwind, he attended a new action film with his friends in the afternoon. While taking his test, Aaron thought the memories of the film were making it hard for him to remember what he had studied in the morning. Aaron's experience is most likely due to

(A) context-dependent learning
(B) anterograde amnesia
(C) proactive interference
(D) retroactive interference
(E) repression

19. During her history exam, Jordan was trying hard to remember the name of the man who assassinated Archduke Franz Ferdinand at the opening of World War I. She knew his last name had two syllables and began with a *P*, but she was unable to retrieve her memory of the whole name. Jordan is experiencing

(A) context-dependent learning
(B) retroactive interference
(C) tip of the tongue
(D) proactive interference
(E) decay

20. Participants who heard a sentence like "The boy carried the older woman's groceries to her car" were better able to recall the sentence when they heard the word *helpful*, which wasn't in the sentence. This is an example of

(A) cued recall
(B) serial recall
(C) free recall
(D) spontaneous recall
(E) semantic recall

21. Robert's grandmother has been diagnosed with alcohol-induced neurocognitive disorder. He asked his psychology professor what the family might expect in terms of his grandmother's behavior. The psychology professor explained to Robert that his grandmother would probably

(A) have trouble remembering her childhood
(B) have difficulty learning new procedures, such as how to use her new microwave
(C) have difficulty learning the names of the hospital staff who are treating her
(D) be unable to recognize Robert and other family members
(E) have difficulty reading

GO ON TO THE NEXT PAGE

22. Henry Molaison, known in the literature as the famous amnesic patient H. M., had difficulty learning new information. This deficit in Molaison's memory functions is the likely result of surgery that produced bilateral damage to his

(A) amygdala
(B) hippocampus
(C) caudate nucleus
(D) putamen
(E) nucleus accumbens

23. The stage of memory that has unlimited capacity and duration is known as

(A) sensory memory
(B) short-term memory
(C) long-term memory
(D) retroactive memory
(E) working memory

24. Strategies for extending the capacity and duration of short-term memory include

(A) primacy and recency
(B) chunking and rehearsal
(C) cramming
(D) reconstruction
(E) priming

25. Which of the following assessments is most dependent on recall as opposed to recognition?

(A) matching
(B) multiple-choice
(C) essay
(D) relearning
(E) true-false

26. Abby was trying to tell her new friend about an incident she remembers from when she was eight years old. To do this successfully, Abby must access her

(A) procedural memory
(B) working memory
(C) episodic memory
(D) semantic memory
(E) anterograde memory

GO ON TO THE NEXT PAGE

27. Juan took his little brother on a fishing trip last summer, and they enjoyed many adventures that Juan likes to relate to his friends. Over time, his friends notice that some of the details of the stories change slightly each time. Juan is likely experiencing

(A) reconstruction
(B) repression
(C) regression
(D) interference
(E) decay

28. According to research on the serial position curve, it is most likely that the superior amount of recall for the first words in a list is the result of

(A) lack of decay
(B) lack of interference
(C) its remaining in short-term memory at the time of recall
(D) reconstruction
(E) chunking

29. Many people form especially vivid memories for distinctive events, such as 9/11 or the assassination of President Kennedy. This phenomenon has been referred to as the formation of

(A) an eidetic memory
(B) an echoic memory
(C) an flashbulb memory
(D) an semantic memory
(E) an confabulated memory

30. Logan works nearly full-time to pay his way through college, so he is in the habit of taking all of his courses in blocks of time rather than spreading them out through the day and evening like most of his classmates do. What might be one of the consequences of Logan's scheduling habits?

(A) His memory for his classes will be superior, because he can concentrate on them without being interrupted by his work activities.
(B) His memory for his classes will be superior, because one class is likely to trigger memories of the others.
(C) There will be no measurable effects. Both approaches to class scheduling are likely to be equally effective.
(D) His memory for his classes will be poor, because he is trying to cram too much information into his memory in short periods of time instead of spacing out his learning.
(E) His memory for his classes will be poor, because there will be big gaps between the times he spends in class and the times he gets to study the material after work.

GO ON TO THE NEXT PAGE

31. Crystal is struggling with memorizing the twelve pairs of cranial nerves for her behavioral neuroscience class. One of her friends suggests that she use mnemonics to help her study. What is her friend suggesting?

(A) Crystal is a visual learner, so she should study images of the cranial nerves instead of their names.
(B) Crystal is a kinesthetic learner, so she should trace the outline of the cranial nerves until she can do this from memory.
(C) Crystal should use flash cards.
(D) Crystal should make sure she doesn't cram.
(E) Crystal should make a funny sentence out of words with the same first letters as the names of the cranial nerves.

32. Miranda's golf coach is making changes to her swing, but Miranda is frustrated by her lack of progress. She produces the new swing form in practice, but under the stress of competition, she reverts back to her original, flawed swing. Which of the following is the best explanation for Miranda's problem?

(A) She is experiencing interference between the memories for the two golf swings.
(B) Not enough time has gone by for memories of the first swing to decay.
(C) A golf swing is a procedural memory, which is automatic and hard to manage consciously.
(D) The primacy of the first golf swing is more powerful than the recency of the second golf swing.
(E) Miranda is practicing too much, producing overlearning.

QUESTIONS 33–43, THINKING

33. Which of the following students is *not* demonstrating the use of metacognition?

(A) A student who reviews questions she missed on the first midterm in a class to help her to avoid making similar mistakes on the next midterm.
(B) A student who turns off his cell phone while studying because he knows he is easily distracted by the "buzz" indicating an update.
(C) A student who takes practice quizzes after each section and uses the feedback to decide whether to review the section or move on.
(D) A student who prepares for a test by reviewing her notes many times.
(E) A student who attempts to link new concepts to material she already knows.

34. Austin won a division championship in tennis. Even though he was seeded rather far down on the list before the tournament, his coach claimed that his win was "no surprise" and that he "knew" Austin was likely to win. Austin's coach's reaction is an example of which of the following types of reasoning?

(A) the self-serving bias
(B) the correspondence bias
(C) the hindsight bias
(D) the representativeness heuristic
(E) the availability heuristic

GO ON TO THE NEXT PAGE

35. According to research on expert performance, which of the following is most likely to result in unusually high levels of performance?

(A) general educational attainment
(B) breadth of experience in related fields
(C) deliberate practice
(D) talent
(E) domain-related knowledge

36. Brandon has developed an algorithm for solving a difficult problem. Compared with the use of heuristics, how would we expect Brandon's algorithm to perform?

(A) It will take more time but is guaranteed to produce a solution.
(B) It will take less time and will guarantee a correct solution.
(C) It will take more time, and the chances of producing a correct solution will be about the same.
(D) It will take less time, and the chances of producing a correct solution will be slightly better.
(E) It will take about the same amount of time, but the chances of obtaining a correct solution will be higher.

37. Which of the following is the best example of the use of a mental set?

(A) You use an unbent paperclip to poke dust out of the case of your computer.
(B) Most doors open when you push them, so we need signs that say "pull" on doors that pull open or people keep pushing them.
(C) You have misplaced your hammer, so you pound a nail into the wall using one of your heavy hiking boots.
(D) A person needing a paperweight to keep papers blowing off a desk doesn't think of using a clean coffee cup.
(E) A person doesn't own a leaf blower, but figures out that a fan will do the job.

38. A physics exam asked students how they might estimate the height of the building by using a barometer. The expected answer was to compare readings taken at the bottom and top of the building. One student responded by saying you can take the barometer to the top of the building, tie a long rope to it, lower it to the bottom, and then measure the length of the rope. This student is avoiding which of the following cognitive problems?

(A) mental set
(B) correspondence bias
(C) self-serving bias
(D) functional fixedness
(E) fundamental attribution error

GO ON TO THE NEXT PAGE

39. Samantha, a graduate student, told her research adviser she wanted to exclude a set of "outlier" participants from her statistical analysis. According to Samantha, their behavior was not valid because the remaining participants acted in ways that confirmed her carefully constructed hypothesis. Which of the following is the most likely response from Samantha's adviser?

(A) Samantha's adviser would tell her to exclude the participants and proceed with her analysis.
(B) Samantha's adviser would caution her about the confirmation bias and instruct her to leave the participants in the analysis.
(C) Samantha's adviser would suggest that she is engaging in the self-serving bias, and she should not exclude the participants.
(D) Samantha's adviser would suggest that she exclude the participants but run a new set that is similar to the participants whose behavior was in line with her hypothesis.
(E) Samantha's adviser would instruct her to discard all of her data and start over.

40. Andrew's professor is refusing to give him an extension on his term paper, even though he was hospitalized following a traffic accident. The professor explains her reasoning by saying "If I make an exception for you, I have to make an exception for everyone with a late paper." Andrew's professor is using which of the following types of reasoning?

(A) a slippery slope fallacy
(B) a brute force argument
(C) a cost-ratio analysis
(D) a utility argument
(E) a self-serving argument

41. Which of the following statements is most consistent with Charles Spearman's concept of g?

(A) Fluid intelligence decreases over the lifespan while crystallized intelligence remains stable.
(B) Children do not show stable scores on standardized intelligence tests until around the age of ten years.
(C) Intelligence in a single individual might differ significantly across domains, such as verbal skills and mathematical reasoning skills.
(D) Genetic influences account for the vast majority of variance in intelligence.
(E) The scores for most individuals on different types of intelligence assessments show high positive correlations.

GO ON TO THE NEXT PAGE

42. Antonio always wants the very best of everything: the best car, the best hamburger in town, and so on. It is likely that in his pattern of decision making, Antonio is a

(A) satisfier
(B) maximizer
(C) minimizer
(D) utilitarian
(E) optimizer

43. Which of the following outlines the classic steps of problem solving?

(A) research options, choose an algorithm, follow steps, complete the process
(B) review past experiences, develop a plan, narrow the options, proceed
(C) understand the problem, make a plan, carry out the plan, review the plan's effect
(D) make a plan, define the problem, evaluate progress, and carry out the plan
(E) define the problem, generate algorithms, select an algorithm, carry out the plan

QUESTIONS 44–55, SENSATION AND PERCEPTION

44. Which sensory modality is associated with the vomeronasal organ?

(A) vision
(B) audition
(C) gustation
(D) olfaction
(E) nociception

45. Which of the following visual depth cues requires the use of both eyes?

(A) linear perspective and interposition
(B) retinal disparity and accommodation
(C) relative size and height in the visual field
(D) motion parallax and shading
(E) texture gradient and accommodation

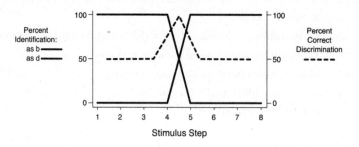

46. What principle of speech perception does the figure above demonstrate?

(A) categorical perception
(B) segmentability
(C) invariance
(D) sine wave perception
(E) prosody

GO ON TO THE NEXT PAGE

47. A wine taster is tasked with tasting expensive wine to see if the wine was tampered with by the addition of an inferior grape. Out of twenty glasses of wine, the taster's results were nine hits, two false alarms, one miss, and eight correct rejections. What can we conclude from these results?

(A) The taster was not capable of detecting the inferior grape better than chance.
(B) The taster had difficulty detecting the inferior grape, and seemed more likely when in doubt to say the wine was tampered with than not.
(C) The taster did a good job of detecting the inferior grape, and seemed more likely when in doubt to say the wine was tampered with than not.
(D) The taster had difficulty detecting the inferior grape, and seemed more likely when in doubt to say the wine had not been tampered with.
(E) The taster did a good job of detecting the inferior grape, and seemed more likely when in doubt to say the wine had not been tampered with.

48. Alyssa is developing a new brand of sports drink, and she is using consumer panels to test her new concoctions. How are her consumer panels likely to respond to drinks with bright, vivid colors?

(A) Consumers will judge the drink as being more bitter.
(B) Consumers will judge the drink as having more intense flavor.
(C) Consumers will find the colors confusing, because we have strong associations between certain tastes and colors.
(D) Consumers will judge the drink as having weaker flavor.
(E) Consumers will misjudge the odor of the drink because they will be distracted by its appearance.

49. A structure that is important in the transduction of sound energy into action potentials is the

(A) Pacinian corpuscle
(B) otolith organ
(C) basilar membrane
(D) semicircular canal
(E) organum vasculosum

GO ON TO THE NEXT PAGE

50. Rebecca sees an illustration of the American flag in her introductory psychology textbook, only instead of red, white, and blue, the flag is colored green, yellow, and black. After staring at the image for a few moments, she glances up at the white wall of her apartment and sees a red, white, and blue afterimage of the flag. Which of the following is the best explanation of her experience?

    (A) By staring at the green, yellow, and black image, she has fatigued visual channels for color, disinhibiting their opposite channels (green for red, etc.).
    (B) She retains a strong iconic memory of the real colors of the flag, which then override the others when she experiences the afterimage.
    (C) Staring at an image for a long time is unnatural, so she has done temporary damage to her visual system.
    (D) The trichromatic theory suggests that she can only hold three colors in memory at one time.
    (E) Her haptic memories maintain the image of the flag in her textbook, but her more dominant echoic memories are activated by looking at the wall.

51. Research on change blindness suggests that large changes in photographs or real-world settings are most likely to occur when

    (A) the changes take place when the person is fixated on the point of change
    (B) the changes take place when the person is using smooth pursuit movements of the eye to scan a scene
    (C) the changes take place during a saccadic eye movement
    (D) there are no masking stimuli between the original and changed scenes
    (E) the person is viewing landscapes rather than people

52. The majority of individuals with color deficiency are

    (A) female dichromats
    (B) male dichromats
    (C) monochromats (no gender difference)
    (D) male tetrachromats
    (E) female tetrachromats

53. When you wear a red sweater in a classroom under fluorescent lights, then walk out into the noon sun, and finally arrive home after dark, your brain "sees" the sweater as being red. Which of the following best explains this experience?

    (A) color contrast
    (B) color constancy
    (C) opponent processes
    (D) achromotopsia
    (E) trichromatic theory

GO ON TO THE NEXT PAGE

54. To focus on an object, Dustin feels that he is actually crossing his eyes. Where in space is the object likely to be?

   (A) close to the horizon
   (B) directly overhead
   (C) very close to Dustin's face
   (D) off to the side, barely within Dustin's peripheral vision
   (E) in the center of his horopter

55. While riding in a car along the central coast of California, a tourist notices that the grapevines next to the road seem to be passing more quickly than the distant rolling hills. This type of depth cue is known as

   (A) occlusion
   (B) retinal disparity
   (C) perspective convergence
   (D) texture gradient
   (E) motion parallax

QUESTIONS 56–81, PHYSIOLOGICAL/BEHAVIORAL NEUROSCIENCE

56. Professor Jarvis is interested in comparing the brain activity that accompanies reading in typical readers with readers with dyslexia. Which of the following technologies is Professor Jarvis most likely to use?

   (A) computerized tomography
   (B) diffusion tensor imaging
   (C) electroencephalogram
   (D) repeated transcranial magnetic stimulation
   (E) functional magnetic resonance imaging

57. Cortisol is secreted by the

   (A) pituitary gland
   (B) hypothalamus
   (C) adrenal gland
   (D) pancreas
   (E) pineal gland

GO ON TO THE NEXT PAGE

58. Jessica's grandmother had a stroke. A physician told the family that the stroke produced significant damage to the third frontal convolution on the left hemisphere, just above the lateral or Sylvian fissure and adjacent to the primary motor cortex. Jessica was able to use her knowledge of neuroanatomy to predict that her grandmother would have which of the following problems?

(A) good comprehension of speech but limited ability to speak
(B) poor comprehension and poor ability to speak
(C) good ability to speak but poor ability to write
(D) good comprehension and speech production, but difficulty repeating sentences
(E) comprehension of language is very poor, but the ability to repeat what is heard is retained

59. Dr. Stark has developed a new drug in her lab that appears to be a dopaminergic antagonist. Which of the following is a possible mode of action for the new drug?

(A) promoting synthesis
(B) enhancing release
(C) decreasing the rate of reuptake
(D) decreasing the storage of dopamine in vesicles
(E) binding with receptors and producing IPSPs

60. Which of the following sets of conditions are you more likely to experience if you have relatives with one of the following conditions? In other words, which of these sets is heritable?

(A) Down syndrome (trisomy 21) and fragile X syndrome
(B) fragile X syndrome and phenylketonuria (PKU)
(C) Klinefelter syndrome and Down syndrome (trisomy 21)
(D) Turner syndrome and Klinefelter syndrome
(E) sickle-cell disease and Turner syndrome

61. Most standard chemotherapy agents are ineffective in the treatment of brain tumors. Which of the following is the best explanation for this phenomenon?

(A) The chemotherapy agents selectively bind to all tissues outside the central nervous system.
(B) The brain absorbs chemotherapy agents too slowly for them to be effective.
(C) The brain is protected from circulating toxins by the blood-brain barrier, formed by astrocytes.
(D) The chemotherapy agents enter the brain, but are deactivated immediately by protective enzymes.
(E) Chemotherapy agents trigger immediate vomiting when they are detected by the area postrema.

GO ON TO THE NEXT PAGE

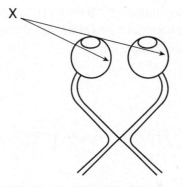

62. Visual information about the X in the picture above will be processed by

(A) the nasal hemiretina of the left eye, the temporal hemiretina of the right eye, and the right hemisphere visual cortex

(B) the nasal hemiretina of the left eye, the temporal hemiretina of the right eye, and the left hemisphere visual cortex

(C) the nasal hemiretinas of both eyes and the left hemisphere visual cortex

(D) the temporal hemiretina of the left eye, the nasal hemiretina of the right eye, and the left hemisphere visual cortex

(E) the temporal hemiretina of the left eye, the nasal hemiretina of the right eye, and the right hemisphere visual cortex

63. Rosa Hoekstra and her colleagues have reported data indicating that symptoms of autism spectrum disorder are nearly 80% heritable. Which of the following conclusions can we draw from this result?

(A) About 80% of an individual's risk of demonstrating symptoms of autism spectrum disorder is inherited.

(B) Across the population, genetics account for about 80% of the variance in symptoms of autism spectrum disorder.

(C) The genes resulting in autism spectrum disorder are probably recessive.

(D) The genes resulting in autism spectrum disorder are probably dominant.

(E) About 20% of an individual's risk of demonstrating symptoms of autism spectrum disorder is due to environmental factors.

64. As the result of a serious automobile accident, Elizabeth has sustained bilateral damage to the orbitofrontal cortex. Which of the following changes in her behavior might she experience as a result?

(A) She will find it difficult to make logical, practical decisions.

(B) She will find it difficult to speak, although her comprehension of others' speech should remain good.

(C) She will find it difficult to form new procedural memories.

(D) She will find it difficult to understand the speech of others, but she will be able to speak clearly and effortlessly.

(E) She will find it difficult to maintain eye contact and detect fear in another person's facial expression.

GO ON TO THE NEXT PAGE

65. According to some researchers, prenatal testosterone plays a significant role in the lateralization of language functions and handedness in humans. This effect of testosterone is an example of hormonal

    (A) activation
    (B) organization
    (C) triggering
    (D) initiation
    (E) facilitation

66. Traditional antipsychotic medications such as the phenothiazines act by

    (A) blocking dopamine receptors
    (B) enhancing dopamine release
    (C) promoting dopamine synthesis
    (D) slowing dopamine reuptake
    (E) promoting the breakdown of dopamine by enzymes

67. Lillian's grandmother is having surgery to remove a brain tumor. The surgeon has warned Lillian and her family that the procedure is seriously life threatening, due to the location of the tumor. Which of the following areas is the most likely location of the tumor?

    (A) occipital lobe
    (B) medulla
    (C) Broca's area
    (D) hippocampus
    (E) amygdala

68. Which of the following neurohormones appear to participate in mating and parenting patterns in rodents?

    (A) cholecystokinin
    (B) substance P
    (C) oxytocin
    (D) endorphins
    (E) insulin

69. Sociobiologists would be most likely to agree with which of the following statements about altruism?

    (A) Altruism occurs when people empathize with others.
    (B) Altruism results from expectations that others will come to a person's aid in the future.
    (C) Altruism occurs because people have internalized a social norm that says it's the right thing to do.
    (D) Altruism occurs because it brings rewards in the form of admiration from others.
    (E) Altruism occurs when it produces a benefit to a genetically related individual.

GO ON TO THE NEXT PAGE

70. Matthew's parents are concerned about the possibility that he has autism spectrum disorder or a hearing problem. He is not responsive to language and has not learned to speak. An audiologist has ruled out an inner ear problem. Which of the following technologies would be most helpful in making a correct diagnosis?

(A) diffusion tensor imaging
(B) brain stimulation
(C) computerized tomography
(D) event-related potentials
(E) positron emission tomography

71. A patient complains of dizziness and problems maintaining her balance. Her physician suspects problems in which of the following areas?

(A) the reticular formation
(B) the red nucleus and the basal ganglia
(C) the cochlear nucleus and the inferior colliculi
(D) the amygdala and nucleus accumbens
(E) the inner ear and the cerebellum

72. Cindy was observing her monkeys' reactions to a fake rubber snake. All but one reacted to the sight of the snake with fear vocalizations, but one did not. Cindy knew that this monkey had experienced bilateral lesions in a previous laboratory, but she didn't know the location. What is the most likely location for the lesion?

(A) nucleus accumbens
(B) hippocampus
(C) amygdala
(D) substantia nigra
(E) caudate nucleus

73. In studies of split brain patients—whose connections between the right and left hemispheres had been severed to reduce seizures—different visual stimuli can be presented to each hemisphere. In one such study, the letters *HE* were presented to the right hemisphere, and the letters *ART* to the left hemisphere. When asked to point to what was seen using the left hand, how would the patient respond?

(A) The patient would point to ART, because that's what the verbal left hemisphere saw.
(B) The patient would point to ART, because the verbal left hemisphere controls the left hand.
(C) The patient would be unable to respond, because the right hemisphere controls the left hand, but the right hemisphere cannot process any language.
(D) The patient would point to HE, because the right hemisphere controls the left hand and the right hemisphere saw HE.
(E) The patient would point to HE, because tactile information is lateralized to the right hemisphere and the right hemisphere saw HE.

GO ON TO THE NEXT PAGE

74. Gabriel was surfing on the coast of California when he saw a large dorsal fin at the peak of a wave coming toward him. Gabriel's heart began pounding and he was breathing very hard as he made for the shore. Which of the following systems was most likely responsible for the changes in heart and breathing rates?

(A) the sympathetic nervous system
(B) the parasympathetic nervous system
(C) the enteric nervous system
(D) the somatic nervous system
(E) the afferent nervous system

75. Alicia was participating in a laboratory experiment using electroencephalography (EEG). The EEG technician observed that Alicia's EEG was dominated by delta waves. In which of the following states was Alicia most likely to be at the time?

(A) wide awake and focused
(B) awake, but probably daydreaming
(C) asleep, and probably experiencing vivid dreams
(D) a relatively light stage of sleep
(E) a very deep stage of sleep

76. Jacqui is having difficulty getting to sleep at night. Her physician recommends that she avoid using her iPad in bed just before she wants to go to sleep. Why might the iPad be interfering with Jacqui's sleep onset?

(A) Using the iPad is stressful, which results in the release of too much melatonin.
(B) The iPad emits blue (short) wavelength light, which breaks down melatonin.
(C) The physician is mistaken; there is no empirical evidence that tablet or smartphone use before bed inhibits sleep onset.
(D) Jacqui must concentrate on using her iPad correctly, which inhibits the release of cortisol.
(E) The iPad emits red (long) wavelength light, which inhibits the suprachiasmatic nucleus.

77. In multiple sclerosis (MS), the immune system

(A) attacks cell bodies, leading to neurodegeneration
(B) attacks dendrites, reducing the amount of incoming information to a cell
(C) attacks the Schwann cells that form myelin in the central nervous system
(D) attacks the oligodendrocytes that form myelin in the central nervous system
(E) attacks Schwann cells in the central nervous system and oligodendrocytes in the peripheral nervous system

GO ON TO THE NEXT PAGE

78. If a recording of the current across a neural membrane changes from –70 mV to –80 mV

    (A)   the cell will reach threshold and initiate an action potential

    (B)   the cell will propagate an action potential to the next node of Ranvier

    (C)   the cell has become hyperpolarized, and is probably in a refractory period

    (D)   the cell has become depolarized, and is probably in a refractory period

    (E)   saltatory conduction has occurred

79. Many poisons found in nature, such as cobra venom and curare (Amazonian dart poison derived from local plants), paralyze organisms by acting at the neuromuscular junction. Which of the following most likely actions do these poisons have?

    (A)   They are cholinergic agonists.

    (B)   They are cholinergic antagonists.

    (C)   They are dopaminergic agonists.

    (D)   They are dopaminergic antagonists.

    (E)   They antagonize glutamate.

80. Amphetamine and cocaine have similar modes of action at the synapse. Both

    (A)   are dopaminergic reuptake inhibitors

    (B)   activate dopaminergic receptors

    (C)   increase the rate of dopamine synthesis

    (D)   block dopaminergic receptors

    (E)   interfere with dopamine storage

81. Students are often cautioned about combining alcohol with other similar drugs, such as benzodiazepines (tranquilizers) and barbiturates. What makes combining these drugs so dangerous?

    (A)   Any combination of drugs can be dangerous. People should use only one drug at a time.

    (B)   All three drugs are agonists for the inhibitory neurochemical GABA.

    (C)   All three drugs are antagonists for the excitatory neurochemical GABA.

    (D)   All three drugs block the excitatory neurochemical glutamate at the receptor.

    (E)   All three drugs act as reuptake inhibitors for dopamine.

GO ON TO THE NEXT PAGE

82. Which of the following best illustrates the best use of a diathesis-stress model?

    (A) Huntington's disease is purely genetic, but produces symptoms that include very high stress.
    (B) People with close family relatives diagnosed with schizophrenia are more likely to be diagnosed themselves, especially when they are exposed to high levels of stress.
    (C) People who begin using cannabis early in adolescence and chronically have a higher risk of developing schizophrenia.
    (D) People diagnosed with schizophrenia respond more negatively to stressful events than do healthy people.
    (E) People with a genetic vulnerability to schizophrenia are more likely to smoke tobacco.

83. Which of the following disorders is likely to be diagnosed when a person experiences simultaneous mood and psychotic symptoms that are either preceded or followed by a period of time with psychotic symptoms without mood problems?

    (A) schizoaffective disorder
    (B) schizophrenia
    (C) brief psychotic disorder
    (D) schizotypal personality disorder
    (E) substance/medication-induced psychotic disorder

84. In spite of reassurances from the physicians with whom he consulted, Daniel remained convinced that he was suffering from a serious but undiagnosed medical condition. It is likely that Daniel might be experiencing symptoms of

    (A) body dysmorphic disorder
    (B) specific phobia
    (C) somatic symptom disorder
    (D) conversion disorder
    (E) panic disorder

85. A cognitive therapist is likely to suspect which of the following factors to be the main cause of a client's depression?

    (A) unresolved childhood conflicts with a parent
    (B) believing that a mistake made at work means that a person is useless
    (C) an underlying genetic predisposition has interacted with high levels of stress
    (D) a chemical imbalance in the nervous system
    (E) exposure to judgmental people

GO ON TO THE NEXT PAGE

86. Biological factors play the largest role in which of the following disorders?

   (A) dissociative identity disorder
   (B) somatic symptom disorder
   (C) anterograde amnesia
   (D) depersonalization disorder
   (E) dissociative amnesia

87. Dr. Scott tells her client that "It looks to me like you are very angry about your work today." Dr. Scott is using a technique that originated in

   (A) psychoanalysis
   (B) cognitive therapy
   (C) behavioral therapy
   (D) humanistic therapy
   (E) rational-emotive therapy

88. Cody, a 25-year-old man, has shown a pervasive pattern of disregard of the rights of others for at least the last ten years, and he feels no remorse when his actions hurt others. It is most likely that Cody would be diagnosed with which of the following personality disorders?

   (A) antisocial
   (B) borderline
   (C) narcissistic
   (D) schizoid
   (E) paranoid

89. Which of the following statements about children with autism spectrum disorder is correct?

   (A) Most children with autism spectrum disorder have above-average intelligence.
   (B) Many children with autism spectrum disorder recover by age eighteen.
   (C) Many children with autism spectrum disorder show little interest in social interactions.
   (D) Most children with autism spectrum disorder outgrow their social difficulties, although some language difficulties may remain throughout life.
   (E) Most children with autism spectrum disorder can be mainstreamed in classrooms with minimal support.

GO ON TO THE NEXT PAGE

90. Linda recently experienced a serious climbing accident that resulted in several wounds. She was surprised when the physician treating her wounds recommended that she begin keeping a journal of her emotional responses to her accident and treatment challenges. Which of the following is the best evaluation of the physician's advice?

(A) The physician is offering sound, scientific advice. Emotional disclosure has been shown to enhance immune function, which should speed the healing of wounds.

(B) The physician's advice is based on popular psychology, but is not scientifically valid. There are no significant effects of emotional disclosure on recovery from trauma.

(C) The physician's advice might be harmful. Linda's best strategy is to think about her accident as little as possible.

(D) The physician's advice is well intentioned, but the emotional disclosure effect only works with psychological trauma, not physical trauma.

(E) The physician should have referred Linda to counseling. Some people do benefit from emotional disclosure, but others have adverse effects. The counselor would be able to tell to which group Linda belongs.

91. Danielle is good friends with a number of individuals who use addictive drugs and encourage her to try them, but she tells them that drug use is illegal and she doesn't want to break the law. According to Freud, it is likely that Danielle has a

(A) strong id
(B) strong ego
(C) strong superego
(D) strong collective unconscious
(E) weak preconscious

92. Destiny had been diagnosed with schizophrenia and she maintains strange physical postures for hours. This type of behavior is known as

(A) mania
(B) catatonia
(C) tardive dyskinesia
(D) flat affect
(E) Korsakoff's syndrome

93. Which of the following is a negative symptom of schizophrenia?

(A) hallucinations
(B) delusions
(C) disorganized speech
(D) avolition
(E) disorganized behavior

GO ON TO THE NEXT PAGE

94. People diagnosed with schizophrenia show an unusually low amount of activity in the

(A) frontal lobes
(B) parietal lobes
(C) occipital lobes
(D) temporal lobes
(E) brain stem

95. Which of the following neurochemical systems have been implicated in the abnormal behaviors seen in patients with schizophrenia?

(A) dopamine and serotonin
(B) dopamine and glutamate
(C) serotonin and norepinephrine
(D) serotonin and oxytocin
(E) GABA and glutamate

96. How do newer antipsychotic medications (e.g., clozapine) compare with traditional antipsychotics (phenothiazines)?

(A) The newer antipsychotics do not produce tardive dyskinesia.
(B) The newer antipsychotics improve negative symptoms, but they are less effective in treating positive symptoms.
(C) The newer antipsychotics treat positive and negative symptoms well, but are more likely to cause tardive dyskinesia.
(D) The newer antipsychotics are more effective in treating negative symptoms.
(E) The newer and traditional antipsychotics are about equally effective in treating symptoms, and have about the same risk of side effects.

97. According to DSM-5, what is the relationship between the symptoms of depression used to diagnose bipolar disorder and those used to diagnose major depressive disorder?

(A) They are the same.
(B) Fewer symptoms are required to be diagnosed with bipolar disorder than to be diagnosed with major depressive disorder.
(C) More symptoms are required to be diagnosed with bipolar disorder than to be diagnosed with major depressive disorder.
(D) Major depressive disorder is characterized by more severe symptoms of depression than is bipolar disorder.
(E) Depressive symptoms must be present for a longer time in order to meet criteria for a diagnosis of major depressive disorder.

GO ON TO THE NEXT PAGE

98. Which of the following disorders is most likely to be treated with lithium carbonate (lithium salts)?

(A) schizophrenia
(B) bipolar disorder
(C) major depressive disorder
(D) panic disorder
(E) conduct disorder

99. Which of the following correctly summarizes demographic variables associated with major depressive disorder?

(A) Major depressive disorder shows no significant difference in rates over the adult lifespan or associated with gender.
(B) Major depressive disorder rates increase over the adult lifespan for both men and women.
(C) Major depressive disorder rates increase over the adult lifespan, and women are more likely to be diagnosed than men.
(D) Major depressive disorder rates decrease over the adult lifespan, and women are more likely to be diagnosed than men.
(E) Major depressive disorder rates are stable over the adult lifespan, and women are more likely to be diagnosed than men.

100. People with untreated major depressive disorder show which of the following abnormalities in their sleep patterns?

(A) They spend too much time in deep (non-REM) sleep.
(B) They spend too much time in REM sleep.
(C) They are unable to initiate any REM sleep.
(D) They initiate REM sleep in normal amounts, but they do not seem to dream.
(E) They enter deep (non-REM) sleep at inappropriate times, such as when driving a car.

101. Electroconvulsive therapy (ECT) is most frequently used to treat

(A) schizophrenia
(B) depression
(C) mania
(D) autism spectrum disorder
(E) antisocial personality disorder

102. Tranquilizers (such as benzodiazepines) and alcohol probably have their main anxiety-reducing effects by

(A) enhancing the inhibitory effects of GABA
(B) suppressing the inhibitory effects of GABA
(C) enhancing the excitatory effects of GABA
(D) suppressing the excitatory effects of GABA
(E) enhancing the inhibitory effects of dopamine

GO ON TO THE NEXT PAGE

103. Dakota reported to his college's health center after experiencing a panic attack while cheering on the college's soccer team at a recent game. The counselor is most likely to tell Dakota

(A) that he definitely has panic disorder, and treatment should begin immediately

(B) that unless he had other attacks in the past, it is premature to diagnose him with panic disorder

(C) it is currently unclear whether he has panic disorder or schizophrenia

(D) that it is likely he has posttraumatic stress disorder (PTSD)

(E) that he probably has agoraphobia

104. The children's rhyme that states "If I step on a crack, I'll break my mother's back" is most similar to reasoning seen in cases of

(A) panic disorder

(B) schizophrenia

(C) bipolar disorder

(D) obsessive-compulsive disorder

(E) posttraumatic stress disorder

105. People diagnosed with posttraumatic stress disorder (PTSD) often show which of the following physical correlates?

(A) smaller hippocampal volume

(B) larger hippocampal volume

(C) reduced white matter integrity

(D) lower levels of amygdala activity

(E) increased responsiveness to benzodiazepines (tranquilizers)

106. Which of the following approaches is *least* consistent with an evidence-based approach to treatment?

(A) I need to read the latest research on the types of cases I'm treating.

(B) I will incorporate my patients' values and expectations into my treatment plans.

(C) I will rely on methods that are consistent with my past practices.

(D) I will evaluate the outcomes of my treatments, and discard those that do not seem to be working.

(E) I will reevaluate techniques that I have used in the past that are thrown into doubt by current research.

107. In the United States, which of the following types of therapists are not currently regulated by the government?

(A) psychiatrists

(B) psychologists with Ph.D. degrees

(C) psychologists with Psy.D. degrees

(D) counselors

(E) life coaches

GO ON TO THE NEXT PAGE

108. Which of the following is true of treatments for autism spectrum disorder?

(A) Medication alone is more effective than applied behavior analysis.
(B) Many children with autism spectrum disorder are prescribed multiple medications that do not have specific government approval for the disorder.
(C) No medications have been approved for the treatment of autism spectrum disorder.
(D) Medication and applied behavior analysis produce about the same quality of outcomes in treating autism spectrum disorder.
(E) Neither medication nor applied behavior analysis improve the functioning of children with autism spectrum disorder.

109. Exposure therapy is very effective in the treatment of

(A) specific phobias
(B) schizophrenia
(C) bipolar disorder
(D) obsessive-compulsive disorder
(E) major depressive disorder

QUESTIONS 110–135, LIFE SPAN DEVELOPMENT

110. Children demonstrate a range of reactivity to novel stimulation early in life. Children who show relatively lower reactivity are more likely to engage in which of the following activities?

(A) reading books
(B) parallel play
(C) climbing a tall tree
(D) completing puzzles
(E) symbolic play

111. Which of the following correctly describes intellectual changes over the life span?

(A) Fluid and crystallized intelligence remain stable.
(B) Fluid and crystallized intelligence decrease gradually.
(C) Fluid intelligence remains stable, whereas crystallized intelligence decreases gradually.
(D) Crystallized intelligence remains stable, whereas fluid intelligence decreases gradually.
(E) Fluid and crystallized intelligence remain stable until around the age of 65, when they both decrease abruptly.

GO ON TO THE NEXT PAGE

112. According to Erik Erikson, which of the following challenges usually occurs at midlife?

(A) identity versus role confusion
(B) intimacy versus isolation
(C) generativity versus stagnation
(D) integrity versus despair
(E) industry versus inferiority

113. Most people find learning a language more difficult after reaching puberty. This change in learning over time is an example of

(A) brain plasticity
(B) brain reorganization
(C) a sensitive period
(D) Kennard's principle
(E) cognitive reserve

114. Brianna's mother describes herself as her children's "best friend," and believes that telling them "no" stunts their emotional development. It is likely that Brianna's mother is using which of the following parenting styles?

(A) authoritative
(B) authoritarian
(C) indulgent
(D) neglecting
(E) abusive

115. Which of the following best illustrates Piaget's concept of class inclusion?

(A) A child looking at four apples and six bananas is able to correctly indicate that there are more fruits than bananas.
(B) A child is able to describe why two differently shaped blobs of clay still have the same volume.
(C) A child is able to change her categorization of bird when she sees a video about ostriches.
(D) A child is able to generalize her concept of butterfly to include a new species described in *National Geographic.*
(E) A child is able to state correctly that pouring fluid into a different-shaped glass does not change the volume of the fluid.

116. Which of the following tasks is most likely to be more difficult for Anna's father than for Anna, who is 23 years old?

(A) playing a fast-paced video game requiring good reaction time
(B) listing animals with names beginning with a certain letter
(C) learning about new discoveries in neuroscience
(D) performing a well-practiced, favorite piece of music
(E) discussing a current event in today's news

GO ON TO THE NEXT PAGE

117. Which of the following children is at the highest risk of child maltreatment?

   (A) a child age ten in a community with high poverty and violence statistics
   (B) a child age ten living in an extended family situation where one member has a serious, chronic illness
   (C) A child age three whose parent is struggling with substance abuse
   (D) A child age three in a community that has strong social ties in spite of high poverty rates
   (E) A child age ten who lives with a nonbiological parent

118. Which of the following is the best example of a child who has developed symbolic thought?

   (A) A child pretends to be a tiger.
   (B) A child uses a play tea set to serve tea.
   (C) A child stops looking for a toy that is removed from sight.
   (D) A child cries when a parent leaves the room.
   (E) A child uses a crayon to draw circles.

119. The theories of Jean Piaget and Erik Erikson could be classified as

   (A) ecological theories
   (B) continuous theories
   (C) discontinuous theories
   (D) cultural theories
   (E) genetic theories

120. In humans, the period between the second and eighth week of development following conception is known as the

   (A) zygote stage
   (B) embryo stage
   (C) fetus stage
   (D) perinatal stage
   (E) teratogen stage

121. Premature infants, born prior to 37 weeks of pregnancy, are at greatest risk for problems in which of the following systems?

   (A) lungs and vision
   (B) heart and hearing
   (C) palate and limbs
   (D) limbs and external genitalia
   (E) heart and limbs

GO ON TO THE NEXT PAGE

122. Which of the following neonatal reflexes causes the baby's toes to spread out in response to stroking the bottom of the foot?

(A) the Moro reflex
(B) the Palmar reflex
(C) the Babinski reflex
(D) the stepping reflex
(E) the rooting reflex

123. Newborn infants are most capable of recognizing their mothers by

(A) touch and vision
(B) vision and voice
(C) voice and smell
(D) touch and smell
(E) touch and voice

124. Compared with adults, infants require which of the following in order to see well?

(A) less color
(B) higher contrast
(C) lower contrast
(D) finer detail
(E) greater distance

125. The nervous system develops from which of the following germ layers in the embryo?

(A) the ectoderm
(B) the mesoderm
(C) the endoderm
(D) the myelenderm
(E) the telenderm

126. On average, most children begin to walk unassisted at about the age of

(A) nine months
(B) twelve months
(C) fifteen months
(D) eighteen months
(E) twenty-four months

127. A child explains to her mother that airplanes pull clouds across the sky and that the Tooth Fairy is real. In which of Piaget's stages is this child likely to be?

(A) sensorimotor stage
(B) preoperational stage
(C) concrete operational stage
(D) formal operational stage
(E) postformal operational stage

GO ON TO THE NEXT PAGE

128. According to information processing theories of development, which of the following abilities reaches adult levels at the earliest age?

    (A) memory formation
    (B) rate of processing information
    (C) judgment of which of two numbers is larger
    (D) focused (selective) attention
    (E) sustained attention

129. Theory of mind (TOM) is generally agreed to be apparent by the age of

    (A) one year
    (B) four years
    (C) seven years
    (D) twelve years
    (E) fifteen years

130. Children who are fearful and shy at early ages have a larger risk for the development of which of the following disorders later in life?

    (A) anxiety and depression
    (B) autism spectrum disorder
    (C) schizophrenia
    (D) conduct disorder
    (E) attention-deficit/hyperactivity disorder (ADHD)

131. A small child watches his mother leave without any sign of distress, and he does not approach her when she returns. According to Ainsworth and her colleagues, what type of attachment is this child showing in regard to his mother?

    (A) secure attachment
    (B) avoidant attachment
    (C) anxious-ambivalent attachment
    (D) disorganized attachment
    (E) failed attachment

132. Compared with children raised by authoritative parents, children raised by authoritarian parents

    (A) have much higher rates of antisocial behavior
    (B) have much higher rates of alcohol and drug abuse
    (C) are more likely to be depressed
    (D) are more likely to be diagnosed with conduct disorder
    (E) are more likely to be diagnosed with attention-deficit/hyperactivity disorder (ADHD)

GO ON TO THE NEXT PAGE

133. Nathaniel rides his skateboard around campus in spite of many signs indicating that skateboarding is prohibited. Nathaniel tells his friends that the rule is more about raising money from fines than any real safety concern, as no skateboarding injuries have been reported on campus for years. According to Kohlberg, Nathaniel is probably using which type of moral reasoning?

(A) preconventional
(B) conventional
(C) postconventional
(D) egocentric
(E) antisocial

134. According to Erik Erikson, the major challenge faced by people in late adulthood is

(A) initiative versus guilt
(B) identity versus role confusion
(C) intimacy versus isolation
(D) generativity versus stagnation
(E) integrity versus despair

135. To which of the following are evolutionary psychologists referring when they discuss the "grandmother effect?"

(A) the human ability to live past reproductive years, possibly providing an advantage by caring for younger family members
(B) the reduction in depression rates seen in older adults, especially women
(C) the tendency for women to postpone childbirth so long that they have relatively little time left as grandmothers
(D) a reduced reliance on multigenerational families accompanying industrialization
(E) the tendency for certain genetic traits to "skip a generation"

QUESTIONS 136–145, PERSONALITY

136. Which of the following psychologists coined the term *superiority complex*?

(A) Alfred Adler
(B) Nancy Chodorow
(C) Carl Jung
(D) Erik Erikson
(E) Albert Bandura

GO ON TO THE NEXT PAGE

137. Matthew realizes that his relationship with Emily is not working, and he plans to break up with her. While getting up the courage to tell her, he begins to shower her with expensive gifts, flowers, and candy. Which of the following Freudian defense mechanisms is most consistent with Matthew's behavior?

(A) displacement
(B) identification
(C) rationalization
(D) reaction formation
(E) repression

138. The popular but not very scientific Myers-Briggs personality test is based on the work of which of the following psychologists?

(A) David Myers
(B) Carl Jung
(C) Austin Briggs
(D) Sigmund Freud
(E) Scott Lilienfeld

139. Mother Teresa's generosity to others dominated her life and reached levels not seen in most people. According to Gordon Allport's theory of personality, Mother Teresa's generosity is best described as

(A) a cardinal trait
(B) a central trait
(C) a secondary trait
(D) a dominant trait
(E) an exemplar trait

140. Not only was Karen Horney one of the first female psychiatrists, but she also worked to extend and adapt the theories of which of the following psychologists?

(A) Wilhelm Wundt
(B) John B. Watson
(C) William James
(D) Sigmund Freud
(E) Max Wertheimer

141. For Carl Rogers, the sense of similarity between the real and ideal selves is

(A) congruence
(B) self-actualization
(C) self-discrepancy
(D) empathy
(E) unconditional positive regard

GO ON TO THE NEXT PAGE

142. A person who is often unreliable and somewhat lazy is likely to score low on items testing which of the Big Five attributes?

(A) openness to experience
(B) conscientiousness
(C) extroversion
(D) agreeableness
(E) neuroticism

143. Shannon is delighted with her high score on her organic chemistry final exam, because she believes that this demonstrates that she is smart enough to go to medical school. Mariah, who also had a high score, is less impressed. She thought the professor was making the test easy because she wanted to improve her upcoming student evaluations. What can we conclude about the personalities of Shannon and Mariah?

(A) Both women have a strong internal locus of control.
(B) Both women have a strong external locus of control.
(C) Shannon has an internal locus of control, but Mariah has an external locus of control.
(D) Shannon has an external locus of control, but Mariah has an internal locus of control.
(E) Both women seem to have vascillating patterns of locus of control.

144. Which of the following Big Five traits seems easiest to identify across the animal kingdom?

(A) openness to experience
(B) conscientiousness
(C) extroversion
(D) agreeableness
(E) neuroticism

145. The heritability of the Big Five personality traits is usually reported to be between 40 and 60%. How should we interpret these findings?

(A) There is no contribution of genetics to the Big Five personality traits.
(B) Genetics account for nearly all of the variance seen in the Big Five personality traits across the population.
(C) Genetics accounts for about half of the influence on an individual's personality.
(D) Genetics seem to have a moderate influence on the variance of the Big Five personality traits across the human population.
(E) There is no contribution of environmental factors to variance in the Big Five personality traits across the human population.

GO ON TO THE NEXT PAGE

146. Many people are under the impression that shark attacks are much more frequent than they really are. You are actually more likely to be killed by falling airplane parts than by a shark. This common misunderstanding arises due to which of the following?

(A) the affect heuristic
(B) the availability heuristic
(C) the representativeness heuristic
(D) the framing effect
(E) the use of algorithms

147. Groups of people sometimes make more risky decisions than the individuals in the group would make on their own, a phenomenon known as "risky shift." Which of the following group process phenomena helps psychologists explain when risky shift will or will not be likely to occur?

(A) social loafing
(B) group polarization
(C) deindividuation
(D) groupthink
(E) social facilitation

148. Which of the following situations would be the most difficult to understand for people with strong just-world beliefs?

(A) A serial murderer receives a life sentence.
(B) A hardworking athlete signs a multimillion-dollar contract.
(C) An average student gets a high-paying position in the family business.
(D) A student who misses most classes flunks an important course.
(E) A home intruder gets attacked and injured by the homeowner's dog.

149. Students working on a group project were rushing to a particular course of action, and did not stop to consider problems with their approach or alternate approaches. This process is an example of possible

(A) group polarization
(B) social facilitation
(C) sunk costs
(D) groupthink
(E) deindividuation

GO ON TO THE NEXT PAGE

150. A runner from Japan competing in the Comrades Marathon in South Africa was attacked along the route by a group of men who stole the runner's expensive shoes. Which of the following terms fits this situation best?

(A) instrumental aggression
(B) relational aggression
(C) maternal aggression
(D) passive-aggression
(E) impulsive aggression

QUESTIONS 151–154 REFER TO THE INFORMATION BELOW.

Justin is having a difficult time adjusting to the life of a first-year dorm resident at a university several hundred miles away from his home. In an effort to feel more comfortable, Justin is working with a therapist to learn more about himself and his reactions to his new situation.

151. Justin's therapist asks him to write down ten things that complete the sentence "I am _____." The results will give Justin and his therapist a snapshot of his

(A) self-esteem
(B) self-concept
(C) self-schema
(D) self awareness
(E) self-enhancement

152. Justin's therapist asks him to think about who he really is and who he wants to become. Which of the following is *not* a reliable source of self-knowledge for Justin?

(A) introspection
(B) observing his own behavior
(C) viewing the reactions of others to his behavior
(D) comparing his behavior with an ideal standard
(E) reading a journal he kept in high school

153. Justin tells his therapist that he just failed an important exam, and that this means that the admissions department at his college probably made a mistake when they admitted him. Justin's therapist tells him that this type of reasoning is most likely due to his

(A) positive illusions
(B) "looking-glass" self
(C) low self-esteem
(D) grandiosity
(E) habit of making downward comparisons

GO ON TO THE NEXT PAGE

154. After a surprise win by Justin's school's football team, he purchases a new school sweatshirt at the campus store and begins wearing it frequently. Justin's therapist suggests that his new sweatshirt is an example of

(A) self-enhancement
(B) upward comparisons
(C) positive illusions
(D) downward comparisons
(E) sandbagging

155. Which of the following researchers demonstrated the power of mutual interdependence in reducing prejudice?

(A) Stanley Milgram
(B) Muzafer Sherif
(C) Leon Festinger
(D) Philip Zimbardo
(E) Bibb Latané

156. Which of the following people is the best example of a low self-monitor?

(A) a person who is the only one in an office to grow a full beard
(B) a person who avoids expressing her actual beliefs because her beliefs conflict with her religion
(C) a person who is opposed to putting bumper stickers on his car, even though his politics are very important to him
(D) a person who buys a hybrid car mainly to impress her friends who are very concerned about the environment
(E) a person who buys a product that is promised to make him look successful

157. Which of the following best illustrates the false consensus effect?

(A) A cohesive group fails to evaluate or question its decisions.
(B) A student believes that all of his peers binge drink every weekend.
(C) A student posts an inappropriate comment on a website because she thinks this is okay to do as long as you are anonymous.
(D) One student involved in a group project thinks it's okay to do less work because the other students care so much about their grades that they'll pick up the slack.
(E) A musical performer sounds fantastic in practice but sometimes performs more poorly during a big, important performance.

158. Ethan is very loud when he is out with his college friends, but he is quiet and soft-spoken in interactions with his professors in class. This distinction reflects Ethan's

(A) self-esteem
(B) self-concept
(C) relational self
(D) collective self
(E) identity role confusion

GO ON TO THE NEXT PAGE

159. The self-reference effect would predict that which of the following groups would remember the most words?

(A) a group studying the size of the letters making up a word
(B) a group judging whether a word rhymed with another word
(C) a group judging whether a word meant the same as another word
(D) a group judging whether a word described themselves
(E) a group judging whether a word described most people

160. Teens often believe that everyone pays more attention to them than is really the case. This phenomenon is known as

(A) the self-reference effect
(B) the spotlight effect
(C) self-awareness
(D) the self-concept
(E) the self-study effect

161. In modern life, we often find ourselves monitored by security cameras in public places. Although we don't know the ultimate effects of this surveillance, classical research usually shows that knowing that you are being watched is likely to

(A) make you behave more ethically than otherwise
(B) enhance deindividuation
(C) compound the spotlight effect
(D) counteract the self-reference effect
(E) lead to social facilitation

162. Commonsense notions about reducing social problems by raising self-esteem

(A) are fully supported by psychological research
(B) are challenged by research showing that the effects of raising self-esteem are short-lived
(C) are challenged by research showing that the effects of raising self-esteem are restricted to the academic setting
(D) are challenged by research showing that self-esteem cannot be changed
(E) are challenged by research showing that antisocial people typically have very high self-esteem

163. According to terror management theory, reminding people of their own mortality

(A) reduces self-esteem
(B) enhances self-esteem
(C) reduces desire for social inclusion
(D) enhances the self-reference effect
(E) reduces the spotlight effect

GO ON TO THE NEXT PAGE

164. People who believe they have limited supplies of willpower

(A) show an exaggerated willpower depletion effect
(B) show no evidence of a willpower depletion effect
(C) have less ability to mobilize glucose stores when faced with temptation
(D) are more likely to be successful dieters than people who do not believe willpower is limited
(E) are advised to test their willpower regularly to build up their capacity

165. Even though you know a particular professor's exams are brutal, you still attribute your friend's failure to his not being smart enough to pass. This willingness to infer a person's disposition from behavior, even in the face of obvious situational factors, is known as the

(A) actor-observer effect
(B) self-serving bias
(C) correspondence bias
(D) defensive bias
(E) in-group bias

166. Even though most universities have very strict rules about hazing, the practice continues. People who have endured hazing to join a group report more value for the group. Psychologists usually explain this phenomenon in terms of

(A) the correspondence bias
(B) the fundamental attribution error
(C) terror management theory
(D) cognitive dissonance
(E) prejudice

167. Highly emotional persuasive messages promising doom and gloom are most effective when

(A) people are using the central route to persuasion
(B) the speaker is addressing a highly intelligent audience
(C) the speaker is addressing an older audience
(D) the speaker is relatively average-looking
(E) the message is followed by an action step the audience can take

168. By definition, a stereotype is an example of

(A) an emotional response
(B) a behavior
(C) a cognition
(D) an attitude
(E) an attribution

GO ON TO THE NEXT PAGE

169. Results from the Implicit Association Test (IAT) have shown that

(A) most people hold similar implicit and explicit attitudes
(B) many people hold divergent implicit and explicit attitudes
(C) explicit attitudes are more predictive of behavior than implicit attitudes
(D) neither implicit nor explicit attitudes predict behavior
(E) people are usually quite self-aware regarding their implicit attitudes

170. When we adopt the behavior of those around us without an explicit direction to do so, we are

(A) obeying
(B) complying
(C) conforming
(D) associating
(E) facilitating

171. Clicking the Like button on an organization's Facebook page often leads to further support of the organization. This persuasive technique is an example of

(A) foot in the door
(B) door in the face
(C) lowballing
(D) obedience
(E) conformity

QUESTIONS 172–180, GENERAL

172. Philosophers and psychologists tackle many of the same questions. Which of the following is more likely to be asked by a philosopher than by a psychologist?

(A) What is the nature of the self?
(B) What is the origin of knowledge?
(C) What is the relationship of body and mind?
(D) Is the universe real?
(E) Do we have free will?

173. Which of the following are *not* typical of an organization following a sociotechnical approach?

(A) internalized regulation
(B) work group autonomy
(C) discretionary behavior
(D) bottom-up participation
(E) close supervision

GO ON TO THE NEXT PAGE

174. Which of the following pairs of psychologists would be most likely to argue about whether experience can be reduced to its basic building blocks?

(A) Carl Rogers and Sigmund Freud
(B) B. F. Skinner and Ulric Neisser
(C) Edward Titchener and Max Wertheimer
(D) William James and Sigmund Freud
(E) Carl Jung and Alfred Adler

175. The "cognitive revolution" was a revolt against which of the following prevailing theoretical approaches in psychology?

(A) psychoanalytic theory
(B) structuralism
(C) functionalism
(D) behaviorism
(E) humanistic psychology

176. Which of the following psychologists demonstrated that relearning is faster than original learning and that spaced trials are more effective than massed trials for learning?

(A) Wilhelm Wundt
(B) Edward Titchener
(C) Edward Thorndike
(D) Hermann von Helmholtz
(E) Hermann Ebbinghaus

177. Which of the following early schools of thought was most directly related to Charles Darwin's theory of evolution?

(A) structuralism
(B) gestalt psychology
(C) functionalism
(D) psychoanalysis
(E) behaviorism

178. Google frequently tops published lists of positive employers. What characteristics are shared by workplaces that are viewed positively by their employees?

(A) the highest pay in the employment sector
(B) reciprocal caring
(C) strongly hierarchical leadership
(D) guaranteed longevity in a position
(E) frequent face-to-face departmental meetings

GO ON TO THE NEXT PAGE

179. About which of the following issues did Freudian and humanistic psychologists disagree most strongly?

    (A) the basic nature of humans as inherently good or not
    (B) the relative contributions of nature and nurture
    (C) whether experience is best seen as a sum of its parts or not
    (D) the importance of using strictly scientific research methods
    (E) the importance of helping people with psychological disorders

180. The majority of psychologists holding a Ph.D. work in which of the following areas?

    (A) business
    (B) elementary and secondary schools
    (C) higher education
    (D) clinical practice settings
    (E) government

QUESTIONS 181–205, MEASUREMENT

181. Dr. Picard measured the friend networks of people on Facebook and displayed his results in graphic form with each friend as a node with lines of various lengths connecting each friend to other people. Dr. Picard is using which of the following research techniques?

    (A) psychodrama
    (B) sociometry
    (C) Delphi method
    (D) nominal group technique
    (E) ethnography

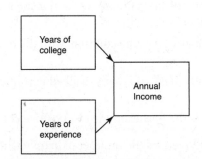

182. A psychologist is interested in the influence of years in school versus years of experience on the annual income in her specialty area. She diagrams the question as shown above. Which type of statistical analysis would she use to answer her research question?

    (A) Chi-square
    (B) regression
    (C) bootstrapping
    (D) analysis of variance (ANOVA)
    (E) factor analysis

GO ON TO THE NEXT PAGE

183. Dr. Estrada is interested in the best way to provide tutoring for high school students studying math. She varies the amount of time available for tutoring, with one group receiving two hours per week and a second group receiving five hours. She also varies the setting, with one group receiving group instruction and the other receiving individual instruction. What type of design is Dr. Estrada using?

(A) a correlational design
(B) a quasi-experimental design
(C) a factorial design
(D) a covariance design
(E) a pretest-posttest design

184. Dr. Colson's data from a newly designed instrument form a normal distribution. Which of the following conclusions can Dr. Colson make from his observations?

(A) The mean of the distribution will be 100 with a standard deviation of 15.
(B) Fifty percent of all scores will fall within one standard deviation of the mean.
(C) The median will be higher than the mean.
(D) The number of scores between one and two standard deviations from the mean will be the same as the number of scores between two and three standard deviations from the mean.
(E) Equal numbers of scores will be found that are either three standard deviations above or three standard deviations below the mean.

185. Olivia is one of the children in a classroom that local university researchers are using for a sociometric study. The researchers conclude that Olivia has "controversial status" based on their analysis. What does this mean?

(A) The other students like Olivia, but the teachers do not.
(B) The teachers like Olivia, but the other students do not.
(C) Olivia receives many disliked nominations, but she is liked by the most popular children in the class.
(D) Olivia is liked by nearly all of the children, with the exception of the most popular ones.
(E) Olivia receives many liked and many disliked nominations.

186. Which of the following is the best example of a positive correlation?

(A) According to Tyler Vigen, as the number of people who drown in swimming pools goes up, more movies starring Nicolas Cage are released by Hollywood.
(B) The more alcohol students drink, the lower their GPA is likely to be.
(C) The number of emergency room visits do not show a systematic relationship with the phases of the moon.
(D) According to Tyler Vigen, the more honey-producing bee colonies there are in the United States, the lower the juvenile arrest rate for marijuana will be.
(E) According to Tyler Vigen, the more farms there are in the United States, the less likely people are to be killed when their truck or van hits a stationary object.

GO ON TO THE NEXT PAGE

187. Which of the following is a "warning signal" that you might not be thinking critically?

(A) I prefer to figure things out for myself instead of being given the right answer.
(B) I do not change my mind if evidence contradicts my original position.
(C) I welcome criticism of my ideas.
(D) I am open to considering alternative explanations.
(E) I avoid using the affect heuristic in my research.

188. Brenda Milner and Suzanne Corkin conducted decades of testing and observation of Henry Molaison, known in the literature as the famous amnesic patient H. M. Which research method was being used by Milner and Corkin?

(A) naturalistic observation
(B) case study
(C) quasi-experiment
(D) correlation
(E) factorial design

189. Dr. Carter is interested in the effects of prenatal exposure to alcohol on infant well-being. To assess these effects, it is likely that Dr. Carter will use

(A) a true experiment
(B) case studies
(C) naturalistic observations
(D) quasi-experimental designs
(E) interviews

190. Dr. Checkov is investigating the effects of caffeine consumption on memory. She assigns students to groups consuming different levels of caffeine in pill form, and then observes their performance on a series of memory tests. Which of the aspects of this experiment serves as the dependent variable?

(A) how much caffeine the participants consume
(B) the participants' performance on memory tests
(C) the comparison of the participants' previous exposure to caffeine and the condition to which they're assigned in the experiment
(D) the participants' current consumption of caffeinated beverages
(E) the participants' attitudes toward caffeine consumption while studying

GO ON TO THE NEXT PAGE

191. Which of the following describes the major difference between a quasi-experiment and a true experiment?

   (A) the number of levels of the independent variable
   (B) the use of parametric versus nonparametric statistics
   (C) the presence of random assignment to groups
   (D) the number of dependent measures
   (E) the use of correlational coefficients

192. One of the stranger measures used in studies of the effects of violent media is the hot sauce paradigm, which asks participants to devise a recipe for hot sauce to be administered (hypothetically) to another participant. Which of the following describes the use of this measure?

   (A) The measure represents an operationalization of the dependent variable, aggression.
   (B) The measure represents an operationalization of the independent variable, aggression.
   (C) The measure is used to control situational variables.
   (D) The measure is used as background for random assignment to groups.
   (E) The measure provides means for conducting strong meta-analyses.

193. Which of the following is one of the advantages of conducting a longitudinal study?

   (A) Longitudinal studies are usually inexpensive to conduct.
   (B) Longitudinal studies can be concluded quickly.
   (C) Longitudinal studies control for cohort effects.
   (D) Longitudinal studies are rarely affected by participants dropping out.
   (E) It is easy to modify research questions during a longitudinal study.

194. Veronica is concerned about a new survey she has developed for her psychology thesis because the Cronbach's alpha for her instrument is .65. What advice do you have for Veronica?

   (A) Proceed with your study, an alpha of .65 is acceptable.
   (B) Revise your instrument, as your alpha shows unacceptable internal consistency.
   (C) Revise your instrument, as your alpha demonstrates problems with test-retest reliability.
   (D) Revise your instrument, as its validity is in doubt.
   (E) Try out an alternate way of evaluating your instrument; Cronbach might be too strict.

GO ON TO THE NEXT PAGE

Joan is designing an intervention aimed at preventing the development of eating disorders, and she wants to present her program to students the year before they are at highest risk for developing an eating disorder. Prior research has shown that a larger gap between interventions and risk for onset makes the intervention less successful. She has the following data provided by the local school districts in her large city.

Age	Number of New Cases
12	4
13	10
14	28
15	6
16	11
17	42

195. Joan computes the average age of onset in her school districts as somewhere between the ages of fifteen and sixteen years, so she plans to develop an intervention appropriate for that age group. Joan is assuming that which of the following measures of central tendency is most appropriate for her project?

(A) mean
(B) median
(C) mode
(D) z-score
(E) t-score

196. Joan examines her data set further, and determines that

(A) it represents a normal distribution of new cases as a function of age
(B) it represents a normal distribution of age as a function of new cases
(C) age and new cases are negatively correlated
(D) the mean, median, and mode are likely to be about the same
(E) the mean and median might be similar, but the distribution appears to be bimodal

197. Joan cannot afford to give her intervention to all age groups. Based on her data and her goals, when would you advise her to present her intervention to students?

(A) at age eleven, before any new cases have had a chance to develop
(B) at age fourteen, before the mean age of onset for eating disorders
(C) at age sixteen, because the largest group of new cases appear at age seventeen
(D) two times, at ages thirteen and sixteen, which would catch the majority of the students at risk at the appropriate times
(E) two times, at eleven and seventeen, when students are both entering and leaving secondary school

GO ON TO THE NEXT PAGE

198. Data about patterns of adult alcohol consumption in the United States collected by the Centers for Disease Control indicate that the modal pattern for Asian adults is "lifetime abstainer." How should we interpret these data?

(A) The most frequent response by Asian adults living in the United States is that they drink no alcohol at all.

(B) The average response by Asian adults living in the United States is that they drink no alcohol at all.

(C) It is likely that the median drinking level for Asians living in the United States is higher than the mean.

(D) The mean level of alcohol drinking for Asians living in the United States is likely to be below the mode.

(E) It is likely that there are several modes in the drinking patterns of Asian adults living in the United States.

199. Josh's fraternity president tells him that the mean GPA of the fraternity members is a 3.0. However, Josh is aware that a small number of the fraternity brothers are academic superstars who maintain 4.0 GPAs. Josh believes that another measure of central tendency might be more accurate. How would you advise him?

(A) Advise Josh that the mean is a good measure, as GPA is typically distributed normally.

(B) Advise Josh that he should ask for any modes and for the median, as these might provide a more accurate measure of central tendency.

(C) Advise Josh that in the distribution of GPA, the mean, median, and mode are very likely to be the same.

(D) Advise Josh that the brothers with the 4.0 GPAs are outliers, and the president has probably already excluded them from the analysis.

(E) Advise Josh that the data set does not allow him to evaluate the usefulness of the mean as a measure of central tendency, so he should stop worrying.

200. Emily has one data set that has a standard deviation of 2.4 and another data set with a standard deviation of 3.6. What can she conclude about her two data sets?

(A) The scores are about equally clustered around the mean.

(B) The scores in the first data set are more tightly clustered around the mean.

(C) The scores in the second data set are more tightly clustered around the mean.

(D) The first data set probably has more outliers than the second.

(E) The second data set probably has more outliers than the first.

201. Most standardized intelligence tests feature a normal distribution of scores. This means that about how many scores will be located within a single standard deviation from the mean?

(A) We do not have sufficient data to make this judgment.

(B) About 34% will fall within one standard deviation from the mean.

(C) About 68% will fall within one standard deviation from the mean.

(D) About 95% will fall within one standard deviation from the mean.

(E) About 47.5% will fall within one standard deviation from the mean.

GO ON TO THE NEXT PAGE

202. Scatter plots are particularly useful ways of graphing

   (A) normal distrubutions
   (B) skewed distributions
   (C) bimodal distributions
   (D) correlations
   (E) quasi-experimental data

203. Isaiah is testing a hypothesis that predicts that use of a new medication will reduce symptoms of bipolar disorder. What will be Isaiah's null hypothesis?

   (A) Bipolar disorder does not respond to any type of medication.
   (B) Bipolar disorder symptoms will worsen following use of the new drug.
   (C) The new drug will have no measurable effects on symptoms of bipolar disorder.
   (D) The new drug will be effective, but side effects will make it unusable.
   (E) The new drug will not be superior to existing treatments for bipolar disorder.

204. Jenna has a rare genetic disorder and she has been approached by a private genetic therapy company to participate in clinical trials. What protections will Jenna have as a research participant?

   (A) Her data will be confidential, which means they will not be shared with her employer or insurance company.
   (B) She will be asked to sign an informed consent.
   (C) The risks of the procedure will be carefully spelled out for Jenna prior to her participation.
   (D) She will be informed that she can leave the experiment at any time.
   (E) Jenna has no protection, as the company has no federal funding and therefore does not fall under government research ethics standards.

205. Animal research in psychology

   (A) no longer occurs
   (B) makes up a very small percentage (7–8%) of published studies in psychology journals
   (C) makes up the majority of published studies in psychology journals
   (D) is not subject to any ethical constraints, unlike the use of human participants
   (E) is regulated in the same way as the cosmetics industry's use of animals

If there is still time remaining, you may review your answers.

1.	B	36.	A	71.	E	106.	C	141.	A	176.	E
2.	A	37.	B	72.	C	107.	E	142.	B	177.	C
3.	B	38.	D	73.	D	108.	B	143.	C	178.	B
4.	C	39.	B	74.	A	109.	A	144.	C	179.	A
5.	A	40.	A	75.	E	110.	C	145.	D	180.	D
6.	D	41.	E	76.	B	111.	D	146.	B	181.	B
7.	A	42.	B	77.	D	112.	C	147.	B	182.	B
8.	E	43.	C	78.	C	113.	C	148.	C	183.	C
9.	A	44.	D	79.	B	114.	C	149.	D	184.	E
10.	C	45.	B	80.	A	115.	A	150.	A	185.	C
11.	B	46.	A	81.	B	116.	A	151.	B	186.	A
12.	A	47.	C	82.	B	117.	C	152.	A	187.	B
13.	C	48.	B	83.	A	118.	A	153.	C	188.	B
14.	C	49.	C	84.	C	119.	C	154.	A	189.	D
15.	A	50.	A	85.	B	120.	B	155.	B	190.	B
16.	B	51.	C	86.	C	121.	A	156.	A	191.	C
17.	D	52.	B	87.	D	122.	C	157.	B	192.	A
18.	D	53.	B	88.	A	123.	C	158.	C	193.	C
19.	C	54.	C	89.	C	124.	B	159.	D	194.	B
20.	A	55.	E	90.	A	125.	A	160.	B	195.	A
21.	C	56.	E	91.	C	126.	B	161.	A	196.	E
22.	B	57.	C	92.	B	127.	B	162.	E	197.	D
23.	C	58.	A	93.	D	128.	D	163.	B	198.	A
24.	B	59.	D	94.	A	129.	B	164.	A	199.	B
25.	C	60.	B	95.	B	130.	A	165.	C	200.	B
26.	C	61.	C	96.	D	131.	B	166.	D	201.	C
27.	A	62.	A	97.	A	132.	C	167.	E	202.	D
28.	B	63.	B	98.	B	133.	C	168.	C	203.	C
29.	C	64.	A	99.	D	134.	E	169.	B	204.	E
30.	D	65.	B	100.	B	135.	A	170.	C	205.	B
31.	E	66.	A	101.	B	136.	A	171.	A		
32.	C	67.	B	102.	A	137.	D	172.	D		
33.	D	68.	C	103.	B	138.	B	173.	E		
34.	C	69.	E	104.	D	139.	A	174.	C		
35.	C	70.	D	105.	A	140.	D	175.	D		

SCORING DIAGNOSTIC TEST 2

To score your second diagnostic test, please compare the answers on your answer sheet with the answers below. Place a check mark next to questions you answered correctly. Place an "X" next to questions you answered incorrectly. Leave questions you did not answer blank.

Answer Explanations

Learning

_____ 1. **(B)** Extinction in operant conditioning occurs when the behavior is no longer followed by the consequence.

_____ 2. **(A)** Learning will happen in most of the other options, but Hull thought drive reduction was important to learning. A hungry child finding candy will reduce her hunger drive.

_____ 3. **(B)** According to the Rescorla-Wagner model, the amount of learning that occurs on each trial is a function of the amount of "surprise" experienced by the learner. The more you know, the less surprised you are, so learning tapers off at asymptote.

_____ 4. **(C)** The rats are experiencing different contingencies. The buzzer is a more reliable signal for the first rat than for the second rat, so the first rat should learn faster.

_____ 5. **(A)** Garcia's taste aversion studies led to interest in animals' predispositions to make certain associations more rapidly than others. We seem to be "prepared" to learn certain things.

_____ 6. **(D)** Insight is sudden.

_____ 7. **(A)** Martin Seligman's experiments with dogs led to his concept of learned helplessness.

Learning Summary	
Number Correct	
Number Incorrect	
Number Blank	

Language

_____ 8. **(E)** One of the most reliable age-related changes in language-learning capacity is decreased sensitivity to differences among phonemes. This is probably one of the reasons that older language learners are more likely than younger language learners to speak with an accent.

_____ 9. **(A)** Pragmatics refers to the practical use of language, which includes knowing when another is done speaking and waiting your turn to speak.

_____ 10. **(C)** Whorf was a strong advocate for the idea that having more vocabulary helps you think differently about a topic.

11. **(B)** In spite of being a language of space and movement, American Sign Language is processed by the brain in ways that are very similar to spoken languages.

12. **(A)** "Semantics" refers to the meaning of words.

13. **(C)** "Recursivity" refers to the quality of taking a limited set of elements (perhaps phonemes or speech sounds) and combining them in a hierarchical fashion to make an unlimited number of novel messages. Most linguists do not believe that animal communicators can produce this unlimited range of utterances.

Language Summary	
Number Correct	
Number Incorrect	
Number Blank	

Memory

14. **(C)** Clustering items to be learned in memory is a very effective strategy. This strategy is evident in free recall, in which the participant can repeat a list of words in any order he or she chooses.

15. **(A)** For a list of the typical length used in serial position curve studies (about twenty or so), the early words on the list are more likely to be recalled (primacy) because they have already been processed into long-term memory and they suffer little interference. The superior recall for the very last words on the list is probably the result of their being maintained in short-term memory at the time of recall. A delay between the presentation of the last word and recall usually abolishes the recency effect, or the superior memory for the last words on a list.

16. **(B)** Baddeley's working memory, an extension of ideas about short-term memory, allows for information from different modalities (vision and audition in this example) to be processed simultaneously.

17. **(D)** This strategy combines spaced trials (superior to massed trials) and emphasis on meaningful, deep processing (superior to shallow processing).

18. **(D)** Retroactive interference occurs when material learned *following* the learning of target material interferes with the processing or retrieval of the target material.

19. **(C)** Tip of the tongue shows us that retrieval is not all or none. We often get bits of data as we search for a target. Do you know the name Jordan is trying to recall? It was Gavrilo Princip, a Bosnian Serb.

20. **(A)** The use of "helpful" served as a cue for the sentence, which illustrated helpfulness, even though the word *helpful* did not appear in the sentence.

21. **(C)** Individuals with this type of neurocognitive disorder, often referred to as Korsakoff's syndrome (although Korsakoff's is a bit broader category) experience anterograde amnesia, or difficulty learning new things.

_____ 22. **(B)** The hippocampus plays an essential role in the formation of new declarative memories.

_____ 23. **(C)** As far as we know, long-term memory is unlimited in terms of learning new things and remembering old things.

_____ 24. **(B)** Chunking can expand the capacity of short-term memory and rehearsal can expand its duration.

_____ 25. **(C)** All of the assessments except the essay are examples of recognition tasks.

_____ 26. **(C)** Our memories for personal experiences make up our episodic memory.

_____ 27. **(A)** Using memories can put them back in a reactivated state that makes them vulnerable to change when they are reconsolidated.

_____ 28. **(B)** We are "fresh" when we begin to process the first words on a list, so they are subject to less interference than the words appearing later in the list.

_____ 29. **(C)** By definition.

_____ 30. **(D)** Logan's schedule is an example of massed learning trials, which produces inferior results compared to the use of spaced learning trials.

_____ 31. **(E)** Mnemonic devices are memory aids that link information to be learned to information that is already well known.

_____ 32. **(C)** Procedural memories quickly become automated, which makes them quite persistent.

Memory Summary	
Number Correct	
Number Incorrect	
Number Blank	

Thinking

_____ 33. **(D)** Metacognition is all about strategies, and while repetition can be useful, it is not as strategic as the other approaches that require students to "customize" their strategies to their own strengths and weaknesses.

_____ 34. **(C)** The coach's "I knew it all along" approach is an example of the hindsight bias.

_____ 35. **(C)** All of these are helpful, but what really separates the expert from the wannabe is a minimum of ten years of regular practice in the expert skill.

_____ 36. **(A)** Algorithms are time-consuming but should guarantee a solution.

_____ 37. **(B)** A mental set can provide a handy shortcut, but if you always solve problems the way you did in the past, you can also miss the obvious. The other choices represent some "outside-the-box" thinking instead of use of a mental set.

_____ 38. **(D)** Functional fixedness results in thinking about a problem a single way, whereas this student demonstrated some creativity. We're not sure the test grader would appreciate this, however.

_____ 39. **(B)** Hopefully, Samantha wouldn't get as far as graduate school without understanding that you have to be very careful about excluding participants, and her egregious behavior is definitely a result of the confirmation bias.

_____ 40. **(A)** Andrew's professor is under no obligation whatsoever to extend an exception to others, but uses this as an excuse to say "no" to Andrew.

_____ 41. **(E)** Spearman's _g_ is not in conflict with the idea that intelligence may occur in multiple domains, but simply assumes so many of them are tightly correlated that a single score predicts most intelligent behavior.

_____ 42. **(B)** Maximizers want the best, but because of this tendency, they might find decision making to be difficult and they are often dissatisfied with the results of their life choices.

_____ 43. **(C)** This is a classic four-step approach to problem solving.

Thinking Summary	
Number Correct	
Number Incorrect	
Number Blank	

Sensation and Perception

_____ 44. **(D)** The "nasal" part here is a giveaway. This structure is part of the olfactory systems of many animals and is used to detect pheromones.

_____ 45. **(B)** Retinal disparity refers to the slightly different view seen by each of the two eyes. Accommodation refers the the extent of "crossing," with more distant objects requiring less or no accomodation.

_____ 46. **(A)** We categorize different versions of the same stimulus (think speech sounds spoken by people with different accents) with an abrupt change at the point where the identification of a category changes.

_____ 47. **(C)** This is a signal detection problem, and the taster's hit and correct rejection scores seem good. False alarms outnumbered misses, suggesting a bias in favor of not wanting to miss a sample of tampered wine.

_____ 48. **(B)** Bright colors associated with taste typically increase ratings of taste or flavor intensity.

_____ 49. **(C)** Hair cells riding on top of the basilar membrane bend in their surrounding fluid, leading to their formation of action potentials.

_____ 50. **(A)** This is a classic demonstration of opponent processes in color vision.

_____ 51. **(C)** We are at most risk of missing a change in the visual field when the change occurs during a saccadic eye movement, during which a person moves both eyes from one point of fixation to the next.

_____ 52. **(B)** The most common form of color deficiency is produced by faulty genes for the long or medium photopigment. Because these genes are located on the X chromosome, this type of color deficiency is sex-linked, or more common in males.

_____ 53. **(B)** By definition.

_____ 54. **(C)** The more "crossed" the eyes are, the closer the point of fixation is to them.

_____ 55. **(E)** This is an example of motion parallax.

Sensation and Perception Summary	
Number Correct	
Number Incorrect	
Number Blank	

Physiological/Behavioral Neuroscience

_____ 56. **(E)** Functional magnetic resonance imaging (fMRI) is best suited of the listed methods to assess brain activity associated with a behavior like reading.

_____ 57. **(C)** Cortisol, a glucocorticoid associated with waking and stress, is released by the adrenal glands.

_____ 58. **(A)** The description of the area affected by the stroke corresponds to Broca's area. Damage to Broca's area tends to leave comprehension relatively intact while impairing speech production.

_____ 59. **(D)** The other alternatives would act to enhance the activity of dopamine at a synapse, which means they would have agonistic instead of antagonistic effects.

_____ 60. **(B)** Fragile X and phenylketonuria (PKU) are definitely heritable, as is sickle-cell anemia. Down syndrome, Klinefelter syndrome, and Turner syndrome are more likely to result from meiosis errors due to parental age.

_____ 61. **(C)** A type of glial cell known as an astrocyte forms a close connection with blood vessels serving the brain, and certain toxins cannot leave the blood vessels at that point. Obviously, any drug considered to be psychoactive moves past the blood-brain barrier into the neural tissue.

_____ 62. **(A)** The nasal hemiretinas are nearest the nose, and the temporal hemiretinas form the lateral half of the retina (toward the temporal lobes). Images to the left of center, assuming the eyes are focused on a point directly ahead, will be processed by the visual cortex in the right hemisphere.

_____ 63. **(B)** Any time you see the word _heritable_, think of populations. Never apply heritability to individuals.

_____ 64. **(A)** The orbitofrontal cortex participates in impulse control and delayed gratification. Individuals with damage to this area often make impulsive, poor decisions.

_____ 65. **(B)** A hormone organizes when it changes structure and activates when it affects the likelihood of behavior without changing the underlying structure, which usually occurs later in life.

_____ 66. **(A)** By definition.

_____ 67. **(B)** All parts of the brain are important, but the medulla is involved with a number of life-sustaining processes, which makes any surgery in this vicinity very dangerous.

_____ 68. **(C)** Oxytocin multitasks, but differences in oxytocin receptor expression in the brains of different species of prairie voles seem to account for differences seen in their mating and parenting behavior.

_____ 69. **(E)** Social psychologists might endorse A through D, but E is the domain of the sociobiologists and their colleagues in evolutionary psychology.

_____ 70. **(D)** Event-related potentials can indicate whether sounds are being processed normally by the brain.

_____ 71. **(E)** The vestibular system of the inner ear and the cerebellum are important for maintaining balance.

_____ 72. **(C)** The amygdala helps us respond appropriately to threat. In the absence of input from the amygdala, an animal might not be scared when it really should be.

_____ 73. **(D)** This is exactly the result reported by Sperry and Gazzaniga. The left hand is controlled by the right hemisphere, which is capable of understanding simple single words like _he_. It is a mistake to think the right hemisphere processes no language at all.

_____ 74. **(A)** Glands and organs are directed by the autonomic nervous system. At times of arousal, the sympathetic division of the autonomic nervous system is running the show.

_____ 75. **(E)** Delta waves are seen during Stages 3 and 4 of non-REM or slow-wave sleep.

_____ 76. **(B)** Melatonin, released only at night by the pineal gland, breaks down very quickly in the presence of light, and in particular, in the presence of the short-wave light that characterizes most electronic devices. In contrast, the firelight enjoyed by our ancestors produces light primarily in the long wavelength (reddish) end of the visible spectrum. Poor melatonin function can disrupt normal sleep patterns.

_____ 77. **(D)** Oligodendrocytes are the glial cells that myelinate the central nervous system, and they are the target of the immune system in multiple sclerosis.

_____ 78. **(C)** Polarization refers to being apart, so this change represents an increase in polarization or a hyperpolarization. Following an action potential, a cell membrane is usually hyperpolarized due to the relatively slow closure of potassium channels. Because it takes much more input to depolarize the cell from –80 mV to threshold than it does to depolarize the cell from –70 mV to threshold, this represents a relative refractory period. The cell is capable of firing again as soon as the sodium channels are reset by a return to a negative recording, but because of the distance to threshold, more than the usual input is needed to fire.

_____ 79. **(B)** Because acetylcholine is the main neurochemical used at the neuromuscular junction, most antagonists produce paralysis. There is a snake in southeast Asia known as "six step," because that's how far a person walks before dying, usually of paralysis of the diaghragm leading to respiratory arrest.

_____ 80. **(A)** By definition. Amphetamines, however, also act by enhancing the release of dopamine from the axon terminal.

_____ 81. **(B)** Alcohol, barbiturates, and benzodiazepines (tranquilizers like Valium) act as agonists at the $GABA_A$ receptor. A combination of these drugs can lead to reduced brain function leading to death.

Physiological/Behavioral Neuroscience Summary	
Number Correct	
Number Incorrect	
Number Blank	

Clinical and Abnormal

_____ 82. **(B)** A diathesis-stress model suggests that genetic predispositions interact with stressful experiences to determine risk for a disorder.

_____ 83. **(A)** This is the new DSM-5 description of schizoaffective disorder.

_____ 84. **(C)** Daniel has symptoms that cannot be explained by current medical causality.

_____ 85. **(B)** According to cognitive therapists, overgeneralizing from one mistake to a global condemnation of the self is typical of people with major depressive disorder.

_____ 86. **(C)** Anterograde amnesia usually results from brain damage.

_____ 87. **(D)** "Reflecting feelings" or serving as a mirror to the client is characteristic of humanistic approaches, like that of Carl Rogers.

_____ 88. **(A)** Cody fits the diagnostic criteria for antisocial personality disorder.

_____ 89. **(C)** Social interaction deficits are among the core symptoms of autism spectrum disorder.

_____ 90. **(A)** Empirical research supports the use of emotional disclosure to help healing.

_____ 91. **(C)** We might make a case for choice B, but the description focuses on Danielle's strong internalization of her cultural norms of right and wrong.

_____ 92. **(B)** By definition. Schizophrenia is not the only disorder in which catatonia occurs, however.

_____ 93. **(D)** Avolition means lack of motivation. The negative symptoms refer to a behavior that is "missing in action." We are supposed to demonstrate motivated behavior, so avolition works as a negative symptom. The reason for distinguishing between positive and negative symptoms is that they seem to have different underlying biological correlates and respond differentially to some medications.

_____ 94. **(A)** Hypofrontality is not unique to schizophrenia, but it might explain some of the bizarre ideation associated with this disorder.

_____ 95. **(B)** Dopamine agonists can produce psychosis and dopamine antagonists reduce psychosis for most patients. Phencyclidine (PCP) is a glutamate antagonist, and produces a rather violent form of psychosis that is nonetheless similar to schizophrenia.

_____ 96. **(D)** The strength of the newer antipsychotics is in their results with negative symptoms. They produce serious side effects, but sometimes this takes a longer time than with the traditional dopamine antagonists like the phenothiazines.

_____ 97. **(A)** There is only one set of symptoms used to diagnose depression within both disorders.

_____ 98. **(B)** Lithium carbonate is one of the very few diagnostic medications in psychopathology. If you have bipolar disorder, you will react to lithium, but if you do not have the disorder, little noticeable change will occur (other than the rather unhealthy side effects).

_____ 99. **(D)** Major depressive disorder decreases over the lifespan, with approximately two-thirds of all patients being female at all adult ages. Prior to puberty, rates of males and females with depression are about the same.

_____ 100. **(B)** Serotonin suppresses REM sleep, so people with depression, who are believed to have low serotonin activity, experience too much REM. They enter REM too early in the night and spend too much time in this stage. Antidepressants boost serotonin activity, hence they suppress REM significantly.

_____ 101. **(B)** Depression found in cases of either bipolar disorder or major depressive disorder is the most likely reason to use ECT.

_____ 102. **(A)** Benzodiazepines and alcohol are GABA agonists, and both reduce anxiety.

_____ 103. **(B)** One panic attack does not panic disorder make. To qualify for panic disorder, a person must experience multiple, frequent attacks accompanied by anxiety about having additional attacks.

_____ 104. **(D)** Many people obsess about harm befalling a loved one, and then engage in useless rituals (stepping around cracks) in an effort to reduce anxiety.

_____ 105. **(A)** Neuroscientists are leaning toward a reduction in hippocampal volume as a result of PTSD, although some consider low hippocampal volume to be a risk factor for PTSD.

_____ 106. **(C)** Just because you've used projective personality tests forever does not mean that they hold up to scientific measures of reliability and validity. We have to be willing to discard approaches if science tells us to do so.

_____ 107. **(E)** Some licensed therapists advertise themselves as coaches, as they find this is stigma reducing for their clients. However, there is nothing to stop anyone from advertising him- or herself as a life coach.

_____ 108. **(B)** A small number of antipsychotics were approved for use with severely impaired children with autism spectrum disorder who are engaging in self-injurious behavior. Nonetheless, many physicians medicate children with autism with a whole host of off-label medications for anxiety, ADHD, and so on.

_____ 109. **(A)** Our favorite is the University of Washington's Spider World, a virtual exposure therapy program for people with specific phobias related to spiders. Eww.

Clinical and Abnormal Summary	
Number Correct	
Number Incorrect	
Number Blank	

Life Span Development

_____ 110. **(C)** Low-reactive children are bold and relatively fearless. In the wrong nurture circumstances, they might have a higher risk for antisocial behavior.

_____ 111. **(D)** Fluid intelligence, like reaction time, describes behavior that requires no previous knowledge or experience. This decreases somewhat over the life span. Crystallized intelligence, which is knowledge based, remains stable as long as individuals remain healthy.

_____ 112. **(C)** Either people are at peace with their life choices to date, and continue to contribute to the world around themselves, or they stagnate.

_____ 113. **(C)** People do indeed retain the ability to learn language after puberty, but their sensitivity to phonology means that they are less likely to speak without an accent.

_____ 114. **(C)** Children have lots of best friends, but they need parents who will step up and set reasonable limits.

_____ 115. **(A)** By definition.

_____ 116. **(A)** As mentioned in question 111, reaction time tends to decrease gradually during adulthood.

_____ 117. **(C)** Most of the circumstances in these answers can be correlated with child maltreatment, but a three-year-old is at higher risk than a ten-year-old.

_____ 118. **(A)** Pretend play in which one object (even the self) can portray another indicates symbolic thinking.

_____ 119. **(C)** Discontinuous theories see stages as changing somewhat abruptly, with behavior at a stage being quite different from what has come before and what will come next.

_____ 120. **(B)** By definition. During this stage, all organs are put in place, and then they mature during the remainder of pregnancy (fetal stage).

_____ 121. **(A)** These systems are among the latest to mature, and their maturation can be challenged by premature birth.

_____ 122. **(C)** This reflex is overwritten as the motor systems mature but can reappear in certain types of brain damage.

_____ 123. **(C)** The fetus starts to hear very well at seven months postconception and new-borns easily recognize their mothers' scent.

_____ 124. **(B)** The infant's visual experience looks blurry by adult standards. Infants need high contrast, like the black letters on this white page, to see well.

_____ 125. **(A)** This germ layer also gives rise to skin, and in the right organisms, to hoof and horn, too.

_____ 126. **(B)** This is average. The usual "window" of normal first-time walking ranges from nine to eighteen months of age.

_____ 127. **(B)** These are magical thinkers who do not yet process cause and effect in logical ways.

_____ 128. **(D)** Surprisingly, children attain adult levels of selective attention (lack of distractibility) in the early years of elementary school. Sustained attention, or ability to stay on task, however, increases gradually into adulthood.

_____ 129. **(B)** This is hotly debated, as some believe tasks have not been found that will demonstrate TOM earlier. However, most psychologists agree that TOM should be in place by age four years.

_____ 130. **(A)** The fearful and shy child is at greater risk for later anxiety and depression than the bold, fearless child.

_____ 131. **(B)** This is the typical behavior shown by avoidantly attached children.

_____ 132. **(C)** Externalizing disorders are about as common among children raised by authoritarian parents as in those raised by authoritative parents, but internalizing disorders like depression are often more frequent.

_____ 133. **(C)** The rights and wrongs are not as important to Kohlberg as the reasoning behind a moral decision. Nathaniel is making an independent judgment of the rule, which is typical of postconventional reasoning.

_____ 134. **(E)** By definition.

_____ 135. **(A)** Human beings are unusual in the animal kingdom for the long amount of time they live past reproductive age. This is one possible advantage for longevity that could impact the passage of genes into future generations.

Life Span Development Summary	
Number Correct	
Number Incorrect	
Number Blank	

Personality

_____ 136. **(A)** "Complex" tells you we are discussing a Freudian, and this was Adler's contribution. Adler is considered a neo-Freudian, although his theories are often quite different from Freud's.

_____ 137. **(D)** When we act in ways that contradict our true feelings, we might be using the defense mechanism of reaction formation.

_____ 138. **(B)** The Myers-Briggs test is based on Jung's personality-type work. If you're a fan of the test, I'm sorry to report that it doesn't do well in analyses of reliability and validity.

_____ 139. **(A)** Allport's cardinal traits are rare and truly dominate a person's life.

_____ 140. **(D)** Horney attempted to modify Freud's theories from a female perspective. She is mentioned frequently in gender study courses.

_____ 141. **(A)** By definition. The other terms are also used by Rogers and other humanistic psychologists, though.

_____ 142. **(B)** By definition. Conscientiousness is the only one of the Big Five traits that predicts stable employment, although people who score low on this dimension do make contributions to work groups by finding shortcuts.

_____ 143. **(C)** People with an internal locus of control believe most of their outcomes are due to their internal characteristics and hard work, whereas people with an external locus of control think outcomes are the results of opportunity or chance.

_____ 144. **(C)** My favorite animal personality work has been done with the octopus. One octopus lab distinguished between shy "Emily Dickinson" and another octopus named "Lucretia McEvil" by the staff. I'd like to see Lucretia.

_____ 145. **(D)** This concept is not restricted to personality but covers any discussion of heritability. Heritability is applied to populations, but never to individuals. With heritability ranging from none (0%, the likelihood of having a heart—we all have one—there is no variation to explain genetically) to absolute (100%, such as the likelihood of Huntington's disease), a measure between 40 and 60% is considered moderate.

Personality Summary	
Number Correct	
Number Incorrect	
Number Blank	

Social

_____ 146. **(B)** According to the availability heuristic, things that are easier to think about seem more likely. We hear news reports about shark attacks (two happened on my local beach this year, but they are actually quite rare), so it is easy to think about shark attacks. When have you ever heard of a person getting killed by falling airplane parts (but it does happen, unfortunately)?

_____ 147. **(B)** It sounds like choice D might be another option, but the "shift" part points to group polarization. In group polarization, people make more extreme decisions after a discussion than they would before a discussion. They don't flip—they just move farther out on the dimension they were on originally.

_____ 148. **(C)** There is a certain amount of just world in the other possibilities, but succeeding just because you were born to the right parents strikes people as a bit unfair.

_____ 149. **(D)** Compare this problem with question 147, and it might help you distinguish between the two concepts. The groupthink literature focuses on failure, but keep in mind some groupthinking groups (e.g., the terrorists who planned 9/11) are sometimes able to meet their goals.

_____ 150. **(A)** Instrumental aggression is goal oriented and relatively impersonal. You have something I want/need, so I use aggression to take it from you.

_____ 151. **(B)** The terms we use to describe ourselves often provide a window to our self-concepts.

_____ 152. **(A)** Introspection for the purposes of self-awareness suffers from the same flaws as introspection as a scientific technique. The other options are based on observation, and are therefore more likely to be reliable.

_____ 153. **(C)** People with low self-esteem often make these overgeneralizations about one failure into a more global problem—I'm not smart enough for college.

_____ 154. **(A)** This is an example of the "bask in reflected glory (BIRG)" method of self-enhancement. People associate themselves with success in efforts to feel more successful. Everybody loves a winner!

_____ 155. **(B)** Sherif's classic Robbers Cave experiments with young boys at summer camp both initiated prejudice between arbitrary groups of campers and then decreased prejudice by bringing the boys together to solve a mutual problem, such as a break in the camp's water supply system.

_____ 156. **(A)** Low self-monitors are less concerned with modifying their behavior to fit their social environments.

_____ 157. **(B)** The "everybody does it" train of thought is usually wrong. Although many college students binge drink, many do not.

_____ 158. **(C)** We modify our behavior somewhat based on the people with whom we're interacting.

_____ 159. **(D)** The self-reference effect (SRE) is very robust, and we encourage you to make use of this strategy as you prepare for your GRE Psychology Test. Relating the concepts in this book to your own experience should make the concepts easier to remember at test time.

_____ 160. **(B)** Teens are often very self-conscious due to the mistaken impression that other people are truly paying attention to them. In truth, other teens are so worried about their own hair and complexions that they have little time or energy to worry about other people's hair and complexions.

_____ 161. **(A)** Simply having a poster featuring two eyes above an honor coffee bar was sufficient in one study to produce more contributions to the coffee fund.

_____ 162. **(E)** Roy Baumeister and his colleagues have been very critical of programs designed to artificially raise self-esteem as a means of reducing social problems. They pointed out that career criminals locked in prisons often have very high self-esteem indeed. They're so good, they feel entitled to take what they want from others.

_____ 163. **(B)** The general idea is that to counteract our fear of mortality, we view our lives as having been meaningful.

_____ 164. **(A)** Cognition can be quite powerful. If you believe you have limited willpower, you tend to use it up by resisting temptation. People who do not believe that willpower is limited do not show a depletion effect.

_____ 165. **(C)** You might have learned that the correspondence bias and the fundamental attribution error are the same things, but social psychologists differentiate between the two. This is a clear example of the correspondence bias. You make dispositional inferences in the face of dominant situational cues. The fundamental attribution error suggests that we fail to see situational contributions at all, which can be one reason for the correspondence bias, but not the only cause.

_____ 166. **(D)** If we had to go through a terrible experience to join a group, that group must be something special.

_____ 167. **(E)** Raising people's emotions can interfere with persuasion unless you provide them with an action step they can take to reduce their arousal.

_____ 168. **(C)** Prejudices are attitudes, stereotypes are cognitions, and discrimination is a behavior.

_____ 169. **(B)** A person might claim to be unprejudiced but still harbor prejudiced attitudes. People who claim to be unprejudiced still seat themselves closer to a person of the same race than to a person of a different race.

_____ 170. **(C)** Conformity occurs in the absence of a direct request.

_____ 171. **(A)** People like to seem consistent. If you can get a person to make a small commitment, he or she might be more willing to make a larger one later.

Social Summary	
Number Correct	
Number Incorrect	
Number Blank	

General

_____ 172. **(D)** The other questions are shared by philosophy and psychology.

_____ 173. **(E)** Close supervision is not a feature of the sociotechnical model.

_____ 174. **(C)** Titchener was a strong proponent of structuralism, whereas Wertheimer was a leading member of the Gestalt school of psychology, which rejected structuralism.

_____ 175. **(D)** Cognitive psychologists began to reject strict behaviorism's reluctance to consider mental or internal processing.

_____ 176. **(E)** These memory phenomena were investigated by Ebbinghaus.

_____ 177. **(C)** Functionalism as described by William James viewed behavior as purposeful. This idea extended Darwin's emphasis on the goals of survival and reproductive success.

_____ 178. **(B)** Google's practice of making all employees stockholders shows care for the workers who in turn invest in the company.

_____ 179. **(A)** Freud had a relatively negative view of humans as being inherently selfish and aggressive, with positive behavior resulting from socialization. In contrast, the humanistic psychologists viewed humans as inherently good and willing to grow and learn. Society for the humanistic psychologist has the potential to do harm in the form of conditional positive regard.

_____ 180. **(D)** The next most frequent choice of employment is in academia, but most Ph.D.s work in clinical practice.

General Summary	
Number Correct	
Number Incorrect	
Number Blank	

Measurement

_____ 181. **(B)** Sociometry is a classic technique for mapping networks of friends.

_____ 182. **(B)** A regression analysis would tell us how much of the variance in annual income resulted from years in college or from years of experience.

_____ 183. **(C)** This experiment is an example of a factorial design, with time spent in tutoring as one factor and group versus individual tutoring as a second factor. The dependent variable is likely to be success on a math test or the equivalent.

_____ 184. **(E)** In a normal curve, each segment will hold the same number of cases.

_____ 185. **(C)** We're left wondering if Olivia isn't something of a bully. Most bullies are disliked by many children, but they are also described as "the coolest kids in class."

_____ 186. **(A)** Please don't review Tyler Vigen's Spurious Correlations website until you're done with the GRE Psychology Test, because you'll spend too much time laughing over his many examples. However, if you end up as a Research Methods T.A., this is a great source for convincing students to avoid making causal attributions based on correlational data.

_____ 187. **(B)** One of the hardest things for a researcher to do is to admit a line of research or former findings are just wrong. Yet this ability is at the core of good science.

_____ 188. **(B)** A case study looks at one or a small number of cases in great depth.

_____ 189. **(D)** One of the major differences between a true experiment and a quasi-experiment is the use of random assignment to groups. Due to ethical concerns, we can't randomly assign pregnant women to drinking and nondrinking groups. We have to take them where we find them, while understanding many individual differences will not be controlled very well.

_____ 190. **(B)** Caffeine probably has lots of effects that could be studied, but in this study, we're interested in outcomes related to memory. The words _effects on_ are the biggest clue.

_____ 191. **(C)** As we mentioned in question 189, we do not have random assignment in a quasi-experiment. People self-select into groups, which means we have much more uncontrolled individual variation than in a true experiment featuring random assignment to groups.

_____ 192. **(A)** This measure has actually been used in a number of studies, but we would need to see how valid it is (does it really predict real-world aggressiveness?).

_____ 193. **(C)** Cross-sectional studies are vulnerable to cohort effects. Being twenty years old in 1975 is very different from being twenty years old in 2015.

_____ 194. **(B)** An alpha of .70 is at the bottom of acceptability for internal consistency. Fortunately, most statistics programs help you highlight individual items that are causing problems. These can then be removed and/or replaced.

_____ 195. **(A)** The mean is the arithmetic average of a data set.

_____ 196. **(E)** We have two peak ages of onset, at ages fourteen and seventeen years.

_____ 197. **(D)** Joan's intervention is best when it is presented within a year of risk of onset, so one year before each mode would be the best use of her resources.

_____ 198. **(A)** The mode describes the most frequent response.

_____ 199. **(B)** A median can do a better job than a mode at describing a data set that is not normally distributed or close to normally distributed. Knowing the modes, too, tells Josh something more about the "typical" behavior of the fraternity brothers.

_____ 200. **(B)** A smaller standard deviation indicates closer clustering of data points around a mean.

_____ 201. **(C)** Thirty-four percent will fall within one standard deviation on either side of the mean, so together, this adds up to 68%.

_____202. **(D)** Scatter plots allow you to graph points representing values for two variables, like height and weight.

_____203. **(C)** If Isaiah's hypothesis is that he will see a measurable effect of the drug on symptoms, the null hypothesis must be that there will be no significant effect on symptoms.

_____204. **(E)** Not all organizations conducting research fall under government guidelines regarding the treatment of research participants. Only organizations that accept federal funding (for research, scholarships, student loans, etc.) are compelled to follow federal standards. We hope that other organizations do so voluntarily, but it's a good idea to read the fine print.

_____205. **(B)** With new brain imaging technologies and other cognitive methods, psychology no longer is as dependent on animal research as it was in the first half of the twentieth century. Most animal research in psychology is done with rodents and invertebrates in the area of behavioral neuroscience.

Measurement Summary	
Number Correct	
Number Incorrect	
Number Blank	

Transfer the data you collected for each section into the chart below for easy reference.

	Number Correct (C)	Number Incorrect (I)	Number Blank	C-(I/4)	75th Percentile Target	Maximum Possible
Learning					5	7
Language					5	6
Memory					12	19
Thinking					8	11
Sensation Perception					8	12
Physio/BN					18	26
Clinical/ Abnormal					18	28
Life Span					18	26
Personality					7	10
Social					18	26
General					6	9
Methods					16	25

Computing Your Total Score	
Add up the totals of the C and I rows above and fill in the total number correct, total number incorrect, and C-(I/4) below. The ETS rounds up for .5 and above, and down for .1 to .4.	
Total Number Correct	
Total Number Incorrect	
Total Raw Score C – (I/4) =	

For copyright reasons, we cannot provide a chart for converting raw scores to scale scores. In addition, the scaled scores differ a bit from one version of the test to another. Please review the latest *GRE Psychology Test Practice Book*, which is free from ETS, to get an idea of how the scaled scores (which are the ones reported to your programs) will look.

We can, however, give you some representative ranges.

Raw Score	Scaled Score	Percentile
175+	800–880	99
163	760	95
154	730	90
147	710	85
138	680	75
134	670	70
125	640	60
117	615	50

PLANNING YOUR STUDY

Review your C-(I/4) scores for each of the topic areas in your results chart. How do they compare with your first diagnostic test results? We hope you are making good progress!

We are assuming that you would like to score as high as possible, but your chances of being admitted to a competitive graduate program are better if you score in the 75th percentile or above. We are using that as an initial target. The relevant C-(I/4) scores for each topic area appear at the bottom of the columns in bold.

Compare your C-(I/4) scores with the target scores. Do you see a pattern? Are there some areas where you are stronger than others? Are your scores consistent across all topic areas? Can you identify any weak areas?

Keeping your strengths and weaknesses in mind, it is time to review once again! To make the best use of your efforts, tackle your weak areas first and give them the most time and attention.

Just a Thought or Two

Here are a few more observations and thoughts to blend with those we already shared. Just tuck 'em in that clever strategy-arsenal you've been building.

- You can expect about a half-dozen or so of those cute little "I only," "II only," and so on question formats. Don't let them throw you. Jennifer Palmer graciously passed along a successful test-taking strategy she used on these GRE items. The format you'll see will be some variation of this: "I only," "II only," "III only," "I and II only," "II and III only." Sometimes you'll see a "I, II, and III." Whatever format you encounter, the key approach is this—*Look at the individual answer choices rather than the combinations!* Take one statement at a time! Here, we'll show you what we mean:

(A) I only
(B) II only
(C) III only
(D) I and II only
(E) II and III only

Start with (A). If it's true then you can eliminate (B), (C), and (E). If it's false you can still eliminate (A) and (D). As Jennifer observed, it's generally more advantageous to decide definitively that a statement is true because that decision allows you to eliminate more answer choices. But since we don't always have that luxury, the strategy is to definitively decide something about one statement and work from there. Let's hear that round of applause for Jennifer! Thanks, Jennifer, for that special sharin'!

- Be familiar enough with your content to be able to apply it in different contexts. There's a major difference between barely hanging onto facts and having the flexibility to apply them in whatever setting a test question gives you. When you can do the latter, it's more fun and you'll feel more confident with any setting a test item presents to you.

- Test yourself on the quick-reference table concepts, names, and terms we've provided. They will help you mentally to organize information, make logical relationships, and check up on any spots that may need a bit more review.

- When reviewing within your selected text, remember the PQRST method. Preview a given section of material originally (like flying quickly and low over a landscape). Then, before you read, phrase in your mind a question you're seeking to answer, much like a detective would. As you read you'll be actively seeking to answer the question you've phrased. Next, self-recite key material. It puts your learning in a different modality— you're hearing as well as seeing. Finally, test yourself by going back to given headings or section titles and seeing what you remember within them. Yeah, it's Preview, Question, Read, Self-Recite, Test, and you'll do just fine.

- Don't forget the importance of moving rapidly through the test items and guessing if you can eliminate even one answer choice.

Practice Tests

5

■■■■■■■■■■■■■■■■■■■■■■■■■■■■■■■■■

This section contains three practice tests. While the diagnostic tests you took earlier attempted to duplicate the real GRE Psychology Test as closely as possible, with the exception of the ordering of the questions, these practice tests focus more on difficult content that you may have missed during your review. For example, there are many questions in the physiological/behavioral neuroscience and methods and measurements sections, as these tend to be the most difficult for many students.

When you score your practice tests, you will be able to see any remaining weak spots in content areas that require more study. These tests also introduce you to the scrambled format of the real test, so that when you finally see the real test, you'll be confident in your abilities to move from one topic area to another seamlessly.

> **HINT**
>
> It doesn't hurt to retake one of the diagnostic or practice tests, so you might want to make a few copies of the blank answer sheets before you mark them all up.

Even though your focus in these practice tests is to find weak content areas, it is still useful to practice your general test-taking skills as you did on the diagnostic tests:

- Try to duplicate the real testing situation as closely as possible.
- Set your timer for 170 minutes (2 hours and 50 minutes).
- Practice your three-pass system.

When you're done with the first practice test, score it and see if any of the content areas seem more challenging than the rest. Brush up on those areas and take the second practice test. Repeat the scoring/review process and then take the third practice test. If you have enough time left before the real test, use your extra copies of the answer sheets and retake as many of the diagnostic and practice tests as you can. Remember, one of the best ways to prepare for a test is to take a test!

ANSWER SHEET
Practice Test 1

1. Ⓐ Ⓑ Ⓒ Ⓓ Ⓔ
2. Ⓐ Ⓑ Ⓒ Ⓓ Ⓔ
3. Ⓐ Ⓑ Ⓒ Ⓓ Ⓔ
4. Ⓐ Ⓑ Ⓒ Ⓓ Ⓔ
5. Ⓐ Ⓑ Ⓒ Ⓓ Ⓔ
6. Ⓐ Ⓑ Ⓒ Ⓓ Ⓔ
7. Ⓐ Ⓑ Ⓒ Ⓓ Ⓔ
8. Ⓐ Ⓑ Ⓒ Ⓓ Ⓔ
9. Ⓐ Ⓑ Ⓒ Ⓓ Ⓔ
10. Ⓐ Ⓑ Ⓒ Ⓓ Ⓔ
11. Ⓐ Ⓑ Ⓒ Ⓓ Ⓔ
12. Ⓐ Ⓑ Ⓒ Ⓓ Ⓔ
13. Ⓐ Ⓑ Ⓒ Ⓓ Ⓔ
14. Ⓐ Ⓑ Ⓒ Ⓓ Ⓔ
15. Ⓐ Ⓑ Ⓒ Ⓓ Ⓔ
16. Ⓐ Ⓑ Ⓒ Ⓓ Ⓔ
17. Ⓐ Ⓑ Ⓒ Ⓓ Ⓔ
18. Ⓐ Ⓑ Ⓒ Ⓓ Ⓔ
19. Ⓐ Ⓑ Ⓒ Ⓓ Ⓔ
20. Ⓐ Ⓑ Ⓒ Ⓓ Ⓔ
21. Ⓐ Ⓑ Ⓒ Ⓓ Ⓔ
22. Ⓐ Ⓑ Ⓒ Ⓓ Ⓔ
23. Ⓐ Ⓑ Ⓒ Ⓓ Ⓔ
24. Ⓐ Ⓑ Ⓒ Ⓓ Ⓔ
25. Ⓐ Ⓑ Ⓒ Ⓓ Ⓔ
26. Ⓐ Ⓑ Ⓒ Ⓓ Ⓔ
27. Ⓐ Ⓑ Ⓒ Ⓓ Ⓔ
28. Ⓐ Ⓑ Ⓒ Ⓓ Ⓔ
29. Ⓐ Ⓑ Ⓒ Ⓓ Ⓔ
30. Ⓐ Ⓑ Ⓒ Ⓓ Ⓔ

31. Ⓐ Ⓑ Ⓒ Ⓓ Ⓔ
32. Ⓐ Ⓑ Ⓒ Ⓓ Ⓔ
33. Ⓐ Ⓑ Ⓒ Ⓓ Ⓔ
34. Ⓐ Ⓑ Ⓒ Ⓓ Ⓔ
35. Ⓐ Ⓑ Ⓒ Ⓓ Ⓔ
36. Ⓐ Ⓑ Ⓒ Ⓓ Ⓔ
37. Ⓐ Ⓑ Ⓒ Ⓓ Ⓔ
38. Ⓐ Ⓑ Ⓒ Ⓓ Ⓔ
39. Ⓐ Ⓑ Ⓒ Ⓓ Ⓔ
40. Ⓐ Ⓑ Ⓒ Ⓓ Ⓔ
41. Ⓐ Ⓑ Ⓒ Ⓓ Ⓔ
42. Ⓐ Ⓑ Ⓒ Ⓓ Ⓔ
43. Ⓐ Ⓑ Ⓒ Ⓓ Ⓔ
44. Ⓐ Ⓑ Ⓒ Ⓓ Ⓔ
45. Ⓐ Ⓑ Ⓒ Ⓓ Ⓔ
46. Ⓐ Ⓑ Ⓒ Ⓓ Ⓔ
47. Ⓐ Ⓑ Ⓒ Ⓓ Ⓔ
48. Ⓐ Ⓑ Ⓒ Ⓓ Ⓔ
49. Ⓐ Ⓑ Ⓒ Ⓓ Ⓔ
50. Ⓐ Ⓑ Ⓒ Ⓓ Ⓔ
51. Ⓐ Ⓑ Ⓒ Ⓓ Ⓔ
52. Ⓐ Ⓑ Ⓒ Ⓓ Ⓔ
53. Ⓐ Ⓑ Ⓒ Ⓓ Ⓔ
54. Ⓐ Ⓑ Ⓒ Ⓓ Ⓔ
55. Ⓐ Ⓑ Ⓒ Ⓓ Ⓔ
56. Ⓐ Ⓑ Ⓒ Ⓓ Ⓔ
57. Ⓐ Ⓑ Ⓒ Ⓓ Ⓔ
58. Ⓐ Ⓑ Ⓒ Ⓓ Ⓔ
59. Ⓐ Ⓑ Ⓒ Ⓓ Ⓔ
60. Ⓐ Ⓑ Ⓒ Ⓓ Ⓔ

61. Ⓐ Ⓑ Ⓒ Ⓓ Ⓔ
62. Ⓐ Ⓑ Ⓒ Ⓓ Ⓔ
63. Ⓐ Ⓑ Ⓒ Ⓓ Ⓔ
64. Ⓐ Ⓑ Ⓒ Ⓓ Ⓔ
65. Ⓐ Ⓑ Ⓒ Ⓓ Ⓔ
66. Ⓐ Ⓑ Ⓒ Ⓓ Ⓔ
67. Ⓐ Ⓑ Ⓒ Ⓓ Ⓔ
68. Ⓐ Ⓑ Ⓒ Ⓓ Ⓔ
69. Ⓐ Ⓑ Ⓒ Ⓓ Ⓔ
70. Ⓐ Ⓑ Ⓒ Ⓓ Ⓔ
71. Ⓐ Ⓑ Ⓒ Ⓓ Ⓔ
72. Ⓐ Ⓑ Ⓒ Ⓓ Ⓔ
73. Ⓐ Ⓑ Ⓒ Ⓓ Ⓔ
74. Ⓐ Ⓑ Ⓒ Ⓓ Ⓔ
75. Ⓐ Ⓑ Ⓒ Ⓓ Ⓔ
76. Ⓐ Ⓑ Ⓒ Ⓓ Ⓔ
77. Ⓐ Ⓑ Ⓒ Ⓓ Ⓔ
78. Ⓐ Ⓑ Ⓒ Ⓓ Ⓔ
79. Ⓐ Ⓑ Ⓒ Ⓓ Ⓔ
80. Ⓐ Ⓑ Ⓒ Ⓓ Ⓔ
81. Ⓐ Ⓑ Ⓒ Ⓓ Ⓔ
82. Ⓐ Ⓑ Ⓒ Ⓓ Ⓔ
83. Ⓐ Ⓑ Ⓒ Ⓓ Ⓔ
84. Ⓐ Ⓑ Ⓒ Ⓓ Ⓔ
85. Ⓐ Ⓑ Ⓒ Ⓓ Ⓔ
86. Ⓐ Ⓑ Ⓒ Ⓓ Ⓔ
87. Ⓐ Ⓑ Ⓒ Ⓓ Ⓔ
88. Ⓐ Ⓑ Ⓒ Ⓓ Ⓔ
89. Ⓐ Ⓑ Ⓒ Ⓓ Ⓔ
90. Ⓐ Ⓑ Ⓒ Ⓓ Ⓔ

91. Ⓐ Ⓑ Ⓒ Ⓓ Ⓔ
92. Ⓐ Ⓑ Ⓒ Ⓓ Ⓔ
93. Ⓐ Ⓑ Ⓒ Ⓓ Ⓔ
94. Ⓐ Ⓑ Ⓒ Ⓓ Ⓔ
95. Ⓐ Ⓑ Ⓒ Ⓓ Ⓔ
96. Ⓐ Ⓑ Ⓒ Ⓓ Ⓔ
97. Ⓐ Ⓑ Ⓒ Ⓓ Ⓔ
98. Ⓐ Ⓑ Ⓒ Ⓓ Ⓔ
99. Ⓐ Ⓑ Ⓒ Ⓓ Ⓔ
100. Ⓐ Ⓑ Ⓒ Ⓓ Ⓔ
101. Ⓐ Ⓑ Ⓒ Ⓓ Ⓔ
102. Ⓐ Ⓑ Ⓒ Ⓓ Ⓔ
103. Ⓐ Ⓑ Ⓒ Ⓓ Ⓔ
104. Ⓐ Ⓑ Ⓒ Ⓓ Ⓔ
105. Ⓐ Ⓑ Ⓒ Ⓓ Ⓔ
106. Ⓐ Ⓑ Ⓒ Ⓓ Ⓔ
107. Ⓐ Ⓑ Ⓒ Ⓓ Ⓔ
108. Ⓐ Ⓑ Ⓒ Ⓓ Ⓔ
109. Ⓐ Ⓑ Ⓒ Ⓓ Ⓔ
110. Ⓐ Ⓑ Ⓒ Ⓓ Ⓔ
111. Ⓐ Ⓑ Ⓒ Ⓓ Ⓔ
112. Ⓐ Ⓑ Ⓒ Ⓓ Ⓔ
113. Ⓐ Ⓑ Ⓒ Ⓓ Ⓔ
114. Ⓐ Ⓑ Ⓒ Ⓓ Ⓔ
115. Ⓐ Ⓑ Ⓒ Ⓓ Ⓔ
116. Ⓐ Ⓑ Ⓒ Ⓓ Ⓔ
117. Ⓐ Ⓑ Ⓒ Ⓓ Ⓔ
118. Ⓐ Ⓑ Ⓒ Ⓓ Ⓔ
119. Ⓐ Ⓑ Ⓒ Ⓓ Ⓔ
120. Ⓐ Ⓑ Ⓒ Ⓓ Ⓔ

ANSWER SHEET
Practice Test 1

121. Ⓐ Ⓑ Ⓒ Ⓓ Ⓔ   145. Ⓐ Ⓑ Ⓒ Ⓓ Ⓔ   169. Ⓐ Ⓑ Ⓒ Ⓓ Ⓔ   193. Ⓐ Ⓑ Ⓒ Ⓓ Ⓔ
122. Ⓐ Ⓑ Ⓒ Ⓓ Ⓔ   146. Ⓐ Ⓑ Ⓒ Ⓓ Ⓔ   170. Ⓐ Ⓑ Ⓒ Ⓓ Ⓔ   194. Ⓐ Ⓑ Ⓒ Ⓓ Ⓔ
123. Ⓐ Ⓑ Ⓒ Ⓓ Ⓔ   147. Ⓐ Ⓑ Ⓒ Ⓓ Ⓔ   171. Ⓐ Ⓑ Ⓒ Ⓓ Ⓔ   195. Ⓐ Ⓑ Ⓒ Ⓓ Ⓔ
124. Ⓐ Ⓑ Ⓒ Ⓓ Ⓔ   148. Ⓐ Ⓑ Ⓒ Ⓓ Ⓔ   172. Ⓐ Ⓑ Ⓒ Ⓓ Ⓔ   196. Ⓐ Ⓑ Ⓒ Ⓓ Ⓔ
125. Ⓐ Ⓑ Ⓒ Ⓓ Ⓔ   149. Ⓐ Ⓑ Ⓒ Ⓓ Ⓔ   173. Ⓐ Ⓑ Ⓒ Ⓓ Ⓔ   197. Ⓐ Ⓑ Ⓒ Ⓓ Ⓔ
126. Ⓐ Ⓑ Ⓒ Ⓓ Ⓔ   150. Ⓐ Ⓑ Ⓒ Ⓓ Ⓔ   174. Ⓐ Ⓑ Ⓒ Ⓓ Ⓔ   198. Ⓐ Ⓑ Ⓒ Ⓓ Ⓔ
127. Ⓐ Ⓑ Ⓒ Ⓓ Ⓔ   151. Ⓐ Ⓑ Ⓒ Ⓓ Ⓔ   175. Ⓐ Ⓑ Ⓒ Ⓓ Ⓔ   199. Ⓐ Ⓑ Ⓒ Ⓓ Ⓔ
128. Ⓐ Ⓑ Ⓒ Ⓓ Ⓔ   152. Ⓐ Ⓑ Ⓒ Ⓓ Ⓔ   176. Ⓐ Ⓑ Ⓒ Ⓓ Ⓔ   200. Ⓐ Ⓑ Ⓒ Ⓓ Ⓔ
129. Ⓐ Ⓑ Ⓒ Ⓓ Ⓔ   153. Ⓐ Ⓑ Ⓒ Ⓓ Ⓔ   177. Ⓐ Ⓑ Ⓒ Ⓓ Ⓔ   201. Ⓐ Ⓑ Ⓒ Ⓓ Ⓔ
130. Ⓐ Ⓑ Ⓒ Ⓓ Ⓔ   154. Ⓐ Ⓑ Ⓒ Ⓓ Ⓔ   178. Ⓐ Ⓑ Ⓒ Ⓓ Ⓔ   202. Ⓐ Ⓑ Ⓒ Ⓓ Ⓔ
131. Ⓐ Ⓑ Ⓒ Ⓓ Ⓔ   155. Ⓐ Ⓑ Ⓒ Ⓓ Ⓔ   179. Ⓐ Ⓑ Ⓒ Ⓓ Ⓔ   203. Ⓐ Ⓑ Ⓒ Ⓓ Ⓔ
132. Ⓐ Ⓑ Ⓒ Ⓓ Ⓔ   156. Ⓐ Ⓑ Ⓒ Ⓓ Ⓔ   180. Ⓐ Ⓑ Ⓒ Ⓓ Ⓔ   204. Ⓐ Ⓑ Ⓒ Ⓓ Ⓔ
133. Ⓐ Ⓑ Ⓒ Ⓓ Ⓔ   157. Ⓐ Ⓑ Ⓒ Ⓓ Ⓔ   181. Ⓐ Ⓑ Ⓒ Ⓓ Ⓔ   205. Ⓐ Ⓑ Ⓒ Ⓓ Ⓔ
134. Ⓐ Ⓑ Ⓒ Ⓓ Ⓔ   158. Ⓐ Ⓑ Ⓒ Ⓓ Ⓔ   182. Ⓐ Ⓑ Ⓒ Ⓓ Ⓔ   206. Ⓐ Ⓑ Ⓒ Ⓓ Ⓔ
135. Ⓐ Ⓑ Ⓒ Ⓓ Ⓔ   159. Ⓐ Ⓑ Ⓒ Ⓓ Ⓔ   183. Ⓐ Ⓑ Ⓒ Ⓓ Ⓔ   207. Ⓐ Ⓑ Ⓒ Ⓓ Ⓔ
136. Ⓐ Ⓑ Ⓒ Ⓓ Ⓔ   160. Ⓐ Ⓑ Ⓒ Ⓓ Ⓔ   184. Ⓐ Ⓑ Ⓒ Ⓓ Ⓔ   208. Ⓐ Ⓑ Ⓒ Ⓓ Ⓔ
137. Ⓐ Ⓑ Ⓒ Ⓓ Ⓔ   161. Ⓐ Ⓑ Ⓒ Ⓓ Ⓔ   185. Ⓐ Ⓑ Ⓒ Ⓓ Ⓔ   209. Ⓐ Ⓑ Ⓒ Ⓓ Ⓔ
138. Ⓐ Ⓑ Ⓒ Ⓓ Ⓔ   162. Ⓐ Ⓑ Ⓒ Ⓓ Ⓔ   186. Ⓐ Ⓑ Ⓒ Ⓓ Ⓔ   210. Ⓐ Ⓑ Ⓒ Ⓓ Ⓔ
139. Ⓐ Ⓑ Ⓒ Ⓓ Ⓔ   163. Ⓐ Ⓑ Ⓒ Ⓓ Ⓔ   187. Ⓐ Ⓑ Ⓒ Ⓓ Ⓔ   211. Ⓐ Ⓑ Ⓒ Ⓓ Ⓔ
140. Ⓐ Ⓑ Ⓒ Ⓓ Ⓔ   164. Ⓐ Ⓑ Ⓒ Ⓓ Ⓔ   188. Ⓐ Ⓑ Ⓒ Ⓓ Ⓔ   212. Ⓐ Ⓑ Ⓒ Ⓓ Ⓔ
141. Ⓐ Ⓑ Ⓒ Ⓓ Ⓔ   165. Ⓐ Ⓑ Ⓒ Ⓓ Ⓔ   189. Ⓐ Ⓑ Ⓒ Ⓓ Ⓔ   213. Ⓐ Ⓑ Ⓒ Ⓓ Ⓔ
142. Ⓐ Ⓑ Ⓒ Ⓓ Ⓔ   166. Ⓐ Ⓑ Ⓒ Ⓓ Ⓔ   190. Ⓐ Ⓑ Ⓒ Ⓓ Ⓔ   214. Ⓐ Ⓑ Ⓒ Ⓓ Ⓔ
143. Ⓐ Ⓑ Ⓒ Ⓓ Ⓔ   167. Ⓐ Ⓑ Ⓒ Ⓓ Ⓔ   191. Ⓐ Ⓑ Ⓒ Ⓓ Ⓔ   215. Ⓐ Ⓑ Ⓒ Ⓓ Ⓔ
144. Ⓐ Ⓑ Ⓒ Ⓓ Ⓔ   168. Ⓐ Ⓑ Ⓒ Ⓓ Ⓔ   192. Ⓐ Ⓑ Ⓒ Ⓓ Ⓔ

Directions: Each of the questions or incomplete statements below is followed by five suggested answers or completions. Select the one that is best in each case and then fill in the corresponding space on the answer sheet.

1. Inability to monitor the movements of one's feet and the absence of feedback regarding their position and relationship to the ground would suggest problems with the

   (A) vestibular sensory system
   (B) kinesthetic sensory system
   (C) cerebellar sensory system
   (D) visceral sensory system
   (E) peripheral sensory system

2. Which of the following is a primary symptom of a patient with Korsakoff's syndrome?

   (A) visual impairment
   (B) sexual dysfunction
   (C) aphasia
   (D) memory impairment
   (E) lack of satiation signals when eating

3. The soldier goes into the heat of battle, and at the moment when he would be expected to fire his weapon, his hand and arm experience total paralysis. What would explain this response?

   (A) somatoform disorder
   (B) reaction formation disorder
   (C) obsessive compulsive disorder
   (D) schizophrenia
   (E) dissociative disorder

4. Which of the following is an example of a negative reinforcer?

   (A) giving a child a cookie
   (B) telling a child that his or her chores do not have to be done that day
   (C) putting $20 in the child's savings account
   (D) slapping the child gently on the wrist
   (E) taking a favorite toy away from the child

GO ON TO THE NEXT PAGE

5. The Big Five Personality Inventory contains or draws from which of the following?

    I. The work of Hans Eysenck
    II. A distillation of personality factor's found in Cattell's 16-PF
    III. Considers extraversion to be a key factor

    (A) I only
    (B) II only
    (C) III only
    (D) I and II
    (E) I, II, and III

6. The law of specific nerve energies refers to

    (A) the fixed amplitude of an action potential
    (B) a receptor's capability to give only one quality of experience (e.g., auditory) regardless of how it was stimulated
    (C) a receptor's capability to give several different qualities of experience (e.g., temperature, pain, and so on), which vary with the quality of the stimulus received
    (D) the fact that a neuron can either excite or inhibit other neurons, but not both
    (E) the lock-and-key system characterizing neurotransmitters and their receptor sites

7. The third stage of labor in childbirth is called

    (A) cervix dilation
    (B) actual newborn emergence
    (C) the afterbirth
    (D) breech
    (E) vertex

8. The writer of an e-mail may put something important in ALL CAPS, or may surround text that needs emphasis **with asterisks**. These two modifications to text replace which aspect of language that is otherwise missing in e-mail?

    (A) prosody
    (B) morphology
    (C) phonology
    (D) semantics
    (E) syntax

9. The standard deviation obtained from a sample distribution of scores is

    (A) an inferential statistic
    (B) a descriptive statistic
    (C) a measure of correlation
    (D) a squared variance
    (E) a measure of central tendency

GO ON TO THE NEXT PAGE

10. What is the primacy effect?

   (A) In a free-recall task, items at the beginning of the study list are more likely to be recalled than items in the middle of the list.
   (B) People from individualistic cultures rate themselves as being above average on many dimensions.
   (C) Infants search for an object where it was previously hidden but not where it is currently hidden.
   (D) It is the ability of someone to focus on one conversation in a noisy room and ignore the background noise.
   (E) The likelihood that a stimulus will evoke a response will increase if the response is followed by a reward.

QUESTIONS 11 AND 12 ARE BASED ON THE FOLLOWING PASSAGE.

One can think of collective behavior from a number of different and unique perspectives. On the one hand, the Marxian model suggests that workers will combine in revolt when their life situations become intolerable. A second perspective, expressed by LeBon, suggests that a crowd takes on characteristics such as impulsiveness and irrationality that are not necessarily characteristic of individual persons within the crowd. A third perspective, held by Freud, sees Oedipal implications in crowd behavior as individuals identify with the crowd leader, expressing a kind of familial love within this identification. Still a fourth perspective is seen in Turner's emphasis on the emergent-norm model—the theory that the ambiguity of a crowd situation prompts the crowd members to adopt as their norm the behavior of a handful of the group's most visible members. Hall adds an additional perspective with the suggestion that crowd behavior tends to violate personal space.

11. Which of the above perspectives would be *least* likely to associate crowd behavior with the immediate, environmental factors?

   (A) Marxian
   (B) LeBon
   (C) Freud
   (D) Turner
   (E) Hall

12. The view that speaks most directly to the concept of territoriality is that of

   (A) Marx
   (B) LeBon
   (C) Freud
   (D) Turner
   (E) Hall

GO ON TO THE NEXT PAGE

13. In which of the following instances would an individual's EEG recording be most likely characterized by alpha wave activity?

   (A) deep sleep
   (B) REM sleep
   (C) eyes closed, in a wakeful but relaxed state
   (D) solving a multiplication problem "in one's head"
   (E) eyes open, in an alert, attentive state

14. "In no case is an animal activity to be interpreted in terms of higher psychological processes, if it can be fairly interpreted in terms of processes which stand lower in the scale of psychological evolution and development." This quotation expresses the

   (A) theory of natural selection (Darwin)
   (B) law of imprinting (Lorenz)
   (C) law of phylogeny (Tinbergen)
   (D) theory of tropisms (Loeb)
   (E) law of parsimony (Morgan)

15. Would it be possible or conceivable that a person diagnosed as abnormal in one culture would be considered quite normal in another?

   (A) No. The diagnostic categories are very specific and consistent across countries and cultures.
   (B) No. There would be no basis for making a judgment different from the diagnosis.
   (C) Yes. Cultures vary in their norms and expectations. Behaviors seen as quite acceptable in one culture could readily be seen as quite abnormal in another.
   (D) No. The diagnostic categories are so loose and elusive that they would catch abnormal behavior in any culture like the strands on a spider web.
   (E) Karen Horney, the sea captain's daughter who traveled from country to country throughout her childhood would say a flat "No!"

16. Which of the following would *not* be characterized as a stimulant?

   (A) caffeine
   (B) barbiturates
   (C) nicotine
   (D) cocaine
   (E) Benzedrine

GO ON TO THE NEXT PAGE

Among theoretical approaches to personality the terms *nomothetic* and *idiographic* serve to identify two basically different avenues. The idiographic approach places emphasis upon the individual person as a unique entity; the nomothetic approach experimentally looks for personality factors and characteristics that are common to people in general.

17. Which of the following points might be made in defense of the idiographic approach?

    (A) The person's unique qualities constitute the essence of his or her personality.
    (B) Correlations designed to find common personality characteristics are essential for progress in the field.
    (C) The function of an organism in response to a specific stimulus is the key to personality study.
    (D) Personality is essentially a matter of physiochemistry and hormonal secretions.
    (E) Id, ego, and superego are the principal factors in personality.

18. Which of the following correctly pairs an advocate of the nomothetic approach with an advocate of the idiographic approach?

    (A) Rogers–Kelly
    (B) Frankl–Perls
    (C) Watson–Skinner
    (D) Maslow–Tolman
    (E) Freud–Adler

19. All of the following terms are associated with the idiographic approach *except*

    (A) individual psychology
    (B) client-centered therapy
    (C) personal construct
    (D) systematic desensitization
    (E) Gestalt therapy

GO ON TO THE NEXT PAGE

20. A child was born with a condition called strabismus, in which the two eyes are misaligned (e.g., cross-eyed). If this is not corrected in childhood, the lack of correspondence between the images on each retina is most likely to permanently affect

    (A) depth perception
    (B) accommodation
    (C) shape constancy
    (D) color constancy
    (E) balance and coordination

21. When individuals use the representativeness heuristic to estimate how likely something or someone is to be a member of some category (based on its similarity to other members of the category), they often ignore how common or uncommon that category is. The resulting error is called the

    (A) base rate fallacy
    (B) primacy effect
    (C) mere exposure effect
    (D) blocking effect
    (E) overregularization error

22. Both Betsy and Bob have brown eyes and are heterozygous for eye color. The statistical likelihood of their producing a brown-eyed child is

    (A) 1 in 4
    (B) 3 in 4
    (C) 2 in 4
    (D) 4 in 4
    (E) 0 in 4

23. Research has related which of the following to maternal stress during pregnancy?

    (A) fetal activity
    (B) reduced IQ
    (C) personality instability
    (D) manic-depression
    (E) psychosis

GO ON TO THE NEXT PAGE

24. Which of the following is *not* part of the brainstem?

   (A) medulla
   (B) pons
   (C) midbrain
   (D) reticular formation
   (E) corpus callosum

25. Memory retrieval is enhanced when a person is in the same situation or environment as during learning. This is called

   (A) state-dependent learning
   (B) elaborative rehearsal
   (C) flashbulb memory
   (D) memory consolidation
   (E) cued recall

26. Each of the scores in a distribution has been multiplied by 7. The standard deviation is

   (A) increased by 7
   (B) increased to 7 times its original value
   (C) increased by its original value divided by 7
   (D) increased by 14
   (E) unchanged from its original value

27. One type of test reliability is the

   (A) degree to which the test measures what it is intended to measure
   (B) degree to which repeated administrations give the same score result
   (C) degree to which the test measures content
   (D) degree to which it is predictive
   (E) degree of thoroughness

28. Most reflexes, like the patellar reflex you exhibit when a doctor taps a hammer on your knee, involve a neural circuit with at least one synapse in the

   (A) cerebellum
   (B) spinal cord
   (C) frontal lobe
   (D) limbic system
   (E) basal ganglia

GO ON TO THE NEXT PAGE

A group of researchers is interested in whether the way people use their hands helps them think. They also want to examine whether any beneficial effects of hand gestures vary depending on someone's gender and cultural background. They recruited twenty male and twenty female participants from three countries (United States, Italy, and Norway) and asked them to solve ten reasoning problems. For half of the problems the participants were allowed to use their hands freely, whereas for the other half of the problems they were asked to sit on their hands, which prevented them from gesturing. The proportion of correct solutions by condition is presented in the following chart:

	Males			Females		
	United States	Italy	Norway	United States	Italy	Norway
Gesture	.78	.72	.69	.81	.67	.71
No gesture	.55	.31	.59	.58	.32	.62

29. Among the variables the researchers manipulated in the experiment, working through a problem with or without gesturing was the only

    (A) independent variable
    (B) within-subjects variable
    (C) between-subjects variable
    (D) control variable
    (E) dependent variable

30. A mixed analysis of variance revealed an interaction between the use of gestures and the participants' cultural background, as indicated by a p value of .02. What is the meaning of a p value of $p = .02$?

    (A) The average proportion of error across all conditions was .02 percent.
    (B) The likelihood that any differences in problem-solving performance among the three cultural backgrounds depending on the presence or absence of gesture is attributed to real effects is 2 percent.
    (C) The likelihood that any differences in problem-solving performance among the three cultural backgrounds depending on the presence or absence of gesture is attributed to chance factors is 2 percent.
    (D) The likelihood that any differences in problem-solving performance among the three cultural backgrounds depending on the presence or absence of gesture is attributed to chance factors is 98 percent.
    (E) The interaction is not significant.

GO ON TO THE NEXT PAGE

31. Based on their analysis, the researchers concluded that participants from Mediterranean cultures are more likely to be affected by the requirement not to use their hands while solving problems, because people from these cultures typically use their hands more when they think and speak. What variable should the researchers have taken into account before reaching such a conclusion?

(A) They should have examined participants from more cultural backgrounds.
(B) They should have measured whether their Italian participants gestured more than participants from the two other cultural backgrounds when they were allowed to use their hands while solving problems.
(C) They should have measured whether their Italian participants used more words than participants from the two other cultural backgrounds when they were allowed to use their hands while solving problems.
(D) They should have measured the handedness of all participants.
(E) They should have examined only male or only female participants.

32. Egbert was joining a fraternity. It was his pledge semester, and part of his initiation was to wrap himself in Christmas tree lights, go to his classes, sit near an electrical outlet, and plug in. As he "lit up" and glowed in each of his classes, we could expect the initiation to have

(A) no effect upon his attraction to the fraternity
(B) a significant positive effect upon his attraction to the fraternity
(C) a very weak positive effect upon his attraction to the fraternity
(D) a significant negative effect upon his attraction to the fraternity
(E) a weak negative effect upon his attraction to the fraternity

33. If Jacqueline wants to reduce hostile, prejudicial attitudes between two groups she cares about, which of the following would you recommend that she try?

(A) simply bring the groups together
(B) engage the groups in competitive activities
(C) develop a superordinate goal
(D) initiate a letter-writing program between the groups
(E) individual psychotherapy

34. Which of the following is central to the stress response?

(A) DNA
(B) TOTE
(C) GABA
(D) ACTH
(E) NMR

GO ON TO THE NEXT PAGE

35. In an experiment, subjects are asked to judge whether a letter is normal or reversed; each item is rotated in one of various angles from upright. The results indicate a positive, linear relationship between the latency to make the decision and the degree of rotation. This result was taken as evidence that mental rotation, like actual movement, takes time, because mental images are

(A) analogical
(B) symbolic
(C) propositional
(D) located in the left hemisphere
(E) located in the right hemisphere

36. Within the Diagnostic and Statistical Manual (DSM-5), under what heading would panic disorder be placed?

(A) schizophrenic disorders
(B) anxiety disorders
(C) somatoform disorders
(D) dissociative disorders
(E) mood disorders

37. All of the following are correct statements *except*

(A) Virtually everybody makes judgments about the normality of other people.
(B) Criteria for judging illness are more value free and clear-cut in medicine than in psychology.
(C) A psychological diagnosis is never based on an individual's personal statement of his or her experience and problem.
(D) Strong classification facilitates sound empirical research.
(E) How the individual is perceived (for example, as patient or as client) will have a significant effect on how he or she is treated.

38. What does the Stroop effect measure?

(A) cognitive dissonance
(B) cognitive interference
(C) group polarization
(D) operant conditioning
(E) observational learning

39. The process of maintaining constancy in the normal internal environment of an organism is called

(A) homeostasis
(B) adaptation
(C) consistency
(D) equivalence
(E) motivation

GO ON TO THE NEXT PAGE

40. Which of the following is produced by tactile stimulation of a newborn's cheek?

    (A) Babkin response
    (B) Babinski response
    (C) Rooting response
    (D) Moro response
    (E) Grasping reflex

41. "With the possible exception of old age, no other phase of individual development is so clearly marked by negative connotations and lack of positive sanctions." This is a reference by Goldblatt to

    (A) age one
    (B) Erikson's age of autonomy versus shame and doubt
    (C) the general preschool period
    (D) early adolescence
    (E) early adulthood

42. As stimulus patterns become increasingly similar, reaction times based on stimulus discrimination

    (A) become shorter
    (B) become longer
    (C) remain unchanged
    (D) become shorter for auditory stimuli but longer for visual stimuli
    (E) become shorter for visual stimuli but longer for auditory stimuli

43. Subjects in a memory experiment were asked to remember a long list of words; to help them, each word was also given in a sentence. For the word *chicken*, some subjects read the sentence "The chicken flew out of the barn when a coyote howled nearby." Other subjects read the sentence "Her mother served roasted chicken and potatoes at every Sunday dinner." Later, subjects were given retrieval cues to help them recall the words on the list. For chicken, the retrieval cue was "a farm animal." The subjects who read the first sentence were more likely to recall chicken than those who read the second sentence. What does this experimental finding demonstrate?

    (A) the generation effect
    (B) encoding specificity
    (C) selective attention
    (D) hindsight bias
    (E) confirmation bias

GO ON TO THE NEXT PAGE

44. George has a very serious case of ochlophobia. What is he intensely afraid of?

(A) water and drowning
(B) crowds
(C) heights
(D) snakes
(E) death

45. Grice's maxims describe the assumptions listeners make about a speaker's intentions; these assumptions are relevant to what topic in psycholinguistics?

(A) prosody
(B) syntax
(C) semantics
(D) phonetics
(E) pragmatics

46. The personality approaches of Cattell and Eysenck rely heavily upon

(A) inner forces (cathexes–anticathexes)
(B) percept and concept
(C) observable action
(D) factor analysis
(E) script and contract

47. Which of the following statements about additive color mixing are true?

I. The primary colors in additive color mixing are blue, green, and red.
II. The primary colors in additive and subtractive color mixing are the same.
III. Additive color mixing refers to the combination of colors when mixing paints.

(A) I only
(B) II only
(C) III only
(D) II and III
(E) I, II, and III

48. When perceiving the distance of a sound, a person must depend heavily on

(A) complexity and resonance
(B) brightness and saturation
(C) dystonia
(D) timbre and loudness
(E) beats

GO ON TO THE NEXT PAGE

49. For simple testing of differences between the means of an experimental and a control group, a researcher would most likely use

(A) chi-square
(B) *t*-test
(C) correlation
(D) regression
(E) *F*-test

50. The term *consolidation* is used in reference to what ability?

(A) object recognition
(B) face recognition
(C) spatial attention
(D) memory
(E) speech perception

51. In research with newborns, the cautious experimental hunch now being advanced is that

(A) fast habituators may be brighter than slow habituators
(B) slow habituators may be brighter than fast habituators
(C) intelligence may be related to the presence and strength of initial reflexes
(D) early onset of pleasant emotions in the newborn means healthy personality later
(E) block design may be an accurate measure of intelligence as early as one month of age

52. What is saltatory conduction?

(A) the method of transmission of an action potential along a myelinated axon
(B) a form of cellular plasticity in which the sensitivity of one neuron to a signal from another is increased
(C) the process by which immature neurons adhere to glial cells in order to migrate to their final location in the brain
(D) neural signaling across electrical synapses, found in the invertebrate brain and in prenatal mammalian brains
(E) when excitation of a neuron or neural system is accompanied by inhibition of another neuron or system

GO ON TO THE NEXT PAGE

53. The "rule of thirds" in schizophrenia means that

    I.   one third of patients will receive treatment and function normally in society
    II. one third of patients will be in and out of the treatment facility across their life span
    III. one third of patients will never be able to leave the treatment facility

    (A) I only
    (B) II only
    (C) III only
    (D) I and II
    (E) I, II, and III

54. In what branch of psychology would you find discussions of fixed-action patterns and releasing stimuli?

    (A) developmental psychology
    (B) behavioral neuroscience
    (C) cognitive neuroscience
    (D) ethology
    (E) animal learning

55. The body's own self-produced "pain killers" are

    (A) epinephrine and norepinephrine
    (B) opium and heroin
    (C) endorphin and enkephalin
    (D) serotonin and acetylcholine
    (E) GABA and ACTH

56. In Adler's approach to personality, the presence of an inferiority complex within a person will be followed by

    (A) heightened sexual activity
    (B) need for maternal love
    (C) desire for peace
    (D) superiority striving
    (E) thanatos

57. Which of the following words or phrases is *least* associated with the work of Clark Hull?

    (A) habit strength
    (B) reaction potential
    (C) drive
    (D) stimulus
    (E) interaction potential

GO ON TO THE NEXT PAGE

58. A political gathering precedes election night by two months. Given a choice of speaking positions on the program, a political candidate would be wise to choose to be

(A) the first speaker
(B) the middle speaker
(C) the last speaker
(D) either the first or the last speaker
(E) in any of the three speaking positions

59. Broca's aphasia is typically associated with brain damage to the

(A) left frontal cortex
(B) right frontal cortex
(C) left temporal cortex
(D) right temporal cortex
(E) right occipital cortex

60. Auditory receptor cells are located in the

(A) anvil
(B) stirrup
(C) cochlea
(D) Eustachian tube
(E) pinna

61. Jane is very worried about her family's finances, her daughter's welfare at college, a very minor mistake she made at work yesterday, and getting to work on time tomorrow. She frequently feels faint, dizzy, sweats, has muscle tension, diarrhea, and elevated heartbeat. As you conclude your clinical notes, you give her the diagnosis of

(A) organic mental disorder
(B) anxiety disorder
(C) mood disorder
(D) dissociative disorder
(E) sexual disorder

62. Sleepwalking and sleep talking

(A) occur primarily during REM sleep
(B) occur primarily during deep sleep
(C) signify hypnagogic activity
(D) correlate strongly with the incidence of alexia
(E) occur far more frequently among women than among men

GO ON TO THE NEXT PAGE

63. Research indicates that Alzheimer's disease is associated with a deficiency in

(A) dopamine
(B) serotonin
(C) epinephrine
(D) acetylcholine
(E) GABA

64. Given a grouping of data that is heterogeneous, you can expect a standard deviation to be

(A) small
(B) large
(C) small if sample size is small
(D) large only if sample size is large
(E) below .9

65. An animal learns that a flash of red light predicts a mild electric shock, and it exhibits freezing behavior in response to the light. Subsequently, the red light is accompanied (simultaneously) with a high-pitched tone, and both are followed by the shock. Finally, the animal is presented with the high-pitched tone *alone*. The animal behaves as if nothing has happened. What phenomenon is illustrated here?

(A) extinction
(B) second-order conditioning
(C) reconditioning
(D) blocking
(E) systematic desensitization

66. "All roses are plants. All plants need water. Therefore all roses need water." This is an example of

I. a syllogism
II. deductive reasoning
III. a premise

(A) I only
(B) II only
(C) III only
(D) I and II
(E) I and III

67. The term *general-to-specific* in child development refers to

(A) visual acuity
(B) auditory sensitivity
(C) motor movements
(D) cortex development
(E) pain sensitivity

GO ON TO THE NEXT PAGE

68. The neonate has well-developed

   (A) temperature-regulating mechanisms
   (B) visual acuity
   (C) immunity to various infections
   (D) lower torso
   (E) auditory acuteness

69. Curare is a toxin used in poison darts and arrows to paralyze prey during hunting. It has its effect by blocking a receptor for a neurotransmitter found in the neuromuscular junction. What is curare?

   (A) acetylcholine agonist
   (B) acetylcholine antagonist
   (C) dopamine agonist
   (D) dopamine antagonist
   (E) none of the above

70. Traci and Donald purchased tickets for a baseball game on Saturday that cost $35 each. A few days later, Traci got an e-mail inviting her and Donald to a friend's birthday party on the same afternoon. Traci wanted to go to the party instead of the baseball game, but they already paid for the tickets and couldn't find anyone to buy them, so they went to the baseball game that afternoon and missed the party. Traci and Donald's decision here illustrates

   (A) a congruence bias
   (B) framing effects
   (C) the sunk cost fallacy
   (D) irrational escalation
   (E) the base rate fallacy

71. What is the difference between panic disorder and anxiety disorder?

   (A) None. They are synonymous.
   (B) In panic disorder, the individual is in a better position to cope than someone in anxiety disorder.
   (C) Panic disorder is a type of anxiety disorder.
   (D) Panic disorder was the former name for today's anxiety disorder classification.
   (E) Both A and D are correct.

72. Any activity in a reinforcement hierarchy is reinforced by an activity above it in the hierarchy and may reinforce any activity below it. This principle was developed by (and named for)

   (A) Watson
   (B) Premack
   (C) Rotter
   (D) Skinner
   (E) Rogers

GO ON TO THE NEXT PAGE

73. Which of the following results from activation of the parasympathetic system?

   (A) respiration increase
   (B) pupil dilation
   (C) heart-rate inhibition
   (D) salivation inhibition
   (E) piloerection

74. The motor primacy principle in development means that

   (A) muscle development precedes neural development
   (B) striated muscle development precedes smooth muscle development
   (C) virtually any motor skill can be learned shortly after birth, if the infant is given sufficient training
   (D) maturation of neuromuscular structures to a given stage precedes ability to respond
   (E) motor development precedes glandular development

75. Innate behavior patterns develop primarily as a function of

   (A) instrumental conditioning
   (B) maturation
   (C) learning
   (D) infant stimulation
   (E) successive approximation

76. Continued improvement in the absence of further practice is known as

   (A) spontaneous recovery
   (B) savings
   (C) incubation
   (D) reminiscence
   (E) recall

77. What type of word is used in studies of context effects on lexical disambiguation during speech comprehension?

   (A) antonym
   (B) homonym
   (C) synonym
   (D) lexonym
   (E) polynym

78. The newborn

   (A) vocalizes socially
   (B) smiles socially
   (C) tracks moving objects behind stationary objects
   (D) has the capability for basic learning
   (E) engages in babbling

GO ON TO THE NEXT PAGE

79. In comparative physical growth curves, females develop

(A) more slowly than males
(B) more rapidly than males
(C) at the same rate as males
(D) more rapidly than males during the first six years and more slowly thereafter
(E) more slowly than males during the first six years and more rapidly thereafter

80. Muscles are prominent and familiar examples of

(A) receptors
(B) affectors
(C) end plates
(D) effectors
(E) ganglia

81. To what does the term *REM rebound* refer?

(A) If REM sleep is disrupted one night, the following night a person will enter REM stages earlier and more often during the night.
(B) When an individual begins taking antidepressants, he or she often experiences a reduction of REM sleep, but after several weeks normal REM cycles return.
(C) During REM sleep, the neurotransmitter systems that normally activate motor neurons are shut down and the individual experiences paralysis of the limbs.
(D) Across different species, the typical amount of REM sleep per day is correlated with the extent of neonatal dependency on adults.
(E) REM sleep allows an animal to scan its environment periodically during a prolonged bout of sleep, which provides protection against predators.

82. Rowell Huesmann and colleagues conducted a longitudinal study beginning with eight-year-old boys who were heavy television viewers of violent programming and eight-year-old boys who were moderate or light television viewers of violent programming. As the researchers followed these two groups across the years, what did they find?

(A) There was no significant difference in violent behavior between the two groups.
(B) Surprisingly, the light viewers were significantly more aggressive than the heavy viewers.
(C) At age thirty, heavy television violence-viewing eight-year-olds were significantly higher than light or moderate viewers in criminality and spousal abuse.
(D) The study was aborted three years after it was initiated for lack of funds.
(E) Only a few boys in either group engaged in violent or criminal acts.

GO ON TO THE NEXT PAGE

83. The words *of*, *the*, and *this* are all examples of

   (A) prepositions
   (B) open-class words
   (C) function words
   (D) count words
   (E) articles

84. If a female human fetus in the early stages of its development received large injections of androgen, which of the following could be expected in the newborn?

   (A) stillbirth
   (B) anoxia
   (C) brain damage
   (D) abnormal, exaggerated female sex characteristics
   (E) abnormal, exaggerated male sex characteristics

85. A circus performer is nine feet tall, with very large hands and feet and a protruding jaw, as the result of an overactive

   (A) thyroid gland
   (B) parathyroid gland
   (C) adrenal gland
   (D) pancreas
   (E) pituitary gland

86. In a "stop smoking" campaign, which of the following persons would be most likely to quit successfully?

   (A) a person who had read statistics on cancer research
   (B) a person who knows the mg tar content of the cigarette
   (C) a person who hears an expert deliver a talk on the subject
   (D) a person who hears one of his or her friends deliver a talk on the subject
   (E) a person who personally delivers a talk on the subject

87. Subjects are read the following list of words: *apple, pear, orange, dinosaur, peach, plum, grapes, banana*. Subjects' memory for these words varied, but *every* subject remembered the word *dinosaur*. What is this an example of?

   (A) primacy effect
   (B) serial position effect
   (C) prototype effect
   (D) spacing effect
   (E) Von Restorff effect

GO ON TO THE NEXT PAGE

88. The general message about early childhood that can be gleaned from personality theorists is that this period is

(A) not very critical to long-term development
(B) critically important to later personality development
(C) critical in the physiological sense but not in the social sense
(D) critical in the social sense but not in the physiological sense
(E) important only in terms of language development

89. Where is the hippocampus?

(A) frontal lobe
(B) temporal lobe
(C) parietal lobe
(D) basal lobe
(E) occipital lobe

90. In *As Good As It Gets*, we see Jack Nicholson in the opening scene washing his hands briskly with a new bar of soap, throwing it in the trash can, unwrapping a new bar, washing briskly and throwing the bar of soap in the trash can. This pattern goes on through several bars of soap. What disorder would you consider central to this observed behavior?

(A) obsessive-compulsive disorder
(B) somatoform disorder
(C) substance-related disorder
(D) major depressive disorder
(E) paranoid schizophrenic disorder

91. The brain and spinal cord compose the

(A) sympathetic nervous system
(B) parasympathetic nervous system
(C) central nervous system
(D) peripheral nervous system
(E) somatic nervous system

92. A desire to guide and contribute to the development of a generation younger than oneself would be characteristic of

(A) generativity
(B) genital stage
(C) self-actualization
(D) narcissism
(E) social interest

GO ON TO THE NEXT PAGE

Assume that a human brain has been split in half, down the midline, and that in the drawing you are viewing the medial surface (the front of the brain is on the left and the back is on the right).

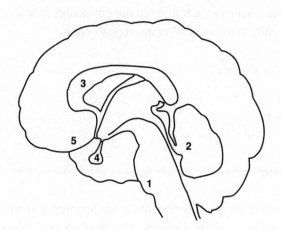

93. Identify the pons.

(A) 1
(B) 2
(C) 3
(D) 4
(E) 5

94. Identify the cerebellum.

(A) 1
(B) 2
(C) 3
(D) 4
(E) 5

95. Identify the corpus callosum.

(A) 1
(B) 2
(C) 3
(D) 4
(E) 5

GO ON TO THE NEXT PAGE

96. There is an epidemic of obesity among young children in the United States. All of the following are true *except*

(A) Type II diabetes has reached down into elementary school children.
(B) Adolescent women are increasingly diagnosed with osteoperosis.
(C) Though anorexia is increasing, bulimia is decreasing.
(D) Hypertension has been found increasingly among children and adolescents.
(E) Girls as young as the third and fourth grade are weight conscious and dieting.

97. Evolution via natural selection is often summarized with the phrase "survival of the fittest." This is misleading because

(A) the phrase makes no mention of genes
(B) fitness cannot be measured
(C) fitness is not constant but rather varies across different environments
(D) reproductive success and not survival is the basis for natural selection
(E) not all traits are shaped by natural selection

98. The socially "good" or "proper" within Freudian theory is conceptually defined as the

(A) id
(B) ego
(C) superego
(D) archetype
(E) preconscious

99. The Reverend Spooner was notorious for making a particular kind of speech error that now bears his name, such as "let us pray for our queer old dean" (instead of dear old queen). What elements of speech are swapped with each other in Spoonerisms such as this?

(A) morphemes
(B) phonemes
(C) memes
(D) monotremes
(E) tonemes

GO ON TO THE NEXT PAGE

100. In evidence-based practice of clinical psychology

(A) psychodynamic techniques have been found superior to behavior techniques

(B) Rogers's client-centered approach has proved more effective than Perls's Gestalt therapy approach

(C) Simplest has proven best—changing behavior by way of reinforcement schedules and plans

(D) Ellis's directive approach—telling patients where they've been engaged in faulty thinking—has proven most effective

(E) effectiveness has been found in several approaches—the professionalism, knowledge, and skill of the practitioner prove to be key

101. What result does the picture superiority effect describe?

(A) It is easier to recall concepts that were studied as pictures than those that were studied as words.

(B) The right hemisphere codes pictures and the left hemisphere codes words.

(C) Attention to pictures is broader than attention to words.

(D) The more often a picture is seen, the more positively subjects will later rate it.

(E) Deductive reasoning is easier when the stimuli are presented as pictures than as words.

102. The learned helplessness theory of depression is the work of

(A) Rotter

(B) Seligman

(C) Maslow

(D) Bandura

(E) Watson

103. An individual's genetic blueprint and environmental experiences together determine the expression of traits known as the

(A) phenotype

(B) genotype

(C) allotype

(D) monotype

(E) exotype

104. Which of the following constitutes a disadvantage of the rooming-in procedure with newborns?

(A) Needs are met with minimal crying.

(B) Trained nurses are easily accessible.

(C) No adjustment is required to handling by several people.

(D) Constant demands are made upon the new mother.

(E) Rigid feeding schedule is adhered to.

GO ON TO THE NEXT PAGE

105. A ground squirrel makes an alarm call when it detects a predator. Although this warns other squirrels of a threat, thereby increasing their chance of survival, the squirrel that sounds the alarm suffers an increased risk of predation. What is likely to be true of the ground squirrel that makes the alarm call?

(A) It is likely to have relatives nearby.
(B) It is likely to be the dominant squirrel in a social hierarchy.
(C) It is likely to be trying to attract a mate.
(D) It is likely to have been raised in social isolation, without a chance to observe safe behaviors.
(E) None of the above.

106. In developmental terminology, PKU refers to

(A) the effects of thalidomide
(B) Down syndrome
(C) sickle cell
(D) a hereditary enzyme deficiency
(E) syphilis in the newborn

107. The Dani people of New Guinea have only two color terms, roughly corresponding to the words *light* and *dark,* in contrast to the many color terms English-speakers know. According to what hypothesis should Dani and Americans perform differently on *nonverbal* color categorization tests?

(A) universal grammar
(B) Whorfian hypothesis
(C) Weber's law
(D) Gestalt theory
(E) critical period hypothesis

108. The person smokes a cigarette and, because of earlier drug administration, becomes nauseous in a technique known as

(A) chaining
(B) therapeutic community
(C) extinction
(D) aversive conditioning
(E) reciprocal inhibition

109. Humans have two copies of each chromosome in most cells (except the gametes). What are species with this pattern called?

(A) diploid
(B) diurnal
(C) dizygotic
(D) diathesis
(E) dichotic

GO ON TO THE NEXT PAGE

110. When we speak of the etiology of a disorder, we are referring to the

   (A) syndrome
   (B) contributing factors
   (C) outcome of treatment
   (D) prognosis for cure
   (E) length of treatment

111. The condition in which a person falls asleep spontaneously and unintentionally is called

   (A) narcolepsy
   (B) epilepsy
   (C) sleep apnea
   (D) insomnia
   (E) delayed sleep phase syndrome

112. According to Piaget, the process through which a young child relates something he or she sees to something he or she already knows is called

   (A) accommodation
   (B) assimilation
   (C) convergence
   (D) concrete operation
   (E) formal operation

113. The phrase *contralateral control* refers to the finding that

   (A) the left half of the brain controls movements on the right side of the body, and vice versa
   (B) anxious attachment styles are more likely to occur in children raised under authoritarian parenting practices
   (C) there is a high correlation between the levels of physical attractiveness of romantic partners
   (D) homeostatic systems, like thermostats, rely on actions that produce consequences that in turn stop or reverse the initial action
   (E) human males are more likely to experience sexual jealousy whereas females are more likely to experience emotional jealousy

114. Ellen was on holiday in Thailand when a disastrous tsunami killed many people. Ellen had frequent nightmares and flashbacks lasting for years. She was experiencing

   (A) generalized anxiety disorder
   (B) posttraumatic stress disorder
   (C) obsessive-compulsive disorder
   (D) panic disorder
   (E) phobic disorder

GO ON TO THE NEXT PAGE

115. Kurt has noticed that his friend, Burt, has stopped going to movies, is wearing worn-looking clothes, and never seems to have his wallet with him when Kurt suggests they grab a bite to eat. Kurt believes that Burt must have lost his job and is trying to hide that from his friend. This conclusion is an example of

(A) unconscious inference
(B) social-identity theory
(C) inductive reasoning
(D) restructuring
(E) rationalization

116. In comparison with centralized networks, which of the following constitutes a distinct advantage of the decentralized communication network?

(A) increased worker productivity
(B) quickly formed interaction stability
(C) more rigid structure
(D) increased independence from other workers
(E) fewer messages required for making a given decision

117. In dual-process models of reasoning, System 1 and System 2 refer to

(A) fast and automatic reasoning versus slow and effortful reasoning
(B) inductive reasoning versus deductive reasoning
(C) availability heuristics versus representativeness heuristics
(D) reliability versus validity
(E) framing versus anchoring

QUESTIONS 118–120 ARE BASED ON THE FOLLOWING CHOICES.

Given a normal distribution with a mean of 68 and a standard deviation of 10, use the following set of choices.

1. .68
2. .84
3. .16
4. .32
5. none of the above

118. What is the probability of a score above 78?

(A) 1
(B) 2
(C) 3
(D) 4
(E) 5

GO ON TO THE NEXT PAGE

119. What is the probability of a score below 48?

(A) 1
(B) 2
(C) 3
(D) 4
(E) 5

120. What is the probability of a score either below 58 or above 78?

(A) 1
(B) 2
(C) 3
(D) 4
(E) 5

121. How many phonemes does the word *chip* have?

(A) 0
(B) 1
(C) 2
(D) 3
(E) 4

122. The method of summated ratings refers to which of the following scales?

(A) Thurstone
(B) Likert
(C) Semantic Differential
(D) Guttman
(E) Bogardus

123. Which of the following structures involved in neuronal communication is *not* technically a part of the neuron?

(A) receptor
(B) myelin sheath
(C) dendrite
(D) axon
(E) synaptic bouton

124. Interpersonal attraction based on rewards and costs is a prominent aspect of the

(A) theory of similarity
(B) theory of complementarity
(C) social exchange theory
(D) theory of cognitive dissonance
(E) distributive justice theory

GO ON TO THE NEXT PAGE

125. The term *universal grammar* is associated with which linguist, who famously challenged behaviorist accounts of language acquisition?

(A) Paul Broca
(B) Ludwig Wittgenstein
(C) Carl Wernicke
(D) Noam Chomsky
(E) Benjamin Whorf

126. In Darley and Latané's "epileptic attack" study, the investigators found that a major determinant in eliciting a helping response was

(A) seeing someone else ask for help
(B) the number of other students that the individual thought had heard the victim
(C) the sex of the victim
(D) the age of the potential helper
(E) the degree of perceived seriousness of the situation

127. Aggression is decreased among members of a species that adopts an assigned status system that governs access to territories, mates, food, and so on. These status structures are referred to as

(A) natural selection
(B) homeostasis
(C) sympathetic systems
(D) dominance hierarchies
(E) competency systems

128. Someone well versed in proxemics would be studying

(A) personal, territorial space
(B) facial expressions
(C) mass communication
(D) brainwashing
(E) nonzero sum games

129. The Young-Helmholtz theory pertains to perception of what property?

(A) pitch
(B) loudness
(C) brightness
(D) color
(E) distance

GO ON TO THE NEXT PAGE

130. Within Newcomb's A-B-X model, if person A likes X, person B likes X, and person A dislikes person B, the triad is said to be

    (A) cooriented
    (B) asymmetric
    (C) congruent
    (D) bipolar
    (E) inoculated

131. In the dual-coding theory of information processing, humans have two, independent information coding systems:

    (A) verbal and nonverbal
    (B) short-term and long-term
    (C) rods and cones
    (D) overt and covert
    (E) episodic and semantic

132. According to the expectancy-value theory

    (A) unattractive women are likely to find attractive male partners
    (B) males and females of equal attractiveness are likely to be matched
    (C) extrovert personality types are likely to pair with introverts
    (D) attitudes will change in the direction of one's behavior
    (E) attractive women are likely to find unattractive male partners

133. When conducting a signal-detection analysis of performance, which of the following is *not* the name given to a response type typically included in the analysis?

    (A) hit
    (B) error
    (C) false alarm
    (D) correct reject
    (E) miss

134. "Sour grapes" is an example of the defense mechanism called

    (A) reaction formation
    (B) compensation
    (C) compartmentalization
    (D) rationalization
    (E) projection

GO ON TO THE NEXT PAGE

135. Reggie is playing a trivia game, and he is asked the question "What comedian performed regularly with Dean Martin early in his career?" Reggie is certain he knows the answer, and even can "feel" the rhythm of the name (two, two-syllable words), and he thinks one of the names starts with a /g/ sound. What is Reggie experiencing?

(A) a source memory failure
(B) the bandwagon effect
(C) the Stroop effect
(D) a tip-of-the-tongue state
(E) the illusion of control

136. Research suggests that an active, outgoing, socially assertive child is most likely to have come from a family background that has been

(A) warm and restrictive
(B) distant and demanding
(C) distant and democratic
(D) warm and permissive
(E) distant and permissive

137. When you view an open door and perceive the door as rectangular, even though the retinal image of that door is trapezoidal, you are experiencing

(A) angle constancy
(B) size constancy
(C) position constancy
(D) shape constancy
(E) rectangular constancy

138. Developmentally speaking, the earliest group in which a person participates is

(A) dyadic
(B) monadic
(C) triadic
(D) quadratic
(E) parallel play group

GO ON TO THE NEXT PAGE

139. Which of the following statements is true about the *subject* of a sentence in English?

    I.   The subject determines the tense of the verb of the sentence.
    II.   The subject is the first noun in the sentence.
    III.   The subject is the noun in the sentence that is most central to the meaning.

    (A) I only
    (B) II only
    (C) III only
    (D) I and II
    (E) I and III

140. Among the features by which we distinguish letters, a three-year-old child is proficient only in

    (A) curvature (U vs. V)
    (B) closedness (O vs. C)
    (C) direction (P vs. d)
    (D) size (a vs. A)
    (E) shape

141. The terms *weights*, *activation*, and *nodes* are all used when talking about

    (A) syntactic structure
    (B) inductive reasoning
    (C) deductive reasoning
    (D) connectionist models
    (E) neuroanatomy

142. All of the following have been found in developmental psychology research *except*

    (A) The degree of maternal responsiveness to a baby's needs affects the quality of the child's attachment to the mother.
    (B) Frequent mother–child separations during the first two or three years can produce anxious attachment.
    (C) The discipline technique of expressing disapproval through love withdrawal has been found to be one of the most effective.
    (D) Failure to form attachments to significant, caretaking persons during childhood relates to the inability to form close personal relationships in adulthood.
    (E) The young child is much more willing to explore strange surroundings when mother is present than when she is not.

GO ON TO THE NEXT PAGE

143. The term *confabulation* refers to a

(A) visual illusion
(B) Gestalt grouping principle
(C) stage in the acquisition of a conditioned response
(D) decision that emerges from a group discussion
(E) memory error

144. All of the following are true *except*

(A) A person with serious anxiety disorder has higher mortality risk than those without the disorder.
(B) Men more readily admit anxiety disorder symptoms than do women.
(C) Compared to the total population, African-American and low-income families have higher incidence of anxiety disorders.
(D) Freud believed anxiety disorders were the product of intense, unresolved conflicts in early childhood.
(E) Fear and anxiety experiences can have an adaptive function.

145. Consider a strand of miniature lights, with 100 bulbs of equal brightness. If 5 of those bulbs suddenly burn out and turn off, an observer will notice the overall change in brightness. However, if those lights are attached to four other fully lit strands, a total of 500 bulbs, when 5 lights burn out, an observer will not notice (although he or she will if many more lights burn out). What important psychophysics principle does this example illustrate?

(A) size constancy
(B) just-noticeable difference
(C) specificity theory
(D) Young-Helmholtz theory
(E) Weber's law

146. Which of the following should be the source of greatest parental concern about a child's emotional health?

(A) frequent laughing
(B) frequent noisiness
(C) long periods of sleep
(D) frequent temper tantrums
(E) frequent game playing

147. Which of the following words or phrases is synonymous with *engram*?

(A) memory trace
(B) visual illusion
(C) morpheme
(D) primary reinforcer
(E) secondary reinforcer

GO ON TO THE NEXT PAGE

148. According to psychoanalytic theory, defense mechanisms develop as a function of

    (A) repression
    (B) depression
    (C) superego
    (D) anxiety
    (E) reaction formation

149. The part of the retina with the most densely packed photoreceptors is the ____ and the part of the retina with no photoreceptors is the ____.

    (A) cone; blind spot
    (B) blind spot; fovea
    (C) fovea; cone
    (D) cone; fovea
    (E) fovea; blind spot

150. The Diagnostic and Statistical Manual (DSM-5)

    (A) has a checklist of symptoms for each disorder
    (B) relies on the MMPI to determine the symptoms
    (C) has a bias-lean toward the projective techniques
    (D) is unlikely to have a further revision in the next five-to-ten years
    (E) was developed by the American Psychological Association

151. Dogs have been trained to make a response when a stimulus is an oval but not when the stimulus is a circle. The animals have been food-deprived and receive food reinforcement for each correct response. On subsequent trials, the oval shape is gradually changed to look more and more circular. At the point where the dogs' previously high level of correct responding becomes random in accuracy, the likely cause of the change is

    (A) satiation
    (B) anxiety
    (C) nondiscriminative stimulus
    (D) figure–ground reversal
    (E) response generalization

GO ON TO THE NEXT PAGE

152. All of the following are true *except*

    (A) The use of ECT (electroconvulsive therapy) has declined in recent years.

    (B) MAO (monoamine oxidase) inhibitors were an early treatment for unipolar depression.

    (C) An increase in the neurotransmitter norepinephrine leads to increased depression.

    (D) Nutraceuticals is a name given to herbal supplements and nature-based hormones.

    (E) Tricyclics preceded the development of selective serotonin reuptake inhibitors (SSRIs) in the treatment of unipolar depression.

153. The inability to acquire and consolidate new memories about personal events is called

    (A) retroactive amnesia

    (B) proactive amnesia

    (C) anterograde amnesia

    (D) infantile amnesia

    (E) implicit amnesia

154. Major criticisms leveled at Freud and psychoanalysis have included the point(s)

    I. that it is not scientific

    II. that its theoretical tenets are not replicable

    III. that it eludes operational definition

    (A) I only

    (B) II only

    (C) III only

    (D) I and II

    (E) I, II, and III

155. While studying for a psychology test, you might do better if you take periodic breaks, interrupting your ongoing studying activities. This advice is based on experimental evidence that interrupted or uncompleted tasks are remembered better than uninterrupted ones, a phenomenon known as

    (A) proactive facilitation

    (B) proactive inhibition

    (C) the Zeigarnik effect

    (D) the von Restorff effect

    (E) serial position effect

GO ON TO THE NEXT PAGE

A pair of psychology professors was interested in whether actually performing an action with one's body (e.g., *swallow*) facilitates the ability to comprehend sentences that refer to this action metaphorically (e.g., *he swallowed his pride*). One of the researchers recruited thirty participants from his introductory psychology course, and asked them to perform each of ten actions; immediately following each action he showed them a sentence that used this action metaphorically on a computer screen and asked them to press a key when they had read and understood the sentence. The other researcher recruited thirty participants from her research methods course, and asked them to perform ten irrelevant actions followed by the same set of metaphorical sentences. Then, the two researchers compared their data.

156. What is a possible confounding variable in this experiment that should have been controlled for?

(A) the possibility that some metaphorical expressions are more abstract than others
(B) the possibility that some subjects may be nonnative speakers of English
(C) the possibility that subjects in one condition may read faster than subjects in the other condition
(D) both (A) and (B)
(E) both (B) and (C)

157. What is the dependent variable in this experiment?

(A) how reliably participants performed the ten actions
(B) how fast participants performed the ten actions
(C) how well participants remembered the sentences at the end of the experiment
(D) how fast participants read the metaphorical sentences
(E) all of the above

158. Before they began their study, the researchers decided that they would reject the null hypothesis if they observed a performance difference between the two groups of subjects that was so large that it could have occurred by chance fewer than 5 in 100 times. The value .05 was the researchers'

(A) *p* value
(B) *t* value
(C) effect size
(D) alpha value
(E) *F* value

GO ON TO THE NEXT PAGE

159. The researchers did not find any significant differences between the two groups. What should they do?

    I.   evaluate the method used in the experiment
    II. consider the possibility of a Type I error
    III. consider the possibility of a Type II error

(A) I only
(B) II only
(C) III only
(D) I and II
(E) I and III

160. The so-called second-generation antidepressants

(A) are the tricyclics
(B) are the monoamine–oxidase inhibitors
(C) are the SSRIs (selective serotonin reuptake inhibitors)
(D) include Elavil
(E) include Tofranil

161. In many models of human memory, iconic memories are described as decaying in under two seconds from the

(A) short-term store
(B) sensory register
(C) hippocampus
(D) long-term store
(E) working memory

162. A friend tells you that she is taking lithium. You immediately conclude that she is suffering from _____ disorder.

(A) unipolar depressive
(B) bipolar depressive
(C) schizophrenic
(D) acute anxiety
(E) paranoia

163. Temporal conditioning

(A) is synonymous with trace conditioning
(B) is synonymous with delayed conditioning
(C) is synonymous with simultaneous conditioning
(D) presents a UCS on a fixed time schedule
(E) utilizes a CS that is in itself inherently rewarding

GO ON TO THE NEXT PAGE

164. All of the following are correct *except*

    (A) Far more men than women commit suicide every year.
    (B) Divorced persons have a higher suicide rate than married persons.
    (C) Serious illness is very rarely a trigger for committing suicide.
    (D) Freud equated suicide with one's death instinct.
    (E) Emphasis has shifted from suicide treatment to suicide prevention.

165. Eleanor Rosch suggested that category membership is determined by similarity of an exemplar to the concept's

    (A) chunk
    (B) schema
    (C) critical features
    (D) prototype
    (E) icon

166. All of the following are true of eating disorders *except*

    (A) Since 1995, African-American women have become much less weight-conscious than white women.
    (B) Eating disorders are prevalent among high-achievement-oriented young women.
    (C) Boredom and depression are two of the triggers for women's eating disorders.
    (D) Recovery is very difficult for women suffering from anorexia nervosa.
    (E) Female weight-consciousness and dieting have "reached down" into early elementary school.

167. *Incorrectly* paired are

    (A) spinal cord–reflex behavior
    (B) medulla–respiration and cardiac activity
    (C) ventricular system–hormonal secretions into the blood
    (D) corpus callosum–communication between left and right cerebral hemispheres
    (E) reticular formation–regulation of sleep/wake cycles

168. As psychologists generally have framed or thought about substance abuse _____. The current trend is _____.

    (A) it tended to be single-substance-related-disorders; polysubstance-related disorders
    (B) it defied any specific substance definition; toward single-substance-related-disorders
    (C) alcoholism was in a class all to itself; toward single-substance drug abuse
    (D) cocaine was in a class all to itself; toward greater emphasis on alcohol abuse
    (E) "speed" was in a class all to itself; toward greater emphasis on alcohol abuse

GO ON TO THE NEXT PAGE

169. The ability to alter one's behavior to be more consistent with long-term goals or with the current context is referred to as

(A) attention
(B) executive control
(C) unilateral control
(D) confabulation
(E) perseveration

170. All of the following are true about schizophrenia *except*

(A) Its symptoms vary widely.
(B) Treatment is always more effective in developed than in developing countries.
(C) There is great variation in responsiveness to treatment.
(D) There is great public fascination surrounding this disorder.
(E) It is frequently mistaken for "split personality" or "multiple personality disorder."

171. During a political campaign, it is common for one to falsely remember a candidate's opinions as more consistent with that candidate's party platform than they really are. The tendency to remember an expected statement instead of an actual statement is an example of

(A) iconic memory
(B) implicit memory
(C) a schema-consistent distortion
(D) a concept prototype
(E) a confirmation bias

QUESTIONS 172 AND 173 ARE BASED ON THE FOLLOWING DIAGRAM.

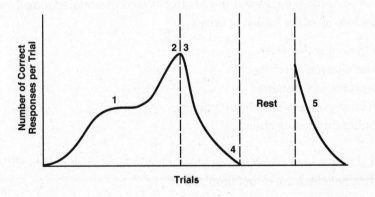

172. In the above diagram, the process of extinction begins at which point?

(A) 1
(B) 2
(C) 3
(D) 4
(E) 5

GO ON TO THE NEXT PAGE

173. What name is given to the phenomenon occurring at point 1?

   (A) asymptote
   (B) extinction
   (C) plateau
   (D) reminiscence
   (E) spontaneous recovery

174. Harry Potter's unprecedented phenomenon characteristics transformed millions of young enthusiasts into hysterical fans. What distinguished these fans and their hysteria from that of individuals suffering from histrionic personality disorder?

   (A) theatrical gestures
   (B) exaggerated mannerisms
   (C) grandiose language
   (D) high emotionality
   (E) none of the above

175. In a study referred to as the "Little Albert" experiment, a child (presumably Albert) was given a white rat to play with, and then the experimenter played a loud noise that scared the child. After several repetitions of this procedure, the child was afraid not only of the white rat, but also of other white objects and other furry objects. This is a famous early example of

   (A) extinction
   (B) spontaneous recovery
   (C) biological preparedness
   (D) reminiscence
   (E) generalization

176. Positive psychology focuses on the positive aspects of stress. Among these benefits, they include all of the following *except*

   (A) developing new skills
   (B) reevaluating priorities
   (C) learning new insights
   (D) focusing on personal shortcomings
   (E) enhancing coping ability

177. Physical exercise has been cited as a major ingredient in personal health. All of the following benefits have been found *except*

   (A) enhanced cardiovascular fitness
   (B) reduced risk of diabetes and respiratory problems
   (C) decreased risk of colon cancer in men
   (D) decreased risk of breast cancer in women
   (E) produces high reactivity to daily stress

GO ON TO THE NEXT PAGE

178. Which of the following would most accurately describe the delusional situation in which a person believes others are talking about him or her?

(A) delusions of sin and guilt
(B) hypochondriacal delusions
(C) delusions of grandeur
(D) nihilistic delusions
(E) delusions of reference

179. Current trends indicate that breast feeding is *most* prevalent among which of the following groups?

(A) lower-class Anglo-American mothers
(B) lower-class African-American mothers
(C) middle-class, well-educated mothers
(D) middle-class, poorly educated mothers
(E) all social strata

180. Kohlberg indicates that at the most primitive level of moral development, morality is decided by

(A) individual rights and social contracts
(B) reward and punishment
(C) individual conscience
(D) social approval or disapproval
(E) religious values

181. In the history of psychology, one of the following could be cited as the first experimentalist.

(A) Plato
(B) Aristotle
(C) Publius
(D) Aquinas
(E) Fechner

182. A peculiar, intoxication-type behavior in which a person loses normal control of one's emotions is characteristic of

(A) fatigue
(B) oxygen starvation
(C) thirst
(D) hunger
(E) sexual deprivation

GO ON TO THE NEXT PAGE

183. To convert a standard deviation into a variance, one must

(A) take the square root of the standard deviation
(B) divide the standard deviation by N
(C) multiply the standard deviation by $1/z$
(D) multiply the standard deviation by N
(E) square the standard deviation

184. Walter Mischel has spoken out very critically against the predictive validity of personality tests. He bases his criticism on

(A) observations he has made during test administrations
(B) a specific situation considered a more powerful behavioral determinant
(C) test makers' inability to distinguish state from trait
(D) low correlation between the Big Five and the 16-PF
(E) a test fad that has outrun its usefulness

185. In applying Mischel's premise, we would expect a child who test-cheats in a school class to be most likely to cheat

(A) when playing games with friends
(B) in another school classroom
(C) at a store
(D) in an agreement with a friend
(E) randomly in virtually any situation

186. Gordon Allport wrote a classic work entitled *The Nature of Prejudice*. In it, he outlined six theories of prejudice. All of the following are among the six *except*

(A) historical–it's always been this way and goes unquestioned
(B) sociocultural; hatred of the city and identifying a group with the city
(C) psychodynamic; frustration/aggression hypothesis
(D) genetic predisposition; inborn characteristics that express prejudice in maturity
(E) earned reputation; it's a just world, therefore people get what they deserve

187. Social psychology makes a distinction between physical distance and functional distance. What forms the basis on which this distinction is made?

  I. Physical distance is most critical in forming relationships.
 II. The key is "next door neighbor"—next door apartment or farmer ten miles away.
III. Functional distance refers to the likelihood of neighbor interaction.

(A) I only
(B) II only
(C) III only
(D) II and III
(E) I, II, and III

GO ON TO THE NEXT PAGE

188. The term *aversive racism* was coined by Dovidio to refer to

    (A) "in your face" racism
    (B) subtle, "polite" racism
    (C) racism observed only in the lab
    (D) philosophical discussion of racism
    (E) specific racial incidents that stand out

QUESTIONS 189–193 ARE BASED ON THE FOLLOWING ANSWER CHOICES.

    (A) Strongly Disagree ____ ____ ____ ____ ____ ____ Strongly Agree
    (B) Check mark the items you agree with
    (C) Good ____ ____ ____ ____ ____ ____ ____ Bad
    (D) Would admit to my family through marriage
    (E) Unidimensional

189. a Likert scale

190. a Guttman scale

191. a Bogardus scale

192. an Osgood scale

193. a Thurstone scale

194. The freshmen came to the university and were invited to a computer dance. It was the impression of each student that they would be date-matched by computer. Actually, as they filed from table to table in the gymnasium, they were being rated for level of attractiveness. After this part of the process they were paired for the dance. Half were paired similarly on the basis of attractiveness and half were paired dissimilarly. After the dance, the researchers did follow-up to determine their level of enjoyment and whether they planned to go out again. Results indicated that

    I. the men who were paired similarly with women wanted to continue; the women did not
    II. the couples paired dissimilarly did not want to continue
    III. both men and women paired similarly wanted to continue

    (A) I only
    (B) II only
    (C) III only
    (D) I and II
    (E) II and III

GO ON TO THE NEXT PAGE

195. Among gender differences found in nonverbal communication, researchers have discovered which of the following?

    I.   When walking, males swing their arms widely; females swing their arms narrowly.

    II. Females cross their legs knee to knee; males cross their legs ankle to knee.

    III. Males are more attune than women to nonverbal communication.

(A) I only

(B) II only

(C) III only

(D) I and II

(E) I, II, and III

196. The soldier who in the heat of battle curls up in a fetal position and cries is demonstrating

(A) phobia

(B) regression

(C) projection

(D) psychosomatic disorder

(E) hypochondriasis

197. A person is completely unresponsive, stares blankly into space, and never moves. She shows symptoms related to

(A) paranoia

(B) schizoaffective

(C) catatonia

(D) residual-type schizophrenia

(E) narcissistic personality disorder

198. In Bandura's behavioral psychotherapy, a withdrawn child in a kindergarten room would be reinforced for

(A) remaining alone

(B) joining the group

(C) drawing a picture

(D) writing his or her name

(E) playing with blocks

199. A team approach to therapy in which the entire life situation and the activities of the patient are brought into the therapeutic plan is known as

(A) milieu therapy

(B) sociotherapy

(C) nondirective therapy

(D) nonanalytical therapy

(E) Gestalt therapy

GO ON TO THE NEXT PAGE

200. An inanimate object would be central to which of the following sexual deviations?

(A) voyeurism
(B) masochism
(C) fetishism
(D) pedophilia
(E) sadism

201. Which of the following could be an example of a *null hypothesis* in a study of male and female performance on an aptitude test?

(A) Males and females will perform equally well on the aptitude test.
(B) Males will perform better than females on the aptitude test.
(C) No males will score below 50% on the aptitude test.
(D) No males will score higher than the highest female score on the aptitude test.
(E) The distribution of test scores for females will be positively skewed.

202. An attitude contains which of the following components?

I. cognitive (knowing)
II. affective (feeling)
III. behavioral (action)

(A) I only
(B) II only
(C) III only
(D) I and II
(E) I, II, and III

203. You have conducted a mail survey and your response rate was 30 percent. What would be your most prominent concern and question?

(A) whether the respondents lied on their survey
(B) whether the survey had been properly pilot-tested
(C) whether some of the questions were too personal
(D) whether nonresponders and responders were equivalent
(E) whether the survey should have been formatted differently

GO ON TO THE NEXT PAGE

204. Jill's favorite basketball team had been doing well in the mid-to-late season. They looked headed for a Conference bid. Then came that fateful game against the Lackluster Mudhens. Jill's team lost badly . . . very, very badly. The score was so lopsided we wouldn't dare tell you how bad it was. In the aftermath of that incredibly bad loss, Jill is most likely to say

(A) "We lost tonight . . . really badly."
(B) "The team lost tonight."
(C) "It wasn't even close."
(D) "We got destroyed."
(E) "We just couldn't do anything right."

205. What does the term *one-way-design* mean?

(A) a one-tailed rather than a two-tailed design
(B) only one independent variable is being manipulated
(C) design has only one condition
(D) design can only be run one way
(E) a nomenclature design

206. Ignatius has a $2 \times 2 \times 3 \times 3$ design. How many variables does he have?

(A) 1
(B) 2
(C) 3
(D) 4
(E) 5

207. From Question 206, how many groups does Ignatius have?

(A) 2
(B) 4
(C) 12
(D) 24
(E) 36

GO ON TO THE NEXT PAGE

QUESTIONS 208 AND 209 ARE BASED ON THE FOLLOWING DESCRIPTION.

In social psychology it often has been said that one can expect far more interactions than main effects. Assume for a moment that we are going to study the onset of prejudice attitudes in young children. We select as our variables

Age: four-year-olds and eight-year-olds

Race: African-American and Anglo-American

Residence neighborhood: integrated or segregated

208. What would constitute a main effect?

   I. a significant difference on the basis of age
   II. a significant difference on the basis of race
   III. a significant difference on the basis of residence neighborhood

   (A) I only
   (B) II only
   (C) III only
   (D) I and II
   (E) I, II, and III

209. What would constitute an interaction effect?

   I. a significant difference found on the basis of age × race
   II. a significant difference found on the basis of race × residence neighborhood
   III. a significant difference found on the basis of age × residence neighborhood

   (A) I only
   (B) II only
   (C) III only
   (D) I and II
   (E) I, II, and III

210. The birthplace of experimental psychology was Leipzig, Germany, in 1879. The scientist who created the lab was

   (A) Fechner
   (B) Wundt
   (C) Helmholtz
   (D) Spirling
   (E) Ammons

GO ON TO THE NEXT PAGE

211. Leipzig, Germany's, psychological research did not get a significant foothold or, perhaps, even a toehold, in the United States. To what would you attribute this failure?

    (A) war
    (B) famine
    (C) introspection
    (D) reflection
    (E) disease

212. Tasha has an understanding of t-tests but does not understand analysis of variance. Rather than taking the time to try to learn analysis of variance, she decides to do a series of t-tests to determine which of four groups were significantly different. What, if any, risk is she running with this decision and procedure?

    (A) no risk at all; response will be equivalent
    (B) very slight risk of a one-tailed distribution error
    (C) risks a major reduction in alpha level (.05 down to .001 or beyond)
    (D) risks a major increase in beta level
    (E) risks a major increase in alpha level (.05 up to .40)

213. What differentiates parametric measures from nonparametric measures?

    (A) simply the presence or absence of the measure
    (B) parametric assumes that the distribution from which samples are drawn is a normal distribution
    (C) nonparametric assumes homogeneity of variance, continuity of measures, and equality of intervals
    (D) nonparametric includes t, F, and r statistics
    (E) nonparametric refers specifically to z statistics

214. The basic altruism model in helping behavior includes:

    I. the action is voluntary
    II. the action is costly (perhaps time, money, personal risk)
    III. the action carries no anticipation of reward

    (A) I only
    (B) II only
    (C) III only
    (D) I and II
    (E) I, II, and III

GO ON TO THE NEXT PAGE

215. We are attracted to perceived similarity. Those to whom we are attracted we perceive as more similar than they really are. These words stem from

(A) Festinger's social comparison theory
(B) Winch's complementarity model
(C) Gergen's behavior exchange model
(D) Aronson's gain-loss model
(E) Bem's androgeny theory

STOP

If there is still time remaining, you may review your answers.

ANSWER KEY
Practice Test 1

1.	B	37.	C	73.	C	109.	A	145.	E	181.	B
2.	D	38.	B	74.	D	110.	B	146.	D	182.	B
3.	A	39.	A	75.	B	111.	A	147.	A	183.	E
4.	B	40.	C	76.	D	112.	B	148.	D	184.	B
5.	E	41.	D	77.	B	113.	A	149.	E	185.	B
6.	B	42.	B	78.	D	114.	B	150.	A	186.	D
7.	C	43.	B	79.	B	115.	C	151.	C	187.	D
8.	A	44.	B	80.	D	116.	A	152.	C	188.	B
9.	B	45.	E	81.	A	117.	A	153.	C	189.	A
10.	A	46.	D	82.	C	118.	C	154.	E	190.	E
11.	C	47.	A	83.	C	119.	E	155.	C	191.	D
12.	E	48.	D	84.	E	120.	D	156.	E	192.	C
13.	C	49.	B	85.	E	121.	D	157.	D	193.	B
14.	E	50.	D	86.	E	122.	B	158.	D	194.	E
15.	C	51.	A	87.	E	123.	B	159.	E	195.	D
16.	B	52.	A	88.	B	124.	C	160.	C	196.	B
17.	A	53.	E	89.	B	125.	D	161.	B	197.	C
18.	E	54.	D	90.	A	126.	B	162.	B	198.	B
19.	D	55.	C	91.	C	127.	D	163.	D	199.	A
20.	A	56.	D	92.	D	128.	A	164.	C	200.	C
21.	A	57.	E	93.	A	129.	D	165.	D	201.	A
22.	B	58.	A	94.	B	130.	B	166.	A	202.	E
23.	A	59.	A	95.	C	131.	A	167.	C	203.	D
24.	E	60.	C	96.	C	132.	B	168.	A	204.	B
25.	A	61.	B	97.	D	133.	B	169.	B	205.	B
26.	B	62.	B	98.	C	134.	D	170.	B	206.	D
27.	B	63.	D	99.	B	135.	D	171.	C	207.	E
28.	B	64.	B	100.	E	136.	D	172.	C	208.	E
29.	B	65.	D	101.	A	137.	D	173.	C	209.	E
30.	C	66.	D	102.	B	138.	A	174.	E	210.	B
31.	B	67.	C	103.	A	139.	A	175.	E	211.	C
32.	B	68.	C	104.	D	140.	B	176.	D	212.	E
33.	C	69.	B	105.	A	141.	D	177.	E	213.	B
34.	D	70.	C	106.	D	142.	C	178.	E	214.	E
35.	A	71.	C	107.	B	143.	E	179.	C	215.	A
36.	B	72.	B	108.	D	144.	B	180.	B		

To score your first practice test, please compare the answers on your answer sheet with the answers below. Place a check mark next to questions you answered correctly. Place an "X" next to questions you answered incorrectly. Leave questions you did not answer blank.

ANSWER EXPLANATIONS

_____ 1. **(B)** The kinesthetic sensory system enables us to monitor the movements and positions of our limbs.

_____ 2. **(D)** Korsakoff's syndrome, which is caused by a thiamine deficiency and is often associated with chronic alcoholism, causes long-term retrograde and antero-grade amnesia.

_____ 3. **(A)** Somatoform disorder relates to instances where a person in a highly stress-ful environment experiences loss of a normal, physiological capability where there is no physiological reason for the loss.

_____ 4. **(B)** Negative reinforcement increases the probability of a desired response by removing something aversive, in this case, the chores.

_____ 5. **(E)** The Big Five is a factor-analytical distillation of Cattell's 16-PF (Personality Factor) Scale; it considers extraversion to be a key factor. The five are extraver-sion (positive emotionality), openness to experience, conscientiousness (con-straint), agreeableness, and neuroticism (negative emotionality).

_____ 6. **(B)** The law of specific nerve energies was first proposed by Johannes Müller in 1826.

_____ 7. **(C)** The three stages, sequentially, are cervix dilation, actual newborn emer-gence, and afterbirth. The third stage involves delivery of the placenta with its accompanying amniotic and chorionic membranes.

_____ 8. **(A)** The term *prosody* refers to the stress or rhythm of speech. Unlike other aspects of speech, it is not readily captured by orthography, which you may have experienced if you ever wrote an ironic or sarcastic e-mail message that was mis-understood by the recipient.

_____ 9. **(B)** The number of scores in a distribution, the measure of central tendency, and the measure of variability are three measures generally called descriptive statistics. On the basis of one's description of the sample, the investigator can make inferences about the probable characteristics of the specific population that could not be measured in its entirety (inferential statistics).

_____ 10. **(A)** In memory, the primacy effect refers to one part of the serial position curve, and is thought to reflect retrieval of well-rehearsed items from long-term mem-ory. Note that the term has also been used in social psychology when discussing impression formation.

_____ 11. **(C)** Freud's perspective places primary emphasis upon the presence of unre-solved personal conflicts brought by the individual to the crowd situation.

_____ 12. **(E)** Hall's concept of personal space is, in effect, a concept of territoriality (i.e., of protecting one's personal "turf").

13. **(C)** Alpha waves refer to one of several frequency bands of EEG activity. Different bands are associated with different states of mental activity, sleep, or pathology. Alpha is predominately observed when a person is in a relaxed state with eyes closed (and also in patients in a coma).

14. **(E)** Referred to as "Morgan's canon," the quotation states a basic interpretative principle in comparative psychology (Morgan's field), although it can be considered a specific case of the principle of parsimony known as Occam's razor.

15. **(C)** Cultures vary dramatically, and what would be considered quite normal in one culture could be considered quite abnormal in another.

16. **(B)** Barbiturates are depressants, not stimulants. It may be helpful to remember that many of the stimulants carry the "-ine" word-ending (another example is amphetamine).

17. **(A)** That a person's unique qualities constitute the essence of his or her personality is a point frequently made in defense of the idiographic approach.

18. **(E)** Freud's psychoanalytic approach is nomothetic and Adler's individual psychology approach is distinctly idiographic.

19. **(D)** Whereas individual psychology, client-centered therapy, personal construct, and Gestalt therapy focus upon individual uniqueness (idiographic), systematic desensitization is a general approach often used in cases of phobia.

20. **(A)** If not corrected, the ability to make comparisons between the two eyes (i.e., retinal disparity) does not develop, and as a result, depth perception will be compromised in some circumstances.

21. **(A)** A common example of the base rate fallacy is when a doctor chooses a very rare diagnosis over a much more common one because the patient's symptoms match the rare diagnosis.

22. **(B)** Heterozygous indicates the presence of genetic potential for either brown-eyed or blue-eyed children. Because brown eyes are a dominant characteristic, only one among the four possible combinations would result in blue eyes.

23. **(A)** Positive correlations have been found between the amount of maternal stress during pregnancy and the extent of fetal activity.

24. **(E)** The corpus callosum is the band of nerve fibers connecting the two cerebral hemispheres; it is part of the forebrain.

25. **(A)** State-dependent learning effects have been noted in comparisons of happy and sad moods, of memory with or without alcohol, and even of underwater versus on-land learning in scuba divers! In all cases, memory retrieval is better when the subject is in the same state as during learning.

26. **(B)** The standard deviation increases by the same multiple as each of the scores in the distribution—in this case, 7.

27. **(B)** Statistical reliability of a test refers to the extent to which repeated administrations will give the same score result. In addition, a test must also have valid-

ity—that is, it must measure that which it was constructed to measure (e.g., intelligence or mechanical aptitude).

28. **(B)** The fact that the brain is not involved in reflexes accounts for the automatic and nearly instantaneous nature of the reflex response.

29. **(B)** Working through a problem with or without gesturing was the only variable that differed within each participant. It is not the only independent variable, because the experiment has two additional between-subjects variables (i.e., gender, cultural background).

30. **(C)** A *p* value is defined as the likelihood that any observed effects in an experiment are attributed to chance/random factors.

31. **(B)** The researchers' conclusion is problematic because they had no measure to establish whether participants from Mediterranean cultures do indeed use their hands more than participants from other cultures when they think and speak.

32. **(B)** Aronson, Mills, and others in the field of cognitive dissonance have found the amount of initiation to be positively correlated with an individual's degree of attraction to a group. Because your fraternity or sorority initiation was rigorous, for example, the group may be more attractive to you than a fraternity or sorority would be to someone who did not have such a rigorous initiation.

33. **(C)** Notably, the "Robber's Cave" research of Sherif would underscore the development of superordinate goals as a positive approach to prejudice-related problems.

34. **(D)** Adrenocorticotropic hormone (ACTH), secreted by the pituitary gland, signals the adrenal gland to secrete corticosteroid hormones. As such, ACTH is a critical component of the "hypothalamic-pituitary-adrenal axis" that controls the stress response.

35. **(A)** Evidence from this, and related experiments (e.g., mental image scanning time), has been used to argue for analogical mental images.

36. **(B)** Within DSM-5, panic disorder would be considered an anxiety disorder.

37. **(C)** A psychological diagnosis is very frequently based on an individual's personal statement of his or her experience and problem.

38. **(B)** The Stroop effect is a measure of interference, specifically between the name of the color a word is printed in and the name of the color the word refers to.

39. **(A)** Homeostatic regulation occurs for body temperature, blood glucose levels, blood concentration, and so on; hormones play an important role in many types of homeostatic regulation in mammals.

40. **(C)** Rooting response, in effect a search for the nipple, is prompted by tactile stimulation of a newborn's cheek.

41. **(D)** Goldblatt is describing the combination of capability and prohibition that besets the early adolescent period of development.

_____ 42. **(B)** For both visual and auditory stimuli, reaction times become longer because stimulus discrimination is more difficult when the patterns are increasingly similar.

_____ 43. **(B)** The term *encoding specificity* describes the finding (such as this) that retrieval efforts are more likely to succeed when the context at recall matches the context at study.

_____ 44. **(B)** George has a very intense fear of crowds (ochlophobia).

_____ 45. **(E)** The study of pragmatics is concerned with our ability to understand the intended meaning of a sentence (beyond the exact words that are uttered).

_____ 46. **(D)** Cattell and Eysenck are prominently concerned with factor analysis—correlation and grouping of traits.

_____ 47. **(A)** The primary colors in additive (light) color mixing are blue, green, and red; the primary colors in subtractive (pigment/paint) color mixing are blue, yellow, and red.

_____ 48. **(D)** Timbre (sound wave complexity) and loudness (sound wave amplitude) are used to determine the distance of a sound.

_____ 49. **(B)** The *t*-test would be used for simple testing of differences between the means of experimental and control groups.

_____ 50. **(D)** Memory consolidation refers to the crystallization of recent information into a more permanent long-term trace. (There is a related term, *reconsolidation*, which refers to the further crystallization that occurs with repeated retrievals of older memories.)

_____ 51. **(A)** The potential relationship between speed of habituation in the infant and intelligence is currently prominent in child psychology research. Initial findings have been promising.

_____ 52. **(A)** The action potential speeds through the insulated axon until it reaches a gap in the myelin, called a node of Ranvier, where it is regenerated and speeds on its way again. This "hopping" of the action potential gets its name from the Latin word *saltare*, which means "to hop" or "leap." (The word *sauté* comes from this same root.)

_____ 53. **(E)** In the "rule of thirds," one third of schizophrenic patients will receive treatment and function normally, one third will be in and out of treatment throughout their lives, and one third will never be able to leave treatment.

_____ 54. **(D)** A central topic in ethology, the scientific study of animal behavior, is the documentation of species-specific instinctual behaviors.

_____ 55. **(C)** For example, it is the rush of endorphins that is central to the pain-relieving effects of acupuncture and to the "runner's high" of the marathoner.

_____ 56. **(D)** Adler believed that the major personality energizer was not a sexual drive (psychoanalytic view) but a superiority striving.

_____ 57. **(E)** Hull is best known for his work on drive theory, as a framework for understanding learning and behavior.

58. **(A)** Two months before election night (a comparatively long time), a political candidate stands the best chance of being remembered if he or she is the first speaker on the program. If, on the other hand, it is the day before the election, being the last speaker is the wisest choice.

59. **(A)** In general, acquired language disorders (aphasias) are associated with left hemisphere damage; Broca's aphasia is usually seen in patients with left frontal lobe damage, whereas Wernicke's aphasia is usually seen in patients with left temporal and parietal lobe damage.

60. **(C)** Auditory receptor cells (called hair cells) in the cochlea transduce sound vibrations into neural impulses.

61. **(B)** Jane's pattern of worrying about minor things and her frequent faintness, dizziness, sweats, muscle tension, diarrhea, and elevated heartbeat, are classic symptoms of generalized anxiety disorder . . . generalized because it has no specific object fear that phobia's have.

62. **(B)** Sleepwalking and sleep talking occur primarily during Stage III and Stage IV sleep; during REM sleep, the sleeper is totally immobile.

63. **(D)** Cell death in Alzheimer's disease has a prominent effect on levels of acetylcholine, a neurotransmitter abundantly present throughout the healthy brain that plays a major role in learning and memory.

64. **(B)** With a heterogeneous data grouping, standard deviation would be large. Homogeneous data would suggest a small standard deviation.

65. **(D)** Conditioning to a CS2 can be blocked if it is presented in conjunction with a previously learned CS1. This effect was an important part of the argument that learning is based on violations of expectations: in this case, the UCS is fully predicted by CS1 so no learning about CS2 occurs.

66. **(D)** This is a syllogism, which is an example of deductive reasoning.

67. **(C)** Massive motor movements (e.g., movements of whole arms or large portions of the body) precede more specific motor movements (e.g., those of wrists or fingers).

68. **(C)** The newborn has a natural immunity that wears off during its first six months of life.

69. **(B)** Curare blocks the nicotinic acetylcholine receptor at the neuromuscular junction when the dart penetrates the muscle.

70. **(C)** The sunk cost fallacy is characterized as an irrational decision, because the price of the tickets should not affect the decision about whether to use them. The money has already been spent and can't be recovered (i.e., it is a sunk cost), so the future decision should only be based on what will maximize happiness (i.e., the birthday party).

71. **(C)** Panic disorders are classified under anxiety disorders in DSM-5.

_____ 72. **(B)** Doing your homework before heading out to a movie is a familiar example of the Premack principle. The movie—being higher on the reinforcement hierarchy—reinforces the activity of homework (which is lower in the hierarchy).

_____ 73. **(C)** The parasympathetic branch of the autonomic nervous system helps calm the body down (e.g., slowing heart rate); all of the other outcomes follow activation of the arousing sympathetic branch.

_____ 74. **(D)** The motor primacy principle refers to maturation as preceding response capability.

_____ 75. **(B)** The terms *innate* and *maturation* both refer to hereditary elements in behavior.

_____ 76. **(D)** In learning theory terminology, reminiscence describes performance improvements without intervening practice on the task.

_____ 77. **(B)** Homonyms are words that sound the same but mean different things (like a river bank and a money bank). When you hear a homonym in a sentence, you use the context (of the sentence and/or the situation) to disambiguate which meaning to select.

_____ 78. **(D)** Such basic learning capability is evident in both the newborn and the late fetal stages of development.

_____ 79. **(B)** This male–female growth differential is especially evident during early adolescence when many girls are embarrassed because they are taller than their male counterparts.

_____ 80. **(D)** Any muscle, gland, or organ that can respond to stimulation from the nervous system is classified as an effector.

_____ 81. **(A)** All of the statements are about REM sleep, but only the first is called REM rebound.

_____ 82. **(C)** The heavy television-violence viewing eight-year-olds were significantly higher than light or moderate viewers in juvenile delinquency at age eighteen and criminality and spousal abuse at age thirty.

_____ 83. **(C)** Function words primarily serve to express grammatical information (not semantic information) in a sentence; they include prepositions, articles, pronouns, conjunctions, auxiliary verbs, and so on.

_____ 84. **(E)** Large injections of androgen (a male sex hormone) have been known to produce abnormal, exaggerated male sex characteristics in the female newborn.

_____ 85. **(E)** Among other things, the pituitary gland secretes growth hormone; overproduction of growth hormone by the pituitary gland causes a condition called acromegaly.

_____ 86. **(E)** A person who delivers a talk on stopping smoking would be most likely to quit successfully. He or she is—through personal involvement—more likely to believe the arguments and experience a consequent behavior change than a person who merely has heard the information passively.

87. **(E)** Dinosaur is the only item on the list that is not a fruit; the Von Restorff effect describes the finding that items that are distinctive or in some way stand out from the others are more likely to be remembered.

88. **(B)** Although some of their explanatory views vary, most personality theorists see early childhood as critically important to later personality development.

89. **(B)** The hippocampus—a key structure in memory formation—is curled up inside the temporal lobe.

90. **(A)** Jack Nicholson's behavior is clearly obsessive-compulsive disorder. He is obsessed by germs and goes through this repeated ritualistic behavior of washing his hands repeatedly with new bars of soap to rid himself of these feared germs.

91. **(C)** The central nervous system comprises the brain and spinal cord; the peripheral nervous system comprises the autonomic and somatic systems.

92. **(A)** This midlife stage is characterized by thought about the next generation.

93. **(A)** The pons is in the hindbrain, on the brain stem.

94. **(B)** The cerebellum is also in the hindbrain, but is posterior to the brainstem.

95. **(C)** The corpus callosum is a bundle of fibers that connects the left and right cerebral hemispheres; in order to split the brain in half (as in this drawing), you have to slice through the corpus callosum. *Note:* In this drawing, 4 is the pituitary gland and 5 is the basal forebrain.

96. **(C)** Both anorexia and bulimia have increased among children and adolescents.

97. **(D)** An individual who survives but who does not reproduce (or whose offspring do not reproduce) will not affect the evolution of the species; therefore, natural selection favors traits that increase reproductive fitness, not survival.

98. **(C)** Within Freud's psychoanalytic theory, moral regulations and restrictions are the province of the superego, which functions in the context of (1) ego ideal or a perfection striving, and (2) conscience or psychological punishment and guilt.

99. **(B)** The phonemes /q/ and /d/ are swapped in this example.

100. **(E)** Several clinical approaches have been found effective. The critical elements are the professionalism, knowledge, and skill of the practitioner.

101. **(A)** The picture superiority effect on memory has been taken as evidence for Paivio's dual coding theory.

102. **(B)** Seligman developed learned helplessness theory, which states that an interpretation of events as being beyond one's control can lead to depression.

103. **(A)** The term *phenotype* refers to the expressed traits (such as appearance and behavior) of an organism; this contrasts with the individual's genotype, which refers to the genetic blueprint.

104. **(D)** Although the rooming-in procedure gives the mother closeness to the newborn and prompt responsiveness to infant needs, the potential price is that of constant demands upon the new mother.

_____ 105. **(A)** Animals are more likely to exhibit seemingly altruistic behavior when relatives are nearby than when they are not; this has been taken as evidence for the theory of kin selection.

_____ 106. **(D)** The acronym PKU refers to phenylketonuria, a defect in the enzyme that metabolizes phenylalanine. Uncorrected by dietetic measures, the disorder can cause brain damage and mental deficiency.

_____ 107. **(B)** Under the Whorfian hypothesis (also known as the Sapir-Whorf hypothesis), the language that one learns affects one's (nonverbal) thought; a controversy continues about the question of color knowledge in the Dani people.

_____ 108. **(D)** This method is aversive conditioning, one of the last resorts therapeutically when other methods have proven ineffective and the problem behavior is a source of pleasure.

_____ 109. **(A)** Most mammals are diploid organisms (in contrast, some reptiles, insects, and amphibians have four copies of each chromosome in most cells).

_____ 110. **(B)** The etiology of a disorder refers to the combination of factors (cognitive, learned, biological, etc.) that contributed to the disorder . . . in effect, the factors that coalesced to "bring it on."

_____ 111. **(A)** A person afflicted with narcolepsy will experience excessive daytime sleepiness and may fall asleep in inappropriate places and without warning. Some estimates of the incidence of narcolepsy are as high as three million people worldwide, and the causes are not yet known.

_____ 112. **(B)** *Assimilation* is a Piagetian term describing the cognitive process of relating a perceived stimulus to the conceptual information that a child already has.

_____ 113. **(A)** The descending fibers from the cerebral motor cortex cross in the brain stem, such that the left side of the brain controls actions of the right side of the body, and vice versa. The term *contralateral*, more generally, refers to relations that cross the vertical axis of the body (in contrast to the term *ipsilateral*).

_____ 114. **(B)** Ellen experienced a traumatic event. Her frequent nightmares and flashbacks lasting for years are symptoms experienced in posttraumatic stress disorder.

_____ 115. **(C)** Kurt has arrived at an uncertain conclusion from a series of observations, the definition of inductive reasoning.

_____ 116. **(A)** Increased worker productivity has been found within decentralized communication networks.

_____ 117. **(A)** These two systems are also referred to as intuition versus reasoning, or association-driven versus rule-driven.

_____ 118. **(C)** Because it is one standard deviation above the mean, the probability of a score above 78 is approximately 16 percent.

_____ 119. **(E)** Below 48 would be a score lower than two standard deviations below the mean, an approximately 2 percent probability.

_____ 120. **(D)** This item refers to the area beyond one standard deviation to each side of the mean—approximately 32 percent.

_____ 121. **(D)** The phonemes (smallest structural units of speech) are /ch/, /i/, and /p/. Notice that there is not a one-to-one correspondence of letters and phonemes: /ch/ is one phoneme but two letters, and the letter _i_ is associated with more than one phoneme (compare the sounds in chip versus kite).

_____ 122. **(B)** The method of summated ratings is part of the Likert scale. It refers to the essential requirement of individual item responses having high positive correlation with overall scale response.

_____ 123. **(B)** The myelin sheath is part of a glial cell that wraps around the axon of a neuron, providing insulation that facilitates the speed of propagation of the action potential.

_____ 124. **(C)** The social exchange theory of interpersonal attraction speaks of continually changing balances between reward and cost in any given interaction.

_____ 125. **(D)** Although all of the above individuals contributed ideas that persist in the contemporary study of language, it was Noam Chomsky who used the term _universal grammar_ to describe the innate language rules he hypothesized to explain language learning.

_____ 126. **(B)** Darley and Latané found that the major determinant in eliciting help was the number of other students that the individual thought had heard the victim.

_____ 127. **(D)** Dominance hierarchies are observed in many species, including fish and birds, and complex dominance hierarchies have been well studied in nonhuman primates. Because access to resources (such as nests and mates) is determined by this social structure, competition and aggression among members of different ranks in the hierarchy is reduced.

_____ 128. **(A)** Proxemics is the study of personal, territorial space. In the American culture, it is believed that each person has a kind of "invisible shield" approximately eighteen inches from his or her body. Anyone who comes closer than this and is not an intimate friend is violating the person's territorial, personal space.

_____ 129. **(D)** The Young-Helmholtz theory holds that activation of each of three visual receptor types (long, medium, and short wavelength) gives rise to the perceptual experience of a corresponding color (red, green, and blue) and that perception of other colors arises from combined activity of more than one receptor.

_____ 130. **(B)** The triad is in a state of asymmetry or imbalance. Symmetry would be achieved if the triad contained an even number of negative (dislike) components. Such would be the case if person A liked person B, person A disliked X, and person B disliked X. Obviously, symmetry would also be attained if the triad contained no negative components—person A liking person B and both of them liking X. For a shorthand heuristic, just remember that an odd number of positives = balance and an odd number of negatives = imbalance.

_____ 131. **(A)** Most strongly associated with the work of Alan Pavio, the dual-coding theory proposes that humans can code incoming information both verbally and nonverbally. One corollary of this theory is that one can improve memory by using both systems.

_____ 132. **(B)** Expectancy-value theory is intrinsic to the social psychology principle of behavior exchange—in effect, a marketplace model. In this formula a person takes the value of a physically attractive partner and multiplies it by their expectancy of obtaining such a partner. This means we tend not to "overshoot" and risk rejection but end up with a partner similar to ourselves in attractiveness.

_____ 133. **(B)** There are two types of errors that are important in a signal detection analysis: misses (not detecting something that is present) and false alarms (reporting the detection of something that is not actually present).

_____ 134. **(D)** One of the classic rationalizations is the "sour grapes" phenomenon. As the story goes, the fox could not reach the grapes he wanted and rationalized that it was just as well because they were sour anyway.

_____ 135. **(D)** In a tip-of-the-tongue (TOT) state, a person fails to retrieve a word (or name) yet feels as if the answer is "close" (on the tip of the tongue). Both Aristotle and William James wrote about this feeling (although Aristotle didn't call it by its current name). By the way, the answer Reggie is looking for is Jerry Lewis.

_____ 136. **(D)** Warmth and permissiveness as well as warmth and authoritative parenting are positively correlated with outgoing, socially assertive characteristics in children, whereas similar correlation is not found for distant, restrictive, demanding, authoritarian family settings.

_____ 137. **(D)** Shape constancy refers to our ability to perceive shapes correctly, and stably, despite variations in the retinal image caused by changes in our viewing angle.

_____ 138. **(A)** The earliest group is the mother–child dyad.

_____ 139. **(A)** The subject of the sentence determines the tense of the verb.

_____ 140. **(B)** The capacity for distinguishing letters on the basis of closedness is characteristic of the three-year-old. More sophisticated distinctions such as curvature will occur later.

_____ 141. **(D)** Connectionist models of memory describe knowledge as a distributed pattern across nodes (or units) that are linked by weighted connections and that are activated during memory retrieval.

_____ 142. **(C)** The work of Hoffman and others indicates that love withdrawal as a discipline technique can produce overdependence upon adult approval. Explaining how the behavior is harmful and undesirable (a reasoning method) has been found to be more effective.

_____ 143. **(E)** Confabulation is a false memory that the individual believes to be true. In some forms of brain damage, confabulations can be very bizarre and fantastic.

_____ 144. **(B)** Women more readily admit anxiety disorder symptoms than do men.

_____ 145. **(E)** Weber's law states that the magnitude of a just-noticeable difference is not absolute but rather is proportional to the intensity of the reference stimulus; in this case, the more lightbulbs that are lit, the more that will need to burn out before the difference is noted.

_____ 146. **(D)** Frequent temper tantrums among children constitute an emotional health signal to be heeded.

_____ 147. **(A)** An engram is a memory trace, often used in reference to the neural representation of learned information. Karl Lashley embarked on a famous "search" for the engram in the early twentieth century, and ended up concluding that there were no localizable memory traces in the cortex.

_____ 148. **(D)** Initiated theoretically within psychoanalysis, defense mechanisms have the function of reducing the anxiety caused by fear that an id impulse may emerge.

_____ 149. **(E)** The fovea, which is the place on the retina where the image of whatever you are looking directly at falls, is densely packed with photoreceptors (specifically cones); the blind spot, which is the point in the retina where the optic nerve forms, has no photoreceptors.

_____ 150. **(A)** The DSM-5 has a checklist of symptoms for each disorder. A person matching a specified number of the checklist symptoms will receive that diagnosis.

_____ 151. **(C)** At a certain point the oval is so close to the circle in shape that it no longer is a distinctive cue as a stimulus. It then has become a nondiscriminative stimulus—lacking the distinctiveness that formerly had given it response strength.

_____ 152. **(C)** An increase in the neurotransmitter norepinephrine leads to a decrease in depression. An increase in serotonin also leads to a decrease in depression.

_____ 153. **(C)** In anterograde amnesia, a patient is unable to explicitly retrieve information acquired after the onset of the disorder. Other forms of memory (e.g., procedural) and memories for events prior to the injury are unaltered.

_____ 154. **(E)** Freud and his psychoanalytic theory have been called unscientific on the grounds that its tenets are not replicable and do not lend themselves to formulating operational definitions that can be scientifically tested.

_____ 155. **(C)** The Zeigarnik effect describes heightened memory for interrupted events. Bluma Zeigarnik began to study this effect after she observed that waiters had better memory for unpaid bills!

_____ 156. **(E)** Because this study uses a between-subjects design without random assignment, it is important to make sure that both groups are native English speakers and that they read equally fast so that any differences in performance are due only to the experimental manipulation and not to baseline differences between the groups.

_____ 157. **(D)** The researchers were interested in measuring whether performing an action with one's body facilitates the ability to understand metaphors that refer to this action. Accordingly, how quickly participants read the sentences was their dependent variable.

_____ 158. **(D)** An experiment's alpha value is the likelihood the experimenter allows for any observed differences in an experiment to be attributed to chance; it is typically decided before data collection.

_____ 159. **(E)** Being unable to detect differences due to an experimental manipulation may be due to methodological problems in a study that did not allow for the hypothesis to be examined with accuracy; the possibility of a Type II error is the likelihood to accept the null hypothesis when it is actually false.

160. **(C)** The so-called second-generation antidepressants are the selective serotonin reuptake inhibitors (SSRIs).

161. **(B)** George Sperling used the "partial-report procedure" to demonstrate that a large amount of visual information can be stored for only a fraction of a second in a "sensory register."

162. **(B)** Lithium is a prominent drug treatment for bipolar depressive disorder.

163. **(D)** A regular, fixed schedule is the critical factor in temporal conditioning.

164. **(C)** Serious illness is frequently a trigger for committing suicide.

165. **(D)** Rosch used category classification reaction times (e.g., Is a penguin a bird?) to demonstrate that an object will be classified as a member of a category on the basis of similarity to the most representative member of the category (i.e., the prototype).

166. **(A)** Since 1995, African-American women have become equally weight-conscious with white women.

167. **(C)** The ventricular system supplies the brain and spinal cord with cerebrospinal fluid.

168. **(A)** Psychologists previously had framed or thought about substance abuse in single-substance terms (e.g., alcohol, specific drugs, etc.). The current trend is polysubstance-related disorders.

169. **(B)** Executive control is associated with prefrontal cortex; patients with damage to this part of the brain often behave in contextually inappropriate ways and fail to achieve stated goals.

170. **(B)** Treatment of schizophrenia has been more effective in developing countries than in developed countries.

171. **(C)** Sir Frederic Bartlett first demonstrated that we distort memories to make them more consistent with our schemas, or expectations.

172. **(C)** At point 3 there began a steady decline in the number of correct responses per trial, indicating that reinforcement had been withdrawn and that the extinction process was underway.

173. **(C)** A temporary leveling in the response acquisition curve is known as a plateau. Such leveling is followed by an increase in the number of correct responses per trial (otherwise it would be called the asymptote).

174. **(E)** Harry Potter fans and their hysterical characteristics are distinct from individuals suffering from histrionic personality disorder only in duration of symptoms. For the fans it is a temporary display of these symptoms.

175. **(E)** Little Albert's fear of things that resembled the furry, white rat is an example of generalization in classical conditioning. This was an experiment conducted by pioneering behaviorist, John Watson.

_____ 176. **(D)** Positive psychology finds within stress the capacity to develop new skills, reevaluate priorities, learn new insights, and enhance coping ability. It does not focus on personal shortcomings.

_____ 177. **(E)** Research finds exercise to be key in lowering the risk of colon cancer in men and breast cancer in women. It also enhances cardiovascular fitness and reduces the risk of diabetes and respiratory problems. It lowers reactivity to daily stress.

_____ 178. **(E)** One's delusional belief that other persons are talking about him or her is known as paranoia or delusions of reference.

_____ 179. **(C)** Middle-class, well-educated mothers are the group most prominently utilizing the breast-feeding method in child rearing. This practice reflects their prominent concern for cognitive–emotional–social development in young children as well as the bonding and significant health/immunity benefits.

_____ 180. **(B)** Kohlberg is a prominent researcher in the area of moral development within children and has been very strongly impressed by the importance of reward and punishment in their moral determinations and decisions.

_____ 181. **(B)** Aristotle was the earliest to focus upon observation, thereby becoming the first "experimental psychologist" long before the field itself was born.

_____ 182. **(B)** An intoxication-type behavior in which a person loses control of his or her emotions is characteristic of oxygen starvation. This result has been produced in experimental settings in which a person inhaled carbon dioxide.

_____ 183. **(E)** Standard deviation can be expressed as the square root of the variance. Therefore, one can obtain a variance by squaring a standard deviation.

_____ 184. **(B)** Walter Mischel criticizes personality tests as having low predictive validity. He bases his claim on his central thesis that a given situation's demands are greater determinants of a person's behavior than his or her personality traits.

_____ 185. **(B)** Applying Mischel's central thesis, one would expect a child who cheats in one school classroom to be more likely to cheat in another school classroom than in a different setting such as a store or with friends. Rationale for this judgment is the similarity of the settings.

_____ 186. **(D)** Allport cites the historical, sociocultural, psychodynamic, earned reputation, and two others—phenomenological (concentric circles in which we relate most closely to those most "like us,") and situational (messages we internalize as children in our homes). He does not cite genetic predisposition.

_____ 187. **(D)** The concept of "next door"—functional distance—is more central than physical distance. It may be your apartment neighbor three steps down the hall or your next door farmer neighbor ten miles away.

_____ 188. **(B)** Dovidio was referring to subtle, "polite" racism. An example would be the restaurant waiter greeting an African-American and an Anglo-American coming for an executive/client dinner and wrongly assuming that the executive is the Anglo-American and the client is the African-American. This wrongful assumption plays out throughout the dinner and bringing the tab.

_____ 189. **(A)** Likert scales are identifiable by their Strongly Disagree to Strongly Agree range. They're frequently used. We bet you've taken a few. So have we!

_____ 190. **(E)** Guttman scaling is associated with unidimensionality. He did not believe it was being attained in scales such as Thurstone, Likert, and Osgood.

_____ 191. **(D)** A Bogardus scale is always social distance in the context of admitting specific groups to one's country, place of work, neighborhood, and family, for example.

_____ 192. **(C)** An Osgood semantic differential scale always uses bipolar adjectives. There may be as many as twenty in a given scale on a given person/group-heading topic.

_____ 193. **(B)** A Thurstone scale always has the instructions to checkmark the items we agree with. What looks so simple in the format is very complex and time-consuming in the scale construction. As many as 200 items, 200 judges sorting them into categories on the basis of degree of pro or anti on the specific topic, and from this process selecting the 20 items that will be on the scale. For every different topic, the entire process has to be done again. Though the most rigorous in its development, it is not in prevalent use currently for reasons of time-efficiency in development.

_____ 194. **(E)** Couples paired dissimilarly did not want to continue, and couples paired similarly did want to continue. Similarity in attractiveness was a strong attraction determinant.

_____ 195. **(D)** When walking, males swing their arms widely; females, narrowly; females cross their legs knee to knee; males, ankle to knee.

_____ 196. **(B)** The soldier curled up in a fetal position and crying is manifesting maladaptive regression behavior.

_____ 197. **(C)** Lack of movement is indicative of catatonia. Muscular rigidity and motionlessness are characteristic of this disorder.

_____ 198. **(B)** In his behavioral psychotherapy settings, Bandura would reinforce a withdrawn child for joining the group.

_____ 199. **(A)** In milieu therapy, the family, close associates, and natural setting become parts of the therapeutic process.

_____ 200. **(C)** Sexual stimulation attained from the sight or closeness of a given object or type of object is characteristic of fetishism.

_____ 201. **(A)** A null hypothesis is most commonly expressed as a statement of the absence of a difference or an experimental effect; evidence *against* the null hypothesis is indicative of a difference between groups.

_____ 202. **(E)** An attitude contains all three components—cognitive, affective, and behavioral.

_____ 203. **(D)** With a 30 percent response rate, the major question is whether the nonresponders are different in some important, qualitative way from those who responded. If they are, the result is biased.

_____ 204. **(B)** Because Jill's favorite team has lost so miserably and so badly, it is natural for her to distance herself from the loss. Where she readily would've said, "We won!" if it had been a victory, she now will most likely say, "The team lost" or "They lost." This demonstrates Cialdini's cutting off reflected failure (CORF). If they had won, her "We won!" would have demonstrated basking in reflected glory (BIRG).

_____ 205. **(B)** The term _one-way design_ means that only one variable is being manipulated.

_____ 206. **(D)** A 2 × 2 × 3 × 3 factorial indicates 4 variables.

_____ 207. **(E)** A 2 × 2 × 3 × 3 factorial indicates 36 groups. You simply multiply the numbers. It's fun!

_____ 208. **(E)** A significant difference found on any one of the three variables—age, race, or residence neighborhood—would constitute a main effect.

_____ 209. **(E)** A significant difference found in all three of the combinations cited—age × race, race × residence neighborhood, and age × residence neighborhood—would constitute an interaction effect. Any of these ___ × ___ would be an interaction effect.

_____ 210. **(B)** Wilhelm Wundt created the first psychological laboratory in Leipzig, Germany, in 1879.

_____ 211. **(C)** Wundt studied the mind by way of introspection, and this technique turned out to be so individual and variable in its results that it lacked the research rigor and replicability required by experimental psychologists in the United States.

_____ 212. **(E)** By running these multiple _t_-tests, Tasha risks a major increase in alpha level (.05 up to .40). This increase will have the net effect of spurious "significant" results.

_____ 213. **(B)** Parametric assumes that the distribution from which samples are drawn is a normal distribution.

_____ 214. **(E)** The altruism model of helping carries all three of the stated action aspects—action that is voluntary, costly, and carries no anticipation of reward.

_____ 215. **(A)** These words describe Festinger's social comparison theory.

EVALUATING YOUR PROGRESS

Before proceeding, make sure you have used your answer sheet to mark each question on the explanation pages with a check mark for correct, an X for incorrect, and a blank for didn't answer.

Unfortunately, when we scramble a test, your job of compiling your results becomes a bit more of a hassle. We recommend that you try one of three ways to proceed:

- If you don't mind flipping pages, simply refer to your marks on the previous explanation pages as you fill out the chart below.
- If you DO mind flipping pages, you can use a copier to make copies of the explanation pages to which you can easily refer as you fill out the chart below.
- If neither of these alternatives works for you, you can transfer your check marks and X's to your answer sheet, and refer to those marks as you fill out the chart below.

Learning (10)	Language (9)	Memory (14)	Thinking (14)
____ 4.	____ 8.	____ 2.	____ 21.
____ 65.	____ 45.	____ 10.	____ 35.
____ 72.	____ 77.	____ 25.	____ 38.
____ 76.	____ 83.	____ 43.	____ 59.
____ 108.	____ 99.	____ 50.	____ 66.
____ 151.	____ 121.	____ 87.	____ 70.
____ 163.	____ 125.	____ 101.	____ 107.
____ 172.	____ 139.	____ 131.	____ 115.
____ 173.	____ 195.	____ 135.	____ 117.
____ 175.	____ Total Correct (C)	____ 143.	____ 141.
____ Total Correct (C)	____ Total Incorrect (I)	____ 147.	____ 165.
____ Total Incorrect (I)	____ Total Blank	____ 153.	____ 169.
____ Total Blank	C – (I/4) = ____	____ 155.	____ 171.
C – (I/4) = ____		____ 161.	____ 204.
		____ Total Correct (C)	____ Total Correct (C)
		____ Total Incorrect (I)	____ Total Incorrect (I)
		____ Total Blank	____ Total Blank
		C – (I/4) = ____	C – (I/4) = ____

Sensation/ Perception (11)	Physiological/ Behavioral Neuroscience (29)	Clinical/ Abnormal (32)	Life Span Development (23)
____ 1.	____ 6.	____ 3.	____ 7.
____ 20.	____ 13.	____ 15.	____ 22.
____ 42.	____ 16.	____ 36.	____ 23.
____ 47.	____ 24.	____ 37.	____ 40.
____ 48.	____ 28.	____ 44.	____ 41.
____ 60.	____ 34.	____ 53.	____ 51.
____ 129.	____ 39.	____ 61.	____ 67.
____ 133.	____ 52.	____ 71.	____ 68.
____ 137.	____ 54.	____ 90.	____ 74.
____ 145.	____ 55.	____ 100.	____ 75.
____ Total Correct (C)	____ 62.	____ 102.	____ 78.
	____ 63.	____ 110.	____ 79.
____ Total Incorrect (I)	____ 69.	____ 111.	____ 84.
	____ 73.	____ 114.	____ 92.
____ Total Blank	____ 80.	____ 144.	____ 104.
	____ 81.	____ 150.	____ 106.
C – (I/4) = ____	____ 85.	____ 152.	____ 112.
	____ 89.	____ 160.	____ 138.
	____ 91.	____ 162.	____ 140.
	____ 93.	____ 164.	____ 142.
	____ 94.	____ 166.	____ 146.
	____ 95.	____ 168.	____ 179.
	____ 97.	____ 170.	____ 180.
	____ 103.	____ 174.	____ Total Correct (C)
	____ 105.	____ 176.	____ Total Incorrect (I)
	____ 109.	____ 177.	____ Total Blank
	____ 113.	____ 178.	C – (I/4) = ____
	____ 123.	____ 182.	
	____ 167.	____ 197.	
	____ Total Correct (C)	____ 198.	
	____ Total Incorrect (I)	____ 199.	
	____ Total Blank	____ 200.	
	C – (I/4) = ____	____ Total Correct (C)	
		____ Total Incorrect (I)	
		____ Total Blank	
		C – (I/4) = ____	

Personality (15)	Social (22)	General/Applied (6)	Methods/ Measurement (30)
____ 5.	____ 11.	____ 9.	____ 26.
____ 17.	____ 12.	____ 14.	____ 27.
____ 18.	____ 32.	____ 57.	____ 29.
____ 19.	____ 33.	____ 181.	____ 30.
____ 46.	____ 58.	____ 210.	____ 31.
____ 56.	____ 82.	____ 211.	____ 49.
____ 88.	____ 86.	____ Total Correct (C)	____ 64.
____ 98.	____ 96.	____ Total Incorrect (I)	____ 118.
____ 134.	____ 116.	____ Total Blank	____ 119.
____ 136.	____ 124.	C – (I/4) = ____	____ 120.
____ 148.	____ 126.		____ 122.
____ 154.	____ 127.		____ 156.
____ 184.	____ 128.		____ 157.
____ 185.	____ 130.		____ 158.
____ 196.	____ 132.		____ 159.
____ Total Correct (C)	____ 186.		____ 183.
____ Total Incorrect (I)	____ 187.		____ 189.
____ Total Blank	____ 188.		____ 190.
C – (I/4) = ____	____ 194.		____ 191.
	____ 202.		____ 192.
	____ 214.		____ 193.
	____ 215.		____ 201.
	____ Total Correct (C)		____ 203.
	____ Total Incorrect (I)		____ 205.
	____ Total Blank		____ 206.
	C – (I/4) = ____		____ 207.
			____ 208.
			____ 209.
			____ 212.
			____ 213.
			____ Total Correct (C)
			____ Total Incorrect (I)
			____ Total Blank
			C – (I/4) = ____

Your next step is to transfer your totals above for each area into this chart:

	Number Correct (C)	Number Incorrect (I)	Number Blank	C-(I/4)	Maximum Possible	Your Percentage: Divide C-(I/4) by the Maximum Possible
Learning					10	
Language					9	
Memory					14	
Thinking					14	
Sensation Perception					11	
Physio/BN					29	
Clinical/ Abnormal					32	
Life Span					23	
Personality					15	
Social					22	
General					6	
Methods					30	

How did you do? Are you able to identify areas that need more work? If so, head back into the review section and use your textbooks and Web resources to brush up on remaining problem areas. When you feel confident, proceed to the next practice test.

ANSWER SHEET
Practice Test 2

1. Ⓐ Ⓑ Ⓒ Ⓓ Ⓔ
2. Ⓐ Ⓑ Ⓒ Ⓓ Ⓔ
3. Ⓐ Ⓑ Ⓒ Ⓓ Ⓔ
4. Ⓐ Ⓑ Ⓒ Ⓓ Ⓔ
5. Ⓐ Ⓑ Ⓒ Ⓓ Ⓔ
6. Ⓐ Ⓑ Ⓒ Ⓓ Ⓔ
7. Ⓐ Ⓑ Ⓒ Ⓓ Ⓔ
8. Ⓐ Ⓑ Ⓒ Ⓓ Ⓔ
9. Ⓐ Ⓑ Ⓒ Ⓓ Ⓔ
10. Ⓐ Ⓑ Ⓒ Ⓓ Ⓔ
11. Ⓐ Ⓑ Ⓒ Ⓓ Ⓔ
12. Ⓐ Ⓑ Ⓒ Ⓓ Ⓔ
13. Ⓐ Ⓑ Ⓒ Ⓓ Ⓔ
14. Ⓐ Ⓑ Ⓒ Ⓓ Ⓔ
15. Ⓐ Ⓑ Ⓒ Ⓓ Ⓔ
16. Ⓐ Ⓑ Ⓒ Ⓓ Ⓔ
17. Ⓐ Ⓑ Ⓒ Ⓓ Ⓔ
18. Ⓐ Ⓑ Ⓒ Ⓓ Ⓔ
19. Ⓐ Ⓑ Ⓒ Ⓓ Ⓔ
20. Ⓐ Ⓑ Ⓒ Ⓓ Ⓔ
21. Ⓐ Ⓑ Ⓒ Ⓓ Ⓔ
22. Ⓐ Ⓑ Ⓒ Ⓓ Ⓔ
23. Ⓐ Ⓑ Ⓒ Ⓓ Ⓔ
24. Ⓐ Ⓑ Ⓒ Ⓓ Ⓔ
25. Ⓐ Ⓑ Ⓒ Ⓓ Ⓔ
26. Ⓐ Ⓑ Ⓒ Ⓓ Ⓔ
27. Ⓐ Ⓑ Ⓒ Ⓓ Ⓔ
28. Ⓐ Ⓑ Ⓒ Ⓓ Ⓔ
29. Ⓐ Ⓑ Ⓒ Ⓓ Ⓔ
30. Ⓐ Ⓑ Ⓒ Ⓓ Ⓔ

31. Ⓐ Ⓑ Ⓒ Ⓓ Ⓔ
32. Ⓐ Ⓑ Ⓒ Ⓓ Ⓔ
33. Ⓐ Ⓑ Ⓒ Ⓓ Ⓔ
34. Ⓐ Ⓑ Ⓒ Ⓓ Ⓔ
35. Ⓐ Ⓑ Ⓒ Ⓓ Ⓔ
36. Ⓐ Ⓑ Ⓒ Ⓓ Ⓔ
37. Ⓐ Ⓑ Ⓒ Ⓓ Ⓔ
38. Ⓐ Ⓑ Ⓒ Ⓓ Ⓔ
39. Ⓐ Ⓑ Ⓒ Ⓓ Ⓔ
40. Ⓐ Ⓑ Ⓒ Ⓓ Ⓔ
41. Ⓐ Ⓑ Ⓒ Ⓓ Ⓔ
42. Ⓐ Ⓑ Ⓒ Ⓓ Ⓔ
43. Ⓐ Ⓑ Ⓒ Ⓓ Ⓔ
44. Ⓐ Ⓑ Ⓒ Ⓓ Ⓔ
45. Ⓐ Ⓑ Ⓒ Ⓓ Ⓔ
46. Ⓐ Ⓑ Ⓒ Ⓓ Ⓔ
47. Ⓐ Ⓑ Ⓒ Ⓓ Ⓔ
48. Ⓐ Ⓑ Ⓒ Ⓓ Ⓔ
49. Ⓐ Ⓑ Ⓒ Ⓓ Ⓔ
50. Ⓐ Ⓑ Ⓒ Ⓓ Ⓔ
51. Ⓐ Ⓑ Ⓒ Ⓓ Ⓔ
52. Ⓐ Ⓑ Ⓒ Ⓓ Ⓔ
53. Ⓐ Ⓑ Ⓒ Ⓓ Ⓔ
54. Ⓐ Ⓑ Ⓒ Ⓓ Ⓔ
55. Ⓐ Ⓑ Ⓒ Ⓓ Ⓔ
56. Ⓐ Ⓑ Ⓒ Ⓓ Ⓔ
57. Ⓐ Ⓑ Ⓒ Ⓓ Ⓔ
58. Ⓐ Ⓑ Ⓒ Ⓓ Ⓔ
59. Ⓐ Ⓑ Ⓒ Ⓓ Ⓔ
60. Ⓐ Ⓑ Ⓒ Ⓓ Ⓔ

61. Ⓐ Ⓑ Ⓒ Ⓓ Ⓔ
62. Ⓐ Ⓑ Ⓒ Ⓓ Ⓔ
63. Ⓐ Ⓑ Ⓒ Ⓓ Ⓔ
64. Ⓐ Ⓑ Ⓒ Ⓓ Ⓔ
65. Ⓐ Ⓑ Ⓒ Ⓓ Ⓔ
66. Ⓐ Ⓑ Ⓒ Ⓓ Ⓔ
67. Ⓐ Ⓑ Ⓒ Ⓓ Ⓔ
68. Ⓐ Ⓑ Ⓒ Ⓓ Ⓔ
69. Ⓐ Ⓑ Ⓒ Ⓓ Ⓔ
70. Ⓐ Ⓑ Ⓒ Ⓓ Ⓔ
71. Ⓐ Ⓑ Ⓒ Ⓓ Ⓔ
72. Ⓐ Ⓑ Ⓒ Ⓓ Ⓔ
73. Ⓐ Ⓑ Ⓒ Ⓓ Ⓔ
74. Ⓐ Ⓑ Ⓒ Ⓓ Ⓔ
75. Ⓐ Ⓑ Ⓒ Ⓓ Ⓔ
76. Ⓐ Ⓑ Ⓒ Ⓓ Ⓔ
77. Ⓐ Ⓑ Ⓒ Ⓓ Ⓔ
78. Ⓐ Ⓑ Ⓒ Ⓓ Ⓔ
79. Ⓐ Ⓑ Ⓒ Ⓓ Ⓔ
80. Ⓐ Ⓑ Ⓒ Ⓓ Ⓔ
81. Ⓐ Ⓑ Ⓒ Ⓓ Ⓔ
82. Ⓐ Ⓑ Ⓒ Ⓓ Ⓔ
83. Ⓐ Ⓑ Ⓒ Ⓓ Ⓔ
84. Ⓐ Ⓑ Ⓒ Ⓓ Ⓔ
85. Ⓐ Ⓑ Ⓒ Ⓓ Ⓔ
86. Ⓐ Ⓑ Ⓒ Ⓓ Ⓔ
87. Ⓐ Ⓑ Ⓒ Ⓓ Ⓔ
88. Ⓐ Ⓑ Ⓒ Ⓓ Ⓔ
89. Ⓐ Ⓑ Ⓒ Ⓓ Ⓔ
90. Ⓐ Ⓑ Ⓒ Ⓓ Ⓔ

91. Ⓐ Ⓑ Ⓒ Ⓓ Ⓔ
92. Ⓐ Ⓑ Ⓒ Ⓓ Ⓔ
93. Ⓐ Ⓑ Ⓒ Ⓓ Ⓔ
94. Ⓐ Ⓑ Ⓒ Ⓓ Ⓔ
95. Ⓐ Ⓑ Ⓒ Ⓓ Ⓔ
96. Ⓐ Ⓑ Ⓒ Ⓓ Ⓔ
97. Ⓐ Ⓑ Ⓒ Ⓓ Ⓔ
98. Ⓐ Ⓑ Ⓒ Ⓓ Ⓔ
99. Ⓐ Ⓑ Ⓒ Ⓓ Ⓔ
100. Ⓐ Ⓑ Ⓒ Ⓓ Ⓔ
101. Ⓐ Ⓑ Ⓒ Ⓓ Ⓔ
102. Ⓐ Ⓑ Ⓒ Ⓓ Ⓔ
103. Ⓐ Ⓑ Ⓒ Ⓓ Ⓔ
104. Ⓐ Ⓑ Ⓒ Ⓓ Ⓔ
105. Ⓐ Ⓑ Ⓒ Ⓓ Ⓔ
106. Ⓐ Ⓑ Ⓒ Ⓓ Ⓔ
107. Ⓐ Ⓑ Ⓒ Ⓓ Ⓔ
108. Ⓐ Ⓑ Ⓒ Ⓓ Ⓔ
109. Ⓐ Ⓑ Ⓒ Ⓓ Ⓔ
110. Ⓐ Ⓑ Ⓒ Ⓓ Ⓔ
111. Ⓐ Ⓑ Ⓒ Ⓓ Ⓔ
112. Ⓐ Ⓑ Ⓒ Ⓓ Ⓔ
113. Ⓐ Ⓑ Ⓒ Ⓓ Ⓔ
114. Ⓐ Ⓑ Ⓒ Ⓓ Ⓔ
115. Ⓐ Ⓑ Ⓒ Ⓓ Ⓔ
116. Ⓐ Ⓑ Ⓒ Ⓓ Ⓔ
117. Ⓐ Ⓑ Ⓒ Ⓓ Ⓔ
118. Ⓐ Ⓑ Ⓒ Ⓓ Ⓔ
119. Ⓐ Ⓑ Ⓒ Ⓓ Ⓔ
120. Ⓐ Ⓑ Ⓒ Ⓓ Ⓔ

121. Ⓐ Ⓑ Ⓒ Ⓓ Ⓔ	145. Ⓐ Ⓑ Ⓒ Ⓓ Ⓔ	169. Ⓐ Ⓑ Ⓒ Ⓓ Ⓔ	193. Ⓐ Ⓑ Ⓒ Ⓓ Ⓔ
122. Ⓐ Ⓑ Ⓒ Ⓓ Ⓔ	146. Ⓐ Ⓑ Ⓒ Ⓓ Ⓔ	170. Ⓐ Ⓑ Ⓒ Ⓓ Ⓔ	194. Ⓐ Ⓑ Ⓒ Ⓓ Ⓔ
123. Ⓐ Ⓑ Ⓒ Ⓓ Ⓔ	147. Ⓐ Ⓑ Ⓒ Ⓓ Ⓔ	171. Ⓐ Ⓑ Ⓒ Ⓓ Ⓔ	195. Ⓐ Ⓑ Ⓒ Ⓓ Ⓔ
124. Ⓐ Ⓑ Ⓒ Ⓓ Ⓔ	148. Ⓐ Ⓑ Ⓒ Ⓓ Ⓔ	172. Ⓐ Ⓑ Ⓒ Ⓓ Ⓔ	196. Ⓐ Ⓑ Ⓒ Ⓓ Ⓔ
125. Ⓐ Ⓑ Ⓒ Ⓓ Ⓔ	149. Ⓐ Ⓑ Ⓒ Ⓓ Ⓔ	173. Ⓐ Ⓑ Ⓒ Ⓓ Ⓔ	197. Ⓐ Ⓑ Ⓒ Ⓓ Ⓔ
126. Ⓐ Ⓑ Ⓒ Ⓓ Ⓔ	150. Ⓐ Ⓑ Ⓒ Ⓓ Ⓔ	174. Ⓐ Ⓑ Ⓒ Ⓓ Ⓔ	198. Ⓐ Ⓑ Ⓒ Ⓓ Ⓔ
127. Ⓐ Ⓑ Ⓒ Ⓓ Ⓔ	151. Ⓐ Ⓑ Ⓒ Ⓓ Ⓔ	175. Ⓐ Ⓑ Ⓒ Ⓓ Ⓔ	199. Ⓐ Ⓑ Ⓒ Ⓓ Ⓔ
128. Ⓐ Ⓑ Ⓒ Ⓓ Ⓔ	152. Ⓐ Ⓑ Ⓒ Ⓓ Ⓔ	176. Ⓐ Ⓑ Ⓒ Ⓓ Ⓔ	200. Ⓐ Ⓑ Ⓒ Ⓓ Ⓔ
129. Ⓐ Ⓑ Ⓒ Ⓓ Ⓔ	153. Ⓐ Ⓑ Ⓒ Ⓓ Ⓔ	177. Ⓐ Ⓑ Ⓒ Ⓓ Ⓔ	201. Ⓐ Ⓑ Ⓒ Ⓓ Ⓔ
130. Ⓐ Ⓑ Ⓒ Ⓓ Ⓔ	154. Ⓐ Ⓑ Ⓒ Ⓓ Ⓔ	178. Ⓐ Ⓑ Ⓒ Ⓓ Ⓔ	202. Ⓐ Ⓑ Ⓒ Ⓓ Ⓔ
131. Ⓐ Ⓑ Ⓒ Ⓓ Ⓔ	155. Ⓐ Ⓑ Ⓒ Ⓓ Ⓔ	179. Ⓐ Ⓑ Ⓒ Ⓓ Ⓔ	203. Ⓐ Ⓑ Ⓒ Ⓓ Ⓔ
132. Ⓐ Ⓑ Ⓒ Ⓓ Ⓔ	156. Ⓐ Ⓑ Ⓒ Ⓓ Ⓔ	180. Ⓐ Ⓑ Ⓒ Ⓓ Ⓔ	204. Ⓐ Ⓑ Ⓒ Ⓓ Ⓔ
133. Ⓐ Ⓑ Ⓒ Ⓓ Ⓔ	157. Ⓐ Ⓑ Ⓒ Ⓓ Ⓔ	181. Ⓐ Ⓑ Ⓒ Ⓓ Ⓔ	205. Ⓐ Ⓑ Ⓒ Ⓓ Ⓔ
134. Ⓐ Ⓑ Ⓒ Ⓓ Ⓔ	158. Ⓐ Ⓑ Ⓒ Ⓓ Ⓔ	182. Ⓐ Ⓑ Ⓒ Ⓓ Ⓔ	206. Ⓐ Ⓑ Ⓒ Ⓓ Ⓔ
135. Ⓐ Ⓑ Ⓒ Ⓓ Ⓔ	159. Ⓐ Ⓑ Ⓒ Ⓓ Ⓔ	183. Ⓐ Ⓑ Ⓒ Ⓓ Ⓔ	207. Ⓐ Ⓑ Ⓒ Ⓓ Ⓔ
136. Ⓐ Ⓑ Ⓒ Ⓓ Ⓔ	160. Ⓐ Ⓑ Ⓒ Ⓓ Ⓔ	184. Ⓐ Ⓑ Ⓒ Ⓓ Ⓔ	208. Ⓐ Ⓑ Ⓒ Ⓓ Ⓔ
137. Ⓐ Ⓑ Ⓒ Ⓓ Ⓔ	161. Ⓐ Ⓑ Ⓒ Ⓓ Ⓔ	185. Ⓐ Ⓑ Ⓒ Ⓓ Ⓔ	209. Ⓐ Ⓑ Ⓒ Ⓓ Ⓔ
138. Ⓐ Ⓑ Ⓒ Ⓓ Ⓔ	162. Ⓐ Ⓑ Ⓒ Ⓓ Ⓔ	186. Ⓐ Ⓑ Ⓒ Ⓓ Ⓔ	210. Ⓐ Ⓑ Ⓒ Ⓓ Ⓔ
139. Ⓐ Ⓑ Ⓒ Ⓓ Ⓔ	163. Ⓐ Ⓑ Ⓒ Ⓓ Ⓔ	187. Ⓐ Ⓑ Ⓒ Ⓓ Ⓔ	211. Ⓐ Ⓑ Ⓒ Ⓓ Ⓔ
140. Ⓐ Ⓑ Ⓒ Ⓓ Ⓔ	164. Ⓐ Ⓑ Ⓒ Ⓓ Ⓔ	188. Ⓐ Ⓑ Ⓒ Ⓓ Ⓔ	212. Ⓐ Ⓑ Ⓒ Ⓓ Ⓔ
141. Ⓐ Ⓑ Ⓒ Ⓓ Ⓔ	165. Ⓐ Ⓑ Ⓒ Ⓓ Ⓔ	189. Ⓐ Ⓑ Ⓒ Ⓓ Ⓔ	213. Ⓐ Ⓑ Ⓒ Ⓓ Ⓔ
142. Ⓐ Ⓑ Ⓒ Ⓓ Ⓔ	166. Ⓐ Ⓑ Ⓒ Ⓓ Ⓔ	190. Ⓐ Ⓑ Ⓒ Ⓓ Ⓔ	214. Ⓐ Ⓑ Ⓒ Ⓓ Ⓔ
143. Ⓐ Ⓑ Ⓒ Ⓓ Ⓔ	167. Ⓐ Ⓑ Ⓒ Ⓓ Ⓔ	191. Ⓐ Ⓑ Ⓒ Ⓓ Ⓔ	215. Ⓐ Ⓑ Ⓒ Ⓓ Ⓔ
144. Ⓐ Ⓑ Ⓒ Ⓓ Ⓔ	168. Ⓐ Ⓑ Ⓒ Ⓓ Ⓔ	192. Ⓐ Ⓑ Ⓒ Ⓓ Ⓔ	

PRACTICE TEST 2

TIME: 170 MINUTES
215 QUESTIONS

Directions: Each of the questions or incomplete statements below is followed by five suggested answers or completions. Select the one that is best in each case and then fill in the corresponding space on the answer sheet.

---

1. According to Paivio's dual-code model of memory, the two types of codes used to store long-term memories are

   (A) visual and auditory
   (B) semantic and syntactic
   (C) semantic and episodic
   (D) implicit and explicit
   (E) verbal and visual

QUESTIONS 2–4 REFER TO THE PARAGRAPH BELOW.

A research team is interested in the relation between traditional measures of intelligence and a divergent production task that taps into creativity (e.g., How many different things can you think to do with a pot besides cooking?). The researchers obtained WISC scores and divergent production (DP) scores from 200 ninth graders. The findings are presented in this frequency table:

WISC Quotient

DP	60-69	70-79	80-89	90-99	100-109	110-119	120-129	130-139	140-149
50-59						1	3		1
40-49						2	4	1	
30-39			2	3	4	11	17	6	2
20-29			1	3	10	23	13	7	
10-19	1		3	9	11	19	7	3	1
0-9	1	3	1	4	10	11	2		

2. What are the numbers in the main body of the table?

   (A) average IQ scores
   (B) average DP scores
   (C) numbers of students
   (D) percentages of students
   (E) proportions of students

GO ON TO THE NEXT PAGE

3. On the basis of this table, it would be most appropriate to make the interpretation that

    (A) IQ and divergent production are independent constructs
    (B) there is an almost perfect negative relationship between IQ and DP
    (C) there is apparently a complete absence of a relationship between IQ and DP
    (D) there is a greater likelihood of DP in the 120–129 IQ range than in the 100–119 range
    (E) there is a greater likelihood of DP in the 100–109 IQ range than in the 130–139 range

4. Interpretations of data such as those presented in this table would rely heavily upon the assumption that the children

    (A) were in the same school
    (B) participated in standardized testing and scoring procedures
    (C) were of the same sex
    (D) received their testing on the same day within the same test setting
    (E) represented all parts of the country

5. Phineas Gage experienced a major personality change after a railroad tamping rod went through his skull. This tragic accident alerted scientists to the role in emotions of the

    (A) frontal lobe
    (B) parietal lobe
    (C) temporal lobe
    (D) occipital lobe
    (E) cerebellum

6. The cerebellum controls which of the following?

    (A) heart rate
    (B) blood pressure
    (C) motor coordination
    (D) language comprehension
    (E) respiration

7. Loftus and her colleagues have found that eyewitness testimony is affected by

    I.   bias in question wording
    II. false information injected into questions
    III. inferences made to fill memory gaps

    (A) I only
    (B) III only
    (C) I and II
    (D) II and III
    (E) I, II, and III

GO ON TO THE NEXT PAGE

8. To what does the phrase *tree diagram* refer?

    (A) a problem-solving strategy
    (B) the structure of a sentence
    (C) a neural circuit
    (D) the Young-Helmholtz theory
    (E) a connectionist memory network

9. Pitch is determined by

    (A) amplitude
    (B) complexity
    (C) frequency
    (D) decibels
    (E) amplification

10. The autokinetic effect is most commonly demonstrated with which of the following stimuli?

    (A) lights flashing on and off in a patterned sequence
    (B) lights rotating around a single, central spot of light
    (C) a circle containing alternating wedges of black and white
    (D) a spot of light in a darkened room
    (E) a steady blue light consistently viewed near dusk

11. A brain wave not evident in the newborn is the

    (A) beta
    (B) alpha
    (C) delta
    (D) theta
    (E) gamma

12. The concept of equipotentiality was formulated on the basis of a systematic experimental program conducted by

    (A) Lindsley
    (B) Tolman
    (C) Lashley
    (D) Skinner
    (E) Terman

GO ON TO THE NEXT PAGE

13. Which of the following is an *incorrect* statement?

(A) Receptive disorders such as agnosia and Wernicke's aphasia most often occur following damage to the posterior cerebral cortex.

(B) Expressive disorders such as apraxia and Broca's aphasia most often occur following damage to the anterior cerebral cortex.

(C) Alexia is a type of visual disorder associated with word blindness.

(D) Apraxia refers to disturbances in audition, commonly called word deafness.

(E) Aphasia describes an inability to produce or comprehend language that is not the result of basic motor or sensory deficits.

14. Perceptual phenomena have been most prominently explored within what tradition?

(A) structuralism

(B) Gestalt

(C) behaviorism

(D) functionalism

(E) eclecticism

15. What do the initials stand for in the term *ROC curve*?

(A) retrograde-obsessive-compulsive

(B) remote-optical-chromatic

(C) respondent-operating-capacity

(D) receiver-operant-characteristic

(E) ratings-of-capability

16. The fact that a cold-blooded animal can remain alive and make coordinated muscle movements for some time after decapitation is possible because of

(A) spinal cord sufficiency for complicated patterns of reflexive behavior

(B) pons activity and increased compensatory functioning

(C) the role of the cerebellum in reflexive behavior

(D) lateral inhibition

(E) negative feedback between antagonist muscle groups

17. A behavioral neuroscientist would be most likely to find the term *reciprocal innervation* in discussions related to

(A) mach bands

(B) obesity

(C) the autonomic nervous system

(D) muscle movements

(E) forgetting

GO ON TO THE NEXT PAGE

18. The capacity for detecting the direction of incoming sound is

(A) referred to as timbre-discrimination
(B) possible only when hearing exists in both ears
(C) frequently termed monaural hearing
(D) explained within the Young-Helmholtz theory of audition
(E) heavily depending on the Meissner receptor

19. Which of the following mobilizes the body by secreting epinephrine in stressful situations?

(A) adrenal cortex
(B) pituitary gland
(C) gonads
(D) pancreas
(E) adrenal medulla

20. Which of the following is an endocrine gland controlling growth and stimulating other endocrine glands?

(A) adrenal
(B) pituitary
(C) thyroid
(D) parathyroid
(E) pineal

21. Experimentation with rats investigating the role of the cerebral cortex in sexual behavior indicates that

(A) sexual behavior survives fairly extensive cortical destruction in male animals
(B) the cerebral cortex is essential for copulation to occur in females
(C) the cerebral cortex is not necessary for the ordering of the sequence that characterizes the pattern of sexual behavior in females
(D) complete cortical destruction has no effect on arousal in male animals
(E) cortical destruction affects motor but not sensory and perceptual functions

22. "A group of individuals capable of interbreeding and producing fertile offspring under natural conditions and thus are reproductively isolated from other such groups," defines the term

(A) phylum
(B) class
(C) order
(D) family
(E) species

GO ON TO THE NEXT PAGE

23. At which of the following ages would you expect clock-time concepts to be mastered initially by a child?

(A) two years
(B) three years
(C) four years
(D) between five and six years
(E) between seven and eight years

24. Reaction time

(A) decreases with age up to approximately forty years
(B) increases with age up to approximately forty years
(C) decreases with age up to approximately thirty years
(D) increases with age up to approximately thirty years
(E) decreases with age throughout the life span

25. Studies of emotion involving transections at various levels of the brain stem in animals reveal that

(A) the integrated "attack reaction" found in normal animals remains intact
(B) organization of intense emotional responses apparently occurs at a level above the midbrain
(C) auditory stimuli retain their normal effectiveness in evoking emotional responses
(D) visual stimuli retain their normal effectiveness in evoking emotional responses
(E) there are no emotional response differences distinguishable from those found in normal animals

26. When Tolman summarized Watson's definition of emotions, he did so in terms of

(A) field theory
(B) law of effect
(C) law of exercise
(D) stimuli and responses
(E) sensations and perceptions

GO ON TO THE NEXT PAGE

27. People with damage to their hippocampus are able to acquire conditioned responses, *except* under circumstances that require the ability to maintain the memory of the CS until the UCS occurs. In which of the following procedures would you expect such a patient to have *difficulty* learning?

    I.   trace conditioning
   II. delayed conditioning
  III. simultaneous conditioning

   (A) I only
   (B) II only
   (C) III only
   (D) I and III
   (E) II and III

28. *Not* among the pictorial cues that permit the perception of stimulus depth is

   (A) texture gradient
   (B) interposition
   (C) relative size
   (D) linear perspective
   (E) convergence

29. Language is hierarchical, with big pieces built out of smaller pieces. In the hierarchy, what is between phrase and morpheme?

   (A) semantic
   (B) sentence
   (C) rhythm
   (D) word
   (E) phoneme

30. Bandura's developmental research

   (A) seriously questions the validity of modeling
   (B) suggests that observation of aggressive models can prompt aggressive behavior by the observer
   (C) suggests that love is a function of "contact comfort"
   (D) suggests that television viewing reduces the incidence of aggressive behavior
   (E) points to the effectiveness of reinforcement in toilet training

GO ON TO THE NEXT PAGE

31. When a testing organization includes instructions to be read verbatim to each test-taking group, the organization is concentrating upon

  (A) dependent variables
  (B) intervening variables
  (C) standardization
  (D) reliability
  (E) validity

32. During the third through the eighth week of pregnancy, the developing child can be accurately referred to as the

  (A) prenate
  (B) zygote
  (C) embryo
  (D) fetus
  (E) blastocyst

33. Developmental research suggests a possible relationship between anxiety in the expectant mother and

  (A) premature birth
  (B) fetal brain damage
  (C) defective hearing
  (D) color blindness
  (E) the incidence of crying behavior in the newborn

34. Experiments with Hopi Indian children have suggested that the point at which a child begins to walk is primarily a function of

  (A) learning
  (B) intelligence
  (C) maturation
  (D) environment
  (E) modeling

35. Research evidence suggests highest aggression among boys who come from which of the following settings?

  (A) mother-and-father-present
  (B) father-absent
  (C) father-present
  (D) mother-present
  (E) parents-deceased

GO ON TO THE NEXT PAGE

36. Through testing procedures that, in effect, ask the newborn what she visually prefers, which of the following is found to be most preferred?

(A) bright-colored triangles
(B) bright-colored squares
(C) pictures of toys
(D) pictures of pets
(E) pictures of the human face

37. Checking a newborn male child via EEG, EMG, EOG, and respiration monitoring, would reveal which of the following?

(A) total absence of REM sleep
(B) some irregularities in respiration
(C) no body movement during sleep
(D) no reflex smiles
(E) no penis erection

38. One meaning of RSVP is "Répondez s'il vouz plait" (reply please). Another meaning of RSVP refers to a method of displaying information in cognitive and perceptual psychology experiments. What does RSVP stand for in this context?

(A) rote serialized verbal protocol
(B) reading-seeing-verbalizing paradigm
(C) rapid visual serial presentation
(D) rate of saturation of vision procedure
(E) none of the above

39. Which of the following would be true of operant conditioning?

(A) The response is elicited by the presence of the unconditioned stimulus.
(B) Reinforcement increases the frequency of the response associated with it.
(C) There is trace presentation of the CS and the UCS.
(D) There is delayed presentation of the CS and the UCS.
(E) There is simultaneous presentation of the CS and the UCS.

40. General knowledge frameworks that help people interpret and remember events are called

(A) chunks
(B) schemas
(C) episodes
(D) propositions
(E) prototypes

GO ON TO THE NEXT PAGE

41. Which of the following is correct?

(A) The correlation coefficient range is –0.05 to +0.05.
(B) +0.40 is greater correlation than –0.40.
(C) Correlation is related to predictability.
(D) Regression coefficients are essential for factor analysis.
(E) Analysis of covariance is not related to correlation.

42. Which of the following most commonly expresses central tendency and variability, respectively?

(A) mode, range
(B) mean, interval
(C) median, range
(D) median, standard deviation
(E) mean, standard deviation

43. The first two years after birth are critical

(A) to self-concept formation
(B) to aptitude formation
(C) to sensory formation
(D) to formation of secondary sexual characteristics
(E) only in the minds of parents

44. Which of the following can be anticipated during the first three months after birth?

(A) shorter periods of wakefulness
(B) the ability to raise the head slightly to look at something
(C) a noticeable lack of any effort to attempt an "answer" when an adult talks to the child
(D) the ability to hold and manipulate a spoon
(E) masturbation

45. A conditioned response has been learned to a specific stimulus. When similar stimuli also evoke the conditioned response, the phenomenon is called

(A) response generalization
(B) stimulus generalization
(C) successive approximation
(D) spreading activation
(E) second-order conditioning

GO ON TO THE NEXT PAGE

46. In social-adjustment terms, early maturity has been found

    (A) advantageous among males
    (B) advantageous among females
    (C) detrimental to males
    (D) detrimental to both males and females
    (E) a source of female prestige and male ridicule

47. The period of the embryo spans the prenatal period from the end of

    (A) second week to end of second month
    (B) first week to end of second month
    (C) third week to end of second month
    (D) first week to end of first month
    (E) third week to end of third month

48. In which of the following classical conditioning procedures would an association be learned most quickly?

    (A) UCS preceding CS by one-half second
    (B) CS preceding UCS by two seconds
    (C) UCS preceding CS by two seconds
    (D) CS preceding UCS by one-half second
    (E) CS preceding UCS by five seconds

49. Which of the following *cannot* occur during the germinal stage?

    (A) death of the zygote before implantation
    (B) glandular imbalance preventing implantation
    (C) implantation in a Fallopian tube
    (D) cell division
    (E) cell mass differentiation into three distinct layers

50. Depth of processing theory provides

    (A) an explanation of memory functioning
    (B) the basics of color vision
    (C) the critical link between neurosis and psychosis
    (D) a taxonomic hierarchy of evolutionary branches
    (E) a simulation theory of emotion

51. Which of the following would *not* be classified as an explicit memory test?

    (A) free recall
    (B) repetition priming
    (C) cued recall
    (D) paired-associate recall
    (E) recognition

GO ON TO THE NEXT PAGE

52. Frenkel and Brunswik conclude that the single most important factor distinguishing prejudiced from tolerant adolescents is

(A) intelligence
(B) aptitude
(C) sexual adjustment
(D) attitude toward authority
(E) vocational choice

53. Moderate anxiety in a child

(A) is detrimental to all learning
(B) may facilitate learning of difficult tasks
(C) may facilitate learning of simple tasks
(D) suggests unhealthy defense against Oedipal conflict
(E) is a function of archetype

54. Which of the following does *not* qualify as a polygenic characteristic?

(A) intelligence
(B) temperament
(C) schizophrenia
(D) blood type
(E) violence proneness

55. Friends become differentiated from strangers during which of the following young ages?

(A) twelve months
(B) six to seven months
(C) one to two months
(D) birth
(E) three to four months

56. Roger Shepard and Steve Kosslyn measured how long people take to mentally rotate or scan visual memories in order to show that

(A) the duration of iconic memories in the sensory register is very brief
(B) visual memories are better remembered than verbal memories
(C) there is a dual-code of both visual and verbal properties of memories
(D) visual memories are stored as images and not as propositions
(E) spatial information is stored in the form of mental maps

GO ON TO THE NEXT PAGE

QUESTIONS 57–59 REFER TO THE FOLLOWING EXPERIMENT.

Fifty children, ages nine and ten, were randomly assigned to two groups, twenty-five children per group. Using a pencil and paper, each subject was given the task of tracing a path around a geometric figure of a star. Normal cues were removed by using a shield between the subject's line of vision and the work area. It was impossible for the subjects to see their hands at work, but they could watch the hands in a mirror that was mounted on the table in front of the immediate work area. A trial began after the subject had been comfortably seated and given the signal to begin work; it concluded when the subject had completed the star-tracing task. A stopwatch monitored the time required for a subject to complete a given trial. Group 1 received one trial per day for seven days; Group 2 received seven trials during a single test session. Comparative tracing time per trial is outlined in the following table.

	Tracing Time (seconds)	
Trial	Group 1	Group 2
1	200	200
2	170	190
3	140	170
4	100	165
5	60	150
6	50	130
7	45	120

57. Important to interpretation of the table data would be a determination that the children in the two groups were equivalent in

(A) verbal IQ
(B) motor ability
(C) art proficiency
(D) mechanical aptitude
(E) degree of introversion

58. The mirror serves to

(A) help the child work more quickly than he could if he were directly observing his work
(B) provide immediate, helpful feedback and knowledge of results
(C) promote stimulus generalization
(D) reorient and move the child beyond familiar habits in eye-hand coordination
(E) provide proactive facilitation

GO ON TO THE NEXT PAGE

59. The results support the statement that

(A) massed practice proved more effective than spaced practice
(B) spaced practice proved more effective than massed practice
(C) practice had no appreciable effect on performance
(D) spaced practice prompted subjects to encounter the effects of forgetting
(E) retroactive aversion operates in star-tracing experiments

60. The heights of kindergarten-aged children

(A) negatively correlate with comparative adult heights
(B) positively correlate with comparative adult heights
(C) in no way relate to comparative adult heights
(D) most strongly correlate with the heights of their mothers
(E) most strongly correlate with the heights of their fathers

61. Kendler's experimentation suggests that in child maturation

(A) mediational processes precede single-unit S-R cognitive mechanisms
(B) single-unit S-R cognitive mechanisms precede mediational processes
(C) single-unit S-R cognitive mechanisms and mediational processes occur at the same developmental point
(D) neither the single-unit S-R cognitive mechanism nor the mediational process occurs until after age six
(E) single unit S-R cognitive mechanisms never occur

62. In the newborn's second year, the rate of growth

(A) is faster than that of the first year
(B) is slower than that of the first year
(C) parallels that of the first year
(D) is faster than that of the fetal period
(E) is faster than that of the embryonic period

63. The mouth opens wide and the head turns to the midline in the

(A) Babinski response
(B) Babkin response
(C) plantar response
(D) Moro response
(E) push-back response

64. The term most closely associated with the work of Tolman is

(A) perceptual learning
(B) sensory preconditioning
(C) reinforcement learning
(D) place learning
(E) contiguity learning

GO ON TO THE NEXT PAGE

65. In Piaget's classification system, the child learns language and the logic of classification and numbers during which period?

(A) sensorimotor
(B) latency
(C) formal operations
(D) concrete operations
(E) assimilation

66. A curve has its most prominent distribution of scores to the left of center and "tails off" to the right. This information would be sufficient to conclude that the curve showed

(A) negative skew
(B) positive skew
(C) normal distribution
(D) bimodal distribution
(E) platikurtic distribution

67. Jacob's therapists have noticed that he demonstrates deficits in social relatedness and communication skills, and often engages in repetitive, ritualistic behaviors. They are most likely to diagnose Jacob with

(A) somatic symptom disorder
(B) attention-deficit/hyperactivity disorder
(C) autism spectrum disorder
(D) antisocial personality disorder
(E) oppositional defiant disorder

68. When performance of an earlier task is interfered with by the learning of a second, more recent task, what has occurred?

(A) proactive facilitation
(B) proactive interference
(C) retroactive facilitation
(D) retroactive interference
(E) negative transference

69. Which of the following developed the "overload theory" of crowding?

(A) Lorenz
(B) Schachter
(C) Aronson
(D) Milgram
(E) Ardrey

GO ON TO THE NEXT PAGE

70. A person is asked to tell a lie for one of the following sums of money. For which sum would the most dissonance be created?

   (A) $1
   (B) $10
   (C) $20
   (D) $25
   (E) $50

71. Which of the following is *not* considered one of the "Big Five" personality traits?

   (A) openness
   (B) conscientiousness
   (C) extraversion
   (D) dominance
   (E) neuroticism

72. The most mature view of sex would be evident in which of the following?

   (A) genital stage
   (B) phallic stage
   (C) anal stage
   (D) puberty
   (E) initiative versus guilt

73. "Man's freedom is absolute and it is his own choices which determine what he shall become, since even refusing to choose constitutes a choice." The preceding view is expressed within

   (A) behaviorism
   (B) psychoanalysis
   (C) ego analysis
   (D) trait theory
   (E) existentialism

74. Which of the following is *not* true of attitudes?

   (A) Your own attitudes seem best to you.
   (B) A common defense against differing attitudes is selective attention.
   (C) A common defense against differing attitudes is rationalization.
   (D) Attitudes require an emotional component.
   (E) Attitudes require a stereotype component.

GO ON TO THE NEXT PAGE

75. A person who judges personality on the basis of facial expression is engaging in

   (A) physiognomy
   (B) phrenology
   (C) trait analysis
   (D) syntonomy
   (E) parataxis

76. An ability that can be expected to continue improving after age thirty-five is

   (A) numerical
   (B) manual
   (C) spatial relations
   (D) verbal comprehension
   (E) associative memory

77. A group of students took a personality test and later were given very general descriptive comments about the test's results. Each student was given the same general description, and the individual students concluded that the description fit their personality very well. This demonstration would be evidence of the

   (A) Freudian effect
   (B) response effect
   (C) Muller/Lyer effect
   (D) rebound effect
   (E) Barnum effect

78. Homans's anticipatory socialization refers to

   (A) downward movement in the social system
   (B) upward movement in the social system
   (C) lateral movement in the social system
   (D) preparation for an older age group within one's own social class
   (E) a child's initial preparation for cooperative play

79. Which of the following is unrelated to the 16-PF?

   (A) 16 personality-factor dimensions
   (B) Cattell
   (C) standardization on normal subjects
   (D) Hathaway
   (E) factor analysis

GO ON TO THE NEXT PAGE

80. A factor analysis approach to personality would be most positively received within which of the following groups?

(A) Cattell, Eysenck, Goldstein
(B) Jung, Freud, Horney
(C) Rogers, Kelly, Allport
(D) Skinner, Watson, Bandura
(E) Sullivan, Erikson, Berne

81. Which of the following makes an accurate distinction between the Strong-Campbell Vocational Interest Blank and the Kuder Preference Record?

(A) success versus failure
(B) differences in administration
(C) occupation emphasis versus broad-area emphasis
(D) male-female distinctions versus unified format
(E) an intelligence factor versus an aptitude factor

82. As a corrections officer—other factors being equivalent—which of the following persons would you consider most likely to be rehabilitated successfully?

(A) person convicted of armed robbery
(B) person who shot and killed another man found making love to the first man's wife
(C) person charged with breaking and entering
(D) person charged with arson
(E) person who shot and killed another person as part of a profit-making contract

83. Mortimer has worn red shirts for years because he likes them. Now red shirts are the "in" thing with his group and he continues to wear them. In Hollander's terms, he is demonstrating

(A) conformity
(B) anticonformity
(C) dissonance
(D) independence
(E) irrelevance

GO ON TO THE NEXT PAGE

84. A salesperson makes a call on a retailer who has been buying a competitor's product line. The salesperson compliments the competitor's store display and asks the retailer whether Company X (the competitor) made it. When the retailer responds "Yes," the salesperson says, "You are very fortunate to have such a display made exclusively for you." The retailer then indicates, "Oh no, Company X doesn't give exclusive display lines"—a fact the salesperson knew in advance. This conversation will continue with the salesperson making subsequent absolute statements about Company X with which the retailer will be forced to disagree. The attitude change technique being utilized draws heavily upon

    (A) Brehm's theory of reactance
    (B) Newcomb's theory of balance
    (C) Goffman's theory of consonance
    (D) Homan's theory of distributive justice
    (E) Adler's theory of superiority striving

85. Imagine that a major attempt is being launched to change household attitudes toward the use of beef liver as a regular mealtime food. The approach is to have the most influential member of each household (a person who currently dislikes beef liver) design and deliver a talk on the prominent advantages of having beef liver as a regular mealtime food. The theory underlying this approach to attitude change would be

    (A) cognitive dissonance
    (B) behavior exchange
    (C) complementarity
    (D) vulnerability
    (E) status congruence

86. It began as a Nobel Prize-winning procedure and ended in disgrace.

    (A) electroconvulsive therapy
    (B) chemotherapy
    (C) individual psychotherapy
    (D) encounter group therapy
    (E) prefrontal lobotomy

87. Which of the following was Adler's conceptual substitution for Freud's libido?

    (A) superiority striving
    (B) social interest
    (C) inferiority feeling
    (D) organ inferiority
    (E) pampering

GO ON TO THE NEXT PAGE

88. Someone well versed in kinesics would be studying

   (A) the meaning of body movements
   (B) personal, territorial space
   (C) mass communication
   (D) brainwashing
   (E) nonzero sum games

89. Jung cites human infant response to mother-closeness and the adult concept of a power beyond himself as examples of

   (A) anima
   (B) animus
   (C) archetype
   (D) prototype
   (E) intuiting

90. The term *gender schema* refers to

   (A) associating words with people
   (B) preponderance of same-sex children in a family
   (C) intelligence test score distributions
   (D) the "gender design" within DNA
   (E) gender-clustering words in memory storage and retrieval

91. Which of the following is most firmly supported by experimental evidence?

   (A) psychoanalysis
   (B) trait theory
   (C) projective testing
   (D) phenomenology
   (E) psychodynamic theory

92. A nonzero sum game refers to a

   (A) recent development in sociograms
   (B) game in which both participants may win
   (C) game in which both participants must lose
   (D) game in which one participant ends up with zero
   (E) game in which one participant may win only if the other participant loses

93. Formulation of dissonance theory was initiated by

   (A) Aronson
   (B) Thurstone
   (C) Festinger
   (D) Heider
   (E) Newcomb

GO ON TO THE NEXT PAGE

94. Borderline disorder would be classified among

   (A) gender dysphoria disorders
   (B) anxiety disorders
   (C) personality disorders
   (D) somatic symptom disorders
   (E) dissociative disorders

95. Believing others intend to harm you is a form of

   (A) anxiety disorder
   (B) catatonic schizophrenia
   (C) paranoid psychosis
   (D) dysthymic disorder
   (E) dissociative disorder

96. Where are you mostly likely to find a pyramidal cell?

   (A) cerebellum
   (B) cerebral cortex
   (C) spinal cord
   (D) neuromuscular junction
   (E) retina

97. Sound vibrations in the ear result in neural impulses in which of the following cortex locations first?

   (A) temporal lobe
   (B) central fissure
   (C) occipital lobe
   (D) parietal lobe
   (E) auditory lobe

98. In stating his view of neurosis as conditioned maladaptive behavior, Eysenck claims that

   (A) extroverts are most likely to become neurotics
   (B) introverts are most likely to develop somatoform disorders
   (C) introverts have greater autonomic reactivity
   (D) phobias persist, once learned, even in the absence of further reinforcement
   (E) parataxic perception must be achieved before therapy can attain significant progress

GO ON TO THE NEXT PAGE

99. Which of the following distinguishes a sedative from a tranquilizer?

(A) cost
(B) drowsiness-inducing characteristics
(C) speed with which it takes effect
(D) anxiety-reducing capacity
(E) mood-elevation properties

100. Syllogisms are an example of what kind of reasoning?

(A) deductive
(B) inductive
(C) evaluative
(D) divergent
(E) heuristic

101. In a working memory experiment, subjects are read a list of six words and are asked to remember them fifteen seconds later. Subjects will do better if the words are short (*tin, lip, tap*) than if the words are long (*peppermint, liberate, forensic*). This finding has been interpreted as evidence for the limited capacity of

(A) working memory
(B) the sensory register
(C) executive control
(D) the phonological loop
(E) the verbal buffer

102. Which of the following distinguishes anxiety from fear?

(A) realistic environmental danger
(B) strength of emotion
(C) galvanic skin response
(D) heart rate
(E) blood pressure

103. The effects of psychotomimetic drugs resemble which one of the following reactions?

(A) depressive
(B) hypermanic
(C) schizophrenic
(D) delirium
(E) somatoform

GO ON TO THE NEXT PAGE

104. Withdrawal reactions include all of the following elements *except*

(A) repression

(B) fantasy

(C) regression

(D) continual wandering—moves without tangible gain

(E) paranoia

105. What causes a neuron's membrane potential to become *more negative* than its resting potential?

(A) EPSP

(B) IPSP

(C) temporal summation

(D) spatial summation

(E) excitation threshold

106. When humans are monitored under conditions that allow the normal light-controlled circadian rhythm to become free running, the duration of the circadian cycle is

(A) under twenty-two hours

(B) between twenty-two and twenty-four hours

(C) between twenty-four and twenty-six hours

(D) over twenty-six hours

(E) incredibly variable across individuals, ranging from as short as eighteen to as long as thirty hours

107. A characteristic of schizophrenia is

(A) heightened awareness of reality

(B) eidetic imagery

(C) withdrawal from interpersonal relationships

(D) psychological "paralysis" in a portion of the body

(E) the "phantom limb" experience

108. Which of the following would encompass the view that a friend or relative's sympathy may serve to feed another's depression?

(A) stress approach

(B) cognitive approach

(C) learned helplessness approach

(D) MAO approach

(E) reduced-reinforcement approach

GO ON TO THE NEXT PAGE

109. The English language has approximately how many phonemes?

(A) 7 ± 2
(B) 26
(C) 40
(D) 40,000
(E) infinite

110. Subjects in an experiment read a list of words (e.g., *stove*) without any instructions to try to remember them. Later, they are shown stimuli such as: "STO—" and they are asked to come up with the first English word they can think of beginning with the indicated letters. Memory for the earlier list is reflected in a greater probability to complete this example with "stove" (compared to subjects who did not see "stove" on the original list). This memory task would be classified as

(A) a free-recall test
(B) a cued-recall test
(C) an implicit memory test
(D) a procedural memory test
(E) a semantic memory test

111. The simplest measure of variability to calculate is known as the

(A) range
(B) standard deviation
(C) variance
(D) stanine
(E) quadrant

112. Intense fear of open places is known as

(A) ochlophobia
(B) acrophobia
(C) claustrophobia
(D) triskaidekaphobia
(E) agoraphobia

113. What does the "all-or-none law" describe?

(A) the process by which the lens of the eye changes shape when focusing on an object
(B) the fixed amplitude of the action potential
(C) a pattern of regular oscillations visible in the EEG waves of a person who is relaxed and awake
(D) the likelihood that infants will search for an out-of-sight object in a location where it was previously hidden
(E) the tendency of group discussions to produce either unanimity or extremely polarized opinions, depending on the degree of group cohesiveness

GO ON TO THE NEXT PAGE

114. Which of the following is *not* a nucleotide composing DNA?

(A) adenine
(B) guanine
(C) thymine
(D) muscarine
(E) cytosine

115. Which one of the following is most likely to set fires?

(A) pyromaniac
(B) ochlomaniac
(C) kleptomaniac
(D) aclomaniac
(E) hypomaniac

116. All of the following are directly related to clinical assessment *except*

(A) MMPI
(B) 16 PF
(C) Osgood Semantic Differential
(D) Rorschach
(E) TAT

117. What brain systems are important for procedural memory?

(A) parietal lobe and hippocampus
(B) hippocampus and basal ganglia
(C) basal ganglia and cerebellum
(D) cerebellum and spinal cord
(E) spinal cord and parietal lobe

118. Transference and resistance are most common in

(A) psychoanalysis
(B) group therapy
(C) behavior therapy
(D) phenomenological therapy
(E) client-centered therapy

119. Each score in a distribution has been increased by 7 (i.e., 7 has been added to every score). What happens to the standard deviation?

(A) it increases by 7
(B) it remains unchanged from its original value
(C) it triples its current value
(D) it increases by 14
(E) it increases by 3.5

GO ON TO THE NEXT PAGE

120. When an English speaker asks a question, the pitch of her voice will rise at the end of the utterance. This is a description of what aspect of language?

(A) phonology
(B) semantics
(C) prosody
(D) syntax
(E) pragmatics

121. The term *mainlining* refers to

(A) use of heroin by the middle class
(B) sniffing heroin
(C) injecting heroin under the skin
(D) smoking heroin
(E) injecting heroin into a vein

122. George has been diagnosed as schizophrenic. Which of the following most likely will be prescribed for him to take?

(A) haloperidol
(B) amphetamines
(C) atropine
(D) dopamine
(E) mescaline

123. The procedure of outlining an experimental problem, stating criteria for making observations, describing measuring instruments and their use in observation, and defining procedures to be used in data analysis is

(A) operational definition
(B) hypothetical construct
(C) logical construct
(D) experimental design
(E) hypothesis

124. The function of a theory is to

(A) prove a hypothesis
(B) establish a law
(C) explain and relate observed facts
(D) develop the steps to be used in experimentation
(E) establish significance levels

GO ON TO THE NEXT PAGE

125. For which of the following forms of sexual problem would treatment be considered most difficult?

    (A) frigidity
    (B) impotence
    (C) fetishism
    (D) pedophilia
    (E) coitus interruptus

126. Depression can cycle with periods of mania in

    (A) sleep disorder
    (B) organic disorder
    (C) bipolar disorder
    (D) schizophrenic disorder
    (E) personality disorder

127. Michelangelo's frustrated desire for closeness with his mother was expressed in painting. This is an example of

    (A) compensation
    (B) rationalization
    (C) sublimation
    (D) projection
    (E) reaction formation

128. Which one of the following persons would be most likely to study and analyze drawings by schizophrenic children?

    (A) Bandura
    (B) Bettelheim
    (C) Szasz
    (D) Skinner
    (E) Adler

129. Which of the following is believed to have an important role in major depressive disorder?

    (A) norepinephrine
    (B) estrogen
    (C) progesterone
    (D) acetylcholine
    (E) potassium chloride

GO ON TO THE NEXT PAGE

130. Assuming a mean of 100 and a standard deviation of 15, what percentage of a group of persons selected randomly can be expected to have IQ scores above 130?

(A) 14 percent
(B) 34 percent
(C) 48 percent
(D) 2 percent
(E) 1 percent

QUESTIONS 131 AND 132 ARE BASED ON THE FOLLOWING SITUATION.

An experimenter plans to study the effects upon comprehension exerted by differences in sex, age, and hair color. Subjects will be equal numbers of males and females, ages twenty-five and forty-five, and either brown-haired or red-haired.

131. The statistical design is

(A) two-factor
(B) four-factor
(C) one-factor
(D) six-factor
(E) three-factor

132. Assuming that the experimenter can somehow obtain the data in a single test session with one score for each subject, she could use

(A) a two-factor factorial design
(B) a three-factor factorial design
(C) a *t*-test for related measures
(D) a *t*-test for unrelated measures
(E) a complex Latin square design

133. *The Psychopathology of Everyday Life* was a prominent work of

(A) Fromm
(B) Rank
(C) Skinner
(D) Freud
(E) Adler

134. The original moron-imbecile-idiot classification of intellectual disability was changed because

(A) the corresponding IQs were inexact
(B) the categories were not sufficiently inclusive
(C) four categories were needed instead of three
(D) unfortunate stereotyping had occurred
(E) five categories were needed instead of three

GO ON TO THE NEXT PAGE

135. Human engineering control principles indicate that a system is best in which the operation of the controls imposes a degree of strain on the operator consistent with the required degree of accuracy. This degree is

(A) below optimum strain
(B) above optimum strain
(C) optimal strain
(D) complete absence of strain
(E) either above optimum or below optimum, depending on the setting

136. Several classical researchers and specific current researchers have used single-subject data gathering (for example, working with children who have stuttering problems). To demonstrate their work to colleagues, the researchers adopt

(A) a parametric measure
(B) a series of t-tests
(C) an F-test
(D) a series of graphs
(E) analysis of variance

QUESTIONS 137–139 ARE BASED ON THE FOLLOWING INFORMATION.

Two judges ranked five beauty contestants as follows:

Contestant	Judge 1	Judge 2
A	1	5
B	2	4
C	3	3
D	4	2
E	5	1

137. Which of the following can be concluded from the above?

(A) A strong positive correlation exists between the judges.
(B) A strong negative correlation exists between the judges.
(C) There is no correlation between the judges.
(D) A moderately positive correlation exists between the judges.
(E) A moderately negative correlation exists between the judges.

GO ON TO THE NEXT PAGE

138. Which of the following methods would be used in computation of the correlation?

(A) Latin Square Design
(B) Spearman Rank-Order Correlation
(C) Point-Biserial Correlation
(D) Simple Analysis of Covariance
(E) Factorial Analysis of Covariance

139. The correlation coefficient that you would be most likely to find would be

(A) +0.5
(B) −0.5
(C) 0.0
(D) −1.0
(E) +1.0

140. In human factors, the term *shape coding* applies to

(A) visual discriminations
(B) dial calibrations
(C) dial color coding
(D) traffic flow between work positions
(E) knob appearance and contour

141. The *method of loci* is an ancient mnemonic technique that improves memory via an elaborative process involving

(A) a counting rhyme
(B) imagery
(C) spaced repetitions
(D) massed repetitions
(E) encoding specificity

142. A situation in which trainees are presented with only the "bare bones" of a managerial situation and are told that participants can get additional information only by asking questions is an example of the

(A) free-association method
(B) leader-behavior method
(C) incident process training method
(D) sensitivity-training
(E) role-playing method

GO ON TO THE NEXT PAGE

PRACTICE TEST 2

143. A company has a screening test that involves responding to letters, memoranda, telephone messages, and other items typical of the contents of an executive's in-basket. This is an example of

(A) an aptitude test
(B) an intelligence test
(C) an achievement test
(D) a sociability measure
(E) an English test

144. Recognizing the difficulty of control in experimental designs, in which of the following could you be assured that variability among subjects has been adequately controlled?

(A) completely randomized design
(B) $2 \times 2 \times 2$ factorial design
(C) point-biserial correlation
(D) test–retest (repeated measures) design
(E) *t*-test

145. A distribution of scores can have more than one

(A) mean
(B) median
(C) variance
(D) standard deviation
(E) mode

146. Which of the following is *not* one of the Gestalt laws describing how we organize our sensory experiences?

(A) law of closure
(B) law of similarity
(C) law of proximity
(D) law of induced motion
(E) law of common fate

147. In a positively skewed distribution, which of the following will move most noticeably in the direction indicated?

(A) mean, to the right
(B) mode, to the left
(C) mean, to the left
(D) median, to the right
(E) median, to the left

GO ON TO THE NEXT PAGE

148. Most scientific investigations of the heritability of personality traits have found that

(A) there is no genetic influence on personality traits
(B) heritability estimates for the Big Five personality traits range from 0% to 20%
(C) heritability estimates for the Big Five personality traits range from 40% to 60%
(D) the only heritable personality trait is neuroticism
(E) the only heritable personality trait is sensation-seeking

QUESTIONS 149–151 ARE BASED ON THE FOLLOWING CHOICES.

(1) paired t-test
(2) t-test for two independent means
(3) one sample t-test
(4) chi-square
(5) treatments-by-levels design

149. The experimenter seeks to determine whether one group of eighteen-year-old boys differs significantly in weight from a second group of eighteen-year-old boys. She would use

(A) 1
(B) 2
(C) 3
(D) 4
(E) 5

150. The experimenter wants to test the effect of child rearing upon identical twins—with one of each twin raised in a foster home and the second of each twin raised in an institution. (IQ scores were obtained for analysis when each group member attained age 15.) Which method would she use?

(A) 1
(B) 2
(C) 3
(D) 4
(E) 5

151. The experimenter wishes to determine whether the weight of a specific group of eighteen-year-old boys is significantly different from the national average for boys this age. Which method would she use?

(A) 1
(B) 2
(C) 3
(D) 4
(E) 5

GO ON TO THE NEXT PAGE

152. Which of the following statements is correct?

    I.   In most right-handed people, the left hemisphere is dominant for language.

    II. In most left-handed people, the left hemisphere is dominant for language.

    III. In most congenitally deaf people, the left hemisphere is dominant for language.

(A) I only

(B) II only

(C) I and II

(D) I and III

(E) I, II, and III

153. Which one of the following could be expected to enhance performance on a vigilance task?

(A) threat of punishment

(B) rest periods

(C) high pay

(D) coworker interaction

(E) background music

154. Most closely associated with the Least Preferred Coworker technique and with the task-centered versus people-centered leader distinction is the work of

(A) Newcomb

(B) Asch

(C) Rokeach

(D) Festinger

(E) Fiedler

155. In the axon terminal of a neuron, neurotransmitters are contained within balloon-like containers called

(A) glial cells

(B) nodes of Ranvier

(C) synaptic vesicles

(D) receptors

(E) axonal cysts

GO ON TO THE NEXT PAGE

156. Research on navigational ability indicates that there are two different methods that an individual can use to learn how to navigate a new environment. What are the names given to these two forms of spatial learning?

(A) survey perspective and route perspective
(B) analogical and symbolic
(C) inductive and deductive
(D) declarative and procedural
(E) covert and overt

157. In McLuhan's framework, television is seen as a

(A) hot medium
(B) moderately intense medium
(C) cool medium
(D) political medium
(E) social medium

158. Bayes's theorem is an example of a system for

(A) prototype formation
(B) divergent production
(C) signal detection theory
(D) deductive reasoning
(E) inductive reasoning

159. The principles of evolution by natural selection cannot be applied to human behavior because

(A) humans have culture
(B) we know that humans do more than try to maximize reproductive success
(C) we do not know everything about humans' evolutionary past
(D) behavior does not fossilize
(E) none of the above: evolutionary principles *can* be applied to human behavior

160. The sympathetic and parasympathetic branches of the autonomic nervous system are characterized, with respect to each other, as

(A) reciprocal systems
(B) parallel systems
(C) redundant systems
(D) orthogonal systems
(E) somatic systems

GO ON TO THE NEXT PAGE

161. Which of the following statements about REM sleep is false?

   (A) The first cycle of REM sleep usually begins more than one hour after falling asleep.
   (B) After drinking alcohol, a person spends less time in REM sleep than he or she otherwise would.
   (C) Sleep terrors and sleepwalking occur during REM sleep.
   (D) Limb muscles are paralyzed during REM sleep.
   (E) Someone awakened during REM sleep is likely to report vivid dream experiences.

162. A piano player is on a flight to an important recital. Because she cannot actually practice, instead she *imagines* playing the piano. What does research indicate about the effectiveness of mental practice for subsequent performance?

   (A) Mental practice actually hinders subsequent performance because there is no feedback.
   (B) Mental practice has no effect on subsequent performance.
   (C) Mental practice helps performance, but not as much as physical practice.
   (D) Mental practice and physical practice both enhance subsequent performance to an equal degree.
   (E) Mental practice has positive effects for experts but negative effects for novices.

163. What neurological disease is associated with the formation of amyloid protein plaques throughout the cerebral cortex?

   (A) Parkinson's disease
   (B) Alzheimer's disease
   (C) autism
   (D) epilepsy
   (E) Huntington's disease

164. With reference to multi-store memory models, which of the following comparisons about the sensory register and the short-term store are correct?

   I. The sensory register can hold less information than the short-term store.
   II. The sensory register can hold information for less time than the short-term store.
   III. The sensory register receives information before the short-term store.

   (A) I only
   (B) II only
   (C) I and III
   (D) II and III
   (E) I, II, and III

GO ON TO THE NEXT PAGE

165. With whom is the linguistic relativity hypothesis associated?

(A) Benjamin Whorf
(B) Noam Chomsky
(C) Carl Wernicke
(D) John Locke
(E) Ernst Weber

166. The concept of a reflex—whereby a stimulus affects the brain, that in turn creates a motor response—was described as a hydraulic system by which seventeenth century philosopher?

(A) René Descartes
(B) George Berkeley
(C) John Locke
(D) David Hume
(E) Immanuel Kant

167. The ability of neurons or brain structures to alter their function as a result of experience or injury is referred to as

(A) accommodation
(B) plasticity
(C) antagonism
(D) assimilation
(E) desensitization

168. The term *alpha male* refers to

(A) an individual who is genetically female but who, due to prenatal androgen abnormalities, is born with external genitals resembling a male
(B) the sole male member of a polygamous mating group
(C) a male with one X and one Y sex chromosome
(D) the group member at the top of a dominance hierarchy
(E) a father with an authoritative parenting style

169. In laboratory studies of memory that compare young subjects to healthy elderly subjects, which type of memory has been reported to show early age-related declines?

(A) procedural memory
(B) semantic memory
(C) remote memory
(D) prospective memory
(E) generic memory

GO ON TO THE NEXT PAGE

170. In signal detection terms, an intrusion error in memory is an example of a

(A) hit
(B) miss
(C) false alarm
(D) correct reject
(E) criterion

171. Prozac is a selective seratonin reuptake inhibitor. This drug would thus be classified as an

(A) agonist
(B) analgesic
(C) antecedent
(D) apraxic
(E) antagonist

172. Keena finds dental work extremely aversive and she has developed a fear of her dentist. One day, she bumps into her dentist's receptionist in the grocery store, and Keena notices that her heart starts racing and her palms begin sweating. Keena's response to her dentist's receptionist is an example of

(A) dishabituation
(B) second-order conditioning
(C) reconditioning
(D) extinction
(E) instrumental conditioning

173. To what does the "magical number seven" refer?

(A) the age at which the critical period for language acquisition ends
(B) the capacity of short-term memory
(C) the number of genes on each human chromosome
(D) the average number of synapses in a reflex arc
(E) none of the above

174. A subject in an experiment is asked to read a series of words presented one at a time, and the voice-onset latency is recorded. Occasionally, a word was preceded by a related word (such as *doctor* preceded by *nurse*). The latency to read words that are preceded by related words is faster on average than the latency to read words preceded by an unrelated word (such as *doctor* preceded by *tomato*). This effect is called

(A) repetition priming
(B) semantic priming
(C) perceptual priming
(D) primacy effect
(E) recency effect

GO ON TO THE NEXT PAGE

175. A major difference between inductive reasoning and deductive reasoning is that

(A) inductive reasoning does not increase one's knowledge base; deductive reasoning does

(B) only humans are known to exhibit inductive reasoning, whereas deductive reasoning is observed more widely in the animal kingdom

(C) inductive reasoning is a form of formal logic; deductive reasoning is not

(D) with deductive reasoning, if the premises are true the conclusion must be true; with inductive reasoning the truth of the conclusion is not guaranteed

(E) deductive reasoning is easier with abstract (symbolic) terms than with concrete examples, whereas the reverse is true for inductive reasoning

176. The notion that there are species-specific biological constraints on learning, attributed to John Garcia, arose from the pattern of _____ in learning.

(A) reconditioning

(B) belongingness

(C) spontaneous recovery

(D) latent learning

(E) long-term potentiation

177. To what does the word *saccade* refer?

(A) propogation of the action potential down a myelinated axon

(B) eye movements

(C) the lateral portion of the hypothalamus

(D) the quality of a sound that distinguishes different types of musical instruments

(E) the eye's transparent outer coating

178. Fixed-action patterns, first described by Niko Tinbergen, are

(A) elicited by a complex arrangement of external stimuli

(B) hormonally induced without reference to external stimuli

(C) elicited by simple, specific external stimuli

(D) synonymous with Watson's concept of nest habits

(E) instrumentally conditioned responses

GO ON TO THE NEXT PAGE

A researcher wants to test the hypothesis that we have analogical (picture-like) representations of word meaning. For example, "The cat is in the hat" would be represented in the mind as a picture of *a crouching cat* hiding inside a hat, ready to jump out and attack. In contrast, in the sentence, "The cat is sleeping," the picture would be more like *a cat lounging* with its legs outstretched on the floor. Importantly, the *cat* looks very different in these two pictures and, thus, would be represented in the mind differently. To test this hypothesis, the researcher asked participants to read sentences on a computer screen (e.g., "The cat is in the hat"). After reading the sentence, one of three different kinds of pictures of an object then appeared: (1) Irrelevant condition: an irrelevant object not in the preceding sentence, like *a hammer*; (2) Match condition: an object that matched the presumed picture of the sentence, like *a crouching cat*; or (3) No Match condition: an object in the sentence that did not match the presumed picture of the sentence, like *a cat lounging*. Participants were required to indicate as quickly as they could and as accurately as they could whether the object pictured on the screen was mentioned in the preceding sentence, by pressing one of two buttons. The reaction time results are as follows:

	Irrelevant	Match	No Match
Reaction Time	700 ms	700 ms	770 ms

179. What is the most reasonable conclusion given by the results?

(A) There is support for the analogical hypothesis because the Irrelevant and Match conditions both have 700 ms reaction times.
(B) The analogical hypothesis is unlikely because it takes a participant longer to respond in the No Match condition than in the Irrelevant condition.
(C) The analogical hypothesis is unlikely because participants take longer to respond in the No Match condition than in the Match condition.
(D) There is support for the analogical hypothesis because participants are quicker to recognize an object in the Match condition than in the No Match condition.
(E) There is support for the analogical hypothesis because participants across conditions respond so quickly.

GO ON TO THE NEXT PAGE

180. Given that the reaction time differences involved in the study are very small, what is the most justified conclusion?

(A) There is no statistically significant difference among the groups.
(B) The researcher should adopt another technique to obtain larger differences among the groups.
(C) The differences found in the data are likely unobtainable if the researcher had simply asked the participants what they think would happen.
(D) The speed of mental processes is too slow to measure.
(E) The speed of mental processes is too fast to measure.

181. In addition to analyzing reaction time data, the researcher also examined each participant's accuracy in object recognition (i.e., whether they answered yes or no correctly that the object was in the preceding sentence). Why was it necessary to analyze accuracy in addition to reaction time?

(A) In this experiment, accuracy is a more important dependent measure than reaction time.
(B) It is possible that reaction time data are irrelevant, if the participant is not performing the task as instructed.
(C) It is possible that reaction time data are unnecessary, if the accuracy measure reveals larger differences across conditions.
(D) In this experiment, the independent variable may have been confounded, and a check of participants' accuracy will reveal this.
(E) It is not necessary to analyze accuracy in addition to reaction time.

182. In reasoning, _____ is a strategy that is more efficient but less accurate than is _____ for reaching a solution.

(A) a syllogism; an algorithm
(B) a heuristic; an algorithm
(C) an algorithm; a syllogism
(C) a proposition; deductive reasoning
(D) a heuristic; inductive reasoning

183. The English and Mandarin Chinese languages utilize different means for distinguishing between two distinct words. In English, different words have different phoneme sequences, but in Mandarin, different words can have the same phoneme sequence but different

(A) pitch
(B) morphemes
(C) syllables
(D) case markings
(E) tenses

GO ON TO THE NEXT PAGE

184. What is the shape of the forgetting curve?

    (A) sinusoidal
    (B) linear
    (C) exponential
    (D) triangular
    (E) quadratic

185. What is the Wada test used to study?

    (A) creativity
    (B) cerebral lateralization
    (C) attachment style
    (D) conformity
    (E) sleep disorders

186. A polysomnogram is used to assess

    (A) the extent of brain damage after a stroke
    (B) changes in the electrical resistance of the skin, associated with fear, anger, and lying
    (C) movement through different stages of sleep
    (D) the point in a scene where an individual is looking (i.e., fixating the eyes)
    (E) regional variations in cerebral blood flow associated with patterns of neural activity

187. According to the definitional theory of word meaning, words can be defined in terms of _____ features.

    (A) probabilistic
    (B) necessary and sufficient
    (C) hierarchically organized
    (D) average
    (E) combinatorial

188. In an example famously popularized by Jerry Fodor, the typical pet fish (a goldfish) does not closely resemble the typical pet (a dog) or the typical fish (a trout). This example has been used to argue against what theory of concepts?

    (A) compositional
    (B) propositional
    (C) analogical
    (D) prototype
    (E) productive

GO ON TO THE NEXT PAGE

189. Carole has a genetic disorder that has led to the complete dysfunction of her umami receptors. What impairment would you expect Carole to have?

(A) an inability to discriminate red and green lights
(B) an inability to discriminate the taste of different cheeses
(C) an inability to localize sounds in space
(D) an inability to discriminate cold from hot temperatures
(E) an inability to interpret stereoscopic cues to depth

190. The terms *informational encapsulation*, *domain specificity*, and *mandatory* are all used in discussions of

(A) phylogeny
(B) post-traumatic stress disorder
(C) modularity
(D) predictive validity
(E) cognitive development

QUESTIONS 191 AND 192 REFER TO THE FOLLOWING SCENARIO.

You are walking down the street with your friend Max, and you pass a man who is easily seven feet tall. Max turns to you and says, "I bet that guy is a professional basketball player."

191. Max's conclusion is based on application of the

(A) representativeness heuristic
(B) frequency heuristic
(C) availability heuristic
(D) anchoring heuristic
(E) familiarity heuristic

192. What error is Max making when he arrives at this conclusion?

(A) congruence bias
(B) confirmation bias
(C) mere exposure effect
(D) outcome bias
(E) base-rate fallacy

193. When Oscar throws a toy at his sister, his mother takes that toy away from Oscar for one hour. By doing this, she hopes he will stop throwing. In learning theory terms, Oscar's mother is applying

(A) classical conditioning
(B) positive reinforcement
(C) partial reinforcement
(D) negative reinforcement
(E) none of the above

GO ON TO THE NEXT PAGE

194. Where would you find a node of Ranvier?

(A) the hypothalamus
(B) inside the ventricles
(C) on a myelinated axon
(D) between the layers of the meninges
(E) on the pituitary gland

195. A principle of neural association, or learning, can be summed up with the expression "Neurons that fire together, wire together." What biological mechanism exhibits this principle?

(A) action potential
(B) temporal summation
(C) salutatory conduction
(D) long-term potentiation
(E) lock-and-key model

196. The term *unconscious inference*, coined by Helmholtz, refers to

(A) the interpretation of a situation that determines what emotional experience a person will have in that situation
(B) the ability to deduce what distal stimulus is most likely to have given rise to a given proximal stimulus
(C) a rule of thumb used to make probability estimates based on the ease of retrieving information about an outcome, rather than on its actual likelihood
(D) the creation of false memory recollections that are believed (often with confidence) when one fails to remember something and fills in this gap
(E) the ability of a person who is blind as a result of a stroke in the visual cortex to report the location of unseen objects

197. Which of the following units is used to describe the frequency, in cycles per second, of any periodic waveform (whether it be visual or auditory)?

(A) alpha
(B) hertz
(C) pitch
(D) amplitude
(E) angle

198. How is an individual's inclusive fitness defined, in evolutionary terms?

(A) the number of years the individual lives
(B) the number of children an individual has
(C) the success of an individual in attracting a mate
(D) the number of copies of an individual's genes that remain in the population
(E) the number of mates an individual has

GO ON TO THE NEXT PAGE

199. What psychologist can be credited with shifting the behaviorist tradition away from a strict focus on overt behavior to a focus on knowledge and mental representations?

(A) Edward Thorndike
(B) B. F. Skinner
(C) John Watson
(D) Edward Tolman
(E) John Garcia

200. Portions of the cell membrane of a neuron that are specialized to allow particular atoms to diffuse across the membrane are called

(A) axons
(B) synapses
(C) nodes of Ranvier
(D) ion channels
(E) dendrites

201. A casino manager programs the slot machines so that they each pay out a large amount of money twenty times per day, apparently randomly, and regardless of how many times someone plays the machine. Someone who gets hooked on playing a machine at this casino is being reinforced on what schedule?

(A) variable interval
(B) variable ratio
(C) fixed interval
(D) fixed ratio
(E) random

202. All of the following statements about antipsychotic drugs are accurate *except*

(A) They reduce the symptoms of patients diagnosed with schizophrenia
(B) For schizophrenic patients they seem less effective than other approaches used alone
(C) Most improvement from drug treatment occurs in the first six months
(D) Symptoms such as hallucinations and delusions are reduced more quickly than flat affect
(E) They carry troublesome side effects resembling Parkinson's disease

GO ON TO THE NEXT PAGE

203. The National Institute of Mental Health conducted long, structured interviews with a representative sample of U.S. citizens. They wanted to discover, in part, how prevalent mental health problems were within the population. In the hundreds of questions that were asked, they discovered that _____ citizens had suffered or currently suffer a significant mental disorder within the past year.

(A) one in twenty-five
(B) one in fifteen
(C) one in twelve
(D) one in nine
(E) one in seven

204. A recent World Health Organization (WHO) study made a twenty-country comparison of mental disorder prevalence during the previous year. Ordering left to right from most-to-least prevalent, select the following accurate statement of WHO findings.

(A) Beijing, Belgium, Netherlands
(B) Japan, Germany, Mexico
(C) Spain, Lebanon, Colombia
(D) Nigeria, United States, Mexico
(E) United States, Ukraine, France

205. De Rougemont (a European social critic) was quoted as saying, "We are in the act of trying out—and failing miserably at it—one of the most pathological experiments that a civilized society has ever imagined, namely, the basing of marriage, which is lasting, upon romance which is a passing fancy." If we put this in the context of loving styles, which of the following would you expect to be most lasting?

(A) companionate
(B) erotic
(C) practical
(D) game playing
(E) narcissistic

GO ON TO THE NEXT PAGE

206. According to Rokeach, we have several levels of belief.

> Primitive: the most basic—one's identity, other unquestioned "givens"
>
> Self: both self-esteem and self-deprecation
>
> Authority: those figures to whom we look for examples and actions
>
> Peripheral: positions and actions we take based on authority examples
>
> Inconsequential: makes absolutely no difference one way or another

The advertiser's dilemma stems from the fact that the products they are selling are, for the most part, in the Inconsequential category. It doesn't matter which brand of toothpaste you buy, for example. What matters is that you use it. Given that dilemma, what do you suppose the advertiser will try to do?

  I.   Link the essential need for this product to Primitive levels of belief
  II. Link the essential need for this product to Self levels of belief
  III. Link the essential need for this product to Authority levels of belief

(A) I only
(B) II only
(C) III only
(D) I and II
(E) I, II, and III

207. What is the difference between affiliation and attraction?

  I.   There is no difference.
  II. Affiliation refers to people we "happen" to be with.
  III. Attraction refers to people we "choose" to be with.

(A) I only
(B) II only
(C) III only
(D) I and III
(E) II and III

208. Which of the following would you consider the most important variables determining whether a person in distress would receive help?

(A) the number of bystanders
(B) having seen a model of helping prior to encountering this person
(C) directness of request for help
(D) degree of hurry the would-be helper is in
(E) all of the above

GO ON TO THE NEXT PAGE

209. Mortimer has just heard the outcome of an event and says he knew all along that it would turn out this way. This is an example of

   (A) common sense
   (B) self-fulfilling prophecy
   (C) the hindsight effect
   (D) the Benson-Roscoe effect
   (E) the Purkinje effect

210. A dispositional view of human nature would be evident in which of the following?

   (A) "Only God could've passed that test!"
   (B) "Megan has charm that works wonders in her pharmaceutical company sales."
   (C) "Ali has a friendly smile."
   (D) "John is so narcissistic that he can't really see or care about the needs of others."
   (E) "If it rains tomorrow Jenn will go to the movies."

211. Festinger and Bem have differing views on the phenomenon Festinger termed *cognitive dissonance*. Where Festinger translates it as _____, Bem sees it as _____.

   (A) self-denial; self-enhancement
   (B) self-justification; self-perception
   (C) self-esteem; self-derogation
   (D) self-abasement; self-illusion
   (E) self-monitoring; self-indulgence

212. You're a teenager and you just did something that you're sure is going to bring down the wrath of God (as in parent) on you when you get home. You go in with fear and trembling. What kind of response from your parent would make it most likely that you will not do that "something" behavior again in the future?

   I.   an unexpectedly mild punishment
   II. a moderately harsh punishment
   III. a very harsh and painful punishment

   (A) I only
   (B) II only
   (C) III only
   (D) I or II
   (E) II or III

GO ON TO THE NEXT PAGE

213. In attribution terms, all of the following are correct *except*

   (A) We attribute our own faux pas (screw-ups) externally, and other people's internally.
   (B) When someone does something spectacular and then does poorly thereafter, we attribute it externally.
   (C) When someone speaks against one's own best interests, we attribute it internally.
   (D) When a nonprize-winning painting is attributed to a man or a woman, it is rated more favorably when attributed to a man.
   (E) When someone believes it's a just world and sees someone who is poor, that individual will make an internal attribution (e.g., that, being a just world, they must be lazy or have done something to deserve it.)

214. How does "foot-in-the-door" differ from "door-in-the-face"?

   I.   Foot-in-the-door is a lot less painful than door-in-the-face.
   II. Foot-in-the-door gets a small initial commitment.
   III. Door-in-the-face requests a large initial commitment.

   (A) I only
   (B) II only
   (C) III only
   (D) I and II
   (E) II and III

215. You went to London and had a marvelous time. Unfortunately, the National Express bus broke down on the way to Heathrow for your departure. You didn't get there in time to make your flight and were faced with spending the night and hoping for better luck tomorrow. As you queued at the nearest hotel, you heard the attendant tell the person in front of you that it would be 200 British pounds for the room (about $400 dollars). Now came your turn. The attendant must have sensed your plight. You were offered a room for 100 British pounds. You were quite relieved, even though it still dug deep into your remaining green pictures of the queen. In social psychology terms you just experienced the

   (A) Maxwell effect
   (B) convenience effect
   (C) contrast effect
   (D) cognitive dissonance effect
   (E) relativity effect

STOP

If there is still time remaining, you may review your answers.

ANSWER KEY
Practice Test 2

1.	E	37.	B	73.	E	109.	C	145.	E	181.	B
2.	C	38.	C	74.	E	110.	C	146.	D	182.	B
3.	D	39.	B	75.	A	111.	A	147.	A	183.	A
4.	B	40.	B	76.	D	112.	E	148.	C	184.	C
5.	A	41.	C	77.	E	113.	B	149.	B	185.	B
6.	C	42.	E	78.	B	114.	D	150.	A	186.	C
7.	E	43.	A	79.	D	115.	A	151.	C	187.	B
8.	B	44.	B	80.	A	116.	C	152.	E	188.	D
9.	C	45.	B	81.	C	117.	C	153.	B	189.	B
10.	D	46.	A	82.	B	118.	A	154.	E	190.	C
11.	B	47.	A	83.	D	119.	B	155.	C	191.	A
12.	C	48.	D	84.	A	120.	C	156.	A	192.	E
13.	D	49.	E	85.	A	121.	E	157.	C	193.	E
14.	B	50.	A	86.	E	122.	A	158.	E	194.	C
15.	D	51.	B	87.	A	123.	D	159.	E	195.	D
16.	A	52.	D	88.	A	124.	C	160.	A	196.	B
17.	D	53.	C	89.	C	125.	D	161.	C	197.	B
18.	B	54.	D	90.	E	126.	C	162.	C	198.	D
19.	E	55.	B	91.	B	127.	C	163.	B	199.	D
20.	B	56.	D	92.	B	128.	B	164.	D	200.	D
21.	A	57.	B	93.	C	129.	A	165.	A	201.	A
22.	E	58.	D	94.	C	130.	D	166.	A	202.	B
23.	D	59.	B	95.	C	131.	E	167.	B	203.	E
24.	C	60.	B	96.	B	132.	B	168.	D	204.	E
25.	B	61.	B	97.	A	133.	D	169.	D	205.	A
26.	D	62.	B	98.	C	134.	D	170.	C	206.	E
27.	A	63.	B	99.	B	135.	C	171.	A	207.	E
28.	E	64.	D	100.	A	136.	D	172.	B	208.	E
29.	D	65.	D	101.	D	137.	B	173.	B	209.	C
30.	B	66.	B	102.	A	138.	B	174.	B	210.	D
31.	C	67.	C	103.	C	139.	D	175.	D	211.	B
32.	C	68.	D	104.	E	140.	E	176.	B	212.	A
33.	E	69.	D	105.	B	141.	B	177.	B	213.	B
34.	C	70.	A	106.	C	142.	C	178.	C	214.	E
35.	C	71.	D	107.	C	143.	A	179.	D	215.	C
36.	E	72.	A	108.	E	144.	D	180.	C		

To score your second practice test, please compare the answers on your answer sheet with the answers below. Place a check mark next to questions you answered correctly. Place an "X" next to questions you answered incorrectly. Leave questions you did not answer blank.

ANSWER EXPLANATIONS

_____ 1. **(E)** Paivio argued that visual codes are used to store sensory information and concrete verbal information, whereas verbal codes are used to store abstract verbal information.

_____ 2. **(C)** A frequency table shows the number of students in each indicated range; for example, of the 200 students studied, 10 had a WISC score between 100 and 109 along with a DP score between 20 and 29.

_____ 3. **(D)** The data in this table indicate a positive relationship between IQ and divergent production, such that students in the 120–129 IQ range score higher on the divergent production test than do students in the 100–119 range.

_____ 4. **(B)** Interpretations of data obtained from standardized test instruments depend on the assumption that standard testing and scoring procedures were followed.

_____ 5. **(A)** The accident severed the connections between the frontal lobe of the cerebral cortex and the limbic system. This alerted scientists to the role of the limbic system in emotions and the moderating influence upon emotional expression exerted by the frontal lobe.

_____ 6. **(C)** Located in the hindbrain (just below the occipital lobe), the cerebellum plays an important role in motor coordination and timing.

_____ 7. **(E)** Loftus and her colleagues found that eyewitness testimony is prominently affected by all of the choices. If, for instance, you asked a witness how fast the white sports car was going when it *hit* the red sedan, you will get a very different speed estimate than if you ask how fast the white sports car was going when it *smashed* into the red sedan.

_____ 8. **(B)** A graphical depiction of the partitioning of a sentence into structural elements is referred to as a tree diagram. For example, a sentence branches into a noun phrase and a verb phrase, the verb phrase further branches into a verb and another noun phrase, and so on.

_____ 9. **(C)** Pitch is the auditory dimension determined by frequency (number of cycles per second).

_____ 10. **(D)** When a stationary spot of light in a darkened room is perceived as moving, the autokinetic effect has occurred.

_____ 11. **(B)** Alpha waves are associated with the relaxed wakeful state in the older child and the adult but do not appear to be present in the newborn. They become evident at approximately six months of age.

_____ 12. **(C)** Basing his conclusion on rigorous experimentation, Lashley stated that equipotentiality showed that different parts of the cortex are interchangeable in their roles in learning (a finding critical in cases of brain damage).

13. **(D)** Apraxia refers to a deficit in skilled (learned) actions or motor sequences. In Greek, *praxis* means work or act, and the prefix *a* means without.

14. **(B)** Gestalt psychologists have most prominently explored perceptual phenomena.

15. **(D)** Receiver-operating-characteristic (ROC) curves are plots of a perceiver's sensitivity, based on signal detection theory. It is a plot of hit against false alarms (saying "yes" when a target is present against saying "yes" when a target is absent) for an individual, as aspects of the procedure are changed.

16. **(A)** The actions of a decapitated animal (which includes removal of the pons and cerebellum!) indicate the complexity of the movements that are under the control of the spinal cord.

17. **(D)** Reciprocal innervation refers to a combination of antagonistic muscle movements, such as those present during walking. This was first described by René Descartes.

18. **(B)** Comparison of the sound waves reaching the two ears (incorporated with knowledge of their position on the head) is critical to determining sound directionality, which is why hearing must exist in both ears.

19. **(E)** The adrenal medulla is the center part of the adrenal gland (surrounded by the adrenal cortex). The adrenal medulla releases epinephrine (adrenalin) and the adrenal cortex releases corticosteroids.

20. **(B)** The pituitary gland is a pea-sized gland that is attached to the bottom of the hypothalamus. It secretes a large number of hormones, some of which function to stimulate other endocrine glands.

21. **(A)** Normal sexual behavior is largely under the control of the hypothalamus and the autonomic nervous system, so damage to the cerebral cortex has little to no effect.

22. **(E)** This quotation is one definition of species, one of the levels of taxonomic classification.

23. **(D)** The normal developmental age range during which a child could be expected to master clock-time concepts would be between five and six years.

24. **(C)** Reaction time decreases with age up to approximately thirty years, beginning a pattern of increase beyond this age.

25. **(B)** Brain stem transections in animals reveal that *organization* of intense emotional responses apparently occurs at a level above the midbrain. Rage reactions, for instance, become bits of disorganized responses.

26. **(D)** Tolman summarized Watson's definition of emotions in terms of stimuli and responses but, of course, took issue with the Watson definition.

27. **(A)** In trace conditioning, there is an interval between the offset of the CS and the onset of the UCS. In both delayed and simultaneous conditioning, the CS and UCS overlap in time, thus obviating the need to maintain the memory of the CS during learning.

_____ 28. **(E)** Although convergence is important for depth perception, it is not a pictorial (or stimulus) cue. It is an oculomotor cue that comes from kinesthetic sensations from the eye muscles about the orientation of the eyes.

_____ 29. **(D)** Sentences are made of phrases that are made of words that are made of morphemes that are made of phonemes.

_____ 30. **(B)** In his work with children, Bandura has found that observation of aggressive models can prompt aggressive behavior by the observer.

_____ 31. **(C)** A verbatim reading of test-taking instructions is indicative of standardization—the effort to be certain that each test taker has an equivalent testing situation.

_____ 32. **(C)** During the third through eighth week of pregnancy, a developing child would be described as being in the embryo stage.

_____ 33. **(E)** Developmental research has found evidence of a relationship between anxiety in the expectant mother and the incidence of crying behavior in the newborn.

_____ 34. **(C)** Hopi Indian children—strapped on their mothers' backs with no opportunity to practice walking skills—were found to walk as early as children who had such practice opportunity. The finding suggested that walking was primarily a function of maturation.

_____ 35. **(C)** Children from father-present home settings have the highest incidence of aggressive behavior—perhaps a function of modeling and paternal discipline.

_____ 36. **(E)** Given a choice among several stimuli, a newborn prefers pictures of the human face.

_____ 37. **(B)** The newborn demonstrates some irregularities in respiration.

_____ 38. **(C)** RSVP refers to a method of displaying information (often text) briefly in sequential order (e.g., during studies of sentence comprehension, when words appear one or two at a time, briefly, and are immediately replaced by the next word in the sentence).

_____ 39. **(B)** In operant conditioning, reinforcement increases the frequency of the response associated with it, and punishment decreases the frequency of the response associated with it.

_____ 40. **(B)** A schema is a general knowledge framework (or collection of facts) that bias our expectations about objects and events in order to help us interpret, organize, and remember those events.

_____ 41. **(C)** Correlation is related to predictability. One indication of this relationship is the predictive validity concept.

_____ 42. **(E)** Mean and standard deviation are the most common expressions of central tendency and variability, respectively.

_____ 43. **(A)** In developmental psychology, the first two years after birth are critical to self-concept formation.

_____ 44. **(B)** In the first three months after birth, a child can be expected to develop the capacity to raise its head to look at something.

_____ 45. **(B)** When stimuli similar to the original CS now elicit the CR, stimulus generalization has occurred.

_____ 46. **(A)** Jones's studies find early maturity advantageous among males.

_____ 47. **(A)** The period of the embryo spans the end of the second week to the end of the second month of pregnancy.

_____ 48. **(D)** Classical conditioning research has found a half-second interval between CS and UCS onset to be most effective.

_____ 49. **(E)** Cell mass differentiation into three distinct layers occurs during the embryonic period.

_____ 50. **(A)** Depth of processing theory describes the importance of the type of encoding for subsequent memory retrieval. For most types of retrieval, performance is enhanced if encoding focuses on meaning and relationships among stimuli compared to encoding focused on surface characteristics.

_____ 51. **(B)** Repetition priming is a measure of implicit memory. Explicit memory tests make reference to a prior learning episode, whereas implicit memory tests do not.

_____ 52. **(D)** Frenkel and Brunswik have found attitudes toward authority to be the single most important factor distinguishing prejudiced from tolerant adolescents.

_____ 53. **(C)** Moderate anxiety in a child may facilitate the learning of simple tasks but will prove detrimental to the learning of difficult tasks.

_____ 54. **(D)** Blood type is a singly determined genetic characteristic.

_____ 55. **(B)** A child's differentiation and consequent fear of strangers generally develops in the sixth-to-seventh month age range.

_____ 56. **(D)** Evidence for mental rotation and scanning with the "mind's eye" supports the idea that visual memories, or images, exist and are processed in ways similar to actual perceived objects.

_____ 57. **(B)** It would be essential for the two groups to be equivalent in motor ability. Otherwise, differences in performance would be meaningless.

_____ 58. **(D)** The child's access only to a mirror to monitor the tracing movements means that feedback is reversed from that which the child normally would receive through direct observation. Therefore, the child must reorient himself and move beyond familiar habits in eye-hand coordination.

_____ 59. **(B)** Group 1 tracing time per trial dropped much more rapidly across trials than tracing time in Group 2—a factor in support of spaced practice as more effective than massed practice in this experimental setting.

_____ 60. **(B)** The heights of kindergarten-aged children are positively correlated with comparative adult heights.

_____ 61. **(B)** Kendler's research suggests that single unit S-R cognitive mechanisms precede mediational processes in a child's conceptual development.

_____ 62. **(B)** In the newborn's second year, rate of growth is slower than in the first year.

_____ 63. **(B)** In the Babkin response, a child's mouth opens wide and its head turns to the midline.

_____ 64. **(D)** Tolman's work is associated with purposive behavior and place learning.

_____ 65. **(D)** In Piaget's classification system, the concrete operations period is the point during which the child learns language and the logic of classification.

_____ 66. **(B)** "Tailing off" to the right would indicate positive skew.

_____ 67. **(C)** Social deficits, communication difficulties, and repetitive, ritualistic behaviors are core symptoms for autism spectrum disorder.

_____ 68. **(D)** When earlier learning is interfered with by later learning, the direction is retroactive and the effect is inhibition.

_____ 69. **(D)** Stanley Milgram has developed the theory of "overload" and has outlined its implications for human behavior in the urban environment. Among those implications is a tendency not to speak to other persons on a city street nor to pick up trash or offer to help a pedestrian in distress. Each of these settings threatens to overload the individual's "system" and capacity to cope. To avoid such overload, the individual limits and restricts inputs.

_____ 70. **(A)** The greatest dissonance would be created by the one-dollar payment. It is the smallest amount of money available in this situation and gives a person the least external justification for telling a lie.

_____ 71. **(D)** The fifth personality trait, missing from this list, is agreeableness.

_____ 72. **(A)** Freud sees a giving-type relationship within the genital stage. At this point, sexual relationships have moved beyond the selfish narcissism characteristic of the phallic stage.

_____ 73. **(E)** Existentialism sees humans as free to make their own choices and, in effect, act as masters of their fates.

_____ 74. **(E)** Attitudes contain cognitive, emotional, and behavioral components. A stereotype component does not constitute a general characteristic of attitudes.

_____ 75. **(A)** Judging personality on the basis of facial expression is an example of physiognomy.

_____ 76. **(D)** Verbal comprehension can be expected to continue improving after age thirty-five while other abilities such as associative memory, spatial relations, and so on, begin gradual declines.

_____ 77. **(E)** When a general description is given—as in astrology—there is an individual tendency to apply the description to oneself. Hence, astrology thrives, as does the Barnum comment that "There's a sucker born every minute."

_____ 78. **(B)** Homans's anticipatory socialization refers to a person's adopting social mores characteristic of a higher social level—toward which that person aspires.

_____ 79. **(D)** McKinley and Hathaway developed the MMPI but had no involvement in the development of the 16-PF scale.

_____ 80. **(A)** Cattell, Eysenck, and Goldstein all espouse factor analytic approaches to the study of personality.

_____ 81. **(C)** The Strong-Campbell interest test makes occupational correlations, and the Kuder preference test puts responses in broad area categories.

_____ 82. **(B)** Persons committing a crime of passion are among those with the least likelihood of committing any subsequent offenses.

_____ 83. **(D)** Mortimer is demonstrating what Hollander calls independence. He wears red shirts when they are both "in" and not "in"—simply because he likes them. Conformity would change systematically in the direction of the "in" style, and anticonformity would change systematically against it.

_____ 84. **(A)** The technique being used was drawing heavily upon Brehm's theory of reactance. In this approach the change agent (salesperson in our example) asserts what the person (e.g., retailer) already agrees with, but the assertion is made in absolute, unqualified-statement terms. Induced to disagree mildly with the unqualified statements, the person is speaking against her own attitude and is weakening support for it. The change agent will then proceed to use the same approach with more strongly held attitudes in the area where change is being sought.

_____ 85. **(A)** The theory underlying this approach to attitude change is cognitive dissonance. In this instance, people who dislike beef liver are being asked to design and deliver a talk on its prominent advantages. Their talk preparation and the talk itself are very much in contrast with their own beliefs about beef liver. Festinger's theory of cognitive dissonance would indicate that their attitude will move in the direction of their behavior. The people who prepare and deliver the talks will themselves develop a more favorable attitude toward beef liver.

_____ 86. **(E)** Prefrontal lobotomy—excision or removal of parts of the prefrontal lobes in severe cases of mental disturbance—has long since become extinct in therapeutic practice.

_____ 87. **(A)** Adler replaced Freud's libido concept with his own concept of superiority striving.

_____ 88. **(A)** Kinesics is the study of nonverbal communication within body movements.

_____ 89. **(C)** Jung viewed archetypes as innate concepts being passed from generation to generation within a species. He placed the infant's natural response to mother closeness in this category.

_____ 90. **(E)** Bem found that persons sex-typed on the Bem Sex Role Inventory tended to recall in gender-clusters rather than randomly when recalling a list of words (the list having equal numbers of gender neutral, masculine, and feminine words). Persons androgynous on the Inventory did not recall words in gender-clusters.

_____ 91. **(B)** Among these personality approaches, trait theory is supported by the largest body of research evidence.

_____ 92. **(B)** In a nonzero sum game, both participants may win or lose simultaneously.

_____ 93. **(C)** Festinger formulated the theory of cognitive dissonance.

_____ 94. **(C)** Borderline disorder, a personality disorder, is characterized by difficulty forming stable relationships.

_____ 95. **(C)** People with paranoid delusions believe that others intend to harm them.

_____ 96. **(B)** Pyramidal cells have a triangular-shaped soma, a long axon, and a large arbor of dendrites that branch off a main "trunk" called an apical dendrite. In the cerebral cortex, 80 percent of the neurons are pyramidal cells, arranged so that the apical dendrite points toward the outer surface of the cortex. They release glutamate, an excitatory neurotransmitter.

_____ 97. **(A)** Primary auditory cortex is located in the most superior portion of the temporal lobe.

_____ 98. **(C)** Eysenck believes introverts have greater autonomic reactivity than extroverts.

_____ 99. **(B)** In contrast to tranquilizers, sedatives have drowsiness-inducing characteristics.

_____ 100. **(A)** A syllogism (two premises followed by a conclusion) is a form of deductive reasoning.

_____ 101. **(D)** The phonological loop rehearses verbal (and other auditory) information by repeating it over and over again (looping it) in the "inner voice." The phonological loop has a limited capacity, defined by the amount of time it takes to cycle through the materials, and so more monosyllabic words can be looped than polysyllabic words.

_____ 102. **(A)** Fear relates to realistic environmental danger; anxiety is, in effect, unrealistic fear.

_____ 103. **(C)** Psychotomimetic drugs (hallucinogens) resemble schizophrenic-type reactions.

_____ 104. **(E)** Repression, fantasy, regression, and continual wandering are among withdrawal reactions, but paranoia is not.

_____ 105. **(B)** An inhibitory post-synaptic potential (IPSP) occurs when a neurotransmitter that binds to the post-synaptic neuron causes the membrane potential to move away from its excitation threshold, thus inhibiting it from firing.

_____ 106. **(C)** Current estimates place the free-running human circadian rhythm at just over twenty-four hours, with very little variability across healthy individuals.

_____ 107. **(C)** The schizophrenic exhibits withdrawal from interpersonal relationships.

_____ 108. **(E)** The reduced-reinforcement model of depression (Lewinsohn and others) indicates that depression is related to a reduction of positive reinforcement in one's environment. Sympathy becomes a reinforcement for the depression itself.

_____ 109. **(C)** The English language has approximately forty different sound-units; because we use an alphabet with only twenty-six characters, some letters correspond to more than one phoneme (e.g., _g_)

_____ 110. **(C)** The word-stem-completion task is an implicit memory test. Performance on this task measures nondeclarative memory processes and is unaltered in patients who have anterograde amnesia.

_____ 111. **(A)** Range is the simplest measure of variability to calculate: maximum minus minimum.

_____ 112. **(E)** Agoraphobia is a neurotic fear of open places.

_____ 113. **(B)** The all-or-none law describes the fact that a neuron, when it reaches its excitation threshold, will produce an action potential of fixed amplitude regardless of the magnitude of stimulation. Neurons signal changes in intensity of stimulation with increased frequency, and not amplitude, of responding.

_____ 114. **(D)** Muscarine, a natural compound found in some mushrooms, acts on certain types of cholinergic receptors.

_____ 115. **(A)** A pyromaniac has an irresistible impulse to set fires.

_____ 116. **(C)** The Osgood Semantic Differential Scale is used primarily in attitude measurement. It is not an instrument for clinical assessment.

_____ 117. **(C)** The basal ganglia and cerebellum are important for procedural memory, such as motor skill learning, visual pattern learning, and so on.

_____ 118. **(A)** Transference and resistance are terms commonly used within psychoanalysis.

_____ 119. **(B)** Though each score in the distribution has been changed through the addition of a constant (the number 7), the variability of the distribution itself is unchanged. Therefore, the standard deviation remains unchanged from its original value.

_____ 120. **(C)** The term _prosody_ refers to the stress or rhythm of speech. Variations in prosody can indicate emotion (e.g., anger) or structure (e.g., questions).

_____ 121. **(E)** Mainlining heroin—injecting into a vein—leads to prominent and rapid increase in dosages and intense, excruciating pain and discomfort upon withdrawal.

_____ 122. **(A)** Antipsychotic agents—chlorpromazine, haloperidol, clozapine, resperidol—have been shown to be effective in cases of schizophrenia. They are believed to suppress the transmission efficiency of the neurotransmitter called dopamine.

_____ 123. **(D)** An experimental design incorporates all aspects of this description.

_____ 124. **(C)** Within a specific problem area, a theory carries the function of explaining and relating observed facts.

_____ 125. **(D)** Of the forms of sexual deviation listed, pedophilia (in which an adult desires or engages in sexual relations with a child) is the most difficult to treat.

_____ 126. **(C)** Bipolar disorder features manic episodes that might be separated by periods of depression.

_____ 127. **(C)** It could be suggested that Michelangelo's frustrated desire for closeness with his mother was expressed in painting. This would be an example of sublimation—redirection of an unacceptable or ungratified impulse into a higher cultural contribution.

_____ 128. **(B)** Bettelheim worked with schizophrenic children and concentrated much effort on study and analysis of their drawings.

_____ 129. **(A)** Norepinephrine and serotonin are the two neurotransmitters credited with a central role in affective disorders such as depression. Several antidepressant drugs facilitate the activity of these neurotransmitters, most notably the "second generation" serotonin reuptake blockers.

_____ 130. **(D)** The score of 130 is two standard deviations above the mean—a point beyond which only about 2 percent of the scores in a distribution will occur.

_____ 131. **(E)** The experiment has a three-factor design—sex, age, hair color.

_____ 132. **(B)** A three-factor factorial design can be used if only one measure (score) is to be analyzed for each subject. If trials were involved, for instance, a four-factor mixed design with repeated measures on one factor would be needed.

_____ 133. **(D)** Freud wrote *The Psychopathology of Everyday Life* to describe the manner in which apparent accidents, slips of the tongue, and the like betray id impulses.

_____ 134. **(D)** Unfortunate stereotyping became associated with the terms *moron*, *imbecile*, and *idiot*, prompting a change to the educable-trainable-nontrainable categories.

_____ 135. **(C)** Human engineering control principles indicate that a system is best in which the operation of the controls imposes optimal strain on the operator consistent with the required degree of accuracy. Optimal strain is not to be confused with painful stress; rather it involves the degree of stimulation necessary for alertness and accuracy.

_____ 136. **(D)** Single-subject researchers utilize a series of graphs to demonstrate the outcome of their treatment condition(s).

_____ 137. **(B)** The fact that the judges' rankings are completely reversed is indicative of a strong (in this case, perfect) negative correlation.

_____ 138. **(B)** The example utilizes rank order and therefore would call upon the Spearman Rank-Order Correlation method for analysis.

_____ 139. **(D)** This correlation coefficient would be –1.0—a perfect negative correlation.

_____ 140. **(E)** The human factor term *shape coding* applies to knob appearance and contour—enabling the operator to locate the correct knob by feel, if necessary.

_____ 141. **(B)** The term *loci* refers to physical locations in a familiar place. When using the method of loci, you imagine placing each to-be-remembered item in one of these locations, and you form a vivid image of that scene. Then, to recall, you simply take a mental walk and retrieve all of the objects.

_____ 142. **(C)** Presenting the "bare bones" of a managerial situation and adding that additional information can only be obtained by asking questions is an example of the incident process-training method in managerial training techniques.

_____ 143. **(A)** A company screening test for executive trainees that involved handling, sorting, and dealing with an array of items in a sample executive in-basket would be an aptitude test.

_____ 144. **(D)** A test–retest, repeated-measures design contains impressive subject variability control because the subjects, in effect, act as their own controls. This relieves the experimenter of the problem, or possibility, that the subjects' backgrounds may somehow contribute to any differences found.

_____ 145. **(E)** If there are two (or more) scores that are tied for most-frequent among a set of scores, the distribution is bimodal (or multi-modal). Under no scenario can a distribution have more than one mean, median, standard deviation, or variance.

_____ 146. **(D)** Induced motion refers to the illusory perception of movement of a stationary object (if the background is moving), but it is not a Gestalt law of organization.

_____ 147. **(A)** Of the central tendency measures, the mean moves most noticeably in the direction of the skew.

_____ 148. **(C)** It appears that there is a substantial genetic influence on temperament and personality; for example, twin studies have found heritability estimates for the Big Five personality traits that range from 40% to 60%.

_____ 149. **(B)** To determine whether a significant difference in weight exists between two randomly selected groups of eighteen-year-olds, a person would use the _t_-test for independent means.

_____ 150. **(A)** Matched pairing has occurred in the initial grouping—an indication that the design will utilize a paired _t_-test for related measures.

_____ 151. **(C)** Comparison with the national average of the weight found in the specific groups of eighteen-year-old boys would utilize the one-sample _t_-test. In this instance, the national average constitutes the population mean.

_____ 152. **(E)** In all of these groups, the left hemisphere is dominant for language in most people. Approximately 60 percent of lefties (compared to 95 percent of right-handed people) are left-hemisphere-dominant for language.

_____ 153. **(B)** Researchers have found that rest periods enhance performance on vigilance tasks.

_____ 154. **(E)** One of the most prominent researchers in the area of leadership, Fiedler has used the Least Preferred Coworker technique to identify task-centered and people-centered leaders.

_____ 155. **(C)** Synaptic vesicles in the axon terminal contain neurotransmitters that are released into the synaptic cleft when an action potential reaches the terminal.

_____ 156. **(A)** The survey perspective refers to a representation of the environment from an arial view. The route perspective refers to a ground-level representation of a path. Both of these perspectives can be used to learn about a new spatial environment, although differences in learning situations and in personal preferences have been reported.

_____ 157. **(C)** McLuhan's framework classifies television as a cool medium—not information intensive, a characteristic required for a hot medium.

_____ 158. **(E)** Bayes's theorem describes a method for calculating the likelihood of a hypothesis, based on a set of facts (prior beliefs and new information). As such, it is an example of inductive reasoning.

_____ 159. **(E)** The field of evolutionary psychology is based on the assumption that the principles of evolution by natural selection can and do explain many aspects of human behavior, such as cooperation, jealousy, and so on.

_____ 160. **(A)** The sympathetic and parasympathetic systems have reciprocal (or opposing) effects on behavior; the sympathetic system prepares the body for action and inhibits "normal" activities (such as digestion and sex), whereas the parasympathetic system returns the body to a resting state after the action has been completed.

_____ 161. **(C)** Sleep terrors and sleepwalking are associated with Stages 3 and 4 (deep sleep); in fact, sleepwalking would be impossible during normal REM sleep, due to the loss of muscle tone.

_____ 162. **(C)** Mental practice has positive effects on learning and performance (even in novices who were just taught a simple piano exercise), although the effects are not as great as the effects of physical practice.

_____ 163. **(B)** All of the above diseases are associated with characteristic neural irregularities, but amyloid plaques observed at autopsy are the hallmark feature of Alzheimer's disease.

_____ 164. **(D)** In multi-store memory models (such as the Atkinson-Shiffrin model), information is initially stored in a sensory register, which has a very large capacity but a very brief duration. Information in the sensory register that is attended to is transferred to the limited-capacity short-term store.

_____ 165. **(A)** Whorf proposed that the language one learns to speak determines how one thinks.

_____ 166. **(A)** René Descartes is credited with drawing the first analogy of the mind as machine, although he allowed for a distinct nonmechanic soul in humans; the other choices are all philosophers who have influenced psychological theorizing in areas of perception, language, memory, and decision-making.

_____ 167. **(B)** Plasticity refers to the ability of the nervous system to change, or more generally, of any ability to change as a result of experience.

_____ 168. **(D)** Many social species form dominance hierarchies, which determine who has access to resources, mates, and territories; the alpha male is at the top of such a group hierarchy.

_____ 169. **(D)** Remembering to remember something in the future (e.g., take a pill twice a day) is one type of memory that may be particularly vulnerable to the effects of normal aging.

_____ 170. **(C)** A false alarm occurs when a subject indicates that a signal is present when it is not; in the case of an intrusion error, the subject indicates that an event occurred when it did not.

_____ 171. **(A)** A drug that inhibits the reuptake of a neurotransmitter by the presynaptic neuron will cause an increase of the neurotransmitter in the synaptic cleft. This increase in the availability of the neurotransmitter would be classified as an agonist.

_____ 172. **(B)** Keena's association of aversive dental procedures with her dentist is an example of a conditioned response, and the further association of the receptionist with the dentist (and thus with the dental procedures) is an example of second- (or higher-) order conditioning.

_____ 173. **(B)** George Miller used the phrase "magical number seven" to refer to the hypothesized capacity of the short-term memory (specifically, seven plus or minus two).

_____ 174. **(B)** Semantic priming is a tool for studying the network of concepts and their relations.

_____ 175. **(D)** This is the key difference between inductive and deductive reasoning.

_____ 176. **(B)** Belongingness refers to the fact the some stimuli seem to belong together (such as tastes with illness, in rats), and are thus easily associated in conditioning, whereas others are not. These patterns of belongingness are thought to be a hard-wired evolutionary adaptation.

_____ 177. **(B)** Saccadic eye movements are quick, simultaneous jumps in eye position; saccades occur when someone makes a spontaneous eye movement around a scene, whereas smooth eye movements are observed when someone tracks a moving object.

_____ 178. **(C)** Tinbergen's fixed-action patterns (e.g., a frog's tongue flick when catching flies) are instinctive (i.e., not learned) action sequences exhibited by all same-sex members of a species. They are elicited by simple, specific external stimuli known as sign or releasing stimuli.

_____ 179. **(D)** The analogical hypothesis predicts that a person holds a mental representation of a sentence that is like a picture of it. When participants see an object (e.g., cat) that _matches_ their stored image (that is, a crouching cat), they are quicker to respond to it than if the object (the cat) matches than does not (one that is lounging).

_____ 180. **(C)** Given that the difference between groups was less than a tenth of a second (70 ms), the mental processes involved are happening outside of conscious awareness. Results indicate the importance of using techniques like this, which are capable of detecting very small differences.

_____ 181. **(B)** It was important to know if participants were answering both as fast as they could and as accurately as they could. Without an analysis of percentage correct, there would be no way to know if participants' responses were as per task instructions, thus calling into question any interpretation of the data. In addition, sometimes manipulations have opposite effects on speed and accuracy, which indicates a strategic tradeoff rather than a change in ability.

_____ 182. **(B)** An algorithm is guaranteed to solve a problem (if there is a solution) but may be very time-consuming; a heuristic is a shortcut that will often work but will occasionally fail to find the right solution.

_____ 183. **(A)** In Mandarin, two words with the same phoneme sequence but different tones (or pitch) can mean entirely different things.

_____ 184. **(C)** Hermann Ebbinghaus first characterized the exponential nature of the forgetting curve.

_____ 185. **(B)** The Wada test is administered prior to neurosurgery, in order to determine which cognitive functions are lateralized to which cerebral hemisphere. In the test, a barbiturate is injected to one cerebral artery at a time, which causes a temporary sedation of only that hemisphere; while the barbiturate is active, the cognitive effects are assessed.

_____ 186. **(C)** A polysomnogram (also called a sleep test) includes recordings of electrical activity (measured on the scalp via electroencephalography), body movements, air flow, heart rate, and eye movements. These measurements are useful in assessing a variety of sleep disorders.

_____ 187. **(B)** According to definitional theories, the meaning of each word or concept is given by a set of features that are essential for membership in that word class. For example, a square is a (1) polygon with (2) four sides of equal length and (3) four equal angles.

_____ 188. **(D)** Fodor has famously pointed out that concepts have compositionality but prototypes, as in this example, do not.

_____ 189. **(B)** Umami is the name given to the newly discovered taste receptors, which are sensitive to glutamate found in meats, cheeses, mushrooms, and anchovies. It is translated in English as *savory*.

_____ 190. **(C)** These (and other features) are all characteristics of putative mental modules; much of cognitive science research is directed at describing the extent to which cognitive systems are or are not modular.

_____ 191. **(A)** The representativeness heuristic is used when making inferences about category membership based on similarity alone: Professional basketball players are tall; the man is tall; therefore, he must be a professional basketball player.

_____ 192. **(E)** Max is neglecting to consider the base rate of being a professional basketball player in the general population: There are very few professional basketball players in the world (and there are lots of really tall people). Even though the person who passed Max was tall, it is still very unlikely that he is a professional basketball player given the base rate of this occupation.

_____ 193. **(E)** Did you pick "negative reinforcement"? Reinforcement causes a behavior to occur more often, not less often, so this is an example of punishment (specifically, negative punishment).

_____ 194. **(C)** Nodes of Ranvier are the gaps between segments of myelin on an axon.

_____ 195. **(D)** Long-term potentiation describes the synaptic changes that occur between two neurons that are stimulated at the same time; for a period following this correlated stimulation, the synapse is said to be "stronger" (i.e., one neuron can more readily excite the other). This is thought to be a neural mechanism of associative learning.

_____ 196. **(B)** Helmholtz proposed that the only way perception could succeed with such impoverished sensory input was if an observer were using prior experience to reason (unconsciously) about the interpretation of a stimulus. The other answers define, in order, appraisal, availability heuristic, confabulation, and blindsight.

_____ 197. **(B)** Frequency is reported in hertz units (Hz); a waveform with a frequency of 5 Hz has five complete oscillations per second.

_____ 198. **(D)** In a view popularized by Richard Dawkins in his book _The Selfish Gene_, evolution acts on genes, not individuals. Fitness, then, does not depend solely on the individual's reproductive success but on the reproductive success of all those who share its genes.

_____ 199. **(D)** Tolman claimed that learning is not a change in behavior but a change in knowledge; latent learning—whereby an animal does not exhibit learning until a later situation—is an example of Tolman's claim.

_____ 200. **(D)** The neuronal membrane contains ion channels, which selectively allow atoms, such as sodium or potassium ions, to pass between the extracellular and intraceullular spaces; the flow of ions through these channels creates both the resting and the action potentials.

_____ 201. **(A)** Interval scales are defined by passage of time, not by number of responses, and in this case, the interval between each reward is variable.

_____ 202. **(B)** Drug treatment has been more effective for schizophrenic patients than other approaches used alone.

_____ 203. **(E)** When the National Institute of Mental Health conducted their extensive interviews, they discovered that one in seven citizens had suffered or currently suffered a significant mental disorder within the past year.

_____ 204. **(E)** Among the twenty countries surveyed, the World Health Organization found mental disorder prevalence to be highest in the United States, notably higher than Ukraine, which was, in turn, notably higher than France.

_____ 205. **(A)** Companionate or friendship love can be expected to be the most enduring. Passionate love and early infatuation cools over time.

_____ 206. **(E)** Faced with the dilemma that for most products it doesn't matter which brand a consumer buys—thereby placing the advertiser in the position of promoting their brand among many in this inconsequential setting—the advertiser tries to link their product to higher levels in the belief spectrum. Rarely can they link to the Primitive level, as London Fog did with a duck wearing a raincoat, but many linkages are made to the Self level (e.g., "Raise your hand if you're SURE!").

_____ 207. **(E)** Affiliation refers to the people we "happen" to be with (in elevators, in professional groups, in college classes, for example). Attraction refers to people we "choose" to be with (the ones to whom we send flowers and Valentines).

_____ 208. **(E)** All of the variables listed have been found central and critical in determining whether a person in distress would receive help. We might expect a model, the directness of request, and how much of a hurry the would-be helper is in to be central. The most surprising one is the number of bystanders. We've always felt more secure in public when there were more people around. Truth is, we are most likely to receive help if only one person is around.

_____ 209. **(C)** Good ol' Mortimer! He knew all along that the event was going to turn out this way. We're all past masters of the hindsight effect.

_____ 210. **(D)** A dispositional view of human nature makes internal-attribution-type judgments about a person or group of people. Saying that "John is so narcissistic that he can't really see or care about the needs of others" hits the dispositional-view-target pretty squarely.

_____ 211. **(B)** Festinger and Bem differ markedly in their views about the phenomenon Festinger termed _cognitive dissonance_. For Festinger it meant a matter of internal self-justification when there was no external justification upon which to draw (like being paid a goodly sum of money to do it). For Bem, it's more a matter of self-perception—the person observes his behavior and infers his attitudes from this behavior, with no experience of conflict. That's Darryl Bem, by the way. Sandra Bem is well known for her androgeny scale.

_____ 212. **(A)** That the wrath of a parent didn't descend on you after you'd done something you considered pretty egregious increases the likelihood that you will not do that "something" again in the future. That's assuming, of course, that you don't belong to the Bloods or a rival gang.

_____ 213. **(B)** When someone does something spectacular and then does poorly thereafter, we attribute it internally. A former baseball pitcher for the Detroit Tigers experienced it vividly. He had a thirty-win season his first year with the Tigers and it was all downhill from there. Commentators and the press got on him saying things like "McLain has a bad attitude," "McLain's lazy," and so on. Beware when you ace that first test in a class! If you slide downward the next round, your professor will lower spectacles and have a word with you.

_____ 214. **(E)** Though a foot-in-the-door may, indeed, be a lot less painful than a door-in-the-face, it here means getting a small initial commitment with designs to return with a whopper of a request later compared with knockin' the socks off with an initial request and then ramping down to something much smaller. For example, the door-in-the-face letter might be a charity asking you for a $200 donation. After you pick yourself up off the floor they then ask whether you could give $25. Ah, relief! Sure!

_____ 215. **(C)** The contrast effect has some resemblance to the door-in-the-face. The Brits are marvelous at queuing (standing in line to wait their turn). Imagine you're standing in line at a UK hotel hoping to get a room. The person just ahead of you has just been told his room will be 200 British pounds (somewhere in the vicinity of $400). When it comes to your turn you're told your room will be 100 British pounds. Though that's still quite a bit of green stuff, you feel quite relieved.

EVALUATING YOUR PROGRESS

Before proceeding, make sure you have used your answer sheet to mark each question on the explanation pages with a check mark for correct, an X for incorrect, and a blank for didn't answer.

Follow the same methods for scoring your test as you did for Practice Test 1. We recommend that you try one of three ways to proceed:

- If you don't mind flipping pages, simply refer to your marks on the previous explanation pages as you fill out the chart below.
- If you DO mind flipping pages, you can use a copier to make copies of the explanation pages to which you can easily refer as you fill out the chart below.
- If neither of these alternatives works for you, you can transfer your check marks and X's to your answer sheet, and refer to those marks as you fill out the chart below.

Learning (12)	Language (6)	Memory (13)	Thinking (12)
_____ 27.	_____ 29.	_____ 1.	_____ 8.
_____ 30.	_____ 109.	_____ 7.	_____ 38.
_____ 39.	_____ 120.	_____ 40.	_____ 56.
_____ 45.	_____ 165.	_____ 50.	_____ 100.
_____ 48.	_____ 183.	_____ 51.	_____ 156.
_____ 64.	_____ 187.	_____ 68.	_____ 162.
_____ 172.	_____ Total Correct (C)	_____ 101.	_____ 174.
_____ 176.	_____ Total Incorrect (I)	_____ 110.	_____ 175.
_____ 178.	_____ Total Blank	_____ 141.	_____ 182.
_____ 193.	C – (I/4) = _____	_____ 164.	_____ 188.
_____ 201.		_____ 169.	_____ 190.
_____ 212.		_____ 173.	_____ 209.
_____ Total Correct (C)		_____ 184.	_____ Total Correct (C)
_____ Total Incorrect (I)		_____ Total Correct (C)	_____ Total Incorrect (I)
_____ Total Blank		_____ Total Incorrect (I)	_____ Total Blank
C – (I/4) = _____		_____ Total Blank	C – (I/4) = _____
		C – (I/4) = _____	

Sensation/ Perception (13)	Physiological/ Behavioral Neuroscience (33)	Clinical/ Abnormal (20)	Life Span Development (21)
____ 9.	____ 5.	____ 53.	____ 11.
____ 10.	____ 6.	____ 67.	____ 23.
____ 14.	____ 13.	____ 82.	____ 24.
____ 15.	____ 16.	____ 94.	____ 32.
____ 18.	____ 17.	____ 95.	____ 33.
____ 28.	____ 19.	____ 102.	____ 34.
____ 146.	____ 20.	____ 103.	____ 35.
____ 153.	____ 21.	____ 107.	____ 36.
____ 170.	____ 22.	____ 108.	____ 37.
____ 177.	____ 25.	____ 112.	____ 43.
____ 189.	____ 54.	____ 115.	____ 44.
____ 196.	____ 96.	____ 116.	____ 46.
____ 197	____ 99.	____ 122.	____ 47.
____ Total Correct (C)	____ 104.	____ 125.	____ 49.
____ Total Incorrect (I)	____ 105.	____ 128.	____ 55.
____ Total Blank	____ 106.	____ 129.	____ 60.
	____ 113.	____ 133.	____ 61.
C – (I/4) = ____	____ 114.	____ 202.	____ 62.
	____ 117.	____ 203.	____ 63.
	____ 121.	____ 204.	____ 65.
	____ 152.	____ Total Correct (C)	____ 76.
	____ 155.	____ Total Incorrect (I)	____ Total Correct (C)
	____ 159.	____ Total Blank	____ Total Incorrect (I)
	____ 160.	C – (I/4) = ____	____ Total Blank
	____ 161.		C – (I/4) = ____
	____ 163.		
	____ 171.		
	____ 105.		
	____ 186.		
	____ 194.		
	____ 195.		
	____ 198.		
	____ 200.		
	____ Total Correct (C)		
	____ Total Incorrect (I)		
	____ Total Blank		
	C – (I/4) = ____		

Personality (14)	Social (25)	General/Applied (12)	Methods/Measurement (32)
___ 71.	___ 52.	___ 12.	___ 2.
___ 72.	___ 69.	___ 26.	___ 3.
___ 73.	___ 70.	___ 81.	___ 4.
___ 75.	___ 74.	___ 86.	___ 31.
___ 77.	___ 78.	___ 91.	___ 41.
___ 79.	___ 83.	___ 134.	___ 42.
___ 80.	___ 84.	___ 135.	___ 57.
___ 87.	___ 85.	___ 140.	___ 58.
___ 89.	___ 88.	___ 142.	___ 59.
___ 91.	___ 90.	___ 154.	___ 66.
___ 98.	___ 92.	___ 167.	___ 111.
___ 118.	___ 93.	___ 199.	___ 119.
___ 127.	___ 157.	___ Total Correct (C)	___ 123.
___ 148.	___ 168.	___ Total Incorrect (I)	___ 124.
___ Total Correct (C)	___ 191.	___ Total Blank	___ 130.
___ Total Incorrect (I)	___ 192.	C – (I/4) = ___	___ 131.
___ Total Blank	___ 205.		___ 132.
C – (I/4) = ___	___ 206.		___ 136.
	___ 207.		___ 137.
	___ 208.		___ 138.
	___ 210.		___ 139.
	___ 211.		___ 143.
	___ 213.		___ 144.
	___ 214.		___ 145.
	___ 215.		___ 147.
	___ Total Correct (C)		___ 149.
	___ Total Incorrect (I)		___ 150.
	___ Total Blank		___ 151.
	C – (I/4) = ___		___ 158.
			___ 179.
			___ 180.
			___ 181.
			___ Total Correct (C)
			___ Total Incorrect (I)
			___ Total Blank
			C – (I/4) = ___

Your next step is to transfer your totals above for each area into this chart:

	Number Correct (C)	Number Incorrect (I)	Number Blank	C-(I/4)	Maximum Possible	Your Percentage: Divide C-(I/4) by the Maximum Possible
Learning					12	
Language					6	
Memory					13	
Thinking					12	
Sensation Perception					13	
Physio/BN					33	
Clinical/ Abnormal					20	
Life Span					21	
Personality					14	
Social					25	
General					12	
Methods					32	

How did you do this time? Are you able to identify areas that need more work? If so, head back into the review section and use your textbooks and Web resources to brush up on remaining problem areas. When you feel confident, proceed to the next and last practice test.

ANSWER SHEET
Practice Test 3

1. Ⓐ Ⓑ Ⓒ Ⓓ Ⓔ	31. Ⓐ Ⓑ Ⓒ Ⓓ Ⓔ	61. Ⓐ Ⓑ Ⓒ Ⓓ Ⓔ	91. Ⓐ Ⓑ Ⓒ Ⓓ Ⓔ
2. Ⓐ Ⓑ Ⓒ Ⓓ Ⓔ	32. Ⓐ Ⓑ Ⓒ Ⓓ Ⓔ	62. Ⓐ Ⓑ Ⓒ Ⓓ Ⓔ	92. Ⓐ Ⓑ Ⓒ Ⓓ Ⓔ
3. Ⓐ Ⓑ Ⓒ Ⓓ Ⓔ	33. Ⓐ Ⓑ Ⓒ Ⓓ Ⓔ	63. Ⓐ Ⓑ Ⓒ Ⓓ Ⓔ	93. Ⓐ Ⓑ Ⓒ Ⓓ Ⓔ
4. Ⓐ Ⓑ Ⓒ Ⓓ Ⓔ	34. Ⓐ Ⓑ Ⓒ Ⓓ Ⓔ	64. Ⓐ Ⓑ Ⓒ Ⓓ Ⓔ	94. Ⓐ Ⓑ Ⓒ Ⓓ Ⓔ
5. Ⓐ Ⓑ Ⓒ Ⓓ Ⓔ	35. Ⓐ Ⓑ Ⓒ Ⓓ Ⓔ	65. Ⓐ Ⓑ Ⓒ Ⓓ Ⓔ	95. Ⓐ Ⓑ Ⓒ Ⓓ Ⓔ
6. Ⓐ Ⓑ Ⓒ Ⓓ Ⓔ	36. Ⓐ Ⓑ Ⓒ Ⓓ Ⓔ	66. Ⓐ Ⓑ Ⓒ Ⓓ Ⓔ	96. Ⓐ Ⓑ Ⓒ Ⓓ Ⓔ
7. Ⓐ Ⓑ Ⓒ Ⓓ Ⓔ	37. Ⓐ Ⓑ Ⓒ Ⓓ Ⓔ	67. Ⓐ Ⓑ Ⓒ Ⓓ Ⓔ	97. Ⓐ Ⓑ Ⓒ Ⓓ Ⓔ
8. Ⓐ Ⓑ Ⓒ Ⓓ Ⓔ	38. Ⓐ Ⓑ Ⓒ Ⓓ Ⓔ	68. Ⓐ Ⓑ Ⓒ Ⓓ Ⓔ	98. Ⓐ Ⓑ Ⓒ Ⓓ Ⓔ
9. Ⓐ Ⓑ Ⓒ Ⓓ Ⓔ	39. Ⓐ Ⓑ Ⓒ Ⓓ Ⓔ	69. Ⓐ Ⓑ Ⓒ Ⓓ Ⓔ	99. Ⓐ Ⓑ Ⓒ Ⓓ Ⓔ
10. Ⓐ Ⓑ Ⓒ Ⓓ Ⓔ	40. Ⓐ Ⓑ Ⓒ Ⓓ Ⓔ	70. Ⓐ Ⓑ Ⓒ Ⓓ Ⓔ	100. Ⓐ Ⓑ Ⓒ Ⓓ Ⓔ
11. Ⓐ Ⓑ Ⓒ Ⓓ Ⓔ	41. Ⓐ Ⓑ Ⓒ Ⓓ Ⓔ	71. Ⓐ Ⓑ Ⓒ Ⓓ Ⓔ	101. Ⓐ Ⓑ Ⓒ Ⓓ Ⓔ
12. Ⓐ Ⓑ Ⓒ Ⓓ Ⓔ	42. Ⓐ Ⓑ Ⓒ Ⓓ Ⓔ	72. Ⓐ Ⓑ Ⓒ Ⓓ Ⓔ	102. Ⓐ Ⓑ Ⓒ Ⓓ Ⓔ
13. Ⓐ Ⓑ Ⓒ Ⓓ Ⓔ	43. Ⓐ Ⓑ Ⓒ Ⓓ Ⓔ	73. Ⓐ Ⓑ Ⓒ Ⓓ Ⓔ	103. Ⓐ Ⓑ Ⓒ Ⓓ Ⓔ
14. Ⓐ Ⓑ Ⓒ Ⓓ Ⓔ	44. Ⓐ Ⓑ Ⓒ Ⓓ Ⓔ	74. Ⓐ Ⓑ Ⓒ Ⓓ Ⓔ	104. Ⓐ Ⓑ Ⓒ Ⓓ Ⓔ
15. Ⓐ Ⓑ Ⓒ Ⓓ Ⓔ	45. Ⓐ Ⓑ Ⓒ Ⓓ Ⓔ	75. Ⓐ Ⓑ Ⓒ Ⓓ Ⓔ	105. Ⓐ Ⓑ Ⓒ Ⓓ Ⓔ
16. Ⓐ Ⓑ Ⓒ Ⓓ Ⓔ	46. Ⓐ Ⓑ Ⓒ Ⓓ Ⓔ	76. Ⓐ Ⓑ Ⓒ Ⓓ Ⓔ	106. Ⓐ Ⓑ Ⓒ Ⓓ Ⓔ
17. Ⓐ Ⓑ Ⓒ Ⓓ Ⓔ	47. Ⓐ Ⓑ Ⓒ Ⓓ Ⓔ	77. Ⓐ Ⓑ Ⓒ Ⓓ Ⓔ	107. Ⓐ Ⓑ Ⓒ Ⓓ Ⓔ
18. Ⓐ Ⓑ Ⓒ Ⓓ Ⓔ	48. Ⓐ Ⓑ Ⓒ Ⓓ Ⓔ	78. Ⓐ Ⓑ Ⓒ Ⓓ Ⓔ	108. Ⓐ Ⓑ Ⓒ Ⓓ Ⓔ
19. Ⓐ Ⓑ Ⓒ Ⓓ Ⓔ	49. Ⓐ Ⓑ Ⓒ Ⓓ Ⓔ	79. Ⓐ Ⓑ Ⓒ Ⓓ Ⓔ	109. Ⓐ Ⓑ Ⓒ Ⓓ Ⓔ
20. Ⓐ Ⓑ Ⓒ Ⓓ Ⓔ	50. Ⓐ Ⓑ Ⓒ Ⓓ Ⓔ	80. Ⓐ Ⓑ Ⓒ Ⓓ Ⓔ	110. Ⓐ Ⓑ Ⓒ Ⓓ Ⓔ
21. Ⓐ Ⓑ Ⓒ Ⓓ Ⓔ	51. Ⓐ Ⓑ Ⓒ Ⓓ Ⓔ	81. Ⓐ Ⓑ Ⓒ Ⓓ Ⓔ	111. Ⓐ Ⓑ Ⓒ Ⓓ Ⓔ
22. Ⓐ Ⓑ Ⓒ Ⓓ Ⓔ	52. Ⓐ Ⓑ Ⓒ Ⓓ Ⓔ	82. Ⓐ Ⓑ Ⓒ Ⓓ Ⓔ	112. Ⓐ Ⓑ Ⓒ Ⓓ Ⓔ
23. Ⓐ Ⓑ Ⓒ Ⓓ Ⓔ	53. Ⓐ Ⓑ Ⓒ Ⓓ Ⓔ	83. Ⓐ Ⓑ Ⓒ Ⓓ Ⓔ	113. Ⓐ Ⓑ Ⓒ Ⓓ Ⓔ
24. Ⓐ Ⓑ Ⓒ Ⓓ Ⓔ	54. Ⓐ Ⓑ Ⓒ Ⓓ Ⓔ	84. Ⓐ Ⓑ Ⓒ Ⓓ Ⓔ	114. Ⓐ Ⓑ Ⓒ Ⓓ Ⓔ
25. Ⓐ Ⓑ Ⓒ Ⓓ Ⓔ	55. Ⓐ Ⓑ Ⓒ Ⓓ Ⓔ	85. Ⓐ Ⓑ Ⓒ Ⓓ Ⓔ	115. Ⓐ Ⓑ Ⓒ Ⓓ Ⓔ
26. Ⓐ Ⓑ Ⓒ Ⓓ Ⓔ	56. Ⓐ Ⓑ Ⓒ Ⓓ Ⓔ	86. Ⓐ Ⓑ Ⓒ Ⓓ Ⓔ	116. Ⓐ Ⓑ Ⓒ Ⓓ Ⓔ
27. Ⓐ Ⓑ Ⓒ Ⓓ Ⓔ	57. Ⓐ Ⓑ Ⓒ Ⓓ Ⓔ	87. Ⓐ Ⓑ Ⓒ Ⓓ Ⓔ	117. Ⓐ Ⓑ Ⓒ Ⓓ Ⓔ
28. Ⓐ Ⓑ Ⓒ Ⓓ Ⓔ	58. Ⓐ Ⓑ Ⓒ Ⓓ Ⓔ	88. Ⓐ Ⓑ Ⓒ Ⓓ Ⓔ	118. Ⓐ Ⓑ Ⓒ Ⓓ Ⓔ
29. Ⓐ Ⓑ Ⓒ Ⓓ Ⓔ	59. Ⓐ Ⓑ Ⓒ Ⓓ Ⓔ	89. Ⓐ Ⓑ Ⓒ Ⓓ Ⓔ	119. Ⓐ Ⓑ Ⓒ Ⓓ Ⓔ
30. Ⓐ Ⓑ Ⓒ Ⓓ Ⓔ	60. Ⓐ Ⓑ Ⓒ Ⓓ Ⓔ	90. Ⓐ Ⓑ Ⓒ Ⓓ Ⓔ	120. Ⓐ Ⓑ Ⓒ Ⓓ Ⓔ

ANSWER SHEET
Practice Test 3

121. Ⓐ Ⓑ Ⓒ Ⓓ Ⓔ   145. Ⓐ Ⓑ Ⓒ Ⓓ Ⓔ   169. Ⓐ Ⓑ Ⓒ Ⓓ Ⓔ   193. Ⓐ Ⓑ Ⓒ Ⓓ Ⓔ
122. Ⓐ Ⓑ Ⓒ Ⓓ Ⓔ   146. Ⓐ Ⓑ Ⓒ Ⓓ Ⓔ   170. Ⓐ Ⓑ Ⓒ Ⓓ Ⓔ   194. Ⓐ Ⓑ Ⓒ Ⓓ Ⓔ
123. Ⓐ Ⓑ Ⓒ Ⓓ Ⓔ   147. Ⓐ Ⓑ Ⓒ Ⓓ Ⓔ   171. Ⓐ Ⓑ Ⓒ Ⓓ Ⓔ   195. Ⓐ Ⓑ Ⓒ Ⓓ Ⓔ
124. Ⓐ Ⓑ Ⓒ Ⓓ Ⓔ   148. Ⓐ Ⓑ Ⓒ Ⓓ Ⓔ   172. Ⓐ Ⓑ Ⓒ Ⓓ Ⓔ   196. Ⓐ Ⓑ Ⓒ Ⓓ Ⓔ
125. Ⓐ Ⓑ Ⓒ Ⓓ Ⓔ   149. Ⓐ Ⓑ Ⓒ Ⓓ Ⓔ   173. Ⓐ Ⓑ Ⓒ Ⓓ Ⓔ   197. Ⓐ Ⓑ Ⓒ Ⓓ Ⓔ
126. Ⓐ Ⓑ Ⓒ Ⓓ Ⓔ   150. Ⓐ Ⓑ Ⓒ Ⓓ Ⓔ   174. Ⓐ Ⓑ Ⓒ Ⓓ Ⓔ   198. Ⓐ Ⓑ Ⓒ Ⓓ Ⓔ
127. Ⓐ Ⓑ Ⓒ Ⓓ Ⓔ   151. Ⓐ Ⓑ Ⓒ Ⓓ Ⓔ   175. Ⓐ Ⓑ Ⓒ Ⓓ Ⓔ   199. Ⓐ Ⓑ Ⓒ Ⓓ Ⓔ
128. Ⓐ Ⓑ Ⓒ Ⓓ Ⓔ   152. Ⓐ Ⓑ Ⓒ Ⓓ Ⓔ   176. Ⓐ Ⓑ Ⓒ Ⓓ Ⓔ   200. Ⓐ Ⓑ Ⓒ Ⓓ Ⓔ
129. Ⓐ Ⓑ Ⓒ Ⓓ Ⓔ   153. Ⓐ Ⓑ Ⓒ Ⓓ Ⓔ   177. Ⓐ Ⓑ Ⓒ Ⓓ Ⓔ   201. Ⓐ Ⓑ Ⓒ Ⓓ Ⓔ
130. Ⓐ Ⓑ Ⓒ Ⓓ Ⓔ   154. Ⓐ Ⓑ Ⓒ Ⓓ Ⓔ   178. Ⓐ Ⓑ Ⓒ Ⓓ Ⓔ   202. Ⓐ Ⓑ Ⓒ Ⓓ Ⓔ
131. Ⓐ Ⓑ Ⓒ Ⓓ Ⓔ   155. Ⓐ Ⓑ Ⓒ Ⓓ Ⓔ   179. Ⓐ Ⓑ Ⓒ Ⓓ Ⓔ   203. Ⓐ Ⓑ Ⓒ Ⓓ Ⓔ
132. Ⓐ Ⓑ Ⓒ Ⓓ Ⓔ   156. Ⓐ Ⓑ Ⓒ Ⓓ Ⓔ   180. Ⓐ Ⓑ Ⓒ Ⓓ Ⓔ   204. Ⓐ Ⓑ Ⓒ Ⓓ Ⓔ
133. Ⓐ Ⓑ Ⓒ Ⓓ Ⓔ   157. Ⓐ Ⓑ Ⓒ Ⓓ Ⓔ   181. Ⓐ Ⓑ Ⓒ Ⓓ Ⓔ   205. Ⓐ Ⓑ Ⓒ Ⓓ Ⓔ
134. Ⓐ Ⓑ Ⓒ Ⓓ Ⓔ   158. Ⓐ Ⓑ Ⓒ Ⓓ Ⓔ   182. Ⓐ Ⓑ Ⓒ Ⓓ Ⓔ   206. Ⓐ Ⓑ Ⓒ Ⓓ Ⓔ
135. Ⓐ Ⓑ Ⓒ Ⓓ Ⓔ   159. Ⓐ Ⓑ Ⓒ Ⓓ Ⓔ   183. Ⓐ Ⓑ Ⓒ Ⓓ Ⓔ   207. Ⓐ Ⓑ Ⓒ Ⓓ Ⓔ
136. Ⓐ Ⓑ Ⓒ Ⓓ Ⓔ   160. Ⓐ Ⓑ Ⓒ Ⓓ Ⓔ   184. Ⓐ Ⓑ Ⓒ Ⓓ Ⓔ   208. Ⓐ Ⓑ Ⓒ Ⓓ Ⓔ
137. Ⓐ Ⓑ Ⓒ Ⓓ Ⓔ   161. Ⓐ Ⓑ Ⓒ Ⓓ Ⓔ   185. Ⓐ Ⓑ Ⓒ Ⓓ Ⓔ   209. Ⓐ Ⓑ Ⓒ Ⓓ Ⓔ
138. Ⓐ Ⓑ Ⓒ Ⓓ Ⓔ   162. Ⓐ Ⓑ Ⓒ Ⓓ Ⓔ   186. Ⓐ Ⓑ Ⓒ Ⓓ Ⓔ   210. Ⓐ Ⓑ Ⓒ Ⓓ Ⓔ
139. Ⓐ Ⓑ Ⓒ Ⓓ Ⓔ   163. Ⓐ Ⓑ Ⓒ Ⓓ Ⓔ   187. Ⓐ Ⓑ Ⓒ Ⓓ Ⓔ   211. Ⓐ Ⓑ Ⓒ Ⓓ Ⓔ
140. Ⓐ Ⓑ Ⓒ Ⓓ Ⓔ   164. Ⓐ Ⓑ Ⓒ Ⓓ Ⓔ   188. Ⓐ Ⓑ Ⓒ Ⓓ Ⓔ   212. Ⓐ Ⓑ Ⓒ Ⓓ Ⓔ
141. Ⓐ Ⓑ Ⓒ Ⓓ Ⓔ   165. Ⓐ Ⓑ Ⓒ Ⓓ Ⓔ   189. Ⓐ Ⓑ Ⓒ Ⓓ Ⓔ   213. Ⓐ Ⓑ Ⓒ Ⓓ Ⓔ
142. Ⓐ Ⓑ Ⓒ Ⓓ Ⓔ   166. Ⓐ Ⓑ Ⓒ Ⓓ Ⓔ   190. Ⓐ Ⓑ Ⓒ Ⓓ Ⓔ   214. Ⓐ Ⓑ Ⓒ Ⓓ Ⓔ
143. Ⓐ Ⓑ Ⓒ Ⓓ Ⓔ   167. Ⓐ Ⓑ Ⓒ Ⓓ Ⓔ   191. Ⓐ Ⓑ Ⓒ Ⓓ Ⓔ   215. Ⓐ Ⓑ Ⓒ Ⓓ Ⓔ
144. Ⓐ Ⓑ Ⓒ Ⓓ Ⓔ   168. Ⓐ Ⓑ Ⓒ Ⓓ Ⓔ   192. Ⓐ Ⓑ Ⓒ Ⓓ Ⓔ

PRACTICE TEST 3

TIME: 170 MINUTES
215 QUESTIONS

Directions: Each of the questions or incomplete statements below is followed by five suggested answers or completions. Select the one that is best in each case and then fill in the corresponding space on the answer sheet.

---

1. In many species, ranging from lizards to lions, and from mice to monkeys, increased physical aggression is associated with high levels of what hormone in the bloodstream?

   (A) testosterone
   (B) melatonin
   (C) oxytocin
   (D) cortisol
   (E) insulin

2. A few years ago, researchers studying communication in a particular species of monkey in Nigeria made the following observation: When an alarm call that normally signaled a leopard was strung together in a sequence with an alarm call that normally signaled an eagle, the resulting sequence elicited group movement (i.e., the sequence meant "let's go!"). If true, this would indicate that these monkeys have a communication system with

   (A) prosody
   (B) phonology
   (C) syntax
   (D) pragmatics
   (E) case marking

3. To which of the following does the phrase "all-or-none" apply?

     I. excitatory post-synaptic potential
    II. inhibitory post-synaptic potential
   III. action potential

   (A) I only
   (B) II only
   (C) III only
   (D) I and II
   (E) I, II, and III

GO ON TO THE NEXT PAGE

4. A patient with which of the following diagnoses would be unable to copy a simple drawing of a horse?

(A) aphasia
(B) agnosia
(C) aplysia
(D) amnesia
(E) alexia

5. Compared with the use of only a starting gun or command, preparatory instructions such as "On your mark, get set, go!"

(A) have no effect upon reaction time
(B) shorten reaction time
(C) lengthen reaction time
(D) shorten reaction time for the experienced runner and lengthening it for the less-experienced one
(E) shorten reaction time for the less-experienced runner and lengthening it for the experienced one

6. Which of the following is part of the parietal lobe of the human brain?

(A) motor cortex
(B) somatosensory cortex
(C) cerebellar cortex
(D) primary auditory cortex
(E) primary visual cortex

7. When talking about sound waves and their perception,

(A) amplitude is to loudness as frequency is to pitch
(B) wavelength is to loudness as frequency is to pitch
(C) amplitude is to pitch as frequency is to loudness
(D) sound wave is to pitch as frequency is to loudness
(E) decibels is to loudness as frequency is to pitch

8. The hormone leptin plays an important signaling function in the regulation of

(A) sexual behavior
(B) aggression
(C) energy intake
(D) sleep–wake cycles
(E) stress reactions

GO ON TO THE NEXT PAGE

9. Remembering the name of the first president of the United States is to remembering the name of your first teacher as semantic memory is to

(A) implicit memory
(B) episodic memory
(C) long-term memory
(D) explicit memory
(E) procedural memory

10. The two-factor theory of emotion was initially proposed by Schachter and Singer, based on an experiment in which they gave subjects an injection, and then they varied both the external cues (i.e., a confederate's behavior) about the context and the information they told subjects about the injection. In actuality, one group received a placebo injection and the other group received an injection of

(A) adrenalin
(B) vitamin C
(C) saline
(D) dopamine
(E) curare

11. In experiments involving learning in a Skinner box, it has been found that, compared with animals receiving normal extinction trials, animals receiving punishment during extinction trials exhibit

(A) fewer total responses prior to complete extinction
(B) more total responses prior to complete extinction
(C) the same total number of responses prior to extinction
(D) an absence of extinction
(E) an absence of spontaneous recovery after extinction

12. Sleep apnea is

(A) the technical name for sleepwalking
(B) cessation of breathing during sleep
(C) non-REM sleep
(D) narcolepsy
(E) insomnia

13. When a neuron is described as "at rest," the intracellular fluid of a neuron has nearly twenty times _____ than does the extracellular fluid surrounding the neuron; this concentration gradient is crucial for the establishment of the resting potential.

(A) less potassium
(B) less calcium
(C) more sodium
(D) more calcium
(E) more potassium

GO ON TO THE NEXT PAGE

14. Memories that are being consciously and actively manipulated, organized, and thought about are part of

    (A) the sensory register
    (B) long-term memory
    (C) working memory
    (D) declarative memory
    (E) explicit memory

15. *Principles of Psychology*, published in 1890, is one of the most influential texts in the history of psychology. Who wrote this detailed account of the human mind and the experimental study thereof?

    (A) William James
    (B) Charles Darwin
    (C) B.F. Skinner
    (D) James Cattell
    (E) Francis Galton

16. A rule of thumb for solving problems that is generally correct but may be imperfect is called

    (A) a heuristic
    (B) a syllogism
    (C) an inference
    (D) a script
    (E) an algorithm

17. The spinal cord does *not*

    (A) relay nerve impulses
    (B) process sensory impulses
    (C) have any function in reflexive behavior
    (D) contain nerve cell bodies
    (E) regulate body temperature

18. According to the Rescorla-Wagner model of classical conditioning, the amount an animal learns in any situation depends on the

    (A) animal's drive to achieve an internal state
    (B) discrepancy between what is expected to happen and what actually happens
    (C) biologically determined belongingness of the stimuli
    (D) number of reinforcing events
    (E) rate of reinforcing events

GO ON TO THE NEXT PAGE

19. What is the physiological mechanism that causes the enhancement of brightness boundaries (i.e., the edge between a light gray and dark gray patch)?

    (A) opponent-process theory
    (B) lateral inhibition
    (C) spatial summation
    (D) sensory adaptation
    (E) mach bands

20. Clive had a stroke resulting in a large lesion in his left occipital cortex. Which of the following statements about his resulting deficits is most likely to be correct?

    (A) Clive will have normal vision with his left eye but impaired vision with his right eye.
    (B) Clive will have normal vision with his right eye but impaired vision with his left eye.
    (C) Clive will have normal vision to the left of fixation but impaired vision to the right of fixation.
    (D) Clive will have normal vision to the right of fixation but impaired vision to the left of fixation.
    (E) Clive will have normal vision above fixation but impaired vision below fixation.

21. Schemata are

    (A) small gaps in the myelin sheath on an axon
    (B) small bones in the middle ear
    (C) primary colors in additive color mixing
    (D) cognitive structures in memory
    (E) procedures used to evaluate Type II error

22. "Any response to a situation will, other things being equal, be more strongly connected with the situation in proportion to the number of times it has been connected with that situation and to the average vigor and duration of the connections." The preceding is a quotation from

    (A) Thorndike's law of exercise
    (B) Lewin's field theory
    (C) Skinner's law of reinforcement
    (D) Markel's law of diminishing returns
    (E) Watson's law of contingency

GO ON TO THE NEXT PAGE

23. Eidetic memory is

    (A) déja vu
    (B) a component of working memory
    (C) a measure of general intelligence
    (D) a mnemonic device
    (E) a vivid visual memory

24. GSR measures

    (A) neuronal membrane potentials
    (B) kinesthetic reflexes
    (C) visual evoked potentials
    (D) cerebral blood flow
    (E) sweat gland activity

25. In a wide range of cultures (e.g., Nigeria, Iran, China, and the United States), men tend to prefer younger mates than do women, whereas women value financial status more than do men. One explanation for these trends is that a woman with an innate preference for wealthy men is more likely to successfully reproduce (and thus pass on her genes to the next generation) because her mate could provide food and other resources; and a man with an innate preference for younger women is likely to have more offspring (and thus pass on his genes). The conjecture that these behavioral preferences arise from reproductive advantages is an example of an approach to psychology known as

    (A) comparative psychology
    (B) ethology
    (C) human factors psychology
    (D) evolutionary psychology
    (E) longitudinal psychology

26. Which of the following sequences correctly describes the typical order of flow of a neural signal?

    (A) soma → dendrite → axon → axon terminal
    (B) dendrite → axon terminal → axon → soma
    (C) axon → axon terminal → soma → dendrite
    (D) axon → axon terminal → dendrite → soma
    (E) dendrite → soma → axon → axon terminal

GO ON TO THE NEXT PAGE

27. The opponent process theory, proposed by Hering, was initially developed in the study of

    (A) color vision
    (B) dream analysis
    (C) forgetting
    (D) groupthink
    (E) cognitive therapy

28. "It was last spring. I had just studied for the Advanced GRE in Psychology and had done quite well on it." This would be an example of

    (A) semantic priming
    (B) encoding specificity
    (C) dual memory
    (D) episodic memory
    (E) repetition priming

QUESTIONS 29–31 REFER TO THE PARAGRAPH BELOW.

A researcher wants to investigate the claim that memory for emotional events is enhanced. She constructs one set of twenty-five words that have no emotional or arousing content (e.g., *tree*) and another set of twenty-five words that are emotionally arousing (e.g., *rape*). All subjects read a list of all fifty words (intermixed). Half of the subjects were given a surprise memory test immediately afterward. Half of the subjects were dismissed, and the following day they took the surprise memory test. In both cases, the memory test was a recognition test of one hundred words (the fifty studied words and fifty unstudied words).

29. The researcher calculated the number of hits on this recognition test minus the number of false alarms for each subject. If a subject is guessing, what is the expected score on this measure?

    (A) −50
    (B) −25
    (C) 0
    (D) +25
    (E) +50

GO ON TO THE NEXT PAGE

30. The researcher calculated the memory scores separately for emotional and neutral words, and the data are in this table:

	Emotional	Neutral
Immediate Test	20	19
Delayed Test	18	12

Based on her statistical analysis of these data, the researcher concludes that enhanced memory for emotional words is evident only after a delay. Which of the following statistical results must be obtained to support this conclusion?

  I.   A significant main effect of testing time (immediate versus delayed) on memory performance

  II. A significant main effect of emotional content (emotional versus neutral) on memory performance

  III. A significant testing-time by emotional-content interaction

(A) I only

(B) II only

(C) III only

(D) II and III

(E) I, II, and III

31. Which of the following scenarios would create a confound in the experiment, such that the interpretation of the emotional effect on memory would be suspect?

(A) Reading the emotional words might activate additional neural structures (e.g., the amygdala) that are connected to memory systems.

(B) Some subjects might suspect there will be a memory test, whereas other subjects might not.

(C) The emotional words might be less common in English usage than are the neutral words.

(D) Memory consolidation is thought to occur while sleeping, so the change in memory after a delay could reflect a sleep effect.

(E) None of the above scenarios presents a confound in this experiment because subjects were randomly assigned to one of the two testing-time conditions.

GO ON TO THE NEXT PAGE

32. Subjects in an experiment are asked to name pictures of common line drawings (e.g., turtle). Later, they are shown the exact same pictures again, and their response latency to rename the pictures is measured. For some subjects, the delay between the first and second naming response was five minutes; for others, it was one hour. What is the most likely result when the latency to name a picture the first time is compared to the latency to name the same picture the second time?

(A) Subjects will be faster to rename the pictures after five minutes, but if the delay is longer than that, there will be no benefit.
(B) Subjects will be slower to rename the pictures after five minutes, but if the delay is longer than that, there will be no benefit.
(C) Subjects will be faster to rename the pictures after five minutes but slower to rename the pictures if the delay is longer than that.
(D) Subjects will be slower to rename the pictures at both the five-minute and one-hour delays.
(E) Subjects will be faster to rename the pictures at both the five-minute and one-hour delays.

33. Which of the following terms refers to a phenomenon studied in the field of psycholinguistics?

(A) garden path effect
(B) cocktail party effect
(C) serial position effect
(D) false consensus effect
(E) misinformation effect

34. After two college roommates have been living together for a year, they find that their menstrual cycles have synchronized. Researchers would attribute this synchrony, in part, to

(A) observational learning
(B) olfactory cues
(C) auditory cues
(D) spatial cues
(E) transmodulation

35. A change in the structure of a gene that leads to minor or major changes in an organism's phenotype is called a

(A) mitosis
(B) meiosis
(C) mastation
(D) stem cell
(E) mutation

GO ON TO THE NEXT PAGE

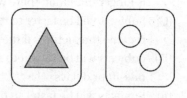

36. The suprachiasmatic nucleus (SCN) of the hypothalamus regulates

(A) circadian rhythms
(B) food intake
(C) sexual behavior
(D) aggression
(E) all of the above

37. The figure here shows two cards from an instrument called the Wisconsin Card Sorting Test. What does this test measure?

(A) set-shifting ability
(B) divergent thinking
(C) spatial memory
(D) working memory span
(E) inductive reasoning

38. The quarterback of a college football team is knocked unconscious on the very last play, just before time expires. The next day he feels fine, but he does not remember any part of the game. This is an example of

(A) anterograde amnesia
(B) proactive amnesia
(C) retrograde amnesia
(D) remote amnesia
(E) infantile amnesia

39. When Roscoe was learning to play piano, his teacher taught him to read the notes on the treble clef staff with the phrase "Every Good Boy Deserves Favor." What did Roscoe's teacher use here?

(A) tip-of-the-tongue phenomenon
(B) mnemonic device
(C) method of loci
(D) semantic priming
(E) partial reinforcement

40. An experimenter measures the abilities of Grace and Jon to detect a flickering light. A signal-detection analysis indicates that Grace and Jon have equal sensitivity (d'), but that Jon has a more lenient decision criterion, such that he has a bias to say "yes" when there is a light present. Which of the following statements is true?

(A) Grace and Jon have an equivalent number of hits.
(B) Grace and Jon have an equivalent number of false alarms.
(C) Jon has more false alarms than does Grace.
(D) Jon has more misses than does Grace.
(E) Jon has more correct rejections than does Grace.

GO ON TO THE NEXT PAGE

41. Aviators are being briefed on a night bombing mission just prior to flight takeoff. They wear special goggles in the lighted briefing room that filter all but red light, and they remove the goggles as they head toward their planes. This procedure has permitted them both to see in the briefing room and to have their eyes dark-adapted as they move out into the night. The goggle-wearing procedure utilizes information about

    (A) trichromatic vision
    (B) rod-versus-cone vision
    (C) complementarity
    (D) eidetic imagery
    (E) negative afterimages

42. Congenital adrenal hyperplasia occurs when the adrenal glands of a fetus produce high levels of androgens. This results in a baby who is

    (A) genetically XY but who has external genitalia resembling that of a boy
    (B) genetically XX but who has external genitalia resembling that of a boy
    (C) genetically XY but who has external genitalia resembling that of a girl
    (D) genetically XX but who has external genitalia resembling that of a girl
    (E) genetically XXY but who has external genitalia resembling that of a girl

43. The "savings method" developed by Ebbinghaus to measure memory performance would today be known by the term

    (A) encoding specificity
    (B) semantic memory
    (C) incidental learning
    (D) deductive reasoning
    (E) implicit memory

44. Kin selection theory can help to explain why some organisms seemed designed to deliver benefits to

    (A) members of other species
    (B) nonrelatives of the same species
    (C) relatives of the same species
    (D) themselves
    (E) none of the above

45. How many morphemes does the word *bakers* have?

    (A) two
    (B) three
    (C) four
    (D) five
    (E) six

GO ON TO THE NEXT PAGE

46. Like many students, Molly usually sits in the same seat every day in her statistics class. On the day of the final exam, she arrives early to class to be certain that she can take her regular seat during the exam. Molly's expectation that she will do better on the exam if she sits in the same seat as when she was learning the material is an example of

    (A) the recency effect
    (B) the primacy effect
    (C) state-dependent learning
    (D) semantic memory
    (E) suggestibility

47. Jenny is holding a yo-yo. Her little brother says "Cool—can I see that?" and she holds it up for him to *see* even though she clearly understood that he really wanted to *hold* the toy. In this situation, Jenny is pretending not to understand what aspect of language?

    (A) phonology
    (B) semantics
    (C) pragmatics
    (D) linguistics
    (E) syntax

48. Decay and interference are two terms that come up in discussions of

    (A) hypnosis
    (B) visual adaptation
    (C) homeostasis
    (D) forgetting
    (E) attachment

49. One error of inductive inference, in which some outcomes are weighted more than others, is called

    (A) the misinformation effect
    (B) confirmation bias
    (C) a false alarm
    (D) functional fixedness
    (E) the von Restorff effect

50. The concepts "rocking chair" and "dentist's chair"

    (A) belong to the same basic level category, but belong to different subordinate and superordinate categories
    (B) belong to the same subordinate category, but belong to different basic level and superordinate categories
    (C) belong to the same superordinate category, but belong to different basic level and subordinate categories
    (D) belong to the same basic level and superordinate categories, but belong to different subordinate categories
    (E) belong to the same subordinate and superordinate categories, but belong to different basic level categories

GO ON TO THE NEXT PAGE

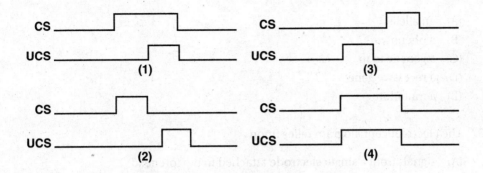

51. The most efficient classical conditioning paradigm is depicted in Figure

    (A) 1
    (B) 2
    (C) 3
    (D) 4
    (E) all are equally efficient

52. The CR is most likely to be inhibitory (i.e., opposite of the UCR) when the conditioning paradigm used is as depicted in Figure

    (A) 1
    (B) 2
    (C) 3
    (D) 4
    (E) none of the above

53. The trace conditioning paradigm is depicted in Figure

    (A) 1
    (B) 2
    (C) 3
    (D) 4
    (E) none of the above

54. The delayed conditioning paradigm is depicted in Figure

    (A) 1
    (B) 2
    (C) 3
    (D) 4
    (E) none of the above

GO ON TO THE NEXT PAGE

55. A particular variant of the DNA sequence at a given locus, or position, on a chromosome is referred to as

(A) an allele
(B) a phenotype
(C) a genetic map
(D) a recessive gene
(E) a mutation

56. The electroencephalogram relies upon

(A) signals from a single electrode attached to the forehead
(B) signals from an array of electrodes attached to various positions on the scalp
(C) an injection of a radioactively labeled glucose molecule into a blood vessel
(D) an injection of a nonradioactive contrast agent into a blood vessel
(E) a frequency rhythm not to exceed six cycles per second

57. Which stage of sleep is commonly referred to as REM sleep?

(A) Stage 1
(B) Stage 2
(C) Stage 3
(D) Stage 4
(E) none of the above

58. The relative contributions of the left and right hemispheres of the brain to language abilities have been studied by examining the performance of epileptic patients who have undergone surgical severing of what structure?

(A) Broca's area
(B) Wernicke's area
(C) hippocampus
(D) cerebellum
(E) corpus callosum

59. The implementation of computational models of cognitive systems that make use of parallel distributed processing principles to mimic neural processing is an example of an approach known as

(A) connectionism
(B) ethology
(C) introspection
(D) symbolism
(E) ontogeny

GO ON TO THE NEXT PAGE

60. If you put your hand on the top of your head, it is resting closest to which surface of the brain?

   (A) coronal
   (B) ventral
   (C) dorsal
   (D) caudal
   (E) raustral

61. If one person in a room yawns, someone who sees or hears this is likely to yawn as well. For this reason, a yawn can be classified as a

   (A) releasing stimulus
   (B) habituator
   (C) conditioned response
   (D) primary reinforcer
   (E) pheromone

62. You would probably experience the Ponzo illusion when looking at

   (A) a set of railroad tracks extending off into the distance
   (B) two parallel lines
   (C) a center circle surrounded by five smaller circles
   (D) a horizontal line intersecting a vertical line
   (E) a three-dimensional box

63. The philosopher Ludwig Wittgenstein drew an analogy between the structure of concepts and the structure of families: members have a resemblance to each other, by virtue of the fact that they share some features, but there is not a single feature that defines the family. This idea—which he called family resemblance—is most closely related to what psychological theory of conceptual structure?

   (A) stereotype theory
   (B) phenotype theory
   (C) allotype theory
   (D) prototype theory
   (E) genotype theory

64. Some researchers have proposed that language learning requires a specialized "language acquisition device" that operates automatically and only on linguistic input. This proposed device is an example of

   (A) a memory trace
   (B) an analogical representation
   (C) a module
   (D) a syllogism
   (E) a domain-general system

GO ON TO THE NEXT PAGE

65. Which of the following types of memory is most affected by anterograde amnesia?

    (A) procedural memory
    (B) implicit memory
    (C) working memory
    (D) short-term memory
    (E) episodic memory

66. A group of subjects reads a list of words, some of which are negative (e.g., *funeral*), some of which are positive (e.g., *friends*), and some of which are neutral (e.g., *spoon*). Subjects in a depressed mood will remember more of the negative words than the positive words, whereas subjects in an elated mood will remember more of the positive words than the negative words. This is called

    (A) the mood congruency effect
    (B) the positivity effect
    (C) emotional contagion
    (D) flashbulb memory
    (E) the consistency bias

67. When a child is put in "time out" by a parent or teacher, the adult has just applied what consequence to change his or her behavior?

    (A) positive reinforcement
    (B) negative reinforcement
    (C) positive punishment
    (D) negative punishment
    (E) avoidance learning

68. The term *spike*, when used to refer to a neuron, is synonymous with

    (A) action potential
    (B) resting potential
    (C) synaptic transmission
    (D) neurotransmitter release
    (E) saltatory conduction

69. In the study of sensory systems, *accommodation* refers to

    (A) the amplification of sound waves by the ossicles
    (B) echolocation during navigation
    (C) the distortion in mechanoreceptors in response to pressure on the skin
    (D) changes in the shape of the lens when focusing on objects at various distances
    (E) a decrease in the intensity of a neural response to continuing sensory stimulation

GO ON TO THE NEXT PAGE

70. Superior performance of chess experts over novices has been reported for memory for the position of chess pieces on a board, if those pieces are arranged in a plausible configuration. What memory principle has been used to explain this difference?

(A) mere exposure effect
(B) chunking
(C) encoding specificity
(D) procedural memory
(E) spacing effect

71. When attempting to judge the properties or traits of all members of some category based on a few exemplars, a heuristic that people often use is called the

(A) frequency heuristic
(B) availability heuristic
(C) representativeness heuristic
(D) framing heuristic
(E) deductive heuristic

72. Pierre is wearing a pair of headphones in a psychology experiment, and a different story is being played to each ear. The researcher asks Pierre to repeat everything he hears in the left ear and to ignore the information in the right ear. Later, Pierre is surprised when the researcher asks him some questions about the input to the right ear. Like most subjects in an experiment like this, Pierre is able to report

I.   if the speaker of the ignored speech stream is male or female
II. if the speaker of the ignored speech stream is speaking Spanish or English
III. if the speaker of the ignored speech stream is talking about school or vacation

(A) I only
(B) II only
(C) I and II
(D) II and III
(E) I, II, and III

73. A central question in the study of mental imagery is the extent to which these mental representations are

(A) declarative or procedural
(B) analogical or symbolic
(C) implicit or explicit
(D) chromatic or achromatic
(E) automatic or effortful

GO ON TO THE NEXT PAGE

74. The term *kinesthesia* is most closely related to the term

  (A) balance
  (B) proprioception
  (C) amnesia
  (D) navigation
  (E) fugue

75. Which of the following structures is *not* part of the hindbrain?

  (A) medulla
  (B) cerebellum
  (C) thalamus
  (D) pons
  (E) all of the above are in the hindbrain

76. As the result of an injury incurred while laying railroad tracks in Vermont, Phineas Gage sustained a massive wound to his

  (A) frontal lobe
  (B) temporal lobe
  (C) occipital lobe
  (D) sagittal lobe
  (E) parietal lobe

77. Which of the following illusions is associated with multistable perception of an ambiguous figure?

  (A) Ponzo illusion
  (B) Ebbinghaus illusion
  (C) Ames room illusion
  (D) Müller-Lyer illusion
  (E) Necker cube illusion

78. *Spontaneous recovery* is a term used to describe

  (A) the return of a classically conditioned response that was previously extinguished after a period of time with no additional exposure to the CS or the UCS
  (B) the emotional response of a child when his or her caregiver leaves the room
  (C) an increase in the speed or accuracy to identify or recognize a stimulus that was recently experienced
  (D) the tendency to perceive exaggerated differences in the brightness of two adjacent visual regions
  (E) the propensity to spend more time in REM sleep one night if deprived of it on previous nights.

GO ON TO THE NEXT PAGE

79. If the occipital lobe of a patient is electrically stimulated during neurosurgery, the patient is most likely to report a

(A) tingling sensation on one side of the body
(B) simple noise such as a click or a hum
(C) detailed personal memory, such as a childhood birthday party
(D) vivid visual experience with no coherent form, such as a color or a flickering light
(E) twitch in a distal extremity such as a finger or a foot

80. The method of loci is an example of

(A) an archetype
(B) cognitive reappraisal
(C) context reinstatement
(D) a goal state
(E) a mnemonic device

81. In a memory experiment, two groups of subjects are given a list of words to read, and later they are given a surprise memory test. When looking at the words, subjects in one group have to decide if each item refers to a living or a nonliving thing; subjects in another group have to decide if each item is printed in uppercase or lowercase. On the subsequent memory test, the latter group performed worse. What effect is demonstrated by this experiment?

(A) memory span
(B) depth of processing
(C) repetition priming
(D) retrograde interference
(E) positive transfer

82. When trying to solve a difficult problem, it can be useful to relate the difficult problem to a simpler problem that has the same formal structure. This process is referred to by the term

(A) heuristic
(B) deduction
(C) mental set
(D) analogy
(E) rehearsal

83. The fatty substance that insulates the axon of a neuron is known as

(A) medulla
(B) magno cells
(C) mach bands
(D) myelin
(E) mendel

GO ON TO THE NEXT PAGE

84. What almond-shaped structure inside the temporal lobe is crucial for the experience and expression of emotions in humans?

(A) amygdala
(B) hippocampus
(C) medulla
(D) androgen
(E) putamen

85. Which of the following effects would *not* be caused by a drug that is classified as an agonist?

(A) increasing the rate of reuptake of the neurotransmitter by the presynaptic cell
(B) increasing the availability of a chemical precursor to a neurotransmitter
(C) decreasing the enzymatic breakdown of a neurotransmitter in the synaptic cleft
(D) mimicking the neurotransmitter action by binding to and activating its receptor
(E) all of the above actions are caused by drugs classified as agonists

86. Which of the following options has one function (closed-class) word and one mass noun?

(A) the oil
(B) yellow banana
(C) her mother
(D) five napkins
(E) dogs bark

87. Francisco receives a salary at the end of each month. His reinforcement schedule is

(A) variable interval
(B) fixed interval
(C) variable ratio
(D) fixed ratio
(E) partial ratio

88. The first well-articulated theory of evolution held that an individual could change his or her traits (or behaviors) depending on how they are used, and then that these changes could be passed on to offspring. Who is credited with this idea?

(A) Charles Darwin
(B) Konrad Lorenz
(C) René Descartes
(D) Jean-Baptiste Lamarck
(E) Ivan Pavlov

GO ON TO THE NEXT PAGE

A researcher hypothesizes that the social deficits observed in children with autism spectrum disorder stem from an inability to recognize emotional expressions. She studies a group of twenty children with a diagnosis of autism spectrum disorder and a group of twenty typically-developing children. She shows each child a series of color photographs of people of various ages and asks each to say the sex of the person in the photograph (male or female) and the emotion expressed on the person's face (anger, surprise, fear, or sadness). The results are given in this table:

	Sex Recognition	Emotion Recognition
Typical children	98	80
Children with autism spectrum disorder	96	40

89. When analyzing these data, the researcher uses an analysis of variance in which the comparison of sex recognition to emotion recognition is a _____ comparison and the comparison of children with autism spectrum disorder to typical children is a _____ comparison.

   (A) within-subjects; between-subjects
   (B) within-subjects; within-subjects
   (C) between-subjects; within-subjects
   (D) between-subjects; between-subjects
   (E) It depends on whether a parametric or nonparametric analysis is conducted.

90. A statistical analysis revealed a significant interaction in the data, allowing the researcher to infer that

   (A) males are more likely to develop autism spectrum disorder than females
   (B) the test of emotion recognition was harder than the test of sex recognition
   (C) the difference in performance between children with autism spectrum disorder and typical children is greater on the emotion-recognition test than on the sex-recognition test
   (D) autism spectrum disorder is associated with damage to the amygdala, a brain structure involved in normal emotional processing
   (E) children with autism spectrum disorder perform worse than typical children on emotion-recognition tests but better than typical children on sex-recognition tests

GO ON TO THE NEXT PAGE

91. Based on this interaction, the researcher wants to conclude that children with autism spectrum disorder do indeed have a selective impairment in emotional ability. What aspect of her data makes this conclusion problematic?

    (A) She did not measure social skills, so she cannot conclude that emotion-recognition deficits cause social problems.
    (B) Because it is impossible to randomly assign children to the autism spectrum disorder or typical groups, she cannot infer that autism spectrum disorder causes impaired emotion recognition.
    (C) Because performance on the sex-recognition test is near 100 percent, it may not have been a sensitive measure of nonemotional deficits.
    (D) Although performance on the emotion-recognition test was worse among children with autism spectrum disorder than typical children, it was still better than chance.
    (E) The performance of children with autism spectrum disorder was more variable than the performance of typical children.

92. In discussions of vision, the term *proximal stimulus* usually refers to

    (A) a color such as black or white that does not have the property of hue
    (B) objects that are in spatial locations quite distant from the observer
    (C) objects that are in spatial locations nearby (i.e., within grasping distance of) the observer
    (D) the pattern of light reflected off any object that strikes the retina
    (E) a stimulus that falls on the blind spot of the retina

93. Which of the following lists of structures compose the HPA axis that controls the stress response?

    (A) hypothalamus, pituitary gland, adrenal gland
    (B) hippocampus, pituitary gland, adrenal gland
    (C) hypothalamus, pineal gland, adrenal gland
    (D) hypothalamus, pituitary gland, amygdala
    (E) hippocampus, pineal gland, amygdala

94. A chemical signal that triggers a behavioral response in another member of the species—such as egg-laying in insects—is called

    (A) an androgen
    (B) a heuristic
    (C) a pheromone
    (D) a meme
    (E) a fixed-action pattern

GO ON TO THE NEXT PAGE

95. As you know, there is a penalty for incorrect answers on the GRE. Therefore, prior to selecting an answer, you should evaluate how confident you are in the answer. Your ability to assess your confidence in the accuracy of a retrieved memory is an example of

    (A) prospective memory
    (B) procedural memory
    (C) semantic memory
    (D) metamemory
    (E) declarative memory

QUESTIONS 96–98 ARE BASED ON THE FOLLOWING INFORMATION.

An experimenter records galvanic skin response (GSR) to study fear conditioning. The subjects were adult males, ages twenty to twenty-five. For this procedure, each subject was attached to GSR monitoring devices, and a shock electrode was placed on each one's left forefinger. Subjects individually received twenty presentations of a tone. In ten of the presentations, the tone was 700 Hz and was followed by electric shock to the left forefinger. In the remaining ten presentations, the tone was 3,500 Hz and was not followed by shock. Presentations were randomized for each subject, making it impossible to predict what tone would be presented on any given trial. GSR to each tonal presentation was recorded, and the results are presented in the following table.

Amplitude of GSR

Trial Block	Tone 1 700 Hz	Tone 2 3,500 Hz
1	10	10
2	8	13
3	6	15
4	5	18
5	4	20

96. Between Tone 1 and Tone 2, GSR across trials shows

    (A) strong positive correlation
    (B) weak positive correlation
    (C) strong negative correlation
    (D) weak negative correlation
    (E) no correlation

GO ON TO THE NEXT PAGE

97. The conditioned stimulus in the experiment was

    (A) shock to left forefinger
    (B) GSR
    (C) age of subjects
    (D) tone
    (E) trials

98. Which of the following phenomena was evident across trial blocks?

    (A) stimulus generalization
    (B) stimulus discrimination
    (C) counterconditioning
    (D) reciprocal inhibition
    (E) extinction

99. Schachter and Singer's research demonstrated the

    (A) prevalence of an anger emotion over emotions of happiness
    (B) validity of the Yerkes-Dodson law
    (C) importance of external cues
    (D) predominance of internal cues
    (E) validity of the Cannon-Washburn theory

100. In contrast with an emotion, a mood is

    (A) more intense and longer in duration
    (B) less intense and shorter in duration
    (C) more intense and shorter in duration
    (D) less intense and longer in duration
    (E) identical in all respects

101. In studying bodily reactions to stress, Hans Selye found the initial reaction to be

    (A) resistance
    (B) exhaustion
    (C) alarm
    (D) ulcers
    (E) migraines

102. The opponent process theory has been prominent in the field of

    (A) vision
    (B) sensory processes
    (C) emotion
    (D) learning
    (E) neurosis

GO ON TO THE NEXT PAGE

103. William James's theory of emotional experience held that

    (A) emotions are primarily a product of learning
    (B) the physical reaction causes the emotional response
    (C) all responses are preceded by cognitive awareness
    (D) emotional patterns are based upon inherited tendencies
    (E) emotional patterns are based upon Gestalt tendencies

104. Research suggests that the sight of a pleasurable object causes which one of the following measurable effects?

    (A) facial tics
    (B) blurred vision
    (C) pupil dilation
    (D) lowered heart rate
    (E) lowered blood pressure

105. *Cannabis sativa* is most commonly known as

    (A) LSD
    (B) heroin
    (C) opium
    (D) marijuana
    (E) milkweed

106. A person performing calculus computations has attained which one of the following stages of cognitive development?

    (A) sensorimotor operations
    (B) formal operations
    (C) preoperational
    (D) concrete operations
    (E) abstract operations

107. Which one of the following terms is not generally used to describe the developmental period from ages two to six?

    (A) pregang age
    (B) age of dominance
    (C) exploration age
    (D) preschool age
    (E) age of solitary, parallel, and associative play

GO ON TO THE NEXT PAGE

108. According to the tenets of family constellation, which one of the following would be most eager for physical demonstrations of attention?

    (A) first-born children
    (B) middle children
    (C) identical twins
    (D) youngest children
    (E) fraternal twins

109. The relationship between a child's intellectual development and the age at which the child first walks is

    (A) strong
    (B) moderate
    (C) nonexistent
    (D) the subject of current investigation, which will probably form the basis for an established theory
    (E) believed by Wechsler to be important

110. The brain of the newborn

    (A) is the least-developed aspect of the child's body
    (B) is fully developed
    (C) will continue to grow in size
    (D) will continue to add brain cells, increasing its total number of cells
    (E) will not permit any reflex activity immediately after birth

111. Which one of the following would most directly affect the development of intelligence?

    (A) diet deficiency in the expectant mother
    (B) smoking by the expectant mother
    (C) premature birth
    (D) Rh factor
    (E) alcoholic beverage intake by the expectant mother

112. One first takes the sum of squared deviations from the mean, divides by the number of scores, and takes the square root to obtain the

    (A) variance
    (B) standard deviation
    (C) z-score
    (D) t-score
    (E) F-score

GO ON TO THE NEXT PAGE

113. Erikson's trust-versus-mistrust stage occurs during

(A) middle childhood
(B) early adulthood
(C) infancy
(D) early childhood
(E) middle adulthood

114. Circular Dial A contains three equidistant sections labeled *hot, safe, cold*; Circular dial B contains clockwise calibrations from zero to 500. Human engineering suggests that

(A) Dial B is easier to interpret
(B) Dial A is easier to interpret
(C) Dials A and B are equivalent as far as ease of interpretation
(D) Dials A and B are both very difficult to interpret
(E) Such information should not be presented on circular dials

115. Which one of the following criteria would be utilized to differentiate "hot" from "cool" media in McLuhan's definitional framework?

(A) verbal message combined with pictures
(B) capacity to present pictures in motion
(C) amount of information conveyed
(D) shock potential of the medium
(E) political potential of the medium

116. A high SSS score indicates that a person is high in

(A) sensation seeking
(B) personality traits found among SS troops in Germany
(C) likelihood to conform even when it means injury to others
(D) sensory susceptibility
(E) satiation sequencing

117. Which one of the following is characteristic of the fetal period?

(A) initial indications of sensitivity to stimulation
(B) human-like physical characteristics beginning to take shape
(C) highest susceptibility to diseases
(D) greatest susceptibility to the effects of thalidomide
(E) initiation of heartbeat

118. Extreme scores in a distribution most prominently affect the

(A) mean
(B) median
(C) mode
(D) semi-interquartile range
(E) negative skew

GO ON TO THE NEXT PAGE

119. Throughout the first three months after birth, there is

    (A) an increase in day sleep and a decrease in night sleep
    (B) a decrease in day sleep and an increase in night sleep
    (C) no change in sleeping schedule
    (D) erratic sleep without identifiable pattern
    (E) increased day sleep for boys, decreased day sleep for girls

120. Menarche refers to the _____ and occurs around _____ years of age.

    (A) appearance of pubic hair; twelve
    (B) acquisition of one's final height; eighteen
    (C) ability to become pregnant; fourteen
    (D) first menstrual period; thirteen
    (E) first incident of secondary sexual characteristics; eleven

121. Stress-resistant individuals differ from their counterparts on which of the following dimensions?

    (A) social and work involvement
    (B) where they were in their family birth order
    (C) intelligence
    (D) family history of schizophrenia incidence
    (E) creativity

122. When the government first began citing statistics correlating lung cancer with cigarette smoking, which of the following statements was a frequent answer from the cigarette manufacturers?

    (A) The tests were biased.
    (B) Representative samples had not been selected.
    (C) The research lacked a control group.
    (D) Correlation does not mean causation.
    (E) Research was performed only on males.

123. A correct sequential or developmental order is represented by

    (A) ego, superego, id
    (B) anal, oral, phallic
    (C) inferiority feeling, superiority striving
    (D) autonomy versus shame and doubt; trust versus mistrust
    (E) parataxic, prototaxic, syntaxic

GO ON TO THE NEXT PAGE

124. Which of the following deficiencies in a pregnant mother would have the most direct and marked effect on brain metabolism and development of learning ability in her newborn?

   (A) vitamin A
   (B) vitamin B
   (C) vitamin C
   (D) vitamin D
   (E) cholesterol

125. Newborns

   (A) cannot discriminate differences in tonal pitch
   (B) have good eye-muscle coordination
   (C) have prominent sphincter-muscle control
   (D) can detect color and shape
   (E) can see faces clearly

126. Severe anoxia at birth most likely will result in damage to the

   (A) brain
   (B) lungs
   (C) heart
   (D) kidneys
   (E) liver

127. According to the concept of coaction,

   (A) Children work faster when another child is present and doing the same task than they would alone.
   (B) Children work more slowly when another child is present and doing the same task than they would alone.
   (C) Children work faster in the presence of an audience than they do when working alone.
   (D) Children work more slowly in the presence of an audience than they do when working alone.
   (E) Children work most effectively when doing two tasks at the same time.

GO ON TO THE NEXT PAGE

Under some conditions, war is necessary to maintain justice. (7.5)
The benefits of war rarely pay for its losses even for the victor. (3.5)
War brings out the best qualities in men. (9.7)
There is no conceivable justification for war. (.2)

128. The above items along with their numbers and decimals are part of

(A) a Likert scale
(B) a Thurstone scale
(C) an Osgood scale
(D) a Bogardus scale
(E) a Remmers scale

129. A subject obtaining a high score on a scale of this type (in comparison with a low-scoring subject) would be

(A) much more pro-war
(B) much less in favor of war
(C) essentially the same in war viewpoint
(D) strongly antiwar
(E) moderately antiwar

130. To be selected for inclusion in this scale, a statement must meet the criterion of

(A) high standard deviation in judge ratings
(B) moderate standard deviation in judge ratings
(C) low standard deviation in judge ratings
(D) high mean rating among judges
(E) low mean rating among judges

131. The numbers in parentheses

(A) represent the mean of ratings assigned to this statement by a large number of judges
(B) represent the mode of ratings assigned to this statement by a large number of judges
(C) represent the average rating assigned to similar statements by a large number of judges
(D) are determined and assigned by the experimenter
(E) are determined and assigned by the subject

GO ON TO THE NEXT PAGE

132. One boy has brown eyes. His twin brother has blue eyes. This information enables a person to conclude that the two

(A) are identical twins
(B) are fraternal twins
(C) exhibit sex-linked hereditary characteristics
(D) are monozygotic
(E) have blue-eyed parents

133. Developmentally, which of the following refers to reduction division?

(A) mitosis
(B) heterosis
(C) parthenogenesis
(D) morphosis
(E) meiosis

134. Which of the following is a correct developmental sequence?

(A) ovum-sperm, blastocyst, zygote
(B) blastocyst, ovum-sperm, zygote
(C) blastocyst, zygote, ovum-sperm
(D) ovum-sperm, zygote, blastocyst
(E) ovum-sperm, placenta, blastocyst

135. Among the following, the most rigorous type of validity is

(A) face
(B) split-half
(C) content
(D) test-retest
(E) predictive

136. Assuming that the correlation between length of eyelashes and number of dates is +.74, which of the following would apply to the process through which the experimenter seeks to determine the number of dates for a specific girl having a given eyelash length?

(A) correlation
(B) regression
(C) significance level
(D) sampling
(E) hypothesis testing

GO ON TO THE NEXT PAGE

137. "Period of adolescent sterility" refers to

   (A) prepubescence in boys
   (B) the time immediately before menarche in girls
   (C) the time immediately after menarche in girls
   (D) an adolescent male's temporary sterility immediately following the attainment of sexual maturity
   (E) the postpubescent period in boys

138. Which one of the following combinations would, by definition, be necessary to have an attitude?

   (A) enduring system, feeling component
   (B) temporary system, cognitive component
   (C) stereotype system, action component
   (D) modification system, behavioral component
   (E) action system, temporary component

139. According to the findings of Lewin, Lippitt, and White, which of the following leadership styles would create the highest group productivity when the leader is absent?

   (A) autocratic
   (B) democratic
   (C) laissez-faire
   (D) laissez-faire or autocratic (equally productive)
   (E) laissez-faire or democratic (equally productive)

140. When two people play nonzero-sum games, there is a tendency for

   (A) cooperation
   (B) competition
   (C) high level of trust
   (D) matrices renovation
   (E) threat potential to enhance cooperation

141. Person A has lied for a $1 payoff while Person B told a similar lie for $20. Person B is

   (A) less likely to believe the lie
   (B) more likely to believe the lie
   (C) equivalent to Person A in belief likelihood
   (D) experiencing more cognitive dissonance
   (E) experiencing more cognitive irrelevance

GO ON TO THE NEXT PAGE

142. When pilots must learn to fly a new type of passenger plane, their transfer to the new set of controls is facilitated most when the new panel

    (A) is similar to but has subtle functional differences from the old panel
    (B) is distinctly different from the old panel in all respects
    (C) looks identical but has some functions that are the exact reverse of what they were in the previous setting
    (D) is an exact right-left reverse of the previous panel
    (E) is an exact copy of the previous panel except that all dial calibrations are reversed

143. Which one of the following statements would *not* be a firmly based criticism of psychoanalysis?

    (A) It is heavily based upon subjective, clinical observation.
    (B) It places an overemphasis upon instinctual behavior.
    (C) It places heavy emphasis upon abnormal behavior.
    (D) It stresses intrapsychic, nonobservable emotions.
    (E) It places primary emphasis upon changing the current problem behavior.

144. As viewed by phenomenologists, which of the following does *not* affect personality in any tangible way?

    (A) past perceptions
    (B) the length of time a person has been exposed to a given perceptual environment
    (C) the person's perceptual outlook brought to the experiencing of external events
    (D) early childhood relationships to family
    (E) archetypal continuities

145. Emotional problems are treated through role-playing techniques in

    (A) psychodrama
    (B) client-centered therapy
    (C) implosive therapy
    (D) logotherapy
    (E) psychoanalysis

GO ON TO THE NEXT PAGE

146. A company wants to utilize an individual intelligence test that (1) will be sensitive to individuals who may do quite well on performance-type tasks but may do poorly on verbal tasks, (2) within its basic formulation evenly represents IQ scores throughout the adulthood age span. Given these guidelines your recommendation would be:

(A) Draw-a-Person Test
(B) Wechsler Adult Intelligence Scale
(C) Stanford-Binet Intelligence Test
(D) Otis-Lennon Test
(E) Minnesota Multiphasic Test

147. During a child's first two years, the child's weight concept is

(A) highly accurate
(B) based entirely on stimulus brightness
(C) based entirely on stimulus shape
(D) based entirely on stimulus size
(E) based entirely on stimulus color

148. Which one of the following is found in newborns?

(A) identical sleep-wakefulness time proportions
(B) almost immediate emotional response to their mothers
(C) fear of strangers
(D) babbling
(E) partial taste sensitivity

149. At what point could a newborn be expected to have the capacity for visually tracking a moving object?

(A) immediately after birth
(B) within a few days after birth
(C) during the second week after birth
(D) at the end of the first month after birth
(E) only shortly before walking occurs

150. In Bandura's experimental work with children, he has demonstrated that

(A) imitation learning occurs through observation
(B) mimicking occurs through reinforcement
(C) toilet training occurs through modeling
(D) toilet training occurs through judicious use of punishment
(E) aggression does not appear to be learned

GO ON TO THE NEXT PAGE

151. Research on infant feeding practices indicates that

(A) there is a clear advantage for breast-fed babies
(B) mothers who breast feed actually tend to be rather tense about sexual matters
(C) most women who try breast feeding soon stop for psychological reasons
(D) the particular methods matter relatively little if the mother is sincere and comfortable with the method
(E) there is a lower incidence of smoking among adults who were breast-fed as infants than among their bottle-fed counterparts

152. The highest incidence of schizophrenia has been found

(A) between fraternal twins
(B) between identical twins
(C) between siblings
(D) in the southeastern United States
(E) in urban areas

153. Relaxation followed by successive approximation to objects formerly feared is

(A) aversive conditioning
(B) fear conditioning
(C) systematic desensitization
(D) implosive therapy
(E) environmental shock therapy

154. Long-term follow-up studies of patients treated through applied behavior analysis techniques indicate

(A) high rates of relapse among practically all patients
(B) high rates of relapse among neurotic patients
(C) high rates of relapse among hypochondriacal patients
(D) few relapses
(E) a low, marginal level of effective life functioning

155. The symptoms of somatic symptom disorder

(A) are unconsciously aimed at obtaining sympathy
(B) do not have any underlying medical cause
(C) result from hallucinations, or false perceptions
(D) are simple to distinguish from symptoms arising from medical conditions
(E) are often mistaken for those of dissociative identity disorder

GO ON TO THE NEXT PAGE

156. Which one of the following statements about IQ scores is true?

   (A) There is a strong correlation of IQ test scores throughout the entire life span.
   (B) The highest validity is found in early IQ test scores.
   (C) There is a negative correlation between early and later test scores.
   (D) The highest reliability and lowest validity are found in early test scores.
   (E) There is virtually no predictive validity between scores obtained prior to age two and those obtained at a later age.

157. In which of the following areas does an older person have the greatest likelihood of demonstrating increases in intelligence?

   (A) digit span
   (B) pursuit rotor
   (C) block design
   (D) spatial relations
   (E) vocabulary

158. Research evidence suggests that in the final aspects of the fetal stage

   (A) extreme pain sensitivity is present
   (B) capability exists only for reflex movements
   (C) capability exists for learning simple responses
   (D) a "quiet period" sets in during which detectable motor movements are very rare
   (E) the basics of newborn vocal sound can be detected

QUESTIONS 159 AND 160 ARE BASED ON THE FOLLOWING STATISTICAL INFORMATION.

   95%—use a z-score of 1.96
   99%—use a z-score of 2.58

159. For one hundred scores on a given test, the mean is seventy-four and the standard deviation, eight. The 95 percent confidence interval for the mean of the population is

   (A) 72.4 to 75.6
   (B) 71.8 to 75
   (C) 70.5 to 73.7
   (D) 71 to 74.2
   (E) 70 to 73.2

GO ON TO THE NEXT PAGE

160. The 99 percent confidence interval for the mean of the population is

(A) 69.8 to 74
(B) 70 to 74.2
(C) 71.9 to 76.1
(D) 72.5 to 76.7
(E) 73 to 77.2

161. A researcher sits beside a playground, carefully observing a small group of children. The method being utilized is

(A) life-history
(B) case-history
(C) laboratory
(D) survey
(E) field-study

162. Enhancing the action of dopamine receptors has what effect on schizophrenic symptoms? Blocking these receptors has what effect on schizophrenic symptoms?

(A) increases/increases
(B) decreases/decreases
(C) increases/decreases
(D) decreases/increases
(E) does not affect/does not affect

163. Which of the following is *not* true of dopamine?

(A) It is a neurotransmitter.
(B) Amphetamines increase its release.
(C) It is implicated as a potential underlying cause in schizophrenia.
(D) It is blocked by antipsychotic drugs.
(E) It is located in the thyroid gland.

164. When a person is secretive about drinking and has occasional "blackouts," that individual is most likely in the

(A) prealcoholic stage
(B) prodromal stage
(C) crucial stage
(D) chronic stage
(E) undifferentiated stage

GO ON TO THE NEXT PAGE

165. Within the current classification system (DSM-5), hypochondriasis would be considered what type of disorder?

(A) psychosexual
(B) dissociative
(C) anxiety
(D) affective
(E) somatoform

166. Childhood accidents are

(A) more prevalent in the second year than in the first year
(B) more prevalent in the first year than in the second year
(C) prevalent with equal incidence in both the first and second years
(D) more prevalent among girls than among boys
(E) more prevalent in the first six months after birth than thereafter

167. Which one of the following elements would invariably be present in Type I error?

(A) rejection of a null hypothesis
(B) acceptance of a null hypothesis
(C) one-tailed test
(D) two-tailed test
(E) establishment of a significance level below .05

168. On a five-item Guttman scale, a person has a score of 3. To fulfill unidimensionality requirements, this person would be in agreement with items

(A) 1, 3, 5
(B) 1, 3, 4
(C) 1, 2, 3
(D) 2, 4, 5
(E) 1, 4, 5

169. Which one of the following would *not* be categorized among personality disorders?

(A) paranoid
(B) schizoid
(C) antisocial
(D) histrionic
(E) neuroleptic

GO ON TO THE NEXT PAGE

170. Which one of the following findings has been voiced in the past few years by notable mental health professionals?

   (A) Lack of warm social approval is in no way related to disease susceptibility.
   (B) Disease prevention is not dependent on diet.
   (C) Disease prevention is not dependent on exercise.
   (D) Married men have a higher death-rate incidence than their divorced male counterparts.
   (E) Geographical locations with the highest heart disease rate also have the highest rates of cancer incidence.

171. A person expressing functional blindness could be experiencing

   (A) a dissociative disorder
   (B) a somatic symptom disorder
   (C) an anxiety disorder
   (D) a mood disorder
   (E) a cyclothymic disorder

172. Which of the following substances is/are included within the classification of substance-related disorders?

   I.   amphetamine
   II. caffeine
   III. cocaine

   (A) I and II
   (B) II and III
   (C) I and III
   (D) I, II, and III
   (E) III only

173. Which of the following would *not* characterize any form of personality disorder?

   (A) emotional shallowness
   (B) antisocial behavior
   (C) incapability of group or individual loyalties
   (D) depression
   (E) rebellion against society

174. Repression : suppression ::

   (A) classical : instrumental
   (B) semiautomatic : automatic
   (C) fixation : regression
   (D) frustration : conflict
   (E) involuntary : voluntary

GO ON TO THE NEXT PAGE

175. Which of the following is the *most* common disorder?

(A) anxiety disorder
(B) somatic symptom disorder
(C) dissociative disorder
(D) factitious disorder
(E) personality disorder

176. Which of the following would be considered the *least* important factor in a therapist's success rate?

(A) personality theory orientation
(B) amount of experience
(C) capacity for empathy
(D) genuineness
(E) warmth

177. The individual is opioid-addicted. The individual is most likely taking which of the following?

(A) cocaine
(B) morphine
(C) clozapine
(D) phenobarbital
(E) methaqualone

178. In a positively skewed distribution, the median is

(A) larger than the mean
(B) equal to the mean
(C) equal to the mode
(D) larger than the mode
(E) actually negatively skewed

179. Given limited funds and a limited time period, which of the following methods might be recommended for dealing with a phobic reaction?

(A) psychoanalysis
(B) transcendental meditation
(C) systematic desensitization
(D) logotherapy
(E) ego analysis

GO ON TO THE NEXT PAGE

180. In the classic Hawthorne plant study at Western Electric, results pointed to the critical importance of

(A) supervisor dominance
(B) employer's concern toward workers
(C) timing and frequency of coffee breaks
(D) employing only females for work in the plant
(E) employing only highly skilled workers

181. The mean of a group of scores is fifty and the standard deviation, ten. If the test scores are normally distributed, approximately what percentage of the people taking this test will score between ten and sixty?

(A) 16 percent
(B) 50 percent
(C) 64 percent
(D) 84 percent
(E) 98 percent

QUESTIONS 182 AND 183 ARE BASED ON THE FOLLOWING PERCENTILE RANKS IN A NORMAL DISTRIBUTION.

(1) 2nd
(2) 16th
(3) 84th
(4) 98th
(5) none of the above

182. Which one of the above percentile ranks would correspond to a z-score of −1.0?

(A) 1
(B) 2
(C) 3
(D) 4
(E) 5

183. Which one of the above percentile ranks would correspond to a z-score of +3.0?

(A) 1
(B) 2
(C) 3
(D) 4
(E) 5

GO ON TO THE NEXT PAGE

184. A test score that has *not* been converted into a form permitting comparison with scores from other tests is known as a

    (A) stanine score
    (B) percentile score
    (C) raw score
    (D) *z*-score
    (E) quartile score

185. The most reliable public opinion polling is that which

    (A) accompanies census bureau statistics
    (B) was done for the Kinsey report
    (C) private firms conduct prior to a political election
    (D) detergent firms conduct concerning product satisfaction
    (E) gasoline companies conduct to learn about driving habits

186. The members of the training group each read several pages of description dealing with a managerial dilemma and the way in which it was dealt with by an individual. The method being used with the group is

    (A) case
    (B) incident
    (C) role playing
    (D) sensitivity training
    (E) free association

187. A company wishes to market a new product and has the natural desire to get large consumer subscription to it. The cognitive dissonance research results of Doob et al. recommend which of the following pricing approaches?

    (A) price initially below the eventual price
    (B) price initially well above the eventual price
    (C) price initially at the eventual price level
    (D) price identically with the largest competitors, regardless of their existing prices
    (E) price regionally rather than nationally set

GO ON TO THE NEXT PAGE

188. In a randomly selected sample, the following distribution was obtained:

Sex	Democrat	Republican
Male	65	35
Female	30	20

To test the hypothesis that the two discrete variables (sex, political party) are independent in the population that yielded the sample, we should use

(A) a t-test
(B) regression statistics
(C) a z-test
(D) chi-square
(E) Duncan's multiple-range test

189. Assuming that a multitude of equal-sized, random samples are gathered from the same infinite population, the mean of each sample is computed, and the means of the different samples are put together to form a new distribution; which one of the following statements about the new distribution is true?

(A) The mean would be greater than the median or the mode.
(B) The distribution would be normal.
(C) The distribution would be positively skewed.
(D) The standard deviation would equal 1.0.
(E) The distribution would be negatively skewed.

190. "The mean of the squared differences from the mean of the distribution" is a definition of

(A) mode
(B) platikurtic
(C) chi-square
(D) variance
(E) t-distribution

191. According to the research of Janis, Kaye, et al., which one of the following activities would be most likely to establish persuasiveness in a written communication?

(A) reading while in a very relaxed position
(B) reading while watching TV
(C) eating while reading
(D) talking while reading
(E) listening to music while reading

GO ON TO THE NEXT PAGE

192. Maslow associated all of these characteristics with self-actualizing people *except*

    (A) spontaneity
    (B) need for privacy
    (C) strong friendships, limited in number
    (D) feelings of kinship and identification with the human race
    (E) notable financial success

193. Under most circumstances, humans like to be liked. Which of the following would give us negative feelings toward someone saying kind things to us?

    (A) compliments
    (B) admiration
    (C) ingratiation
    (D) special caring
    (E) willingness to help

194. All of the following could be said of companionate love *except*

    (A) it is characterized by affection
    (B) it is erotic and passionate
    (C) it is enhanced by self-disclosure
    (D) it is premised on equity
    (E) it has the quality of friendship

195. You are the mayor of a large city. You want desperately to develop a sense of positive feeling and positive interaction among groups that traditionally have been hostile to one another. One option you might consider for effectiveness is

    (A) simply bringing the groups together
    (B) setting a superordinate goal
    (C) sponsoring "feel good" ad boards across the city
    (D) establishing tough law-and-order measures
    (E) airing several television commercials

196. When two hostile countries heighten the blunt name-calling and smears of each other and any chance of averting war seems impossible, which of the following might have a chance for success?

    (A) bringing together the foreign ministers of each country for a last-minute discussion
    (B) scheduling a meeting of the two leaders
    (C) an Osgood-developed program named GRIT
    (D) building up arms levels on both sides
    (E) calling a truce for an indefinite period

GO ON TO THE NEXT PAGE

197. The term *copycat violence* has sometimes been used in relation to media productions. To what does it refer?

    I.   Different media outlets trying to "one-up" each other in violence for ratings

    II.   An overall network pattern of increasing violence-laden programming in the year after such programming has received high ratings

    III.   Viewers acting out the violent acts they have seen within the programming

(A) I only

(B) II only

(C) III only

(D) I and II

(E) II and III

198. Which of the following influences is found in the childhood backgrounds of adults with a high achievement need?

(A) encouragement of curiosity

(B) encouragement of creativity

(C) encouragement of independence

(D) frequent frustrations

(E) encouragement of aggression

199. Perceptually, to "wait 'til Christmas" would be the longest wait for the

(A) preschool child

(B) elementary-school child

(C) teenager

(D) college-age adult

(E) middle-age adult

200. The Gestalt school of psychology subscribes to the basic principle that

(A) only overt behavior can be studied scientifically

(B) behavior or experience equals more than the sum of its parts

(C) psychology must concern itself only with studying our adjustment to our environment

(D) thanatos-eros forms the primary conflict to be studied within psychology

(E) conscious experience cannot be a legitimate area for scientific investigation

201. Which of the following is an apparent bodily response to the emotions of resentment and hostility?

(A) lower heart rate

(B) lower blood pressure

(C) heightened auditory sensitivity

(D) lower breathing rate

(E) increased stomach acidity

GO ON TO THE NEXT PAGE

202. Elizabeth Loftus has reported that the testimony given by eyewitnesses in a trial is

(A) very accurate when the event is highly emotionally charged
(B) very accurate when the event is surprising or unexpected
(C) susceptible to errors from post-event misinformation or suggestions
(D) inaccurate because witnesses fail to pay attention to critical details
(E) not weighed heavily by jurors in reaching a verdict

203. Which of the following is *not* true of emotion?

(A) A linkage has been noticed between specific facial expressions and resulting emotions.
(B) Expecting to experience a given emotion can result in the emotion actually being experienced.
(C) Opponent process theory suggests that the opposite of a given emotion may follow its being experienced.
(D) There appears to be no relationship between ulcers and emotional state.
(E) The James-Lange theory suggests we are afraid because we run.

204. One would expect reversal shifts to be accomplished most easily and most rapidly within which of the following groups?

(A) rats
(B) dogs
(C) two-year-old children
(D) seven-year-old children
(E) ten-year-old children

205. A cryptarithmetic problem widely used in the study of human problem solving has been

(A) A + B = C
(B) Alpha + Beta = Kappa
(C) DONALD + GERALD = ROBERT
(D) MARY + SUSAN = ELIZABETH
(E) Alpha = Gamma + Beta

206. On the basis of Schachter's research, one might conclude that

(A) misery loves any kind of company
(B) misery loves any kind of miserable company
(C) misery loves only miserable company in the same situational circumstances
(D) familiarity breeds prejudicial contempt
(E) likes attract, opposites repel

GO ON TO THE NEXT PAGE

207. In Rogers' view, through interaction with one's environment, a portion of the phenomenal field becomes differentiated and known as the

   (A) archetype
   (B) script
   (C) superego
   (D) frame of orientation
   (E) self-concept

208. When the performance of an individual is enhanced by the mere presence of others, the phenomenon is called

   (A) reactive facilitation
   (B) cognitive dissonance
   (C) conformity
   (D) social facilitation
   (E) complementarity

209. A person is highly competitive, cannot relax, feels a great sense of time urgency, and frequently becomes impatient or irritated with others. In stress and heart disease terms this person would be characterized as

   (A) Type X
   (B) Type A
   (C) Type Y
   (D) Type B
   (E) Type H

210. All of the following are true of attitudes *except*

   (A) predispositions to respond
   (B) relatively stable
   (C) an emotional component
   (D) unconditioned
   (E) a cognitive component

211. Aggression displacement suggests that the farther removed an object or person is from the source of frustration the

   (A) lower the frustration
   (B) lower the cooperation
   (C) higher the inhibition
   (D) greater the cooperation
   (E) greater the likelihood of aggressive actions

GO ON TO THE NEXT PAGE

212. Which of the following is an *incorrect* statement relating to suicide?

    (A) There is a higher incidence of suicide among churchgoers.
    (B) The family of the suicide victim frequently attempts to conceal the cause of death.
    (C) The lowest likelihood of suicide is among persons who talk about doing it.
    (D) There is a higher incidence of suicide among divorced persons and persons living alone.
    (E) There is a higher incidence of suicide among persons believing in life after death.

213. An experimenter wishes to determine the effects of different shock intensities on GSR. She believes, however, that it will be essential to counterbalance the shock intensities by having one group receive high intensity first, a second group receive medium intensity first, and so on. The statistical design within which she has organized the experiment is

    (A) Two-Factor Mixed ANOVA
    (B) Pearson Product Moment Correlation
    (C) *t*-test
    (D) point-biserial correlation
    (E) Latin Square

214. Believing that the CIA and the attorney general are out to get him, a man comes out of his apartment only at night after painstaking efforts to be certain he is not being followed. This is a case of

    (A) paranoid schizophrenia
    (B) paranoid personality disorder
    (C) dissociative reaction
    (D) anxiety reaction
    (E) obsessive-compulsive reaction

215. The statistic that deals most prominently with the terms *observed frequency, expected frequency,* and *contingency tables* is

    (A) *t*
    (B) *z*
    (C) chi-square
    (D) analysis of covariance
    (E) point-biserial correlation

If there is still time remaining, you may review your answers.

ANSWER KEY
Practice Test 3

1.	A	37.	A	73.	B	109.	C	145.	A	181.	D
2.	C	38.	C	74.	B	110.	C	146.	B	182.	B
3.	C	39.	B	75.	C	111.	A	147.	D	183.	E
4.	B	40.	C	76.	A	112.	B	148.	E	184.	C
5.	B	41.	B	77.	E	113.	C	149.	B	185.	C
6.	B	42.	B	78.	A	114.	B	150.	A	186.	A
7.	A	43.	E	79.	D	115.	C	151.	D	187.	C
8.	C	44.	C	80.	E	116.	A	152.	B	188.	D
9.	B	45.	B	81.	B	117.	A	153.	C	189.	B
10.	A	46.	C	82.	D	118.	A	154.	D	190.	D
11.	C	47.	C	83.	D	119.	B	155.	B	191.	C
12.	B	48.	D	84.	A	120.	D	156.	E	192.	E
13.	E	49.	B	85.	A	121.	A	157.	E	193.	C
14.	C	50.	D	86.	A	122.	D	158.	C	194.	B
15.	A	51.	A	87.	B	123.	C	159.	A	195.	B
16.	A	52.	C	88.	A	124.	B	160.	C	196.	C
17.	E	53.	B	89.	A	125.	D	161.	E	197.	C
18.	B	54.	A	90.	C	126.	A	162.	C	198.	C
19.	B	55.	A	91.	C	127.	A	163.	E	199.	A
20.	C	56.	B	92.	D	128.	B	164.	B	200.	B
21.	D	57.	E	93.	A	129.	A	165.	E	201.	E
22.	A	58.	E	94.	C	130.	C	166.	A	202.	C
23.	E	59.	A	95.	D	131.	A	167.	A	203.	D
24.	E	60.	C	96.	C	132.	B	168.	C	204.	E
25.	D	61.	A	97.	D	133.	E	169.	E	205.	C
26.	E	62.	A	98.	B	134.	D	170.	E	206.	C
27.	A	63.	D	99.	C	135.	E	171.	B	207.	E
28.	D	64.	C	100.	D	136.	B	172.	D	208.	D
29.	C	65.	E	101.	C	137.	C	173.	D	209.	B
30.	C	66.	A	102.	C	138.	A	174.	E	210.	D
31.	C	67.	D	103.	B	139.	B	175.	A	211.	E
32.	E	68.	A	104.	C	140.	B	176.	A	212.	C
33.	A	69.	D	105.	D	141.	A	177.	B	213.	E
34.	B	70.	B	106.	B	142.	B	178.	D	214.	B
35.	E	71.	C	107.	B	143.	E	179.	C	215.	C
36.	A	72.	A	108.	B	144.	E	180.	B		

To score your third and final practice test, please compare the answers on your answer sheet with the answers below. Place a check mark next to questions you answered correctly. Place an "X" next to questions you answered incorrectly. Leave questions you did not answer blank.

ANSWER EXPLANATIONS

_____ 1. **(A)** Testosterone, a steroid hormone released from the testes of males and the ovaries of females, is associated with physical aggression in many species; however, in humans this relation is not totally clear-cut.

_____ 2. **(C)** Much of the scientific community was excited by this apparent demonstration of a simple syntax in a natural nonhuman communication system.

_____ 3. **(C)** An action potential, once initiated, always reaches the same amplitude, leading it to be described as "all-or-none." In contrast, EPSPs and IPSPs are referred to as graded potentials, because they can vary in amplitude (depending on the amount of neurotransmitter that binds to the post-synaptic receptors).

_____ 4. **(B)** Patients with visual agnosia are unable to perceive and recognize objects they see (although their memory and language faculties are otherwise intact). All of the other terms (except aplysia, which is a simple sea slug used in studies of cellular learning) refer to different neuropsychological disorders that do not affect visual perception.

_____ 5. **(B)** Preparatory instruction serves to shorten reaction time.

_____ 6. **(B)** Information about bodily sensations (touch, temperature, pain, position) is received (initially) in the parietal cortex, just posterior to the central sulcus separating the frontal and parietal lobes.

_____ 7. **(A)** The two properties of a waveform discussed in reference to sound are amplitude (the height of the waveform) and frequency (which is related to the length of the waveform but technically refers to the number of wave peaks per second). Note that frequency/wavelength in vision is related to color perception.

_____ 8. **(C)** Leptin is released by fat cells in the body and is recognized by brain centers as a signal of satiety; mutations in the leptin gene lead to a constant desire for food (and thus obesity).

_____ 9. **(B)** Endel Tulving first distinguished semantic memory of facts, meanings, and general knowledge from episodic memory of personal events tied to specific experiences.

_____ 10. **(A)** Half of the subjects received an injection of adrenalin (epinephrine), to mimic the body's normal response to an arousing situation. The experiment demonstrated that the experience of emotions depends on a cognitive assessment of a physiological response—subjects who were not given an explanation for their physiological state mimicked the confederate's behavior (elated or angry).

_____ 11. **(C)** Skinner found that punishment during extinction trials produces the same total number of responses as found in extinction trials without punishment.

_____ 12. **(B)** An individual with sleep apnea is typically unaware of difficulty breathing during the night; polysomnograms (sleep tests) can be used to definitively diagnose sleep apnea.

_____ 13. **(E)** The large difference in the concentration of potassium (K+) ions inside (relative to outside) the neuron helps to create the electrical gradient referred to as the resting potential.

_____ 14. **(C)** Information transferred to working memory from either the sensory register or long-term memory can be rehearsed, reorganized, and manipulated.

_____ 15. **(A)** James, credited with setting up the first experimental psychology lab (at Harvard in 1875), spent over a decade writing this textbook on experimental psychology.

_____ 16. **(A)** A general problem-solving strategy or rule of thumb is called a heuristic, whereas an algorithm is a methodical (but more time-consuming) recipe for successfully solving a problem.

_____ 17. **(E)** Regulation of body temperature is associated with the hypothalamus.

_____ 18. **(B)** The Rescorla-Wagner model provides a powerful explanation of many learning phenomena, such as blocking, by introducing the notion of "surprise" into the learning equation.

_____ 19. **(B)** When a photoreceptor is stimulated, it excites some nerve cells but inhibits other, neighboring nerve cells. As a result of this lateral inhibition, a dark patch right next to a light patch will look even darker (at the edge).

_____ 20. **(C)** Primary visual cortex (in the occipital lobe) is organized with respect to visual field (not eye): Visual information from the left part of space (relative to where the eyes are focused) is received by the right occipital cortex and information from the right part of space is received by the left occipital cortex. Damage to the left occipital cortex, as in Clive's case, will cause a visual impairment in the right side of space.

_____ 21. **(D)** Schemata (the plural of _schema_) are abstract mental structures that represent one's understanding of some aspect of the world. Another way to say that you know how to go about driving a car would be to say that you have a schema for driving a car. It is an abstract representation of the real-world event of driving a car.

_____ 22. **(A)** Edward Thorndike's law of exercise stated that stimulus–response associations are strengthened through repetition; this can be contrasted with his law of effect, which focused on outcomes rather than repetition.

_____ 23. **(E)** Similar in meaning to the phrase "photographic memory," eidetic memory can also be applied to extremely vivid memories in other modalities (e.g., sound).

_____ 24. **(E)** The galvanic skin response (GSR) is a measure of changes in the electrical resistance of the skin, caused by a change in sweat gland activity. Changes in GSR occur with changes in emotional states, although in a nonspecific manner (i.e., the GSR response looks similar in response to fear, anger, sexual arousal, and so on).

_____ 25. **(D)** Evolutionary psychologists apply the basic tenets of natural selection to psychological traits, as they consider how the survival demands that our early human ancestors faced in their hunting and gathering societies may have shaped our behaviors, emotions, and preferences.

_____ 26. **(E)** Excitatory potentials on the neuron's dendrites spread to the soma and trigger an action potential, which propagates down the axon to the axon terminal, where neurotransmitters are released into the synaptic cleft.

_____ 27. **(A)** According to the opponent process theory, activation of one member of an antagonistic pair (red/green, yellow/blue, black/white) automatically inhibits the other. This theory provides an account of negative afterimage effects. Although the theory was originally developed to explain color vision, the notion of antagonistic states was subsequently applied to other sensory systems and even to more complex psychological states (e.g., emotion, motivation, addiction).

_____ 28. **(D)** Episodic memories make reference to a specific time and place.

_____ 29. **(C)** If a subject is guessing, he or she should say "old" to half of the studied words and to half of the unstudied words. Thus, of the fifty studied words, he or she would be expected to have twenty-five hits (saying "old" to an old item), and of the fifty unstudied words, he or she would be expected to have twenty-five false alarms (saying "old" to a new item). Hits minus false alarms would therefore be zero. Note that some subjects might be guessing, but have a bias to say "new"; they would have fewer than twenty-five hits and fewer than twenty-five false alarms, but the expected difference would still be zero.

_____ 30. **(C)** Although the analysis may reveal either of the stated main effects, the only outcome that is required for the researcher's conclusion is the interaction. The significant interaction would indicate that the effect of emotional content varies as a function of testing time.

_____ 31. **(C)** If the emotional words are less common than the neutral words, the memory effect attributed to emotional content might instead be an example of enhanced recognition memory for uncommon words.

_____ 32. **(E)** This is an example of an experiment measuring repetition priming, which is defined as an improvement in the speed or accuracy to detect, recognize, or produce some item as a result of a prior encounter with that item. Repetition priming effects can be quite long-lasting; facilitation of picture-naming latency (such as in this case) has been reported to persist for months!

_____ 33. **(A)** The garden path effect—namely, that readers/listeners can be misled early in a sentence about the meaning and thus need to reevaluate as the sentence goes on—illustrates that sentence comprehension is an incremental (gradual) process (e.g., The man who whistles tunes pianos).

_____ 34. **(B)** The olfactory sense is credited with the phenomenon of menstrual synchrony.

_____ 35. **(E)** Mutations are changes to the sequence of nucleotides that compose our DNA, and they create variations in the gene pool that are the target of natural selection.

_____ 36. **(A)** The suprachiasmatic nucleus controls circadian rhythms (i.e., our daily biological clock). The SCN receives input from the eyes, which is why light exposure affects our sleep–wake cycles.

_____ 37. **(A)** The Wisconsin Card Sorting Test (WCST) requires subjects to place multidimensional cards into piles based on a single sorting rule (e.g., shape), and then measures their ability to switch to a new rule (e.g., number of items). The test was developed to measure executive control deficits in brain-damaged patients.

_____ 38. **(C)** Retrograde amnesia (which is a common consequence of a concussion as in this example), is a loss of memory for events prior to the onset of head trauma or brain damage. It is contrasted with anterograde amnesia, which is an inability to learn and remember events that occur after the onset of head trauma.

_____ 39. **(B)** The term _mnemonic device_ refers to any method for improving memory. Many mnemonics work by making meaningless information more meaningful, as in this case: The arbitrary order of EGBDF can be remembered with this more meaningful phrase.

_____ 40. **(C)** If Jon has a greater bias to say "yes" but not greater sensitivity, he will have more false alarms and hits (the two responses that involve saying "yes") and fewer misses and false rejects than will Grace.

_____ 41. **(B)** Rods are insensitive to long-wavelength (red) light. In a normally lit briefing room, the rods would be active and therefore become saturated and then would not function well on the night flight. But, with goggles that only allow long-wavelength (red) light to reach the eyes, vision is still possible (with the cones) yet does not saturate the rods, leaving the pilots ready for their night flight. This example is related to the Purkinje shift: under low light levels, color sensitivity shifts away from the red end of the spectrum.

_____ 42. **(B)** An increased level of prenatal male sex hormones results in the development of a clitoris in a genetic girl (i.e., XX) that resembles the penis of a boy.

_____ 43. **(E)** Ebbinghaus measured the effect of prior exposure on the amount of time required to relearn a list of words, and he distinguished this from conscious recollection. This mirrors the contemporary distinction between implicit and explicit memory.

_____ 44. **(C)** Kin selection theory accounts for altruistic behavior by explaining that behaviors that help a genetic relative are favored by evolution.

_____ 45. **(B)** Bakers has three meaning-units (morphemes): _bake_ + _er_ (one who does) + _s_ (more than one).

_____ 46. **(C)** State-dependent learning refers to the finding that people remember more when they are retrieving information in the same _context_ as when they learned that information. The context can be a physiological state (e.g., alcohol), an emotional state (e.g., depression), or an environmental state (e.g., a specific room, or seat in a room!).

_____ 47. **(C)** Pragmatics describes the ability for people to communicate more than that which is explicitly stated.

_____ 48. **(D)** In the study of forgetting, interference theory and decay theory have been contrasted and debated for many decades.

_____ 49. **(B)** Confirmation bias refers to the tendency to pay more attention to outcomes that are consistent with our views than those that oppose them. This bias is problematic for inductive reasoning, where individual observations are used to reach general conclusions. A bias to attend to some observations and ignore others can lead to the wrong conclusion.

_____ 50. **(D)** Using terminology most directly associated with psychologist Eleanor Rosch, a basic level category groups members that are most similar to each other and least similar to members of other categories; most practically, these are more common category labels and are easier to produce or verify. In this case, the two terms both belong to the basic level category of "chair" and the superordinate category of "furniture," but to two different subordinate categories.

_____ 51. **(A)** Delayed conditioning, depicted in Figure 1, is the most efficient classical conditioning paradigm: The CS precedes the UCS, but the two stimuli overlap in time.

_____ 52. **(C)** When the UCS precedes the CS, called backward conditioning, the CS signals the end of the UCS and therefore can produce an inhibitory CR.

_____ 53. **(B)** As with the delayed paradigm, in the trace paradigm the CS precedes the UCS, but there is an interval between the offset of the CS and the onset of the UCS that requires the formation of a memory trace of the CS in order to learn.

_____ 54. **(A)** See answer to question 51.

_____ 55. **(A)** In humans, who have two copies of each chromosome, there are two alleles for each gene that can either be the same (heterozygous) or different (homozygous).

_____ 56. **(B)** EEG recordings are obtained from electrodes placed on various locations on the scalp; depending on the purpose, the number of electrodes can range from just over a dozen (in clinical tests) to over two hundred (in research labs where signal localization is of special interest).

_____ 57. **(E)** There are five stages of sleep: Stages 1–4 and a fifth stage known as REM, or paradoxical, sleep.

_____ 58. **(E)** The corpus callosum is the large white-matter (axon) tract that connects the two cerebral hemispheres; in patients who have had the corpus callosum sectioned to alleviate epileptic seizures, information presented to the left visual field (right hemisphere) cannot reach the left hemisphere areas traditionally associated with language.

_____ 59. **(A)** Connectionism refers broadly to any effort to understand cognitive processes as a result of interactions among interconnected elements in a network. In the 1980s a particular form of connectionism known as parallel distributed processing was popularized by Rumelhart and McClelland.

_____ 60. **(C)** In humans, the dorsal surface of the brain is the superior (top) surface. Note that the word _dorsal_ comes from the root _dorsum_ meaning back, which you can remember by thinking of the dorsal fin of a shark, emerging in the water from the top of its back.

_____ 61. **(A)** A releasing stimulus (or sign stimulus) triggers an instinctive behavioral sequence called a fixed-action pattern. Another way in which yawning is like a fixed-action pattern is that once started, a yawn is quite difficult to stop.

_____ 62. **(A)** The Ponzo illusion arises because of our experience with objects (such as railroad tracks) moving off into the distance. Because we believe the distance between the tracks remains constant, our perception of objects of equal (retinal) size lying across different parts of the track is that the closer object is smaller than the distant object.

_____ 63. **(D)** Prototype theory describes concepts as a set of exemplars related to a central prototype; the more any given exemplar resembles this prototype, the "better" an example of the concept it is. Prototype theory is contrasted with the definitional theory of concepts.

_____ 64. **(C)** As described in the question, the language acquisition device has many of the features considered definitional of a mental module (e.g., domain-specificity, automaticity). The term _module_ is used widely throughout cognitive science, and is associated with the work of Jerry Fodor.

_____ 65. **(E)** Anterograde amnesia (such as that reported in patient H.M.) is an inability to form new episodic memories. (There is some debate about the ability to form new semantic/generic memories, but the relative sparing of the other memory types listed is uncontroversial.)

_____ 66. **(A)** The mood congruency effect is a specific example of encoding specificity (the way you encode an event affects how you will retrieve it) because subjects in a sad mood likely encode events differently than subjects in a happy mood.

_____ 67. **(D)** Negative punishment (or, punishment by contingent withdrawal) decreases a response by following it with the removal of something favorable.

_____ 68. **(A)** If you plot the neuron's membrane potential over a fairly long time scale, each action potential will look like a spike, of fixed amplitude and with almost no duration (because it is so brief), on this plot.

_____ 69. **(D)** Muscles in the eye make the lens flatter for distant-object viewing and rounder for near-object viewing, to allow for proper focusing of the image on the retina. A decrease in the ability for accommodation is an inevitable consequence of aging (and cause for bifocals or reading glasses).

_____ 70. **(B)** Because chess experts have a vocabulary of chess positions, they can group single elements into stored patterns in order to increase their apparent memory span (in the same way that television experts can remember the letter string HBOESPNABC as HBO–ESPN–ABC).

71. **(C)** When applying the representativeness heuristic, one assumes that each individual (or exemplar) is equally representative of a category despite the fact that categories are often not uniform.

72. **(A)** In a dichotic listening experiment like this, low-level perceptual discriminations can be made (such as the high- versus low-frequency difference that distinguishes female and male speech), but higher-level conceptual discriminations that require accessing the meaning of the input typically cannot. (A well-known exception to this rule is when one hears one's own name.)

73. **(B)** Analogical representations share some characteristics with the things they represent whereas symbolic representations are arbitrary. Most researchers now believe that mental images are better described as analogical than symbolic, although there are differences between imagery and perception.

74. **(B)** The terms *kinesthesia* and *proprioception* are both used to refer to our ability to sense the position of different parts of our body.

75. **(C)** The hindbrain comprises three structures: the medulla, the pons, and the cerebellum. The thalamus is part of the forebrain.

76. **(A)** A long metal rod entered Gage's head underneath his eye and exited in the front of his head, passing through (and thus destroying) the frontal lobe of his brain. Note that there is no such thing as a sagittal lobe.

77. **(E)** The Necker cube is an ambiguous representation of a cube. It can be perceived with equivalent ease in each of two interpretations, and because these are not stable, we tend to experience the cube "flipping" between the two. All of the other named illusions produce a single, stable, perceptual experience (that differs from objective reality).

78. **(A)** A classically conditioned response can be extinguished by presenting a CS without a UCS, but after an interval of time with neither stimulus, presenting a CS will elicit the extinguished CR. Spontaneous recovery might allow the learner to "check" if the CS is still uninformative in a new setting.

79. **(D)** The occipital lobe is responsible for our sense of vision, and electrical stimulation of neurons there creates poorly formed visual sensations.

80. **(E)** The method of loci is a mnemonic technique based on imagery. An ordered list of objects can be remembered better (and longer) if you imagine placing each object at a familiar location on a route around your college campus.

81. **(B)** The finding that attention to meaning of words (deep processing) leads to better memory than attention to their superficial characteristics (shallow processing) is an example of the depth of processing effect.

82. **(D)** Finding an appropriate analogy is an important tool in problem solving, as demonstrated in experiments where subjects' ability to solve a problem was improved if they previously read a story involving the solution to an analogous problem.

_____ 83. **(D)** Glial cells wrap around the axon of neurons to form myelin, which speeds the propagation of the action potential down an axon.

_____ 84. **(A)** The amygdala is an evolutionarily ancient subcortical structure in the forebrain, which plays a role in emotional learning, experience, and expression.

_____ 85. **(A)** A drug that increases the rate of reuptake of a neurotransmitter will have the effect of decreasing the response of a postsynaptic cell (because less neurotransmitter will be available to stimulate the cell) and thus will be classified as an antagonist, not an agonist.

_____ 86. **(A)** Function (or closed-class) words—like _the_—are the finite set of words in a language that play largely structural roles rather than conveying specific content (e.g., prepositions, articles); they are contrasted with content (or open-class) words such as common nouns, descriptive adjectives and adverbs, and most verbs. Mass nouns—like _oil_—refer to objects that are not individuated and counted, but rather refer to an unbounded mass; they are contrasted with count nouns.

_____ 87. **(B)** Reinforcement at a constant time interval is called fixed interval.

_____ 88. **(A)** Although a core principle of what is now called Lamarckian evolution—inheritance of acquired characteristics—was not substantiated, the notion that the evolution of species is shaped by the environment is a central tenet of Darwin's theory of evolution by natural selection.

_____ 89. **(A)** Sex recognition and emotion recognition were both measured in every subject, so the comparison of the two can be made within subjects; however, each subject was classified as either having autism spectrum disorder or not, so that comparison must be made between subjects.

_____ 90. **(C)** The significant interaction indicates that the difference between typical children and children with autism spectrum disorder varies across the two tests; choice (E) also describes an interaction, although inspection of the data does not support that interpretation.

_____ 91. **(C)** These data exhibit a "ceiling effect": performance on the sex-recognition test is nearly perfect. In such cases, it is possible that a real deficit in that ability would go undetected. These data could also be interpreted as indicating that children with autism spectrum disorder show bigger impairments on more difficult visual tests, instead of indicating a deficit specific to emotional processing.

_____ 92. **(D)** The term _proximal stimulus_ refers to the information about a stimulus that actually reaches the sensory receptors (in the case of vision, on the retina); a major question in the study of perception is how an observer reconstructs or infers the actual (distal) stimulus from the fairly limited proximal stimulus.

_____ 93. **(A)** The HPA axis is the neuroendocrine system that controls the release of hormones critical to the stress response (e.g., cortisol).

_____ 94. **(C)** Other examples of pheromones are alarm pheromones that trigger flight in bees, trail pheromones that attract and guide ants to a food source, and territorial pheromones that signal territories in dogs.

_____ 95. **(D)** Metamemory is also the ability that guides your belief about when you have studied enough. Have you?

_____ 96. **(C)** As the amplitude of GSR increases across trial blocks for tone 2, a corresponding pattern of response decrease across trial blocks is evident for tone 1—events indicative of strong negative correlation.

_____ 97. **(D)** The conditioned stimulus in the experiment was tone.

_____ 98. **(B)** Stimulus discrimination was evident across trial blocks. The pattern described in the explanation accompanying question 5 gives strong indication that the subjects were making prominent discrimination between the two tones.

_____ 99. **(C)** These epinephrine studies vividly demonstrated the potential effects of external suggestion upon experienced emotion.

_____ 100. **(D)** As distinguished from emotions, moods last longer and are less intense.

_____ 101. **(C)** Selye developed the concept of the general adaptation syndrome. The body's reaction under stress occurs in the three major stages—alarm reaction, resistance, and exhaustion.

_____ 102. **(C)** The opponent process theory—principally Solomon's—states that the brain functions to suppress emotional responses. Therefore, when an emotional response occurs (for example, fear) its opposite (sociability) is subsequently experienced—in effect, functioning to counterbalance. In the area of drugs this helps explain why the initial "high" or "rush" that is experienced becomes very minimal with continued use, and its opposite, depression, becomes more pronounced afterward. Stronger dosages are likely to be taken subsequently to counteract this negative experience—a vicious cycle.

_____ 103. **(B)** The James-Lange theory expresses the view that physical reaction prompts emotional response rather than vice versa.

_____ 104. **(C)** Pupil dilation is a prominent current measure of pleasurable object perception.

_____ 105. **(D)** *Cannabis sativa* is a technical name for marijuana.

_____ 106. **(B)** In Piaget's system, calculus computations have the cognitive complexity of formal operations.

_____ 107. **(B)** Although the period from ages two to six has been called pregang, preschool, exploration, and the time of solitary-parallel-associative-play sequence, it has not been called a period of dominance.

_____ 108. **(B)** In family constellation aspects of personality theory, the middle child is often described as the forgotten child (an Adler concept), therefore the prime candidate for receptiveness to physical demonstrations of attention.

_____ 109. **(C)** The age of initial walking in no way relates to a child's intelligence.

_____ 110. **(C)** Though it will not gain brain cells, the brain of the newborn will continue to grow in size after birth.

_____ 111. **(A)** Maternal diet deficiency during the embryonic period could be critically detrimental to the development of intelligence.

_____ 112. **(B)** A standard deviation is obtained by summing squared deviations from the mean, dividing by the number of scores and taking the square root.

_____ 113. **(C)** Erikson's trust-versus-mistrust stage occurs in the earliest mother-child social interaction related to feeding.

_____ 114. **(B)** Human engineers consider a three-section circular dial easier to interpret than the strictly numerical circular dial.

_____ 115. **(C)** The amount of information conveyed distinguishes "hot" from "cool" media in McLuhan's definitional framework. Books and articles are considered "hot" media, but TV is a "cool" medium.

_____ 116. **(A)** SSS is Zuckerman's sensation-seeking scale. It has been found that people differ dramatically in their sensation-seeking tendencies, and the scale has prominent utility in marriage compatibility.

_____ 117. **(A)** Researchers have found indications of sensitivity to stimulation during the fetal period.

_____ 118. **(A)** The mean is most dramatically affected by extreme scores because it is, in effect, an average.

_____ 119. **(B)** During the first three months after birth, the newborn shows a noticeable increase in night sleep and a decrease in day sleep.

_____ 120. **(D)** Menarche refers to the first menstrual period and occurs around thirteen years of age.

_____ 121. **(A)** Researchers such as Kobasa have found that stress-resistant executives differ from their counterparts on three dimensions—they feel more in control of their life events, have stronger social and work involvement, and have a positive attitude toward challenge and change.

_____ 122. **(D)** It was in the cigarette manufacturers' best interests to suggest that correlation does not mean causation but, rather, only shows a relationship between two observed events.

_____ 123. **(C)** Adler believed that inferiority feelings develop early in life through interaction with adults. Superiority striving is the consequence.

_____ 124. **(B)** Several B vitamins serve as coenzymes in brain metabolism; vitamin B deficiencies in pregnant women have been found to impair the learning abilities of their children.

_____ 125. **(D)** Stimulus discrimination research with newborns suggests that the infants can detect both color and shape.

_____ 126. **(A)** Severe anoxia at birth (interruption of oxygen supply) could result in brain damage.

_____ 127. **(A)** According to the concept of coaction, a child works faster when in the presence of another child performing the same task. This concept—along with the concept of audience effects—is known by the more general term *social facilitation*.

_____ 128. **(B)** These statements are part of a Thurstone scale designed to measure attitudes toward war.

_____ 129. **(A)** A high-scoring subject would be more pro-war than a low-scoring subject.

_____ 130. **(C)** To be acceptable for inclusion in a Thurstone scale, an item must have low variability (low standard deviation) in judge ratings.

_____ 131. **(A)** The numbers in parentheses reflect the mean of all judge ratings of this statement.

_____ 132. **(B)** Only two separate zygotes could produce one brown-eyed and one blue-eyed twin (fraternal twins).

_____ 133. **(E)** Meiosis refers to reduction division in which chromosome pairs separate, with one set going to one new cell and the remaining set to the other.

_____ 134. **(D)** Ovum-sperm, zygote, blastocyst is a correct developmental sequence.

_____ 135. **(E)** Predictive validity is the most rigorous form of validity. It is because the GRE has predictive validity that you and your "ancestors" have had to take it.

_____ 136. **(B)** Regression would deal with establishing the best prediction for an individual case based on a known general correlation.

_____ 137. **(C)** Immediately after menarche, a girl is incapable of conception—the time period known as adolescent sterility.

_____ 138. **(A)** Attitudes are enduring systems that contain both cognitive (knowledge) and affective (feeling) components manifested in behavior.

_____ 139. **(B)** Democratic leadership groups proved most productive in a leader-absent setting.

_____ 140. **(B)** In the nonzero-sum game, where both persons can experience simultaneous gains or losses, there is a tendency for competition to develop.

_____ 141. **(A)** The person receiving $20 is less likely to believe the lie because that person has more external justification ($20) for telling it—and consequently, less cognitive dissonance than a person receiving only $1.

_____ 142. **(B)** In contrast to a similar panel with subtle functional differences or identical controls with exact reversal in function, a pilot would experience more success and less interference in learning a new panel that was distinctly different from the old panel in all respects.

_____ 143. **(E)** Psychoanalysis focuses upon the early childhood bases underlying personality problems rather than the current behavioral symptoms.

_____ 144. **(E)** Only Jung speaks of archetypal continuities, and concept is totally foreign to phenomenologists.

_____ 145. **(A)** Treating emotional problems through role playing is a primary aspect of psychodrama.

_____ 146. **(B)** The intelligence test that would be suitable to the specifications of performance/verbal distinctions and evenly representative of IQ throughout the adult age span would be the Wechsler Adult Intelligence Scale. It has a separate IQ computation for verbal and for performance, and its standardization process is such that it is not locked in by a formula such as MA/CA $\times$ 100, where CA is Chronological Age, which would unfairly lower IQ representation in the older age range.

_____ 147. **(D)** During the first two years of development, a child bases his weight concept on stimulus size. A large box, therefore, is seen as heavier than a small box.

_____ 148. **(E)** Newborns have a partially developed taste sensitivity and corresponding taste preferences that will change as their sensitivity develops further.

_____ 149. **(B)** The capacity for visually tracking a moving object appears in the newborn a few days after birth.

_____ 150. **(A)** Bandura's research has centered upon observational learning and points to the strength of imitation learning achieved by children through the observation process.

_____ 151. **(D)** The mother's sincerity and warmth in the child relationship overshadows the feeding method in importance.

_____ 152. **(B)** In Kallmann's studies, the highest incidence of schizophrenia was found in identical twins—evidence frequently cited to prove the disorder's hereditary characteristics.

_____ 153. **(C)** Systematic desensitization in the Wolpe approach involves substituting a relaxation response for fear in the presence of a formerly feared object.

_____ 154. **(D)** In follow-up studies of patients treated through applied behavior analysis techniques, few relapses to problem behavior have been found.

_____ 155. **(B)** Detectable unexplainable physiological symptoms such as pain are present in somatic symptom disorder.

_____ 156. **(E)** Scores obtained prior to age two are most aptly called the Developmental Quotient, which bears no predictive validity for the later Intelligence Quotient.

_____ 157. **(E)** The vocabulary or verbal information areas offer the greatest possibility for an older person to demonstrate increases in intelligence.

_____ 158. **(C)** Classical conditioning has been achieved late in the fetal stage, demonstrating that the fetus has a capacity for learning simple responses.

_____ 159. **(A)** A basic confidence interval formula determines the lower limit by subtracting the (z-score times the standard deviation/the square root of _N_) from the mean of the distribution. The upper limit is obtained by adding the same quantity expressed in parentheses to the mean.

_____ 160. **(C)** See Question 159.

_____ 161. **(E)** Such observation of a natural setting is characteristic of the field-study method.

_____ 162. **(C)** Increasing the action of dopamine receptors increases schizophrenic symptoms; blocking the receptors relieves schizophrenic symptoms. This has led researchers to suspect a central role of dopamine in schizophrenia.

_____ 163. **(E)** Dopamine is a neurotransmitter located in the limbic system. Snyder has found that low doses of amphetamines make the schizophrenic symptoms even more obvious. When the release of dopamine is blocked by antipsychotic or neuroleptic drugs, the schizophrenic symptoms are relieved.

_____ 164. **(B)** The prodromal stage is characterized by secretive drinking and possible "blackouts." It is preceded by the prealcoholic stage, which involves social drinking and stress drinking. Crucial and chronic stages follow it.

_____ 165. **(E)** Somatoform disorders have physical symptoms for which no organic basis can be found. For example, the soldier who, in the heat of battle, develops paralysis in his right arm (thereby unable to fire his rifle) would be demonstrating a somatoform disorder.

_____ 166. **(A)** Childhood accidents are more prevalent in the second year than in the first—which is at least partially attributable to the youngster's increased mobility.

_____ 167. **(A)** Type I error would be mistaken rejection of a null hypothesis. Type II error is mistaken acceptance of a null hypothesis.

_____ 168. **(C)** Guttman's concept of unidimensionality would require a score of 3 to reflect agreement with items 1, 2, and 3.

_____ 169. **(E)** Neuroleptic is a medication-induced movement disorder.

_____ 170. **(E)** Mental health professionals find that the geographical locations with the highest heart-disease rates also have the highest rates of cancer incidence.

_____ 171. **(B)** Functional blindness—not traceable to a physiological cause—could be a somatic symptom disorder.

_____ 172. **(D)** Amphetamines, caffeine, and cocaine are all included within substance-related disorders.

_____ 173. **(D)** Although personality disorders encompass emotional shallowness, antisocial behavior, absence of group or individual loyalties, and rebellion against society, they do not include depression.

_____ 174. **(E)** In Freudian theory, repression constitutes a kind of involuntary absence from consciousness; suppression, on the other hand, involves a voluntary act of removal from consciousness. ("I'm not going to think about that anymore!")

_____ 175. **(A)** Anxiety disorders are the most commonly found disorders, and dissociative disorders are among the most rare.

_____ 176. **(A)** The therapist's personal qualities and experience are considered far more important factors in therapeutic success than the therapist's personality theory orientation.

_____ 177. **(B)** The only opioid in this drug listing is morphine.

_____ 178. **(D)** In a skewed distribution, the median moves in the direction of the skew, and the mode occurs at the distribution's high point. The mean moves more exaggeratedly in the tail direction than does the median.

_____ 179. **(C)** Systematic desensitization is the method in this listing used for directly treating problem behavior without concern for its underlying cause.

_____ 180. **(B)** The Hawthorne plant study at Western Electric launched the human relations movement in American industry. It pointed convincingly to the relationship between supervisory attention and concern for workers and resulting work output.

_____ 181. **(D)** Being within four standard deviations below the mean encompasses virtually all scores on that side of the distribution (50 percent). The score of sixty is one standard deviation above the mean (approximately an additional 34 percent), resulting in a combined 84 percent.

_____ 182. **(B)** Approximately 16 percent of the scores in a distribution would occur beyond a point that is one standard deviation below the mean.

_____ 183. **(E)** For all practical purposes, this point (three standard deviations above the mean) would encompass all distribution scores—essentially a 100th percentile, which is not among your answer choices.

_____ 184. **(C)** Raw scores are not in a form that permits comparison with performance on other test measures.

_____ 185. **(C)** The most reliable public opinion polling is that of private organizations conducted prior to a political election. Such firms are heavily staffed for such polling because they know there will be a "day of reckoning" when their findings will be confirmed or disproved.

_____ 186. **(A)** Having participants read several pages of description relating the problems and dilemmas of a specific manager would be an example of using the case method.

_____ 187. **(C)** Research studies indicate that the product should be priced initially at the eventual price level rather than at a discount price. In systematic studies, this recommendation has been demonstrated repeatedly.

_____ 188. **(D)** Determining that two discrete variables are independent within a population on the basis of the sample data would be a mission of chi-square.

_____ 189. **(B)** The distribution of sample means would be a normal distribution.

_____ 190. **(D)** Variance is defined as the average/mean of the squared differences from the mean of the distribution.

_____ 191. **(C)** Eating while reading was found to enhance the persuasiveness of the material being read. Thus, a salesman taking a client to lunch is right on target.

_____ 192. **(E)** Maslow did not associate the characteristic of notable financial success with self-actualizing people.

_____ 193. **(C)** When a person ingratiates us, they are saying nice things to us with an ulterior motive. When we detect that it is, indeed, ingratiation, it backfires on the one who ingratiated.

_____ 194. **(B)** Companionate love is affectionate, enhanced by self-disclosure, premised on equity, and has the quality of friendship. It is a love that endures after the heat of passion has cooled.

_____ 195. **(B)** As a mayor of a large city wishing to instill positive feelings between groups that traditionally have been hostile to one another, you might consider setting a superordinate goal that transcends any one group—a goal that groups will have to work together to accomplish.

_____ 196. **(C)** Charles Osgood developed an approach designed to reduce the level of hostilities between two countries. It is named Graduated and Reciprocated Initiatives in Tension-Reduction (GRIT). Clearly it depends on the reciprocal willingness of the respective countries' leaders.

_____ 197. **(C)** The term _copycat violence_ refers to viewers acting out the violent acts they have seen within the programming. Teen suicides after the movie _Deer Hunter_ were but one of several instances of this tragic phenomenon.

_____ 198. **(C)** Encouragement of independence has been found in the childhood backgrounds of persons with high achievement need.

_____ 199. **(A)** A unit of time (day, month, and so on) seems longest when it is being perceived by a young child. Hey, we've all been there…we thought it was an eternity!

_____ 200. **(B)** A basic Gestalt tenet is that behavior is more than the sum of its parts.

_____ 201. **(E)** There appears to be a relationship between increased stomach acids and the presence of resentment-hostility emotions within a person.

_____ 202. **(C)** Loftus has repeatedly demonstrated the contamination of memories by subtle suggestions prior to recollection, resulting in memory distortions that could have profound personal, social, and legal implications.

_____ 203. **(D)** There definitely has been a relationship found between ulcers and emotional state—the physical symptoms (ulcers) having been brought on by the psychological state (prolonged stress, for example).

_____ 204. **(E)** The well-known Kendler and Kendler studies found that reversal shifts are performed more quickly and more easily among older children than among younger children or animals.

_____ 205. **(C)** Attributable to Bartlett in England, this cryptarithmetic problem has found wide usage in the study of human problem solving both in this country and abroad.

_____ 206. **(C)** Schachter found that persons experiencing fear of an upcoming event preferred the company of others having a similar fear based on their scheduling to experience the same threatening event. If given a choice of associating with other persons not scheduled to experience the event, they preferred to be alone.

_____ 207. **(E)** Rogers emphasizes the self-concept—differentiation of a portion of one's phenomenal field.

_____ 208. **(D)** Social facilitation refers to performance enhancement prompted by the mere presence of others (e.g., "I play better with an audience.").

_____ 209. **(B)** Friedman and Rosenman set out the behavior characteristics of Type A people. These individuals are high risk in relation to the likelihood of heart attacks. Very competitive, impatient, and time-driven, these individuals cannot relax, and they experience quite a bit of underlying hostility. Their counterpart is Type B behavior characteristics, which encompass relaxing without feelings of guilt, patience, and little evidence of hostility.

_____ 210. **(D)** Attitudes are learned, not unconditioned.

_____ 211. **(E)** With greater distance from the source of frustration comes lower inhibition and, consequently, greater likelihood of aggressive actions.

_____ 212. **(C)** At one time, talking about suicide was believed to indicate low likelihood of its occurrence. On the basis of research, this belief is no longer considered valid.

_____ 213. **(E)** The Latin Square experimental design sets up controls for the order in which treatments are received.

_____ 214. **(B)** The setting vividly describes a paranoid personality disorder.

_____ 215. **(C)** _Observed frequency, expected frequency,_ and _contingency tables_ are terms relating to the chi-square statistic.

EVALUATING YOUR PROGRESS

Before proceeding, make sure you have used your answer sheet to mark each question on the explanation pages with a check mark for correct, an X for incorrect, and a blank for didn't answer.

Follow the same methods for scoring your test as you did for Practice Tests 1 and 2. We recommend that you try one of three ways to proceed:

- If you don't mind flipping pages, simply refer to your marks on the previous explanation pages as you fill out the chart below.
- If you DO mind flipping pages, you can use a copier to make copies of the explanation pages to which you can easily refer as you fill out the chart below.
- If neither of these alternatives works for you, you can transfer your check marks and X's to your answer sheet, and refer to those marks as you fill out the chart below.

Learning (13)	Language (7)	Memory (16)	Thinking (14)
_____ 11.	_____ 2.	_____ 9.	_____ 5.
_____ 18.	_____ 4.	_____ 14.	_____ 16.
_____ 51.	_____ 33.	_____ 23.	_____ 21.
_____ 52.	_____ 45.	_____ 28.	_____ 37.
_____ 53.	_____ 47.	_____ 32.	_____ 49.
_____ 54.	_____ 64.	_____ 38.	_____ 50.
_____ 61.	_____ 86.	_____ 39.	_____ 59.
_____ 67.	_____ Total Correct (C)	_____ 43.	_____ 63.
_____ 78.		_____ 46.	_____ 70.
_____ 87.	_____ Total Incorrect (I)	_____ 48.	_____ 71.
_____ 97.	_____ Total Blank	_____ 65.	_____ 73.
_____ 98.		_____ 66.	_____ 82.
_____ 150.	C – (I/4) = _____	_____ 80.	_____ 156.
_____ Total Correct (C)		_____ 81.	_____ 205.
_____ Total Incorrect (I)		_____ 95.	_____ Total Correct (C)
_____ Total Blank		_____ 202.	_____ Total Incorrect (I)
C – (I/4) = _____		_____ Total Correct (C)	_____ Total Blank
		_____ Total Incorrect (I)	C – (I/4) = _____
		_____ Total Blank	
		C – (I/4) = _____	

Sensation/ Perception (12)	Physiological/ Behavioral Neuroscience (37)	Clinical/ Abnormal (21)	Life Span Development (27)
____ 7.	____ 1.	____ 143.	____ 42.
____ 19.	____ 3.	____ 145.	____ 106.
____ 27.	____ 6.	____ 146.	____ 107.
____ 40.	____ 8.	____ 152.	____ 108.
____ 41.	____ 12.	____ 153.	____ 109.
____ 62.	____ 13.	____ 154.	____ 110.
____ 69.	____ 17.	____ 155.	____ 111.
____ 72.	____ 20.	____ 162.	____ 113.
____ 77.	____ 24.	____ 164.	____ 117.
____ 92.	____ 26.	____ 165.	____ 119.
____ 102.	____ 34.	____ 169.	____ 120.
____ 200.	____ 35.	____ 170.	____ 124.
____ Total Correct (C)	____ 36.	____ 171.	____ 125.
____ Total Incorrect (I)	____ 44.	____ 172.	____ 126.
____ Total Blank	____ 55.	____ 173.	____ 127.
C – (I/4) = ____	____ 56.	____ 175.	____ 133.
	____ 57.	____ 176.	____ 134.
	____ 58.	____ 177.	____ 137.
	____ 60.	____ 179.	____ 147.
	____ 68.	____ 212.	____ 148.
	____ 74.	____ 214.	____ 149.
	____ 75.	____ Total Correct (C)	____ 151.
	____ 76.	____ Total Incorrect (I)	____ 157.
	____ 79.	____ Total Blank	____ 158.
	____ 83.	C – (I/4) = ____	____ 166.
	____ 84.		____ 199.
	____ 85.		____ 204.
	____ 88.		____ Total Correct (C)
	____ 93.		____ Total Incorrect (I)
	____ 94.		____ Total Blank
	____ 101.		C – (I/4) = ____
	____ 104.		
	____ 105.		
	____ 121.		
	____ 132.		
	____ 163.		
	____ 201.		
	____ Total Correct (C)		
	____ Total Incorrect (I)		
	____ Total Blank		
	C – (I/4) = ____		

Personality (7)	Social (23)	General/Applied (7)	Methods/ Measurement (32)
____ 116.	____ 10.	____ 15.	____ 29.
____ 123.	____ 25.	____ 22.	____ 30.
____ 144.	____ 99.	____ 114.	____ 31.
____ 174.	____ 100.	____ 139.	____ 89.
____ 175.	____ 103.	____ 142.	____ 90.
____ 207.	____ 115.	____ 180.	____ 91.
____ 209.	____ 138.	____ 186.	____ 96.
Total Correct (C)	____ 140.	Total Correct (C)	____ 112.
____ 141.	____ 118.
____ Total Incorrect (I)	____ 187.	____ Total Incorrect (I)	____ 122.
____ 191.	____ 128.
____ Total Blank	____ 192.	____ Total Blank	____ 129.
____ 193.	____ 130.
C – (I/4) = ____	____ 194.	C – (I/4) = ____	____ 131.
____ 195.	____ 135.
____ 196.	____ 136.
____ 197.	____ 159.
____ 198.	____ 160.
____ 203.	____ 161.
____ 206.	____ 167.
____ 208.	____ 168.
____ 210.	____ 178.
____ 211.	____ 181.
____ Total Correct (C)	____ 182.
____ 183.
____ Total Incorrect (I)	____ 184.
____ 185.
____ Total Blank	____ 188.
____ 189.
C – (I/4) = ____	____ 190.
____ 213.
____ 215.
____ Total Correct (C)
____ Total Incorrect (I)
____ Total Blank
C – (I/4) = ____

Your next step is to transfer your totals above for each area into this chart:

	Number Correct (C)	Number Incorrect (I)	Number Blank	C-(I/4)	Maximum Possible	Your Percentage: Divide C-(I/4) by the Maximum Possible
Learning					13	
Language					7	
Memory					16	
Thinking					14	
Sensation Perception					12	
Physio/BN					37	
Clinical/ Abnormal					21	
Life Span					27	
Personality					7	
Social					23	
General					7	
Methods					32	

How did you do this time? Are you able to identify areas that need more work? If so, head back into the review section and use your textbooks and Web resources to brush up on remaining problem areas. We hope by this point, you are feeling very confident and well-prepared for your GRE Psychology Test. But if you need more practice, go ahead and try completing the diagnostic and practice tests again.

Index

lobes, 135, 139
lock-and-key model, 134, 138
Locke, John, 96, 184
Loewi, Otto, 132, 134
logotherapy, 167, 172, 186, 191
long-term potentiation, 96, 136, 142
Lorenz, Konrad, 152, 154–155
love, theories of, 212, 221
LSD, 145, 149

M

magnetic resonance imaging (MRI), 136, 141
MAO (monoamine oxidase) inhibitors, 147, 150, 168
marijuana, 145
McGaugh, James L., 133, 134
McGuire's inoculation theory, 214
measurement
    of attitude, 195–198, 220
    of brain function, 136, 140–142
    of child development, 174
    of emotion, 207
    of hearing, 121
    of personality, 192–194
    of sensation, 116–118
    and thought, 108
media elite, 213
medical therapies, 173
medulla, 135, 139
Meichenbaum, Donald, 168
melatonin, 135, 140
memory, 101–103, 101–106, 133
Mendel, Gregor, 152, 153–155
mental representations of thought, 107, 109
mescaline, 146
metabolic measuring techniques, 136, 141
methadone, 145
methamphetamines, 146, 149
methodology in psychology, 235–246
midbrain, 135, 139
Minnesota Multiphasic Personality Inventory (MMPI), 192–193
MMPI (Minnesota Multiphasic Personality Inventory), 192–193
mnemonics, 103
models of thought, 109
molecular genetics, 154–155, 155
monoamine oxidase (MAO) inhibitors, 150, 168
mood-altering drugs, 136, 143–150
morphemes, 98
Motherese, 99
motivation, 198–203
motor and sensory homunculus, 136, 141
motor development, 175
motor neurons, 134, 138
MRI (magnetic resonance imaging), 136, 141
multi-modal therapy, 168, 172

multiple-choice questions, 9–10
multiple intelligences, 110–111
Multiple Sclerosis, 137
muscle atonia, 136, 142
myelin sheath, 134, 137–138

N

narcolepsy, 136, 142
narcotic drugs, 136, 145, 149
natural injury, 136, 141
naturalistic approach, 174
nature/nurture issues, 111
need-press theory, 203
needs hierarchy theory, 202
negative after-image, 120
nerve impulses, 137–138
nerves, cranial, 126–127
nervous system, 134, 138, 206
neural function, 132–133
neural plasticity, 136, 142–143
neurobiology of memory, 104, 106
neurocognitive disorders, 160
neurodevelopmental disorders, 158
neuromodulators, 138
neurons, 134, 137–144
neuroticism, 185, 187
neurotransmitters, 132, 138
Newell, Allen, 106
nicotine, 147
nodes of Ranvier, 134, 137–138
nominal use of numbers, 235, 240
nonphysiological motives, 202
nonregulatory physiological mechanisms and motivation, 201
nonverbal behavior, 206
nonverbal communication, 213, 222
noradrenalin, 135
norepinephrine, 134, 138
normal distribution, 240
null hypothesis, 235–236
numbers, 235, 240

O

obedience, 223
observational learning, 165, 172
obsessive-compulsive disorders, 158
occipital lobes, 135, 139
oculomotor nerves, 126
olfaction (smell), 117, 122–123
olfactory nerves, 126
one-tailed tests, 241
openness, 185, 187
operant conditioning, 94–95
opiates, 136, 145, 149
opium, 145, 149
opponent-process, 203, 204

Opponent-Process Theory, 119–120
optic nerves, 126
optimal-state theories, 202–203
ordinal use of numbers, 235, 240
organizational psychology, 227–230, 231
ovaries, 135, 140
overload concept, 224
oxytocin, 135, 139

P

pain-relief drugs, 149
pain senses, 123–125
pancreas, 135, 140
parameter-statistic distinction, 237, 240
paraphilic disorders, 160
parapraxes, 188
parasympathetic nervous system, 138
parathyroid, 135, 139
parietal lobes, 135, 139
Parkinson's disease, 139, 142
Pavlov, Ivan, 94
PCP, 146
Pearson Product-Moment Correlation, 243
Peck's stage elaboration, 182
peptides, 134, 138
percentile ranking, 239, 241
perception, 116–131, 128–131
perceptual constancies, 129–130
perceptual expectation, 130
perceptual organization, 130–131
peripheral nervous system, 138
Perls, Fritz, 167
personal attributes, 209
personal construct personality theory, 186, 191
personality, 183–194, 218
    disorders, 160, 162
    testing, 192–194
    theorists, 188–192
personology traits, 187, 192
persuasion, 214–215, 222
PET (positron emission tomography), 135, 140–141
phenomenological theories of personality, 184, 186–187, 190–191
phenomenological therapies, 166–168, 172
phenothiazine drugs, 148
phoneme, 98
phonology, 98
physiological regulatory mechanism and motivation, 201
Piaget, Jean, 174–175, 176–177
Piagetian stages, 179
pineal gland, 140, 142
pituitary gland, 135, 139
pleasure centers, 202
pleasure drugs, 149
pleasure-pain, 202
Point-Biserial Correlation, 244

polling, 196–197
polysomnogram, 135, 142
pons, 135, 139
positive psychology traits, 187
positive reinforcement, 95
positron emission tomography (PET), 135, 140–141
practical intelligence, 111
pragmatic therapy, 169–170, 173
preconscious, 188
prejudice, 217–218, 224
Premack principle, 95
prenatal and postnatal influences on intelligence, 112
prenatal developmental stages, 175, 178
preparing for GRE, 6–8
pressure (touch), 123–125
primal therapy, 170, 173
probability, 239, 241
problem solving, 109, 113–115
process model for workers, 229
product model for workers, 229
professional journals, 246
projection, 193
propositions, 98
proprioception, 124
proxemics, 213, 222
proximity, 208
psilocybin, 146
psyche, divisions of, 188
psychedelic drugs, 136, 145–146, 149
psychoanalysis, 163, 171, 226
psychoanalytic motivation, 202
psychoanalytic theories of personality, 184, 186, 188
psychodrama, 170, 174
psychodynamic analysis, 163–164, 171
psychodynamic model of abnormalities, 157
psychodynamic theory of personality, 184, 186, 189–190
psycholinguistics, 100, 106
psychological drives, 199
psychopathology, 156–157, 192–193
psychosexual stages, 188
psychosocial theory, 177, 184, 186
psychotic disorders, 158
psychotomimetic drugs, 149
punishment, 96
purkinje effect, 119

R

radical behaviorist personality theory, 186, 190
Ramon y Cajal, Santiago, 132, 134
random sampling, 237
Ranvier, nodes of, 134, 137–138
rapid eye-movement sleep (REM), 135, 142
rational-emotive therapy, 167, 172
ratios, 235, 240
reactance theory, 220

reality therapy, 170, 173

reasoning, types, 107, 108

receiver-operating characteristics (ROC) curves, 117–118

receptors, 116, 123–125, 134, 138

reciprocal inhibition personality theory, 186, 190

recording techniques of brain function, 135, 140–142

reflected glory, 224

reflexes, 132, 179

registration procedure for GRE, 1

regression, 241

reinforcement, 95–96

REM (rapid eye-movement sleep), 135, 142

representations of thought, 109

resting potential, 134, 137

reticular formation, 135, 139, 142

reuptake and breakdown, 134, 138

rewardingness, 209

Rhine, J. B., 128, 130

right hemisphere, 135, 139

risk-taking, 223

ROC (receiver-operating characteristics) curves, 117–118

Rogers, Carl, 167

Role Construct Repertory Test, 167

roles and status, 218–219, 224

Rorschach Inkblot Test, 193, 194

Rutherford's Frequency Theory, 120–121

S

saltatory conduction, 134, 138

sampling statistics, 236–237

Schachter epinephrine studies, 204

schizophrenia, 158, 161

school and applied psychology, 234

scientific method, 235–246

scoring of GRE, 2

self-actualization personality theory, 186

self-perception theory, 220

self-reference effect, 6

semantic differential scale, 196

semantics, 98

sensation, dimensions of, 116–118, 127

sensation seeking, 203

senses, 117

sensitivity of skin, 125

sensitization, 94

sensory capabilities, 180

sensory code, 117

sensory neurons, 134, 138

separation anxiety, 179

serotonin, 134, 138

serotonin reuptake inhibitors, 147, 150, 168

sex drive, 199, 201

sexual disorders, 159

Sherrington, Charles, 125, 132, 141

signal-detection theory, 117–118

significance levels, 241, 245

similarity, 208

Simon, Herbert, 106

single stimulus factor, 220

situational context cues, 204

skew, 241

skin and skin senses, 117, 123–127

sleep and sleep disorders, 135, 142

sleep/wake disorders, 159, 162

smell (olfaction), 117, 122–123

social and personality development, 177–178

social cognition, 220

social-comparison and attraction, 211

social Darwinism, 154

social distance scale, 196

social drives, 199

social exchange theory, 210–211

social identity theory, 224

socialization, 223

social personality theory, 186, 190

social psychology, 194–225

social role theory, 219

social stimulation need, 207

sociobiology, 154, 155

sociopsychoanalytic personality theory, 186, 190

soma, 134, 137

somatic symptom disorders, 159

spatial summation, 134, 137

Spearman Rank-Order Correlation, 243

Spearman's Two Factor Theory, 110

specificity theory, 117

specific nerve energies, 117

Spencer, W. Alden, 133

spinal accessory nerves, 127

spinal cord, 134, 138

Stanford-Binet test, 110

statistical inference, 237

statistics, 112, 236–246

status and roles, 218–219, 224

Sternberg, R., 110

Stevens' Law, 117–118, 127

stimulants, 136, 146–147, 149

stimulus, 127–128

stress and emotions, 205, 207–208

stress management, 8

stressor-related disorders, 159

structuralism, 225

structural recording techniques, 135

substance P, 134, 138

substance-related disorders, 160

substantia nigra, 139

successive approximations, 95

sulcus, 135, 139

suprachiasmatic nucleus of hypothalamus, 135, 142

surgical ablation, 135, 141–142

sympathetic nervous system, 138